25

THE CHURCHES, IRELAND AND THE IRISH

THE CHURCHES, IRELAND AND THE IRISH

PAPERS READ AT
THE 1987 SUMMER MEETING AND
THE 1988 WINTER MEETING OF
THE ECCLESIASTICAL HISTORY SOCIETY

EDITED BY

W. J. SHEILS AND
DIANA WOOD

PUBLISHED FOR
THE ECCLESIASTICAL HISTORY SOCIETY

BY

BASIL BLACKWELL

1989

© Ecclesiastical History Society 1989

First published 1989

Basil Blackwell Ltd
108 Cowley Road, Oxford OX4 1 JF, UK

Basil Blackwell Inc.
432 Park Avenue South, Suite 1503,
New York, NY 10016, USA

British Library Cataloguing in Publication Data
Ecclesiastical History Society, *Summer meeting* (*1987:*
    St. Patrick's College, Maynooth, Ireland).
    The Churches, Ireland and the Irish.
    1. Ireland. Christian church, history
    I. Title II. Sheils, W. J. (William J.) III. Wood, Diana
    IV. Ecclesiastical History Society, *Winter Meeting*
    (*1988: King's College, London.*)
    274.15
    ISBN 0-631-16114-7

Library of Congress Cataloging-in-Publication Data
Ecclesiastical History Society. Summer Meeting
    (1987 : Patrick's college, Maynooth)
    The Churches, Ireland, and the Irish.

    (Studies in church history; 25)
    Includes index.
    1. Ireland – Church history – Congresses.
2. Northern Ireland – Church history – Congresses.
3. Irish – Foreign countries – Religion –
Congresses. 4. Scots-Irish – Foreign countries
– Religion – Congresses. I. Sheils, W. J.
II. Wood, Diana, 1940-   . III. Ecclesiastical History Society. Winter Meeting (1988 :
King's College, London) IV. Title. V. Series.
BR792.E25   1987   280'.09415   88-7718
ISBN 0-631-16114-7

Typeset by Joshua Associates Limited, Oxford
Printed in Great Britain by Billing and Sons Ltd, Worcester

CONTENTS

CONTENTS

vi

CONTENTS

PREFACE

The Ecclesiastical History Society chose to hold its first summer conference outside of the United Kingdom at St Patrick's College, Maynooth in
the summer of 1987 and the President for the year, Professor J. A. Watt,
provided as the theme 'The Churches and the Irish and the Irish in
Churches at home and abroad'. The Society is grateful to St Patrick's
College for the hospitality it provided, and also to the Provost of Trinity
College, Dublin for the welcome he extended to the Society during a visit
to that institution. The venue at Maynooth provided a pleasant meeting-
place for scholars from both sides of the Irish Sea and further afield, as well
as for historians from both north and south of the border. The opportunity thus provided was taken both by members of the Society belonging
to many of the Churches represented in Ireland and by those without particular religious affiliations. The papers published here represent a selection of those offered for discussion on that occasion and also during the
winter meeting of the Society at King's College, London, where once
again the college extended its customary hospitality.

W. J. Sheils
Diana Wood

LIST OF CONTRIBUTORS

J. A. WATT (*President*)
Professor of History, University of Newcastle-upon-Tyne

BERNARD ASPINWALL
Senior Lecturer in History, Glasgow University

DOMINIC AIDAN BELLENGER
Monk of Downside Abbey

BRENDAN BRADSHAW
Lecturer in History, University of Cambridge

MICHAEL A. J. BURROWS
Curate, Parish of Douglas, Cork

JUDITH F. CHAMP
Lecturer in Ecclesiastical History, King's College, London

AIDAN CLARKE
Erasmus Smith's Professor of Modern History, University of Dublin

PAUL COLLINS
Research Scholar, School of Social Sciences, Australian National
University, Canberra

BARNADETTE CUNNINGHAM
Assistant Librarian, Dublin Diocesan Library

BRIAN EAGAR
Research Assistant, University College, Dublin

OWEN DUDLEY EDWARDS
Reader in American and Commonwealth History, University of
Edinburgh

DECLAN GAFFNEY
Research Student, Trinity College, Dublin

RAYMOND GILLESPIE
Dublin

DAVID HEMPTON
Lecturer in History, Queen's University, Belfast

MYRTLE HILL
Junior Fellow, Institute of Irish Studies, Queen's University, Belfast

R. F. G. HOLMES
Principal, Union Theological College, Belfast

DONAL A. KERR
Professor of Ecclesiastical History, St Patrick's College, Maynooth

COLM LENNON
Lecturer in Modern History, St Patrick's College, Maynooth

HUGH McLEOD
Lecturer in Modern Church History, University of Birmingham

STUART MEWS
Lecturer in Religious Studies, University of Lancaster

HIS EMINENCE CARDINAL TOMÁS Ó FIAICH
Archbishop of Armagh

T. C. F. STUNT
History Master, Stowe School

RORY M. SWEETMAN
Research Student, Peterhouse, Cambridge

RALPH WALLER
Chaplain, Westminster College, Oxford

KATHERINE WALSH
Universitätsdozent, Institut für Geschichte, Salzburg

C. PETER WILLIAMS
Vice-Principal, Trinity College, Bristol

INTRODUCTION

I RELAND's experience of Christianity and its influence on other
countries has been of wonderful richness and diversity. Celtic Christianity with its monasticism and its role in evangelization and cultural
renaissance abroad, the conversion of the Hiberno-Norse, the establishment of a colonial Church, and the stresses of the Reformation give
distinctiveness to the Irish medieval past. The creation of the Church of
Ireland, the settlements of Presbyterians, and that persecution of the
majority which ensured the identification of Irish nationalism with
Catholicism made religion fundamental to the whole evolution of Irish
society. The Irish Churches remain profoundly marked by their past.
Historians have their own role to play in the healing of old wounds and
laying the intellectual foundations for mutual understanding.

It is, however, not the least important feature of the history of the Irish
Churches that they have so often transcended sectarian strife in important
movements of reform and renewal within their own traditions. Some of
the more impressive fruits of these movements have manifested themselves in the spread and fostering of Christianity in the Third World.
Overseas, however, it has been continuously heavy emigration which has
left its mark, transformingly profound, on the Christianity of other
countries, especially in Britain, North America, and Australia.

It is eminently fitting that the Society should have chosen Ireland as the
location of its first conference outside the United Kingdom. For the Irish
Christian traditions, at home, in Britain, and overseas, from Patrick to our
own time, offer a fascination for historians of Christianity world-wide,
out of all proportion to the size and geographical position of the country.

Of course, conferences, of their nature inevitably restricted, cannot do
full justice to all aspects of such a wide-ranging theme. But the papers
published in this volume have chronological breadth, a variety of
approach, and a diversity of topic. Each of Ireland's main Christian
traditions figures prominently. Over a quarter of the papers treat of the
Irish presence in, and influence on, Churches outside Ireland. The conferences at Maynooth in July 1987 and at King's College, London in
January 1988 brought together historians from different countries and
academic institutions, who were members of different churches and of
none. Professional history in Ireland has long been intercultural and

non-sectarian. The Ecclesiastical History Society was privileged to witness that academic ecumenism in action and, I trust, in its own way, to help to maintain and forward it.

J. A. Watt
President for 1987–88

THE WILD AND WOOLLY WEST:
EARLY IRISH CHRISTIANITY AND
LATIN ORTHODOXY*

by BRENDAN BRADSHAW

IN recent historiography a rather unlikely alliance has emerged which is concerned to normalize Early Irish Christianity by emphasizing its links with the religious culture of Western Europe. One wing of the alliance represents a historiographical tradition that originated in the debates of the Reformation with the introduction of a formidable Aunt Sally by the erudite ecclesiastical historian Archbishop Ussher, who purported to discover in the Early Irish Church a form of Christianity in conformity with the Pure Word of God, uncorrupted by papal accretions. Ussher's *A Discourse of the Religion anciently professed by the Scottish and Irish* initiated a debate that has reverberated down the centuries around the issue of which of the two major post-Reformation Christian traditions may claim Early Irish Christianity for its heritage.[1] The debate continues to echo, even in these ecumenical times, in a Roman Catholic tradition of writing about the history of the Early Irish Church which emphasizes its links with Roman Orthodoxy—which were, in reality, tenuous and tension-ridden—and glosses over its highly characteristic idiosyncrasies.[2] More recently that tradition has received unlikely and, indeed, unwitting support in consequence of the development of a revisionist trend in Celtic historical studies against a perception of Celtic Ireland that originated in the romantic movement of the nineteenth century and that was taken over *holus-bolus* by the cultural nationalists. This romantic-nationalist interpretation pivots upon an ethnographic antithesis between the Celt

---

* I wish to thank Richard Sharpe for much useful comment on this paper, not all of which, unfortunately, I felt able to take to heart.

[1] James Ussher, *A Discourse of the Religion Anciently Professed by the Irish and British* (London, 1631). Ussher's thesis, expressed in the dedicatory epistle, is that 'the religion professed by the ancient bishops, priests, monks and other Christians in this land, was for substance the very same with that which now by public authority is maintained therein against the foreign doctrine brought thither in latter times by the bishop of Rome's followers'.

[2] For a recent example in this tradition see P. J. Corish, *The Irish Catholic Experience: A Historical Survey* (Dublin, 1985). Corish provides an admirable survey which, however, is written on the assumption that the history of the 'Irish Catholic experience' is equivalent to the history of the Irish Christian experience with the history of Irish Protestantism left out. As an example of the work of the previous generation of Catholic scholars see John Ryan, 'The Early Irish Church and The Holy See', *Studies* 49 (1960), pp. 1–16; 50 (1961), pp. 165–74.

and the other races of Western Europe which endows the former with singular qualities of spirit and of heart and interprets Early Irish Christianity accordingly. By way of antidote modern scholarship has taken to emphasizing external influences and the European context as the key to an understanding of the historical development of Christianity in Ireland, playing up its debt to the Latin West and playing down the claims made on its behalf as the light of Dark Age Europe.[3]

It may seem inordinately perverse, therefore, to devote an essay at this juncture to exploring the idiosyncratic quality of Early Irish Christianity. Perhaps it may be as well to stress at the outset, however, that the purpose in doing so is neither ideological nor polemical. The intention is not to seek to reinstate the claims of Celtic religion to a special spiritual superiority, still less to recover its heritage for Protestantism. Nor, indeed, is the purpose simply to insist on the fact of difference, for that would be to state the obvious: ultimately the oddity of Early Irish Christianity seems to be acknowledged even by the revisionists.[4] The purpose is rather to attempt to establish the specific nature of the difference with a view to placing on the historical agenda two problems which seem to be among the most interesting which the history of the period poses: how are the Irish oddities to be explained and what are their implications for the subsequent history of Christianity in Ireland?

I

As a missionary and bishop of the Latin Church of late antiquity St Patrick would have found the Irish Church disconcertingly odd as it emerged in its developed form in the seventh century. Its oddness related to four principal features which provide the substance of the discussion which follows. One was its institutional structure. It seems that at some point in the aftermath of the phase of evangelization the Celtic Church abandoned the Latin system of territorial organization based on the unit of

---

[3] A good-humoured exercise in revisionism is provided in Patrick Sims-Williams, 'The Visionary Celt: The Construction of an Ethnic Preconception', *Cambridge Medieval Celtic Studies*, 11 (1986), pp. 71–96. Similar concerns inform two recent collections of essays, though not all of the contributors adopt the revisionist perspective: ed. Dorothy Whitelock, Rosamund McKitterick and David Dumville, *Ireland in Early Medieval Europe: Studies in Memory of Kathleen Hughes* (Cambridge, 1982), hereinafter cited as *Hughes Studies*; Proinsías Ní Chatháin and Michael Richter, *Irland und Europa, die Kirche im Frühmittelalter* (Stuttgart, 1984). That the romantic tradition continues to flourish is evident from a number of the contributions to Peter O'Driscoll (ed.), *The Celtic Consciousness* (Portlaoise and Edinburgh, 1982).
[4] See for instance the foreword in *Hughes Studies* pp. 1–8 at p. 2.

the diocese. Instead a loose disaggregated system evolved, based on the great monastic 'families' that were developing at the same time, and which now became patrons to collectivities of dispersed local churches—significantly, the nearest equivalent to the notion of family in the Irish language is a derivative of *monasterium*, i. e. *muinntir*. Accordingly, the abbot came to replace the bishop as the *locus* of power in the Celtic Church, the latter assuming a special but subordinate role as dispenser of the sacrament of Holy Orders.[5] This is the 'strange and unaccustomed order' that the Venerable Bede notes in recounting the sixth century mission of the Celtic Church to Scotland in his *Ecclesiastical History*. In doing so he registers the shock of an orthodox Latin churchman on encountering the institutional form of the Celtic Church.[6]

The second disconcerting feature of Early Irish Christianity relates to what historians nowadays call collective mentality. The mental gap that opened up between Celtic and Latin Christianity finds an apt illustration in the comparison between the religious outlook revealed in St Patrick's own writings and that reflected in the biographies by Irish monks who wrote up the saint's Life two centuries later with a view to the promotion of his cult as National Apostle.

The attractiveness of the personality that emerges from the *Confession* and the *Letter to the soldiers of Coroticus* has to do in large part with the psychological tension produced by a religious outlook that combines profound reverence for the public role which the saint felt called upon to occupy with a profound sense of his personal unworthiness. The terms in which the dilemma is perceived and resolved by Patrick are highly relevant to the present discussion since they illuminate a frame of mind

---

[5] The institutional development of the Early Irish Church was unravelled in Kathleen Hughes, *The Church in Early Irish Society*, London, 1966, esp. caps 5–8. For a survey of the long quest for the European source of Celtic Ireland's monastic ecclesiastical structure see Edward James, 'Ireland and Western Gaul in the Merovingian Period' in *Hughes Studies*, pp. 362–86. The discussion remains highly speculative and inconclusive. It seems that more progress is likely to be made by starting the search elsewhere, namely with the socio-political structures of Early Irish society—which was, of course, the starting point which Kathleen Hughes adopted, e.g. her remark on the ecclesiastical legislation of the Early Irish Church: 'The job of the seventh-century "Irish" canonists was to apply the native law to the Church. In so doing they produced an Irish Church with a unique constitution', *Early Christian Ireland: Introduction to the Sources* (London, 1972), pp. 67–80 at p. 77.

[6] *Venerabilis Bedae Historiae Ecclesiasticae Gentis Anglorum*, III, iiii: 'Habere autem solet ipsa insula Iona rectorem semper abbatem presbyterum, cuius iuri et omnis provincia et ipsi etiam episcopi ordine inusitato debeant esse subiecti, iuxta exemplum primi doctoris illius, qui non episcopus sed presbyter et monachus.' The sixteenth-century English version by Thomas Stapleton reinforces the sense of shock by translating *ordine inusitato* as 'strange and unaccustomed order', ed. Philip Hereford, *The Ecclesiastical History of the English People* (London, 1935).

conditioned by the Hellenization of the Christian gospel. One horn of Patrick's dilemma reflects the strongly institutional outlook of Latin Christianity, its ecclesial mentality, dominated by consciousness of the hierarchically ordered and governed society that comprises the adherents of the Christian religion, the Church. Hence the 'churchly awareness' which permeates Patrick's writings, reflected especially in the awesome consciousness which he displays of his own status as a bishop and of his office as leader and defender of a community of Christians—the attitude graphically reflected in the *Letter to Coroticus*.[7] The other side of the dilemma reflects a perception of the gospel message of salvation through Jesus that has been filtered through the conceptual framework of Hellenic, specifically Neoplatonic, soteriology. Thus Patrick's crushing sense of personal unworthiness in which lack of moral purity and lack of learning weigh equally upon him—this *leitmotiv* of the *Confession* is announced in the opening sentence, 'I, Patrick, a sinner, the most uncultivated of men, the least of all the faithful and utterly despicable to many . . .'. Patrick's means of sustaining, and indeed of resolving, his predicament is to resort to another characteristic feature of the frame of reference of Hellenic Christianity. He invokes the concept of providential grace: the power of God acting, whether upon the life of the individual or the histories of nations, in a hidden and 'instrumental' way, ordering them to his salvific purpose. The theme of the *Confession* is precisely that of God's providential grace operating through the instrumentality of the misfortunes and fortunate occurrences of the saint's life, to make of him 'the letter of Christ for salvation to the ends of the earth';[8] significantly, the *Confession* has no dramatic miracles to relate, only interior illuminations which enable Patrick to perceive and to cooperate in God's providential designs mediated through the instrumentality of human history.[9] The religious

[7] For the Patrician texts, i.e. the *Confession* and the *Letter to the Soldiers of Coroticus* see A. B. E. Hood (ed. and transl.), *St. Patrick: His Writings and Muirchú's Life* (London, 1978); for the early hagiography see Ludwig Bieler (ed. and transl.), *The Patrician Texts in the Book of Armagh* (Dublin, Institute for Advanced Studies 1979); Whitley Stokes (ed. and transl.), *Vita Tripartita*, 2 vols, *RS* (1887); for commentary see Hughes, *Sources*, pp. 219–47; Eoin MacNeill, *Saint Patrick*, ed. John Ryan (Dublin 1964); D. A. Binchy, 'Patrick and his Biographers Ancient and Modern', *Studia Hibernica*, 2 (1962), pp. 7–173; D. O'Donoghue, 'The Spirituality of St. Patrick', *Studies*, 50 (1961), pp. 152–64; for an interesting parallel with the Hellenic outlook of St Patrick see the remarks on Gregory of Tours in Raymond Van Dam, *Leadership and Community in Late Antique Gaul* (Berkeley, Los Angeles, and London, 1985), pp. 224–9.

[8] Ludwig Bieler (ed.), *Libri Epistolarum Sancti Patricii Episcopi* (Dublin, 1952), *Confessio*, 11, 'Quanto magis nos adpetere debeamus, qui sumus, inquit, epistola Christi in salutem usque ad ultimum terrae.'

[9] For a comprehensive account of the emergence of Christianity from Judaism and its development within the cultural and intellectual framework of the Greco-Roman world see W. H. C.

consciousness revealed in the writings of Patrick, therefore, is characterized by three dominant perceptions: an institutional view of the Church as the hierarchically organized Christian community; a moral evaluation of his personal condition as sinful and ignorant; an interiorized and instrumental view of supernatural power as mediated in a hidden mysterious way through providential grace. These perceptions explain the affinity, rightly noted, between Patrick's *Confession* and that of the 'doctor of the West'.[10] And that affinity in turn confirms the categorization of Patrick, the zealous churchman, humble 'rustic' and confessor of the hidden *mirabilia Dei*, as a representative of the Hellenized Christianity of the Latin West.

The contrast provided by the figure proposed for veneration as National Apostle is all the more revealing for the fact that the early biographies show familiarity with the saint's two authentic writings. By the manipulation of these—through excision and embellishment—and by the incorporation of material presumably drawn from a living hagiographical tradition, the early biographers effected a startling metamorphosis.[11] Too often the result has been dismissed as a distortion and a caricature.[12] In fact what was achieved was the transformation of a Latin confessor-bishop into a credible patron saint of the seventh-century Celtic Church. The interest of the latter is that he provides, in striking ways, the antithesis of the former. To begin with the self-conscious ecclesiastic. The biblical antithesis between priest and prophet provides an apt analogy here.[13] True, the early biographers are careful to emphasize Patrick's episcopal consecration. But the *persona* does not fit the office. The Patrick of the hagiographers conforms to the behaviour-pattern of the inspired holy man: perpetually wandering in the company of a small band of disciples; confronting the protagonists of false religion rather than exercising the

---

Frend, *The Rise of Christianity* (London, 1984); for the assimilation of the notion of providence from Stoic philosophy see Henry Chadwick, *Early Christian Thought and the Classical Tradition* (Oxford, 1966), esp. cap. 4; for an exposition of St Augustine's highly influential ideas on the subject see R. A. Markus, *Saeculum: History and Society in the Theology of St. Augustine* (Cambridge, 1970).

[10] On St Augustine's *Confession* see Peter Brown, *Augustine of Hippo: a biography* (London, 1969), pp. 158–81. For the affinity noted between Patrick and Augustine see Corish, *The Irish Catholic Experience*, pp. 14–15.

[11] See above, note 7.

[12] e.g. Brian de Breffny, *In the Steps of St. Patrick* (London, 1982), pp. 71-110. Cf. Ludwig Bieler, *The Life and Legend of St. Patrick* (Dublin, 1948), pp. 92-125.

[13] The distinction between the priestly and the prophetic traditions of Judaism is often made in situating Jesus in the context of Old Testament religion by associating him with the latter tradition.

pastoral care of a Christian community; pronouncing curses and blessings and performing miracles; withdrawing into wildernesses and high places to pray, mortify the flesh, and to enter into direct contact with the other world. The second antithesis relates to Patrick's personality. Here the abject self-deprecation of the *Confession* is discarded. Instead the saint takes on the character traits of another familiar biblical type, the angelic messenger: remote, indomitable, self-possessed, but, for all that, compassionate and beneficent. The third contrast is with the figure of Patrick as the confessor of the *mirabilia Dei*. Against the Hellenic perception which the *Confession* reflects, of the divine power as mediated interiorly and instrumentally through providential grace, the perception of the Patrician hagiography is of the divine power as mediated charismatically, i.e. directly and personally through the wonder-working gifts possessed by the servant of God, specifically, in this case, by Patrick himself. It is scarcely necessary to draw attention, yet again, to the biblical resonance of the hagiographical Patrick in this respect also.

The transformation of the real Patrick into the cult figure of seventh-century hagiography serves, therefore, to draw attention to a more profound transformation at the level of religious consciousness. The interest of the latter for present purposes lies in the process of 'de-Hellenization' that it reflects. The institutional, philosophical and instrumental-mediatory perceptions that dominated Hellenic Christianity, and Patrick's authentic writings, here give way to a religious outlook more redolent of the ethos of the Judaeo-Christian scriptures themselves—inspirational, transcendental, charismatic. Two questions arise in consequence. One, which must be reserved for brief consideration later, concerns how such a value-shift is to be explained. The other concerns its practical implications for the religion of early medieval Ireland and for the relationship of the Early Irish Church to Latin Orthodoxy. These latter issues take the discussion to a consideration of the third general feature that removes Early Irish Christianity from the ambience of Latin Orthodoxy, the form of spirituality which it developed. Analysis here reveals a striking correspondence between the dominant perceptions of the Patrician hagiography and the dominant devotional modes of Celtic religion while at the same time confirming the antithesis earlier observed with Latin Orthodoxy.

II

As might be expected, monasticism, the central institution of the Early Irish Church, looms large again in this context as the supreme embodiment of Celtic spiritual values. In the first place, the antithesis between the institutional mentality of Latin orthodoxy and the inspirational outlook of the Celtic Church finds no better expression than the contrast between the monastic movements which each generated. The Venerable Bede may here also be invoked as an early witness to the incompatibility of the two systems. In a well-known passage describing the collapse of St Colman's experiment in integrating English and Irish monks in a common monastic foundation at Inishboffin he pinpoints a central feature of Irish monastic culture that was to prove a source of scandal to Latin authors over some four centuries. This was the *consuetudo peregrinandi*, the inveterate propensity of the Celtic monks for wandering. Nothing could have been more calculated to affront the Benedictine ideology of order, discipline, and stability: the rule of St Benedict opens with a classification of monastic 'types' in which the vagrant (*gyrovagus*) is placed fourth and last, so contemptible as not even to merit discussion.[14] On the other hand the *peregrinatio* was a compelling ideal of the Irish monastic movement, nurtured by a rich and varied literature, ranging from Adamnān's classic *Life of Columcille* to the sermons of St Columbanus.[15] All that could be said on this vast subject must here be reduced to a few relevant comments. One, to stress the inspirational character of the ideal, is that unsolicitous self-abandonment in the quest for God was of its essence—slipping moorings on to the high seas in a tiny coracle without oars or rudder, like the Irish monks who came to land on the coast of Cornwall in 891, wishing, as the Anglo-Saxon chronicler says, 'for the love of God to be on pilgrimage,

---

[14] Benedict almost certainly derived his classification, as he derived much else, from Cassian: in this case from *Conference xviii*, 'On the Three Sorts of Monks'. The aditional 'fourth sort', not provided by the Egyptian Father, is that of the *gyrovagus*. Although the date at which the Benedictine rule took final form is uncertain there is no doubt that the fourfold typology was part of the original sixth-century version and was central to the Benedictine conception of stability and discipline. While it is true that a number of alternatives to the Benedictine rule were in operation in Gaul in the seventh century what is significant for present purposes is the successful promotion of Benedictinism as the form of monasticism peculiarly associated with the Roman see, most specially through the public approbation accorded to St. Benedict by Pope Gregory the Great in his *Dialogue II*. Cassian's *Conference xviii* and *The Rule of St. Benedict* are reproduced in translation in Owen Chadwick, *Western Asceticism* (The Library of Christian Classics 12, London, 1958).

[15] The theme is especially prominent in Columban hagiography: the Irish *Life* opens with an excursus designed to ground the ideal in scripture, Whitley Stokes (ed. and transl.), *Lives of the Saints from the Book of Lismore* (Oxford, 1890), lines 655–1119. See also Kathleen Hughes, 'An Irish Litany of Pilgrim Saints compiled c. 800', *An Bol*, 77 (1959), p. 321; *idem*, 'The changing Theory and Practice of Irish Pilgrimage', *JEH* 11 (1960), pp. 143–51; E. G. Bowen, 'The Irish Sea in the Age of Saints', *Studia Celtica*, 4 (1960), pp. 56–71; T. M. Charles-Edwards, 'The Social Background to Irish Peregrinatio', *Celtica*, 11 (1976), pp. 43–59.

they cared not whither'.[16] The second, to avoid a common reductionism, is that while the spirituality of the *peregrinatio* subsumed the missionary impulse, it comprehended the full range of apostolates in which the spiritual energies of the Irish monks found an outlet: the trek of the missionaries into darkest Europe; the retreat of the anchorites into the wilderness in search of solitude; the tramping of evangelists and pastors along the highways and byways of Ireland and Celtic Scotland.[17] A final comment concerns the biblical resonance, yet again, of the Celtic perception—found in the lifestyle of Jesus and of the Old Testament prophets, and in St Paul's ascetic ideal of the *hospes mundi*—none of which was lost on Irish monastic commentators.[18] The compelling force of the *peregrinatio*, therefore, as an ideal and a practice provides a graphic illustration of the inspirational character of Early Irish spirituality and of the antithetical implications of such an outlook in relation to the monastic culture of Western Christendom. By way of reinforcing those points it must suffice simply to note, before moving on, two other manifestations of the inspirational style of the Irish monastic movement. One is the monastic rules that it generated, principally that of St Columbanus: much concerned to inculcate the spirit; less concerned with the practical details; selective in their treatment and unsystematic; utterly removed from the sober, practical, and comprehensive code elaborated by the institutionally-minded St Benedict.[19] The second is the physical disposition of the Irish monastic sites: weakly delineated, randomly ordered, pluriform—usually possessing more than one chapel—quasi-anchoritic, with proliferating beehive cells, altogether an affront to the formality, order, and communality of the Benedictine foundations—and altogether a delight to the latter-day romantic.[20] A revealing throwaway comment by St Columbanus may serve as an

---

[16] Quoted in Hughes, 'Irish Pilgrimage', p. 143.

[17] A sketch of the Celtic itinerant apostolate in action is provided by Bede in his account of St Aidan's apostolate in the north of England, *Ecclesiastical History*, III. v.

[18] For a general discussion of pilgrimage see *Catholic Encyclopaedia*.

[19] e.g. *Regula Monachorum* in *Sancti Columbani Opera*, ed. and transl. G. S. M. Walker (Dublin, 1957), pp. 122–42; 'Rule of Ailbe', ed. J. O'Neill, *Eriú*, 3 (1907), pp. 92–115; 'The Teaching of Máel-Ruain', ed. E. J. Gwynn, *Hermathena*, 44 (2nd supp. vol., 1927), pp. 1–63; 'Rule of the Célí Dé' in *ibid.*, pp. 64–87; John Ryan, *Irish Monasticism* (Dublin, 1931), section III, *passim*. Apropos Hughes comments: 'Irish monasticism had diverged from the common stock before the Benedictine rule spread, and it is more enlightening to compare it with the very early monasticism of the desert; its asceticism, variety of practice and absence of clear legislation are all similar', *Sources*, p. 90.

[20] However, a recent study convincingly discerns a basic pattern beneath the apparent jumble: Michael Herrity, 'The layout of Irish early Christian monasteries', *Irland und Europa*, pp. 105–116.

epilogue to the foregoing discussion which has sought to relate the anti-thesis between the institutional and inspirational perceptions of Latin and Celtic Christianity to the forms of monastic culture generated in the two regions. Defending the spontaneous, free-floating style of one of his lengthy letters to the brethren Columbanus remarks, *'amor non tenet ordinem'*.[21]

Moving on from a consideration of the inspirational to the transcend-ental quality of Celtic spirituality, the topic of Early Christian Ireland's ascetic tradition presents itself. Here the embarrassing prospect of an Irish heresy must be confronted. The subject may be approached by way of an idiosyncrasy of the Irish monastic schools. This was their attachment to the literal-historical method of biblical exegesis long after it had been ousted elsewhere in the West by the spiritual-allegorical method favoured by St Augustine.[22] Heretical implications arise here because the Irish literal-historical tradition of biblical commentary fed off an earlier one derived directly from St Augustine's great opponent Pelagius. And it is sig-nificant also that the one philosopher-theologian of genius to emerge from early medieval Ireland, John Scotus (Eriugena), displayed the kind of theological concerns—the freedom of the will, the universality of grace—that serve to situate him towards the Pelagian end of the spectrum over against St Augustine.[23] Nevertheless, the Pelagian strain in Early Irish Christianity has not to do with doctrinal heterodoxy. True, Scotus's sys-tem was to be condemned centuries after his death, but not on the grounds of Pelagianism. And the exegetes of the Irish monastic schools displayed little interest in such doctrinal refinements. On the contrary, their interest in the Pelagian tradition of biblical commentary arose from the fact that the literal-historical method lent itself to the exposition of scripture as *ascesis*, i.e. concerned with holiness of life, rather than as *gnosis*, i.e.

---

[21] *Sancti Columbani Opera*, p. 34 l. 33 (Epistola III).

[22] Martin McNamara, 'Tradition and Creativity in Early Irish Psalter Study', *Irland und Europa*, pp. 338–89; Joseph F. Kelly, 'Pelagius, Pelagianism and the Early Christian Irish', *Mediaevalia*, 6 (1978), 99–124; idem, 'The Hiberno-Latin Study of the Gospel of Luke', in Martin McNamara (ed.), *Biblical Studies: The Medieval Irish Contribution*, pp. 10–29; Brian Grogan, 'Eschatological Teaching of the Early Irish Church', in *ibid.*, pp. 46–58.

[23] Kelly, 'Pelagius, Pelagianism and the Early Christian Irish' which stresses the non-theological nature of the Irish interest in Pelagius. Despite his different concerns Kelly's findings seem to corroborate the view expressed here of the source of Irish interest in Pelagius. His analysis highlights the idiosyncrasy of the Early Irish exegetical tradition in relation to the Latin main-stream, arising significantly, in part from a preference for St Matthew and the Catholic epistles over against St Paul, Kelly, 'Hiberno-Latin Theology', in Heinz Löwe (ed.), *Die Iren und Europa in frühen Mittelalter*, 2 (Stuttgart, 1982), pp. 549–67. For Eriugena see John J. O'Meara, *Eriugena* (Dublin, 1969); ed. John J. O'Meara and Ludwig Bieler, *The Mind of Eriugena* (Dublin, 1973).

concerned with spiritual mysteries, the approach to which the spiritual-allegorical method lent itself.[24] Here, indeed, lies the key to the nature of the Irish heresy. It was not concerned with soteriology as such, with the debate about the relationship between saving grace and human free will that so exercised Pelagius and St Augustine. Irish heterodoxy lay in the realm of praxis, not of doctrine. Specifically it concerned the practice of Christian holiness. And it is here that the transcendental element in Early Irish spirituality manifests itself.

Consideration of this question returns the discussion to the original antithesis between the real and the hagiographical Patrick, in particular to the contrast between the saint's humble avowal of ignorance and sinfulness and the angelic personality attributed to him as National Apostle. Behind that contrast may be glimpsed the different perceptions of sanctity that informed the writings of Patrick and of his early biographers. Of the former little need be said. As earlier suggested, Patrick's attitude reflects the familiar Hellenic-Neoplatonic notion of sanctity as an inner moral transformation, the attainment of a state of perfect virtue (justice) and truth (wisdom).[24] To recover the contrasting Celtic pereception the task is to identify the conventions of the hagiographical literature through which its ideal of holiness are conveyed. In this regard an initial negative point may help to clear the way. It concerns the lack of sensitivity which the *genre* displays to the Hellenic moral ideal. The Celtic saints behave no better in this regard than the holy men of the Old Testament: they are frequently irascible, sometimes violent, and not above deceit. Their holiness, therefore, as depicted in the hagiography, is established by others means. Two principal conventions are involved. One is the device of epiphanies. Through these the veil is lifted on the outward reality to reveal its spiritual significance. The relevant feature of the convention for present purposes is the way in which the tropes that are utilized transform human sanctity into an angelic state. Thus the monastic settlements, sanctified by the presence of holy people, are depicted as teeming with holy angels instead:

> For this do I love Derry,
> It is gentle; it is bright;
> And hosts of angels fill it
> From head to end.[25]

---

[24] Above, note 9. In the formation of a Hellenic-Christian ideal of holiness the spiritual teaching of the early third century Fathers, Clement of Alexandria and Origen, was especially influential, on whom see Henry Chadwick, *Early Christian Thought*, pp. 31–94.

[25] W. Reeves (ed.), *The Life of St. Columba* (Dublin, 1857), Bk. III, *passim*.

And in describing the epiphanies of individual saints the corporeal being is transformed into an angelic presence, radiating ethereal light: the darkened monastic chapel is suffused with brightness as the saint enters to keep the night vigil—a scene classically represented in Adamnān's poignant account of Columcille's death.[26] The second convention provides a dramatic contrast. Its purpose is to portray holiness as visibly embodied in the person of the saint. It does so by depicting an emaciated and lacerated ascetic. The feature that needs to be emphasized in this regard is the extremity of the ascetic regime that is endorsed by means of a sometimes whimsical hyperbole. The Celtic saint, according to the hagiography, does not simply fast, pray, keep vigil, and discipline the flesh. He observes a total fast from food or drink throughout the whole of the three periods of Lent; he prays for so long with outstretched arms that the birds come and nest in his hands; he keeps vigil standing up to his neck in ice-cold water, and when he sleeps he does so on the bare earth with a stone for a pillow; he wears chains that bite into his flesh and produce suppurating sores. To dismiss such tropes as hagiographical histrionics and nothing more would be to miss the point. They reflect an ascetical ideal that is far removed from the balanced discipline approved by Latin orthodoxy but amply attested elsewhere on the desert fringes of Hellenic Christianity and aptly described as a 'ritual of desolidarization'.[27] By means of these two conventions, therefore, the hagiography provides a statement in counterpoint of the Celtic

---

[26] *Ibid.*, Bk. III, cap. 23.

[27] For examples of the hagiography see Whitley Stokes (ed.), *Lives of the Saints from the Book of Lismore* (Oxford, 1890); ed. C. Plummer, *Vitae Sanctorum Hiberniae*, 2 vols (Oxford, 1910); ed. W. W. Heist, *Vitae Sanctorum Hiberniae* (Brussels, 1965). For commentary see Robin Flower, *The Irish Tradition* (Oxford, 1947), pp. 24–66; Hughes, *Sources*, pp. 219–47. A recent writer suggests that the stress on radical austerity does not enter the hagiography until the eleventh and twelfth centuries: Peter O'Dwyer, *Céli Dé: Spiritual Reform in Ireland 750–900* (Dublin, 1981), p. 60. This is simply not in accordance with the facts. It is, indeed, the case that *one* tradition within the 'culdee' movement of reform represents a reaction against severe asceticism but the evidence points at the same time to a tradition within the reform movement which endorses the radical ascetic ideal, *ibid.*, pp. 68–80, 108–11. Cf. Pádraig Ó Fiannachta, 'The Spirituality of the Céilí Dé', in Michael Maher (ed.), *Irish Spirituality* (Dublin, 1982), pp. 22–32. On the asceticism of the Christian East see Peter Brown, *Society and the Holy in Late Antiquity* (London, 1982), pp. 103–52, 166–95 (the phrase 'ritual of desolidarization' occurs on p. 181). On the moderating influence of Hellenism on (eastern) biblical asceticism—a process in which the teaching of Clement of Alexandria and Origen is once more vital—see J. A. McGuckin, 'Christian Asceticism and the Early School of Alexandria', *SCH* 22 (1985), pp. 25–39; for an illuminating case-study of the conflict between Celtic and Hellenic ascetic ideals in the context of a conflict between Celtic and Benedictine monasticism see Julia M. H. Smith, 'Celtic Asceticism and Carolingian Authority in Early medieval Brittany', *SCH* 22, pp. 53–63. On the opposition of Orthodoxy to Eastern asceticism see Frend, *The Rise of Christianity*, pp. 252–6.

perception of holiness: an ascetical transformation, culminating in a state of angelic perfection in which the spirit utterly transcends the claims of the flesh.

The impact of this transcendent perception on the devotional life of the Early Irish Church may now finally be considered. The first point in this regard serves to resume the topic that initiated the discussion, the Pelagian strain in Early Irish Christianity. Further classification of its significance is now possible. Earlier its lack of doctrinal implications was emphasized and it was associated instead with Pelagianism as praxis, with the emphasis of Pelagian biblical exegesis upon the radical demands of the evangelical way of life.[28] However, a distinction between the two must be drawn at that level also. In its obsessions with moral perfectionism the Pelagian heresy of good works constituted a characteristically Hellenic heterodoxy. It will now be clear that moral perfection was not the Celtic obsession. By reason of its ascetical orientation, therefore, the Celtic heresy of good works constitutes a unique deviation from Latin orthodoxy. It remains to note the evidence of this ascetic orientation in the forms of piety that developed within Early Irish Christianity. Three dominant themes may be singled out here which indicate the pervasiveness of the ascetic ideal and which also hold a special long-term significance. One is the theme of sacrifice associated in Celtic spirituality with the central Christian mystery: the devotional literature presents Christ as a hero who did not flinch from the ordeal of personal destruction to save his people—the emphasis is on heroic suffering rather than on atonement or resurrection; and Eucharistic devotion revolves upon Christ's act of self-immolation—the Irish word for the Eucharistic liturgy derives from *offerendum*, i.e. *aifreann*.[29] The second is the related theme of martyrdom. Significantly, Early Irish Christianity failed to generate a cult of martyrs as such: it had no martyrs to boast of itself, and the Roman cult failed to catch on for reasons that are, perhaps, beginning to become clear. Its cult of martyrdom, therefore, represents the attempt of the Celtic Church to develop a spirituality—or spiritual ideology—in which this supreme act of sacrifice could be set before the Celtic Christian as a practicable ideal: thus the threefold typology of martyrdom on which the cult hinged, viz. red martyrdom which is to shed one's blood for Christ; white martyrdom which is to undertake the self-immolation of the ascetic life; *glas* (blue) martyrdom which is the

---

[28] Above, pp. 9–10.
[29] W. Godel, 'Irisches Beten im frühen Mittelalten', *Zeitschrift für katolische Theologie*, 85 (1963), pp. 61–321, 389–439; in English translation in *Milltown Studies*, 4 (1979), 60–99.

mortified state of the penitent.[30] The third theme is that of penance, more especially the mortification required of the repentant sinner in accordance with the system of the Irish Penitentials.[31] The impress of the ascetic ideal is obvious here in the notorious prescriptions of the *Penitentials* — forty days on bread and water for the lesser sins of thought. More interestingly, perhaps, if less obviously, the ascetic bias can also be seen in the discussion of the vices: avarice, the obverse of justice, is given relatively short shrift; lust, the obverse of virginity, is dealt with in excruciating detail, from childish obscenities to the more exotic perversions—such, as one scandalized late Victorian protested, as might have 'dimly floated through our minds in our darkest moments'.[32] In these three themes of sacrifice, martyrdom, and penance the ascetic ideal of Early Irish Christianity finds its most potent expression. They pervade its devotional literature and practice, lending them a stark, heroic bleakness that is often remarked upon. Nevertheless the picture needs to be balanced since the starkness was relieved by an attractively humane, if not quite humanistic, current which is equally often remarked upon. Attention must, therefore, be drawn to that aspect in conclusion.

The more humane aspect of the Celtic ascetic tradition reveals itself in three main features. One is in pastoral practice, represented, as it happens, by the penitential system. Even though, as already noted, the system has acquired notoriety as the embodiment of the severe Celtic penitential ideal, it also provides a landmark in the development of a compassionate pastoral approach towards personal sin in the Latin West. This was by means of the practice of 'commutation' through which a substantial reduction of the prescribed penance could be obtained by recourse to a holy ascetic as *anamchara* (soul-friend) with a view to restoration to sacramental communion—the practice of private confession was to be the permanent legacy of the Irish penitential system to the Western Church.[33] Secondly, Celtic asceticism was humanized by a strongly affective

---

[30] See Clare Stancliffe, 'Red, White and Blue Martyrdom', in *Hughes Studies*, pp. 21–46. Stancliffe convincingly elucidates the tricolour typology as a distinctively Irish development, which drew upon Patristic ascetic theology. The author makes out a good case for translating the third of the colour terms, *glas*, as blue in this instance rather than the more usual green. A good case can also be made out for grey but the word seems strictly untranslateable.

[31] L. Bieler (ed. and transl.), *The Irish Penitentials* (Dublin, 1963); ed. D. Binchy, 'The Old-Irish Table of Penitential Commutations', *Ériu*, 19 (1962), 47–72. For commentary see Hughes, *Sources*, pp. 82–9.

[32] Quoted Hughes, *Sources*, p. 84.

[33] *Ibid.*, pp. 82–9; O'Dwyer, *Céli Dé*, pp. 90–5; Ó Fiannachta, 'The Spirituality of the Céili Dé', pp. 22–32 at pp. 27–9.

devotional current. Its cult of the feminine provides a remarkable example of this, focussed on devotion to Mary and to a number of native monastic foundresses through whom the feminine attributes—mercy, tenderness, motherhood—were affirmed; St Ita is depicted suckling the infant Jesus in her hermitage in one well-known devotional poem.[34] Another, no less remarkable, expression of ascetic affective devotion is found in the celebration of nature. The ascetic's delight in the beauty of physical creation and in communion with the animal kingdom is expressed in a body of literature too voluminous and too well-known to be treated here, except to emphasize the novelty of such sensibilities at this period in the devotional history of the Christian West—Franciscanism several centuries before St Francis, in fact.[35] The third humanizing feature of the tradition is its saving grace of wit. Clearly the Celtic monks found the notion of holy folly a highly congenial one: one literary trope associates the holy man with the madman as companion and *alter ego*. [36] And the comic perspective keeps breaking through elsewhere: in the hagiography in recurring irony reminiscent of the saga literature, and in the imaginative buffoonery of the voyage tales;[37] in the visual arts in the animal caricatures and in the cartoons inserted unobtrusively among the abstract decorative motifs, as, for instance, in the Chi Rho initial, which constitutes one of the glories of the Book of Kells and which contains a cartoon half hidden in its base depicting two mice engaged in a tug-o'-war with an altar bread to a gallery of two mild-looking cats each carrying another mouse on its back. The distinctiveness of the Celtic ascetic tradition lies, therefore, not only in the extremity of the ascetic ideal which it affirms but also in the disposition which it reveals to aspire towards an asceticism with a human face.

* * *

The third and final contrast between Celtic and Latin spirituality hinges on the charismatic quality of Early Irish Christianity. It brings to

---

[34] Hughes, *Sources*, pp. 226–9, 232–4. The poem is reproduced in Gerard Murphy (ed. and transl.), *Early Irish Lyrics* (Oxford, 1957), pp. 26–9; Peter O'Dwyer, *Devotion to Mary in Ireland, 700–1100* (Dublin, 1976).

[35] Flower, *The Irish Tradition*, pp. 42–66; O'Dwyer, *Céli Dé*, pp. 184–91; Myles Dillon, 'Early Lyric Poetry' in James Carney (ed.), *Early Irish Poetry* (Dublin, 1969); Gerard Murphy, *Early Irish Lyrics*, pp. xiii–xx.

[36] Flower, *The Irish Tradition*, pp. 63–7.

[37] Hughes, *Sources*, pp. 210–16; Myles Dillon and Nora K. Chadwick, *The Celtic Realms* (London, 1967), pp. 188–96. The most famous example of the *genre* is, of course, *Navigatio Sancti Brendani Abbatis*, ed. C. Selmer (Notre Dame, 1959).

the fore an aspect of that spiritual culture implicit in much of the discussion so far, the cult of the saints. The point of the contrast does not lie, of course, in the absence of a saintly cult in Latin orthodoxy: the rise of such a cult represents, in fact, one of the most striking aspects of the transition of the Christian West from Late Antiquity to the early medieval period.[38] The point lies rather in differences which a comparison of the two cults reveals, and more especially in the implications of such differences for the phenomenon with which the cult of the saints was closely associated, the manifestation of miraculous power. In the latter regard three contrasting features have special significance. One relates to the sanctoral canon, the criterion which gave admission to the ranks of the saints. The contrast here is between Celtic ascetics and Latin martyrs, in effect, between a cult of living saints and one of dead saints. Martyrs required neither *vita* nor *gesta* to authenticate their claims: what mattered was death for the faith—their saintly careers were entirely posthumous affairs.[39] The second contrast arises in regard to the respective calendars or rolls of the saints. Comparison of these reveals a striking asymmetry in regard to what might be called saintly demography. The effect of the cult in Ireland was to produce a proliferation of local saints, a veritable population explosion, giving rise to the sobriquet of the *insula sanctorum* much vaunted ever since. The effect of the cult in Europe by contrast was gradually to obliterate the memory of local saints in favour of a colonial elite of Roman martyrs. The rise of the cult, therefore, was accompanied paradoxically by a contraction of the saintly population.[40] The key to the strategy was the device of relics. By the translation and dissemination of these a martyr elite were able to colonize a very wide territory indeed, from Rome to westernmost Gaul,[41] but not, significantly, to Ireland where the

---

[38] The subject has been illuminatingly analysed from the perspective of religious anthropology in two works by Peter Brown. *The Cult of the Saints* (London, 1981); *idem*, *Society and the Holy in Late Antiquity* (London, 1982). What follows is much indebted to these works.

[39] Brown, *The Cult of the Saints*, pp. 69–85. A fascinating sidelight on the situation depicted by Brown is provided by the early history of the monastery of Redon on the Breton border to which the dissertation of Caroline Brett has recently drawn attention, 'The Monks of Redon in Ninth Century Brittany: *Gesta Sanctorum Rotonensium* and *Vita Conuuoionis*' (Cambridge PhD. thesis, 1986). The prize relic procured by the monastery was the body of St Marcellinus, pope and martyr, about whose life nothing was then or is now known!

[40] Brown, *Society and the Holy*, pp. 166–95, esp. 178 seq. The effect of the arrival of the relics of Pope Marcellinus at Redon was to oust the cult of Bishop Hypotemius, whose body had earlier been stolen by the monks from his patronal church at Angers. Commenting on both episodes Dr Brett remarks on Redon's 'lack of confidence in the native saints of Brittany', p. 387.

[41] The advent of Marcellinus at Redon highlights the pervasiveness not only of the cult of relics but specifically the cult of the Roman martyrs. The rise of the relic cult in Late Antique Gaul is analysed in Van Dam, *Leadership and Community*, pt IV.

saints remained tenaciously native and local.[42] The third contrast relates to the saints' shrines, the centres of the cult. The difference here has to do with ways of establishing the credentials of the shrine as an authentic *locus* of the saint's presence. In Ireland the shrine was authenticated by recourse to local tradition associating the place with the life of the saint, e.g. a well where the saint had reputedly baptized, a retreat where reputedly divine visitations had been vouchsafed, and so on. At Latin shrines, in contrast, the method was to provide a material sign of the saint's spiritual presence in the form of his corporeal remains or other relics—any association of the living saint with the place was quite irrelevant.[43]

It remains to consider the significance of all of this for the function which the cult was ultimately intended to serve, the attraction of saintly patronage in the solicitation of benefits from on high. Here the key lies in a more fundamental contrast to which those just elaborated point: the contrast between an ecclesiastically ordered Latin cult and a popular Celtic one. The rise of the martyrs bears the signs of a clerical bid for jurisdiction over the area of miraculous power. The martyrs were peculiarly susceptible to ecclesiastical management both on ideological grounds—their deaths testifying to the truth of the Church—and for the practical reason that the hierarchy generally gained possession of their tombs.[44] The martyrs' relics were, therefore, at the Church's disposal and were, in fact, disseminated by means of a network of ecclesiastical patronage. Not surprisingly, in the circumstances, the shrines associated with the cult were invariably located at major ecclesiastical centres, cathedrals, basilicas, abbey churches.[45] The Celtic cult on the other hand remained in popular lay control: based on popular esteem for the ascetic life; dependent on popular tradition rather than on ecclesiastical management for its

---

[42] It is clear that while Ireland was influenced by the relic cult as it pertained to local saints, the cult of the Roman martyrs made very little impact. Dr Richard Sharpe has analysed what looks to have been the crucial episode in the attempt to introduce the classic cult of the Roman martyrs to Ireland, i.e. as a strategy for promoting the jurisidictional hegemony of the church that possessed the martyrs' relics. He shows that the attempt to assert a metropolitan primacy for Armagh by the introduction of Roman relics late in the seventh century was abortive. Armagh soon reverted to the traditional claim of a Patrician *paruchia* comprehending all Ireland, i.e. a claim based on a special association with the career of St Patrick rather than on the possession of relics. In fact Armagh did not possess the relics of St Patrick; its claims to a Patrician *paruchia* were based on tradition: Sharpe, 'Armagh and Rome in the Seventh Century', *Irland und Europa*, pp. 58–72. Cf. Charles Doherty, 'The use of Relics in Early Christian Ireland', *ibid.*, pp. 89–101.

[43] Brown, *The Cult of the Saints*, pp. 86–104.

[44] *Ibid.*, pp. 23–49.

[45] *Ibid.*, pp. 86–127. Cf. Van Dam, *Leadership and Community*, pp. 230–55.

dissemination; focussed on the local country-side and on non-ecclesiastical centres as its physical location. This contrast, it will be clear, was reflected yet again in the processes whereby saintly patronage was obtained. In short, by means of the martyr cult the Latin Church was enabled to constitute itself as mediator between the saint and his client and, thereby, as the immediate, terrestrial mediator of miraculous power. As in the dispensation of grace the hierarchy assumed the function of custodian of the heavenly keys. In Early Christian Ireland, in contrast, miraculous power remained a charismatic gift, dispensed at a multitude of rural shrines by means of immediate and direct interaction between sainted ascetics and their local clients.

*   *   *

In case the foregoing lengthy excursus on Celtic spirituality has obscured the wood for the trees a summary sketch of the wood may be useful before proceeding. Two themes have shaped the discussion. One is the correspondence that can be discerned between the specific content of the spiritual culture—the ideals which it articulates and the practices in which they are embodied—and the religious outlook reflected in the Patrician hagiography, which has been earlier epitomized as inspirational, transcendental, and charismatic in nature. The effect of the demonstration has been to throw three distinctive features of Celtic spirituality into high relief: firstly, the monastic movement as manifesting the Celtic inspirational approach to religion in its spontaneity, improvidence, and, above all, in its predilection for pilgrimage;[46] secondly, Celtic ascetic piety as reflecting the transcendental orientation of Celtic religion in its aspiration towards the spiritualization of the flesh through sacrifice, martyrdom (holiness of life), and penance;[47] finally, the cult of the saints as reflecting the charismatic quality of Celtic religion in its popular, traditional, and local orientation.[48] The second shaping theme has been the contrast which precisely these features highlight between Celtic spirituality and the religious culture of Latin Orthodoxy. Thus the inspirational ethos of Celtic monasticism is set off against the institutional ideology of the Benedictine rule with its passion for discipline, order, and stability.[49]

[46] Above pp. 6–9.
[47] Above pp. 9–13.
[48] Above pp. 14–17.
[49] Above pp. 2–6.

Similarly, the transcendent Celtic perception of Christian holiness, as a state of ascetic perfection, contrasts with the philosophized Latin perception directed towards moral virtue.[50] Finally, the charismatic Celtic cult of the saints, focussed upon a proliferating population of wonder-working ascetics, is at odds with the sacramentalized Latin cult, Church-centred, mediated through the hierarchy, and focussed upon the relics of the Roman martyrs.[51] Set over against the spirituality of Latin orthodoxy, therefore, the spirituality of Early Christian Ireland constitutes a highly idiosyncratic *scala perfectionis.*

III

To complete this comparative analysis a fourth point of contrast between Celtic Christianity and Latin Orthodoxy remains to be considered. It relates to the cultural effervescence which in Ireland accompanied the process of Christianization. The contrast here derives from two remarkable aspects of Ireland's reception of Latin Christianity. One is the success with which Celtic society resisted acculturation on coming within the ambience of the Latin Church. The other is the creative vitality with which, nevertheless, it responded to the experience. Contrary to what is sometimes supposed, the cultural distinctiveness of Early Christian Ireland does not constitute a measure of its adherence to an inveterate paganism. Rather it reflects the success of Celtic society in adopting a Christian mould without abandoning the native culture or hiding it in remote fastnesses, as occurred elsewhere in Northern Europe in face of the advance of the indomitable Latin-Christian alliance.[52] Herein lies the achievement that has won for early medieval Ireland the title of a Golden Age.

As the process of Christianization advanced a creative interaction can be observed taking place across the entire cultural range between the civilization of the Latin West and the barbaric Celtic cultural tradition. Probably the most spectacular example is provided by the cross-fertilization of the Celtic (La Tène) and various Latin-Christian styles to produce Early Christian Ireland's unique artistic tradition in manuscript illumination, in metal-work, in monumental sculpture and, when finally the Irish took to building in stone, in Romanesque architecture.[53] Less well known,

---

[50] Above pp. 3–5.
[51] Above pp. 14–17.
[52] Brown, *Cult of the Saints*, pp. 113–27.
[53] Françoise Henry, *Irish Art in the Early Christian Period to AD 800* (London, 1965), *idem*, *Irish Art during the Viking invasions, 800–1020 AD* (London, 1967); *idem*, *Irish Art in the Romanesque Period, 1020–1170 AD* (London, 1970); Hughes, *Sources*, pp. 259–63.

perhaps, but ultimately more revealing and significant is the achievement in the field of literature. Christianity brought literacy to Ireland but the literary culture developed in the Irish monastic schools was an emphatically native produce—even the script was distinctively Celtic.[54] Two features of the literary culture have a special relevance. One is the assimilation and, thereby, the preservation of the ancient pagan oral lore: the data of Celtic pseudo-history and genealogy were moulded to harmonize with the Judaeo-Christian scheme, providing, in effect, a 'second stream'— or, at least, a tributary—of salvation history, in the manner of the Greek Fathers' baptism of Hellenic philosophy.[55] The second feature is the baptism of the vernacular by its use as the medium of a Christian literature—a development with which it was to take the Latin West half a millennium to catch up. Vernacular *genres* of hagiography and of Christian narrative tales—voyages and visions—were vigorously cultivated.[56] But the crowning achievement was a religious lyric poetry, unique at this period in the keen sensitivity it displays to the world of nature.[57] A final sphere of creative interaction was the domain of learning. What was remarkable in this regard was firstly the survival of the ancient druidic caste as the desacralized custodians of the native scholarly heritage: as such providing a tradition of lay scholarship unique in the Christian West where learning became a clerical monopoly, a tradition all the more remarkable for having developed by means of clerical sponsorship—as the legend of Columcille's dramatic intervention at the Convention of Drom Ceatt must at least be taken to indicate.[58] Turning to the Celtic tradition of Christian scholarship itself, its distinctiveness appears in two features. One, earlier remarked upon, is the predilection of Celtic scholars for the literal-historical method of biblical exegesis, against the tide in favour of the spiritual-allegorical method which set elsewhere in the West under

---

[54] Timothy O'Neill, *The Irish Hand, Scribes and their Manuscripts from the Earliest Times to the Seventeenth Century* (Portlaoise, 1984).

[55] James Carney, 'The Impact of Christianity', in Myles Dillon (ed.), *Early Irish Society* (Dublin, 1954), pp. 66–78; M. A. O'Brien, 'Irish Origin-Legends', *ibid.*, pp. 36–51; D. A. Binchey, 'The Background of Early Irish Literature', *Studies*, 50 (1961), pp. 1–18. Cf. Máire Herbert, 'The Irish *Sex Aetates Mundi*: First Editions', *Cambridge Medieval Celtic Studies*, 11 (1986), pp. 97–112.

[56] Hughes, *Sources*, pp. 210–16, 219–47. See also n. 37 above. An incidental illustration of the strength of the vernacular is provided by the increasing use of Irish in monastic chronicles over the early medieval period to an extent that substantially anticipates the *Anglo-Saxon Chronicle* which has been regarded as a unique specimen of vernacular usage in Western Europe: David Dumville, 'Latin and Irish in the Annals of Ulster, AD 431–1050', *Hughes Studies*, pp. 320–41.

[57] Above, note 35.

[58] Hughes, *Sources*, pp. 77–8, 165–6.

the influence of St Augustine.[59] The other is the striking absence of a school of philosophical theology. True, Celtic Christianity can boast one philosopher of consummate genius, John Scotus (fl. 815–75), hailed as 'the most considerable philosopher in the West between Augustine and Thomas Aquinas'.[60] But his lonely eminence serves only to emphasize the absence of a Celtic philosophical-theological tradition with which he might be associated. No doubt, as the venerable legend of '*oileān na naomh is na n-ollamh*' asserts, Early Christian Ireland teemed with scholars, as it teemed with saints, but the scholars were manuscript copyists, rhetoricians, computists, skilled in Latin, and biblical exegetes; they were not, in any serious way, philosophers or theologians.[61]

IV

On this note of apparent anti-climax the extended comparison of Latin and Celtic Christianity which is our main concern must come to a close. It will be clear from the context, of course, that the anti-climax is more apparent than real. In the light of the cultural and intellectual effervescence just described the absence of a Celtic tradition of philosophical theology leaves the glow of the Golden Age undimmed. Precisely for that reason, however, the lacuna seems all the more worthy of attention. It raises in a particularly useful way the questions to which this study must finally and briefly proceed; how are the idiosyncrasies of early Irish Christianity to be explained and what is their long-term significance?

As to how the oddities of Celtic religion are to be explained, the value of raising that question in the context of the particular case just mentioned is that it serves to expose the superficiality of a two-tier cultural model

---

[59] Above pp. 9–10.

[60] On Eriugena see above, note 23. The assessment of Eriugena's significance is in O'Meara, *Eriugena*, p. vii.

[61] This is incidentally illustrated by the omission of any discussion of philosophical or theological activities from even the most competent surveys of Early Irish Christian scholarship, e.g. Brian Ó Cuív (ed.), *Seven Centuries of Irish Learning, 1000–17000* (Cork, 1971); Hughes, *The Church in Early Irish Society*, cap. 21; *idem*, *Sources*, *passim*. One recent scholar does indeed speak of a tradition of 'Hiberno-Latin theology' but the reference is to the cultivation of biblical studies: Joseph F. Kelly, 'Hiberno-Latin Theology', in Heinz Löwe (ed.), *Die Iren und Europa im frühen Mittelalter* (Stuttgart, 1982), pp. 549–67. Kelly, in fact, characterizes the approach of the Irish monastic schools to biblical exegesis as 'non-speculative'. Elsewhere it is characterized as 'imaginative': Robert E. McNally, 'The Imagination and Early Irish Biblical Exegesis', *Annuale Mediaevalia*, 10 (1969), pp. 5–27. The juxtaposition of 'non-speculative' and 'imaginative' highlights an important quality of the cast of mind reflected in the intellectual tradition of Early Christian Ireland.

often assumed to apply to discrepancies between the ethos of Irish society and that of the European mainstream. This explains cultural differences in terms of lag and retarded development in Ireland in view of the island's geographical location on the remote European fringe.[62] Patently such an explanation does not apply in the present case: the interest of the lacuna is that it occurs amidst abundant evidence of cultural vitality and sophistication. Significantly, the puzzle becomes susceptible to a more positive explanation by abandoning the two-tier model and taking the comparison to highlight a characteristic feature of an indigenous Celtic culture: its predilection for concrete and imaginative modes of thought—and, hence, for historical and literary modes of expression—as against abstract, speculative reflection.[63] The question arises, therefore, as to whether the idiosyncracies of Early Irish Christianity are to be explained as features of a distinctive Christian culture or as 'popular', that is to say primitive and debased, forms of Latin Christianity. It remains to press the claims of the former.

Here it is necessary to return *ad fontes*, to the circumstances which conditioned the reception of the Christian religion in early medieval Ireland. In this respect two factors, long recognized as influential, now emerge as crucially determinative in the light of interpretative insights gained from social anthropology. One has to do with the fact that the dissemination of Christianity in Ireland was neither preceded by nor accompanied by a Roman conquest: by exception in Western Europe the island remained beyond the long reach of the Roman imperial system. The implications of this circumstance can now be better understood by reference to recent work which brilliantly demonstrates the extent to which Latin Christianity presupposed a process of socialization within the socio-political system of Roman Late Antiquity.[64] Lacking the experience of Romanization Irish society lacked the social moulds and the mental frame of reference to which Latin Christianity was relevant, and which, indeed, provided the cultural infrastructure on which it was established. Two closely related consequences follow. The cultural environment of early medieval Ireland

---

[62] For a devastating critique of the two-tier model as a basis for the interpretation of the religious culture of Christianity see Brown, *The Cult of the Saints*, pp. 12–22; *idem*, *Society and the Holy*, caps 1–3.

[63] It may be added that the Judaeo-Christian scriptures for the most part reflect the same cast of thought.

[64] Brown, *The Cult of the Saints*, pp. 119–27 and *passim*. Brown's case is strengthened by recent work which demonstrates substantial continuity between the culture of Latin Late Antiquity and that of (barbaric) Early Medieval Europe: Pierre Riché, *Education and Culture in the Barbarian West*, transl. J. J. Contreni (Columbia, South Carolina, 1976).

did not provide conditions in which Latin Christianity could easily take root. By the same token, however, that environment was distinctly propitious to the de-Hellenization of the Christian Gospel. The other determining factor has to do with the decisive historical juncture at which the process of Christianization took place. This occurred just as the Goidelic (Q-Celtic) colonizers gained dominance over their rivals (P-Celts and Picts) and with it cultural hegemony.[65] The adoption of Christianity by the ruling kindreds of this vigorous and expanding society must ultimately explain its successful dissemination throughout the island and, at the same time, the transmutation of Latin Christianity into a distinctively Gaelic idiom—all of which, no doubt, explains, in turn, the remarkable fact that the process of conversion produced no martyrs. To say so much, of course, is merely to state a thesis. To demonstrate it would require undertaking in respect of Early Irish Christianity what has been so brilliantly achieved for the religious culture of Western Europe in the period of transmission between Late Antiquity and early medieval times:[66] an analysis of the way in which Christianity, by adapting itself to the social moulds and mental environment of a barbaric Celtic culture, was both itself transformed as well as precipitating a profound transformation of the indigenous culture. Such a project is beyond the scope of the present study. However, by drawing attention to the claims of Early Irish Christianity to be studied as a distinct cultural phenomenon, the study attempted here may serve to put the larger project on the historical agenda.

The long-term significance of the thesis just proposed must finally be pondered. Once again the failure of Early Irish Christianity to generate a school of philosophical theology provides an instructive starting point. That is because the same lacuna can be observed as a feature of Irish Christianity throughout its long history: occasional luminaries brighten the scene but the Irish contribution to Christian theology could scarcely be described as distinguished. An interesting perspective is thus provided on the question of continuity raised at the outset. The brunt of this essay argues—at least by implication—against two conceptions of a continuous Christian tradition in Ireland which were formulated in the polemical debates of the Reformation era: the one which forces Early Irish Christianity into the Roman mould; the other which presents it as a fore-runner of

---

[65] Gearóid MacNiocaill, *Ireland before the Vikings* (Dublin, 1972), caps 1–4; M. A. O'Brien, 'Irish Origin-Legends'.

[66] Brown, *The Cult of the Saints*, cap. 1 and *passim*; *idem*, *Society and the Holy*, esp. caps 1, 6, 8.

Protestantism. The effect of the case in point is to reopen the prospect of continuity by shifting the perspective from ecclesiology to that of religious culture. The question is to what extent was the course of Irish Christian history permanently conditioned by the circumstances and the nature of the original experience? Of course that question could be satisfactorily answered only by means of an analysis of the dynamics of Irish Christian history as it unfolded in the course of over fifteen centuries. Again here this essay will have served its purpose if it succeeds in placing the question on the historical agenda. Meanwhile, it is interesting to observe that at the two major turning points in the history of Western Christianity, the sixteenth century Reformation and the nineteenth century onset of secularization, the pattern of development in Ireland defied the trend elsewhere in Western Europe. How very Irish?

Queens' College, Cambridge

TRISTERNAGH PRIORY: THE ESTABLISHMENT OF A COLONIAL MONASTIC HOUSE IN THE LORDSHIP OF MEATH (c 1200)

by BRIAN EAGAR

THIS paper is concerned with the establishment of a monastic house in a recently colonized area by the lord responsible for the settlement of the land. The importance of the priory to the local economy will be examined in the forty years after its foundation, when settlement in the area was stabilizing and the initial flow of settlers appears to have stopped. The role of the monastery in the process of colonization will be studied and the priory considered as an instrument of colonization. The paper will also attempt to establish the nature of the relationship between the founder of the house and the priory in the latter's early years of existence.

The priory founded at Tristernagh at the end of the twelfth century was an Augustinian house, dedicated to the Blessed Virgin Mary. The Augustinians were not a new order introduced to Ireland as a result of the arrival of the Anglo-Normans after 1169. They had been introduced to the country as a result of the efforts of Saint Malachy, bishop of Armagh, in the 1140s. Many previously unreformed early Christian monasteries adopted the rule of Saint Augustine. The Gaelic rulers sponsored the reform of the Church by founding and patronizing monastic houses of the new continental orders, such as the Cistercians and Augustinians.[1]

The Augustinians were an attractive proposition for the Gaelic lords as they did not require large territorial grants as did the Cistercians. The same attraction was there for the Anglo-Norman lords, especially those who had not received large fiefs.[2] The Augustinian houses could be supported by the grants of tithes and churches. These did not affect the lord's ability to take full profit from his lands. The ecclesiastical revenues were not the lord's to exploit.

Both Gaelic and Anglo-Norman lords appear to have been anxious to support the Church and to secure their future after death by giving as generously as they could to religious houses. The foundation of a monastery was a

[1] John Watt, *The Church in medieval Ireland* (Dublin, 1972), pp. 19–22.
[2] C. A. Empey, 'The sacred and the secular: the Augustinian priory of Kells in Ossery, 1193–1541', *Irish Historical Studies*, 24 (1984), pp. 131–51.

particularly important undertaking and was likely to ensure for the lord the thanks and prayers of the monks both before and after his death. This generosity should not be seen as a cynical gesture. The lords and their tenants do seem to have been motivated by true religious feeling.[3] They made significant grants to the monastic houses and the social range of people that were involved in the granting of rights and land to the monasteries is perhaps an indication of the sincerity of the grantors.

The foundation of Tristernagh Priory

The exact date of the foundation of the Augustinian priory at Tristernagh is not known and the precise identity of its founder is unclear. The house appears to have been founded at the end of the twelfth century by a Geoffrey de Costentin. It seems likely that the founder was the son of the Geoffrey de Costentin who received a fief from Hugh de Lacy at the time of the initial subinfeudation of the lordship of Meath. The date of death of the first Geoffrey de Costentin is not known, but it seems unlikely that, since he was a grown man when he came to Ireland in the 1170s, he was still alive in 1232 when the death of a Geoffrey de Costentin is recorded.[4] The monastery was one of two Augustinian houses in modern County Westmeath. The priory was located on the west bank of Lough Iron, in the barony of Moygoish, and was about 16 kilometres north-east of an important settlement at Loughsewdy.[5] Very little of the fabric of the monastery has survived and what does remain appears to date from the fourteenth century.[6]

The priory was founded very shortly after the area was initially occupied in 1192. A motte was constructed at Kilbixy in that year. In Ireland, the establishment of such a military fortification has been seen to be evidence of the first serious attempt to occupy the area.[7] Clearly Geoffrey de Costentin was anxious to introduce the Augustinian order into the region and to see them established there. The order was particularly concerned with the development of the pastoral element of the areas that were put under its control.[8] The Anglo-Norman lords were very interested in

---

[3] *Registrum cartarum monasterii B.V. Mariae de Tristernagh . . . : register of the priory of . . . Tristernagh*, ed. M. V. Clarke (Irish Manuscripts Commission, Dublin, 1941), pt 1, no. 1.

[4] *Ibid.*, pp. vii–xi.

[5] G. H. Orpen, *Ireland under the Normans*, 4 vols (Oxford, 1911–20), 2, pp. 80–1, 88–9.

[6] H. G. Leask, *Irish Churches and Monastic buildings*, 3 vols (Dundalk, 1955–60), 2, p. 153.

[7] R. F. Frame, *Colonial Ireland, 1169–1369* (Dublin, 1981), pp. 72–3.

[8] C. H. Lawrence, *Medieval Monasticism* (London, 1984), pp. 140–2.

seeing the emergence of a parochial structure and the fact that this did not exist before 1159 gave the lords an extra incentive to patronize monastic houses.[9]

The lands, churches, and rights granted to the priory at Tristernagh were the result of the generosity of the founding lord and his tenants. One of the results of this was that the possessions of the priory mirrored, almost completely, the territorial extent of the de Costentin lordship. These possessions offer a glimpse of the extent of the territorial control of the Anglo-Normans in that part of the lordship of Meath which, at the time of the foundation of the priory, was beginning to see settlement by the new colonial population.

The founder

The de Costentin family came to Ireland from Bonby in Lincolnshire. They left England after their association with the unsuccessful revolt of the Earl of Chester and others.[10] By 1176 Geoffrey de Costentin was in Ireland and appears to have received his initial land grant from Richard fitz Gilbert de Clare (known as Strongbow), but within a year he had also received a grant from Hugh de Lacy, lord of Meath. These lands were to form the core of his Irish lands. They were located around Kilbixy and Rathconrath. A later confirmation by Hugh de Lacy's son, Walter, to Geoffrey de Costentin of this fief gave more detail. Geoffrey held 5 knights' fees in the fief of Kilbixy with the castle there and 15 knights' fees in the lands of Conmacne for the service of four knights. The nature of this grant, 20 knights' fees for the service of only four knights, is an indication of the frontier nature of the de Costentin fief.[11] Geoffrey also received more land at Balrothery near Dublin, in a more peaceful area.[12] By the end of the first quarter of the thirteenth century, Geoffrey, son of the original settler, was a man of considerable importance. He was the constable of the castles of Loughsewdy and *Inchelleffer* in the lordship of Meath until 1216 and in 1229 he was the keeper of the vacant and richest see in Ireland, the diocese of Dublin.[13]

[9] A. J. Otway-Ruthven, 'Parochial development in the rural deanery of Skreen', *JRSAI* 94 (1964), pp. 111–22.
[10] *Reg. Tristernagh*, pp. vii–xi.
[11] *Ibid.*
[12] *Ibid.*
[13] *Ibid.*

Sources

The major source for this study is a register, drawn up in the fourteenth century, and edited in the 1930s by Maud Clarke.[14] The material in this register consists of charters, confirmations of charters, papal confirmations of the churches held by the priory, and some agreements involving the priory. The majority of these documents can be dated to the period 1192–*c.* 1235. For this reason this study will consider the first forty years of the priory's existence.

No document survives that can be clearly identified as a foundation charter. Two documents are given the title of charter of foundation, but there are internal difficulties in both that suggest that neither is, in reality, a foundation charter. In spite of this, both provide important information on the early relationship between the founder, Geoffrey de Costentin, and the priory.[15] One of the documents,[16] in addition to listing the majority of the grants made to the new monastery, also gives detailed rules for the election of a new prior after the death of Henry, the first prior of Tristernagh.[17] It is unusual to find this type of provision in such a document. The charter states that the founder gives up all his rights in the election and confirmation of the prior. In normal circumstances the founder reserved for himself rights as patron, both in the provision of a licence for an election and in confirming the choice of the canons.[18] It is difficult to know what de Costentin had in mind when he included this right to allow free elections of the priors. It has been suggested that he was engaged in a sham.[19] The provisions for the choice of the successor are apparently copied from the charter of Bishop Simon de Rochford of Meath (1192–1227).[20] The insertion of the words 'statui item quod ad patronum pertinet' is described as a clumsy attempt to adapt the episcopal grant so as to exclude the patronal rights which the founder would wish to reserve.[21] Whatever de Costentin's purpose, the effect was to include in a document held by the priory, the right to a free election. As the founder, de Costentin would have almost certainly had an influence over the canons that would undoubtedly have influenced them in their choice.

[14] See above footnote 3.
[15] *Reg. Tristernagh*, pt 1 nos. 1 and 2.
[16] *Ibid.*, pt 1 no. 1.
[17] *Ibid.*, pp. xii–xiii.
[18] *Ibid.*
[19] *Ibid.*
[20] *Ibid.*, pt 2 no. 8.
[21] *Ibid.*, pp. xii–xiii.

The priory and its locality

The charters of the register of Tristernagh priory reveal the range of grants obtained by the Augustinians. The priory held churches, tithes, lands, mills, fishponds, and common pasture of woodland. The main property of the house was situated in the western part of modern County Westmeath and in modern County Longford. It has a presence in the lands immediately around the priory and further holdings at Balrothery in modern county Dublin and in Dublin city.[22] The extent of these holdings was directly linked to the size of the fiefs of Geoffrey de Costentin and his tenants. In addition to all these rights, the priory was also granted the right to hold a free court for their tenants. The priory would have been able to dominate the area because of its substantial landed holdings and the number of churches that it controlled in the region. The control of the tithes gave it a major stake in the landed produce of the region and in the livestock that must have been an extremely important part of the economy of this part of the lordship of Ireland.[23] The priory could count among its benefactors and supporters many of the prominent families in the lordship of Meath: the de Lacy lords of Meath, the de la Mares, the Flemings, and the Tuits. It was an important new house and received almost 1500 medieval acres of land in the first forty years of its existence.

The priory was given control of three mills and the right to construct another.[24] By this means the priory was placed very closely in contact with the tenants, who were required to bring to the mills all the corn that they wanted to be milled. This monopoly was an extremely valuable one and control of mills was often the subject of arguments and of litigation in the courts.[25] The interest of the priory in ensuring that they maintained full control over the mills can be seen from the grant that they received from John Tuit to bring water by canal to their house at Tristernagh to power the mills there and presumably to ensure that the priory had a steady supply of flowing water.[26] The later confirmations of this grant and a later

[22] *Ibid.*, pt 1 no. 1, this gives a good indication of the range of the priory's holdings.
[23] For the importance of pastorialism see K. W. Nicholls, *Gaelic and Gaelicised Ireland in the Middle Ages* (Dublin, 1972), cap. 6.
[24] *Reg. Tristernagh*, pt 1 nos. 1, 9, and 54.
[25] J. F. Lydon, 'The Mills at Ardee', *Journal of the County Louth Archaeological Society* 19 (1979), pp. 259–60.
[26] *Calender of the Carew manuscripts preserved in the archiepiscopal library at Lambeth*, ed. J. S. Brewer and W. Bullen, 6 vols (London, 1867–73), 6 (Book of Howth), p. 401.

requirement that the priors construct two bridges over the canal clearly suggests that the canal was a reality.[27] The willingness of the community at Tristernagh to undertake such a project says much about their attachment to the area and their desire to realize its resources. This feature may also be seen in the grants that the priory obtained to the rights of common pasture and of free use of woodland. Tristernagh was not a passive foundation. The monks went out and sought to increase their holdings by means of offering incentives to laymen, in the form of money, for grants of land. While very similar to a policy of outright purchase, the charters seek to disguise it as money given by the priory to the grantor for his kindness.[28] Some of the sums of money involved were quite considerable. Twenty marks was paid to Adam de Ledewych for a grant of two carucates of his demesne land at *Slewin*. The desire of the priory to get land is obvious from the fact that it still had to pay an annual rent of 4 marks for this land.[29]

The various possessions of the priory by *c*. 1235 may be divided into three categories: landed holdings, land rights and buildings, and churches and tithes. If these are examined in a little detail the importance of the priory to its locality is more easily seen and understood.

The landed holdings came to the priory in various sizes, from about 4 carucates (ploughlands) at Tristernagh and 10 carucates in Connacht to the tofts and small plots of land at Kilbixy.[30] Some of the grants are impossible to quantify.[31] These holdings, such as the land of *Glyn*, also reflect the importance of the pre-Norman territorial boundaries to the Anglo-Normans of the region. Hugh Tyrel granted to the priory all the land of the fee at *Portloman* called *Corworan*. No need was felt to measure or describe the acreage of the grant, which must have been known to both parties in the grant. The Anglo-Normans adopted the territorial boundaries that had been used by the Gaelic population.[32]

Not all the grants were in the large units of carucates. The priory received grants of twelve, ten, and eighteen acres.[33] Some of these holdings are described as having been measured by loyal and trusted men; a reflection of the high degree of organization in the area at the beginning of the thirteenth century.

---

[27] *Ibid.*
[28] *Reg. Tristernagh*, pt 1 nos. 18, 38, 44, and 51.
[29] *Ibid.*, no. 38.
[30] *Ibid.*, no. 1.
[31] *Ibid.*, no. 87.
[32] *Ibid.*, no. 48, and see also R. F. Frame, *Colonial Ireland 1169–1369* (Dublin, 1981), pp. 70–1.
[33] *Reg. Tristernagh*, pt 1 nos. 29, 32, and 47.

In the majority of cases, the grants give no indication of the type of land that was being granted to the priory, but there are several examples where this is not the case. Eadricus the weaver granted a toft at Kilbixy and land in the fields of that vill to the priory.[34] A further example is the grant by Herbert de la Mare of the wood of *Derfad* (Derrad) and 6 perches of the Red Moor.[35] In general, however, this lack of information makes it impossible to state with any accuracy the intensity of arable farming in the area. The existence of mills, and of one charter with some evidence of the nature of agriculture are the only real material which can be used. The charter lists the tithes that are to be derived from the *tuath* (petty kingdom) of Moygoish. The tithes listed are as follows: the tithes of grain, hay, flax, wool, cheese, the produce of mills and fisheries, the fruits of trees, the dung of sheep, the tithe of all young animals, and what may be honey.[36] This suggests that the agriculture in the area was mixed, with a balance between arable and pastoral farming.

The second type of possession concerned land rights and buildings granted to the priory. In addition to the mills, the community received the *aula lapidea* (stone hall) that pertained to the chapel of Kilbretan.[37] The priory also obtained rights to fisheries on the rivers that were a basic part of the natural geography of the area.[38] Perhaps the most important land rights that were granted to the priory were the rights to free common in the woods of some of their benefactors. These were not granted freely by any lord and the number of animals that were to be allowed to avail of the free common and pannage rights was detailed in the charters. Thomas de Stoks made a grant of free common for 24 draught animals and 40 pigs in the wood of Corkry to the priory, which also received the rights of heyboyts and husboyts for building and other purposes.[39] These were invaluable rights as wood was an essential of life. It was necessary for cooking, building, and for heating in winter. Many agricultural implements were made of wood as were items of domestic use.

The priory did not get free use of all these rights. One grant, in particular, is very significant. Geoffrey de Costentin, the founder, granted a fishery called *Karodothan* to the priory for which the community was

---

[34] *Ibid.*, no. 1.
[35] *Ibid.*, no. 74.
[36] *Ibid.*, pt 2 no. 9.
[37] *Ibid.*, no. 27.
[38] *Ibid.*, pt 1 nos. 1, 4, 38, and 47.
[39] *Ibid.*, no. 51.

required to pay an annual rent to de Costentin of 500 eels.[40] This rent was important as can be seen from an inquisition of 1253, in which the rent owed from Kilbixy to the lords of Meath was detailed. It included a rent of 2400 eels,[41] of which the rent of Tristernagh priory was an important part.

The final group is the churches and ecclesiastical rights accumulated in the period before 1235. Two papal confirmations allow an assessment to be made of the rate of acquisition. The confirmation of 1221 reveals that the priory already controlled the following churches: Balrothery, Kilbixy, *Tyrcloghir*, *Rathewyn*, *Glyn*, *Crosheyn*, *Kylleo*, *Kenkile*, and *Leen*.[42] Of these only the first was not to be found in the area in which the priory was located. These churches and the tithes that were associated with them were an important source of revenue for Tristernagh. The priory also received tithes of land in areas where they did not hold churches. The founder, Geoffrey de Costentin, granted to the community all the tithes of 5 knights' fees in Conmacne.[43] The freedom and ease with which grants of tithes were made is a reflection of the change brought to the area as a result of the arrival of the Anglo-Normans and the role of the priory in this process. The parochial system had not begun to develop properly in Ireland before 1169 and its gradual introduction to the country was the result of the actions of Anglo-Norman lords. They alienated churches to monastic houses and granted to those houses the tithes of the lands under their control. The result of this was the creation of a parochial system that was very closely linked to the holdings of the Anglo-Norman lords. It has been shown that in the eastern parts of the country which came under strong colonial control, the knight's fee was coincident with the manor and this was, in turn, coincident with the parish.[44] This system can be seen in its initial stages in the lands around Tristernagh. The monastic house was active in the creation of a parochial system in this area. The episcopal confirmations from the bishops of Meath and Ardagh can be seen as a reflection of their support for this continuation of the process of church reform, a process begun in the early twelfth century.[45]

It can be seen that the priory had a considerable involvement in the region and must have been in a position to have had a significant impact on the population, both Gaelic and Anglo-Norman. The only other area

[40] *Ibid.*, no. 4.
[41] *Calendar of documents relating to Ireland*, ed. H. S. Sweetman, 5 vols (London, 1875–86), 2, no. 146.
[42] *Reg. Triosternagh*, pt 2 no. 42.
[43] *Ibid.*, no. 37.
[44] A. J. Otway-Ruthven, *A History of Medieval Ireland* (2 edn, London, 1980), pp. 119–21.
[45] *Reg. Tristernagh*, pt 2 nos. 15, 16, and 26 are examples of such confirmations.

where the priory was influential was at Balrothery, close to Dublin. The church there was controlled by the priory although the amount of land held by it was small, as might be expected in an area that was already densely settled.[46] Some of Geoffrey de Costentin's demesne land was held by the priory and the initial holding was swapped for another at a different location on the demesne. The main holding there was of half a carucate, but little is known about the nature of the land except for the information of one charter. In the year 1210, Walkelin Flanders granted land at *Port-argyl* to the priory. In return for this he was to receive from it while he lived 6½ marks for clothes, 18 quarters of wheat for bread, 4 gallons of beer per day, 6 sheep, 6 pigs, 200 eels for food for his bread, and hay and fodder for two horses.[47]

The monastery as an instrument of colonization

What was the role of Tristernagh priory in the colonization of this part of the western half of the lordship of Meath? The house was founded very shortly after its founder had established his initial foothold in the land by the construction of a motte. De Costentin clearly saw a role for the priory in the development and exploitation of his large grant in the region. It provided the means of establishing a parochial system quickly and would be part of the colonial presence in the area. The Augustinians were known for their ability and willingness to concern themselves with the spiritual welfare of those under their care and in Wales they had been entrusted with the task of bringing areas into line with European religious norms.[48]

The range of the priory's holdings in the area meant that its influence was far-reaching. An example of the nature of this influence is revealed in a charter of Fulc Flanders dating from *c.* 1210.[49] In this he stated that any chaplains that he presented to the chapel under his advowson at *Tinewine-muk* were to be presented for approval to the prior at Tristernagh. The chaplain was to be obedient to the prior in all things. More importantly, however, Fulc pledged to come with all his men to the priory on three occasions during the year, bringing blessed bread and wax. The three times were the day and night of Christmas, Easter, and the feast of the

---

[46] Material in *Calender of Archbishop Alen's register, c.1172–1534; prepared and edited from the original in the registry of the united dioceses of Dublin and Glendalough and Kildare*, ed. Charles MacNeill; index by Liam Price (RSAI Dublin, 1950), esp. pp. 175–8.

[47] *Reg. Tristernagh*, pt 1 no. 87.

[48] R. R. Davies, *Conquest, Coexistence and Change: Wales, 1063–1415* (Oxford, 1987), p. 195.

[49] *Reg. Tristernagh*, pt 1 no. 15.

person to whom the house was dedicated, the Blessed Virgin Mary, 25 March. These were the three most important occasions in the religious life of the priory and the presence of one of the benefactors with his men (who could include some Gaelic tenants) is evidence of the significance of the priory as a means of bringing to the local population the values and practices of a European monastic order, an order introduced into the area by one of the colonial lords.

The introduction of the parochial system was another effective method of bringing to the area the new system and ideas of the colonists. Tithe had to be paid by all men both native and colonial and the decision about the allocation of the tithe was that of the new lord of the land. The payment of tithe may be seen as a symbol of the acceptance of the new order by the native population.

The creation of a new monastic house brought new men into the region. These men were an addition to the colonial population and their sympathies and associations were with the Anglo-Normans. In terms of language, the monks would have been closer to the new lords, the values that they held were similar and they came as instruments of reform with the full support of the bishops of the region, both Gaelic and Anglo-Norman. The closeness of the priory to the new colonial order in the area and the wide range of land and resources that it controlled made its influence difficult to avoid.

One point in particular which seems to mark Tristernagh as being an important and almost exclusively colonial institution is the fact that it does not appear to have received any land grants from the native population. It is known that to the west and north of the lands controlled by the priory, Gaelic lords were still free and independent. It can be assumed that within parts of the lordship of Meath Gaelic tenants were still in possession of land.[50] In other parts of the country, monastic houses received grants from both Gaelic tenants and independent lords.[51] There is no evidence that this was the case for the priory at Tristernagh. All its benefactors appear to have been part of the new colonial order.

---

[50] R. F. Frame, *Colonial Ireland*, pp. 82–3.
[51] See *Chartularies of St. Mary's Abbey, Dublin . . . and annals of Ireland, 1162–1370*, ed. J. T. Gilbert (2 vols, 1884–6).

The founder

The priory of Tristernagh was founded as a result of the generosity of Geoffrey de Costentin. He provided the monks with the site of its buildings, 24 carucates of land in the western part of the lordship of Meath and Connacht, other holdings, a half carucate in Balrothery, mills and sites of mills, and fisheries. He also gave the priory tithes and possibly as many as seven churches.[52] These holdings and rights formed the core of the priory's wealth. In return for this what did de Costentin get from the priory? His religious motivation was to secure the prayers of the monks for the souls of himself, his wife, his father and mother, and all his ancestors.[53] He made some effort, however unwillingly, to give the priory a large degree of control over its own affairs.[54]

Geoffrey de Costentin saw the Augustinians as the ideal means of aiding his effort to consolidate the substantial holdings that he had received. They would be part of the new colonial society, not cut off from it like the Cistercians. They had wide experience in Wales and Scotland in grafting themselves on to an older church and the means which they used, working through the parochial system, was a further incentive to de Costentin. He wished, as did so many other Anglo-Norman lords, to bring the parish network to his lands. For the Augustinians it was a natural part of everyday life.

He offered protection to the priory. Its location, so close to his *caput* at Kilbixy gave a physical security to the monks and clearly associated the priory with his own secular lordship. His initiative was an incentive to others to give their patronage to the new monastic house. The monks' only job was to secure a future for the de Costentins in heaven and to establish themselves in the region. The evidence of canal building suggests that they did the latter at least.

Conclusions

The priory at Tristernagh was one of the many foundations by the Anglo-Normans in the sixty years after they established themselves in Ireland. It was not located in the heartland of the lordship of Ireland, but on the periphery. It was founded for both religious and political reasons by

[52] *Reg. Tristernagh*, pt 2 nos. 1, 10, 31, 33, 34, 35, and 36.
[53] *Ibid.*, pt 1 no. 1.
[54] *Ibid.*

Geoffrey de Costentin. He saw the priory as a symbol of his allegiance to God and as a means of bringing reform to the Church in the lands that he had been granted. In this he was aided by the bishops of the region. He also saw the priory as an instrument of colonization that would help consolidate his holding in the area. The priory would reinforce his lordship and aid the development of the resources of the region.

Tristernagh priory is merely a case study of one such monastic house. Its charters enable the importance of the priory to the region to be seen in the generation after its foundation. It was a colonial priory and, as such, was similar to Augustinian houses in Wales and Scotland. As such it was part of the process of change that was the consequence of the arrival of new lords and a reformed Church in the western parts of Christian Europe.

University College, Dublin

THE CHURCH AND THE TWO NATIONS
IN LATE MEDIEVAL ARMAGH
(PRESIDENTIAL ADDRESS)

by J. A. WATT

PERHAPS I can best introduce my paper, explain its nature and state my objective in writing it, by describing it as another step towards completing the second part of a study of which my book *The Church and the Two Nations in Medieval Ireland* was the first part.[1] The study which concluded with the Statute of Kilkenny of 1366 needs extending chronologically by at least a century. More importantly, the nature of the analysis itself needs to be deepened. The 'Two Nations' book began with asking a fairly simple and limited question: what was the relationship of the ecclesiastical and civil powers within the English-settled parts of Ireland—in short, English law and the Irish Church. But it ended raising a more complex and more fundamental question about the overall effects on the Church of the establishment in Ireland of an English colony which was not coterminous with the country as a whole and whose strength and influence declined in the later middle ages. There may have been a more or less satisfactory answer in the book to the restricted question. There was, at best, no more than a tentative beginning to an answer to the more fundamental one.

At least, however, the more searching question is posed to give direction to further research. This paper will be looking at certain aspects of the interaction of the churchmen of the English colony with those of Gaelic Ireland in the first half of the fifteenth century and that in one particular province. I choose Armagh, not primarily because it is the senior Irish see, through whose history pass all the main themes of Irish ecclesiastical history, from Patrick down to his present *coarb* (successor). Late medieval Armagh chooses itself for investigation because of the existence of a source unique in Ireland, the Armagh registers. Episcopal registers do not otherwise exist, not even for Dublin, the most Anglicized of the Irish dioceses. The Armagh registers begin with that of Milo Sweetman, who became archbishop in 1361, and continue in broken sequence down to George Dowdall in the mid-sixteenth century. For a study of the ecclesiastical consequences of the ethnic, cultural, and political divide between native

---

[1] In *Cambridge Studies in Medieval Life and Thought*, ser. 3, 3 (1970).

Irish and English colonists, which is the central, all-conditioning reality of medieval Irish society, they are of unparalleled importance.

They are not, however, the easiest of materials to use. I am reminded of an observation made by that master of medieval episcopal records, C. R. Cheney: 'Records, like the little children of long ago, only speak when they are spoken to, and they will not talk to strangers.'[2] I am by now no stranger to the Armagh registers, but I am not yet sure they are talking to me—at any rate, in the way I should like them to.

Perhaps I may be allowed a brief word on their nature, which is more by way of personal impression than technical exposition. A. Hamilton-Thompson once spoke of a typical English episcopal register as an *indigesta moles*.[3] By comparison, the other part of the same quotation from Ovid, is the more apt for the Armagh registers—*chaos rudis*.[4] The judgement of the editors of the only register so far to achieve a full, scholarly edition, Archbishop John Mey's register, is that it is not an episcopal register at all, but 'a collection of miscellaneous notes and drafts by William Somerwell in his various capacities as notary and registrar preparatory to the production of instruments and their enregistration where appropriate'.[5] This might well apply, *mutatis mutandis* to other collections. Many of these 'miscellaneous working papers' are simply examples of common forms and other documents useful for notarial purposes. They do not therefore necessarily provide a wholly satisfactory basis for the systematic study of an administrative unit. Nor would they meet Dr David Smith's criterion of document selection in English registers, 'it is really only business closely related to the appointment of clergy that is guaranteed a place in episcopal registers'.[6] No such guarantee operates in the Armagh registers.

There is, however, a greater methodological hazard. To quote Professor Roberts and Dr Quigley again, 'In Mey's register there is a complete

---

[2] 'The records of medieval England', in *Medieval Texts and Studies* (Oxford, 1973), p. 8.

[3] 'The registers of the archbishops of York', *YAJ* 22 (1936), p. 256.

[4] '. . . quem dixere chaos: rudis indigesta moles / nec quicquam nisi pondus iners congestaque eodem / non bene iunc tarum discordia semina rerum'. *Metamorphoses*, 1. 7-9. '. . . well named chaos, a raw and undivided mass / Naught but a lifeless bulk, with warring seeds / Of ill-joined elements compressed together'. Loeb edn and transl. by F. M. Miller (1971), pp. 2-3.

[5] *Registrum Iohannis Mey. The Register of John Mey Archbishop of Armagh, 1433-1456*, ed. W. G. H. Quigley and E. F. D. Roberts (Belfast, 1972), p. xli.

[6] D. M. Smith, *Guide to Bishops' Registers of England and Wales* (1981), p. ix. Closer perhaps to the Armagh registers is Hamilton Thompson's summary: 'The primary object of an episcopal register was to preserve the common forms upon which the extensive correspondence of a diocesan chancery was conducted, together with such necessary records of business as had to be preserved for future reference.' 'Documents relating to the visitations of the diocese and province of York, 1407-1452', *Miscellanea* (SS 127, 1916), p. 134.

absence of any detectable principle or purpose, either of chronological arrangement or diplomatic category, in the entries on its folios.'[7] This is true of the series as a whole. This may well have been the case in the original order and selection of the documents. But it is almost certainly the consequence of regatherings and redistributions made when the records were bound in the seventeenth century. Much material has been lost. Extensive material from one pontificate has been bound in with the volume identified with another.

For this paper I have used four registers. Each has its own individuality and I will conclude this introductory section of my paper with a brief word of general description. That of Nicholas Fleming (1404-16) is not too far distant from an English-style episcopal register.[8] It is quite short, some 245 Fleming documents in all, which seem to constitute slightly more than half of the original, and much of it is in its correct order. The lost material is not spread evenly over the whole period; material tends to be concentrated in a limited number of years. The register labelled with the name of John Swayne (1418-39) is of a very different type.[9] It is a composite of four very different parts: a first section is a miscellany of episcopal *acta*, some of them from earlier periods; the second part is of no direct Irish relevance, being documents of the Council of Constance; the third part is made up of working papers of John Prene, *officialis* of the court of Armagh, and are of the period 1425-39. The last section is a compilation of documents largely concerned with summonses to parliaments and other civil business, and was apparently compiled during Archbishop Mey's time (1444-56). Prene (1439-43)[10] succeeded Swayne. His register is mostly records from Mey's time or from Archbishop John Bole's (1457-71) who has not achieved a separate volume of his own. The Prene material itself is relatively slight and seems to owe as much to the notary William Somerwell as does Mey's register. The authoritative comments of Roberts and Quigley on this last collection have already been noticed. None of these four collections can offer anything approaching a complete record for the particular archbishop under whose name it passes. But

[7] *Reg. Mey*, p. xxvi.
[8] H. J. Lawlor, 'A Calendar of the Register of Archbishop Fleming', *PRIA* 30 C (1912-13), pp. 94-190. Trinity College, Dublin MS 557/2 (transcripts of the originals made by W. Reeves).
[9] *The Register of John Swayne*, ed. D. A. Chart (Belfast, 1935).
[10] No edition or calendar yet in print. A typescript calendar compiled by W. Reeves is in the National Library of Ireland, Dublin. Another was drawn up by Quigley and Roberts, 'A Study in the structure and history of the registers of Archbishops Prene and Mey together with an edition of the register of Mey and a calendar of the register of Prene' (Ph.D. Queen's Univ., Belfast, 1955).

taken together, covering the period 1404–1456,[11] with all their omissions and deficiencies, they supplement each other tolerably well. We must not allow ourselves to be frightened by the textual perils nor for matter of that, by the technicalities of notaries and canon lawyers. They may slow our progress. But they offer to us the possibility of reconstructing the administrative structures of a diocese and a province, the structures by means of which, within the framework of which, the Church sustained its pastoral function. And that is a possibility which no other single medieval Irish source offers us. It is a possibility that might even tempt us to formulate another question, perhaps even more ambitious than my two earlier ones: how fared the spiritual mission in the prevailing circumstances? Was it a casualty of the cultural divide and its accompanying enmity between the two nations?

The reality of that divide and enmity is writ large in Armagh records. Dr K. Walsh has been reminding us lately of Archbishop Richard Fitzralph's concern about the 'confrontation of the two nations in traditional hatred' and his pastoral concern about the moral climate it created.[12] It was his successor Milo Sweetman who put that concern on permanent record in a provincial constitution making it obligatory on all bishops to work for peace between English and Irish, with suspension and *ipso facto* excommunication for any bishop who sowed discord between the two nations.[13] The registers contain entries which make it clear that the Statute of Kilkenny with its restrictive and discriminatory legislation against Irish-born clergy and religious living and working the English areas, was no dead letter. The registers contain examples of such clergy purchasing charters of English liberty which made them free, in the words of the grant, of all Irish servitude and gave them licence to minister among the

---

[11] A. Gwynn's pioneering study, *The Medieval Province of Armagh* (Dundalk, 1946), is concerned primarily with the period from 1470 down to the Reformation.

[12] K. Walsh, *A Fourteenth-Century Scholar and Primate: Richard FitzRalph in Oxford, Avignon and Armagh* (Oxford, 1981), pp. 341–45.

[13] As recorded in provincial constitutions in Swayne's register: 'Item ad instar Milonis auctoritate presentis concilii statuimus et ordinamus sub poena inobedientie et excommunicationis quod unusquisque episcopus suffraganeorum nostrorum pro pace reformanda, tenenda et conservanda inter Anglicos et Hibernicos provincie nostre Ardmachane secundum possibilitatem suam laboret, et pacem inter eos predicet, et ad pacem tenendam omnes subditos uos et singulos per omnes censuras ecclesiasticas compellat. Si quis autem seminator discordie inter predictos Anglicos et Hibernicos ut predicitur fuerit, quod absit, non solum a pontificalibus sit suspensus, sed ipse quisque fuerit excommunicetur ipso facto.' First printed by W. Reeves, *Acts of Archbishop Colton in his metropolitical visitation of the diocese of Derry* (Irish Archaeological Soc., Dublin, 1850), p. xvii.

English.[14] The Cistercians of Mellifont were fined for admitting to profession a native Irishman.[15] The archbishops were regularly instructed to order their dean and chapter to send proctors to the parliaments and great councils of colonial Ireland. Just as routinely, they wrote back to say that it was not the practice to summon them 'since they were pure Irish (*meri Hibernici*) living among the Irish to whom it was neither customary nor proper for the king's council to reveal its secrets'.[16]

The most striking indicator of the division, however, is its permanent institutionalization into its two ethnic parts. The registers accept an administrative division according to nation.[17] *Inter Hibernicos* lay three deaneries: Armagh itself, Tullaghoge in what is now County Tyrone, the traditional inauguration site of the O'Neills and at the heart of their territory, and Erthir or Orior, O'Hanlon country in south County Armagh. *Inter Anglicos* were the three deaneries of Drogheda, Ardee, and Dundalk in County Louth. In this area were what in English law constituted the diocesan *temporalia*, the manors of Dromiskin and Termonfeckin.

Before it is considered how the archbishops coped with this division, we should ask who these archbishops were. Mention of their names earlier—Fleming, Swayne, Prene, Mey—has already revealed that they were not Gaelic Irish. But neither were they English—or at least, in the ethnically-sensitive language of medieval Ireland, they were not 'English of England'; they were 'English of Ireland',[18] men of the middle nation, to use another ethnic label known in medieval Ireland.[19] This distinguishes them from their Dublin contemporaries who came to their see fresh from England, totally unversed in the ways of medieval Ireland. Thomas

---

[14] An example, from Swayne's *Register*, is given in the full, J. A. Watt, '*Ecclesia inter Anglicos et inter Hibernicos*: confrontation and coexistence in the medieval diocese and province of Armagh' in *The English in Medieval Ireland*, ed. J. F. Lydon (Dublin, 1984), pp. 48–9.

[15] C. Conway, *The story of Mellifont* (Dublin, 1958), p. 117.

[16] ... decanus et capitulum sunt meri Hibernici et inter Hibernicos conversantes quibus consilium regium nec consuevit nec decuit secreta consilia relevare'. *Fleming reg.* T.C.D. MS 557/2, p. 359.

[17] Studied in more detail, Watt, *Ecclesia inter Anglicos et inter Hibernicos*. Cf. A. Lynch, 'The archdeacons of Armagh 1417–71', *Journal of the County Louth Archaeol. Hist. Soc.* 19 (1979), pp. 218–26.

[18] A distinction made, for example, in Statute of Kilkenny (1366), c. 14, forbidding the reception of native Irishmen into religious houses in the English areas, 'mes resceuient gentes Engleis sanz auoir consideracion les queux ilz soient neez en Engleterre ou en Irland'. *Statutes and Ordinances and Acts of the Parliament of Ireland: King John to Henry V.* H. F. Berry (Dublin, 1907), pp. 444–6.

[19] J. F. Lydon, 'The middle nation' in *The English in medieval Ireland*, pp. 1–26; A. Cosgrove, 'Hiberniores ipsis Hibernicis' in *Studies in Irish history presented to R. Dudley Edwards*, ed. A. Cosgrove and D. McCartney (Dublin, 1979), pp. 1–14.

Cranley (1397-1417) had been fellow of Merton, Warden of New College and Chancellor of the University. It is perhaps not surprising that DNB says of him, in the language of late Victorian England, 'he experienced considerable difficulty in performing his duties in consequence of the opposition of the natives' (and they were just the colonists).[20] Richard Talbot (1417-49), a younger son of the fourth baron Talbot and younger brother of John Talbot, the future earl of Shrewsbury, was dean of Chichester when appointed to Dublin.[21] Michael Tregury (1449-71) was another former academic: fellow of Exeter College and first Rector of the short-lived, English-established University of Caen.[22] The four Armagh archbishops all had some previous connexion with the province, most typically by holding benefices in the diocese of Meath. Prene, as has been mentioned, was *officialis* of Armagh when appointed. Mey held a similar position in Meath. Fleming, Prene, and Mey were Oxford graduates,[23] Swayne probably of a Continental university.[24]

All four were papally provided to the see. Fleming had taken his predecessor's resignation to Rome in 1404 and found himself nominated. Swayne was also on the spot in 1418, in Constance, to be chosen by Martin V. More precise details of the procedure by which archbishops were selected are not to be found in the registers. Was the Crown, either directly or indirectly through its lieutenant in Ireland, involved in the selection process? Fleming's difficulty in getting possession of his manors for lack of the correct documentation from the Papal Curia makes it clear that the Crown was involved at least in the final stages. It is to be assumed that he would not get possession if he was unacceptable and also that he would be required, in the procedure demanded of papal nominees to English sees, to renounce the offending clauses in the papal letters concerning *temporalia* and the alleged papal right to confer them. Was the selection simply an English and colonial matter? Were the *meri Hibernici* of the Armagh chapter involved at all?

Indeed they were, unlikely though this might seem. In two of the four vacancies which occurred in the period with which we are concerned, the

---

[20] *DNB* 5, pp. 17-18 (R. L. Poole); Emden (O), 1, pp. 510-11.
[21] J. H. Bernard, 'Richard Talbot archbishop and chancellor, 1418-1449', *PRIA* 35 C (1918-20), pp. 218-29; Emden (O), 3, pp. 1845-6.
[22] Emden (O), 3, pp. 1894-5.
[23] Fleming and Prene are listed in Emden (O), 3, p. 2176; 3, pp. 1515-16. As elect of Armagh, Mey is described as 'bacallarius in utroque iure' in *Mey reg.* no. 285.
[24] The most helpful biographical study is K. Walsh, 'The Roman career of John Swayne, arch-bishop of Armagh 1418-1439', *Seanchas Ardmhacha*, 11 (1983-4), pp. 1-21.

chapter sought to select its own candidate to put to the Papal Curia for confirmation as archbishop of Armagh.

On the death of Nicholas Fleming in 1416, the Armagh chapter chose Richard Talbot, dean of Chichester and brother of the recently arrived chief governor, Lord Furnival, otherwise John Talbot. This selection came to nothing because Dublin having become vacant, Richard Talbot was appointed to that see. The chapter, having been informed of this, met in Armagh cathedral in October 1417, reinforced with proctors of Edward Dantsey, bishop of Meath, and of Henry, abbot of Mellifont, and elected the chancellor of St Patrick's Dublin, Robert Fitzhugh and publicly announced so, using the Irish language. The chapter then sent two proctors to Dublin to seek Fitzhugh's assent and this was given. The Council of Constance (or the Pope if one had been elected) was asked to approve the choice. Martin V had other ideas; Fitzhugh was passed over in circumstances that remain unknown, and John Swayne was appointed. Despite this lack of success, it is clear that the legitimacy of the chapter's role was recognized in English Ireland and that the native Irish chapter was not averse to choosing outside its own ranks and outside its own Gaelic milieu.[25]

This was not, however, the end of the chapter's interest in having Richard Talbot for its bishop. Notarial documentation of a similar character from the period of the vacancy between Prene and Mey in 1443 confirms that assessment of the situation. Again the chapter selected Talbot, by now after twenty-seven years as archbishop of Dublin, three terms of office as chancellor of the civil administration based in Dublin, and five terms of office as chief governor, Ireland's most prominent prelate. Somerwell's notarial instruments in Mey's register are quite precise. Within a month of Prene's death, the chapter had secured Talbot's assent to the proposed move from Dublin to Armagh. He had made it clear that royal assent was also necessary and so the dean and chapter wrote to Henry VI to ask for it. Owen O'Neill, chief of the Irish of Ulster, also wrote in support.[26] In the event, again for reasons unrecorded in the registers, John Mey was chosen by the Pope and Talbot remained in Dublin until his death in 1449. The election of Talbot in 1416, of Robert Fitzhugh in 1417, and the postulation of Archbishop Talbot in 1443 were those of a Gaelic Irish chapter. There is no reason to believe, or even to suspect, that these choices were forced on them. That they chose as they did, albeit

[25] *Swayne reg.*, ed. Chart, pp. 32–4.
[26] *Mey reg.*, nos 283, 187–9.

unsuccessfully, is sufficient evidence in itself, even if there were no other, to suggest that we should be thinking of the relationship between the nations in late medieval Armagh as symbiotic rather than purely disjunctive.

In saying this I am not of course seeking to minimize the reality and importance of the 'two nations' divide. The two societies each had their distinctive way of relating to their clergy. The English way was expressed most characteristically in the law. The legal system imposed constraints within which churchmen were required to act: episcopal *temporalia* were rigorously subject to state control; the ecclesiastical courts functioned only within defined jurisdictional limits and were subject to writs of prohibition by means of which the limits were enforced; benefit of clergy was permitted only in a curtailed and severely controlled form; lay patrons presented to benefices in the procedures which normally gave the laity a dominant voice; prelates were required to impose canonical sanction on those clergy who did not pay their parliamentary taxes and to sequestrate the benefices of those in debt to the State. No cleric was too mighty to be brought to account by the civil power, as Edward Dantsey, bishop of Meath, was to discover, as was Michael Tregury, archbishop of Dublin. Dantsey was a member of the Irish council and had served a term as deputy lieutenant. In 1427, accused by one of his own clergy of stealing some sort of drinking vessel, the bishop found himself brought before the circuit judges. On their report to the chief governor, the matter was brought to parliament wherein the bishop, in accordance with established procedure, asked in the name of ecclesiastical liberty for the case to be remitted to his metropolitan before whom he would establish his innocence by purgation. This was granted and in St Peter's church, Trim, in the presence of Archbishop John Swayne, suitable and sufficient compurgators testified to the bishop's innocence and the archbishop pronounced him discharged. The verdict was then reported to, and accepted by, parliament.[27] Tregury's case was somewhat different. He stood accused of causing a disturbance among the citizens of Drogheda by provocatively allowing his cross-bearer to exhibit the head of the Dublin primatial cross in Armagh province. He made his purgation in the Franciscan house in Drogheda before James Butler, fourth earl of Ormond, the deputy, and his council.[28]

Gaelic Ireland had no parallel system of state control of the clergy. Yet

[27] *Swayne reg.*, pp. 66–8.
[28] *Mey reg.*, no. 405.

Gaelic society had its own characteristic relationship with its clergy. *Inter Hibernicos*, the distinctive feature was the network of kin-relationships that decided who held the different ecclesiastical establishments—parishes, tenure of church lands, religious houses, even the tenure of sacred objects like the bell of St Patrick—and conditioning in turn the composition of cathedral chapters and succession to bishoprics. The professional clerical families, for the continuation of which clerical marriage was a *sine qua non*, with their kindred links with ruling families, dominated the Gaelic ecclesiastical world. One example must suffice to illustrate the general point and I make it with material published by Fr Canice Mooney in his all-too short study *The Church in Gaelic Ireland: Thirteenth to Fifteenth Centuries* (Dublin, 1969). The MacCawells were a clerical dynasty of the Clogher diocese, the chief ruling family of which was the Maguires of Fermanagh. Art MacCawell was bishop of Clogher from 1390 to 1432. One of his sons became a canon of Clogher, a grandson, Pierce Maguire, dispensed as the son of a priest *super defectu natalium*, was provided to the see by Eugenius IV and ruled it from 1433 to 1447, a great grandson was bishop of Clogher from 1505 to 1515. Many other members of the family held lesser offices in the diocese. There is nothing in the Armagh registers to suggest that these bishops were unacceptable as suffragans. Indeed, as we will see, another of them was consecrated by Archbishop Mey in St Peter's, Drogheda, in 1449. Fr Canice claimed this bishop, Ros Maguire, had ten children.[29]

The law of the English state, then, and the customary practices of Gaelic Ireland formed the working environment of the archbishops of Armagh. There was a third dimension. They worked more especially within the structures of canon law. That law and the custom of the *ecclesia Ardmachana* called the archbishops to a tripartite office. They were primates—'tenens omnium ecclesiarum tocius Hibernie primatus'—in Armagh terminology. But it was a primacy more honoured in the breach than the observance. They were metropolitans: the province of Armagh consisted of ten suffragan sees (nine after the union of Down and Connor became effective in the 1450s).[30] All save Meath, Down, and Connor were *inter Hibernicos* and normally ruled by Irish bishops. They were the ordinaries of a diocese with a frontier, as has already been indicated, between two different types of society. Any analysis of how these prelates

---

[29] *Church in Gaelic Ireland*, pp. 57–8.
[30] On this union, Watt, 'The papacy and Ireland in the fifteenth century' in *The Church, Politics and Patronage in the Fifteenth Century*, ed. R. B. Dobson (Gloucester, 1984), pp. 140–2.

came to terms with the particular circumstances of their *milieu* must take account of each of these three dimensions of their office.

The primacy is the least important of the three aspects. Which is not to say that it is unimportant.[31] But by the fifteenth century it was already abundantly clear that the claim of 'a primacy over all the churches of the whole of Ireland' was untenable, at any rate so far as jurisdiction was concerned. By the mid-thirteenth century the Papacy had ruled that Dublin and Cashel were autonomous provinces, though allowing that Tuam was subject to the primacy of Armagh. The fifteenth-century registers have documentation showing that this subjection, manifested in the form of a claim to primatial visitation, was still upheld, but contain no evidence that such visitation ever took place. Dublin had gone on to assert, from the early fourteenth century, a vigorous primatial claim of its own. This rivalry had nothing to do with 'two nations' relationships. Its effects were felt in colonial Ireland, particularly in the political sphere. As a consequence of what Armagh considered Dublin's usurpation of its status, archbishops of Armagh refused to attend any official function in the Dublin province because they would be prevented from having the primatial cross borne before them. As this included parliament, and it was relatively rare for them to be held outside the Dublin province, this led to a certain distancing of Armagh from the civil administration. This led Edward III to try to impose a solution. He had recently coaxed Canterbury and York into a compromise, with the adoption of the 'primas totius Angliae' and 'primas Angliae' titles and thought he could persuade Archbishop Milo Sweetman to follow suit. The papacy declined to offer a solution. The registers testify to the persistent refusal of the archbishops to attend Dublin based parliaments. When John Mey was appointed deputy to the lord lieutenant in September 1453 he made it clear that he expected to be allowed to have his cross carried before him wherever in Ireland he thought it appropriate.[32] It is extremely doubtful if the citizens of Dublin, let alone the archbishop and clergy, would have tolerated this, for the cross-bearing issue was as much a civic matter in Dublin as it was in Drogheda. It is not surprising that Mey's deputyship was brief and ineffectual.

The relationship between the metropolitan and his suffragans is a matter of much more moment, not least in the 'two nations' context. The law of the medieval church did not attempt to define universally valid

---

[31] I have examined this in more detail, 'The disputed primacy of the medieval Irish Church', forthcoming in the *Proceedings of the Seventh Conference of Medieval Canon Law, Cambridge 1984*.

[32] *Mey reg.*, no. 399.

norms for the jurisdiction of metropolitans. Its tendency was more towards safeguarding the rights of individual bishops and thereafter leaving the matter of metropolitan authority to the custom of local churches. Armagh's own claim was not over-modest. A conventional Armagh chancery phrase of Mey's time echoed the terminology of the papal chancery in claiming it was *mater et magistra huius regionis omnium ecclesiarum*. What this meant in practice is revealed in the registers. Close study of them, especially in the period of about a century from Milo Sweetman to John Mey, makes clear what was the understood relationship in the province between its metropolitan and his suffragans. For the tex-tual reasons already indicated the record is patchy. And practice did not always (need it be said?) match theory. But the archbishops exercised authority over the whole province, not just the English part of it. Not always wholly adequately, not always unchallenged, not always equally effectively at the same time in every part of the province, but with pastoral responsibility and the authority of the acknowledged canon law.

A comprehensive study of metropolitan jurisdiction (no such study exists for medieval Ireland and it is only Armagh, with its registers, that offers the possibility of one) would require a detailed investigation of the relationship of each archbishop with each of his dioceses. Obviously, no such study is possible here. One must aim instead to a summary of the main elements of the relationship, with appropriate illustrations.

Records of episcopal consecrations are very few. But whether con-secrated by the archbishop of Armagh or not, the suffragans were required to take an oath of canonical obedience to him, including a promise to obey the provincial constitutions and to attend provincial councils. There is no reason to assume there was any widespread evasion of this obligation. Fleming's register, for example, records such oaths sworn by Richard Bayl (Dromore, 1408) and his successor in 1410, John MacCormack (Raphoe, 1416), and Con O'Farrell (Ardagh, 1419).[33] Nor can it be assumed that the suffragans' obligation to attend provincial councils was widely ignored. It is clear from the registers that such councils were held frequently, appar-ently always in St Peter's, Drogheda. All suffragans without exception were summoned and, though there survive many more lists of who was summoned than of who actually came, when the scattered register evid-ence is assembled, there can be no doubt that such councils were well attended, either in person or by proxy, with archbishops severely repri-manding absentees. These were genuinely provincial assemblies wherein

---

[33] *Cal. reg. Fleming*, nos 86, 87, 88, 90; TCD MS 557/2, pp. 116-19.

the metropolitan with his brethren legislated, judged, admonished, and exhorted in fulfilment of their corporate pastoral charge.[34] In the later fourteenth and early fifteenth centuries, the Armagh provincial constitutions were codified and repromulgated, all clergy being ordered to possess them and expound them to the laity as appropriate at stated times of the year. There is a particularly full, composite set in the Swayne register.[35]

An important claim by the archbishop was for the custody of the suffragan sees during vacancy. This included custody of the *temporalia* as well as the spiritual jurisdiction in all the Irish dioceses. This did not apply in Meath, Down, and Connor, however; being in the English law area, their temporalities were in the hands of the Crown during vacancy. In Meath the archdeacon of Kells successfully asserted a claim to the spiritual custodianship, though Armagh did not recognize this as anything but a *de facto* situation. Elsewhere it seems to have been implemented through the archbishops very sensibly allowing their jurisdiction to be exercised by local men appointed as commissaries. In cases of prolonged vacancy as happened frequently in Dromore diocese, for example, this could be a particularly important matter.

Occasionally it was thought necessary to vindicate the custodial right. In October 1397 Archbishop John Colton went in person to Derry to make a very firm and successful assertion of his right as metropolitan to be *iudex ordinarius* of the Derry diocese *sede vacante*, forcing the dean and chapter to accept this 'most ancient custom . . .' observed inviolably from time out of mind and causing to be drawn up an impressive set of notarial deeds to register exactly every studied assertion of his temporary position of bishop of Derry.[36] The deeds have an importance beyond the limited issue of metropolitan jurisdiction. They afford a unique insight into the exercise of episcopal jurisdiction in medieval Gaelic Ireland. Colton was accompanied by a team of Armagh clergy of both nationalities. It included Maurice O'Corry, dean of Armagh, and a future dean, member of another prominent Armagh clerical family. This was Thomas O'Loughran who had been the interpreter when in Drogheda in March 1395 Niall Og O'Neill had sworn liege homage to Richard II.[37] The Derry erenachs, as

[34] There is a typical example of the nature and limitations of the evidence for the provincial council of 1427, *Swayne reg.*, pp. 61-3, 73-5, 78, 120.

[35] *Swayne reg.*, pp. 8-16, 17-18.

[36] Reeves, *Acts of Archbishop Colton in his metropolitical visitation of the diocese of Derry*. Analysis, Watt, 'John Colton, Justiciar of Ireland (1382) and Archbishop of Armagh (1383-1404)', *England and Ireland in the later middle ages*, ed. J. F. Lydon (Dublin, 1981), pp. 204-11.

[37] E. Curtis, *Richard II in Ireland, 1394-5 and submission of the Irish chiefs* (Oxford, 1927), *De instrumentis tangentibus Hiberniam*, VIII, p. 69.

they were obliged to do by the terms of their holding of church lands, provided the party with food for men and horses, accommodation, fresh horses, and night watchmen. Colton performed a variety of episcopal duties: reconsecrating churches and cemeteries polluted by the shedding of blood, confirming erenagh charters, hearing marriage cases, conducting a searching visitation of the Derry houses of Augustinian canons, condemning local lords for seizing church lands. The excommunicated canons of the chapter were absolved on swearing to acknowledge metropolitan right. John Colton celebrated Mass outside the parish church of Clooney (whose rector was dean of Derry and had supported Colton throughout) because the church itself was too small to accommodate 'the thousands of people who had gathered out of respect for their father', the archbishop.

Another area of metropolitan jurisdiction which has left its mark on the registers was the disciplining of bishops for gross misconduct. Milo Sweetman made heroic efforts to reform Richard O'Reilly, bishop of Kilmore,[38] and Simon, Dominican bishop of Derry.[39] Swayne, after personal visitation of Derry in 1429 forced Bishop Donald Omeraich to make purgation before him that he would cease his immoral and criminal behaviour.[40] John Prene tried, condemned, and recommended to the Papacy for deposition, John Sely, Benedictine bishop of Down, following his visitation of that diocese in 1440.[41]

For visitation of suffragan sees, the evidence is of very variable quality and it is not possible to form any precise view as to the exact frequency and regularity for each diocese. But it was taken seriously. In the period of Fleming[42] and Swayne, for example, it would seem that no diocese was left unvisited. The evidence suggests that Meath was the most regularly visited but the frequency of reference is because every visitation provoked a lengthy and acrimonious dispute about procurations. The most significant evidence of Swayne's concern for visitation comes from the years 1434 and 1435. Between May and October 1434, he arranged visitations—to be done by commissaries, it is to be noted—for Dromore, Derry, Connor, and Down, as well as his own diocese.[43] Between June and August 1435, he did

---

[38] *Cal. reg. Sweetman*, nos 68–78, 99 (1366–8).

[39] *Cal. reg. Sweetman*, no. 16 (1369); no. 14 (1380).

[40] *Swayne reg.*, pp. 117–18.

[41] Cf. 'Papacy and Ireland in the Fifteenth Century', pp. 140–1.

[42] Kilmore (1409); Derry (1410); Dromore (1411); Ardagh (1416). *Cal. reg. Fleming*, nos 107; 127; 147; 128; 256.

[43] *Swayne reg.*, p. 149.

the same for Raphoe, Clogher, Kilmore, Clonmacnois, and Ardagh.[44] Thus the whole province was covered. Not every archbishop arranged for every visitation to be done by commissaries and it would not be true to say that the only visitations performed by the archbishops in person were in the dioceses *inter Anglicos*.

There remains to mention one last aspect of metropolitan jurisdiction: the Armagh court of audience claimed an appellate jurisdiction over the province as a whole. It also operated a system of *tuitio*, tuitorial procedure whereby litigants at the Papal Curia secured the protection of their persons, property and office pending the hearing of their appeals in Rome. In a period of much Rome-running, this protection was in demand from all parts of the province. It also operated when appeal was made from a suffragan to metropolitan.[45]

It is not often that any source other than the registers reveals anything of the relationship of metropolitan and suffragan. But under the year 1449 the *Annals of Ulster*, a work of Maguire provenance, recorded the consecration as bishop of Clogher of Ross Maguire, son of Thomas Maguire, king of the Irish of Fermanagh. It took place about New Year, in St Peter's Drogheda. The annalist comments: 'and not often before had there been celebrated a *bainnriugad* [literally, espousal; marriage] more lavish'.[46] The celebration over, however, it was not long before Archbishop Mey was reminding the new bishop that he was in breach of the oath he had recently sworn in that he had failed to promulgate censures against a local lord, Hugh MacMahon, as ordered by the provincial council. Then the archbishop began to receive appeals: the abbot and community of the Augustinians of St Mary, Clogher, complaining that Ross had deprived them unjustly of an endowment granted by his predecessor after a fire in the monastery; the dean of Clones whose church had been put under interdict because he refused to pay his bishop a sum to which he was not entitled. There was an accusation that he was unjustly favouring a relative in tenure of church land. In 1450 Mey conducted a visitation in person and was unhappy about one of his decisions being ignored. He was even more unhappy about non-payment of procurations and eventually put the diocese under interdict.[47] Clearly the euphoria of the consecration day had

---

[44] *Swayne reg.*, pp. 157–8.
[45] Characteristic examples can be studied by following the Index *Mey reg.* s.v. Courts, ecclesiastical (appeals; appeals, tuitorial).
[46] *Annala Uladh: Annals of Ulster*, ed. W. M. Hennessy, 4 vols (Dublin, 1887–1901), 3, pp. 162–5.
[47] *Mey reg.*, nos 153, 232, 264, 273, 382.

not lasted very long. But perhaps for that impression we should blame the registers—of their nature they tend to caricature the Christian life into a series of legal tussles.

Few of the documents in Swayne's register are dated from Armagh itself. They are mostly dated from places *inter Anglicos*. Some historians have seen this as an indication that he seldom, if ever, set foot in that part of his diocese which lay *inter Hibernicos*. Others have gone further to generalize that this was true of all archbishops of Armagh. It was not. It is most evidently not so in the case of John Mey who took canonical possession of his see in his cathedral of Armagh on 9 July 1444 and proceeded immediately to the first of his personally conducted visitations of the deaneries of Erthir and Tullahoge and of Armagh itself.[48] Thereafter, his visits to Armagh were quite frequent.[49] His involvement with his diocese *inter Hibernicos* was considerable. It is not possible here to pursue the detail of this involvement. It is, however, manifested in particularly striking fashion in the second half of the year 1455. Even a brief review provides graphic evidence of the relationship, ecclesiastical and political, of the archbishop to his diocese *inter Hibernicos*.

The review must begin with an entry in the Annals of Ulster recording how, on 1 July 1455:

> O'Neill, that is Henry, son of Owen, son of Niall Og O'Neill, was this year made king over Ulster . . . Ua Cathain and Mag Uidhir and Mag Mathgamna and all the O'Neill clans and the successor of St Patrick went with him to Tulach-Og and he was made king there honourably, by the will of God and men.[50]

This is the first record we have of the presence of the primate at an O'Neill inauguration of the kingship stone, blessed according to legend by St Patrick himself. Archbishop Mey moved on to Armagh and began a visitation. It proceeded in a routine sort of way for the first fortnight in August—hearing cases of clerical indiscipline, lifting canonical censures, deciding property cases, scrutinizing titles to benefices, and conducting a visitation of the Augustinians of SS Peter and Paul, reform of which house he had initiated ten years earlier. The one extraordinary feature took place on 4 August in the hall of SS Peter and Paul where Mey was staying. His register records that Owen, by now old and frail, had recently resigned the

---

[48] *Cal. Prene* (Quigley and Roberts), no. 102; *Cal. Prene* (Reeves), no. 99.
[49] Summarized in an Appendix to '*Ecclesia inter Anglicos et inter Hibernicos*', pp. 61-4.
[50] *Ann. Ulster*, 3, pp. 184-5.

headship of the O'Neills. His eldest son, Henry, therefore presented himself before the archbishop as chief-elect, asserting that 'his election and institution into his temporal lordship pertained to his lord primate and so he sought institution and confirmation from the same lord'. Archbishop Mey, praising Henry as a good man and useful for his Church and the people of Ulster, declared ratified his position as chief (*capitaneus*) of the O'Neill *nacio*. This took place in the presence of a very large crowd of clergy and laity, no one of whom dissented.[51] We have here, then, apparently, a new procedure for choosing the O'Neill. First, traditional inauguration at Tullahoge, then the confirmation by the successor of St Patrick. The innovation of the second, confirmatory part being introduced, without doubt, because of succession uncertainties. Henry's father's reign had been violently contested, with his losing the headship twice, for long periods,[52] and renewal of strife was always possible. Primatial confirmation stamped the succession with legitimacy. It also, incidentally, helped to establish the principle of primogeniture.

Henry O'Neill, then, thought he needed the archbishop's support. The archbishop was sure he needed the O'Neills'. He had strong grievances against all of them, of a strength which had led in November 1454 to his placing the diocese *inter Hibernicos* under interdict.[53] His complaint was of O'Neill harrassment of clergy, ecclesiastical tenants, and his officials, and of obstruction to his conduct of visitation. Mey wanted guarantees that such aggressions would cease and that Henry O'Neill would be in practice what he was supposed to be in theory, the protector of the church of Armagh. This role made of him the archbishop's *brachium seculare* —for caption of excommunicates, for police action against priests' concubines, and for protection of the archbishop's commissaries and stewards in the collection of his dues.

Mey was back in Armagh for the second half of November 1455. He was busy with continuing and tidying up matters connected with the July visitation. The chief business, however, was the ratification of an agreement with Henry O'Neill. Mey had kept his side of the bargain in July, now in November Henry was called on to agree to his. Mey specified the terms: O'Neill was to uphold the church of Armagh in its full liberty and defend

---

[51] Full references, with some previously unpublished texts, '*Ecclesia inter Anglicos et inter Hibernicos*', Appendix, pp. 61-3.

[52] Accession, 1410; deposed, 1414; restored, 1419; dep. 1421; rest. 1432. Detail from *A new history of Ireland*, ed. T. W. Moody et al. (Oxford, 1984), p. 212.

[53] *Mey reg.*, no. 343.

it to the best of his ability; he was to assist in the collection of the archbishop's dues when, wherever, and as often as asked to do so; he was not to
impose any degree of servitude on any church or its tenants or on priests
or their property, either directly or indirectly, but should defend them to
the best of his ability; this should apply especially to Armagh; visitation,
and free movement of the archbishop's representatives, should not be hindered. For his services, O'Neill was to receive a *pencio*, forfeitable if he
failed to honour his obligations. All this was agreed in the church of the
monastery of SS Peter and Paul, Armagh, in the presence of a great assembly of onlookers and witnesses.[54]

My attempt at conversation with the Armagh registers is, for the
moment at least, at an end. It is time to sum up, briefly, what they seem to
be saying in answer to the three questions I posed.

The first of these was about the relationship of the ecclesiastical and
civil powers in the English parts of Ireland. By the fifteenth century, colonial Ireland had changed in a very important way to differentiate it from
England. Centuries of intermarriage and acculturation with the Irish
population had sharpened the difference between the English of Ireland
and the English of England. Nevertheless, institutionally speaking, colonial Ireland was still recognizably in the fifteenth century what it had been
in the thirteenth century: a smaller England oversea. And so far as the
Church was concerned, English law continued to exercise a powerful
influence, this influence had two distinctive features: ecclesiastical institutions operated within limits determined by the lay power; the lay power
was still attempting, at least sporadically, to enforce discriminatory legislation against Irish clergy ministering *inter Anglicos*.

My second question was about relationships across the frontier
between the two nations. One important dimension of that subject concerns the relationships of the archbishops with the leading Ulster ruling
family, the O'Neills. On one level, the registers record an apparently
stormy relationship—of seized church lands, of exploited ecclesiastical
tenants, of excommunications defied and interdicts ignored, of solemn
agreements lightly broken: a sorry tale of defiance and disorder. But that is
only the negative side of the story. On another level, there is evidence of
positive relationships in major matters. John Colton acting as the trusted
adviser of the O'Neills in the crisis days of the submissions to Richard II,
the O'Neill intervention in the succession to John Prene, Mey's actions in

---

[54] Texts from Prene's Register in K. Simms, 'The concordat between Primate John Mey and
Henry O'Neill (1455)', *Archivium Hibernicum* 34 (1976-7), pp. 71-82.

easing the succession of Henry O'Neill after the abdication of his father, are but the most striking illustrations of relationships that transcended the cultural divide in an enduring constructive liaison of Church and lay powers.

How fared the pastoral ministry on levels other than that of public policy? The registers reveal the ordinary, routine working of ecclesiastical institutions. They show, all of them, quite unambiguously a remarkable *modus vivendi* between the *ecclesia inter Anglicos* and the *ecclesia inter Hibernicos*. Or perhaps, more accurately, how the archbishops exercised their authority, both ordinary and metropolitan. They did so in different ways according to whether their subjects lived *inter Hibernicos* or *inter Anglicos*. Appropriate structures had been devised and they worked, albeit often imperfectly; they provided a framework for Christian ministry that bridged the divide between the two nations. It was no small achievement to construct and maintain such a system and historians should not undervalue it.

University of Newcastle upon Tyne

FIFTEENTH-CENTURY IRISH PROVINCIAL LEGISLATION AND PASTORAL CARE

by MICHAEL A. J. BURROWS

I T is rewarding, if usually fairly difficult, to discover to what extent the views of medieval bishops on matters of devotion and church discipline impinged upon the spiritual lives of ordinary lay people. In the case of Ireland, provincial legislation probably provides the best available means by which to attempt this. Although the most important pastoral relationship within the Church was always that of priest and people in the parish, both parties were under the guiding hand and oversight of the bishop. It is to this ancient episcopal role as overseer, in the pastoral context, that the surviving sources direct us most.

After even a cursory look at the most obvious available source, the Armagh archiepiscopal registers,[1] we can conclude that provincial synods were held regularly by the archbishops, and attended by their suffragans, the archdeacons, and representatives of the chapters of the province, along with interested lay notables. Further details of the composition of these bodies are hard to obtain, but the important points are that synods were attended, despite the division of the province into territories inter Anglicos and inter Hibernicos, by the majority of the suffragans or, when necessary, their proctors and that they tended to precede the archbishop's metropolitan visitation.[2] Ideally, therefore, provincial synods should have been held every three years, but ideal conditions rarely existed in medieval Armagh. However, if circumstances were reasonably favourable, regular assemblies do seem to have been held, despite the dangers of travel across Ulster and the frequent references to attacks on those who were journeying to meet the primate.[3] The Italian primate Octavian (1479–1513), who

---

[1] Concerning the scope of these registers, see *Registrum Johannis Mey: The Register of John Mey, Archbishop of Armagh, 1443–1456*, ed. W. G. H. Quigley and E. F. D. Roberts (Belfast, 1972), pp. ix–xii, xxxvii–xlii; A. O. Gwynn, *The Medieval Province of Armagh, 1470–1545* (Dundalk, 1946), p. 20.

[2] J. Watt, "'Ecclesia inter Anglicos et inter Hibernicos': Confrontation and Coexistence in the Medieval Diocese and Province of Armagh' in *The English in Medieval Ireland*, ed. J. F. Lydon (Dublin, 1984), pp. 56–7.

[3] Regarding travel through Armagh *inter Hibernicos*, see K. Simms, 'The Concordat between Primate Mey and Henry O'Neill', *Archivium Hibernicum*, 34 (1977), p. 77. In his efforts to ensure that his agents might have a peaceful passage across Ulster, the primate showed himself to be entirely dependent on the good will of the Gaelic rulers, especially the O'Neills—see J. Watt, *The Church in Medieval Ireland* (Dublin, 1972), p. 204.

had something of a reputation as a reformer, has left us, for example, evidence of provincial synods in 1480, 1483, 1486, 1489, 1492, 1495, 1504, and 1507. He may well have held other councils, his register being defective particularly for his later years.[4]

Unlike being present at parliament, which the Anglo-Irish primates regarded as an unsuitable role for representatives of their chapter of 'rebellious' Irish in Armagh—declaring that political secrets ought not to be made known to disloyal subjects of the king—there were no racial limits on attendance at provincial councils.[5] All were seen to be equally open to the guidance of the Holy Spirit. In 1495, the higher clergy of the province were described as 'being of one mind in the Holy Ghost'.[6] This, one presumes, applies as much to members of the wayward, persistently O'Neill-influenced, Armagh chapter as to the archdeacon of Armagh who, living in Louth and working with the archbishop in the territory *inter Anglicos*, was generally very much under the primate's thumb.[7] Synods tended to be held in St Peter's, Drogheda, in effect the pro-cathedral of the predominantly Anglo-Irish archbishops of the time,[8] and they began with High Mass *de Spiritu Sancto*, at which the primate was both celebrant and preacher. After the Mass, a solemn *Veni Creator* was sung, a roll was taken, and any proxies who were present presented their credentials. Then the council went into session and would continue thus for approximately three days.[9] We know that this was the procedure for holding councils in Armagh and it is safe to assume that similar procedures were followed in Dublin, Cashel, and Tuam as well.

Much of the impact of the legislation produced during these synods depended on the diligence of the individual primates in following up the

---

[4] Gwynn, *Medieval Province*, pp. 7 *seq.*, 20; W. Reeves, *Memoir of Octavian del Palacio, Archbishop of Armagh* (Dublin, 1875).

[5] Watt, "'Ecclesia inter Anglicos et inter Hibernicos'", pp. 49–50; Trinity College Dublin MS 557/2, p. 359 (an extract from the register of archbishop Fleming); D. A. Chart, *A Calendar of the Register of John Swayne, Archbishop of Armagh* (Belfast, 1935), p. 53.

[6] Fr Colmcille, 'Some Documents from the Old Abbey of Mellifont', *Journal of the County Louth Archaeological Society*, 134 (1953–6), p. 58.

[7] A. Lynch, 'The Archdeacons of Armagh, 1417–1471', *ibid.*, 19 (1979), pp. 218–26; cf. K. Simms, 'The Archbishops of Armagh and the O'Neills, 1347–1471', *Irish Historical Studies*, 19 (1974–5), pp. 38–55, *passim.*

[8] Gwynn, *Medieval Province*, pp. 20, 73–5; cf. his *Anglo-Irish Church Life: Fourteenth and Fifteenth Centuries* (Dublin, 1968), p. 30.

[9] Chart, *Register of Swayne*, pp. 73–5; L. P. Murray and A. Gwynn, 'A Calendar of the Register of Archbishop Cromer', *Journal of the County Louth Archaeological Society*, 8 (1933–6), p. 340, and 10 (1941–4), p. 121; A. Stephens, *Provincial Synod of Armagh: Opinion of Counsel on behalf of the Lord Primate* (Dublin, 1864), pp. 34, 44 *seq.*

work of the councils with personal visitations of large portions of their province. This was the test of how effective a primate's authority over the day-to-day pastoral mission in the province actually was. The account of the Armagh synod of 1411 seems to have its climax in the words: 'procedendum esse ad visitationem nostram metropoliticam'.[10] The question of whether suffragans held their own diocesan synods to add impetus to the implementation of provincial legislation as well as to discuss such matters as taxation[11] remains a difficult issue. Certainly there were times when the archbishop of Armagh held annual assemblies of the clergy *inter Anglicos* of his own diocese and these assemblies produced precepts related, for example, to minor matters of liturgy. By Archbishop Cromer's time (1521–43), a definite distinction was made between diocesan synods held to discuss purely ecclesiastical affairs and those held to discuss the clerical contribution to royal subsidies. The former were held in June or July (Cromer had sixteen of them) and the latter in December.[12] In the dioceses *inter Hibernicos* the question of discussing royal subsidies did not arise, but local bishops may well have been anxious to hold clerical gatherings where, for example, they could promote the cults of popular local saints in their dioceses just as, on a provincial level, the archbishops promoted the cults of saints who had a special significance in the religious tradition of the province in general.

Some of the provincial legislation of this period is not at all remarkable; for example, Anglo-Irish primate after Anglo-Irish primate seem to repeat the decrees of their predecessors in the matter of clerical concubinage, which remained such a persistent problem in the church *inter Hibernicos*. We cannot assume, however, that unorthodox standards of clerical morality necessarily were a hindrance to the pastoral mission in Gaelic Ireland: there is little sign of any special social stigma attached to concubinage there. In this matter the primates had to accept that all they could do was to fulminate on deaf ears, even in the case of many of the province's bishops themselves.[13] Despite such keenly-felt variations in culture and in social *mores* within the province, however, there remains plenty of legislation which gives us clear glimpses of the effective role of

[10] Stephens, *Provincial Synod*, pp. 45, 59.
[11] See J. F. Lydon, 'The Church and Taxation in Fourteenth-century Ireland', *Proceedings of the Irish Catholic Historical Committee* (1964), pp. 3–10.
[12] M. V. Clarke, *Medieval Representation and Consent* (London, 1936), pp. 57–8.
[13] K. Nicholls, *Gaelic and Gaelicised Ireland in the Middle Ages* (Dublin, 1972), p. 92; Gwynn, *Medieval Province*, pp. 165–6; S. G. Ellis, *Tudor Ireland* (London, 1985), p. 187; A. Lynch, 'Religion in Late Medieval Ireland', *Archivium Hibernicum*, 36 (1981), p. 8.

the Church in specific pastoral situations on both sides of the so-called racial frontier.

Before considering a few themes from surviving legislation, it must be stressed that this material, rich as it is in what it offers to students of pastoral care, is by no means easy to consult or use. No scholar has yet attempted to provide an all-embracing edition of the texts of Irish provincial legislation, with the notable exception of Aubrey Gwynn in the case of Dublin.[14] At least he had a coherent series of texts to use: other sets of legislation vary greatly in their dates and places of origin. For example, we have almost no legislation produced in the synods of Armagh in the middle decades of the fifteenth century, exactly at the time when Cashel evidence is at its richest. But, even if the legislation is scattered in place and time, there is room for a systematic study of dominant themes. A collection of late medieval Irish provincial legislation would not be beyond the scope of a single volume and would reduce our dependence on defective works such as D. A. Chart's calendar of the register of archbishop John Swayne,[15] or Wilkins' *Concilia Magnae Britanniae et Hiberniae* (1737),[16] the latter being our most up-to-date edition of the important Cashel legislation of 1453. Furthermore, there have been few more serious sins of omission in recent times than the delay in producing critical editions of the remaining Armagh registers comparable to that provided by Drs Quigley and Roberts in the case of archbishop John Mey.[17] There is not even a printed calendar available of the registers of Prene and Octavian and, in cases where we do have such calendars, we are still indebted to pioneering but now clearly inadequate work carried out by Chart and H. J. Lawlor half a century and more ago.[18] To be more specific at this point, Chart at times imposes the historical thinking of his day to an unfortunate if understandable extent upon the documents which he translates. A single example of this must suffice here. The Statutes of Kilkenny (1366) condemn a game which was long assumed to be an exclusively Gaelic form of hurling. An Armagh constitution, almost certainly produced by archbishop Nicholas Fleming in 1411, condemns what seems to have been a similar game as being primarily a source of disorder in the community:

---

[14] A. Gwynn, 'Provincial and Diocesan Decrees of the Diocese of Dublin during the Anglo-Norman Period', *Archivium Hibernicum*, 11 (1944), pp. 31–117.

[15] See note 5 above.

[16] *Wilkins*.

[17] See note 1 above.

[18] Among H. J. Lawlor's papers see especially 'A Calendar of the Register of Archbishop Fleming', *PRIA* 30, C (1912), pp. 94–190.

Because by a certain game called ... galbardy ... mortal sins and beatings and often homicides are committed, the archbishop prohibits the faithful from playing that reprehensible game in the future. ...[19]

Chart, working in the early 1930s, and influenced no doubt by the prevailing opinion regarding the intention of the Kilkenny statutes, went so far as to suggest an equation between 'galbardy' and hurling in his calendar. This sort of thinking could easily lead to an assumption that both the Statutes of Kilkenny and the legislation of an Anglo-Irish primate were intended to be seen as 'anti Irish'.[20] It is better to compare this constitution, not the only such directive to come from a late medieval Armagh synod, with that of the Cashel synod of 1453 ordering the clergy not to play football as this could serve as an example of disorder to their flocks.[21] Even in Dublin itself, archbishop Rokeby found it necessary, at a provincial council in 1518, to prohibit the playing of football by the clergy.[22] All over contemporary Europe, efforts were being made to make the clergy live more exemplary lives and Ireland was no exception.[23]

We now turn to consider a few specific themes in fifteenth-century provincial legislation, aiming thereby to investigate the problem of whether episcopal policy could have had any significant impact on the spiritual life of the ordinary believer.

One occasion when any Christian might possibly have had contact with his bishop was at confirmation. Fleming's constitutions of 1411 specified that bishops were to hold regular confirmations of the children around their dioceses 'if they can safely approach them'.[24] This provision is important for two reasons. First of all, it suggests that bishops were not

---

[19] Fleming's legislation is translated in Chart, *Register of Swayne*, pp. 8–18. For this constitution see pp. 12–13. I have discussed the question of the precise dating of sections of this legislation and considered the implications of the textual problems raised by it at some length in my thesis, 'The Irish Episcopate and Pastoral Care, 1318–1534' (Dublin University M.Litt., 1986), pp. 61 *seq.*

[20] Chart, *Register of Swayne*, p. 12; E. Curtis, *History of Medieval Ireland* (Dublin, 1923), pp. 283–4. Curtis speaks of the spirit of the Kilkenny statutes as being 'Anti-Gaelic' and believes that they led to 'a real outlawry of the *mere* Irish'. See also J. F. Lydon, *The Lordship of Ireland in the Middle Ages* (Dublin, 1972), pp. 221–2; also his *Ireland in the Later Middle Ages* (Dublin, 1973), pp. 95–7.

[21] The Cashel legislation is available in full in *Wilkins*, 3, pp. 565 *seq.*

[22] H. J. Lawlor, 'A Calendar of the Liber Ruber of the Diocese of Ossory', *PRIA* 27, C (1908–9), p. 165.

[23] Nicholls, *Gaelic and Gaelicised Ireland*, p. 100; A. Gwynn, 'The Origins of the Anglo-Irish Theatre', *Studies*, 28 (1939), pp. 268–9.

[24] Chart, *Register of Swayne*, p. 10; Lydon, *Lordship*, p. 107.

always able to approach the people of their dioceses in safety—an indication of the disturbed state of the racially-divided province. Secondly, it suggests that confirmation was not seen as an absolute necessity: in cases of need it could be dispensed with. This reminds one of the situation in most of contemporary western Christendom where confirmation certainly seems to have been a neglected rite. The whole issue of the theology of confirmation in the middle ages remains very much an uncharted field.[25] No one has yet discovered any hard evidence of a fifteenth-century Irish bishop actually holding a confirmation: it seems to be the one sacrament concerning which the available sources reveal absolutely nothing.[26]

Throughout the middle ages, the Easter festival was the one occasion when the average layman would have received (as opposed to merely being present at) the Eucharist. The 1411 legislation stresses the importance of the Holy Week devotions in preparing the people for coming to the altar at Easter 'as very clean vessels'. The primate spoke out concerning what seems to have been a persistent superstition which interfered with the solemnity of Good Friday:

> Because in many places of Armagh province that . . . perverse vulgar error has crept in that the flesh of a hare on the Feast of Preparation (i.e. Good Friday) is an excellent medicine against various diseases, the archbishop inhibits the faithful . . . from hunting . . . the hare on that holy day.[27]

The provincial council of Cashel, meeting at Limerick in 1453, went so far as to lay down that those who did not confess their sins and receive the sacrament annually were to be deprived of Christian burial.[28]

Constitutions such as those of 1411 concerning basic matters of general Christian discipline were supposed to be explained to the people four times a year, in the vernacular, 'on the greater festivals' and for this purpose parish clergy were supposed to have their own copies of the legislation. How useful it would be to have even a little evidence concerning parochial preaching in fifteenth-century Ireland. We only know that Armagh clergy were supposed to possess a tract entitled *Ignorantia Sacerdotum* (which had been mentioned as long ago as 1281 in a constitution of

---

[25] See *Bishops: but What Kind?*, ed. P. Moore (London, 1982), p. 31.
[26] FitzRalph's episcopal experience in this area in England in the 1340s is considered in K. Walsh, *a Fourteenth-century Scholar and Primate: Richard FitzRalph in Oxford, Avignon and Armagh* (Oxford, 1981), pp. 230-1.
[27] Chart, *Register of Swayne*, p. 12.
[28] See J. Begley, *The Diocese of Limerick* (Dublin, 1906), 1, p. 294.

Archbishop Peckam of Canterbury), dealing with basic matters of faith such as the Creed, the seven sacraments, and the ten commandments. This material was to be used for vernacular sermons on the great festivals.[29]

One of the obvious ways in which the personal spirituality of different archbishops might have affected their people was through changes or adjustments in the prescribed observances of saints' days. Some changes were in line with the mainstream of European liturgical development: in 1460 the octave (as opposed to the actual day) of Corpus Christi was ordered to be observed in Armagh. On a more local level, Archbishop Fleming in 1411 ordered the feasts of Feghin (patron saint of the Termon-feckin area) and Ronan to be observed throughout his diocese while the feasts of Patrick, Brigid and Columba were cited, as on previous occasions, as demanding full observation in the entire province. This is only one of many examples of an Anglo-Irish archbishop promoting the cults of native saints.[30] There was a theological side to this which needs to be remembered. Anglo-Irish and Gaelic prelates celebrated the saints' days together, with no doubt as to the fact that they were all potential members of the same communion of saints. Despite various ordinances controlling the activities of Irish 'enemies' in the city of Dublin, not only the Irish parliament and the Dublin assembly, but also the Armagh provincial council of 1495, following the lead of a Dublin provincial council in 1494, were quick to produce a dictum that sanctions could be imposed on those molesting any persons going to Holy Trinity specifically for the purpose of a pilgrimage to visit the shrine of Dublin's patron saint, Lawrence O'Toole, and the other famous relics there.[31] Moreover, despite the intrinsic Irishness of the cult of St Lawrence, the bishops present at the Dublin provincial council just mentioned were willing to boost it even in a sensitive political climate.[32] The fact that these prelates were representatives of a colonial culture which was being continually eroded by things Gaelic

[29] Watt, *Church in Medieval Ireland*, pp. 210–11; for the text of *Ignorantia Sacerdotum*, see *Councils and Synods with Other Documents relating to the English Church*, ed. C. R. Cheney (Oxford, 1964), 2, pt 2, pp. 900–5.

[30] Chart, *Register of Swayne*, p. 13; A. Lynch, 'The Province and Diocese of Armagh, 1417–1471' (University College Dublin MA thesis, 1979), p. 40.

[31] Lydon, *Lordship*, pp. 94–5, 115; *Calendar of the Ancient Records of Dublin*, ed. J. T. Gilbert (Dublin, 1889), 1, p. 383; H. J. Lawlor, 'A Calendar of the Liber Niger and Liber Albus of Christ Church, Dublin', *PRIA*, 27, C (1908–9), pp. 25–6; 'Calendar of Christ Church Deeds', *Appendix to 20th Report of the Deputy Keeper of the Public Records in Ireland*, nos. 361–2; Reeves, *Memoir of Octavian*, p. 13; National Library of Ireland MS 98, fol. 98.

[32] For further details regarding the Dublin council of 1494 (including the attendance levels at its various sessions), see *Registrum Diocesis Dublinensis: A Sixteenth-Century Dublin Precedent Book*, ed. N. White (Dublin, 1959), pp. v, 28 *seq.*

did not matter in such a case. There is no hint in any of this of the subtle change to an attitude which considered the Gaelic Irish to be too barbarous and uncivilized to be acknowledged as truly Christian—an attitude which began to manifest itself with the increase in humanist learning among the English in Ireland early in the next century and which was to be of profound significance when the time came to consider strategies by which to impose the Henrician Reformation upon Ireland. The attitudes towards the Gaelic way of life expressed by the English archbishop of Armagh, Kite (1513-21), who was a Cambridge humanist and very much Wolsey's right hand man in Ireland, during his brief period of residence in his diocese are a case in point.[33] Yet, during our period, neither nation seems yet to have regarded the other as, in practice, unchristian or, by its very nature, uncivilized. The O'Neills never had any difficulties over recognizing an English or Anglo-Irish archbishop as coarb of Patrick (with all that that title meant) in terms of spiritualities, nor did the prelate in question ever object to being perceived in such terms, although disputes and lack of trust regarding temporalities often soured pastoral relationships.[34] In this connection, it is interesting to note that, apart from a few bizarre cases, the term 'heretic' had really only a technical meaning in medieval Ireland. 'Heresy' was usually to disregard the rights of the Church by encroaching upon its possessions. In retaliation, the Church placed the offender in the position of a heretic. He was declared to be unentitled to hold property and the faithful were encouraged to prey, crusader-like, upon his goods. In Raphoe, in 1410, the bishop was supported by his Anglo-Irish metropolitan in acting against the 'heresy' of certain unnamed lords who had occupied ecclesiastical lands.

> The archbishop commands the bishop . . . to pronounce sentence of excommunication and interdict on Sundays and festivals with cross erect, bells and candles, on . . . (the offenders concerned) . . . praying that the Lord Jesus will bring them back to the catholic faith. . . .[35]

---

[33] On Kite see Gwynn, *Medieval Province*, pp. 43 *seq.*; *DNB*; *A New History of Ireland*, ed. A. Cosgrove (Oxford, 1987), 2, pp. 658-9. Reformation strategy in Ireland is considered in B. Bradshaw, 'Sword, Word and Strategy in the Reformation in Ireland', *HJ* 21 (1978), pp. 475-502 and see especially pp. 480 *seq.*

[34] Simms, 'Archbishops of Armagh and the O'Neills', *passim*; Watt, '"Ecclesia inter Anglicos et inter Hibernicos"', pp. 52-5, 61; K. Simms, '"The King's Friend": O'Neill, the Crown and the Earldom of Ulster' in *England and Ireland in the Later Middle Ages*, ed. J. F. Lydon (Dublin, 1981), pp. 224-5.

[35] Lawlor, 'Calendar of the Register of Fleming', pp. 131-2; cf. Simms, 'Archbishops of Armagh and the O'Neills', p. 42.

The Armagh synods seem constantly to refer to problems raised by situations of this sort. 'Heresy' remained primarily a temporal matter and to be, as bishop, the guardian of doctrine meant very logically that one had to be the zealous guardian of one's temporalities as well.

The lack of an enduring university helped to spare Ireland the type of atmosphere in which conventional 'heresy' could have arisen. But learning can also help to maintain the stability of the faith and to counter superstition. The whole question of clerical education in medieval Ireland still remains an uncharted field. Archbishop FitzSimons of Dublin took a significant step at his provincial council of 1494. This assembly granted a seven-year subsidy from each of the dioceses of the Dublin province for the support of theological lecturers in St Patrick's University, Dublin. It was hoped that these payments would suffice 'until other provision is made for the lecturers'.[36] Was an attempt being made to revive the university established *c.* 1321, by Archbishop Bicknor, possibly as a centre for the provision of higher degrees in theology as opposed to a more basic training for ordination? It is all too easy to assume that the *studium* established by Bicknor was more or less stillborn and lacked any sort of institutional continuity. It is time that someone re-examined Aubrey Gwynn's long-accepted views on this particular subject, particularly his assumption that the native Irish who were willing to travel to Oxford in significant numbers would have been unwilling to attend an English-administered *studium* in Dublin.[37]

Amid the one hundred and twenty-one constitutions of the Cashel council of 1453 presided over by Archbishop John Cantwell, an Oxford-trained Anglo-Irish canon lawyer,[38] there are a few clues as to the nature of theological training in a more Gaelicized environment. Here we evidently find ourselves on a more basic and practical educational level. It appears that there were recognized clerical teachers who ran small-scale seminaries, based in their own homes, which were attended by ordinands in accordance with a system based on the Gaelic concept of fosterage. However, the synod believed that certain persons, especially those of noble

---

[36] C. MacNeill, *A Calendar of Archbishop Alen's Register* (Dublin, 1949), p. 260; F. McGrath, *Education in Ancient and Medieval Ireland* (Dublin, 1979), pp. 221-2; W. Monck Mason, *The History and Antiquities of the Collegiate and Cathedral Church of Saint Patrick, near Dublin* (Dublin, 1820), p. 101.

[37] A. Gwynn, 'The Medieval University of Saint Patrick's, Dublin', *Studies*, 27 (1938), pp. 199-212, 437-54; McGrath, *Education*, pp. 216 *seq.*; Walsh, *Richard FitzRalph*, pp. 10-13.

[38] Emden (o), 1, p. 351; St. J. Seymour, *Pre-Reformation Archbishops of Cashel* (Dublin, 1910), pp. 57-58.

birth, who were unable to attend university in Ireland, were using these schools to gain some form of literary education without having any real intention of being ordained. It was enacted that no-one was to attend the schools unless he had a real commitment to being ordained. Ordinations were to take place as soon as training was over. No cleric was to take the son of a nobleman into his house for fosterage without episcopal licence.[39] Did the synod intend that the bishops should impose some sort of test of vocation on would-be ordinands?: 'vocation' being a term that historians traditionally seem shy of using in connection with the medieval Irish clergy.

The question of the training of the secular clergy was not the only critical problem confronted at the synod of 1453. Once again we see signs of the presence of a FitzRalph-like attitude towards the ministry of the friars, who were alleged to be intruding upon areas that were properly the pastoral concern for the parish clergy.[40] In Armagh, in 1411, Archbishop Fleming had attempted to reduce tension by allowing mendicants to preach and to hear confessions, but only through a strict system of episcopal licences. Those who had made confessions to unlicensed mendicants were ordered to confess this to their parish priests, and the Easter communion was always to be preceded by confession to the *pastor in parochia*.[41] This was in line with the principles expressed long before in the Lateran IV canon *omnis utriusque sexus*, which stressed the importance of confession to one's *proprius sacerdos*. The intention of the canon was that a penitent should have as his confessor one who knew him well, rather than go to a stranger, such as a friar, from whom it might be possible to obtain an absolution more easily. However, a vast amount of controversy was generated throughout the middle ages by those who sought to define what exactly the phrase *proprius sacerdos* meant.[42]

The Cashel council of 1453, however, produced a much tougher defence of the rights of the secular clergy *vis-à-vis* those of the mendicants. It was declared to be a mortal sin merely to hear the sermons of an unlicensed friar. This rigorous approach may have been an offshoot of the anti-mendicant campaign of the controversialist Philip Norreys, a disciple of FitzRalph's, who was to become dean of St Patrick's, Dublin, in 1457. It

---

[39] *Wilkins*, 3, pp. 565 ff. See also McGrath, *Education*, pp. 170 *seq.*; Nicholls, *Gaelic and Gaelicised Ireland*, p. 99; Begley, *Diocese of Limerick*, p. 293.

[40] Cf. Walsh, *Richard FitzRalph*, pp. 349 *seq.*

[41] Chart, *Register of Swayne*, pp. 8–9.

[42] Walsh, *Richard FitzRalph*, pp. 332, 344, 371, 416, 423, 424, 429.

was Norreys who described the friars as 'anti-Christs and disciples of Mahomet'.[43]

One major aspect of the relationship between pastors and people concerns the nature of church buildings themselves. Not only the quality of liturgy, but also the very appearance of church buildings, contribute to a sense of the numinous and of the holy among the people. The 1453 legislation lays down a detailed code concerning church furnishings. We hear so much about how the alleged economic growth of the fifteenth century was manifested in the building of observant friaries and tower houses.[44] We might forget that greater prosperity could also produce, on a more personal level, a desire to benefit one's soul by presenting gifts for use in one's own parish church. Perhaps the legislation of 1453 was endeavouring to channel such munificence towards the purchase of the most useful available articles. The synod ordered that the laity of a parish, apart from their traditional obligations to maintain the nave of the church, should also provide certain articles for use in the liturgy at their own expense. These were a missal, a silver chalice, an alb, a stole, a chasuble, a surplice, and a font *inter alia*. Mention is also made of vestries. Moves were clearly being made to replace tin chalices with silver; an expensive task for a small congregation but one which might be undertaken as a pious gesture by wealthy individuals. As late as 1518, attempts were still being made at a Dublin provincial council to abolish the use of tin chalices.[45] The 1453 legislation also prescribed that each parish church was to possess three statues; one of Christ on the cross, one of the Blessed Virgin, and one of the patron saint of the church concerned. There was to be a suitable vessel for holding the reserved sacrament, and a bell was always to be rung during processions when the eucharistic elements were carried about. The synod also decreed that the offices were to be said publicly in all parishes on Sundays, festivals, and at least three week days. The church bell was to be tolled three times before each such service. Beneficed clergy who did not recite their offices were to be deprived by their ordinaries if they refused to change

---

[43] For Norreys and his anti-mendicant campaign see Walsh, *Richard FitzRalph*, p. 360; E. Bolster, *History of the Diocese of Cork* (Shannon, 1972), 1, p. 476; Emden (o), 2, pp. 1365–6; E. Fitzmaurice and A. Little, *Materials for the History of the Franciscan Province of Ireland* (Manchester, 1920), pp. xxix, 172 *seq.*, 191; St. J. Seymour, *Anglo-Irish Literature, 1200–1582* (Cambridge, 1929), p. 40; H. J. Lawlor, *The Fasti of Saint Patrick's Cathedral, Dublin* (Dundalk, 1930), p. 43.

[44] A. Cosgrove, *Late Medieval Ireland, 1370–1541* (Dublin, 1981), p. 93; C. T. Cairns, *Irish Tower Houses—A Co. Tipperary Case Study* (Athlone, 1987), pp. 3 *seq.*

[45] Lawlor, 'Calendar of the Liber Ruber of Ossory', p. 165.

their ways. In the cathedrals of the province, no-one was to be admitted as a dignitary to the choir unless he was able to sing.

Another delicate problem faced by the synod of 1453 involved the custom of parishioners placing their valuables in the church, or within the walls of the churchyard, for safe keeping in a society which clearly had its many violent moments.[46] Churches were being used as repositories for the storage of grain although, on occasions, the sanctuary was violated by those who sought to plunder the corn, and such a situation could easily lead to violence within the churchyard. The synod, in the course of several references to the question of violence, ordered that those who shed blood in a churchyard should pay a fine to the bishop. It also prohibited the people from threshing in the church buildings themselves! This whole matter adds some strength to Professor Lydon's contention that religion sat lightly on the medieval Irish layman.[47] He had, perhaps, too easy a familiarity with his parish church, which was so much the centre of all aspects of life in the medieval community. The various Gaelic lords who, time after time, invaded the lands of the primates in Armagh had a similarly casual approach to the possessions of the Church.[48] The ultimate spiritual relevance and authority of the Church was never denied but it was often tempting to exploit its possessions, not out of any defined anti-clericalism but because of simple pragmatism. The addition of many new furnishings to the churches of Cashel in the mid-fifteenth century, in accordance with the comprehensive guidelines set out in the legislation of 1453, may have enhanced the sense of the beauty of holiness within them and contributed to a greater sense of awe and mystery, and less of a sense of casualness, among those who visited them.

This paper, all in all, has aimed at being straightforward and exploratory. We have examined how, while an adequate approach to this subject remains so difficult without modern editions of the more vital texts, a definitive edition of all surviving late medieval provincial legislation would not in fact be an impractical suggestion. Furthermore, an attempt has been made to make certain suggestions relating to the pastoral role of prelates in guiding the life of that ephemeral figure, the common man,

---

[46] This, of course, was no new problem in Ireland—see A. T. Lucas, 'The Plundering and Burning of Churches in Ireland, 7th to 16th century' in *North Munster Studies*, ed. E. Rynne (Limerick, 1967), pp. 172-229 for a wide-ranging discussion of the question of sanctuary, especially with regard to lay property.

[47] Lydon, *Lordship*, p. 114.

[48] 'Watt, "Ecclesia inter Anglicos et inter Hibernicos"', pp. 51-3; also his *Church in Medieval Ireland*, pp. 204-5.

exploring some themes which have been neglected even in recent work and which must be seen from a theological as well as from an historical perspective. To give specific examples, we have the contemporary understanding of confirmation, the nature of vocation, the question of what was deemed to be 'heresy', and the dominant concept of the communion of saints. One might have added the question of the Church's teaching regarding marriage in the context of medieval Anglo-Irish and Gaelic society but this issue, while demanding an entire paper to itself, has fortunately received significant treatment from other writers in the course of recent years.[49] Today a theological perspective on church history is something very necessary in Irish scholarship—to quote one of our leading ecclesiastical historians:

> One can only regret the curious dichotomy in Ireland between the professional study of theology and the study of the humanities in the general university world, for in this task of exploring a heritage theology and the humanities need one another.[50]

This challenging comment could hardly be more pertinent to any subject than to the theme which has been explored in this paper.

Trinity College, Dublin

Additional Note

Much of this paper is based upon impressions gained through perusal of the contents of the surviving Armagh registers themselves. Nineteenth-century transcripts of all these registers, prepared by William Reeves, are conveniently available in the library of Trinity College, Dublin, MSS 557/1-13, and these provide an indispensable aid to students of medieval pastoral care, given the continued lack of printed editions of all but one of the registers involved.

[49] See especially A. Cosgrove, 'Marriage in Medieval Ireland' in *Marriage in Ireland*, ed. A. Cosgrove (Dublin, 1985), pp. 25-50; K. Simms, 'The Legal Position of Irishwomen in the Later Middle Ages', *Irish Jurist*, 10 (1975), pp. 96-111.
[50] P. J. Corish, *The Irish Catholic Experience* (Dublin, 1985), p. viii.

FROM 'VICTIMS' OF THE MELK REFORM TO APOSTLES OF THE COUNTER-REFORMATION: THE IRISH REGULAR CLERGY IN THE HABSBURG DOMINIONS

by KATHERINE WALSH

IN a lengthy and favourable review of Pádraig A. Breathnach's edition and analysis of the legendary account of the foundation of the Irish monastery at Regensburg, *Libellus de fundacione ecclesie consecrati Petri*, Daniel Binchy remarked of the history of the Schottenklöster that, whatever interest it might have for German medievalists, it 'is a mere footnote—or perhaps rather a postscript—to the remarkable story of the early Irish missions to Europe'.[1] However, Binchy greatly over-estimated the interest of German-speaking medievalists in the case of that particular Schottenkloster which is central to the present paper, namely that in Vienna. Since the well-documented but overtly apologetic study by Patrick Barry, which appeared in 1927,[2] the Viennese Schottenkloster has been studied mainly by members of its own monastic community,[3] and by scholars pursuing the sort of questions with which local and economic historians generally turn to the archives of formerly rich and powerful monastic landlords. The *raison d'être*, aspirations and fears, triumphs and failures of adherents to a particular monastic tradition are of marginal interest to students of land tenure and administration. Hence it seems appropriate to take a fresh look at the reasons why Irish monks found that

---

[1] *Celtica*, 14 (1981), pp. 155–64, at 164. Cf. P. A. Breathnach, *Die Regensburger Schottenlegende— Libellus de fundacione ecclesie consecrati Petri. Untersuchungen und Textausgabe — Münchener Beiträge zur Mediavistik und Renaissance-Forschung*, 17 (Munich, 1977).

[2] P. J. Barry, *Die Zustände im Wiener Schottenkloster vor der Reform des Jahres 1418* (D.Phil. thesis, Munich, 1926, publ. Aichach, 1927). The value of this study lies above all in the comprehensive survey of the internal sources for the history of the monastery, but lack of familiarity with central issues, e.g. university organization and papal administrative procedures, diminishes the value of its interpretations.

[3] Cf. *800 Jahre Schottenabtei*, a special issue of *Religion, Wissenschaft, Kultur. Vierteljahrsschrift der Wiener Katholischen Akademie*, 11 (1960), Folge 1, containing the jubilee lectures delivered in 1958, especially the contributions by H. Hantsch and H. Peichl; C. R. Rapf, *Das Schotten-Stift* (*Wiener Geschichtsbücher*, 13, Vienna, Hamburg, 1974); H. Ferenczy, *Das Schottenstift und seine Kunstwerke. Mit 58 Farbtafeln und 100 Schwarzweißbildern von Christoph Merth* (Vienna, 1980); W. Berger, *Die Wiener Schotten* (Vienna, 1962), is an informative guidebook without academic pretensions, and the standard work still remains Ernest Hauswirth, *Abriß einer Geschichte der Benedictiner-Abtei Unserer Lieben Frau zu den Schotten in Wien* (Vienna, 1858).

there was no longer a place for them in early fifteenth-century Vienna, with a view to providing a tentative answer to a related question, which cannot be discussed in detail here: why was it possible for Irish regular clergy, especially mendicant friars, to be warmly welcomed back to the lands of the *Casa de Austria* two centuries later?

The traditional explanation for the collapse of the Irish Benedictine community in Vienna and the exodus of the monks under protest can be summarized briefly. A significant stream of reformed Benedictine monasticism, the *Consuetudines* of Subiaco which had been largely inspired by monks from Germany,[4] had already been introduced in the Austrian monastery at Melk—some fifty miles west of Vienna and guardian of the tomb of St Colman, an Irish pilgrim to Palestine murdered in the area in 1012.[5] During the later stages of the Council of Constance the monks of the Subiaco observance obtained the approval of the newly elected pope Martin V and of the temporal ruler concerned, Duke Albrecht V of Austria, for their intention to conduct a visitation of the Irish monastery in Vienna. They wished to introduce their reform and also to ensure that the community would no longer be restricted to monks of Irish origin, as the original foundation charter and statutes of the Viennese Schottenkloster had stipulated. The reformers sought to introduce German monks, in order to bring the community back to full strength, after a catastrophic fire in 1410 had caused both the alienation of convent property and a sharp decline in numbers.[6]

The visitation took place during the first week of August 1418. The Irish community was larger than that of any other Schottenkloster in German lands at the time: it consisted of the abbot, Thomas (III) O'Crosscraid,

---

[4] Cf. Barbara Frank, 'Subiaco, ein Reformkonvent des späten Mittelalters. Zur Verfassung und Zusammensetzung der Sublacenser Mönchsgemeinschaft in der Zeit von 1362 bis 1514', *QFIAB* 52 (1972), pp. 515–656. For a brief summary of the older literature cf. M. Heimbucher, *Die Orden und Kongregationen der katholischen Kirche*, 1 (Paderborn, Munich, Vienna, 3, 1933), pp. 219 seq.

[5] On Coloman, cf. *LThK* 3 (1959), coll. 7–8; Acta SS Oct. VI (1794), coll. 342–62; A. Riedl, 'Der Kult des hl. Koloman in Melk und anderswo', *Jahresbericht des Stiftes Melk*, 101 (Melk, 1959), pp. 3–22. Soon after their foundation, the Irish monks in Vienna were placed in charge of a chapel dedicated to St Coloman, who had meanwhile become a locally venerated patron saint of lower Austria, cf. Rapf, *Schotten-Stift*, p. 11.

[6] For a survey of this material cf. Barry, *Wiener Schottenkloster*, esp. pp. 22–47; Rapf, *Schotten-Stift*, pp. 25–7, though it should at this early stage be pointed out that Rapf is an ardent proponent of the theory that the Irish monks were an alien, and a spent force in Vienna. However, many of the charters he cites refute the case he is trying to make. For a more impartial view of the problem cf. L. Hammermayer, 'Die irischen Benediktiner-"Schottenklöster" in Deutschland und ihr institutioneller Zusammenschluß vom 12. bis 16. Jahrhundert', *StMBO* 87 (1976), pp. 249–338, esp. 286–7.

and six monks, several of whom had unquestionably Irish names such as Patrick and Fintan. These refused to accept German monks on the grounds that this would be a source of danger and scandal, and that it would alter the entire character of their foundation and religious observance. But they soon recognized that they were powerless to resist, drew the consequences, and abandoned their Viennese convent for ever, though they were later to regret this over-hasty reaction. Abbot Thomas subsequently became abbot of the Irish convent in Würzburg, where he died in 1437.[7]

The principal charges against the Irish community—both at the time of their dispersal and in the subsequent historiography of the German community which took over the monastery in 1418 and have maintained it to the present day—were lack of vocations, general decline, and the failure to observe the rule of chastity. The tag *quod qui haberet uxorem, quaereret eam ad Scotos* gained wide currency, and it has since been subject to a variety of interpretations.[8] A further charge, which acquired a prominent place in subsequence German historiography, was that the Irish monks were allegedly perceived by the local Viennese population as an alien body, ignorant of the German language and customs, and that they therefore had to be removed. This latter argument was clearly a compulsive one for the German successors of the Irish community.[9] The new occupants needed it as justification and defence against the charge that they were mere usurpers. But the available evidence indicates that this argument was the least tenable of all, and it is irreconcilable with the intensive involvement of the fourteenth-century Irish abbots in political and academic affairs, and in central issues of ecclesiastical policy.

It must be recalled that when the Babenberg Markgrave of Austria and Duke of Bavaria, Henry II (Jasomirgott) transferred his residence from Regensburg to Vienna in 1155 he invited a community of Irish monks to follow him and gave them their present site, about four hundred paces outside the then existing city wall. In the foundation charter issued on 22 April 1161 he stipulated that the convent should be the exclusive

---

[7] Cf. *Cal. Pap. Let.* 7, p. 452; ASV, Reg. Lat. 261, fol. 31. On resigning the abbey in Vienna he had been guaranteed an annuity of 80 gold ducats. His successor, the first German abbot of the Viennese Schotten-community, Nicholas (III) von Respitz, a monk of the Subiaco observance, successfully petitioned in 1426 to have this burden relieved, on the grounds that his predecessor was now adequately provided for, whereas his own community had suffered heavy losses as a result of the Hussite invasions.

[8] Cf. below, pp. 84–5.

[9] In the sense of German-speaking inhabitants of the Holy Roman Empire, and including the Austrian lands.

preserve of Irish monks: *Solos eligimus Scottos.*[10] Twelfth-century Vienna was something of a crossroads for crusaders, merchants, and pilgrims, and the newly established ruler wanted a hospital convent to receive them. Hence it is not a mere coincidence that the Irish church in Kiev, founded to provide pastoral care for German traders in the Ukraine, was staffed initially by Irish monks from Vienna. But the Babenberg duke intended even more—he established a 'court' convent, which was to be both a memorial to the elevation of his territories to the status of a duchy, and at the same time a mausoleum for the deceased members of his family—as was later to be the case with the Escorial for the Spanish and the Capuchin church in Vienna for the Austrian branch of the Habsburgs. This political function of the Viennese foundation helps to explain the need for independence from the mother convent at Regensburg, which was to be a source of friction in the early years of its existence. It also helps to clarify why the Schottenkloster in Vienna, unlike similar foundations elsewhere, neither expected nor received financial support from Ireland.[11]

The Babenberg rulers and their Habsburg successors established the convent on a firm financial footing in the usual manner, by assigning it property and the income from a number of parishes, to which it had the right of presentation, and many of which were subsequently incorporated into the monastery. A Viennese dissertation submitted in 1952 shows that the Irish monks normally adopted the common practice of appointing a parish priest who was *not* a member of their community, whereas they took over themselves the care of the parish of St Mary attached to their convent.[12] Hence the decision was based on considerations of distance from their convent and not, as otherwise might be assumed, the consequence of a language barrier. Both J. A. Watt and the present author have argued on various occasions that the alleged language barrier in the later medieval province of Armagh was not a formidable obstacle to

---

[10] Cf. Ernest Hauswirth, *Urkunden der Benedictiner-Abtei Unserer Lieben Frau zu den Schotten in Wien vom Jahre 1158 bis 1418* — *Fontes Rerum Austriacarum*, II, Abt. 18 (Vienna, 1859), no. 4; a facsimile of the charter is reproduced in Ferenczy, *Schottenstift*, p. 25. On the Babenberg rulers, and their interest in the Irish foundation in Vienna cf. K. Lechner, *Die Babenberger. Markgrafen und Herzoge von Österreich 976-1246* (Vienna, Cologne, Graz, 1976), *ad indicem.*

[11] Cf. paper by Tomás O'Fiaich in the present volume, for the financial support which some Irish communities, especially Regensburg and Würzburg, received from ruling circles in Munster. On the Irish community in Kiev cf. the literature cited in Hammermayer, 'Die irischen Benediktiner', p. 259, also Władysław Abraham, *Powstanie organizacyi kościoła łacinskiego na Rusi*, I (Lemberg [Lłow], 1904), pp. 64–71.

[12] B. Weiss, *Die Pfarren des Stiftes Schotten von der Gründung des Stiftes bis zur Glaubensspaltung* (D.Phil. thesis, Vienna, 1952).

communication among those who genuinely sought contact—the willing-ness and ability of medieval administrators to learn a language other than their own should not be underestimated, and references to interpreters at peace negotiations are frequent.[13]

The impressive range of Latin and German charters, which were edited by Ernest Hauswirth in 1859,[14] document the extent to which the Irish community was in close contact with all sections of Viennese society: individuals and families from all callings, trades, and professions chose to make their will in the convent or have it witnessed by one of the monks; they donated money, lands, houses, rents, vineyards, and miscellaneous property, presumably in gratitude for spiritual and legal advice. All this may be more a testimony to the monks' business acumen than to their selfless piety, but it indicates that they were not perceived by the population as alien and undesirable. In a charter of 28 February 1200 the Babenberg Duke Leopold VI, who later died on crusade, men-tioned the Irish monks as requiring his special protection, because they were *exules et simplices.*[15] They were unquestionably exiles, but—at least in terms of their acquisition of property—they did not remain *simplices* for very long. By 1200 they owned property in thirty-one places in Lower Austria, and they have been estimated as landlords of up to one-fifth of all dwelling houses in fourteenth-century Vienna. A comparison of the extant property lists for 1322 and 1377 shows that in the later fourteenth century they were still expanding. Now they were extending their property beyond the original concentration in areas north of the Danube to include regions south of the river as well.[16] It is difficult to

[13] Cf. K. Simms, 'The concordat between Primate John Mey and Henry O'Neill, 1455', *Archivium Hibernicum*, 34 (1976-7), pp. 71-82; *idem*, 'The King's friend: O'Neill, the Crown and the earldom of Ulster' in *England and Ireland in the later middle ages. Essays in honour of Jocelyn Otway-Ruthven*, ed. J. F. Lydon (Dublin, 1981), pp. 214-36; *idem*, *From Kings to Warlords. The changing political structure of Gaelic Ireland in the Later Middle Ages* (Studies in Celtic History, 7, Woodbridge, Suffolk, 1987); J. A. Watt, 'John Colton, Justiciar of Ireland (1382) and Arch-bishop of Armagh (1383-1404) in *England and Ireland*, pp. 196-213; *idem*, '*Ecclesia inter Anglicos et inter Hibernicos*: confrontation and coexistence in the medieval diocese and province of Armagh', *The English in Medieval Ireland. Proceedings of the first joint meeting of the Royal Irish Academy and the British Academy, Dublin, 1982*, ed. J. F. Lydon (Dublin, 1984), pp. 46-64.

[14] See above note 10.

[15] Hauswirth, *Urkunden*, no. 11; lists of property from the early years of the monastery have not survived, but for subsequent additions cfr. K. Janacek, 'Zur Besitzgeschichte des Wiener Schottenklosters', *Jahrbuch des Vereines für Geschichte der Stadt Wien*, 5-6 (1946-7), pp. 24-92.

[16] Much of the evidence for this development is contained in the unpublished thesis of B. Weiss, *Die Pfarren*, and in S. Petrin, *Das Urbar des Wiener Schottenklosters über dessen außerstädtischen Besitz vom Jahre 1376* (unpublished: Staatsprüfungsarbeit am Institut für Österreichische

avoid the impression that the Irish monks were being handsomely rewarded for services rendered.

What were these services? On the one hand the Irish abbots in Vienna emerge as delegates of successive popes and of the territorial rulers with wide powers of investigation and supervision in ecclesiastical matters in Moravia and Hungary. These activities were not always guaranteed to enhance their popularity and may have been a crucial factor in their fate in 1418. On the other hand they played a prominent role in the foundation of the University of Vienna in 1365 and of its theological faculty in 1384, and furthermore acted as delegates to the older university in Prague. In addition they frequently acted as peace-makers between the citizens of Vienna and the territorial rulers—again an indication of closer integration than is normally assumed.

A substantial body of Moravian charters and the corresponding material in the papal registers document the regular involvement of the Irish abbots in disputes between the secular and regular clergy in the diocese of Olomouc, concerning *ius patronatus*, tithes, monastic exemptions, and privileges. The earliest of these date from 1246, and in a series of letters Popes Innocent IV and Alexander IV issued commissions to Abbot Felix and, after the latter's death in 1247, to Philip, abbot of the Irish convent in Vienna 1248–68.[17] In 1246 Felix was to give judgement in a dispute about tithes involving the Cistercian abbot of Welehrad,[18] the Cistercian nuns at Tišnowic (Porta Coeli)[19] and other religious communities in

---

Geschichtsforschung, Vienna, 1962); K. Lechner, 'Ein unbekanntes Urbar des Wiener Schottenklosters aus dem Jahre 1322', *MIÖG* 68 (1960), pp. 402–33.

[17] The most reliable lists of the Irish abbots are given in Rapf, *Schotten-Stift*, p. 107; Ferenczy, *Schottenstift*, pp. 15, 30. As Philip's successor, Joannes I, does not figure in the records until the late summer of 1269, there is some doubt as to the actual date of Philip's death.

[18] *Cod. Dip. et ep. Moraviae*, 3, no. LXXXVII, p. 63. On Velehrad, south-east of Brno, which was founded in 1205 from Plasy, cf. L. H. Cottineau, *Répertoire topo-bibliographique des abbayes et prieurés*, 2 (Macon, 1939), col. 3440; J. Nevěřil, 'Beitrag zur Geschichte der Zisterzienser-Niederlassung in Welehrad', *LXI. Jahresbericht des k. k. Staatsgymnasiums mit deutscher Unterrichtssprache in Ung. Hradisch für das Schuljahr 1914–1915*, pp. 3–32. The most important feature of this contribution is the printing of an historical chronicle of the monastery to 1737, then located in the Cistercian abbey of Osseg (dioc. Prague), which indicates the succession of abbots. These were a mixed group, with some members of the German *natio*, while the majority in the period under discussion came from Bohemia, Moravia, Poland, and Italy. On the desecration of the monastery and murder of the abbot and remaining monks in 1421 at the hands of Jan Žižka's troops cf. T. [Pater Tescelin] Halusa, 'Das Martyrium der Cistercienser-Mönche in Welehrad', *Cistercienser-Chronik*, 9 (1897), pp. 13–16.

[19] Cf. Cottineau, *Répertoire*, 1, col. 1448 [Himmelpforte]. The convent is situated a short distance north-west of Brno, and its church has a magnificent Romanesque portal which gave

southern Moravia in the region of Brno. Both Felix and his successors had to deal with a lengthy dispute, which continued into the fourteenth century between the Cistercian abbess of Tišnowic and the provost of the church of SS Peter and Paul in Brno, which in 1298 attained the status of a collegiate church with a chapter of canons.[20] As patron of the church the abbess claimed the right of presentation and secured the support of successive Irish abbots, in their capacity as papal judges delegate, and consequently papal approval for the claim. The nuns, who had considerable property in Brno,[21] clearly represented a predominantly Slav element in Tišnowic and in the mixed city of Brno, and among the formidable opponents with whom they had to contend in defence of their *ius patronatus* was Peter von Aspelt. Peter, who rose from personal physician to the emperor Rudolf von Habsburg to become archbishop of Mainz and chancellor of the Holy Roman Empire,[22] acquired numerous benefices in Vienna, and in Bohemia and Moravia, including the provostship of SS Peter and Paul in Brno, and in this case the nuns' resistance had little chance of success.[23]

These are the earliest indications that the Irish abbots had acquired particular responsibility for the Cistercian communities in the diocese of Olomouc, at first on an *ad hoc* basis, then formally as protector and conservator of their privileges from 1309 onwards. On 4 September 1309 Pope Clement V had appointed the abbot of St Peter in Erfurt[24] as

---

the abbey its popular name, cf. J. E. Wocel, *Die Kirche des ehemaligen Cistercienser-Nonnenklosters Porta Coeli zu Tisnovic* (Vienna, 1859); T. Halusa, 'Einige Stunden in Mährisch-Himmelpforten', *Cistercienser-Chronik*, 8 (1896), pp. 200–9, summarizes previous specialized research.

[20] *Cod. Dip. et ep. Moraviae*, 3, no. CCXLII, pp. 226–7, dated 8 January 1257, is the earliest recorded indication of the Irish abbots' involvement in the Brno disputes. Cf. further B. Bretholz, *Geschichte der Stadt Brünn bis 1411* (Brünn, 1911), esp. pp. 170 *seq*.

[21] *Ibid.*, p. 160.

[22] On Peter von Aspelt cf. J. Heidemann, *Peter von Aspelt als Kirchenfürst und Staatsmann* (Berlin, 1875); A. Hessel, *Jahrbücher des Deutschen Reichs unter König Albrecht I. von Habsburg* (Munich, 1931), esp. pp. 136 *seq.*; F. Bock, *Reichsidee und Nationalstaaten vom Untergang des alten Reiches bis zur Kündigung des deutsch-englischen Bündnisses im Jahre 1341* (Munich, 1943), *ad indicem*; M. Arens, *Die Reichspolitik des Erzbischofs von Mainz, Peter von Aspelt, 1306–1320* (unpublished D.Phil. thesis, Freiburg i. Br., 1949); E. Schubert, 'Kurfürsten und Wahlkönigtum. Die Wahlen von 1308, 1314 und 1346 und der Kurverein von Rhens', *Balduin von Luxemburg, Erzbischof von Trier—Kurfürst des Reiches 1285–1354. Festschrift aus Anlass des 700. Geburtsjahres*, ed. Franz-Josef Heyen *et al.* (Mainz, 1985), pp. 103–17.

[23] For important documents concerning his Bohemian benefices, including the valuable provostship of Vyšehrad which he managed to retain even after becoming bishop, cf. *Actenstücke zur Geschichte des Deutschen Reiches unter den Königen Rudolf I und Albrecht I*, ed. F. Kaltenbrunner (*Mitteilungen aus dem Vaticanischen Archive*, 1, Vienna, 1889), *ad indicem*, and esp. p. 493.

[24] Cf. Cottineau, *Répertoire*, 1, coll. 1061 *seq.*; this foundation is not to be confused with the Irish Benedictine monastery, the Schottenkloster of St James in Erfurt, cf. Hammermayer, 'Die irischen Benediktiner', pp. 296.

protector of the Cistercian communities. For geographical reasons the latter wished to transfer responsibility for the Moravian convents to his brother abbot in Vienna, and this was duly approved in a charter of Bishop Konrad of Olomouc, on 27 February 1320, which lists all the communities of Cistercian monks and nuns for whom the Irish abbots were to be responsible.[25] By the time of abbot Philip (1248–68/9) the status of the Irish abbots was clearly high: he is the first who is known to have obtained the right to the pontificalia, i.e. to mitre and crozier, and a seal dated 1261 depicts him as such. In a charter issued by King Přmysl Ottokar II of Bohemia on 17 October 1258, confirming the rights of the abbess of Tišnowic, Abbot Philip headed the list of witnesses[26]—one of the many occasions on which the Irish abbots may have backed the wrong horse and unwittingly helped to pave the way for their own downfall.[27]

Vatican material tells a similar story with regard to the involvement of the Irish abbots in church affairs in Hungary, where they acted as conservators for the bishop of Veszprém, and in Meissen in Saxony.[28] Clearly the abbots of the Viennese Schottenkloster enjoyed a special position in more ways than one, and by virtue of their activities as papal delegates in Hungary and Moravia they made themselves indispensable, carving out for themselves an area of jurisdiction which put even that of the canons of Klosterneuburg in the shade.[29] The Irish abbots usually acted in response to a papal commission: in 1320 Abbot Johannes issued charters and described himself as *Judex et conservator . . . a sede apostolica deputatus.*[30] He had his own personal notary and a chancery staff to issue his documents; the seals of the convent and the personal seal of the abbot began to take on the definitive form which was to be adopted by the German community after 1418.[31] Under the title *principalis et perpetuus Conservator Monasteriorum Cisterciensis Ordinis a Sede Apostolica specialiter deputatus* Abbot Clement

---

[25] *Cod. Dip. et ep. Moraviae*, 15 (Nachträge, 1207–1408), no. XXXIII, pp. 25–7.

[26] *Ibid.*, 3, no. CCLXX, pp. 260–1. For Philip's seal cf. Rapf, *Abriß*, p. 133 n. 278.

[27] The conflict of interests already became clear in the lifetime of abbot Philip, when he endeavoured to protect the parochial rights of the Schottenkloster in Vienna against the parish of St Stephen. One of the papal judges delegate appointed in 1265 to deal with the issue was the provost of Brno, cf. Hauswirth, *Abriß*, p. 10 and *Cod. Dip. et ep. Moraviae*, 3, no. CCLXIX, pp. 259–60.

[28] Cf. esp. *Acta Pataviensia Austriaca. Vatikanische Akten zur Geschichte des Bistums Passau und der Herzöge von Österreich (1342–1378)*, I, *Klemens VI (1342–1352)*, ed. J. Lenzenweger (*Publikationen des Österreichischen Kulturinstituts in Rom* II/4, 1, Vienna, 1974), *passim*.

[29] *Ibid.*, p. 236.

[30] *Cod. Dip. et ep. Moraviae*, 6, no. CLXVIII, pp. 129–30.

[31] *Ibid.*, 5, no. CXLI, pp. 146–7 (30 September 1302); cf. A. Zelenka and W. Sauer, *Die Wappen der Wiener Schottenäbte* (Vienna, 1971), p. 3.

(1349–72), who will figure again below as one of the founding fathers of the University of Vienna, was authorized to impose all customary ecclesiastical sanctions against those who violate or alienate monastic property.[32] These sanctions included the right to excommunicate, a right which the Irish abbots were prepared to exercise on a number of occasions.

Under Clement's successor, Donatus (1372–80), a new range of duties was added, namely the protection and supervision of the cathedral chapter of Olomouc, also *ex delegacione sedis apostolice.* In this capacity the Irish abbots were as active as in their obligations towards the Cistercians, and they handed down a number of decisions concerning appointments to dignities in the cathedral of Olomouc and in the collegiate church of Kroměříž.[33] Here Abbot Henry made another potentially dangerous mistake. In a sentence dated 4 March 1399 he excommunicated—among others, who are all described as oppressors of the Church in the diocese of Olomouc—Markgrave Jobst (Jodok) of Moravia, a nephew of the Emperor Charles IV and a serious candidate for the German kingship ten years later.[34] Nevertheless the prestige of the Irish abbots appeared undiminished, and on 28 September 1407, when the Habsburg Duke Leopold IV negotiated a settlement with Jodok of Moravia, the last Irish abbot Thomas O'Crosscraid witnessed the deed (in the German language) as third on the list, immediately after the ruler and his chancellor Berthold von Wehingen[35]—the Irish abbot was clearly still a person of consequence at court in Vienna.

The long-lived abbot Clement (1349–72) played a decisive part in the negotiations leading up to the foundation of the University of Vienna, and he had a prominent place on the list of prelates who witnessed the foundation charter on 12 March 1365.[36] In return for his assistance the founder, Duke Rudolf IV (the 'Stifter'), who appears to have consulted Clement on

---

[32] *Cod. Dip. et ep. Moraviae*, 9, no. CCCIX, p. 239, 12 August 1363; *ibid.*, 7, no. DVII, p. 371, contains a similar authorization from Clement VI for the abbot of the Viennese Schottenkloster, 9 October 1343.

[33] *Ibid.*, 10, no. CCXXXVII, p. 250; *ibid.*, 12, no. LXXXV, pp. 70 f.; ASV, Reg. Lat. 30, fols 178ʳ–179ʳ; Reg. Lat. 89, fol. 100ʳ⁻ᵛ; *Cal. Pap. Let.* 4, p. xxiii.

[34] *Cod. Dip. et ep. Moraviae*, 12, no. DXXIV, pp. 455–64. For an assessment of Markgrave Jodok cf. most recently J. Spěváček, *Václav IV. 1361–1419 k předpokladům husitské revoluce* (Prague, 1986), *ad indicem.*

[35] *Cod. Dip. et ep. Moraviae*, 13, no. CCCCLXXXIX, pp. 522–4. On Berthold von Wehingen, and his place in Habsburg ecclesiastical policy cf. A. A. Strnad, 'Kanzler und Kirchenfürst. Streiflichter zu einem Lebensbilde Bertholds von Wehingen', *Jahrbuch des Stifies Klosterneuburg*, 12, n.s. 3 (1963), pp. 79–109.

[36] For the text cf. A. Lhotsky, *Die Wiener Artistenfakultät 1365–1497* (*SB der Österreichischen Akademie der Wissenschaften, phil.-hist. Klasse*, 247/2, Graz, Vienna, Cologne, 1965), pp. 207–22.

matters of a more political nature as well, took the abbey and its monks under his special protection.[37] Clement's successor Donald played a similar role in the preparations for the erection of the theological faculty in the early 1380s. In 1383 he was elected, as eighth in the line, rector of the young foundation, and he managed to establish the integration of the abbey into the ceremonial of the university. The convent had a geographical advantage: originally a university quarter was planned between the Schottenkloster and the Hofburg, and the convent was situated about 1300 metres, or $\frac{3}{4}$ mile from the *Collegium ducale*, which was the core of the university. Donald, as abbot and rector, ensured that on three major feasts the university assembled for mass in the Schottenkloster—on foundation day, 12 March, which was also the feast of one of the patron saints of the abbey, St Gregory; on 21 March the feast of St Benedict, when the abbot also had the right to nominate the preacher;[38] and on 8 September, the Marian feast which gave the abbey its name, 'Unsere liebe Frau zu den Schotten'.[39] A further indication that the integration of convent and university was taken for granted occurs in a marginal remark in the acts of the faculty of arts for 29 May 1401. It was decided that the bell should sound to summon members for meetings of Congregation so as to allow sufficient time for members to come from the Schottenkloster.[40] The spontaneity of the phraseology, even in the relatively formal acts of university corporations, confirms the assumption that the Schottenkloster was expected to be a major catchment area for members of Congregation. The convent had its own school at least since the early fourteenth century—payment to the schoolmaster in 1330 amounted to a barrel of wine and 24 pence.[41] The monks were indeed represented in the university, though the matriculation records indicate that the majority of academics from the Schottenkloster were not, as

---

[37] Cf. R. Kink, *Geschichte der kaiserlichen Universität zu Wien* (Vienna, 1854), 2, p. 22; on Rudolf's ecclesiastical and intellectual policies cf. A. A. Strnad, 'Libertas Ecclesiae und fürstliche Bistumspolitik', *Römische Historische Mitteilungen*, 6–7 (1964), pp. 72–112.

[38] Cf. Kink, *Universität zu Wien*, 2, p. 88; Barry, *Wiener Schottenkloster*, pp. 25–6; Rapf, *Schotten-Stift*, pp. 25, 46. On the modification of Duke Rudolf's original plan for a *quartier latin* near the Hofburg, cf. Lhotsky, *Wiener Artistenfakultät*, pp. 62 *seq.*

[39] Barry, *Wiener Schottenkloster*, p. 25 n. 52, printed the relevant extract from the university statutes for 5 October 1385.

[40] *Acta Facultatis Artium Universitatis Vindobonensis 1385–1416*, ed. P. Uiblein (*Publikationen des Instituts für Österreichische Geschichtsforschung*, 6. Reihe 2. Abteilung, Graz, Vienna, Cologne, 1968), p. 195, l. 6. For further evidence of the central importance of the abbots Patricius (1400–1) and Thomas (1403–18), *ibid. ad indicem.*

[41] Hauswirth, *Urkunden*, no. 166, pp. 190–1.

might have been expected, theologians. They were to be found among the ranks of the canon lawyers.[42]

Apart from the *de iure* position of the Irish abbots, as leading prelates in the regional assembly,[43] they were useful collaborators in the plans for the foundation of a university with a theological faculty, because of their good connections with the only existing university in Central Europe, that at Prague. Given the present state of research, these contacts are difficult to document with precision, but they are presumably to be explained through the Irish abbots' involvement with the regular clergy in Moravia. Abbot Donald's contacts with Prague however, depended more specifically on his position in Vienna as rector of the university,[44] when he went to Prague as member of a commission whose objective was the defence of academic rights and privileges, especially with regard to the faculties of arts.[45] At this stage there was still no reason to assume that cosmopolitan academic life in Prague faced an uncertain future.

Although the prime mover in the downfall of the Irish community in 1418 was a distinguished member of the university of Vienna, namely Nicholas of Dinkelsbühl,[46] the last Irish abbot clearly enjoyed the confidence both of the university as a corporate body, and of the bishop of Passau as ordinary of the diocese in the years leading up to the final crisis. On 7 July 1413 the bishop of Passau granted an indulgence to all who were prepared to help the convent repair the serious damage caused by the fire of 1410, in which they had lost so many valuables, and especially most of their books.[47] Two years earlier, on 17 August 1411 in a decision which—

---

[42] Cf. *Die Matrikel der Universität Wien*, I Band, 1377–1450 (*Publikationen des Instituts für Österreichische Geschichtsforschung*, 6. Reihe, 1. Abteilung, Graz, Cologne, 1956), *passim*. Nor was the new reform community after 1418 more prominent in Viennese theological circles. In the period up to 1508 they never provided a dean of the faculty of theology, and references to the abbey in the *Acta* of that faculty are restricted to the annual nomination of the statutory preacher for 8 September, cf. *Die Akten der Theologischen Fakultät der Universität Wien (1396–1508)*, ed. P. Uiblein (Vienna, 1978), *ad indicem*, and pp. xxv–xxxi for the list of deans.

[43] i.e. 'landständisch'. This involvement in worldly affairs, especially in the case of abbot Clement (1349–72), was mentioned frequently in the criticism expressed by the later German community, without apparently noting the incongruity. Cf. C. Rapf, 'Die Abtbischöfe des Wiener Schottenstiftes im 17. Jahrhundert', *Festschrift Franz Loidl zum 65. Geburtstag*, ed. V. Flieder (Vienna, 1970), 1, pp. 255–300.

[44] Cf. H. Peichl, 'Die Beziehungen des Schottenstiftes zur Wiener Universität seit deren Gründung', *800 Jahre Schottenabtei*, pp. 63 *seq.*

[45] *Ibid.*; Barry, *Wiener Schottenkloster*, p. 24, confused Donald's office of rector with that of dean of the arts faculty. The full text of the statutes of the Faculty of Arts in Vienna from 1 April 1389 is printed in Lhotsky, *Wiener Artistenfakultät*, pp. 223–62.

[46] Cf. A. Madre, *Nikolaus von Dinkelsbühl, Leben und Schriften. Ein Beitrag zur theologischen Literaturgeschichte* (*Beiträge*, xl/4, Münster, 1965); *Die Akten der Theologischen Fakultät*, *ad indicem*.

[47] Hauswirth, *Urkunden*, no. 437, p. 540; *Idem*, *Abriß*, p. 25.

viewed with the benefit of hindsight—would prove no good service to the Irish monks, John XXIII appointed Abbot Thomas, together with the bishops of Olomouc and Regensburg, as protectors and conservators of the University of Vienna, and therefore responsible for judicial procedures involving its members.[48] It might be argued in Thomas' defence that in 1411 the popes of the Pisan line seemed a force for conciliation, and that in this case he could not have foreseen that he was opting for the wrong, and losing side. However a subsequent document indicates that Irish monks in south German convents[49] continued to adhere to Baldassarre Cossa long after the writing must have appeared on the wall. On 9 January 1415 Cormac, abbot of the Irish Benedictine community in Constance, sought—and on paper obtained—from the still-Pope John XXIII the priory of Weih-St. Peter outside the walls of Regensburg *in commendam*, because the income from his abbatial *mensa* was insufficient.[50]

It is well known that supporters of the deposed John XXIII—unless they had powerful protection[51]—were harshly treated, and the Irish Benedictines in Vienna were no exception. Their principal antagonist was Nicholas Prunczlein (Brüntzler), better known as Nicholas of Dinkelsbühl, because he carefully avoided having his family name publicized beyond the pages of the matriculation record.[52] Nicholas was one of the most prominent theologians in the early university. A student of Heinrich Hembuche of Langenstein and Heinrich Totting of Oyta,[53] he acted on a number of occasions as dean of the faculty of theology, and as rector was a

---

[48] Kink, *Universität zu Wien*, 1, pp. 138, 152.

[49] Dietrich von Niem's Anglo-Irish contact, John Swayne, acted in a similar vein, cf. K. Walsh, 'The Roman Career of John Swayne, Archbishop of Armagh 1418-1439: plans for an Irish hospice in Rome', *Seanchas Ardmhacha*, 11 (1983-4), pp. 1-21.

[50] ASV, Reg. Lat. 181, fol. 93ʳ-94ᵛ; *Cal. Pap. Reg.* 6, p. 487. On Weih-St. Peter cf. G. A. Renz, 'Beiträge zur Geschichte der Schottenabtei St. Jakob und des Priorats Weih-St. Peter in Regensburg', *StMBO* 16-8 (1895-97). For his presence at the Council of Constance and at the Benedictine chapter at Petershausen, cf. Barry, *Wiener Schottenkloster*, p. 38. For an earlier grant of Weih-St. Peter to an Irish monk from Vienna, cf. n. 60.

[51] Walsh, 'Swayne', esp. pp. 14 *seq*.

[52] The offending entry 'Nycolaus Prunczlein' (under 14 April 1385) is to be found on p. 18 of the printed edition, *Die Matrikel . . . Wien*.

[53] Cf. H. Pruckner, *Studien zu den astrologischen Schriften des Heinrich von Langenstein* (*Studien der Bibliothek Warburg*, 14, Berlin, 1933); J. Lang, *Die Christologie bei Heinrich von Langenstein. Eine dogmenhistorische Untersuchung* (*Freiburger Theologische Studien*, 85, Freiburg, Basel, Vienna, 1966); T. Hohmann, *Heinrichs von Langenstein 'Unterscheidung der Geister' lateinisch und deutsch. Texte und Untersuchungen zu Übersetzungsliteratur aus der Wiener Schule* (*Münchener Texte und Untersuchungen zur deutschen Literatur des Mittelalters*), 63 (Zurich, Munich, 1977); A. Lang, *Heinrich Totting von Oyta. Ein Beitrag zur Entstehungsgeschichte der ersten deutschen Universitäten und zur Problemgeschichte der Spätscholastik* (*Beiträge*, 33, Münster, 1937).

canon of the chapter of All Saints at St Stephen and tutor to the young Duke Albrecht V, whom he then represented at the Council of Constance.[54] Though not himself a Benedictine, Nicholas supported the *Consuetudines Sublacenses* and the reform at Melk, where he lectured in theology for several years.[55] He was also an enthusiastic devotee of the new forms of corporative thinking which dominated the conciliar era. Supporters of the conciliar movement believed that the age of corporate decision-making had come, and that power now rested in the College of Cardinals, the universities, the plenum of conciliar assemblies, and the *natio*. Nicholas, who got some votes in the papal election of 1417, was an ardent supporter of the new territorial concept of the German *natio*, and he clashed with the Irish monks in Vienna, who tried to defend their own more exclusive concept, which was not territorial but restricted to their own monastic community and ethos. Even apart from the increasing difficulty in obtaining suitable new recruits of Irish parentage, this no longer seemed opportune. In the circumstances it is difficult to establish whether or not the decision to act against the Irish community in Vienna came from Albrecht V personally or—more probably—was due to the initiative of Nicholas of Dinkelsbühl. When the duke petitioned Martin V to order a visitation of the convent on the lines laid down at the Benedictine general chapter held at Petershausen near Constance during the Council, the proposals for the reorganization of the Schottenkloster were drawn up by none other than Nicholas of Dinkelsbühl.[56]

Nicholas' attitude to the Irish monks is perhaps more easily explained if it is recalled that he was a pupil of Heinrich of Langenstein, who is to be remembered among other things for having brought the standard of theological teaching in Vienna to something of which his native university, Paris, need not have been ashamed. He also came to know the vernacular version of the account of the Hungarian knight George Grissaphan's

---

[54] Cf. G. Koller, *Princeps in Ecclesia. Untersuchungen zur Kirchenpolitik Herzog Albrechts V. von Österreich* (AÖG 124, Vienna, 1964), esp. pp. 62 ff.

[55] *Ibid.*, pp. 78 *seq.*; Madre, *Nikolaus von Dinkelsbuhl*, esp. pp. 99–125 on the significance of the *Lectura Mellicensis*. For the reform cf. J. Zeller, 'Das Provinzialkapitel im Stifte Petershausen im Jahre 1417, ein Beitrag zur Geschichte der Reformen im Benediktinerorden zur Zeit des Konstanzer Konzils', *StMBO* n.s. 10 (1922), pp. 1 *seq.* Nicholas presented a copy of his *Questiones in libros sententiarum*, written in his own hand, to the German post-1418 community at the Schottenkloster, now Cod. 274, cf. *Catalogus Codicum manu scriptorum qui in bibliotheca Monasterii B.M.V. ad Scotos Vindobonae servantur . . .*, ed. P. Albertus Hübl (Vindobonae et Lipsiae, 1899), p. 303.

[56] Printed in Anselm Schramb, *Chronicon Mellicense* (Vienna, 1702), pp. 308 ff. Cf. Koller, *Princeps*, pp. 63 ff.; Hammermayer, 'Die irischen Benediktiner', p. 287.

pilgrimage to the purgatory of St Patrick, and he voiced serious criticism both of George's visions and of the cult of St Patrick's Purgatory.[57] In view of the sudden, successful, and geographically persistent circulation of vernacular versions of the account of George's travels in the south-east German–Austrian–Bohemian area during the later fourteenth century, the question should be raised: were Irish monks responsible for boosting the publicity campaign for the *Puragorium sancti Patricii* in an area in which they were linguistically competent? And was this yet another possible reason for their sudden unpopularity in the early fifteenth century, when a more sophisticated theological school in Vienna could take up arms against the spirituality of the Irish monks in the same way as reforming circles around Duke Albrecht V protested against their *consuetudines* and their life-style? Was this a component in the fabrication of the legend of an alien community with an alien culture?

In this context a further provocative hypothesis suggests itself. Unfortunately we know all too little about the theological opinions held by these Irish monks. The indulgence suggests that they lost books in the fire of 1410, and they may have taken others with them in 1418. There is little in the present library at the Schottenkloster which reflects their literary production.[58] However we do know that Nicholas of Dinkelsbühl was one of the most enthusiastic proponents of the Immaculate Conception of the Blessed Virgin, which was then a controversial issue in the schools and among the religious orders.[59] Reservations were widespread, and many serious theologians viewed the matter with considerable scepticism. If the Irish monks shared these reservations, then it may cautiously be suggested that this could have been a further element in Nicholas' campaign against them.

---

[57] Cf. Hohmann, *Langenstein*, pp. 44; L. L. Hammerich, 'Eine Pilgerfahrt des XIV. Jahrhunderts nach dem Fegfeuer des H. Patrizius', *Zeitschrift für deutsche Philologie*, 53 (1928), pp. 25–40; idem, ed. *Visiones Georgii, Visiones quas in purgatorio sancti Patricii vidit Georgius miles de Ungeria A.D. MCCCLIII* (*Det Kgl. Danske Videnskabernes Selskab. Historisk-filologiske Meddelelser*, 18/2, Copenhagen, 1930). No copy of the *Visiones* has survived with a known provenance from the Viennese Schottenkloster, but there was a text of the visions of purgatory experienced by the Irish knight Tun(g)dale, in a 13th-century codex, cf. Hübl, *Catalogus*, Cod. 189, pp. 203 seq. Cf. P. Dinzelbacher, *Vision und Visionsliteratur im Mittelalter* (*Monographien zur Geschichte des Mittelalters*, 23, Stuttgart, 1981), *ad incidem*.

[58] Cf. Hübl, *Catalogus*, passim—with excellent indices. It has also been suggested that the Irish monks took archival records with them in 1418, cf. W. Latzke, 'Das Archiv der Benediktinerabtei Unserer Lieben Frau zu den Schotten in Wien', *Mitteilungen des Österreichischen Staatsarchivs*, 28 (1975), pp. 291–318, at p. 297.

[59] Cf. K. Binder, *Die Lehre des Nikolaus von Dinkelsbühl über die unbefleckte Empfängnis im Licht der Kontroverse* (*Wiener Beiträge zur Theologie*, 31, Vienna, 1970).

Despite the prominence of the later Irish abbots and the responsible tasks they performed, one abbot does not constitute a spiritually intact monastic community. What about the rest of the monks? Were they integrated, or did they experience a sense of alienation from the local population? The evidence of the papal registers at the turn of the fifteenth century indicates that the Irish community was weak in numbers, and that it was surviving with the help of dispensations for illegitimacy. It also shows that the links with Ireland were still strong, especially with particular dioceses, such as Killaloe, and that there was some mobility of personnel among the several Schottenklöster. Furthermore we learn that monks of the Irish community in Vienna had, by the 1390s, begun to seek alternative opportunities for themselves: on 10 April 1395 Patrick O'Higgins, OSB Vienna, was to be examined in Latin by the bishop of Freising—the same Berthold of Wehingen mentioned earlier as chancellor to Leopold IV of Austria—so that he could take over the priory of Weih-St. Peter outside Regensburg, the Pope having satisfied himself that Patrick is *professus et natione Scotus.*[60] Eimear O'Dowd was permitted on 20 November 1396 to become Cistercian abbot at Bective, County Meath, despite the fact that he was a professed Benedictine of the Viennese Schottenkloster.[61] Thomas O'Kelly was not a Benedictine, but he had studied in Vienna and presumably lived at the Schottenkloster,[62] and he received a canonry at Killaloe on 31 August 1399.[63] On 5 September 1399 Thady O'Kyne, OSB Vienna, was given a dispensation to hold benefices normally held by secular clerics, and to exchange them as often as he wished. He was clearly preparing to abandon the *stabilitas loci* of the Viennese convent. A year earlier on 1 September 1398 he had been appointed a papal chaplain. This appointment was essentially an honorary sinecure, but it carried special privileges and exemptions.[64] In a retrospective from 29 October

---

[60] ASV, Reg. Lat. 38, fol. 115ʳ; *Cal. Pap. Let.* 4, p. 522. On Berthold of Wehingen supra n. 35.

[61] ... *alterius coloris et forme regularis habitus*, ASV, Reg. Lat. 44, fol. 273ʳ-274ʳ; *Cal. Pap. Let.* 5, p. 23. Apart from other considerations, the appointment of a member of the Gaelic Irish *natio* was clearly at variance with a ruling of the English king Richard II. Cf. A. Gwynn and R. N. Hadcock, *Medieval Religious Houses, Ireland* (London, 1970), p. 128.

[62] Frater Johannes O'Kelly (Okvallii), monk of the Viennese Schottenkloster, was matriculated in the Nacio Saxorum on 14 April 1398, together with the future abbot Thomas Ocosstraid (*sic*), Donaldus Ograda Ybernicus, and one Donatus Maclancada, for whom neither a nationality nor a monastic affiliation is mentioned, cf. *Die Matrikel . . . Wien*, p. 52.

[63] ASV, Reg. Lat. 54, fol. 146ʳ; *Cal. Pap. Let.* 5, pp. 184-5. His links with the Schottenkloster are indicated by the fact that the executory mandates customary in such cases were sent to the abbot in Vienna and to the archdeacon of Killaloe.

[64] ASV, Reg. Vat. 316, fol. 234ᵛ; Reg. Lat. 54, fol. 218ʳ; Reg. Lat. 68, fol. 64ᵛ-65ʳ; *Cal. Pap. Let.* 4, p. 408; v, pp. 186, 213.

1429 we learn that Donatus O'Grada, a former Benedictine in Vienna who had abandoned habit and order, was accused of financial peculation involving church lands in Killaloe.[65]

This random sample shows that the community was populated to the end by recruits with genuinely Gaelic Irish names. How did all these come to be in Vienna at a time when ideals of *peregrinatio* and crusade were dying out, and when—by all accounts—the Irish communities were finding it increasingly difficult to secure suitable recruits from Ireland? Barry assumed that these foundations recruited very young boys from Ireland and cited the Regensburg visitation protocol of 1452: *fuerunt ibi quinque iuvenes ydiote nec literam nec theutonicum scientes.*[66] The evidence adduced in this paper for the administrative and legal expertise of the Irish abbots in Vienna, and for the integration of the convent with the local community, university, and territorial ruler suggests that these reproaches were scarcely applicable in the Viennese Schottenkloster during the crisis of 1418. However the reference to *uxores*, also mentioned earlier in this paper and in contemporary criticism by no means limited to the Irish convent in Vienna, suggests another possibility. The various versions of this tag in circulation have often been interpreted as meaning that the monks drew on the services of strange women, and that the sober citizen whose wife had gone astray might be well advised to look for her in the Schottenkloster. But it is well known that the Gaelic Irish Church operated a form of clerical marriage, and recent legal and genealogical research has done much to illuminate the trend in the Church *inter Hibernicos* for the clerical profession to become subject to traditional pressures of hereditary family right.[67] Episcopal succession lists and some abbatial appointments indicate that clerical marriage, and succession from father to son or near relative was an integral part of the system. The ecclesiastical family was a fully accepted fact of Irish medieval society. Though permissible, and even desirable under Gaelic customary law, it was clearly at variance with established canon law.[68] It worked with the help of a

---

[65] ASV, Reg. Lat. 285, fol. 304ᵛ-305ᵛ; *Cal. Pap. Let.* 8, p. 81. It is not clear whether he is identical with the Donaldus O'Grada, who matriculated in Vienna thirty years earlier. The clan also contained one Donnchadh O'Grada, who was lector in the Franciscan house at Nenagh, Co. Tipperary, in 1371. Cf. J. A. Watt, 'Gaelic polity and cultural identity', *A New History of Ireland, 2, Medieval Ireland 1169-1534*, ed. A. Cosgrove (Oxford, 1987), p. 337.

[66] Cited in Barry, *Wiener Schottenkloster*, p. 54.

[67] For a useful recent summary of this, partly based on unpublished research by Kenneth Nicholls, cf. Watt, 'Gaelic Polity', pp. 335 *seq.*; A. Cosgrove, 'Marriage in medieval Ireland', *Marriage in Ireland*, ed. A. Cosgrove (Dublin, 1985), pp. 25-50.

[68] Cf. B. Schimmelpfennig, 'Zölibat und Lage der "Priestersöhne" vom 11. bis 14. Jahrhundert', *HZ* 227 (1978), pp. 1-44.

system of papal dispensation which recognized the pressures—and indeed some of the advantages—of a stable system of kin relationships, and thus permitted the sons of priests to be ordained and accept major ecclesiastical appointments, including bishoprics. Hence a clerical caste was established as an hereditary professional elite, and the custom was not restricted exclusively to the secular clergy. However, the evidence for it in religious houses in Gaelic Ireland is quantitatively and qualitatively less satisfactory than for prominent episcopal families such as the O'Farrell in Ardagh and the O'Gráda, who built up an ecclesiastical empire in the dioceses of Cashel, Tuam, and Elphin.[69] One example for the regular clergy is relevant to the present discussion: on 17 August 1349 John O'Carroll, a professed Benedictine of the Schottenkloster in Vienna, received a papal dispensation permitting him to be eligible for election as abbot of that monastery, despite his illegitimacy as the son of a priest.[70] In his petition he stressed that there was such a lack of regular clergy in the area that some monasteries were being governed by secular clerics—an understandable and widespread phenomenon after the Black Death. Between 1346 and 1349 three abbots were elected, but died in quick succession, and John O'Carroll clearly had hopes, though he reckoned without the longevity of Abbot Clement.[71] In view of the preponderance of members of Gaelic families in the Viennese convent to the end, and in view of their obvious determination to preserve a traditional Gaelic cultural identity far from their home country, it may be suggested that Gaelic customs of clerical marriage—which were regarded as socially acceptable and not morally reprehensible—were employed in the battle for survival of the Irish monastic community in Vienna, and possibly elsewhere within the *Germania Sacra*. Unfortunately the prosopographical sample is too thin to permit more than a hypothesis that the Viennese Schottenkloster attempted to solve its recruitment problems internally and along Gaelic lines, and that uncanonical wives (drawn from the daughters of clerical families or fresh imports from Ireland?) were the *uxores* to whom the reformers took such exception, and rejected in 1418 as alien practice.

Hence the last Irish monks in Vienna were not victims of a conspiracy

---

[69] Watt, 'Gaelic Polity', pp. 336–9, and the most reliable version of the episcopal lists in *HBC*[3] for the dioceses *inter Hibernicos*.

[70] ASV, Reg. Suppl. 19, fol. 116ʳ; Reg. Vat. 198, fol. 84ʳ. The former is printed in *Acta Pataviensia Austriaca*, p. 616, under the name 'Okernil'.

[71] See above n. 17. The frequent references in capitular legislation and registers of the mendicant orders to the need to lower standards for ordination, in order to attract new recruits after the Black Death, supports O'Carroll's claim.

to eject them solely because they were foreigners. But they *were* victims of a combination of disadvantageous circumstances, which were linked with the fact that they did not fit into the current ecclesiastical concept of the German *natio* and of the *Princeps in ecclesia*. [72] Despite their function as a court convent, and despite the undisputed political and cultural prestige of the last abbot, Thomas O'Crosscraid (whose seal continued to be used until 1534), [73] Duke Albrecht V allowed himself to be convinced that they were a spent force. Among the factors that told against them were—apart from the possibility of alien marriage customs as a not particularly successful solution to their recruitment problems—their identification with elements which in the aftermath of the Council of Constance were anathema to the policy leaders of the German Church and *natio*. On the one hand they clearly supported John XXIII and on the other—and this may have been even more damaging—were perceived as identifying themselves with Slav elements in the monastic communities of pre-Hussite Bohemia and Moravia. This tendency was much more likely to arouse suspicion in the early fifteenth century than it would have done in the more open climate a century earlier, when the Irish abbots intervened freely in support of the culturally and racially mixed communities of Cistercian monks at Welehrad and Saar, and the nuns at Tišnowic, [74] as well as in the more obviously German-dominated community of Cistercian nuns at Oslowan. [75] In these cases, and in their often critical treatment of members of the chapters of Olomouc and Kroměříž towards the end of the century, it is highly improbable that the abbots of the Viennese Schottenkloster were consciously pursuing an 'anti-German' policy, or even aware of such a possibility. But they did have a weakness for the underdog, and were adamant in defence of the rights of rural monastic communities, where names like Bohuslava, Ludmilla, and Vaclav (Wenceslaus) occur frequently in the records, against the possibly intimidating sophistication of prelates and canons in Olomouc and Brno. [76] These

[72] For a theoretical discussion of this concept cf. Koller, *Princeps*, pp. 58.

[73] Zelenka and Sauer, *Die Wappen*, pp. 3, 10 *seq.*

[74] Cottineau, *Répertoire*, 2, cols 2151, 2569 *seq.*

[75] This emerges from the consistent occurrence of German names of the abbess of Oslowan in *Cod. Dip. et ep. Moraviae* for the 13th and 14th century, *passim*. Oslowan also held extensive property in Brno and the *ius patronatus* of the parish church of St James in the city. The latter involved the nuns in a constant struggle between the provost of SS Peter and Paul (who also claimed this *ius patronatus*) and the papacy, *ibid.* and Bretholz, *Geschichte der Stadt Brünn*, pp. 161 ff.

[76] The names of the provosts cited in *Cod. Dip. et ep. Moraviae*, and the list of families represented in the chapter at Brno in the 14th century, cited in Bretholz, *Geschichte der Stadt Brünn*, p. 160, suggest that here the German element dominated.

contacts may well be an indication that the Irish abbots did experience a sense of alienation from their German-speaking neighbours, and were thus inclined to identify with another element often perceived to be alien. Friendly contacts in an area of potential religious dissent during the early stages of the Hussite upheaval *may* have mitigated against the Irish monks in Vienna, and would have increased the suspicion of a Nicholas of Dinkelsbühl, who emerges as the prime architect of their removal.

The related question alluded to in the title can only be posed as a hypothesis here: its exposition would require a separate, and very different essay. However the manner in which the Irish community in Vienna came to a sudden and—as the evidence indicates—up to the last minute unexpected end in 1418 is illustrative of the thinking of corporate groupings about the identity and function of the *natio*. Once confessional pluralism became an established fact in the sixteenth century the basis for thinking in identity-groups shifted from the national to the confessional unit. The 'Mauerkirche'[77] had to permit older barriers to be dismantled, in order to stabilize newer supranational structures of the Counter-Reformation. Hence when Fr Florence Conry and his small band of Franciscans set up their new headquarters in Louvain in the early seventeenth century,[78] with the support of King Philip III of Spain and especially that of regents, the archducal pair Albrecht VII and Isabella, questions of allegiance to a *natio* had lost much of their relevance as a component of ecclesiastical policy. Therefore the Irish friars could be employed beyond their own original purpose of establishing a training ground for the Irish mission at home, to become agents of the Counter-Reformation in the Habsburg lands, especially in Prague, where their role as a religious and intellectual force from their foundation in 1629 until the suppression under the Emperor Joseph II was recognized in pre-1948 Czech historiography.[79]

---

[77] F. Heer, *Die Dritte Kraft. Der europäische Humanismus zwischen den Fronten des konfessionellen Zeitalters* (Frankfurt am Main, 1960), favours this term.

[78] *Louvain Papers 1606-1827*, ed. B. Jennings. Prepared for publication and indexed by C. Giblin (Irish Manuscripts Commission, Dublin, 1968), no. 153, pp. 112 *seq. et ad indicem*. The archives of the convent are now lodged in the University Library, Prague.

[79] E. Winter, *Tausend Jahre Geisteskampf im Sudetenraum. Das religiöse Ringen zweier Völker* (Salzburg, Leipzig, 1938), pp. 243 *seq.*; *idem*, *Frühaufklärung. Der Kampf gegen den Konfessionalismus in Mittel- und Osteuropa und die deutsch-slawische Begegnung* (*Beiträge zur Geschichte des religiösen und wissenschaftlichen Denkens*, 6, Berlin DDR, 1966), pp. 165, with extensive references to Czech sources and literature. A more popular summary of the same material is to be found in *idem*, *Barock, Absolutismus und Aufklärung in der Donaumonarchie* (Vienna, 1971), p. 45.

Now they are remembered only for a street, the Hibernska, and for the fact that an Irish Franciscan vegetable garden was the first place where potatoes were successfully grown in Central Europe.

Universität Salzburg

IRISH MONKS IN GERMANY IN
THE LATE MIDDLE AGES

by TOMÁS Ó FIAICH

Introduction

EVERYONE has some acquaintance with the Irish missionaries and scholars who from the sixth until the ninth century abandoned their homeland to go on a *peregrinatio pro Christi nomine* and left a lasting imprint on the history of many countries in Western Europe. They included St Columba of Iona, Apostle of Scotland († 597), St Aidan of Lindisfarne, Apostle of Northern England († 651), St Columbanus of Luxeuil and Bobbio († 615), St Gall, after whom Sankt Gallen in Switzerland is named († *c.*630), St Fursey († 650) and St Fiachra († 670) of northeast France, St Feuillen († 652) of Belgium, St Kilian and his companions of Würzburg († 689), St Fergal or Virgilius of Salzburg († 784), whose twelfth centenary was celebrated four years ago, and several others.

Perhaps not so well known to the ordinary people but certainly familiar to students of medieval philosophy and literature are the names of the ninth-century scholars who were driven by the Viking attacks on the Irish monasteries to seek refuge on the Continent. They made a notable contribution to the Carolingian Renaissance just before 800 and for a few generations afterwards, scholars like Dicuil the geographer, Dungal of St Denis, and Dungal of Pavia (who was charged by Charlemagne with the organization of education in Italy), Clemens Scottus (master of the Palace School), and the two outstanding personalities among them: Eriugena of Laon, their greatest philosopher, and Sedulius Scottus of Liège, their most notable poet.

Both of those groups, the saints and the scholars, laid the foundation of lasting links between Ireland and the continental mainland which have never entirely disappeared until the present time. But it is not about either of the two groups already mentioned but about a third group of Irish monks on the continent that I wish to write. They were a later, lesser-known, and narrower group. For nearly 500 years, from the eleventh century until the sixteenth century, they provided an extensive Irish presence on the continent, and were the only group of Irish monasteries then outside Ireland. Unlike the two earlier movements which had been strongest in the Romance-speaking parts of Europe, this third movement

89

turned to the Germanic parts, to modern Germany and Austria. In a sense it was the last fling of Irish monasticism abroad, before it finally petered out at the Reformation.

The name Schottenkloster

Why were these Irish foundations in Germany called *Schottenklöster*, a name which has caused a vast amount of confusion ever since and was partly responsible for the expulsion of the Irish? When St Patrick arrived in Ireland in the fifth century, the country was known to Roman writers since the previous century as Scotia (and its inhabitants as Scotti)—even Irish dogs were called *Scottici canes*. In addition the earlier Latin name, Hibernia, first met in Julius Caesar, lived on. The two names continued in use side by side for several centuries, but the usual name for an Irishman in early Christian literature was Scottus. Hence whenever this name is applied to someone on the continent between the fifth and the twelfth century, he is always an Irishman. Thus the ninth-century scholars Clemens Scottus, Thomas Scottus, Sedulius Scottus, Johannes Scottus Eriugena, were all Irish, as was David Scottus, the historiographer of Emperor Henry V, at the beginning of the twelfth century. Wherever a *Monasterium Scottorum* was founded (as at Péronne in north-eastern France), it was meant for *Irish* monks.

Around the time of St Patrick, however, an Irish colony had been founded in south-west Scotland which ultimately brought the names Scotia and Scottus across the channel. This exclusive use of Scotia for Scotland first becomes common from the twelfth century on, after the Norman invasion of Ireland; hence the great thirteenth-century Franciscan scholar and philosopher, Duns Scottus, was almost certainly born in Scotland, even though the Irish of a later era claimed him as their own. From that time on, Hibernia is the normal Latin name for Ireland, and Scotia is the name for Scotland.

But when seventeenth-century scholars began to research the early saints of Western Europe, some of them wrongly took the Scotti as Scotch rather than Irish. Propagandists from Scotland naturally promoted such an interpretation. This grave error has not been completely eradicated down to the present time. For instance, at the entrance to the parish church at Lagny near Paris, where St Fursey founded his last monastery, you will still find him described as a 'moine écossais', even though he probably never set foot on Scottish soil in his life.[1] In the crypt of the Neumünster in Würzburg, where

---

[1] Since this lecture was delivered I had occasion to visit Lagny again and found that the *écossais* has now been corrected to *irlandais*.

St Kilian and his two companions were martyred, you can still read on the plaque erected in 1853: 'Traveller, pause here, the most venerable spot in Franconia. Here died the first messengers of the Faith in the land of the Franks, who arrived two years earlier from Scotland' (*aus Schottland*). The inscription should of course read 'from Ireland'.

In the last century when German scholars began to investigate the Schottenklöster scientifically for the first time they invented the term *Iro-schotten* to mean the Scotti who came from Ireland. I think 'Schotto-Iren' would have been a better term. But that term, the Scotch-Irish, is now an emotive one, as it is sometimes used in Northern Ireland and in U.S.A. to denote Northern Protestants of Scotch ancestry. So there is plenty of ambiguity about the terminology, but we shall not go astray if we remember that up to the Reformation the Schottenklöster were Irish monasteries, and only from then on were some of them handed over to monks from Scotland.

Beginnings

The founder of the Scottenklöster movement was an Irishman named Muireadhach Mac Robhartaigh, usually known under the latinized form of his name Marianus Scottus. The Mac Groarty family was prominent in County Donegal for centuries, and the names Mac Groarty and Roarty are still common there today—there are 32 people of these names in the current Irish provincial telephone directory and all but one are living in County Donegal. The family were hereditary custodians of the earliest manuscript of Irish provenance now on Irish soil, the Cathach, a copy of the Psalter which may have been written by St Columba in the sixth century, was certainly believed subsequently to have been written by him, and was carried into battle over the centuries by his O'Donnell kinsmen in order to bring them victory through the power of the saint. The name Domhnall Mac Robhartaigh can still be read on the silver case made in the eleventh century for this ancient manuscript and he was then abbot of Kells and successor of St Columba. The Mac Robhartaigh who came to Germany was his kinsman, but he must be carefully distinguished from another Irish monk in Germany at the same time, the chronicler Maelbride of Mainz, who also latinized his name as Marianus Scottus.

We are fortunate to possess a pretty full life of Mac Robhartaigh written by an Irish monk of Regensburg in the twelfth century. According to this *Vita Mariani* he set out on a pilgrimage to Rome in 1067 with two companions John and Candidus. Another source says he had seven, all from the north of Ireland. They spent a year *en route* in the monastery on the Michelsberg in Bamberg, where they took the Benedictine habit, and then moved on to Regensburg. Here they were persuaded by a fellow-countryman named Muircheartach who had been living for nearly twenty years as an *inclusus* beside the nunnery of Obermünster to go no further on the way to Rome, but to settle in Regensburg instead. In 1076 the small group of monks was settled at the house called Weih-Sankt-Peter. Soon there was not sufficient room in Weih-Sankt-Peter for all the novices who came out from Ireland and about 1089 they purchased a piece of ground for a new monastery in honour of St James. It was set up in 1090 with Domnus as its first abbot—perhaps his Irish name was Fear Domhnach, the same name as that of the scribe of the Book of Armagh, or Tigerna[n]. We have still some letters written by the monks about 1090 to Wratislaw, King of Bohemia, asking for an escort for their representatives to Poland. John settled down at Gottweich under its founder Altmann, and Candidus went on pilgrimage to Jerusalem and died there. Another of the monks, accompanied only by a boy, travelled as far as Kiev where the King of Rus resided. He received rich presents towards the building from the King and his nobles, and brought back several wagons loaded with furs, worth a hundred silver marks, when he returned with a group of Regensburg merchants. With the proceeds the monastic buildings were completed and the church roofed. It was consecrated in 1111, the year in which the present-day Irish dioceses were set up, with boundaries which have changed very little since. This monastery of St James in Regensburg became the mother-house of ten Benedictine abbeys and priories in the Germanic part of Europe and the abbot of St James became the superior of the abbots and monks of the other Schottenklöster, who formed a separate congregation within the Benedictine Order.

When we come to study the location of the other Schottenklöster, we notice that most were in towns and on the trade and pilgrim routes that led to Rome and Jerusalem. The monks engaged in the *Cura Animarum*. Unlike the Irish missionaries of earlier centuries, they always maintained a close connection with Ireland. The third abbot of Regensburg, Giolla Críost Mac Carthaigh, of the royal house of Munster, journeyed home to Ireland about 1150 accompanied by four of his monks including a builder named Konrad. He was splendidly received by Conchubhar Slaparsalach ['Dirty Shoes'] O'Brien, King of Thomond, and given gifts totalling 200 marks. With this money the buildings in Regensburg were extended and beautified. When the money ran out Abbot Mac Carthaigh returned on a second visit and was equally successful in fund-raising. He seemed likely to be chosen as archbishop of Cashel but died suddenly and was buried before St Patrick's altar in Cashel. We must remember that Cormac's chapel was being built on the Rock in those years by King Cormac Mac Carthaigh, and Abbot Giolla Críost Mac Carthaigh of Regensburg was probably closely related to him. Art historians have often pointed out some German features in the romanesque architecture of Cormac's chapel and I would not be surprised if master-builder Konrad gave a hand at the building.

Giolla Críost was succeeded as abbot by Gregory, the prior, and during his long reign of over 30 years he rebuilt the church, apart from the towers, and added a cloister. Despite several disastrous fires in the monastery, the twelfth-century church still remains basically as it was erected. Its great glory is, of course, the famous Schottenportal, which presents an amazing mixture of animals and human figures whose full significance still baffles scholars. Just as art experts have found German influence in Cashel, so have they found Irish influence in the two doorways of St James in Regensburg.

Daughter Houses

The first daughter-house of Regensburg was founded at Würzburg in 1134 (or 1139 according to another source). It was an obvious place for a new Irish monastery, having the tomb of St Kilian to which a steady stream of Irish pilgrims had travelled since the seventh century. In fact we know that a small group of Irish monks were already there before 1100 with Giolla na Naomh, bishop of Glendalough, at their head, but we cannot say if they were then Benedictines. At any rate Bishop Embricho of Würzburg founded a new monastery on the Girberg at the edge of the city in 1134 and Abbot Giolla Críost sent monks from Regensburg to staff it. It too was dedicated to St James and its first abbot was a scholarly Irishman, Macharius. We cannot be sure what Irish name this represents—perhaps Mochonna or Mochua or some other name beginning in M, or perhaps it was just a pun on the surname Mac Cárthaigh.

The *Vita Mariani* again provides several anecdotes to emphasize his sanctity. For instance it tells how on one occasion he was visiting the bishop who insisted on offering him a bowl of wine in honour of St Kilian. The saintly abbot was a most untypical Irishman—he would never take strong drink. Now he was torn between abstinence and obedience, but having prayed over the wine he asked the bishop to taste it first. Christ's miracle at Cana was reversed, the contents were pure water, but when the bishop upbraided the butler he was assured that genuine wine had been poured into the bowl.

Macharius died in 1153 and Trithemius records the epitaph on his tomb in Würzburg: *Hic jacet Macharius, primus abbas huius loci, per quem omnipotens Deus vinum in aquam convertit.* There is a fine effigy of him from 1615 on his tomb in the Marienkapelle with a beaker of wine, crozier, and flowing habit—a tall, stout, strong, and tough-looking Irishman. It was Macharius who received into the Würzburg monastery the Irish chronicler David Scottus, historiographer of Emperor Henry V.

Macharius was succeeded in Würzburg by Gregory, probably the later abbot of Regensburg. The whole list of abbots down to the sixteenth century has been preserved, but there are chronological problems about the first few, just as at Regensburg.

After the foundation of the first daughter-house at Würzburg a great number of other daughter-houses followed in quick succession. The second was probably St Aegidius of Nürnberg, which grew out of the appointment of Abbot Carus or Deocarus of Regensburg as chaplain to the Hohenstaufen Emperor Konrad III (1138-52) and his wife Gertrude. About 1140 the Emperor handed over the Aegidiuskapelle to him. When Carus died about 1145 he was buried not in Regensburg but in this little chapel in Nürnberg built twenty years earlier in honour of St Aegidius. Abbot Declan then combined the two posts of Abbot of Regensburg and Chaplain at the Court of Nürnberg and it was he who brought monks from Regensburg and Würzburg to the Schottenkloster of Nürnberg about 1145-6 and, from 1150, added to the small chapel of St Aegidius the large romanesque basilica. We shall return to it later.

About the same time another Schottenkloster was taking shape on the Bodensee—St James's at Konstanz. In 1142 monks from Regensburg were invited by Bishop Henry to set up a new foundation there and the first abbot bore the Latin name of Macrobius. Reeves thinks his Irish name might have been Maelsuthain [suthain = aeternus], but Brian Boru's secretary, Maelsuthain Ó Cerbaill, latinized his name as Calvus Perennis.

The 1150s saw the despatch of a colony of Irish monks from Regensburg to Vienna, whither they were invited by Henry, duke of Austria, who had formerly been duke of Bavaria and had resided in Regensburg. The abbey was dedicated to Our Lady. Their first abbot was Sanctinus, which may be a Latinization of Giolla na Naomh. He arrived with twenty-four companions and, as many of the merchants in Vienna had come from Regensburg, the Irish monks found themselves at home. The foundation is usually dated to 1156 and the founder, Duke Henry Jasomirgott, still rests under the high altar.

Duke Henry's great rival, the old Duke Guelph of Suabia, set up a monastery dedicated to St Nicholas at Memmingen, just south of Ulm, in 1167. His only son had died of the plague and he erected the monastery in his memory. In addition he had murdered the bishop of Augsburg and wished to do penance. The Irish Muiredach (latinized Maurus) was first abbot, and twelve companions accompanied him from Regensburg in 1187.

Before the death of Abbot Gregory in Regensburg in 1204, one further foundation had been made from it. This was at Eichstätt where the Praepositus of the Chapter, Walbrun, handed over a church which he had built in honour of the Holy Cross and seventeen acres of land for the new priory of Holy Cross. Gerard, prior of Weih-Sankt-Peter, and six companions took up residence there in 1183. Twelve was the normal number to accompany the abbot in a new foundation but it was sometimes doubled as in Vienna and sometimes halved as in Eichstätt.

The Schottenkloster of Erfurt was probably founded about the end of the century but we are not sure of the exact year. We find that Trínót [— Trinitas] abbot of St James, Erfurt, attended a chapter of abbots of the Schottenklöster held at Regensburg in 1214. Archbishop Siegfried of Mainz confirmed the subjection of the Schottenkloster of Erfurt to the abbot of St James, Regensburg in 1225. It is the only Schottenkloster which was situated in what is now East Germany.

Of later origin is the Schottenkloster of Kelheim, south-west of Regensburg, at the confluence of the Altmuhl and the Danube. Duke Otto of Bavaria, in memory of his father who was murdered there in 1231, built a religious house and placed it as a priory under the superintendence of the abbot of St James, Regensburg. It was subsequently referred to as the hospital of St John and Souls' House but did not remain too long in Irish hands.

One final foundation which is sometimes said to have been linked to the Schottenklöster was at Oels in Silesia, but there is no record of the prior or abbot there being present at any chapter. It is reported in ruins in 1505 and no one could then remember a monk from Ireland in it. The Irish were so long forgotten that the monastery was described by the local dukes as 'formerly belonging to the Wendish brethren, of the Order of St Benedict', i.e. another lost tribe like the Irish! Nobody knows if there was a tenth house; and if Oels was never formally set up, there were perhaps only eight houses apart from the two Regensburg ones.

Outside German-speaking lands the Schottenklöster Congregation founded two small priories in Ireland, presumably to act as recruiting centres for novices and collecting depots for material aid. They were set up not as daughter-houses of Regensburg but of Würzburg. One of these was on the Rock of Cashel, a second was in West Cork at Roscarberry, then better known as Ros Ailithir (Ros of the Pilgrims). We have two briefs of Pope Innocent IV dated 1248 empowering the abbot of St James to reform these Irish houses. A century later Cornelius, the prior, and the whole convent of the Benedictine monastery of St Mary of Ross professed obedience to 'Philippo, abbati monasterii S. Jacobi Hibernicorum jam dicti ordinis extra muros Herbipolenses per se venienti' on his visitation of 1353. A similar profession was made by Prior Odo of Ross to Abbot Domhnall of Würzburg who in 1378 'venit per se, licet hoc per alium facere potuisset, et in nostro monasterio suum officium exercuit' and in another document of 1454 the Ross prior asks Würzburg for a visitation. That made twelve houses in all (six abbeys and six priories) linked together in the Congregation of the Schottenklöster; the original two Regensburg houses (Weih-Sankt-Peter and St James), the eight daughter-houses of St James of Regensburg in Central Europe, and the two daughter-houses founded from St James of Würzburg in Ireland.

For a short period in the twelfth and thirteenth centuries an extra foundation was added, when the Vienna monks opened a house as far east as Kiev. It never grew into a full monastery but the priests attached to it carried out pastoral work among German merchants and their families. Unfortunately the Mongol invasions forced the Irish to abandon Kiev in 1241, the most easterly outpost reached by Irish ecclesiastics until our own time.

All the Schottenklöster were subject to St James of Regensburg, but they sometimes tried to get more independence. Erfurt was particularly unsettled and its talkative monks merited a verse from the thirteenth-century Nicholas of Bibra: 'Sunt et ibi Scotti, qui cum fuerint bene poti, Sanctum Brandanum proclamunt esse decanum, In grege Sanctorum, vel quod Deus ipse deorum Brandani sit frater et ejus Brigida mater.' Vienna was constantly striving to throw off its subjection and its charters never mention the monatery of Regensburg. A document of Pope Lucius III in 1185 laid down that the superiors of the Irish houses should present themselves annually at St James's to receive the abbot's sentence on all irregularities they had incurred. Pope Innocent III at the Fourth Lateran Council in 1215 prescribed that the Schottenklöster should constitute one monastic congregation and should hold a chapter every three years presided over by the abbot of St James, who was also to act as Visitor-General of the monasteries. In 1225 King Henry granted him the right to bear in his coat of arms half of the Imperial Eagle. He was declared subject to no superior except Pope and Emperor. In 1230 the ecclesiastical court of Passau annulled the election of the abbot in Vienna because it had not been directed by the abbot of St James, Regensburg.

Perhaps what is most remarkable about this group of Irish Benedictine monasteries is that they existed at all. They were certainly the most distinguished group of Irish Benedictine houses in history, and St James of Regensburg one of the great mother houses of medieval monasticism. At home in Ireland the Benedictines never had many houses or monks in medieval times as compared with the Cistercians or even with the Canons Regular or the Mendicant Orders. This gave rise to the gibe that it was because the motto of the Benedictines was the one word: PAX.

Development

A separate paper on each of these houses would be required in order to cover its history over the next few centuries. Here I can only hint at a few general features:

1. The twelfth century was their most prosperous period. They received great numbers of recruits from Ireland, as is shown by the speed with which they opened new daughter-houses. They must have numbered well over one hundred monks. They also received very generous donations from secular rulers both in Ireland and Germany and this allowed them to build fine churches and monastic buildings shortly after their foundation. Outside the cities and towns where their monasteries were, they served the *Cura Animarum* of many parishes in villages and small towns and owned farms and houses there, but as wealth increased, numbers declined. Thus as late as 1332 the Vienna monks bought a mortgage on 38 houses in the city for 65 pounds. A charter of Emperor Sigismund (1422) lists among the possessions of Regensburg—7 mills, 100 vineyards, 3 fisheries, 4 chapels, 8 manses, and 70 denominations of land, but there were probably less than half a dozen Irish monks in Regensburg in that year.

2. Although Muireadhach Mac Robhartaigh and his companions were from the north of Ireland, the predominance passed quickly to the south, and most of the monks in the Schottenklöster from then on seem to have come from Munster. This was the inevitable result of having the two Irish priories in Munster. Even after the Anglo-Norman invasion of Ireland, however, the monks came almost exclusively from the Old Irish part of

the population, not from the Norman Irish. Apart from one Burke, the names which have so far been published from their archives are typical Gaelic family names like O'Carroll, O'Driscoll, O'Dowd, O'Donoghue, O'Grady, O'Hickey, O'Donovan, Kelly, Clancy, and so on.

3. Many of the early inmates of the Schottenklöster were famed for their sanctity and learning. Apart from the founders like Marianus and Macharius it is useful to recall the cult of the *Drei elende Heiligen* of Etting and the other three of Griesstetten whom some scholars have taken to be members of the Irish community in nearby Eichstätt and Regensburg.

The learning of the first generation is also beyond dispute. From the twelfth- and thirteenth-century Regensburg community came three important texts which have some significance in Irish history:

(a) *The Vision of Tnugdal* (or Tundale), the last of the notable Irish pieces of vision literature beginning with the vision of Fursey in the seventh century, all of which prepared the way for Dante's *Inferno*;

(b) *The Life of Marianus Scottus*, composed about 1185, and recently edited by Pádraig Breatnach;

(c) *The Libellus de fundacione ecclesie Consecrati Petri* (Weih-Sankt-Peter), composed in the 1250s, and much less trustworthy as a historical source.

In Vienna the library received gifts of books from Irish monks Malachy, Patrick, Maelcoilm—Gospels and a Missal, works of Gregory the Great and Bede, and a Treatise on Preaching. The Vienna monks had a scriptorium which also produced charters for other abbeys. Under the second Irish abbot, Fionán (1169–95), historical writing began there and continued for a whole century. A manuscript in the Austrian National Library in Vienna includes the *Annales Scotorum* for the period from 1178 to 1224 and a *Continuatio Scotorum* from 1225 to 1233. With the death of Abbot Thomas II in 1286, historical writing there comes to an end. Abbot Clemens (1349–72) was a witness to the document founding Vienna University in 1365, and Abbot Domhnall (1380–92) was eighth rector of the University in 1383, helping to set up the theology faculty in the following year. Abbot Mathew O'Driscoll at the end of the century had studied law in Oxford, Vienna, and Passau. The last Irish abbot, Thomas III (1403–18), was superintendent of the University before his return to Regensburg.

At least some of the Schottenklöster had schools attached to them. Thus we hear how an outbreak of the plague in Nürnberg in 1362 caused a drastic fall in the number of pupils. St James's in Regensburg also had a school and probably Our Lady's Monastery in Vienna.

4. After the initial burst of enthusiasm the supply of Irish recruits quickly fell off and some of the Schottenklöster began to accept German novices. Probably the unsettled conditions in Ireland following the Norman invasion and the constant warfare between Gael and Gall affected recruitment from home. At the time of the Vienna enquiry in 1418 it had only seven Irish monks, but that was more than any other Schottenkloster.

There was undoubtedly a fall in standards as well as a fall in numbers, and it was even suggested that some monks were sent from Ireland to Germany because their superiors wanted to get rid of them. Before mentioning the allegations made against the Irish monks it is necessary to say that these accusations are unlikely to be fully objective since they come from men who had their eyes set on the Irish properties or were trying to justify their confiscation afterwards. They saw no reason why foreigners, now few in number, should continue to occupy valuable property in Germany. Yet even when allowance is made for self-interest, it would seem that some of the allegations made against the Irish (e.g. of ignorance, lack of numbers, immorality, and neglect of their property and duties) must have had a certain foundation. We must remember, too, that we have no defence from the Irish side. They were probably no better and no worse than their German contemporaries.

Decline

During the fourteenth century allegations were often made that the new arrivals from Ireland, now few in number, neglected to learn the vernacular and therefore were useless in pulpit or confessional; that the monastic property was squandered and the buildings falling into ruin. By 1400 the three small priories at Memmingen, Eichstätt, and Kelheim had quietly disappeared.

In the fifteenth century the cry for reform went up on all sides, and the Schottenklöster did not escape notice. A German visitation of Regensburg in 1453 referred to the five novices recently arrived from Ireland as: *quinque iuvenes idiotae, nec litteram nec Theutonicum scientes* ['five young eejits, unlettered, and ignorant of German']. In Nürnberg we hear that the Irish ran a tavern in the monastery which was popular with women, so that it became a proverbial saying there: *Uxor amissa in monasterio Scottorum quaeri debet* ['if a wife is lost, look for her in the Schottenkloster'].

In 1411 or 1412 there was a visitation of Nürnberg monastery and the abbot was urged to seek new blood from Ireland. Three young novices arrived, without education or experience, and after a short period they made off. The monks of St Aegidius continued to carouse late into the night *more Scottico*; in the morning they were so drunk that they could not say Mass. Monks from Fulda were brought in to reform them and the abbot went again to Ireland for novices and returned with four. But these soon declared they had not come all the way from Ireland to practice mortification but to live as they pleased [*non propter abstinentiam . . . sed propter liberam voluntatem vivendi*]. The abbot then appealed to the Margrave of Nürnberg for protection against the Fulda monks and forced them to withdraw.

In 1418, some German monks from Reichenbach near Stuttgart were introduced into St Aegidius's monastery in Nürnberg. They claimed that everything was in a terrible condition: the abbot's mitre and staff had been pawned; there were only two volumes in the library; and for processions the monks had to borrow vestments from the Dominicans. The German monks stayed on and linked the monastery with the Bursfeld congregation. The few remaining Irish monks left and thus Nürnberg was lost to the Schottenklöster without a fight. At the Reformation the monastery became the Melanchthon-Gymnasium and the church a Lutheran one. Destroyed by fire in 1696 and by bombs in 1945 the Aegidiuskirche has changed in character, but the side-chapels of St Eucharius and St Wolfgang preserve the Romanesque features of the twelfth-century Schottenkloster.

In the same year, 1418, Vienna passed out of Irish hands. A sixteenth-century compiler of its history says the building was in ruins and the bells had been pawned. The monks were selfish and useless, engaged in worldly occupations, trading in furs and skins and Jewish wares. They got up public dances and sports with ball-playing and boat-tilting [hielten offentliche däntz und lustspiel mit palnschlagen, stangenschuppfen]. It is not clear whether the ball-game was football or handball, or perhaps more likely hurling since the Irish priories were in Cork and Tipperary! They pawned the chalices, vestments, and bells. It was impossible to reform their wicked and crooked lives. When they were finally expelled, the monks were like devils who had been exorcized. They blasphemed and threatened; one wanted to rush into this monastery and another into that one.

Pope Martin V appointed visitors for Vienna in 1418 but Abbot Thomas refused to let them in, 'quia nos interficeremus eos vel interficeremur ab eis'. He had six other Irish in the community: Lorcan, Patrick, Donncha, Cathal, Maurice, and Fintan. But they soon recognized the game was up and asked only for travelling expenses and a safe conduct to Regensburg. Hormayr's *Geschichte von Wien* says that when they were replaced by other priests they returned by night and drove them out and proclaimed that they would not surrender to Emperor, Pope, or people. But they had to yield and go to Regensburg. 'We can and will live only with monks of our own nation.' In 1448 Pope Nicholas V confirmed the now reformed Schottenkloster of Vienna as independent of Regensburg.

The Irish monks held their ground longer in Würzburg, Erfurt, Konstanz, and the two houses in Regensburg. Würzburg had few Irish monks in the fifteenth century, sometimes no one but the abbot. Thomas the abbot (1483–94), *praefuit in magna paupertate.* His second successor Philip, the thirty-second and last Irish abbot, died in 1497, and the monastery was handed over by the bishop with papal authority to German monks from St Stephen's, Würzburg. The first German abbot was Kilian Kraus from Ochsenfurth and the next was the celebrated scholar Trithemius, who wrote a history of the monastery. He is reputed to have been the prototype of Dr Faustus. Later, as we shall see, monks from Scotland would recover it. Thus by 1500 the seven houses which survived in 1400 had been reduced to four, and the only one which had a community was St James of Regensburg, which appointed superiors for the other houses.

End

For these four Schottenklöster, two at Regensburg, and one each at Konstanz and Erfurt, the end came through the arrival of monks from Scotland who claimed these foundations had originally belonged to their nation and that the Irish were intruders. In 1514, an Imperial visitation of Regensburg resulted in the arrest of Walther, the last Irish abbot. A certain Scotch priest named John Thomson from Dunfermline, who had become friendly with Pope Leo X in Rome, secured a document from him dated 31 July 1515 handing over St James of Regensburg to 'the Scottish monks who had founded it', and appointing Thomson himself as superior. The Pope's knowledge of Irish history was obviously no greater than his theological sensitivity in granting an indulgence for the re-building of St Peter's Basilica. Paradoxically Thomson was not a Benedictine at all, but with the backing of King James of Scotland he brought out a community of Scottish Benedictines from Dunfermline and a new era in the history of St James's had begun. Being 'Abbot General' of St James, Thomson now proceeded to appoint Scots superiors of the other houses also.

When you visit the historic old church in Regensburg today you will notice that apart from the strange image of Rydan the porter, and the two twelfth-century doorways there is almost nothing else to remind you that for over 400 years it was an Irish church served by Irish priests. All the tombs in the church are now of the Scottish abbots of the sixteenth and seventeenth centuries. There must have been tombs—modest perhaps but with at least names and dates like the two surviving in the cloister of Joannes (d. 1343) and Matheus (d. 1396)—of the Irishmen who preceded them. The Irish made only one attempt to recover the building—through an appeal to Rome in 1653-4—and though the Austrian Cardinals supported them, Pope Innocent IV decided against them. The other Schottenkloster in Regensburg was destroyed in the wars of the mid-sixteenth century and Konstanz was badly damaged, while Erfurt was without Scots monks for many years.

After about half a century of poverty the monastery of St James at Regensburg began to prosper again towards the end of the sixteenth century with its Abbot Ninian Winzet and his community from Scotland, and it became a noted gathering-place for Scottish Catholics exiled by the Reformation. Bishop Lesley of Ross arrived in Nürnberg in 1578 to demand the 'return' of Saint Aegidius which had been turned into a Lyceum after the Reformation, but he failed in his efforts. Another attempt, by Abbot Ninian in 1581, was also a failure. In Vienna their attempts to get 'back' the Schottenkloster also failed. But in Erfurt and Konstanz the Scotch had been successful and in Würzburg Abbot John Whyte (Winzet's successor as abbot of Regensburg), got the Schottenkloster for monks from Scotland in 1595. According to a later story the local bishop, the famous Julius Echter, took a vow, when in danger of death, to hand it over.

In 1624 the Scottish abbots appealed to Emperor Ferdinand II to give them the Vienna Schottenkloster and were turned down. In 1654 a few Irish Benedictines appealed unsuccessfully to Rome for half the places in the same Schottenkloster. The Scotch made their last attempt under Emperor Leopold I in the second half of the seventeenth century, but with the Turks at the gates of Vienna he had more important things on his mind than Scottish disputes. So the oldest monastery in Vienna passed into the hands of Austrian Benedictines from Melk. It was ironic that they came from an abbey which had grown to fame through its possession of the body of St Colman of Ireland. In that way the Schottenkloster of Vienna now remains the only one which is still a Benedictine abbey, though with no Irishman in the community.

The Scottish Benedictines held on to Erfurt and Konstanz until the eighteenth century and to Würzburg and Regensburg until the nineteenth. In Erfurt the church is still called the Schottenkirche, while in Konstanz a little old chapel off the Schottenstrasse was still known as the Schottenkapelle when I last visited the city in 1973. It was then no longer in use.

The Würzburg monastery was secularized in 1803 but its handful of monks remained in or near Würzburg at parish work till the last died in 1839. The relics of the first abbot Macharius, whom the Scottish monks had 'promoted' into a great saint, were removed in 1803 to Our Lady's Church, the Marienkirche. After the terrible air-raid of 1945 they were transferred elsewhere for safety and lost! The well-known sculptor, Michael Amberg, brought them to light again in 1984.

Only the choir of the old church of the Schottenkloster remained in use in the nineteenth century; the rest was desecrated. In 1860 Niedermayer wrote: 'the eastern part has been rebuilt as a concerthall; the beautiful western part serves as an army storeroom. On the graves of the Irish abbots and monks there are vehicles full of baggage and ammunition.' It was 1904 before it was all in use again as a church. Then on St Patrick's eve and morning 1945, only two months before the end of the war, Würzburg was devastated and the Schottenkirche was destroyed. Only the two towers, minus their spires, and the Gothic choir remained. The Salesians opened a hostel for boys on the site of the Schottenkloster in 1951 and Bishop Doepfner (later Cardinal) blessed the reconstructed church in 1956, the first church on German soil dedicated to St John Bosco. The archives of the Würzburg Schottenkloster were almost completely destroyed.

St James of Regensburg remained even longer in Scotch hands, down to 1862. Then it became the major seminary of the diocese of Regensburg and remains so today, having already given the diocese over 3,000 priests. The last Scottish Benedictine in it, Dom Anselm Robertson, helped to found Fort Augustus Abbey in Scotland, overlooking Loch Ness, in the 1870s, and did not die until the beginning of the present century in 1900. The last seminarian, Donald Mackintosh, survived as a Scotch parish priest until 1927. That brings the heritage of Muireadhach Mac Robhartaigh very close to us. The archives came safely through the war and are now housed in a splendid new building beside the Obermünster. The earliest document I saw there was dated 1 May 1248.

When I first visited Regensburg in 1960, I found one thing puzzling. Under the high altar of St James's Church, now attached to the seminary, is a shrine containing relics with the inscription 'Mercherdach'. In the sacristy of the minor seminary, now removed to the Mercherdachskapelle beside the Obermünster, was a shrine containing the relics of the same hermit! The priests were obviously embarrassed as they showed me the two shrines. I believe the Germans found it difficult to distinguish between the two Gaelic names Muireadhach and Muircheartach, and that the bones in St James's church are really those of Muireadhach Mac Robhartaigh, founder of the first Schottenkloster. In 1984 the well-known Regensburg historian, Dr Paul Mai, told me he agreed with this and that the inscription on the Reliquary in St James would be corrected. May these relics of the founder of the Schottenklöster movement long remain as a symbol of the close links between Ireland and Germany.

So the Schottenklöster, which were once a bone of contention between the Irish and the Scots, now belong to neither. Each had some of them for nearly four centuries, the Irish from the twelfth to the fifteenth, the Scots from the sixteenth to the nineteenth. There is still much work to be done in their archives and many problems about them still remain unsolved. Let us hope that Irish and Scots can now share them eagerly as a subject for historical research.

Armagh

VARIETIES OF UNIFORMITY:
THE FIRST CENTURY OF THE CHURCH OF IRELAND

by AIDAN CLARKE

THE historiographical background to this paper is provided by a recent dramatic change of perspective in the study of the Reformation in Ireland. Traditionally the failure of Protestant reform has been explained in ways that amounted to determinism. In its crudest expression, this involved the self-sufficient premise that the Catholic faith was so deeply ingrained in the Irish as to be unshakable. More subtly, it assumed a set of equations, of Protestantism with English conquest and Catholicism with national resistance, that acted to consolidate the faith. In the 1970s, these simplicities were questioned. Dr Bradshaw and Dr Canny argued that religious reform had made sufficient headway in its initial phase to suggest that the replacement of Catholicism by Protestantism was at least within the bounds of possibility, and raised a fresh question; why did this not happen? That the debate which followed was inconclusive was due in part to an inability to shake off an old habit of circular thought, so that the issue has remained one of deciding whether Protestantism failed because Catholicism succeeded, or Catholicism succeeded because Protestantism failed. Both Dr Robinson-Hammerstein, when she observed that 'Ireland is the only country in which the Counter-Reformation succeeded against the will of the Head of State',[1] and Dr Bottigheimer, when he insisted that the failure of the Reformation must 'concentrate our attention on the nature and limits of political authority',[2] implied that what needs to be explained is how actions were deprived of their effect. The alternative possibility is that the actions themselves were inherently ineffectual. The premise of this paper is that the failure of Protestantism and the success of Catholicism were the necessary condition, but not the sufficient cause, of each other, and its object is simply to recall attention to the existence of very practical reasons why the Church of Ireland should have evolved as it did in the hundred years or so between the

---

[1] H. Hammerstein-Robinson, 'The Continental Education of Irish students in the reign of Queen Elizabeth I', *Historical studies*, 8, ed. T. Desmond Williams (Dublin, 1971), p. 153.
[2] Karl Bottigheimer, 'The failure of the Reformation in Ireland: *une question bien posée*', *JEH*, 36 (1986), p. 207.

first and second Acts of Uniformity; that is, from an inclusive Church, claiming the allegiance of the entire community, to one that excluded all but a privileged minority.

The term Church of Ireland was first used in the 1536 Act of Supremacy, but the continuous institutional history of that Church began in 1560 when it was established by statute under the direction of the same Viceroy who had presided over the restoration of Roman Catholicism only three years previously. Although there was no ambiguity of intention, circumstances prevented this settlement from being recognized as a final resolution of the confused developments of the preceding decades, during which Henry had reconstituted ecclesiastical authority and ordered the suppression of the religious orders, Edwardian proclamations had introduced new articles of belief and substituted a vernacular communion service for the mass, and Marian legislation had restored the old order. In England, Elizabeth's compromise settlement, with its theology of grace, mixed liturgy and traditional structure, clearly involved the reconciliation of various brands of Protestantism, rather than any attempt to accommodate Catholic opinion, but the arrangements were not officially interpreted on the Catholic side as signalling an irreversible breach with Rome. The pressures which had produced it seemed resistible, and as late as 1564, after the Convocation of the English Church had adopted the Thirty Nine Articles, the Cardinal Protector of Ireland advised the newly consecrated archbishop of Armagh that 'the Queen would turn shortly to the Catholic faith'.[3] It was with reluctance that the papacy receded from this view in the later 1560s,[4] and that tentativeness of response was mirrored in Ireland, where the hierarchy itself acted without consistency. Of the five bishops who were presented with the oath of supremacy, three subscribed, and two demurred.[5] Bishops from both the pre-Reformation and Marian periods found it possible to remain in office alongside those who had no papal sanction for their appointments. That they were willing to do so, of course, justified the lower clergy and the laity in likewise evading the necessity to choose; that they were able to do so rested upon a dual equivocation: their own, and that of the Established Church itself. The adaptability of both parties is neatly expressed in the case of Roger Skiddy, who was elevated to the see of Cork in the Roman communion so late in Mary's

[3] E. P. Shirley, *Original Letters and Papers* (London, 1851), p. 174.
[4] F. M. Jones, *The Counter-Reformation* (Dublin, 1967), pp. 11–13.
[5] The figure includes O Fihely of Leighlin who took the oath in England in 1559. *CalSPI 1509–73*, p. 154.

reign that his investiture was prevented by the Queen's death, but who was reappointed by Elizabeth and consecrated in the Church of Ireland.[6]

Official equivocation, however, was not accommodatory. It is true that the statutory arrangements of 1560 were concerned only with authority, through the reassertion of royal supremacy;[7] and with liturgy, through the enforcement of uniform observance of the form of worship contained in the Book of Common Prayer.[8] But seven years later the clergy were presented with a statement of what it was that they were required to believe, in the form of Twelve Articles.[9] These marked the first departure from the set practice of proceeding step by step with the Church of England, for the model chosen was not the Thirty Nine Articles, but an earlier draft prepared by Archbishop Parker which was less elaborate and avoided precise definition.[10] The attraction of this alternative, however, was not that it allowed any latitude in the Catholic direction, but that it made it possible to broaden the base of Protestantism. The absence of strong doctrinal disagreements in the internal history of the Reformation Church in Ireland rested upon an early agreement to differ. At most, four members of the Irish hierarchy were of consequence in the mid-1560s: two of them felt sufficiently strongly to intervene in the vestiarian controversy and to protest against the deprivation of English clergy for offences which, though technical, bespoke extremism. Daly of Kildare confined himself to restrained reproaches,[11] but Loftus of Armagh did not trouble to mince his words and his denunciation of 'mixed and mingled religion' elucidates the Irish Articles.[12] Their imprecise and undifferentiated Protestantism meant that the Church of Ireland need not follow the English Church in incorporating 'the monuments, tokens and leavings of papistry; for as long as any of them remains, there remains also occasion of relapse into the abolished superstititon of Anti-Christ'. The evidence suggests that this unconcealed disapproval of the Thirty Nine Articles did not represent a fully agreed position, for the influential Bishop Brady of

---

[6] J. Morrin (ed.), *Calendar of the Patent and Close Rolls of Chancery in Ireland, of the reigns of Henry VIII, Edward VI, Mary, and Elizabeth* (Dublin, 1861), pp. 377, 472.

[7] 2 Eliz cap. 1, 4.

[8] 2 Eliz cap. 2.

[9] *A brefe Declaration of certein Principall Articles of Religion* (Dublin, 1566/7). Reprinted in C. R. Elrington, *The Life of the Most Rev. James Ussher* (Dublin, 1848), Appendix 3, pp. xx–xxix.

[10] Parker's 'Eleven Articles' were converted into twelve by numbering the two paragraphs of Article XI separately. Otherwise, the formularies are identical. Charles Hardwick, *A History of the Articles of Religion* (Cambridge, 1859), pp. 120–3, 181–2, 337–9.

[11] Shirley, *Original Letters*, pp. 203–5.

[12] *Ibid.*, pp. 214–21.

Meath seems not to have concurred, but this was the way that the Church of Ireland went, and as it did so the initial vagueness of the Credo was increasingly informed by a predestinarian emphasis. When it finally came to codifying the beliefs of the Irish Church, during a meeting of Convocation in 1615, these tendencies were fused into a set of 104 Articles which were unmistakably to the theological left of the Church of England: they pointedly omitted the English article dealing with consecration, incorporated the doctrine of reprobation, and identified the Pope as Anti-Christ.[13]

Differences of situation no doubt contributed to this trend. It was natural for a powerful, alien minority to value most highly those elements in its religious position that were most distinctive, and to stress areas of difference rather than similarity. But the tendency, if at first diffuse, was concentrated and systematized after the early 1590s through the influence of the newly founded Trinity College, Dublin. The impulses behind that foundation were confused, and to an unrealized extent in rivalry with one another. The effective thrust derived from the need to create local access to the higher educational opportunities that were increasingly necessary to secular careers and were observably drawing both Catholic and Protestant youth from Ireland.[14] It was the notion of the university as both desirable amenity and instrument of anglicization that engaged official and local support, but the promotion of the scheme was affected by a long-standing ecclesiastical ambition to create adequate provision for the training of a qualified ministry, and its final shape was significantly influenced by the puritan view of the university as serving religious rather than secular ends—as 'the seed and fry of the holy ministry throughout the realm', in the words of the second Provost.[15] In the event, Trinity was planned and nurtured by Cambridge graduates of doubtfully orthodox persuasion whose interest lay in the formation of a puritan style clergy, and who imbued lay education with the same spirit of antagonism towards traditionalist approaches.[16]

---

[13] Elrington, Life of Ussher, Appendix 4, pp. xxxi-l. Alan Ford, The Protestant Reformation in Ireland, 1590-1641 (Frankfurt am Main, 1985), pp. 194-201. R. Buick Knox, James Ussher, Archbishop of Armagh (Cardiff, 1967), pp. 16-23.

[14] Sir James Croft, 'A Discourse for the Reformation of Ireland', Irish Manuscripts Commission, Analecta Hibernica, 4 (Dublin, 1931), p. 315. J. Lodge (ed.), Desiderata Curiosa Hibernica, 2 vols (Dublin, 1772), 2, pp. 28-9. J. W. Stubbs, Archbishop Adam Loftus and the foundation of Trinity College, Dublin (Dublin, 1892), pp. 4-5. W. A. Phillips (ed.), History of the Church of Ireland, 3 vols (Oxford, 1933-4), 2, p. 421.

[15] [Walter Travers], Ecclesiasticus Discipline (Heidelburg, 1574), p. 144.

[16] H. F. Kearney, Scholars and Gentlemen (London, 1970), pp. 66-70. Ford, Protestant Reformation, pp. 76-9.

This carefully contrived deflection of the university's purpose is reveal-ing, because it hints at the Church of Ireland's central problem, at its prime dilemma, and at its crucial uncertainty of direction. The central problem arose from the fact that the legislation of 1560 had not been designed to create a new Church, but to change the nature of an existing one. The Church as statutorily established, and as brought under new management through a small number of strategic episcopal appointments in the 1560s,[17] was structurally and organizationally, in terms of member-ship and staffing, the old Church. The legislation was intended to take over a going concern. In consequence, the Church both incorporated those clergy who were prepared to conform and inherited the complex community entanglements of the past. From the outset, its personnel con-sisted of a largely unreconstructed clergy and its internal administration was complicated extensively by rights of lay patronage and by lay control of its property. This position was not, of course, unique. In England also an established clergy required reformation, and the laity was intrusive, but the circumstances were very different: the pressures of community involvement in Church affairs worked in the opposite direction where lay influence opposed rather than supported change. In Ireland, the assimil-ated clergy were at best unfruitful, at worst fifth-columnists, and they were entrenched and protected in their positions by the fact that both appointments procedures and resources were controlled by fellow dissen-tients.

It was in this area that the prime dilemma lay. Personnel, institutional forms, and physical structures could be taken over, but statute could not create a social reality. In law, everyone in Ireland was required to act as a member of the Church established by Parliament. In practice, few did so. It was the plain duty of both Church and State to enforce the Statute of Uniformity. In practice, there were limitations. The most obvious, and the most frankly conceded, were geo-political. Where the Government's writ did not easily run, that is to say, in three-quarters of the dioceses, no attempt was made to substitute a new Protestant hierarchy. Initially, the existing bishops were simply treated as office-holders in the Established Church, and it was their individual responses that defined the govern-ment's relationships outside the Dublin region. The result was to create a rough distinction between those dioceses in which episcopal authority acknowledged royal authority, and those in which it failed to do so.[18] The

---

[17] Kildare (1560, 1564), Armagh (1562), Meath (1563), and Dublin (1567).
[18] R. D. Edwards, *Church and State in Tudor Ireland* (Dublin, 1935), pp. 187–90.

force of this distinction, however, was largely secular. In Ireland, as in England, bishops were government agents as well as ecclesiastical dignitaries. Their functions were threefold: to reform the clergy, to teach wholesome doctrine and 'to serve their country or commonwealth as magistrates'.[19] The most that was expected of the majority of those who were treated as bishops of the Church of Ireland in its early years was that they should do the last. The extreme case was the archbishop of Tuam, who took the oath of supremacy but retained the old liturgy, and used it even in the presence of the Lord Deputy himself.[20] But Tuam was the only member of the episcopacy outside the Dublin region who was required to take the oath. For practical purposes, it was better not to put the hierarchy to the test, but simply to construe a willingness to accept state authority as implying acceptance of the royal supremacy. The effect was to create three ecclesiastical zones: one in which religious reform could not be enforced in any respect; one in which the Act of Supremacy could be said to operate, but not the Act of Uniformity; and one in which the adequacy of state authority seemed to make it feasible to implement both. It was in this last zone, more than covered by the dioceses of Dublin, Meath, and Kildare, that the State and Church establishment confronted the dilemma of deciding whether to aim at an outward conformity coercively imposed, or at a willing compliance moved by authentic conversion. The dilemma related to means, of course, for outward conformity was not envisioned as a permanent condition, but as the prelude to inner belief, as a preparation for conversion.

At bottom, perhaps, the difference of approach was philosophically based, and ranged those who believed in the force of reason, and who looked to churchmen to produce their own congregations evangelistically, against those who believed in the enforcement of truth, and who looked to the State to provide congregations by vigorously implementing the penal clauses of the Act of Uniformity. The division was obscured and complicated, however, by a related disagreement between those who thought that anglicization was a necessary condition of Protestantism and those who saw Protestantism as a means of anglicization. It was reasonable to hold that social reconstruction and religious reform must await the thorough conquest that would make them possible, but it was not unreasonable to argue that piecemeal reform might be achieved in the

---

[19] Sir Henry Sidney's words: Shirley, *Original Letters*, p. 265.
[20] M. V. Ronan, *The Reformation in Ireland under Elizabeth, 1558-80* (Dublin, 1930), p. 214. P. F. Moran, *History of the Catholic Archbishops of Dublin* (Dublin, 1864), p. 86.

meantime, whether by persuasion or coercion. In short, questions of method and timing were distinguishable from one another. Some of those who placed their trust in coercion believed that religious action should be postponed, but some did not: similarly, some of those who wished to tackle the religious task immediately thought in terms of persuasion, but some did not.[21]

Thus uncertainty of purpose arose from a fundamental inability to settle the operational questions of method and timing. It is tempting to diagnose a paralysis of the collective will, brought about by unresolved problems with large philosophical dimensions and expressing itself in inconsistent and unsystematic activity which allowed the Reformation to fail by default. But the point can be easily overstressed. Although both government and Church had conceptual difficulties, the divergences on strategy were reduced in importance by the fact that, whether the emphasis was placed on conversion or persuasion, on the short term or the long run, the remedy was the same. Everyone who seriously considered the fundamental requirements of religious progress reached the same prosaic conclusion: that what was necessary was an adequate ministry, and that this could be obtained only by providing Church livings that would meet the professional expectations of such men, if they could be found, or produced.[22] At bottom, that is to say, were the interrelated problems of human and material resources.

The reciprocating connection of the two was epitomized in a recurring dispute which arose from proposals to use the assets of the supernumary cathedral of St Patrick's in Dublin to fund a university.[23] The opponents of the scheme were those who stood to lose from it, but their arguments had force. They maintained, in effect, that there was no point in producing an educated clergy if there were no livings worth their attention and protested that the liquidation of St Patrick's would eliminate the only adequately paid positions and the only worthwhile pool of patronage in the Dublin diocese.[24] The problem disclosed by these arguments was not confined to the lower clergy. One of the dioceses in the small group

---

[21] B. Bradshaw, 'Sword, word and strategy in the Reformation in Ireland', *HJ*, 21 (1978), pp. 475–502. N. Canny, 'Why the Reformation failed in Ireland: *une question mal posée*', *JEH*, 30 (1979), pp. 423–50. Bottigheimer, 'The failure of the Reformation', pp. 196–207.

[22] *Irish Manuscripts Commission: Calendar of the Irish Patent Rolls of James I* (Dublin, 1966), pp. 396, 399.

[23] Richard Bagwell, *Ireland under the Tudors*, 3 vols (London, 1885–90), 3, pp. 131–5.

[24] W. M. Brady (ed.), *State Papers concerning the Irish Church in the time of Queen Elizabeth* (London, 1868), pp. 93–6.

chosen as the core of the government's Dublin centred initial thrust was Kildare, where Elizabeth's first episcopal appointment was made. In certain respects, the anguished experience of the Scots appointee, Alexander Craik, as a stranger propounding a strange religion in a strange tongue, might serve as a paradigm of one aspect of the history of the Church of Ireland, but the problem that defeated him was financial: within a few years, he was in prison for failing to pay his first fruits to the Crown.[25] His punishment did not prove exemplary. Two decades later, the Solicitor General reported that only the self styled 'scarecrow bishop of Ossory' had paid what was due.[26]

The resource problems, human and material, were not separable, and not easily soluble, for they proceeded from an inherited interlocking of the structural fabric of the Church with the community which made it almost impossible for the Church to act independently of those who bore it no goodwill. The Commission for Ecclesiastical Causes, to which the Queen's spiritual powers as Supreme Governor were formally delegated in 1564, quickly discovered that the procedural arrangements for imposing lay uniformity, relying as they did on the collaboration of local juries, were inoperable in the Pale.[27] Clerical uniformity was no easier to achieve. It is a familiar measure of the degree of failure that in Meath in 1576, after thirteen years in office, Bishop Brady reported that only fifteen of his clergy were both competent and reasonably provided for.[28] Most obviously, the problem was one of personnel: though Brady was, on the evidence, the best pastoral bishop in the Church—a believer in persuasion who preached regularly in Gaelic, established a free school, visited his clergy conscientiously and employed a chaplain to assist him in their reform[29]—he had made few inroads on their traditionalism. They had warned him, he observed early on, that 'they be old bottles and cannot away with this new wine',[30] and so it had proved. But the mesh which protected them in their congregation-less cares was the network of lay intrusion upon ecclesiastical arrangements. Roughly speaking, one half of the livings in Brady's care were in the royal gift, but all of them had been granted on long term leases to laymen who enjoyed both the use and

[25] Shirley, *Original Letters*, pp. 95-7, 106-8, 122-3.
[26] Brady, *State Papers*, ppl. 25, 115. Exemptions had been granted to the Archbishops of Dublin and Armagh.
[27] Shirley, *Original Letters*, pp. 194-7.
[28] Brady, *State Papers*, pp. 14-19.
[29] Shirley, *Original Letters*, pp. 317-20. *Analecta Hibernica*, 4, p. 300.
[30] Shirley, *Original Letters*, p. 162.

income of the property and the right to appoint an incumbent without any stipulations as to salary or status; a quarter of the livings were nominally under episcopal control, but they had been similarly alienated by previous bishops; the remaining quarter were in the full possession of laymen. The consequence was that the human resources that Brady had at his disposal to evangelize the laity of Meath consisted in great part of ill paid, ignorant, crypto-Catholic curates. Most were not merely Irish, but monoglots; they lived on alterage payments and what they earned from 'masses, dirges, shrivings and such like trumpery'.[31] He could neither replace them, nor choose their successors when they died. It was open to him to refuse to accept a nomination 'for want of learning, lewdness of life, or corruption in religion',[32] but in practice the patron's control of parochial resources made the sanction extremely difficult to impose. The choice was between an unsatisfactory appointment or none at all. The consequential abuses could be spectacular. A Commission of Faculties sent to Ireland shortly after Brady's survey of Meath discovered instances of laymen, and even children, in occupation of livings in Meath itself.[33] Further afield, this was more common, perhaps even commonplace. In the Dublin region, the result was either, at best, that the official Church presence was token, or, at worst, that a Catholic clergy was actually being maintained within the structure of the establishment. 'There is scant a minister to be found among them', claimed the prebends of St Patrick's.[34] Thus the ability of the Church to manage its own affairs, to advance its interests and perform its minimal functions was subverted by the influence of interests which ran counter, not so much perhaps to the Reformation in the first instance, as to ecclesiastical autonomy.

Moreover, the appropriation and misuse of church resources was not exclusively a private or secular activity. The government itself, for instance, supplemented the income of a lay Lord Chancellor by making him Dean of St Patrick's,[35] met part of the expenses of the Lord Deputyship from the profits of three rectories and the tithes of five parishes,[36] and proposed that the Lord President of Munster should double up as rector

---

[31] Brady, *State Papers*, p. 16.
[32] Shirley, *Original Letters*, pp. 317–20.
[33] Brady, *State Papers*, p. 33.
[34] *Ibid.*, p. 94.
[35] Phillips, *Church of Ireland*, 2, pp. 345, 350.
[36] 'Book of Entry of divers reports and letters concerning the state of the Kingdom of Ireland upon the view of certain Commissioners sent thither by King James in the year 1622', BL MS 4756, f. 19.

of Dungarvan.[37] More generally, government leasing policy never incorporated adequate conditions to protect the interests of the Church, and no effective restrictions were placed upon the way in which churchmen managed those resources that did remain within their control. The position of the churchman, as an ex officio landholder administering property in trust for his successors, had always been open to abuse, but the Protestant cleric, with a family to support and a posterity to provide for, had greater needs and greater temptation, and some succumbed. The normal way of diverting ecclesiastical resources was through grants of long term, low rent leases in return for large entry fines. If the appropriate assents could be obtained, from the Dean and Chapter or patron and ordinary as the case might be, land could be alienated in perpetuity.[38] But alienation, though it excited deep suspicion, seems only exceptionally to have been used as a means of family aggrandisement:[39] more commonly, it was resorted to as a means of supplementing income. Bishops, Cathedral Chapters and clergy all found incomes too low and utilized what capital assets they controlled to cover routine expenses. Bishops in particular, as representatives of Queen as well as Church, needed to maintain a certain style. Brady felt that he must keep open house 'unless I should utterly discredit both myself and my doctrine', and the Council confirmed that 'feeding of the poor, and keeping good hospitality' were part of an 'effectual ministry'.[40] Lay pressure for leases, granted sometimes 'without reserving of any rent at all',[41] and government intervention to procure beneficial leases to reward favourites contributed further to a process of asset-stripping that sacrificed the future to the present. As the Solicitor-General observed severely in the 1580s, it 'tendeth greatly to endamage the religion of our successors'.[42] But the solution he suggested, a restriction to twenty-year leases, evaded the real problem: alienation of resources was not merely a cause of impoverishment, but a result of it. There were other symptoms too, of which the most pervasive was perhaps pluralism which existed at all levels, from the cut-price curate travelling (as it was said) 'like a lackey to three or four churches in a morning',[43] to the Primate doubling up as Dean of St Patrick's.[44]

[37] Nicholas White to Cecil, 10 March 1569, P.R.O., S.P., Ire., 63/27.44.
[38] BL MS 4756, f. 21ᵛ.
[39] Shirley, *Original letters*, pp. 236–7.
[40] *Ibid.*, pp. 189, 317–21.
[41] BL MS 4756, f. 21ᵛ.
[42] Brady, *State Papers*, p. 111.
[43] *Ibid.*, p. 94.
[44] Shirley, *Original Letters*, p. 296.

These were the faults of the centre, of the core dioceses. The initial strategy had been to concentrate on the confined area in which state authority could enforce ecclesiastical change by suppressing Catholic worship, compelling attendance at Protestant services, and both appointing and supporting bishops competent to undertake the internal overhaul of the Church that was needed to provide those services for the community at large. Lack of resources and control subverted the design. In Dublin city itself, some progress in nominal conformity was possible:[45] outside it, neither Church nor State possessed the organization to achieve the reform of the clergy, let alone the conformity of the laity.

But the exercise was at least technically realizable in the anglicized Dublin region. Continuity of both institutions and officers could be managed where the Church was already organized on the parochial model that the Established Church had adopted. Beyond the Pale, this condition existed only imperfectly: the dominant religious institutions of the Gaelic Irish were provided by the religious orders whose flexibility allowed each lineage to make its own spiritual provision. Church structures followed socio-political divisions, and were usually integrated to the extent that ecclesiastical offices and property had been largely secularized under the influence of ruling families. Although the familiar apparatus of territorial parishes existed nominally in such areas, the Church as a social institution had assumed a form which rendered it unassimilable to the Established Church.[46] For that reason, the gradual extension of political control in the Tudor period was not accompanied by a corresponding extension of religious control. The State Church could not achieve institutional continuity. It could establish a presence only by using religious structures which had never functioned in the normal way to supplant those which had evolved to meet local needs. It could succeed only by excluding rather than absorbing the pastoral clergy, and transforming the accustomed routines of religious observance. In most places, at most times, this was a quite impracticable task. Whereas in the Pale existing patterns were disturbed by State intrusion, and Catholic survival seems to have involved a movement of the regular clergy from a supplementary to a leading role in spiritual life, elsewhere

---

[45] Even David Wolfe conceded the point: 'they go perforce to the communion and sermons of the heretics', he reported. Ronan, *Reformation in Ireland*, p. 480.

[46] John Bossy, 'The Counter-Reformation and the people of Catholic Ireland', *Historical Studies*, 8, pp. 155–70. Aidan Clarke, 'Colonial Identity in early seventeenth-century Ireland', T. W. Moody (ed.), *Historical Studies 11: Nationality and the Pursuit of National Independence* (Belfast, 1978), pp. 57–72.

the traditional arrangements remained in working order even when the Established Church managed to gain a footing.

That footing was rarely firm. Not only was it difficult to find suitable appointees, but suitability itself was not always defined in religious terms. An Act of 1570, requiring the establishment of free schools in each diocese, illustrates the situation nicely.[47] In the long term, it provided that the appointment of schoolmasters should be the responsibility of the bishops; in the short term, it reserved that function to the Lord Deputy in every diocese except Armagh, Dublin, Kildare, and Meath. Among those who were not to be trusted with this sensitive task were three bishops appointed within the Dublin archdiocese itself only three years before, and the reasons are not hard to find. Daniel Kavanagh's chief qualification for Leighlin had been that he was 'an apt man, for his alliance in the diocese, to be minister of justice'.[48] Similar considerations influenced the appointment of John Devereux to succeed his uncle in Ferns, despite the fact that he had already been deprived of the deanery of Ferns for 'confessed whoredom'.[49] The new bishop of Ossory, Christopher Gaffney, seems not to have regarded his consecration as valid, for he made arrangements to have his clergy obtain their orders from his papally appointed rival.[50] Thus attempts to establish a presence on the basis of some sort of expedient and beneficial alliance with local interests paid poor spiritual dividends.

The only areas in which some progress was reported was in a number of port towns which were parochially organized and English speaking, and in which the Government made some effort to appoint authentic protestants. The distinctiveness of these situations was acknowledged in the Act of 1569 which reserved to the Lord Deputy the right to make all ecclesiastical appointments in Munster and Connacht for the ensuing ten years, for it excepted the Cathedral Churches of Cashel, Cork, Limerick, and Waterford.[51] Beyond the town walls, however, the resource problems were insuperable. Marmaduke Middleton, who occupied Waterford and Lismore for three years (1579–82), found his diocese worth less than £30 a year, 'and all the spiritual living in temporal men's hands so sure linked that they cannot be redeemed'.[52] His contemporary in Cork, Cloyne, and

[47] 12 Eliz cap. 1.
[48] Shirley, *Original Letters*, pp. 292, 298.
[49] *Ibid.*, pp. 265–6, 271.
[50] Brady, *State Papers*, p. 32.
[51] 11 Eliz cap. 6.
[52] Brady, *State Papers*, p. 41.

Ross, Matthew Sheyne, derived an income of £70 from Cork and Cloyne, and five marks from Ross—that being the rent reserved when Roger Skiddy alienated the entire assets of the see for £40.[53] Middleton resorted to long leases to raise money. Sheyne's solution was more radical: in 1578, he publicly confessed to simony, explaining 'that except he sold the livings of his collation he were not able to live, his bishopric was so poor'.[54]

The intractability of making over the existing Church to Protestantism did not diminish as time passed, but new needs arose which diverted attention to more congenial tasks, for Protestant settlement produced congregations which required genuine services and created a stock from which future clergy might be drawn. The result was an alteration of direction and emphasis, a process at once of contraction and increasing purposiveness. Contraction was inherent in the circumstances. As death gradually eliminated the transitional generation of clergy, at first in the Dublin area, later elsewhere, it was often possible to ensure that they were either replaced by true conformists or not replaced, so that the Church establishment shrank and its ambivalent elements decreased. This development was associated with a more fundamental change of character which was part of a broader trend obscured in Ireland by the peculiarity of the local situation. Throughout much of Europe religion was ceasing to be what it had always been, an agreed body of inherited assumptions and practices sanctioned by social convention, and was becoming a matter of inquiry, disagreement, and choice. Authority, structure, theology, doctrine, and liturgy had become variables, and the clergy were becoming controversialists, who needed to be able to defend their own positions and attack those of their opponents, to expound truth and disclose error in a way not previously required. Capability of this kind could come only from specialized education which was unavailable in Ireland and rare among the Irish clergy. In the early 1560s, a papally inspired survey concluded that not more than ten had theological qualifications, and none was competent in canon law.[55] On both sides, the official response was the same: Brady and others pressed for a local university,[56] and Pius IV ordered the leaders of his Church to found one.[57] Progress was slow, but in Ireland as elsewhere the gradual introduction of a learned clergy brought

---

[53] E. Bolster, *A History of the Diocese of Cork from the Reformation to the Penal Era* (Cork, 1982), p. 72.
[54] Brady, *State Papers*, p. 31.
[55] P. F. Moran (ed.), *Spicilegium Ossoriense* (Dublin, 1874), pp. 32–8. E. Hogan (ed.), *Ibernia Ignatiana* (Dublin, 1880), p. 13.
[56] Shirley, *Original letters*, pp. 162, 201–2, 256.
[57] Moran, *Spicilegium Ossoriense*, pp. 32–8.

changes of both social role and identification. Where the medieval priest had been a peasant among peasants, his successor was increasingly likely to be a professional gentleman whose formation set him apart from the people, even if he had originated from among them. In the Church of Ireland, this development was exaggerated, both by the importation of clergy from England and by the contracting community involvement of the Church as it settled for minority status and shed its inheritance of doubtful clergy who had been brought into the State Church by the momentum of events. The first transitional generation might stumble along, making the minimal adaptations required by their local circumstances, but the position of their successors was quite different. They were conformists by choice, having committed themselves to a new system of recruitment and a new order of ordination. But the population pool from which such men could be drawn was too small to provide a full complement of clergy. Although the proportion of Trinity graduates who entered the Church was very high, probably more than half,[58] the supply fell far short of the demand and it was impossible to attract clergy from outside the country in sufficient numbers to make up the deficiency. An inquiry conducted in 1622 revealed that there were only 380 certified preaching ministers distributed over the 2492 parishes that comprised the Church of Ireland.[59] Their privileged status worked to intensify existing trends for, with few exceptions, the educated clergy commanded the better livings and gravitated towards sympathetic patronage, ready-made congregations, and settled conditions, rather than towards the evangelical frontier. For the most part, they found benefices within the Pale, leaving the remoter and poorer parishes to be served, if at all, by reading ministers, unlearned men who read prescribed homilies to what congregations they could muster.

The overall tendency is clear: as the Church consolidated itself and established its Protestantism unequivocally, its alienation from the community increased. In fact, as the number of Protestant settlers grew the 'prime dilemma' was operationally resolved. The creation of congregations was achieved neither by coercion nor by persuasion, but by immigration, and the Church confined itself to the manageable task of providing properly for the spiritual needs of those who were already Protestant. Although there was no formal abandonment of the claim to absolute inclusiveness, ecclesiastical practice became exclusivist. So too, of course, was doctrine, and a simple equation was there to be made: the

[58] Ford, *Protestant Reformation*, p. 78.
[59] BL MS 4756, f. 19.

application of predestinarian doctrine to the Irish situation allowed for the easy identification of the elect of God with the elite of colonialism, and generated a sense of spiritual superiority which reinforced the strong conviction of social and cultural superiority which the settlers already felt. The inherent conflict of interest is evident: where privilege rested upon Protestantism, the unwelcome logic of the successful realization of the official policy of total conversion was the elimination of privilege. The Church's ideological contribution to the community it served was to resolve that conflict by aligning duty with interest, for the direction in which its doctrine became most distinctive was in its identification of the Roman Church with Anti-Christ and its members with the reprobate who were beyond redemption. Thus privilege itself was predestined.[60]

The early seventeenth century saw a process of consolidation in which the Church, now for the first time confident in its Protestantism, made better episcopal appointments, prepared an elaborate set of Articles of belief which confirmed its independence of the Church of England, and officially pressed for the proscription of Catholicism. But no systematic effort to arrange for the reception of Catholics was made, and the Church's considerable intellectual energies were directed towards Protestant theological controversy rather than towards debate with Catholics:[61] it was grossly understaffed and remained under-financed, and Protestant laymen proved as rapacious and as stubborn in clinging to Church property as their Catholic counterparts. But it was not the continuing inability to make inroads upon Catholicism that distinguished this phase so much as the fact that the scale of operations to which the Church had been reduced proved too small to enable it to cope effectively with the expansion of Protestantism itself. As the Church came to terms with its situation, the situation changed, and the Church proved incapable of responding—organizing, regulating, and absorbing the relatively enormous extension of its responsibilities in Ulster. Though there was no difficulty in fitting the Ulster establishment into the national framework of the Church, the reality was that the arrival of new patrons and the tapping of fresh sources of clergy largely by-passed the existing patterns of influence and control, and there was a pronounced tendency for settlers and their clergy to continue their associations with the Church of Scotland

---

[60] Ford, *Protestant Reformation*, cap. 8.
[61] Philomena Kilroy, 'Puritanism in Ireland in the Seventeenth Century' (National University of Ireland, MA thesis, 1973); 'Sermons and Pamphlet Literature in the Irish Reformed Church', *Archivium Hibernicum*, 23 (1975), pp. 110-21.

rather than to develop new ones with the Dublin-centred Church of Ireland. Even English settlers in the north were drawn into this ambience. Elsewhere, the situation was reproduced in miniature, as bishops freshly exported from England without reference to Dublin relied on their established connections and drew help from the region or university they knew best.[62] In most places outside the Dublin area, the Church fragmented, but it was only in Ulster, with its aberrant Scottish orientation that this decentralization assumed lasting significance.

The Church of Ireland was not merely an inefficient host, but also an accommodating one, Calvinist inclined, tolerant of liturgical unorthodoxy, and with Articles that omitted to provide for the consecration of bishops and the ordering of priests and deacons. The Scots, who were accustomed to follow Presbyterian practice within an episcopal framework, were able to import this arrangement to Ireland, where any Protestant was a welcome addition to the common front against Catholicism. Thus, under the nominal cover of the Established Church, Protestantism diversified, until the 1630s. Then, a new Lord Deputy, Wentworth, abruptly reaffirmed the Church's original objective of universal membership, devised a long term strategy based on a clear-sighted recognition of the resource difficulties and the priorities they dictated, and set about doing what had needed to be done for seventy years—repossessing Church assets and using them to endow a national framework of spiritual provision capable of serving the entire community. The result was a systematic programme of depriving laymen of both property and influence through legal process, intimidation, and cajolement. By moral and immoral suasion of all kinds, Wentworth fought for the Church's independence of the laity. But the issue was complicated by recent alterations of emphasis in the doctrine of the English Church, involving both a retreat from predestinarianism and revisions of liturgy in the direction of traditionalism. Wentworth set out to bring the divergent Irish Church into conformity by securing the adoption of the Thirty Nine Articles and the English Canons of 1604, and, having done so, to make that conformity uniform.[63]

This comprehensive attack, upon both vested interest and established beliefs and practices, with its attendant implication of subordination to

[62] Ford, *Protestant Reformation*, cap. 5, 7.
[63] H. F. Kearney, *Strafford in Ireland, 1633-41* (Manchester, 1959), cap. 10. Buick Knox, *James Ussher*, pp. 44-53. T. W. Moody, F. X. Martin, F. J. Byrne (eds), *A New History of Ireland*, 3, pp. 256-9.

the English Church,[64] excited hostility throughout the Protestant community, and made it effectively impossible for the Scots in Ulster to remain within the Church of Ireland. But remain they must, if they wished to remain in Ireland, for Wentworth would not tolerate a divided or ambiguous Protestant presence: the evidence of Catholic attitudes made it plain that that would destroy the moral authority needed to sustain a conversion programme.[65] In the face of rebellion in Scotland, on the eve of rebellion in Ireland and civil war in England, the Church's original role as a comprehensive association of the entire community was being restated with a new clarity and an unprecedented practicality, and the consequences were felt by Protestants long before they could begin to affect Catholics.

The catharsis of the 1640s and 1650s obliterated Wentworth's anachronistic vision. By the 1660s the proliferation of beliefs and the excesses of believers had discredited the very notion of uniformity. The only practicable course was to define orthodoxy and protect it from its rivals. In Ireland, the pressures in that direction were reinforced by a dramatic change in the status of the historic principle that the inadmissibility of Catholicism was justified by the innate disloyalty of Catholics, who could not be loyal to spiritual and temporal masters at the same time. Recent events had revealed that the connections between religious belief and political obedience were less simple than they had seemed: the theory could no longer be employed without acute Protestant embarrassment, and practice was pragmatic rather than dogmatic. Division of opinion existed. It formed the crude basis of the expropriation and redistribution of Irish land that had taken place in the 1650s, and determined the way in which political power was distributed in the 1660s. It was fundamental to the colonial system, and its survival was necessary.

When a revised Act of Uniformity was passed in 1666, the Church of Ireland discarded its century-old tradition;[66] the concern now was to purge the Church of non-conformists and the legal fiction that the

---

[64] Archbishop Ussher feared a canonical equivalent to Poyning's Act, 'giving the Church of England such superintendence over us, that nothing shall be law here that was not first allowed there, and afterward, that we must reform nothing here, that there had obtained a confirmation'. F. R. Bolton, *The Caroline Tradition in the Church of Ireland* (London, 1958), pp. 13–14.

[65] Arguments exploiting the diversity of Protestant opinion, familiar in England from the work of Robert Parsons, were most systematically employed in Ireland by Henry Fitzsimons, S.J. For a succinct example, see *Words of comfort to Persecuted Catholics*, ed. E. Hogan (Dublin, 1881), pp. 13–15.

[66] 17/18 Car II, session 2, cap. 6.

Church and the community were co-extensive was silently abandoned. The Restoration Church settlement took for granted the existence both of Catholics and of divisions within Protestantism and evolved a three-tiered structure of fully privileged members of the Church of Ireland, less privileged Presbyterians, and unprivileged Catholics. These three tiers mirrored the evolution of the Church in its first century. The lowest reflected its failure to convert the people of Ireland; the middle reflected its inability to assert effective jurisdiction over the Scots immigrants; the highest realized its continuous inclination towards elitism. The connections seem plain. The unsuccessful attempt to create the fictitious statutory Church of Ireland resulted only in the slow development of a Dublin-centred core of authentic Protestantism, adequate to its miniature pastoral tasks, but so scaled down as to be incapable of integrating the Scots, so that failure was cumulative. The consequence of the failure to take over Catholicism was the failure to contain Protestantism. By the standards of those who instituted it, the Church of Ireland failed, not once, but twice.

Trinity College, Dublin

THE RISE OF RECUSANCY AMONG THE
DUBLIN PATRICIANS, 1580-1613

by COLM LENNON

'HE mayor, aldermen, merchants and inhabitants of Dublin are notorious papists, hating the English nation and government', wrote a state official in 1596. It was noted about the same time that, by contrast, there had been scarcely six of that ilk to be found there in the early years of Queen Elizabeth's reign.[1] While grossly mistaken in perceiving a conjunction of religious dissidence and political disaffection, this commentator on late sixteenth-century Dublin correctly identified a steady trend towards adherence to the older religion on the part of the leading citizens and others. Within a decade the assertion was publicly confirmed, at least in the case of the aldermen. More than half of that elite group of senior city councillors were convicted of recusant offences and suffered imprisonment and heavy fines.[2] And by 1613 the much-feared merging of the religious and political discontents of Dubliners seemed to be closer to becoming a reality. The freemen chose as their members in the forthcoming parliament two avowed Catholics. The election of Aldermen Thomas Allen and Francis Taylor (which was later overturned by state intervention) was regarded as a deliberate effort by the civic body to defend cherished liberties, including that of conscience, through determined recusancy.[3]

Government charting of the growth of convinced Catholicism among the Dublin patricians from the later 1590s tended to magnify the part played by the newly-arrived seminary priests.[4] While registering their influence, this brief study of the alienation of the aristocratic majority from the Established Church will advert to the force of the leading citizens' social and cultural ascendancy within their community. Manifestations of the slow disengagement of the urban lords and their families from the forms and institutions of the Church of Ireland may be seen as

---

[1] 'Memorandum of the state of Ireland', November 1596, PRO, SP 63/195/52; *CalSPI, 1600*, p. 295.
[2] See *CalSPI, 1603-6*, pp. 348-9, 352-3, 391, 401-2; *HMC Egmont MSS* 1, pt 1 (1905), pp. 30-1.
[3] See *CalSPI, 1611-14*, pp. 305, 360-23, 441-2, 445.
[4] See, for example, Archbishop Loftus and others to the Privy Council, 31 October 1598: PRO, SP 63/202/3, 35; William Paule to Cecil, 2 February 1598: PRO, SP 63/202(1)/45; same to Archbishop Loftus, 17 January 1598: PRO, SP 63/202(1)/17(1).

the impact of the quashing of rebellion in the early 1580s is assessed. When the Jacobean administration imposed a policy of rigorous enforcement of the Reformation statutes upon leading Dubliners, their general predisposition towards the conservation of the traditional religion developed into a self-assured form of Counter-Reformation Catholicism, and a very brief review of the reasons for this will conclude the paper.

Who were these patricians and why were they so important in determining the pace of religious change, or lack of it, in the heart of the English Pale in the later Tudor period? Under the auspices of the English crown they forged for themselves a formidable power-base in the institution of the bench of twenty-four aldermen, from among whom was elected the mayor.[5] Affluent and predominantly mercantile, this privileged coterie of some seventy families consolidated its social exclusivity through marriage with fellow-patricians and with gentry from neighbouring counties, and by investment in urban and rural properties.[6] Aware of their position as political loyalists, social arbiters, and religious exemplars, Church and State authorities were anxious to foster the gradual implementation of the Reformation laws of 1560 without disturbing too convulsively the *ad hoc* ecclesiastical influence of which the civil leaders disposed.[7] Among the examples which may be cited is that of the patronage given by households in city and county to unreformed priests, some of whom were engaged in educating the residents' and their neighbours' children.[8] The parish churches of Dublin continued to body forth in their funerary monuments and chantry chapels the pride and piety of the older patrician families.[9] Even after the parochial buildings had been absorbed within the Established Church system, the rights to tithes and other ecclesiastical dues in most of the parishes of the Dublin archdiocese were at the disposal of patrician and gentry farmers.[10] Also in lay possession were the

[5] See R. Dudley Edwards, 'The beginning of municipal government in Dublin', *Dublin Historical Record*, 1 (1938-9), pp. 2-10; Colm Lennon, 'Civil privilege, state policy and the growth of recusancy: the patriciate of Dublin in the age of Reformation, 1548-1613' (Ph.D. thesis, National University of Ireland, Maynooth, 1987), pp. 40-84.

[6] Lennon, 'Patriciate of Dublin, 1548-1613', pp. 85-135.

[7] *Ibid.*, pp. 214-15.

[8] Cf. Patrick McGrath and Joy Rowe, 'The Marian priests in Elizabethan England', *Recusant History* (1984), pp. 110-20; Lennon, 'Patriciate of Dublin, 1548-1613', pp. 228-32.

[9] Ralph Loeber, 'Sculptured memorials to the dead in early seventeenth Ireland: a survey from "Monumenta Eblanae" and other sources', *PRIA* 81, C (1981), pp. 267-95; Myles V. Ronan, 'Religious customs of Dublin medieval guilds', *IER* 5 series, 26 (1925), pp. 255-47, 364-85.

[10] See 'Archbishop Bulkeley's visitation of Dublin, 1630', ed. Myles V. Ronan, *Archivium Hibernicum*, 8 (1941), pp. 56-98.

income and properties of the religious fraternities which the royal government had failed to suppress in Ireland, and which continued to dispose of much wealth to be directed towards spiritual uses.[11]

The government's hopes for the sapping of these continuous links between Dublin patrician families and the personnel, institutions, and customs of the older religious establishment in the first two decades of Elizabeth's reign rested largely on a very small nucleus of enthusiastic native Protestants. Their leavening influence would be felt among their peers through normal social intercourse, but especially through the proven commitment of these local reformers to educational and evangelizing initiatives. Aldermen John Challoner, John Ussher the elder, and Walter Ball, who all served on the court of High Commission, were dedicated to the progress of the Reformation at urban and national levels from at least 1560.[12] Ussher was particularly prominent in working for a university in Dublin and he set up a printing press in his city house for the dissemination of Irish-language versions of Protestant texts.[13] A tight nexus of marriage alliances among the offspring of these reformers helped to strengthen their identity, but also perhaps in its severe endogamy served to isolate these families from the municipal mainstream which contained the broad mass of uncommitted patricians.[14] It may also have been that the fragmentation of families such as Ball and Ussher into Catholic and Protestant branches, due to government vacillation in the implementation of reform, vitiated the force of native Dublin Protestantism. A major part of this placatory policy in the decades after 1560 was reform through education, particularly at university level.[15] A proposal to found a college based on the site and revenues of St Patrick's cathedral in 1570, which was supported by a small humanist circle in Dublin headed by the city recorder, James Stanihurst, was thwarted, and this marked the failure of a moderate type of reform in religion and society under the tactful

---

[11] See Ronan, 'Dublin medieval guilds'; Henry F. Berry, 'The history of the religious guild of St Anne', *PRIA* 25 C (1904), pp. 21–106.

[12] The history of the families of Ball and Ussher has been documented in two works edited by W. Ball Wright, *Ball family memoirs* (York, 1908), and *The Ussher memoirs* (London, 1889). For Challoner, see *Calendar of Fiants, Ireland, Elizabeth*, 34, 1059, 1238, 1811, 2605, 2848; Dublin, City Hall, City Archive, MR5/vi/2b; vii/11b.

[13] Ussher to Cecil, 1568: PRO, SP 63/17/10; John T. Gilbert, *History of the city of Dublin*, 3 vols (Dublin, 1884–9), I, pp. 382–5.

[14] Details of the marriage connections between these families are to be found in Wright, *Ball family memoirs* and *Ussher memoirs*; see also Lennon, 'Patriciate of Dublin, 1548–1613', pp. 220–1.

[15] See Timothy Corcoran, *State policy in Irish education* (Dublin, 1916).

patronage of a well-disposed viceroy, Sir Henry Sidney.[16] The college would undoubtedly have attracted the attendance of the youth of many of the gentry families of the Pale and the merchant patriciates of the towns in a way that Trinity College, founded twenty years later, failed to do to any great extent as a result of the major change in religious attitudes wrought in the interim.

The effect of the political side of the European Catholic resurgence upon events in Ireland helped to cause the slow transformation in the religious disposition of the patrician majority from the later 1570s onwards.[17] A small group of citizens, as convinced in their Catholicism as the Protestants were in their confession, stimulated through their militancy the large middle group of uncommitted or loosely-committed patricians to take measures to defend what was seen increasingly clearly as a Catholic heritage.[18] James Eustace, head of a prestigious gentry family in the southern marches of the Pale, rose in short-lived rebellion for the restoration of Catholicism in 1580.[19] Although disappointed by the lack of assistance from his fellow gentlemen, he received material and moral support from two leading aldermen, the father and son, Christopher and Walter Sedgrave, and two members of the Fitzsimon family, William, a prosperous merchant in Dublin, and Michael, a schoolmaster.[20] Details of arms-supplying and other forms of aid to the viscount from these prominent Dubliners were revealed in 1583 as the state authorities conducted a reign of terror in the Pale as a reaction to revolt and conspiracy. Although Walter Sedgrave and William Fitzsimon escaped punishment after their arrests, over twenty other gentlemen (including later Michael Fitzsimon, son of Alderman Thomas) were executed for their involvement.[21] Between many of their families and those of the patriciate there were matrimonial ties. Religious divisions within families were exacerbated by the tension generated in the early

---

[16] See R. Dudley Edwards, 'Ireland, Elizabeth and the Counter-Reformation' in S. T. Bindoff *et al.* (eds), *Elizabethan government and society* (London, 1961), pp. 315–39; Colm Lennon, 'Recusancy and the Dublin Stanyhursts', *Archivium Hibernicum*, 33 (1975), pp. 101–10.

[17] For the background, see S. G. Ellis, *Tudor Ireland* (London, 1985), pp. 278–83.

[18] Lennon, 'Patriciate of Dublin, 1548–1613', pp. 251–4.

[19] David Mathew, *The Celtic peoples and Renaissance Europe* (London, 1933), cap. 10; Ellis, *Tudor Ireland*, pp. 221–3, 282–3.

[20] 'Confession of Christopher Barnewall', 28 June 1580: PRO, SP 63/102/114(1); 'Confirmation of Barnewall's confession by Teig Rowe', 24 July 1583: PRO, SP 63/103/36(3); 'Additional confession of Christopher Barnewall', 28 August 1583: PRO, SP 63/104/38(1).

[21] P. Woulfe, 'Some martyrs of the Pale' in Myles V. Ronan (ed.), *Catholic emancipation centenary record* (Dublin, 1929), pp. 30–5; John Brady, 'Some Irish scholars of the sixteenth century', *Studies*, 37 (1948), pp. 226–31.

1580s. It was in this climate that Alderman Walter Ball proceeded against his mother, Margaret, and her chaplain, embarrassed as he was by her overt recusancy during his mayoralty, and the elderly matron was reported by Catholic writers to have died in prison for her beliefs in 1584.[22] In that year as a result of the continuing prosecution of the Munster and Pale rebels the captive Archbishop Dermot O'Hurley was secretly executed in Dublin, and a cult of his martyrdom sprang up among some pious women.[23] An Irish Catholic martyrology which found expression later in the works of Revd Henry Fitzsimon, S.J., another member of the municipal family, and others had its genesis in this period, and clearly the attitudes of Dubliners contributed greatly to the making of this religious historiography.[24]

Signs of the supplanting of the older Christianity of the patrician families by a more vigorous Catholicism in the later 1580s and 1590s are to be found in their changing choice of academic training for their children, their selection of marriage partners for family members, and their disposal of the ecclesiastical resources under their control. While young people from Dublin aristocratic households had traditionally migrated for further education to the English universities and law-schools in large numbers, there was also a well-founded pattern of travel to the continent by scholars in search of learning.[25] The reputations of Leonard Fitzsimon and David Delahide in Douai in the early Elizabethan period were well established among their fellow-citizens, for example.[26] After 1580, however, there was a significant increase in the numbers of students going to continental colleges.[27] What made the choice of academies in France, Spain, and the Low Countries significant was the scholars' parents full realization that the curricula were designed to instil strong Catholic beliefs and a desire to communicate them through missionary activity. While some entrants to seminary courses were mature scholars who had decided upon career paths for themselves, most of the Dublin students were in their teens or early twenties and

---

[22] Patrick F. Moran (ed.), *Spicilegium Ossoriense*, 3 vols (Dublin, 1874–84), I, pp. 105–6.

[23] David Rothe, *Analecta sacra*, ed. Patrick F. Moran (Dublin, 1884), pp. 43–5.

[24] An early account of Archbishop O'Hurley's interrogation and death was printed in Richard Verstegan, *Theatrum Crudelitatum* (Antwerp, 1587); Henry Fitzsimon, *Catalogus praecipuorum sanctorum Hiberniae* (Liege, 1619).

[25] Liam Miller and Ellen Power (eds), *Holinshed's Irish Chronicle* (New York, 1979), pp. 98, 101; Brady, 'Some Irish scholars', pp. 226–30; Helga Hammerstein, 'Aspects of the continental education of Irish scholars in the reign of Elizabeth I', *Historical Studies*, 8 (1971), pp. 140–3.

[26] Brady, 'Some Irish scholars', pp. 226–30.

[27] Hammerstein, 'Continental education of Irish scholars'.

had been directed thereto by their parents.[28] In the area of marriage alliances it is evident in the latter half of Elizabeth's reign that the sons and daughters of those patricians who can be clearly identified as recusant from their later bearing were married into families whose religious orientation was similar. Thus about twenty years later than its Protestant counterpart a Catholic marital network was woven, but this encompassed a much broader range of Dublin patrician families, especially those with county seats to the north of the metropolis.[29]

The resources of ecclesiastical patronage and property which were under lay control after the Reformation were withheld from the officials of the Established Church when the shift towards more positive Catholic commitment took place after the early 1580s. Rectorial tithes in particular were unavailable to clerics in most cures in the archdiocese into the seventeenth century.[30] In some cases continuity can be traced from the granting of lands in the aftermath of the Henrician dissolutions to the archiepiscopal visitation in 1630. In Baldoyle parish, for example, in 1630 a great-grandson of the original Fitzsimon grantee farmed the tithes of forty pounds, out of which the Protestant curate received thirty-four shillings. The vast majority of the parishioners repaired, not to the ruined parish church, but to the residence of the Fitzsimon lord to attend Mass.[31] The largest of the surviving religious guilds, that of St Anne in St Audoen's parish, also served to channel funds into a newly-established Catholic church structure in the seventeenth century. The guild's masters from the late Elizabethan years were all aldermen who were publicly revealed as recusants after 1605, and a majority of the bench of twenty-four were members of that fraternity.[32] A salient feature of the officers' activities from the early 1590s was the resisting of legal challenges to guild privileges from state officials, as was the careful shepherding of revenues from the extensive lands, most of which, according to government sources, went towards the support of seminary priests.[33]

Despite the recently-discovered religious certitude of the majority of leading Dubliners and their quiet disengagement from the Church of

---

[28] Edmund Hogan (ed.), *Ibernia Ignatiana* (Dublin, 1880), pp. 19, 228–9.
[29] Dublin, Genealogical Office, MSS 47–8; Lennon, 'Patriciate of Dublin, 1548–1613', pp. 263–4.
[30] 'Archbishop Bulkeley's visitation, 1630', pp. 60–98.
[31] *Ibid.*, p. 65.
[32] Dublin, Royal Irish Academy, Haliday MSS, 12 D 1, pp. 6, 34, 35, 38, 45; Berry, 'Religious guild of St Anne', pp. 94–5.
[33] Lennon, 'Patriciate of Dublin, 1548–1613', pp. 266–8.

Ireland, there is little evidence to suggest that they were other than politically loyal during the critical years of national warfare at the turn of the century. As we have seen, some government officials at that time suspected that, with the incitement of the newly-arrived Catholic missioners, religious fervour could foment disloyalty, especially in a period of economic hardship.[34] The vast majority of the councillors were content to represent their grievances to the English court in the time-honoured form of an embassy, eschewing the course of rebellion which characterized the response of many southern towns to the end of the Nine Years' War and Queen Elizabeth's death.[35] It was in fact the new Jacobean administration with its insistence on religious conformity on the part of the patriciate which caused the majority to go beyond mere dissent from the official orthodoxy to a more all-embracing Catholicism. Credal confidence was forged in the tribunals of the mid-1600s, in cases such as those of the seven aldermen who were penalized in 1603 for breaches of the Act of Uniformity,[36] and that of Alderman John Shelton who was ejected from the mayoralty by order of the government for refusing to take the Oath of Supremacy in November 1604.[37] The faith of these recusants was observed by members of the Society of Jesus, such as Henry Fitzsimon and Christopher Hollywood, to be simple and unquestioning, and they resolved to inform it with a dimension of more sophisticated theological argument.[38]

The sustained campaign of the royal administrators against recusancy among the civic leaders, conducted for several months in 1605-6, provided the occasion for the concurrence of dogged belief and deepening knowledge which the priests desired. Twenty-two substantial citizens were brought before the prerogative court of Castle Chamber on grounds of their refusal to obey mandates addressed to each individually, ordering them to accompany the Lord Deputy to divine service.[39] The court, which could order imprisonment at pleasure and impose large fines, was the instrument used by the State to break the non-conformity of the Dublin patricians whose example was crucial in

---

[34] See note 4 above.
[35] For details of embassies, see 'The humble petition of the mayor and commons of Dublin', June 1957: PRO, SP 63/199/127(1); *CalSPI, 1603-6*, p. 228. On the subject of the recusancy revolt, see Anthony J. Sheehan, 'The recusancy revolt of 1603: a reinterpretation', *Archivium Hibernicum*, 38 (1983), pp. 3-13.
[36] *CalSPI, 1601-3*, pp. 566-9; Hogan (ed.), *Ibernia Ignatiana*, pp. 109-10, 112-13, 117-18, 119-20.
[37] *CalSPI, 1603-6*, pp. 212-13.
[38] Hogan, *Ibernia Ignatiana*, pp. 113, 196.
[39] *CalSPI, 1603-6*, pp. 348-9, 353-4, 391, 401-2; *HMC Egmont MSS*, 1, pt 1 (1905), pp. 30-1.

both city and country.[40] The head of the Jesuit mission, Christopher Hollywood, anticipating the trials, assembled the patricians and gave them guidance on the issues which would be raised in questioning.[41] The answers which the citizens gave at their hearings testify to the coherence of their defence, and the ever-vigilant Hollywood was ready to confirm the doubts of individuals in the cells of the castle if Protestant ministers attempted to dissuade them from their course.[42] The outcome was a victory for the corporate resistance of the aldermen, whose fines were reduced if not remitted, and whose legal prosecution was called into question due to the manner of procedure against them by mandates.[43] The use of compulsion helped to foment more ingrained opposition on the part of most to the forms of the Established Church. After 1606 many reports suggest that the practice of Catholicism became much more open and that the priests, far from complying with the proclamation of their banishment, were more active than ever in the city and its environs.[44] Mass-houses were established in most of the parishes of Dublin in the residences of prominent citizens such as Alderman Patrick Browne of Browne's Castle.[45] A public building which attracted Mass-congregations was the hall of St Anne's Guild, an institution whose patrician members continued to operate actively, farming revenues and issuing leases, despite several judicial investigations of its charter.[46]

For the Catholic majority among the patricians of Dublin their assurance of the rightness of their religious stance was transposed into a peaceful campaign for the defence of valued political and economic liberties which were being threatened with extinction by the state. Issues such as customs rights and merchant guild privileges combined with that of liberty of conscience to form a set of principles of conservatism among the city lords after 1606. To their use of the established forms of representation of grievances, such as missions to court, the principal councillors could bring their new-found confidence.[47] As in the case of the religious mandates of 1605, the government made use of the

[40] See Herbert Wood, 'The Court of Castle Chamber', *PRIA* 32 C (1913-16), pp. 152-70.
[41] Hogan, *Ibernia Ignatiana*, pp. 130, 183, 194-7.
[42] *Ibid.*, pp. 183, 194-7, 201-2.
[43] *CalSPI, 1603-6*, pp. 362-3, 365, 373-4, 390, 405-6, 413-15, 445-52, 457, 463.
[44] *CalSPI, 1608-10*, pp. 284, 310.
[45] Barnaby Rich, *A new descreiption of Ireland* (London, 1610), p. 67; Myles V. Ronan, 'Religious life in old Dublin', *Dublin Historical Record*, 2 (1939-40), pp. 106-7.
[46] Dublin, Royal Irish Academy, Haliday MSS, 12 D 1, pp. 24-32, 37, 48, 56-7, 62-4.
[47] For a discussion of the political and economic aspects, see Lennon, 'Patriciate of Dublin, 1548-1613', pp. 316-28.

prerogative to circumvent statutory law to remove the merchants' exemption from customs dues in 1611,[48] and contemporaneously a bout of repressive actions to enforce religious conformity was initiated. Foreign travel for scholars was banned, priests were again declared banished, and the Oath of Supremacy was imposed on municipal office-holders.[49] A meeting of parliament to legislate for many of these matters was planned, and in order to intimidate possible opponents the administration in Dublin Castle was empowered to execute at least one Catholic bishop. Chosen for exemplary punishment was the aged bishop of Down and Connor, Conor O'Devaney, along with a priest, Patrick O'Loughran. Both were charged with treasonable dealings with the attainted earl of Tyrone and convicted.[50] The occasion of the executions served as a great Catholic demonstration by the residents of Dublin and surrounding districts, many hundreds of whom followed the procession to the gallows. Prominent among those who witnessed the final ordeal of the bishop and priest were many of the patricians and their wives. Lord Deputy Chichester was forced to admit that the executions had effects opposite to those desired in that the dead ones were accounted martyrs.[51]

The election of the two noted Catholic members of parliament for Dublin in 1613 shows that the foremost citizens had decided on a radical course in defence of their political and religious rights. Instead of choosing Protestants to represent them, they perceived that religious affirmation was itself at issue. They did display flexibility in allying with their Protestant fellows in later conflicts over municipal jurisdiction with the State,[52] but the Catholic cause, increasingly drawing its intrepidity from the European Counter-Reformation, by 1613 had become a rallying point for the preservation of a communal heritage. Religious conservatism had been revealed in the last two decades of the sixteenth century as a result of the oppression of Catholic militants. The merging of secular discontents and religious recusancy took place in the early years of the seventeenth century due to the official Protestant attitude that political and other liberties were detrimental, if not dangerous, when possessed by Catholics. The

---

[48] *CalSPI, 1611–14*, p. 114.

[49] *Ibid.*, pp. 96–7; R. R. Steele (ed.), *A bibliography of royal proclamations of the Tudor and Stuart sovereigns*, 2 vols (Oxford, 1910), 2, nos 198, 203.

[50] The main sources for these events are: Barnaby Rich, *A Catholicke conference* (London, 1612), fols 3ᵛ-6ʳ; Rothe, *Analecta*, ed. Moran, pp. cxviii–cxxi; Moran (ed.), *Spicilegium Ossoriense*, 1, pp. 122–3, 123–6.

[51] *CalSPI, 1611–14*, p. 244.

[52] See Lennon, 'Patriciate of Dublin, 1548-1613', pp. 344–6.

forcing of consciences exacerbated the state of civic resentment caused by curtailment of privileges. Confirmed by the seminary priests, their kins-folk, inspirited by the defence mounted against the mandates, and un-troubled by the weak efforts of the Church of Ireland clergy to win acceptance, the recusant patricians of Dublin took their stand in the name of an old religious faith which dovetailed with venerable municipal traditions and institutions.

St Patrick's College, Maynooth

GEOFFREY KEATING'S
EOCHAIR SGIATH AN AIFRINN AND THE
CATHOLIC REFORMATION IN IRELAND

by BERNADETTE CUNNINGHAM

THE name of Geoffrey Keating is familiar to generations of students of Irish language and literature. His prose works are fine examples of seventeenth-century Irish writing. He was credited by scholars of Irish with having saved from oblivion many stories of the Gaelic heroes of old in his magnum opus, the *Foras Feasa ar Éirinn*, a compendium of knowledge on the history of Ireland.[1] Writing in the early part of the seventeenth century, when the native Irish system of learning and patronage of scholars was disintegrating, Keating synopsized many manuscript sources for the history of Ireland into a flowing text full of stories and curiosities. His writings were frequently transcribed and are preserved in countless manuscript copies.

Keating's literary stature has meant that his tracts were more read for their language and style than studied for their content and it may appear curious at first sight to discover that this father figure of early Irish history and the preserver of the Irish language also wrote two theological tracts, on a continental Catholic Reformation model.[2] This should come as no surprise to anyone familiar with Keating's background. Although subsequently hailed as a champion of Gaelic Ireland, Keating was not a product of that society. In fact he was of Anglo-Norman (Old English) descent. He was ordained as a secular priest and was educated at two of the continental colleges set up to train Irishmen for the priesthood, Bordeaux and Rheims, where he came under English Jesuit influence. The precise dates of his sojourn on the continent are not known, but pre-date 1619. It is thought he was born about 1570 and died about 1644, spending most of his life as a priest working in Munster.[3]

---

[1] Geoffrey Keating, *Foras Feasa ar Éirinn: the History of Ireland*, ed. David Comyn and P. S. Dineen, 4 vols (London, Irish Texts Society, 1902–14).

[2] Geoffrey Keating [Seathrun Céitinn], *Eochair-Sgiath an Aifrinn . . . an Explanatory Defence of the Mass . . .*, ed. Patrick O'Brien (Dublin, 1898); Geoffrey Keating, *Trí Bhior Ghaoithe an Bháis*, ed. Osborn Bergin (Dublin, 1931).

[3] *Selections from the Zoilomastix of O'Sullivan Beare*, ed. T. J. O'Donnell (Dublin, Irish Manuscripts Commission, 1960), p. 22; *Calendar of State Papers Ireland, 1615–25*, p. 318. Donnchadh O Corráin, 'Seathrún Céitinn (c.1580–c.1664): an cúlra stairiúil', *Dúchas, 1983, 1984, 1985* (Dublin, 1986), pp. 56–68.

Keating's history of Ireland revealed some of the particular preoccupations of an Old English secular priest in early seventeenth-century Ireland. A bias towards the perspective of a diocesan priest can be noted, for example, in the particular emphasis placed on the Synod of Kells of 1152 which had divided Ireland into the four archdioceses of Armagh, Dublin, Cashel, and Tuam. By stressing their antiquity Keating gave the diocesan and parochial structures recommended by Trent a 'genealogy' dating back several centuries even though the Tridentine recommendations were not yet fully a reality in the Ireland of his day. This interpretative framework was not a mere academic exercise, but was part of Keating's argument for the continuity of the Catholic Church since its foundation by Patrick. Protestant writers such as James Ussher, archbishop of Armagh, contended that the Church of Patrick had become corrupt, and had been restored to its original purity by the reformation as represented in Ireland by the Anglican Church. Keating's chronological framework dated that reform to the twelfth century when he considered that the elimination of abuses had gone hand in hand with the establishment of the archdiocesan structure in its modern form. Keating's historical writing, therefore, presented readers with an alternative model for Irish church history to that provided either by Ussher on the one hand, or the religious orders on the other. He did not refute these other historical interpretations, merely ignored them.[4]

I

Keating's theological writings, on the other hand, were in a more controversial mould. This is particularly true of his earliest work, the *Eochair-Sgiath an Aifrinn*, an exposition and defence of the Mass. His later work, *Trí Bhior Ghaoithe an Bháis* [*The Three Shafts of Death*], a treatise on purgatory and death, was more 'popular' in tone. Keating prefaced the *Eochair-Sgiath an Aifrinn* by saying that the arguments of Luther and Calvin were not worth refuting, but that since they had gone beyond the bounds of truth and right he was moved to defend the Catholic Church, and he chose to do that through a defence of the Mass, one of the main issues of theological dispute in the Reformation era.[5] Both tracts are curious, not because

---

[4] Keating, *Foras Feasa*, 3, pp. 299-307, 357. On Keating as historian see Bernadette Cunningham, 'Seventeenth-century Interpretations of the Past: the Case of Geoffrey Keating', *Irish Historical Studies*, 25 (1986), pp. 116-128.

[5] Keating, *Eochair-Sgiath*, p. 19.

they are untypical of continental European writings of the Counter-Reformation era, but rather because they are the only works of their kind known to exist in the Irish language in the seventeenth century.

Keating's tract on the Mass, written about forty years after the Tridentine decree, was less an original contribution to a continental theological debate than a distillation of current teaching for an Irish audience. An introductory chapter outlined the three conditions of the true Church: unity, catholicity, and holiness, and gave the author's reasons for writing. Chapter one illustrated, by reference to the words of early popes and other early church fathers, especially Saint Ambrose, Saint Augustine, Pope Leo I, Gregory, Bede, Anselm, and others, that the Mass originated at the time of the Apostles and had been in existence ever since. It defined the essential elements of the sacrament of the Mass as being: to bless the bread and wine, to offer them to the Father Almighty, and to receive the body and blood of Christ under the form of bread and wine, and Keating reaffirmed that only a priest had the authority to say Mass. The second and third chapters were devoted to proving that the Mass was a sacrifice. It presented the purpose of the Mass as being to commemorate the passion, a spiritual food for the souls of the living and a benefit to the souls in purgatory. He distinguished different types of sacrifice; the figurative sacrifice of Christ in the death of Abel, the sacrifice on the cross, and the sacramental sacrifice, under the form of bread and wine. Keating asserted that the Mass was a sacrifice under this last sacramental form and not, as he claimed the heretic stated, under the second form.

Chapter four concentrated on the etymology of the Latin word 'Missa'. That he was translating from a Latin source is suggested by the inclusion of this chapter, for he failed to offer an explanation of the Irish word for Mass, 'Aifreann'. He did not get far with his explanation and concluded that it is not necessarily odd that there were different words for the Mass in different languages, as Liturgia in Greek, Aifreann in Irish, and Mass in English. Chapter five discussed the vestments and the objects associated with the altar. Chapter six analysed the liturgical elements preceding the canon of the mass. Four chapters were devoted to the canon of the Mass. Chapter nine dealt with the Real Presence quoting *exempla* to illustrate that the bread does in fact change into the body and blood of Christ. There followed three chapters on Confession with stories from the *Magnum Speculum Exemplorum*, and the *Scala Coeli*.[6] Chapters fourteen and fifteen dealt with Communion, giving an account of the ten reasons of the

---

[6] Padraig Ó Fiannachta, 'Scéalta ón *Magnum Speculum Exemplorum*', *IER* 99 (1963), pp. 177–84.

Catholic Church why the Body of Christ was not given to the laity under the form of wine, and an account of the way it was laid down that the penitent should receive the body of Christ. In a further digression, chapter seventeen discussed purgatory in order to show that the Mass benefited the souls in purgatory. Finally, chapter eighteen gave an account of the regulations on the frequency with which Mass should be said or heard, where it should be heard, and by whom it should be heard.

The discussion was presented throughout as disproving the contentions of Luther and Calvin. Keating's arguments were supported by evidence drawn from Scripture and the early Church Fathers. Although making frequent general reference to the arguments of Luther and Calvin, he only rarely gave specific citations or direct quotations from their works. He argued that whereas the writings of the Fathers tended to substantiate each other, the writings of Luther frequently contradicted those of Calvin and vice versa. He was particularly pleased when he found something which he could impute to Calvin but which could be contradicted by reference solely to Scripture, and he referred more than once to the illogicality of a church expounding a doctrine on the basis of scripture alone, but then making church laws about Sunday observance and the like.[7] One gets the impression he enjoyed the disputation.

II

In European terms, of course, a tract on the Mass was nothing new. Following Lutheran and Calvinist criticisms and in particular the denial that the Mass was a sacrifice, or that transubstantiation occurred, Catholic tracts in defence of the Mass appeared as early as 1520. The Council of Trent, meeting at intervals between 1546 and 1562 dealt with the theme of the Eucharist in sections, at different stages of the Council proceedings. It dealt with the sacrament and the Real Presence; Communion, and the canon of the Mass, and in particular, the Mass as sacrifice. This almost accidental division of themes, prompted by external conditions to which the Tridentine discussions were a response, was perpetuated with little modification in most later tracts drawing on the Tridentine decree, and Keating's tract was no exception.[8] The drawing together of the diverse

---

[7] Keating's citations included Calvin's *Institutes*, 4, cap. 18 and Luther's *Treatise on the New Testament* and his *Table Talk*, Keating, *Eochair-Sgiath*, pp. 7-9, 3, 15-16.

[8] Josef A. Jungmann, *The Mass, an Historical, Theological and Pastoral Survey* (Collegeville, 1976), pp. 83-7.

themes in one coherent discussion took centuries rather than years to achieve.

Keating's tract then was clearly within this Tridentine mould, its most distinguishing characteristic being that it was in the Irish language. Unlike many of the Irish language catechetical writings of members of religious orders it was not circulated in printed form in the early modern period. Rather, it circulated in manuscript only, and the earliest extant copy is dated 1657. The text continued to be transcribed regularly down to the middle of the nineteenth century.[9] Four of the fourteen manuscripts which pre-date 1715 are known to have been in the hands of clergy. We may perhaps deduce from this that some clergy felt it worth the trouble and expense of acquiring copies. Curiously though, at least one scribe sought to improve the text and supplied the Latin original of quotations, followed by a full translation, where Keating had merely synopsized the argument. Somebody wanted to use the text and found it inadequate.[10] He was probably the exception rather than the rule, but it does warn one against underestimating the reception accorded this text by the Gaelic Irish intellectual elite, even though the intellectual environment which originally produced it had little enough in common with that of the scribes on whom it depended for transmission.

III

The context of theological writing in Irish into which we have to place Keating's tract on the Mass is that shaped by the efforts of the Irish Franciscans, mainly based at Louvain, who in the early seventeenth century published a series of catechisms which conveyed the essence of the Tridentine catechism to an Irish audience.[11] They printed devotional

---

[9] National Library of Ireland, MS G 49, is the earliest known extant copy. For subsequent copies see Richard J. Hayes, *Manuscript Sources for the History of Irish Civilization* (Boston, 1965), 2, pp. 653–9, and *Manuscript sources for the History of Irish Civilization, first supplement* (Boston, 1979), 1, p. 383.

[10] Pádraig Ó Fiannachta, 'Aiteanna as Bhíobla aistrithe ag Seán O Maolchonaire', *IER* 97 (1962), p. 382; Ó Fiannachta, 'Eochair-Sgiath an Aifrinn' in *Dúchas, 1983, 1984, 1985*, pp. 33–42. Ó Fiannachta, 'Seán Mhac Torna I Mhaoilchonaire agus *Eochair-Sgiath an Aifrinn*', *Eigse*, 10 (1962–3), pp. 198–207.

[11] For a summary of this catechetical tradition see Patrick Wallace, 'Irish Catechesis: the Heritage of James Butler II, Archbishop of Cashel, 1774–1791' (Ph.D. thesis, Catholic University of America, 1975), pp. 77–88. The earliest printed catechisms in Irish were Bonaventure O hEodhasa, *An Teagasg Criosdaidhe* (Antwerp, 1611), ed. Fearghal Mac Raghnaill (Dublin, 1976); Theobald Stapleton [Teabóid Gallduff], *Catechismus, seu doctrina Christiana, Latina Hibernica, per modum dialogi inter Magistrum et discipulum . . .* (Brussels, 1639) (Reflex facsimile, Dublin,

works, translations of continental works adapted for Irish consumption, and they also collected material on the history of Ireland and the lives of early Irish saints.[12] The first of these catechisms, Bonaventure O hEodhasa's *Teagasg Críosdaighe*, like any other derived from Canisius and Bellarmine, was based around the Creed, the Our Father, the Commandments, and the sacraments. Among the sacraments it taught that the essential elements of the Mass were that it be performed by a priest, with bread and wine, over which words ordained by Christ were said, and that the priest must have the intention of performing the sacrament. It conveyed the law of the Church on the laity receiving Communion in the form of bread only, and laid down the regulations regarding frequency.

There was no significant doctrinal difference from what Keating held— but the Catechism version was just a brief statement of doctrine in a work devoted largely to other matters, in contrast to Keating's detailed disputation focusing solely on the Mass. It is significant that in its short treatment of the Mass this first Franciscan catechism twice resorted to the advice that that in case of difficulty in understanding what was taught the reader should remember that God could do more than the reader could understand.[13]

Later catechetical efforts further simplified the text, as expectations of what could be taught were repeatedly modified. In 1639, an Old English diocesan priest from Kilkenny, Theobald Stapleton, published a catechism with parallel text in Irish and Latin. In his introduction Stapleton addressed parish priests, patrons, parents, preachers, and confessors, asking them to see to the catechesis of those in their care, and reminding them of the indulgence to be gained for each person to whom they taught the catechism. He argued that despite the many learned doctors of theology and the other arts in Ireland, nothing was more lacking than a simple catechism in the ordinary language of the people which was clear, concise, simple, and intelligible, and which the common people could understand. With undeniable logic he argued the case for the use of the

---

Irish Manuscripts Commission, 1945); Anthony Gearnon, *Parrthas an Anama* (Louvain, 1645), ed. Anselm Ó Fachtma (Dublin, 1953); John Dowley, *Suim Bhunadhasach an Teagaisg Chriosdaidhe* (Louvain, 1663); Froinsias Ó Maolmhuaidh, *Lucerna Fidelium* (Rome, 1676), ed. Pádraig Ó Súilleabháin (Dublin, 1962).

[12] For an overview of these writings see Brian Ó Cuív, 'The Irish Language in the Early Modern Period' in T. W. Moody, F. X. Martin, F. J. Byrne (eds), *A New History of Ireland*, 3 (Oxford, 1976), pp. 529-34.

[13] Ian Green, 'For Children in Yeeres and Children in Understanding', *JEH* 37 (1986), p. 402; Ó HEodhasa, *Teagasg Criosdaidhe*, pp. 79-83.

vernacular, asking how the poor simple lay Irishman could understand a sermon in Latin, English, French, or any other foreign language, unless he first learnt that language. He regretted that so many Irish speakers were taught to say their prayers in broken Latin, repeating them 'like a parrot', not knowing what they were saying.[14]

Stapleton's allegations on the poor state of catechesis in Ireland in 1639 were probably accurate, and the Franciscans too came to realize that there were problems of communication that were rooted in tradition. Florence Conry, in his translation from Spanish of *Desiderius*, in 1616 had explained that in an attempt to open the door of the true faith to the ordinary person in Ireland he used the wooden key of the simple language rather than the golden key of the literary language of the bardic schools.[15] Thus one of the difficulties of the dissemination of Counter-Reformation literature in Gaelic Ireland is revealed. The intermediaries between continental ideas and the Irish Catholics were by and large the remnants of a literary elite, who were conscious of compromising their literary standards in the attempt to reach a wider audience. It was an audience which had not previously been addressed by what Stapleton described as the 'Aos Ealaine', Ireland's literary elite.[16] It was the values of the Catholic Reformation which first motivated that elite to make contact in writing with lower social orders.

Some years after Stapleton's discouraging remarks, a Franciscan, Anthony Gearnon, echoed his realization of the people's ignorance of the faith. Gearnon's *Parrthas an Anma* was largely a simplification of the 1611 O hEodhasa catechism, reformulated in question and answer form. It proved to be one of the most popular publications in Irish in the seventeenth century and the prayer book section was frequently copied and circulated in manuscript form through the seventeenth and eighteenth centuries.[17]

Keating's *Eochair-Sgiath an Aifrinn* was in a rather different league. It made no apology about its language or form. Clearly, Keating was addressing an audience whom he felt comfortable about addressing. The intended audience was obviously an Irish speaking, literate minority. Its detailed discussion of the Mass might suggest that it was designed to be a manual for the use of the clergy. However in the section on confession he

---

[14] Stapleton, *Catechismus*, preface.
[15] Flaithrí Ó Maolchonaire [Florence Conry], *Desiderius, otherwise called Sgáthán an Chrábhaidh* (Louvain, 1616), ed. T. F. O'Rahilly (Dublin, 1941), p. 2.
[16] Stapleton, *Catechismus*, preface, sig. b2.
[17] Gearnon, *Parrthas an Anama*; Wallace, 'Irish Catechesis', pp. 83–4.

suggested that if the reader should require more detail on confession he would get detailed explanation from a wise father confessor.[18] This suggests that the tract was not in fact primarily addressed to the clergy but rather the educated laity, and in this it contrasted with the bulk of other Catholic Reformation literature in Irish. We must conclude either that Keating was addressing a very small learned elite as his deliberately chosen audience, or that he had wildly misjudged the nature of the Irish audience to which he directed his theological works.

His readers were treated to a discourse which denigrated Luther and Calvin. While a continentally-trained author might automatically proceed in such a manner, its relevance to the contemporary Irish situation would have been limited enough. Many questions arise. How well known were the teachings of Calvin and Luther among the Irish speaking audience Keating was addressing or even to Keating himself? Why did Keating present his work on the Mass as a hard-hitting refutation of Protestant writers, rather than merely conveying Tridentine teachings on the Mass to an Irish audience? The body of the work certainly appears more influenced by the continental preoccupation with denigrating Protestant authors and the academic model of the disputation rather than with the more particular concerns of the Catholic community within Ireland.

But yet this may not be the whole story. The introductory chapter may have had particular relevance to the Ireland of the early seventeenth century. Without mentioning Ireland specifically it drew attention to the distinction between ecclesiastical and secular authority, denied by the Protestants but supported, in Keating's view, by the biblical authority indicated in 'Reddite quae sunt Caesaris, Caesari; et quae sunt Dei, Deo'. Keating presented the Mass to his readers as the central tenet of Catholicism as contrasted with Protestantism, arguing that those who outlawed the Mass outlawed God. He presented the Mass as a touchstone of loyalty, stating baldly that he who was not loyal to the Mass was a heretic. He added to this a defence of the clergy, complaining that in the present climate priests and brothers were treated as woodkerne and criminals, but, he argued, if it was a crime to be a priest then was God not wrong to show love to Aaron, Moses, and Melchisidech, and of course Christ himself, all of whom were priests.[19]

Keating's work on the Mass was perhaps closer in form to the work of the Jesuit, Henry Fitzsimon, a fellow Old Englishman, than to the work of

---

[18] Keating, *Eochair-Sgiath*, p. 93.
[19] *Ibid.*, pp. 16-17.

the Franciscan catechetical writers. Fitzsimon's own tract on the Mass, presented as a refutation of the arguments of Mr John Ryder, was published at Louvain in 1611. Both were comprehensive treatises on the Mass, quoting from a wide variety of sources, making many of the same points. Although their approaches were not identical it would appear at least that they had both taken to heart the words of St Thomas Aquinas, quoted by Fitzsimon that 'it is more meritorious to indoctrine many preachers and pastors than to be alone one of the ferventest and most beneficial'.[20]

One might say that the only thing distinctively Irish about Keating's tract on the Mass was the language in which it was written. Keating did not draw on any native Irish material for his examples. His one Irish example was a scientific example drawn from Giraldus Cambrensis about fossilized wood in Lough Neagh. Giraldus was not an Irish writer, but was in fact the only source of information on Ireland which would have circulated on the continent before the Franciscans and others got to work on alternative versions of the Irish past.

This continental bias in the sources of Keating's theological work contrasted with his historical writings in which he was at pains to illustrate the virtues of the Catholic community, both native Irish and Old English, from the coming of St Patrick, using Irish sources. In his later theological tract, *Trí Bhior Ghaoithe an Bháis*, he had come to reflect some aspects of Irish society in his writing, giving Irish as well as Biblical examples to illustrate his arguments on funerals, wakes, and burial customs. In this later tract too, Keating incorporated Irish verse in support of his arguments.[21] By contrast his attempt in *Eochair-Sgiath an Aifrinn* to provide a mnemonic for confession based on the letters of the word IUDAS is a clumsy attempt to render into Irish a mnemonic which obviously originated in a Latin text. His equivalent Irish words actually spelt IFDDL,[22] and were a direct translation from Latin, inadequately adapted for its intended audience.

IV

The rationale for a treatise on the mass, in continental terms, is clear, since the Catholic Reformation advocated catechetical teaching designed

---

[20] Henry Fitzsimon, *The Justification and Exposition of the Divine Sacrifice of the Mass* (Douai, 1611), sig. e2–e2ᵛ.
[21] Keating, *Three Shafts*, pp. xii, 180–1.
[22] Keating, *Eochair-Sgiath*, p. 91.

to promote the use of the sacraments within a parochial framework. A central focus of that catechesis was the promotion of an appreciation of the Mass. The way in which the Old English writers, Keating and Fitzsimon, presented their treatises on the Mass underlined in no uncertain way that in promoting an understanding of the Mass as central to Catholicism, and in refutation of Protestantism, they understood the significance of the fact that in early seventeenth-century Ireland 'to be a Catholic . . . was to know why one was not a Protestant'.[23]

Fitzsimon's tract on the Mass could possibly be regarded as little more than one more contribution to the controversial writing indulged in by some Old English writers, including Ryder, Ussher, and Sibthorpe, but Keating's tract differed from any of these. Written in Irish, it must have been intended for a different audience from that of the controversial writing in English. Whether it enhanced the position of the Mass within the Catholic community is another question entirely. Richard O'Ferrall, a Capuchin, writing to Rome in 1658 on the state of the Irish Church mentioned the good work of the Franciscan authors in counteracting ignorance, increasing holiness, and preserving the Irish language, but did not mention Keating in this regard.[24] This may, however, have been because of a bias against secular clergy, or Old English authors, rather than concrete evidence that Keating's tract was not widely known.

On the other hand there is folklore evidence that stories from Keating's *Eochair-Sgiath an Aifrinn* survived for over three centuries in the folk memory in Connacht.[25] This would perhaps suggest that though written on the continental model of a 'disputation' in the early seventeenth century, it may have subsequently fulfilled its secondary role as a handbook for the clergy and provided material for many a sermon. While not written with the education of the illiterate populace in mind, it may in the long run have contributed to popular beliefs on the Mass and confession. The early manuscript tradition also suggests a parallel secular motive for the transcription of Keating's tract. Three of the pre-1715 manuscripts which contained portions of the tract also contained other works by Munster authors, including selections from the poetic dispute known as the Contention of the Bards. Perhaps the finer points of theology may not have counted for much, but the Munster scribes knew a good argument when

---

[23] P. J. Corish, *The Irish Catholic Experience: a Historical Survey* (Dublin, 1985), p. 105.
[24] Richard O'Ferrall and Robert O'Connell, *Commentarius Rinuccinianus*, ed. Stanislaus Kavanagh (Dublin, Irish Manuscripts Commission, 1944), 5, pp. 490–1.
[25] Mrs T. Concannon, *The Blessed Eucharist in Irish History* (Dublin, 1932), p. xxii.

they heard one. A Munster priest, triumphing over Luther and Calvin, whoever they might be, was probably just as good as a Munster poet, Tadhg Mac Daire Mac Bruidheadha, triumphing over the mythical northern poet, Torna, in a debate over the superiority of the southern half of Ireland over the northern half. When these manuscripts were being transcribed the Calvinist Presbyterians were in the ascendant in Ulster, and undertones of a new cultural rivalry may have served to link the two texts which had originally emerged from very different contexts.[26]

In the short term context of the early seventeenth-century Irish church, the very form and extent of *Eochair-Sgiath an Aifrinn* illustrates best of all perhaps, the yawning gap between the illusions of a seminarian as to what might be achieved and the reality at home. The transmission of ideas from one cultural environment to another was more difficult to achieve than was realized at first by these early seventeenth-century authors. Transmission of ideas and concepts from a literate to a largely oral culture had special problems. While the Franciscan, Aodh Mac Aingil, might have rejoiced in the illiteracy of the laity, which preserved them from exposure to heresy, the proponents of the Catholic Reformation in Ireland encountered near insurmountable problems of communicating new ideas to a largely unreceptive laity.[27] Geoffrey Keating's choice of following in the Jesuit tradition of catering almost exclusively for the needs of the gentry and clergy, may not have been that much less influential in the development of popular piety than the possibly more direct, but not necessarily more successful, efforts of the Franciscan catechists.

Dublin Diocesan Library

[26] Royal Irish Academy, MS 23 H 18; NLI, microfilm P 471 (Stonyhurst College MSS); Maynooth, O'Curry MS 14. For the 'Contention of the Bards' see Lambert McKenna (ed.), *Iomarbhagh na bhFileadh*, 2 vols (London, ITS, 1929).

[27] Aodh Mac Aingil [Hugh MacCaghwell], *Scathán Shacramuinte na hAithridhe* (Louvain, 1618), ed. Canice Mooney (Dublin, 1952), p. 94; Wallace, 'Irish Catechesis', p. 78.

THE PRACTICE OF RELIGIOUS CONTROVERSY
IN DUBLIN, 1600-1641

by DECLAN GAFFNEY

The name controversy, I confess, is the name of a disease; but necessary ... to be known first, to make a readier way for the cure; and he that cares not which way disputes about religion go, brands himself with the palpable neglect of his faith and religion. Not as though all were equally interested in the study of controversies, but that everyone may be ready to give an answer to every man that asks him a reason of the hope that is in him.[1]

JOSUA Hoyle, the author of these words, was well qualified to expand upon the nature of religious controversy. In 1622 he had succeeded James Ussher as professor of Theological Controversies in Trinity College, Dublin, a position Ussher had taken up on its foundation in 1607.[2] Much of what Hoyle says might have been echoed by the Roman Catholic polemicists of the day. A training in religious controversy was essential to clergy on both sides of the confessional divide; the ability to refute the arguments of one's doctrinal opponents came into play not only in the composition of polemical literature and the conduct of public disputations, but also in preaching and in private conversion-seeking. As Hoyle points out, public controversy was also intended to go some way towards providing the educated members of the faithful with a surer grasp of the principles of their religion, and of the unassailability of those principles.[3]

At the same time Hoyle's characterization of controversy as a 'disease' as well as a duty is typical of the reservations on the subject expressed by Protestant polemicists of the day. An over-studious concern with disputed theological points might undermine the efficiency of public preaching as

---

[1] Josua Hoyle, 'Preface to the reader' in *A Rejoynder to Malone's Reply* (Dublin, 1641).
[2] R. B. MacDowell and D. A. Webb, *Trinity College Dublin: an Academic History* (Cambridge, 1982), pp. 12–13.
[3] Thus the post of professor of Theological Controversies carried with it a public lectureship on controversies at Christchurch Cathedral, Dublin. Cf. J. W. Stubbs, *The History of the University of Dublin* (Dublin, 1887), p. 49 and *The Whole Works of . . . James Ussher, Archbishop of Armagh, with a life of the Author . . .*, by C. R. Elrington (Dublin, 1864) [hereafter *UWW*], I, p. 18. The standard modern biography of Ussher is R. Buick Knox, *James Ussher, Archbishop of Armagh* (Cardiff, 1967).

a means of conversion. James Ussher warned recently-ordained clergy-men to 'meddle with controversies and doubtful points as little as may be in your public preaching, lest you puzzle your hearers or engage them in wrangling disputations, and so hinder their conversion, which is the main design of preaching'.[4] Ussher was also aware of the dangers of exposing the more lukewarm and the more enthusiastic among the Protestant laity to 'doubtful points'. As he explained to Laud in 1631, his book on Gotteschalcus, a contribution to the debate on predestination, had been published in Latin because he thought it 'not convenient that the common people should trouble themselves with questions of this nature'.[5] Thus the first polemical work in Latin published in Dublin during this period was not only not intended for the Irish public, it was not, strictly speaking, intended for public consumption at all. This policy of 'containment' was not confined to themes which were liable to raise disagreements among Protestants. Ussher's first book, *De ecclesiarum successione*, was also never published in English, although it was directed purely against Catholic doctrines. Works such as these were more likely to be read by fellow theologians, both Catholic and Protestant, than by laymen of either denomination.[6] It is important, in dealing with the practice of controversy to distinguish between texts aimed at a learned audience and those aimed simply at the educated public.

The intended audience for the works considered in this paper were the English speaking Catholics of the Pale, where the circumstances of religious life in the early seventeenth century demanded a less rarefied approach to the defence of the reformed faith. Throughout this period, Dublin was supplied with a predominantly native Catholic clergy, educated on the continent and including several highly qualified controversialists. Henry Fitzsimon SJ had been educated at Oxford and at Douai, and had lectured in metaphysics at Louvain, before returning to Ireland in 1598. He had the distinct advantage of being a convert from

---

[4] Richard Parr, *The Life of James Ussher, Archbishop of Armagh* (London, 1686), p. 387.

[5] *CalSPI 1625-32*, p. 618. The work in question is *Gotteschalci, et praedestinationae controversie historia* (Dublin, 1631) in *UWW* 4. This statement needs to be considered in the context of the royal Declaration against controversies of 1628, which was particularly concerned with discouraging works on predestination. A few months later Laud, as bishop of London, secured the withdrawal of George Downhame's *Treatise of the certainty of perseverance* (Dublin, 1631). See *CalSPI 1625-32*, p. 633; *DNB* and footnote 34 below.

[6] *De Christianorum Ecclesiarum . . . Continua Successione et Statu* (London, 1613) in *UWW* 2. For two Catholic replies to this work by Irish authors see Richard Stanihurst, *Brevis Praemunitio . . .* (Paris, 1618) and the second edition of *De Investigenda Verra Ecclesia* (Antwerp, 1619) by Christopher Holywood (Sacrobosco). Cf. *UWW* 15, p. 148.

what he himself termed 'puritanism', and was familiar enough with differences of opinion within the Anglican Church to put them to good use in his dispute with the Dean of St Patrick's Cathedral, John Rider. Christopher Holywood, superior of the Jesuit mission in Ireland, had lectured at Padua and had published a defence of Bellarmine at Antwerp in 1607, a work which was used by Ussher in his lectures at Trinity. The English priest Paul Harris, who wrote under the pseudonym Paulus Veridicus, had been educated at Cambridge as well as at the university of Seville before coming to Dublin in the early years of the seventeenth century.[7]

Protestant divinity was, of necessity, defensive. The motivation behind Ussher's polemical writings of the 1620s was the same as that which led him, as archbishop of Armagh, to encourage the bishops and clergy of his province to 'deal with the Popish recusants, that if possible they might make them understand their errors, which way, in a country where there are no penal laws to restrain the public profession of the religion, was the best if not the only means that could be used'.[8] Proselytising was the unwelcome alternative to the suppression which under more favourable circumstances it would have supplemented. Henri Meylan's observation *'Qui dit propagande, dit aussi polemique'* applies to seventeenth-century Ireland as well as to sixteenth-century France.[9] Propagation of the faith went hand in hand with its public defence.

An important advantage on the side of the Church of Ireland was the tight control of the Irish press. As shall become clear, the press was not the only means, perhaps not even the most important means by which polemical activity was pursued, and the printed remains of religious controversies in Dublin are probably only the tip of the iceberg. None the less, Catholic polemicists were hindered in their activities by their inability to engage in a pamphlet war on equal terms. For most of the seventeenth century the press in Ireland constituted a monopoly. The King's Printer's Patent, issued to John Franckton in 1604 and renewed in 1609, as well as granting the monopolies on prayer books and proclamations normally associated with the position of official printer, also granted him sole right to print, publish, sell, and bind books in Ireland.[10] In 1618, the Patent was

---

[7] On FitzSimon, see the texts collected in *Words of Comfort to Persecuted Catholics, written in exile 1607*, ed., with a sketch of his life, by Edmund Hogan SJ (Dublin, 1881). For Paul Harris see *Tanner Letters*, ed. Charles MacNeill (Dublin, 1943), p. 89; Rev. John Brady, 'Father Paul Harris, who was he?' in *Repertorium Novum*, 2 (1960), p. 376; *DNB*.

[8] Parr, *Life of Ussher*, p. 39.

[9] *Aspects de la Propagande Religieuse* (*Travaux d'Humanisme et Renaissance* 28, Geneva, 1957), p. xiv.

[10] For the role of the King's Printers' patent in Ireland see M. Pollard, 'Control of the press in

aquired by the Stationers' Company of London, whose first official act in Ireland was to issue a printed power of attorney authorizing the Company's deputies to seize 'all popish and prohibited books, volumes, pictures, and other things forfeit, or to become forfeited', a typical example of the role of official printers as censors.[11]

The representatives of the Company were in contact with James Ussher as early as June 1618, when he wrote to the historian William Camden 'The Company of Stationers in London are now erecting a factory for books and a press among us here: Mr Felix Kingston and some others are sent over for that purpose.'[12] In fact, John Franckton was still officially King's Printer at this stage, and the Stationers' Company did not begin printing in Dublin, under their imprint of the 'Society of Stationers, Dublin', until after Franckton's death in 1620. While religious books had formed only a small part of Franckton's sporadic output as King's Printer, the new holders of the patent seem to have decided on a policy of publishing the works of Protestant divines. This may reflect the perception on the part of the Stationers' Company of the duties involved in being King's Printers to a Protestant monarch in a Protestant outpost such as Ireland; or it may have been based on the assumption that the increase of the Protestant population due to the plantation policies of James I would lead to a corresponding increase in the market for religious books.[13] At the same time the Stationers' Company also began to print polemical works directed at Old English Catholics, perhaps under Ussher's influence.

A plan to reprint Ussher's *De ecclesiarum successione*, mentioned in Ussher's letter to Camden of June 1618, seems to have been shelved, perhaps because Ussher was to keep the presses busy with other works over the next few years. While most of the religious works printed by the Society of Stationers were sermons by such prominent figures as Christopher Hampton, archbishop of Armagh, sold in pamphlet form or in collections, three substantial polemical works appeared between 1622 and 1625. *A Friendly Advertisement to the Pretended Catholics of Ireland* by Sir

---

Ireland through the King's Printer's patent 1600–1800', *Irish Booklore*, 5, pp. 79–96. I am grateful to Ms Pollard for making available to me some of her valuable unpublished work on the Dublin press in the early seventeenth century.

[11] The Stationers' Company already had an interest in Ireland before the acquisition of the patent, as they had contributed to the levies of contributions for the Londonderry plantation from 1613 to 1616. See *Londonderry and the London companies, being a survey and other documents . . . by Sir Thomas Phillips* (Belfast, 1928), pp. 135–7.

[12] *UWW* 15, p. 135.

[13] Pollard, 'Control of the Press', p. 80.

Christopher Sibthorp, justice of the King's Bench, was a rather clumsy attempt to encourage Catholics to take the oath of supremacy. Included in the same volume was James Ussher's *A Letter to Sir Christopher Sibthorp, Knight*, the first edition of the work which was later known as *A Discourse concerning the Religion of the Ancient Irish and British*. Ussher's *An Answer to an Irish Jesuit* of 1624 was the first printed instalment of the controversy with William Malone (the last instalment, Josua Hoyle's *Rejoynder*, was not to appear until 1641). In 1625 appeared Ussher's *A Briefe Declaration of the Universalitie of the Church of Christ delivered in a Sermon at Wainsted*.[14]

All of these works went into second printings. This does not tell us how many copies were distributed, but it argues for an amount of public interest greater than that generated by other works published by the Society of Stationers, as does the extent of the polemical activity which resulted from their publication. Ussher's *Answer to a Jesuit* was to generate well over a thousand pages of printed controversial material, and went through three editions before 1631. Christopher Sibthorp defended his *Friendly Advertisement* with two pamphlets in 1625 and 1627; the second of these was also printed twice, and Sibthorp prepared a revised edition of both these pamphlets (including a new piece directed against William Malone) which was not printed, presumably due to the author's death in 1632.[15]

In the second of his three pamphlets, *A Reply to a Popish Adversary*, Christopher Sibthorp refers to 'the Presse which some say the Papists have . . . in this kingdom',[16] but this is the only reference to a Catholic printing press in Ireland in the polemical literature of the time, and Sibthorp significantly fails to repeat the statement in his *A Surreplication to a Popish*

---

[14] By no means all of the printing for the Irish market was done in Dublin. The second edition of *An Answer to a Jesuit* (1625) carries the imprint of the Dublin Society of Stationers, but is in fact a London printing, and in many copies is bound with the second edition of the Wanstead sermon, which carries a London imprint. The first edition of this sermon was also a London printing, but both these editions must have been distributed in Dublin as Paul Harris, writing from Dublin in 1627, referred to the sermon as having been 'twice printed': *A Briefe Confutation* (St Omer, 1627), p. 1. The fact that the Dublin press carried out some printing for the English market during the 1620s hardly makes matters any clearer (Pollard, 'Control of the press', p. 80; *CalSPI 1625–32*, p. 633), and in general the imprint of texts of this period cannot be taken as firmly establishing where they were to be sold. The justification for treating the above-mentioned texts in an Irish context lies, therefore, not in the fact that they were printed in Dublin (as most of them were), but in the expressed intentions of the authors and the reactions on the part of contemporaries.

[15] Christopher Sibthorp, *A Reply to a Popish Adversary* (Dublin, 1625) and *A Surreplication to a Popish Adversary* (Dublin, 1627). Sibthorp's copy of these two pamphlets, with corrections for the printer, and bound with the manuscript of a reply to Malone is in T.C.D. library, shelf-mark BBH.11.28.

[16] Sibthorp, *A Reply*, p. 4.

Adversary of 1627. C. W. Dugan speculated around the turn of this century that Henry FitzSimon's *A Catholic Confutation*, which appeared in 1608 with a Rouen imprint, had been printed in Dublin, but it is now generally accepted that the place of printing was Douai.[17] However, although FitzSimon's book was not printed in Dublin, an offer was made by his polemical opponent John Rider to place the Dublin press at his disposal.[18] (FitzSimon's book was a reply to Rider's *Friendly Caveat* of 1602, itself a reply to a manuscript of FitzSimon's, who was at the time imprisoned in Dublin Castle, a circumstance which seems to have done little to hinder his activities as a polemicist and converter.) Rider's offer to assist FitzSimon in the publication of his reply is not as surprising as it might sound. The debate between Rider and FitzSimon had been set up with a certain amount of official approval, and FitzSimon had already been allowed to conduct theological disputations from his cell.

FitzSimon's reasons for rejecting Rider's offer are made clear by a letter from Rider in December 1603, in which he told him that the use of the press 'will be granted you I doubt not, provided . . . I may print with you in the same volume, sheete and page'.[19] The obvious implication was that FitzSimon's text would be divided up and printed with Rider's refutations appearing on the same page, a common enough technique in the presentation of religious controversy at the time but one which would place Fitz-Simon at a distinct disadvantage.

The only Catholic writer to have work published in Dublin during this period was Fr Paul Harris, who was involved in the bitter dispute between the secular clergy of Dublin and the Franciscan archbishop Thomas Fleming in the 1630s. The details of this dispute fall outside the scope of this paper, but the Dublin government took an active interest in the hostilities, seeing them as useful in furthering the division within the Pale between the largely Old English and loyalist secular clergy and laity and the Regulars, whose social composition and continental connections marked them out as politically untrustworthy.[20] Between 1632 and 1635 Harris scored an important coup by managing to have a series of anti-Regular

[17] *A Catalogue of Early Dublin Printed Books 1601-1700*, comp. by E. R. MacC. Dix with an introduction by C. W. Dugan (Dublin, 1898), p. 6; cf. A. F. Allison and D. M. Rogers, *A Catalogue of Catholic Books in English 1558-1640* (Bognor Regis, 1956).

[18] Henry FitzSimon, *A Reply to Mr Rider's Rescript* (Douai 1608), p. 22.

[19] *Ibid.*, p. 22.

[20] H. F. Kearney, 'Ecclesiastical Politics and the Counter-Reformation in Ireland, 1618-1648', *JEH* 2 (1960), pp. 202-12; W. D. O'Connell, 'The Cahill propositions, 1629', *IER* 5 series, 62 (1943), pp. 118-23.

pamphlets printed in Dublin,[21] and it seems very unlikely that this was done without official approval, if not encouragement. Ussher sent a copy of one of Harris's pamphlets to his friend Samuel Ward in 1637, despite having been attacked in print by Harris some years previously, and Harris seems to have presented a bound copy of his anti-Regular pamphlets to the library of Trinity College, Dublin.[22]

Unless he was attacking fellow-Catholics, publishing abroad was the only opportunity for a Catholic writer to get his work into print, but it was a slow process. FitzSimon's *Catholic Confutation* was printed at Douai six years after Rider's *Friendly Caveat*, the text to which it was intended as a reply. William Malone managed to print his *Reply to Mr Ussher's Answer* in 1627, within three years of the publiction of Ussher's *Answer to a Jesuit*, but it seems unlikely that the book reached Ireland before 1629 or 1630.[23] Paul Harris's *A Briefe Confutation*, directed against Ussher's Wanstead sermon of 1624, was printed in 1627 at St Omer; however, a letter of 1629 from William Bedell (at that time Provost of Trinity College, Dublin) to Samuel Ward makes it clear that Harris's text was being distributed in manuscript form before being printed. In the printed version Harris claimed somewhat disingenuously that he had written his reply with the intention of communicating it directly to Ussher, and had only resorted to the printing press as a result of Ussher's absence from Ireland. This was of course, no more than a device to justify the *ad hominem* tone of the work; the manuscript was intended for circulation. Bedell wrote 'this fellow hath set abroad a scoffing, railing, pamphlet against my Lord Primate's Wainsted sermon', and added 'I hear it is now in print.'[24] This implies that two years after being printed, Harris's pamphlet was more easily available in manuscript than print in Dublin.

The distribution of a manuscript is, of course, impossible to quantify, but within the educated Old English community of the Pale a fairly small number of copies would probably serve to have an effect on public opinion. Certainly Sir Christopher Sibthorp took the manuscript replies to his *Friendly Advertisement* seriously enough to respond in print. One can only speculate about the means by which a manuscript was 'published'. What is evident, however, is that the issuing of a manuscript was considered a public act.

---

[21] *STC* 12808 to 12812.
[22] *UWW* 16, p. 9.
[23] See below footnote 32.
[24] *Tanner Letters*, p. 89.

Harris was probably the most prolific Catholic polemicist in Dublin. Apart from his anti-Regular pamphlets and his *Briefe Confutation*, he engaged Bedell in a manuscript controversy between 1629 and 1633, when he revived the thirty-year-old arguments of William Alabaster, a sometime convert to the Church of Rome.[25] The title of one of Bedell's contributions gives us an indication of the extent of material generated by this controversy: 'A Defence of the Answer to Mr Alabaster's Four Demands against a Treatise entitled "The Catholic's Reply upon Bedell's Answer to Mr Alabaster's Four Demands".'[26] Harris was also the author of the most extensive polemical manuscript to survive from the period, a 200 folio reply to Ussher's *Letter to Sir Christopher Sibthorp, Knight*, the first comprehensive Catholic attempt to deal with Ussher's claim that the religion of the early Irish was 'for substance the same as that which is now by public authority maintained in this kingdom'.[27]

The longest and best documented religious controversy in Dublin at this time was that which involved James Ussher and the Jesuit William Malone, and a look at the circumstances surrounding it gives some idea of the concerns of both Catholic and Protestant polemicists. In 1617 or 1618, Malone issued a manuscript challenge to the Protestant divines of Ireland at the instigation of Sir Pierce Crosby, a Protestant.[28] This challenge, later printed by Ussher in *An Answer to a Jesuit*, presents two different types of question. Given that Protestants acknowledge that the Church retained its original purity of doctrine and discipline for four or five hundred years after the death of Christ, Malone asks 'what bishop of Rome did first alter that religion . . . ? In what pope's day was the true religion overthrown in Rome?' Malone then goes on to ask 'how can your religion be true, which disalloweth so many chiefe articles, which the saints and fathers of that primitive church did hold to be true?' which allows him to introduce the standard topics of tradition, the real presence, auricular confession and so on.[29]

The task of replying was given to Ussher, the natural choice as professor of Theological Controversies at Trinity. Ussher agreed to the terms of

---

[25] *Ibid.*, pp. 89, 114, 106.
[26] *A True Relation of the Life and Death of William Bedell*, ed. Thomas Wharton Jones, C Ser. NS 4 (1872), p. v.
[27] National Library, Dublin MS 16250. Unfortunately, there is no trace of a reply to this work, nor indeed any evidence that it was ever circulated.
[28] William Malone, Preface to *A Reply to Mr James Ussher his answer* (Douai, 1627).
[29] The challenge is printed in the preliminaries to Ussher's *An Answere to a challenge issued by a Jesuit in Ireland* (Dublin, 1624).

Malone's challenge, and composed a manuscript reply to the first question, which he refers to as the 'general challenge'.[30] In doing so, he was accepting that the 'general challenge' established a framework, or at least a pre-condition for the treatment of the more specific disputed points. Presumably Ussher sent a manuscript of his answer to the 'general challenge' to Malone in the expectation that Malone would issue a general reply, but Malone did not do so. By 1621 Ussher had decided to expand his answer to take in the specific points raised in Malone's challenge and to print the results. In a letter of that year he said that he had put off the printing of the second part of his answer until he returned from his visitation of the diocese of Meath, to which he had recently been presented. This suggests that the first part of the answer was already printed or at least in the printer's hands.[31] However, the first edition of Ussher's *Answer to a Jesuit* appeared in 1624, three years later; and three years after that Malone's *A Reply to Mr Ussher's Answer* was printed at Douai. Copies of the work were seized by the customs in England, and it seems likely that the book did not arrive in Ireland until 1629 or 1630.[32] When Malone's book finally appeared in Dublin, it was decided to issue a collective rejoinder by a team of Church of Ireland divines, under Ussher's patronage. The plan was quickly modified, however, and George Synge's *A Rejoynder to the Reply published by the Jesuits* appeared in 1632, closely followed by Roger Puttocke's *A Rejoynder unto Friar Malone*.

Synge's reply is concerned with Malone's 'general challenge', and Puttock's with the first of the specific questions, concerning church traditions. The original intention had thus presumably been to allot the task of replying to each chapter of Malone's book to a different author while retaining the structure established by Ussher's original. Considering that Synge's *Rejoynder* alone runs to over 400 pages, the proposed collective reply would have been a mammoth enterprise. Synge explained that his part of the work was rushed out because some proof-sheets had been leaked to the Catholic side before the printing was finished, and a Catholic reply was already in preparation.[33] The great collective rejoinder never appeared. During the lord deputyship of Wentworth the limited resources of the Dublin press were largely taken up with official business;

[30] Ussher, *An Answer to a . . . Jesuit*, p. 2.

[31] *UWW* 16, p. 9. Ussher was still working on the answer in March 1622: *Tanner Letters*, pp. 61–2.

[32] Synge and Puttock (and later Hoyle) all claim that the task of replying to Malone began as soon as his book appeared in Dublin and was completed within a few months.

[33] Synge, Preface to *A Rejoynder*.

moreover Laud's determination to enforce the Declaration against Controversies prefixed to the 1628 edition of the 39 Articles (which he had already demonstrated in the case of George Downham's *Treatise on the Certainty of Perseverance*) may have impeded the publication of the later sections, particularly after the reception of the 39 Articles in Ireland. It was not until 1641 that Josua Hoyle's *Rejoynder*, the last contribution to the controversy, made a belated and inauspicious appearance.[34]

Malone's text also raised Catholic eyebrows on the continent and in England. This was due not to anything in the body of the *Reply*, but to its dedication. Ussher had dedicated his *Answer to a Jesuit* to James I, presumably in gratitude for the see of Meath, and Malone followed suit by dedicating his *Reply* to Charles I. The terms in which the dedication was couched seemed to some Catholics to come dangerously close to according the King the right to act as judge in matters of religious controversies. '[S]eeing that my adversary hath already brought this controversy into the highest court . . . I think myself necessarily obliged to undergo the trial of my cause in the same lists, and to submit the right thereof unto the censure of your most excellent wisdom.'[35] In fact, such appeals to secular authority on the part of Catholic controversialists were nothing new. A similar strategy had been adopted by Malone's fellow Jesuit, Henry Fitz-Simon, a quarter of a century earlier when he offered to engage John Rider in public disputation with the Viceroy, the Council, and even the members of the university acting as referees. As FitzSimon emphasized, their role was to be strictly limited to judging 'whether for the consent of antiquity in Mr Rider's case or mine, he or I had perverted, dissembled, or denied the effect and substance of the authors' minds in our allegations'. This was effectively to shift the subject of the controversy from the doctrinal questions at issue to the honesty of one's opponent's use of sources, thus turning a theological debate into something like a libel action. Like FitzSimon, Malone was appealing to Charles to judge not his

---

[34] See above footnote 5. In March 1635 Ussher wrote to Samuel Ward: 'Malone's reply hath been long since answered touching that matter [i.e. "the power of the keys *in ordine ad remissionem culpae*"] but the innovation which you write of beginneth to be as prevalent here as it is with you, which giveth no small stop (if not an absolute impediment) to the publication.' (*Tanner Letters*, p. 115.) It is tempting to identify the innovation referred to with Laud's attempt to impose episcopal licensing by imprimatur of printed works which had already been successful at Cambridge, where Ward was master of Sidney Sussex college. See Franklin B. Williams, Jr., 'The Laudian Imprimatur', *The Library*, 5 series 15 (1960), which identifies Dublin books carrying an imprimatur.

[35] Malone, *A Reply*, p. 3. For the reactions to Malone's work on the continent see *Wadding Papers 1614-38*, ed. B. Jennings OFM (Dublin, 1953), pp. 265-7, 274.

faith but his good faith. In doing so he was offering a demonstration of allegiance to the crown, however rhetorical.[36]

Malone's demonstration of loyalty may have gone too far for some Catholics, but it drew only scorn from George Synge, who wrote 'Ireland may rejoice that she hath found a Jesuit, that giveth Princes judgement in spiritual matters, when the whole world . . . cannot produce another, that will allow them an independent temporal jurisdiction' and proceeded to give a catalogue of Jesuit treachery in France and in England.[37] The loyalty of Jesuits was one matter, however, that of Old English Catholics another. Malone had quoted freely from the works of Ussher and Sibthorp, who had both paid testimony to the loyalty of the Catholics of the Pale (who formed, after all, their intended audience), but neither would have accepted the conclusion drawn from their writings by Malone: 'the free exercise of our religion is our strongest tie and union to your crown'.[38] For Synge, as for Ussher, it was despite rather than because of their religion that Catholics were trustworthy subjects. 'That they have not revolted from their obedience, we impute to their pious inclinations and native fidelity, not to popish doctrines, which in these particulars they have scorned and abhorred.'[39] This amounted to no more than saying that a faithful subject could not be a true Catholic, rather than that a true Catholic could not be a faithful subject.

It was not only in relation to the question of the loyalty of Catholics that this kind of doublethink came into operation. A topic taken up in several of the polemical works mentioned was that of the possibility of salvation for Catholics, an aspect of the broader question as to whether the Roman Catholic Church could be classed as a 'true Church'. In his Wanstead sermon Ussher agreed that it was possible for Catholics to be saved despite the apostasy of their Church, on the grounds that that apostasy was confined to doctrines to which the majority of Catholics did

---

[36] 'Father Henry FitzSimon S.J.', *IER* 8 (1873), p. 188. In offering to submit themselves to the judgement of the bearers of civil authority, Malone and FitzSimon were following the example set by the disputation on the Eucharist held at Fontainebleau in 1600 between Philippe du Plessis-Mornay and Jacques Davy du Perron, bishop of Evreux. At Fontainebleau Mornay was defending not only the Calvinist doctrine of the Eucharist, but his own reputation, having been accused of falsifying and misquoting patristic sources, and this enabled judges to be appointed, who found against Mornay (R. Patry, *Philipe de Plessis-Mornay* (Paris, 1933), pp. 388–94). The example of the Fontainebleau disputation is appealed to by FitzSimon, *A Reply to Mr Rider's Rescript*, p. 6.

[37] Synge, *A Rejoynder to the Reply published by the Jesuits under the Name of William Malone. The First Part*, pp. 4–5.

[38] Malone, *A Reply to Mr James Ussher his Answer*, p. 3.

[39] Synge, *A Rejoynder*, p. 5.

not assent. It was possible, for instance, to argue that most of the Catholic laity were simply unaware of the full implications of the doctrine of transubstantiation, to which they could not possibly give their rational assent. The apostasy was on the part of the pastors, not the flock.[40] Although in this sermon Ussher had been concerned with the salvation of pre-Reformation Catholics, the sermon was obviously regarded as topical enough to be published in Dublin, where it drew the reply already referred to from Paul Harris.

As Harris pointed out, it was difficult to adopt this position without either acknowledging the Roman Catholic Church as a true Church (and thus undermining one's own polemical position) or else throwing aside the concept of a Church altogether. False doctrine could not be confined to the clergy without corrupting the body of the Church, as, for both Protestants and Catholics, the Church was either the unity of pastors and faithful or was nothing at all. The necessity for membership of a true Church as a precondition for salvation was acknowledged by both. Either the Roman Catholic Church was a true Church or it was not, and Ussher was simply refusing to draw the implications of his own premisses.[41]

These implications had, in fact, been drawn by William Bedell several years earlier, before he left England to come to Dublin as Provost of Trinity College.[42] For Bedell, there was no difficulty in acknowledging the Church of Rome as a true Church, nor indeed in acknowledging the ministry of Catholic priests.[43] That Bedell was prepared to go this far, and that Ussher was not (at least in public) is an indication, not so much of basic theological differences between the two men, as of the relative weight accorded by them to controversy and instruction. In 1630 Bedell, by then bishop of Kilmore, wrote to Samuel Ward that he and Ussher were agreed that 'the differences between us and the Church (or court, rather) of Rome were not in faith (which we had in common) but in certain additions foreign to it, which by corrupt custom were crept in'.[44] For Bedell this approach to the corruption of the Catholic Church provoked serious reservations about the practice of controversy. 'Faith is

[40] James Ussher, *A Briefe Declaration of the University of the Church of Christ in a Sermon preached before the King at Wainsted* (London, 1624).
[41] Harris, *A Briefe Confutation.*
[42] See 'The copies of certain letters . . . between Master J. Wadesworth and W. Bedell' in Gilbert Burnet's *The life of William Bedell* (London, 1685), especially pp. 358 *seq.* These letters were first published in 1624.
[43] Burnet, *Life of Bedell*, pp. 156–65.
[44] *Tanner Letters*, p. 89.

not logic . . . many errors and much ignorance, so it be not affected, may stand with true faith in Christ.'[45] Catholics who remained unaware of the more complex areas of their Church's theology might retain a pure faith even while assenting to superstition and error; if their ignorance of theology was what saved them from apostasy, it was unlikely that theological controversy would serve to bring them into the fold of the Church of Ireland. By the same token, the value of an understanding of controversies to lay members of the Church of Ireland was questionable. The public defence of the faith might be a duty for churchmen, but among the laity too great an interest in controversies was more likely to be a source of faction. Bedell's position can thus be seen as the direct opposite to that expressed by Josua Hoyle in the quotation which began this paper. 'He that cannot give true definition of the soul, is not for that without a soul; so he that defines not faith truly, yet may have true faith.'[46]

It was, in fact, the view that the Roman Catholic Church was a true Church which brought Bedell into disagreement with Hoyle during Bedell's time as Provost of Trinity College.[47] While in England this view was used to support the historical continuity between the pre-Reformation Church and the Anglican Church, in an Irish context it tended to raise questions about the measures to be adopted towards the Catholic population. For Bedell the weakness of the controversial approach lay not only in its tendency to overstep its intended function and reproduce itself endlessly, but in its failure to make use of the common ground provided by the uncorrupted elements in the religion of the uneducated.

While the themes addressed in religious controversy in early seventeenth-century Dublin were not particularly Irish (even Ussher's work on the early Irish Church falling into a well-defined tradition in Anglican thought) the influence of the circumstances under which controversy was practised need to be borne in mind. The polemical works published in English in Dublin were intended for a largely Catholic audience. The same cannot usually be said for the works of English polemicists of the same period, even where the alleged target is Roman Catholic doctrine. In aiming their works at Catholics, Protestant polemicists had to adapt to suit the readership, which could mean moderating or reinforcing particular points. Thus, in none of Ussher's vernacular polemical works does he identify the Papacy with Antichrist as he had done in his first book *De*

---

[45] Burnet, *Life of Bedell*, p. 157.
[46] *Ibid.*, p. 122.
[47] *A true Relation of the life and death of . . . William Bedell*, pp. 28–9.

Ecclesiarum Successione. At the same time he refused to acknowledge the Church of Rome as a true Church, yet in private conversation he and Bedell found themselves in substantial agreement on this question. This inconsistency is revealing; in seeking to gain an insight into the theological views of Protestant churchmen in Ireland it is important to remember that much of what they wrote was influenced by the difficulties inherent in the task of attacking Catholicism without attacking Catholics.

Trinity College, Dublin

THE PRESBYTERIAN REVOLUTION
IN ULSTER, 1660–1690

by RAYMOND GILLESPIE

I N early 1642 a Scottish army under the command of Robert Munroe
arrived in Ulster as part of a scheme to defeat the native Irish rebellion
which had begun late in the previous year. The conquest was not to be
purely a military one. As a contemporary historian of Presbyterianism,
Patrick Adair, observed 'it is certain God made that army instrumental for
bringing church governments, according to His own institutions, to Ireland . . . and for spreading the covenants'.[1] The form of church government was that of the Presbyterian Church of Scotland, and in June 1642
the chaplains and officers established the first presbytery in Ireland at
Carrickfergus. Sub-presbyteries, or meetings, were created for Antrim,
Down and the Route, in north Antrim in 1654, for the Laggan in east
Donegal in 1657, and for Tyrone in 1659. Within these units the Church
was divided into geographical parishes each with its own minister. This
establishment of a parallel structure rivalling that of the Anglican Church,
but without the king at its head, is what has been termed the 'presbyterian
revolution'.[2] It supported the Presbyterian claim to be 'the Church of Ireland', a claim which was to bring it into conflict with the civil and ecclesiastical authorities in the late seventeenth century. In order to further
underpin this claim the reformed church began to move out of its Ulster
base by the 1670s. The Laggan presbytery ordained William Cock and
William Liston for work in Clonmel and Waterford in 1673 and was
active in Tipperary, Longford, and Sligo by 1676. Its advice to some
Dublin ministers was to form themselves into a group who were 'subject
to the meeting in the north'. The presbytery of Tyrone also supplied
Dublin.[3]

This revolution did not take place in a vacuum. Adair described their

---

[1] Patrick Adair, *A True Narrative of the Rise and Progress of the Presbyterian Church in Ireland*, ed.
W. D. Killen (Belfast, 1866), pp. 90–4.
[2] Edward Furgol, 'The military and ministers as agents of Presbyterian imperialism in England
and Ireland, 1640–8' in John Dwyer, R. A. Mason, A. Murdoch (eds), *New Perspectives on the
Politics and Culture of Early Modern Scotland* (Edinburgh, 1982), pp. 95–115; H. Trevor Roper,
'Scotland and the Puritan Revolution' in H. Trevor Roper, *Religion, Reformation and Social
Change* (London, 1967), pp. 329–444; Adair, *True Narrative*, pp. 214–15.
[3] NIPRO, D1759/1E/2, pp. 65, 213–14, 218, 225, 242, 244; D1759/1A/2, p. 48.

work not as a new development but 'a more full reformation' of Ireland. From 1605 Scots, many with Presbyterian backgrounds, had been settling in Ulster as part either of the plantation scheme or of the informal settlement of Antrim and Down. However, like many cultural traits in a colonial environment religious structures and practices were modified by the migration. Local liturgical and theological accommodations had been made with the Anglican Church, not a difficult operation since the Church of Ireland was strongly Calvinist in the early seventeenth century and many Anglican cures were occupied by Presbyterian clergy. In other Anglican churches in County Down Presbyterians came for the sermon but not the reading of the service, while in Belfast in the 1640s Adair discovered the Presbyterian minister, Mr Black, using the *Book of Common Prayer*. Private baptism, specifically forbidden in Presbyterian polity, was also practised. There were some objectors to this situation, especially after 1619 when the Articles of Perth in Scotland forced many of the more puritanical Presbyterians to migrate to Ireland, but these men, such as Robert Blair at Bangor, were in a minority.[4]

The essence of the Presbyterian revolution of the 1640s was the creation of a new structure, based on the Scottish model and later codified in a modified form in the Westminster Form of Church Government of 1645. Thus the full title of the official contemporary history of the revolution was 'A true narrative of the rise and progress of the Presbyterian government in the north of Ireland'.[5] Subscription to this divinely ordained system of government was seen as central. In 1675 when Mr Barclay arrived in Cork the Laggan presbytery wrote 'to desire that as he is in his judgement a Presbyterian as he would really show himself to be such by testifying his submission unto the advice of his brethren and subordination to the courts and judicatories of Jesus Christ established among us', and in Antrim a new congregation was founded at Glenavy in 1673 because the people 'profess subjection to Presbyterian government'.[6] Making this revolution a reality was not as simple as the creation of presbyteries by an invading army. The relationship between the various elements within the Presbyterian system of government, the kirk Session, the presbytery and, from the late seventeenth century the Synod of Ulster had

[4] M. Perceval Maxwell, *The Scottish Migration to Ulster in the Reign of James I* (London, 1975), pp. 252–73; Finlay Holmes, *Our Presbyterian Heritage* (Belfast, 1985), pp. 10–20. On Anglican theology Alan Ford, *The Protestant Reformation in Ireland* (Frankfurt am Main, 1985), pp. 193–242; Adair, *True Narrative*, pp. 99–100.

[5] Adair, *True Narrative*, p. 1 note 1 gives the full title.

[6] NIPRO, D1759/1A/2, p. 92; D1759/1E/1, p. 163.

to be worked out in a society where they were a new innovation. The establishment of the 'Presbyterian revolution' was not simply the result of the events of the 1640s but continued throughout the late seventeenth century as the roles of the elements in that revolution were defined.

The basic element in the Presbyterian system of government was the Session, the body of elders presided over by the minister. The Session was the expression of the local Presbyterian community as well as of the Church. This was all the more significant given that the Presbyterian communities of late seventeenth-century Ulster were very localized affairs. The early seventeenth-century settlement had delineated regions of Scottish influence and these were refined almost down to townland level as a result of internal population movements. A survey of the Rawdon estate in County Down in 1712, for example, shows that certain areas of the estate were almost entirely Presbyterian while others were entirely Anglican. Again in the 1690s one commentator noted that the Scots in Ulster were 'generally very frugal, industrious, very national and very helpful to each other against a third'.[7] This geographical cohesion was reinforced by a social cohesion, for one commentator of the 1680s noted that Presbyterians were generally drawn from men who owned land below the value of £3 to £4 a year.[8] For these communities the Session provided a way of enforcing church attendance and other ecclesiastical matters, and also a forum for dispensing charity and resolving disputes within the community, such as slander, debt, and local brawls. It was an extremely efficient method of social control because it operated from within the community itself with the elders acting as its officials as opposed to paid officials. The Templepatrick Session managed in 1647–8 to despatch over eighty cases—well up on the average of a contemporary Scottish Session and certainly more than any ecclesiastical court.[9]

The Session also provided an important contact with the outside world through other sessions and the hierarchy of presbytery and Synod. In late seventeenth-century Ulster society, such contacts were vital. Internal population mobility was high, the settlement grew as waves of settlers

[7] Philip Robinson, *The Plantation of Ulster* (Dublin, 1985), pp. 109–14; Henry E. Huntington Library, California, Hastings MSS Boxes 75, 77 (I am grateful to Prof. N. Canny for drawing my attention to these surveys); BL Add. MS 2902, fol. 218.

[8] *CalSPD 1684–5*, p. 261.

[9] W. T. Latimer, 'The Old Session Book of Templepatrick Presbyterian Church', *JRSAI* 25 (1895), pp. 130–4; 31 (1901), pp. 162–75, 259–72 (original in NIPRO, CR4/12B/1); L. M. Smith, 'Church and Secular Courts in Cromwellian Scotland' in Dwyer, Mason, Murdoch, *New Perspectives*, p. 130.

were enticed to Ulster by offers of cheap land and rapid upward social mobility. As a result social networks were usually poorly cemented and business contacts were often of dubious reliability. Here the Session was invaluable. Backgrounds of suspect new arrivals could be checked through the certificates which they would have to bring from their home Session to gain admission to the new congregation, and their behaviour was monitored by the elders. Local excommunicants could be isolated since these were announced in all pulpits in the region after sentence had occurred. The hierarchy of the local congregation also provided a framework for the local social hierarchy, the elders being men of considerable social standing in a society where the traditional criteria of social status were of dubious applicability because of rapid social mobility following migration.[10]

In some ways the local Session modified the strict rules of Westminster to suit local circumstances. The Westminster Directory for Public Worship specifically forbade sponsors at baptism, yet sponsors were the norm in Ulster Presbyterianism, reflecting the need to build up new kinship networks to replace those broken in the migration process.[11] Similarly, in Ulster there is a near absence of one of the preoccupations of the Scottish Sessions, witchcraft. This does not mean that there was no magic, white or otherwise, practised among Ulster Presbyterians and disapproved of by the Church. In the 1670s the General Committee of the Church issued an edict against sorcery and in November 1699 the minister of Enniskillen asked the Laggan presbytery for 'advice what he should do with persons that used charmers and charms in curing the sick'. This lack of concern was not because the beliefs about witchcraft had been jettisoned from the settlers mental baggage in the migration, but because the intensity of emotion which promoted witch hunts was absent. The settler community was a minority in the settlement and could not afford splits.[12]

The Session also provided a focus for the local community among the Scots settlers. As Bishop King of Derry observed of the Presbyterians 'the

---

[10] J. M. Barclay, *The Ruling Eldership in Irish Presbyterianism* (Belfast, 1963), pp. 22–65; Raymond Gillespie, *Colonial Ulster* (Cork, 1985), pp. 113–20. The use of Communion tokens by Presbyterians was also seen as a mark of social approval: Joseph Boyse, *A Vindication of the Remarks on the Bishop of Derry's Discourse* (Dublin, 1695), pp. 53–4.

[11] J. M. Barclay, *The Westminster Formularies in Irish Presbyterianism* (Belfast, 1956), pp. 44–5. The use of godparents was denied in Joseph Boyse, *Remarks on a Late Discourse of William Lord Bishop of Derry* (Dublin, 1694), pp. 67–9.

[12] NIPRO, D1759/1A/2, p. 72; D1759/1E/2, n.p.

arts by which they keep up their party are to take no apprentices that will not engage to go to the meetings with them, to employ none nor trade with any that are not of their own sort'.[13] Members of a congregation were also expected to take other members as their followers and one army officer was condemned by the Templepatrick Session in 1647 for having 'some Irish under him' who did not come to church. An elder was appointed to speak to him 'that either he will put them away from him or else cause them to keep the church'.[14] Late seventeenth-century Presbyterian worship was also a meeting of the community as well as a meeting for worship. Services in the 1660s and 1670s were held in secular settings. As Adair commented of the late 1660s the clergy 'took liberty to preach more publicly in barns and such places in their parishes where the bulk of the people met'. There was also little outward participation by the congregation in the worship itself. The minister acted as the mouthpiece of the congregation, he prayed, read, and preached. Psalms were sung by the minister giving out the line and the congregation singing it. Worship lacked what Bishop King of Derry described as the 'language of gestures'.[15] If an individual was not spiritually minded it would be easy to become left out of the whole proceedings.

When meeting houses were built in the late seventeenth century they reflected the link between Church and community. Pews became the property of individual families and so the meeting house became symbolic of the community. The divisions within the meeting house reflected the geographical divisions of the community. When the people of Drumcar in County Tyrone petitioned the presbytery for a meeting house in 1672 it advised 'that they should build an aisle for themselves in that [Termonmagurk] house'. The community of Drumcar was to remain distinct even at worship. In the case of Templepatrick the church was divided into north and south sides to reflect the division of the parish by a river.[16]

The close identification of Church and community had both advantages and problems. One difficulty was that Presbyterianism became as much a social as a religious phenomenon. As Bishop King of Derry noted

[13] Printed in R. H. Murray, *Revolutionary Ireland and its Settlement* (London, 1911), p. 366.
[14] Latimer, 'Session Book', *JRSAI* 31 (1901), p. 271.
[15] The main sources for Presbyterian worship are in William King, *A Discourse Concerning the Inventions of Men in the Worship of God* (Dublin, 1694): the quotation is from p. 140; Robert Craghead, *An Answer to a Late Work Entitled A Discourse the Inventions of Men . . .* (Edinburgh, 1664); Boyse, *A Vindication*; Boyse, *Remarks* and other pamphlets by these men in 1694/5.
[16] NIPRO, D1759/1E/1, pp. 4, 30, 34; D1759/1E/2, p. 115; Latimer, 'Session Book', *JRSAI* 31 (1901), p. 265.

of his diocese in 1693 'The religion of this country is rather a national faction than conscience as I have found by many experiments and I doubt where it would end.' In one tract he calculated that of 30,000 dissenters in his diocese only about 6,000 attended Sunday worship.[17] His fears were well founded. The statistics quoted for church attendance, catechetical knowledge, and access to the sacraments by the Presbyterian Joseph Boyse in 1696 were indeed dismal.[18] According to Boyse of the 2,400-strong congregation at Derry only 600, or a quarter, could repeat the 'Assembly's catechism'. Again at a Holy Communion Service at Derry out of about 2,400 of a congregation 984 received communion. While this appears impressive it should be noted that communion services were held infrequently, usually once a year, and it was normal practice for people from many congregations to attend such a service.[19] Boyse himself estimated that on such an occasion up to two-thirds would be 'strangers'. Even allowing one-third of the communicants to be 'strangers' this would mean that only a quarter of the home congregation would have been communicants.

The advantage of the close identification of Church and community was that it was resilient to the periodic persecution of Presbyterians which occurred throughout the late seventeenth century. To effectively break a local congregation a whole local community would have to be broken. The impossibility of achieving this was appreciated by the duke of Ormonde when he observed in 1683 that closing meeting houses 'is no better than scattering a flock of crows that will soon assemble again, and possibly it were better to leave them alone than to let them see the impotence of the government upon which they will presume'.[20]

Against this background of a strong local base for the Presbyterian revolution, in which social factors reinforced the aims of the Church, a second, and in some ways competing, institution, the presbytery was emerging. The origins of the various presbyteries of late seventeenth-century Ulster lay in the four meetings established by the presbytery of Ulster in the 1650s. According to Adair these meetings were not to be full

---

[17] TCD, King Lyons MSS No. 264 King to Samuel Foley, 21 March 1693; William King, *A Second Admonition to the Dissenting Inhabitants of the Diocese of Derry* (Dublin, 1695), p. 4. This explains in part the divergence between the austerity preached by Presbyterians and the 'riotous living' of their followers: John Hanly (ed.), *The Letters of Saint Oliver Plunkett, 1625–81* (Dublin, 1979), p. 394.

[18] Boyse, *A Vindication*, pp. 2, 19; Boyse, *Remarks*, p. 136.

[19] For another large communion service *CalSPI 1669–70*, p. 148; on frequency of Communion, Boyse, *A Vindication*, pp. 15–16.

[20] HMC, *Report on Ormonde MSS*, new series 5, p. 102.

presbyteries but sub-meetings. They were to deal with local matters of discipline when requested by congregations and to licence preachers until the full presbytery met. They could not enter expectants on trial nor allow them to be ordained, and the meetings had no existence apart from the presbytery itself.[21] However by the 1670s these meetings were acting as full presbyteries, a power which they took as a matter of necessity since the original presbytery of Ulster did not meet after 1660 because of government opposition. Some thought was given in the late 1680s to regularizing the position by making the Antrim meeting a full presbytery but nothing was done.[22] The composition of the presbyteries varied. In practice, however, they were clerically dominated. In Antrim lay men were not admitted until 1687.[23] In the meetings of the Laggan presbytery between 1672 to 1679 laymen were admitted but there were occasions when no elders were present and on only five occasions were there ten or more, whereas it was unusual for clerical attendance to fall below ten. Over these years the average lay attendance at the presbytery was 5.6 while the clergy averaged ten. There was also a considerable turnover in laymen while the clerical group remained substantially the same.

The main concern of the presbyteries was the supply and maintenance of ministers. This was a vital area for the success of the Presbyterian revolution. The minister acted as broker between the local community and the wider world, and it was he who would convey and enforce the decisions of presbytery and Synod in the Session. It was part of his role, according to the Antrim meeting, to refute divisive principles by sound knowledge and holy conversation.[24] This was of considerable importance given the role the Church was trying to develop. On one level it was trying to paint a moderate picture of itself, since the denial of the headship of the Church to the King had raised suspicions about Presbyterian loyalty which appeared to be confirmed by events in Scotland. The duke of Ormonde claimed in 1678 that they were as bad as Catholics and the Catholic Bishop Nicholas French argued that Presbyterians were more dangerous than Catholics.[25] The Irish Presbyterian clergy were at pains to prove their moderation and loyalty, in contrast to the more radical Covenanters in

---

[21] Adair, *True Narrative*, p. 214.

[22] NIPRO, D1759/1A/2, p. 312.

[23] *Ibid.*, D1759/1A/2, pp. 320, 338.

[24] *Ibid.*, D1759/1A/2, p. 218.

[25] Bodleian Library, Oxford, Carte MS 70, fols 521-2, Nicholas French, *The Settlement and sale of Ireland* in S. H. B[indon], *The Historical Works of Dr French*, 2 vols (Dublin, 1846), 2, pp. 119-20; David Miller, *Queen's Rebels* (Dublin, 1978), pp. 7-24.

Scotland, and were quick to disassociate themselves from the Covenanter disturbances in Scotland during 1679.[26] To make this picture convincing it was also important to control popular belief in the almost magical effect of the covenants. As Daniel O'Neill noted in 1660 when action against the Covenant in Ulster was being rumoured 'my countrymen of Ulster will mutiny against such an injury to the Dagon',[27] the Old Testament allusion revealing the magical quality the Covenant had assumed. Again in Antrim in the 1680s it was commented that 'the people will not omit christening with their own minister supposing the children to be christened into the solemn league and covenant'.[28]

Clergy, however, were in short supply. Using the number of English, Irish, and Scots households in Ulster in 1660, as reflected in the hearth money rolls, as indicative of the number of Anglican, Catholic, and Presbyterian families, the number of Presbyterian clergy varied from a ratio of 1 to 31 families in the area of the Route to 1 to 201 in the presbytery of Antrim. Comparative material is difficult to come by, but in the area of the Laggan meeting the ratio of ministers to families was 1:130 while in the roughly equivalent diocese of Derry the Anglican ratio was 1:31 and the Catholic ratio was between 1:105 and 1:120, depending on assumptions about the size of the native population. Such estimates can only be tentative because of the nature of the sources but the supply of clergy was certainly limited.[29] The demography of the settler community was such that there were relatively few children of the age for training and the ready availability of cheap land meant that there were other opportunities outside the Church. Repeated but unsuccessful attempts were made to establish a philosophy school at Antrim to train clergy. In at least one case in the 1680s it failed for want of pupils.[30] The Irish Church was dependent on clergy from Scotland and they were not always easy to come by.

The supply of ministers was also a matter of considerable concern to

---

[26] *CalSPD 1679-80*, pp. 576-7; Bodl., Carte 45, fols 220, 221, 274, 348, 530, 543; Osmond Airey (ed.), *Essex Papers*, 1 (C series, London, 1890), pp. 34, 37-8.

[27] Edward Berwick, *Rawdon Letters* (n.p., 1819), p. 150. The biblical reference is to Judges 16: 23 and 1 Sam. 5: 1-5.

[28] TCD, MS 883/1, p. 189.

[29] I am indebted to W. A. Macafee, University of Ulster, for allowing me to see his important unpublished paper on the population of seventeenth-century Ulster, from which I have estimated the number of households. Clergy figures are from T. W. Moody and J. G. Simms (eds), *The Bishopric of Derry and the Irish Society*, 2 vols (Dublin, 1968-83), 1, pp. 326-9 (Anglican); Benigius Millet, 'Archbishop O'Reilly's Report on the State of the Church in Ireland in 1660', *Collectanea Hibernica*, 2 (1959), pp. 105-14 (Catholic); J. S. Reid, *History of the Presbyterian Church in Ireland*, 3 vols (Belfast, 1867), 2, pp. 267-9 (Presbyterian).

[30] NIPRO, D1759/1A/2, pp. 161, 183, 252.

local congregations since the minister was the central figure at worship, administering the sacraments and presiding over the Session. Without a minister the Session could not meet and local organization would collapse. In at least one case at Islandmagee in the 1650s special permission had to be given for the Session to meet without a minister because local discipline was non-existent.[31] There was considerable local demand for clergy. In 1675 the appearance of one man from Scotland saw three congregations fighting for him.[32] In this situation clerical stipends became a contentious issue. Under the Commonwealth most Ulster Presbyterian clergy had a stipend of about £80 a year. With the restoration of the Church of Ireland and the withdrawal of Exchequer support for ministers' maintenance non-conformist clerical incomes fell to about £30 a year, and sometimes less, with some benefits such as a house or supply of grain. The issue of the clergy's remuneration was a crucial one for the success of the Presbyterian system and it was one on which the presbytery and Session were to come into conflict almost immediately.[33]

From the early 1670s the presbyteries of the Laggan and Antrim took a close interest in the maintenance paid to clergy, writing to all the Sessions asking for an account of the position locally. Although returns were slow to come in it soon became apparent that many clergy were not being paid what was promised by the Session or the promised amount was insufficient. The presbytery took it upon itself to rectify this situation. The first line of attack was to write to the congregation. If that failed a minister of the presbytery was sent to 'speak' with a meeting of the heads of the families in the congregation. Should this fail there were two further options. If the local landlord was a Presbyterian or was sympathetic the 'secular arm' could be evoked. If all else failed the minister could be declared 'transportable', that is free to accept any call he would be offered. The most important case was that of the Strabane congregation in 1676–7 which had repeatedly failed to provide what the presbytery regarded a satisfactory maintenance for their minister Robert Wilson. The presbytery declared him 'transportable' and he was offered a call to Termonmagurk. The case of the Strabane Session was that 'the business of his [the minister's] maintenance might be left to be agreed upon betwixt himself and them'. The presbytery condemned such a suggestion and declared that the 'transportability should stand'.[34]

---

[31] *Ibid.*, D1759/1A/1, pp. 56, 65.

[32] *Ibid.*, D1759/1E/1, pp. 171, 188, 192, 194.

[33] T. C. Barnard, *Cromwellian Ireland* (Oxford, 1975), pp. 155–8, 166–7.

[34] NIPRO, D1759/1E/1, pp. 252–3.

The presbytery had asserted its right to control an essential element in the establishment of a Presbyterian structure. The independence of the powerfully based local Session was difficult to curtail. In January 1693 the Laggan presbytery claimed the right to vet the elders for the individual Sessions. They had not done this before except in an isolated case in 1678 when one minister had asked for his elders to be approved by the presbytery. The practice never developed, even after 1711 when the Synod of Ulster required it. The Session with its strong community links was not prepared to give up the right to appoint its own elders.[35]

The third element in the Presbyterian revolution was the last to appear, the Synod of Ulster. Originally the governing body for Ulster Presbyterianism was the presbytery of Ulster established at Carrickfergus, but this did not meet after 1660. By the 1670s, however, the various presbyteries decided they needed to agree standard theological matters in an Irish context, especially ordination rules and the practice as to marriage. They established a 'General Committee' with the limited brief 'to consult as a committee for the welfare of the people as a whole and to recommend to the various meetings such steps as their present exigencies demanded'.[36] It does not seem to have had any general coordinating role in representing Presbyterianism, and the various presbyteries kept their own agents in Dublin to represent their interests.[37] By the 1670s some attempt was being made by this General Committee to establish some sort of authority over the individual presbyteries. The Antrim meeting objected and the Laggan noted 'we do not agree to that overture in the minutes of the General Committee which speaks of constituting a General Committee with power over the meetings'. However the Committee continued to meet and develop its functions and by the late 1680s, probably encouraged by James II's Declarations of Indulgence, consideration was being given as to whether a General Synod should be set up. The Antrim meeting objected. Again in March 1689 the General Committee proposed a meeting of a General Synod and suggested April of that year. Reluctantly this was agreed but the meeting was postponed by political events.[38]

By 1690 when the General Synod was constituted in the wake of William III's landing in Ireland much of this opposition seems to have lessened. The Synod had two advantages that the General Committee did

[35] NIPRO, D1759/1E/1, pp. 303–4.
[36] Adair, *True Narrative*, p. 293.
[37] NIPRO, D1759/1A/2, pp. 329, 313; D1759/1E/1, p. 64.
[38] *Ibid.*, D1759/1A/2, pp. 59, 64, 420; D1759/1E/1, p. 323.

not have. First there was a sense that the revolution was nearing its completion and that the Irish Church was firmly and distinctly established. The production of the official history of the establishment of the Presbyterian Church government by Patrick Adair was one sign that they felt that they had almost achieved their end. Moreover the Church in the 1690s received a major boost in the form of possibly the largest single immigration of Scots during the century. As the Jacobite author of the *Light to the Blind* noted of the Ulster landlords 'their tenants for the most part were Roman Catholics until after the battle of the Boyne ... when Scottish men came over into the north with their families and effects and settled there so that they are at this present the greater proportion of the inhabitants of Ulster'.[39] These were men used to the discipline and organization of the Scottish Church and prepared to accept it in Ireland. Secondly, the Synod had money at its disposal in the form of the *Regium Donum*. When the royal grant had first been made in 1675 its disposal had been left to Sir Arthur Forbes. Now with the regrant of 1690 its disposal was in the hands of a group of Presbyterian ministers acting as trustees, and its allocation was one of the items discussed at the General Committee which was to become the Synod of Ulster.[40]

It was thus left to the Synod to tidy up the loose ends of the revolution. In 1697 they ordered 'that some particular minister be appointed by this Synod to overlook the Acts of the General Assembly of the Church of Scotland and draw out what may be applicable to us in this Church', and in 1698 they attempted to ensure complete uniformity by introducing a new element into Irish Presbyterianism—an obligation to subscribe to the Westminster Confession of Faith.[41]

The strength of Irish Presbyterianism in the eighteenth century lay in the fact that it had a coherent organization. That organization was not easily achieved. It was by no means inevitable that the Presbyterian revolution begun in the 1640s would be successful. There was no guarantee that the presbytery would establish firm control over the Sessions in its care, indeed a Calvinistic form of Congregationalism was a real possibility in the late seventeenth century and tendencies in this direction had been noticed as early as the 1630s.[42] The presbyteries had been on the look out for such a development and condemned it wherever it arose. In 1683, for

---

[39] J. T. Gilbert (ed.), *A Jacobite Narrative of the War in Ireland* (Dublin, 1892), p. 556.
[40] NIPRO, D1759/1A/2, pp. 414–15; for the *Regium Donum* J. C. Beckett, *Protestant Dissent in Ireland, 1687–1780* (London, 1948), pp. 106–8.
[41] *Records of the General Synod of Ulster*, 3 vols (Belfast, 1890–8), 1, pp. 22, 34.
[42] Holmes, *Presbyterian Heritage*, p. 28.

example, when the Islandmagee congregation did not pay its 'collection for pious uses' the presbytery demanded they 'are to show their reason for declining it or the Meeting will take course with them for their seeming independency'.[43] The intricate relationships of the various elements in the revolution had to be worked out as each group established the boundaries of its power within a rapidly changing colonial environment. It is the history of these complex social relationships that is one of the most intriguing features of late seventeenth-century Ulster Presbyterianism.

Dublin

[43] NIPRO, D1759/1A/2, p. 188.

UNITED IRISHMEN AND UNIONISTS:
IRISH PRESBYTERIANS, 1791 AND 1886

by R. F. G. HOLMES

WHEN Gladstone decided, some time in 1885,[1] that the only way to achieve 'social order'[2] in Ireland was to concede Home Rule, he was disappointed to find that among his most implacable and vociferous opponents were the Irish Presbyterians. In vain he was to remind them that their ancestors had been United Irishmen in the 1790s, the founding fathers of Irish republicanism. His appeal to them to 'retain and maintain the tradition of their sires' fell on deaf ears.[3]

It seemed to Gladstone as it has seemed to Irish nationalists and to some historians that the Irish Presbyterians had turned their political coats, that the grandsons of the United Irishmen had repudiated the principles of their grandfathers. Lecky, in his monumental *History of Ireland in the Eighteenth Century*, writing in the context of the Home Rule crisis, expressed his magisterial opinion that 'the defection of the Presbyterians from the movement of which they were the main originators, and the great and enduring change which took place in their sentiments . . . are facts of the deepest importance in Irish history and deserve very careful and detailed examination'.[4]

That some Irish Presbyterians were among the 'main originators' of the United Irish movement in the 1790s is undeniable. As early as 1787 the duke of Rutland, Irish Lord Lieutenant, observed that 'The province of Ulster is filled with dissenters, who are in general very factious—great levellers and republicans.'[5] A decade later, Wolfe Tone, urging the French to mount an invasion of Ireland, claimed that the Irish Presbyterians were 'to a man sincere republicans and devoted to the cause of liberty and of France'.[6] That sharp observer of the Irish scene, Castlereagh, himself baptized an Irish Presbyterian, could later describe 'the Presbyterians of Ireland' as 'having partaken so deeply, first of the popular, and since the

---

[1] For Gladstone's conversion to Home Rule see J. Loughlin, *Gladstone, Home Rule and the Ulster Question, 1882–93* (Dublin, 1986), pp. 35–52.
[2] *The Witness*, 9 April 1886.
[3] J. J. Shaw, *Mr Gladstone's Two Irish Policies, 1869 and 1886* (London, 1888), pp. 7–9.
[4] W. E. H. Lecky, *A History of Ireland in the Eighteenth Century* (London, 1892), 4, p. 403.
[5] HMC, *Rutland MSS* 3, p. 421.
[6] T. W. Tone, *Life of Theobald Wolfe Tone etc.* (Washington, 1826), 2, p. 186.

democratic, politics of the country as to be an object much more of jealousy than of support to the government.[7]

We ought not to be astonished to find Irish Presbyterians in such a role. As A. T. Q. Stewart has observed: 'The Presbyterian is happiest when he is being a radical',[8]

> The austere doctrines of Calvinism, the simplicity of his worship, the democratic government of his Church, the memory of the martyred Covenanters, and the Scottish unwillingness to yield or to dissemble—all these incline him to that difficult and cantankerous disposition which is characteristic of a certain kind of political radicalism.[9]

In Ireland in the eighteenth century Presbyterians could scarcely escape being radicals. They numbered some ten per cent of the Irish population but a much larger proportion, perhaps as much as a third, of the population of Ulster, where they were concentrated. This was because they were the descendants of successive waves of seventeenth-century immigrants from Scotland, and their Presbyterianism had contributed to their persistently distinctive identity in Ireland. It had also brought them, as dissenters, various disabilities, which, though less oppressive than those suffered by Roman Catholics, were irritating. They resented having to pay tithes to support what they regarded as an incompletely reformed prelatical Established Church, while the ordained status of their own ministers was not recognized, and the legality of their marriages called in question. The defection of many of their own gentry to the Protestant establishment had enhanced the leadership role of their ministers, in an age when the pulpit was an unrivalled platform of influence.

Although an 'adventurous seeking of better accommodation'[10] had brought most of the seventeenth-century Scots immigrants to Ireland it is also true that they had been encouraged to come to augment and support the English colony in Ireland, one result of James VI's translation to the throne of England. 'Your Lordship knows', the Revd William Bruce reminded Castlereagh,

---

[7] Castlereagh to Addington, 21 July 1802, *Memoirs and Correspondence of Castlereagh*, ed. Marquess of Londonderry (London, 1848–53), 4, p. 224.
[8] A. T. Q. Stewart, *The Narrow Ground* (London, 1977), p. 83.
[9] *Ibid.*
[10] R. Blair, *Autobiography and Life*, ed. T. McCrie (Edinburgh, 1886), p. 57.

that we are not dissenters in the same sense as the Puritans of England and their descendants but were planted here by Government as a separate Church and never belonged to the Church of Ireland but zealously and effectually co-operated with it in the settlement, reformation and preservation of this kingdom.[11]

In the great crises for the future of British rule in Ireland in the seventeenth century they had played their part, but they had not shared fully in the rewards of victory. The Test Act of 1704, officially 'to prevent the further growth of Popery', had removed from office the Presbyterian majorities on the Belfast and Londonderry corporations. Although the path to public life was never completely closed to Presbyterians—they never lost the right to sit in parliament and after 1719 a succession of indemnity acts suspended discriminatory legislation against them—in fact few of them had the resources or influence to enable them to do so. They were very conscious of being second class citizens, excluded from the Protestant Ascendancy which, as Wolfe Tone claimed, 'held almost the whole landed property of the country in their hands ... all the offices and appointments in the Church, the army, the law, and every department of state, to the utter exclusion of the other two sects i.e. the Roman Catholics and dissenters'.[12]

Of course the majority of Irish Presbyterians were much more conscious of their economic, than of their political, grievances. Most of them were tenant farmers and many of them had come from Scotland after the Williamite victory to take up land offered at low rents. When leases of twenty or thirty years were renewed there were heavy 'fines' for renewals and steep increases in rent. This process continued throughout the eighteenth century, quintupling rents in some cases,[13] without any corresponding rise in prices. Natural calamities—poor summers, bad harvests, epidemics of livestock disease—exacerbated the situation. Ireland had disappointed the expectations of these late seventeenth-century immigrants and they began to look further west towards colonial America. In 1718 the diaspora began and continued throughout the century. Sometimes ministers and most of their congregations emigrated together, as when Thomas Clark led three hundred members of his congregation of Seceders at Cahans, County Monaghan to America in 1764.[14]

[11] *Castlereagh*, 3, pp. 266–9.
[12] *Tone*, 2, pp. 182–3.
[13] R. J. Dickson, *Ulster Emigration to Colonial America, 1718–1785* (London, 1966), pp. 29–30, 69 seq.
[14] *Ibid.*, p. 177.

The economic situation in eighteenth-century Ulster was complicated by proto-industrialization which contributed both to population increase, in spite of emigration, and social conflict. An ancient indigenous textile industry was stimulated by immigrants from the north of England and later by Huguenot refugees from France. Irish linen, imported duty-free in Britain, commanded an expanding market and production increased rapidly to meet demand.[15] This expanding linen industry spawned both a new class of peasant weavers, who depended less and less upon agriculture for their livelihoods, and therefore were less dependent on their landlords, and a new mercantile elite, many of them Presbyterians, who began to challenge the traditional monopoly of political power enjoyed by landowners.[16]

The expansion of linen manufacturing and trade required and promoted the development of markets and towns and improvements in communications. Road and bridge building increased both local rates and demands for tenant farmers to provide obligatory days of labour on the roads.[17] Their response was to take collective action in such groups as the Hearts of Oak, who could assemble thousands of men to intimidate local clergy and gentry in order to reduce their demands upon them.[18]

Later in the century, when Lord Donegall used the opportunity of renewal of leases on his extensive estates in County Antrim to raise rents and demand stiff fines, some of his tenants followed the example of the Hearts of Oak in combining as Hearts of Steel to resist evictions and what they considered to be excessive rent increases.[19] Though their raison d'etre and aims were different from the Hearts of Oak they both represented and articulated the grievances of the poorer sort of tenant farmers, many of whom were Presbyterians. Recent research has emphasized that they were not revolutionaries; their aims were limited, local, and conservative. They were what Hobsbawm has called 'primitive rebels',[20] but they represented a tradition of collective aggressive action which could be mobilized for revolutionary purposes.

That leadership came eventually from the Society of United Irishmen which originated in Belfast in 1791 as a pressure group for radical change in Ireland which, when the path to constitutional reform seemed blocked

---

[15] W. H. Crawford and B. Trainor, *Aspects of Irish Social History 1750–1800* (Belfast, 1969), p. 74.
[16] *Ibid.*, p. 32.
[17] *Ibid.*, p. 36.
[18] J. S. Donnelly, 'Hearts of Oak, Hearts of Steel', *Studia Hibernica*, 21 (1981), pp. 8–12.
[19] *Ibid.*, pp. 27 *seq.*; A. Canavan, 'Hearts of Steel' (MA thesis, Queen's University Belfast, 1982).
[20] E. J. Hobsbawm, *Primitive Rebels* (Manchester, 1965).

in 1795, became a revolutionary conspiracy. Belfast was both the capital of Presbyterian Ulster and the commercial centre of the linen industry. It was poised to take off as a great industrial centre; it was in 1791 that William Ritchie of Glasgow began to build ships there.[21] It was also becoming distinguished by a vibrant intellectual life in which Presbyterian ministers, doctors, and businessmen played prominent parts.[22] They were influenced by contemporary European Enlightenment ideas which some of them had imbibed as students in the Scottish universities. Men like Francis Hutcheson, himself an Ulsterman and son of the manse, taught them that political and social questions were ultimately moral questions, that they had a responsibility to establish a just political order which would provide for 'the greatest good of the greatest number', that

> when the common rights of the community are trampled upon . . . then as the governor is plainly perfidious to his trust, he has forfeited all the power committed. In every sort of government the people has this right of defending themselves against the abuse of power.[23]

The implications for the manifestly unjust Irish situation were inescapable.

The Ulster Presbyterian intelligentsia were naturally whigs in politics and they were enthusiastic supporters of the opposition or reform party in the Irish parliament, led by men like the duke of Leinster and the earl of Charlemont in the Lords and Henry Grattan and Henry Flood in the Commons. They sympathized keenly with the American colonists in their fight for independence. Although Irish Presbyterian and Scotch-Irish historians have traditionally tended to exaggerate the contribution of Ulster Scots settlers to the colonists' cause, the example of some of them and, even more, the occasion of their struggle, had significant repercussions in Ireland.

The American war led to the formation of local defence corps or Volunteers, the first company being formed in Belfast in 1778. After some initial hesitation the Irish government gave them recognition, but they retained a measure of independence and their alliance with and support for the 'reformers' in parliament contributed to their dramatic if short-lived success.[24] Confronted by the demands of the Irish parliament,

[21] R. B. McDowell, *Ireland in the age of Imperialism and Revolution* (Oxford, 1979), p. 35.
[22] *Ibid.*, pp. 35–7.
[23] F. Hutcheson, *A short Introduction to Moral Philosophy* (Glasgow, 1747), p. 303.
[24] P. D. H. Smyth, 'The Volunteers and Parliament', *Penal Era and Golden Age*, eds T. Bartlett and D. W. Haydon (Belfast, 1979), pp. 113–36.

supported by thousands of armed Volunteers, British governments, in the context of the disastrous American war, made concessions. In 1779 restrictions on Irish trade, popularly believed to have damaged the Irish economy, were removed and, three years later, limitations on the independence of the Irish parliament, going back to Poynings' law (1494) were repealed.

This triumph was illusory, for the Irish executive remained responsible to the Westminster government and the 'independent' Irish parliament remained unrepresentative and conservative. An assembly of placemen and representatives of rotten boroughs was unlikely to pursue radical reforms. In vain the Volunteers called for parliamentary reform but now parliament, which had used the Volunteers as a weapon against the British government, questioned the right of a military force to dictate to the legislature. Divisions soon appeared among the Volunteers. Their chairman, the earl of Charlemont, reveals in his memoirs his lack of enthusiasm for further reform.[25] The first stage in the constitutional movement for reform was over, conservative reformers were satisfied, radicals were not, and many Presbyterians were radicals. They had participated wholeheartedly in the Volunteer movement, ministers acting as officers in some companies, in the words of one of them, William Steel Dickson, 'The rusty black was exchanged for the glowing scarlet and the title of reverend for that of captain.'[26] Real advances had been made, Roman Catholics and dissenters had been relieved of some disabilities but the Irish Protestant Ascendancy parliament shrank from radical measures of Catholic emancipation as they shrank from any real democratization of the legislature itself.

The early stages of the revolution in France revived hopes that the most venerable oppressive regimes could be overthrown. The day of liberty had dawned in America and in France, why not in Ireland? The mild reformism of the Northern Whig club, founded in Belfast in 1789 by the earl of Charlemont and his Presbyterian ally, Dr Alexander Haliday, seemed too tame for more ardent reformers like another, younger Presbyterian physician, Dr William Drennan, who, like Haliday, was a son of the manse.[27] Drennan, who had returned from his studies in Glasgow and Edinburgh in time to be caught up in the Volunteering excitement, was

---

[25] HMC, *Charlemont, Manuscripts and Correspondence*.
[26] W. S. Dickson, *Narrative of the Confinement and Exile of the Rev. William Steel Dickson, DD* (Dublin, 1812), pp. 9–10.
[27] A. T. Q. Stewart, 'A stable unseen power: Dr William Drennan and the origins of the United Irishmen', *Essays presented to Michael Roberts*, eds J. Bossy and P. Jupp, pp. 80–92.

soon impatient with the pace and limited objectives of the reform movement. Their aims, he believed, should be an immediate reform of parliament and the union of Presbyterians and Roman Catholics to overthrow the Protestant Ascendancy. In his correspondence with the Revd William Bruce, the young minister of Belfast's First Presbyterian congregation, he outlined his plans for a secret society or brotherhood to take the lead in achieving these aims.[28]

It was not until 1791 that the first Society of United Irishmen was founded in Belfast by a group of Presbyterians inspired by events in France and influenced by Thomas Paine's *Rights of Man*, which became the Koran of the Belfast radicals, according to Wolfe Tone.[29] Drennan, who had moved to Dublin, was the first president of the Society in the capital city, which was founded by a committee of 18 Protestants and Roman Catholics.[30]

The United Irishmen were not, at first, revolutionaries. They were propagandists. The Belfast group published a newspaper, the *Northern Star*, to propagate their ideas. Their first policy statement, which appeared in the *Star*, was vague: 'to make all Irishmen Citizens ... we gladly look forward to a people united in a fellowship of freedom; to a parliament the express image of the people, to a prosperity established on civil, political and religious liberty; to peace ...'.[31] When they did spell out their objectives they were characteristic of contemporary radical programmes: universal manhood suffrage, annual parliaments, payment for MPs, Catholic emancipation.[32]

Catholic emancipation proved to be a divisive issue, even in reforming circles. Drennan's friend and correspondent, the Revd William Bruce, found the prospect of immediate emancipation alarming. At a Belfast town meeting in January 1792 he argued for gradualism in the process of reform and attacked the United Irishmen as an oath-bound society.[33] The champions of full and immediate emancipation won the debate but the division between reformers and radicals had been revealed.[34]

A year later, in 1793, another Presbyterian minister and erstwhile

---

[28] NIPRO, D 553, Drennan to Bruce, n.d.
[29] F. MacDermott, *Theobald Wolfe Tone* (Tralee, 1968), p. 73.
[30] Drennan to S. McTier, Nov. 1791, *The Drennan Letters*, ed. D. A. Chart (Belfast, 1931), pp. 62–3.
[31] M. Elliott, *Partners in Revolution. The United Irishmen and France* (Yale, 1982), pp. 26–7.
[32] *The Northern Star*, 1, no. 3.
[33] *Belfast News Letter* (*BNL*), 31 January 1792.
[34] *Ibid.*

reformer, Robert Black of Derry, launched a public attack upon 'seditious spirits who wished to overturn the constitution', warning them that such a course would 'expose its leaders to the punishment and infamy due to an act of such atrocious folly'.[35] He claimed to be speaking for 'the sober and rational part of the community', but Drennan was disgusted, attributing Black's 'harangue', as he called it, to the recent increase in *regium donum* payments for Presbyterian ministers.[36] Drennan considered that the ministers had been gagged,[37] but the synod, at its annual meetings in 1793, in its address to the lord lieutenant, called for parliamentary reform and Catholic emancipation though it assured him that the members of synod approved only of constitutional means of obtaining reform, 'rejecting with abhorrence every idea of popular tumult or foreign aid'.[38]

Circumstances were to force the United Irishmen to resort to both. They found themselves unable to arouse the same kind of irresistible public opinion that the Volunteers had achieved a decade before; plans to hold a great national convention to call for reform failed. Drennan's sister, Martha McTier, commented gloomily: 'There is a tide in the affairs of men and the Irishmen have lost it.'[39] The behaviour of men like Black and Bruce showed that Presbyterians who had been reformers were distancing themselves from their more radical brethren.

Traditionally, British policy in Ireland had always oscillated between coercion and conciliation and in the context of the war with France coercive policies began to be adopted. Drennan was charged with issuing a seditious libel and, though acquitted, became an observer of events.[40] Drennan's prosecution was only one of several which put leading United Irishmen, like the Presbyterian landlord, Archibald Hamilton Rowan, into prison and drove others, including Wolfe Tone and Napper Tandy, into exile. Increasingly coercive government policies drove persisting United Irishmen underground and, ultimately, into rebellion, when, in alliance with the French, they tried to bring revolution to Ireland. To mount a successful rebellion, with or without French help, they had to ignite the explosive force of peasant discontent and this they attempted to do. A manifesto drafted by a United Irish committee in County Down in 1795

---

[35] *BNL* 27 January 1793.
[36] Drennan to S. McTier, 31 January 1793, *Letters*, p. 125.
[37] *Ibid.*
[38] *Records of the General Synod of Ulster, 1691–1820* (*RGSU*), 3, p. 157.
[39] M. McTier to Drennan, 1 April 1793, *Letters*, p. 147.
[40] *Ibid.*, pp. xii–xiii.

promised abolition of tithes and parish rates and new and equitable con-
tracts between tenants and landlords.[41]

The situation was complicated by the fact that, in mid-Ulster in the
1790s, peasant discontent and economic rivalry were erupting in
sectarian conflict. Protestant peasants had begun to feel themselves
threatened by the improving prosperity and increasing self-confidence
of Roman Catholics who had invaded the linen industry, thus challenging Protestant profits and prospects. They had also been admitted to
the ranks of some Volunteer corps and been given instruction in drill
and the use of arms. Friction led to incidents and incidents led to collective action in the formation of groups like the Peep o'Day Boys and
the Defenders. Protestant Peep o'Day Boys raided Catholic homes, looking for arms and damaging looms, and Catholic Defenders retaliated.
The Defenders multiplied and improved their organization and, after a
Defender attack upon a group of armed Protestants in an inn at the
Diamond in County Armagh in 1795, the Protestants organized themselves in Orange societies or lodges.[42]

Recent research has shown that the Defenders were not simply anti-
Protestant paramilitaries, but were subversives inspired by a mixture of
contemporary revolutionary ideology and traditional Catholic millenial-
ism with its promise of deliverance and liberation.[43] The Orange Order
was cast therefore in a counter-revolutionary role and the gentry in mid-
Ulster were quick to recognize its value to protect them and their interests
and preserve their influence in a rapidly changing society.

This was a great blow to the United Irish hopes of uniting the rural
population of all denominations in a crusade to overthrow the existing
order. The United Irishmen were discovering that it was easier to proclaim the unity of 'Protestant, Catholic and Dissenter', than to achieve
it in practice. There was another problem. As Maureen Wall has written:

The brutal truth was that the policy of equal rights for all, and the
brotherhood of Irishmen, if pushed to its logical conclusions, would
inevitably lead to Catholic superiority, and naturally no Protestant
could contemplate such a prospect without very grave misgivings

---

[41] Crawford and Trainor, pp. 181–2.
[42] D. W. Miller, 'The Armagh Troubles', *Irish Peasants*, ed. S. Clark and J. S. Donnelly,
pp. 155–89.
[43] T. Bartlett, 'Defenders and Defenderism', *Irish Historical Studies*, 24 (1985), pp. 373 *seq.*

indeed. This was the fundamental weakness of the whole United Irish position.[44]

Marianne Elliott has also emphasized this weakness in the United Irish position; she believes that they recognized it themselves and that 'their insistence on the need for French military assistance stemmed as much from their fears of how the Catholic lower classes would conduct themselves in a rebellion as from their desire for independence from British rule'.[45] Nevertheless they were forced into an alliance with the Catholic Defenders and it was the alliance of United Irishmen and Defenders on one side and Orangemen and gentry on the other which ensured that the rebellion of 1798 was not only a civil war with Irishmen fighting Irishmen but a sectarian war, except perhaps in Antrim and Down.

The Presbyterian historian, Latimer, judged that 'Those Protestants who hated the Catholic more than the landlord became Orangemen, and those who hated the landlord more than the Catholic became United Irishmen.'[46] For Protestant read Presbyterian. His judgement has been repeated in essence by a Marxist historian of Anglo-Irish relations, Strauss, who described the Ulster Presbyterians at the end of the eighteenth century as being faced by 'the alternative of fighting the Catholic peasants on the side of the landlords or of fighting the landlords with the help of the Catholic masses'.[47]

In fact Presbyterians fought on both sides. Some fought as rebels, chiefly but not only, in Antrim and Down while others wore the uniform of the Yeomanry in Fermanagh, Tyrone, Derry, and Armagh.[48] Perhaps as many as thirty ministers and eighteen licentiates were involved in some active way, though only one minister, James Porter of Greyabbey, and one licentiate, Archibald Warwick, were executed.[49] Some, like William Steel Dickson and Sinclare Kelburn, were imprisoned and others, like John Glendy of Maghera, were forced into exile. In the nineteenth century, after the triumph of Old Light orthodoxy in Irish Presbyterianism, Presbyterian historians like W. D. Killen and W. T. Latimer were inclined to

[44] M. Wall, 'The United Irishmen', *Historical Studies*, 5, ed. J. L. McCracken (London, 1965), p. 134.

[45] Elliott, p. xvii.

[46] W. T. Latimer, *A History of the Irish Presbyterians* (Belfast, 1902), p. 391.

[47] E. Strauss, *Irish Nationalism and British Democracy* (London, 1951), p. 25.

[48] R. Musgrave, *Memoirs of the different Rebellions in Ireland* (Dublin, 1802), 1, pp. 237-8; 2, pp. 93-110.

[49] Latimer, p. 399; D. W. Miller, 'Presbyterianism and "Modernization" in Ulster', *PP* 80 (1980), p. 77.

identify the rebels of 1798 with the New Light or liberal theological party.[50] However there is evidence that many rank and file Presbyterian rebels in 1798 were motivated by a very conservative theological outlook.

The Covenanting tradition was strong in Ulster Presbyterianism, much stronger than the small cluster of Reformed Presbyterian or Covenanting congregations would suggest. It went back to the apocalyptic preaching, a century before, of men like Alexander Peden, who prophesied divine deliverance for God's covenanted people through the agency of the French.[51] Sermons of Covenanting preachers were being reprinted in the late eighteenth century and a hagiographic pamphlet about Peden was circulating in the north of Ireland.[52] Millennialist preaching was prevalent with the fall of the Bastille and the overthrow of Church and State in France interpreted as signs of the end of the age. In a sermon preached before the Synod of Ulster in 1793, entitled *The Obligation upon Christians and especially ministers to be exemplary in their lives, particularly at this important period, when the Prophecies are seemingly about to be fulfilled in the Fall of Antichrist*, the Revd T. L. Birch, who was to be imprisoned for his alleged part in the rebellion, asked the members of the synod, 'Have we indeed the distinguished honour of being the soldiers to be employed by the *Great Captain of our Salvation in that glorious Conflict*, in which he is finally to defeat *the Devil and all his Agents*?'[53] It is not surprising that some Ulster Presbyterians saw the rebellion as a crusade to overthrow an uncovenanted king and an apostate Church to bring in the kingdom of the Christ of the Covenants.

This, of course, was not the official view of the Synod. Having postponed its annual meeting in 1798 until the end of August, the Synod reiterated its 1793 position—reform was right, rebellion wrong. In its loyal address it repudiated 'the inexcusable crimes' of a 'few unworthy members of our Body' while beseeching His Majesty 'to accept the faithful Exertions of those who have withstood the torrent of Popular fury and the Seductions of Sophistical Philosophy, as an atonement for their deluded Brethren'.[54]

The rebellion did nothing to heal divisions between Roman Catholics

---

[50] *Ibid.*, pp. 77–9; J. S. Reid, *History of the Presbyterian Church in Ireland*, ed. W. D. Killen (Belfast, 1867), 3, pp. 391–8; Latimer, p. 401.

[51] Miller, 'Modernization', p. 81.

[52] *Ibid.*, pp. 71–2, 81.

[53] T. L. Birch, *A Sermon . . . Preached before the Very Reverend the Synod of Ulster* (Belfast, 1794), p. 32.

[54] *RGSU* 1798, pp. 208–9.

and Protestants of all kinds in Ireland. Presbyterian rebels at Antrim felt betrayed by the non-arrival of their Defender comrades[55] and a northern Catholic told a visitor to Ulster that 'he thanked God that he didn't belong to the black-hearted breed of Presbyterians—didn't they sell the pass upon us at Ballynahinch'.[56] According to that visitor, an English dissenting minister who made a tour of the north of Ireland in 1812, 'Catholics accused Presbyterians of leading them into the rebellion and, when they had got them fairly engaged in it, leaving them to shift for themselves'.[57] This was also the view of James McKey, a loyalist correspondent of Lord Downshire, who blamed 'the Presbyterian ministers and rich republican shopkeepers' for having led the lower orders into rebellion—'They had caused the rising but since it has broken out their courage failed and self was predominant.'[58] McKey judged, however, that 'we will have a much more settled country in a short time than ever your lordship saw it. For some years past there was something brooding in the minds of the republicans and now that it has broke out, and that they could not succeed, they will become loyal subjects'.[59]

McKey was certainly right so far as the Presbyterians were concerned. The experience of the rebellion and the sufferings of those suspected of being rebels made a deep impression upon minds accustomed to interpret disaster as divine judgement. Reports of massacres of Protestants in the rebellion in the south revived old fears and suspicions. A sense of disillusionment is expressed in the verses of the folk poet James Orr, who was himself forced to flee to America,[60] and what Norman Vance has called 'a note of melancholy retrospect' resounds in Drennan's poem 'Glendaloch', in which he presents the ancient monument as the memorial and mausoleum of Ireland's disappointed hopes:

> Yon mould'ring pillar, 'midst the gloom,
> Finger of Time! shall point her tomb . . .[61]

Castlereagh as Irish chief secretary pursued a policy of encouraging loyalism and unionism among the Presbyterians. A number of corre-

[55] T. Pakenham, *The Year of Liberty* (London, 1972), p. 249.
[56] J. Gamble, *A View of Society and Manners in the North of Ireland in the Summer and Autumn of 1812* (London, 1813), pp. 116–17.
[57] *Ibid.*, pp. 115–16.
[58] McKey to Downshire, 15 June 1798; NIPRO D601/F/244.
[59] *Ibid.*
[60] D. H. Akenson and W. H. Crawford, *James Orr, Bard of Ballycarry* (Belfast, 1977), pp. 10–17.
[61] N. Vance, 'Celts, Carthaginians and Constitutions: Anglo-Irish Literary Relations, 1780–1820', *Irish Historical Studies*, 22 (1981), p. 231.

spondents, including his former secretary, Alexander Knox, and Presbyterian ministers Black and Bruce gave advice and kept him informed about the situation on the ground. Knox advised him that

> this is perhaps a more favourable moment for forming a salutary connection between the government and the Presbyterian body of Ulster than may arrive again. The republicanism of that part of Ireland is checked and repressed by the cruelties of Roman Catholics in the late rebellion and by the despotism of Bonaparte. They are therefore in a humour for acquiescing in the views of government beyond which they ever were or (should the opportunity be missed) may be hereafter.[62]

The means which Castlereagh, guided by Knox and Black, adopted to achieve his ends involved a massively increased *regium donum* for ministers, but given on new terms. It was to be paid to ministers as individuals and not as a block grant to the Synod. The agent who distributed the payments was no longer to be appointed by the Synod, but by the government and at a large salary. Black himself was given the office. Ministers who took an oath of allegiance were to receive grants of £100, £75, or £50 a year according to the size of their congregations.[63] This was a huge subvention, considering that the Synod had been trying, in the eighteenth century, to ensure that ministers had a minimum stipend of £40 a year. Knox believed that these arrangements would turn the Presbyterian ministers into 'a subordinate ecclesiastical aristocracy, whose feelings must be those of zealous loyalty and whose influence upon their people will be as surely sedative when it should be so, and exciting when it should be so, as it was the direct reverse before'.[64] In other words the object was to turn Presbyterian ministers into a conservative social force.

Drennan prophesied that many Presbyterians would become Methodists, Independents, or even Deists.[65] Though some members of general Synod congregations may have joined the covenanters or seceders, there were no mass defections. Nor did the Synod lose its old spirit of independence altogether. When, a few years later, Castlereagh threatened to have the *regium donum* withdrawn if the Synod persisted in its plans to adopt for ministerial training the newly founded Belfast Academical Institution,

---

[62] Knox to Castlereagh, 15 July 1803, *Castlereagh*, 4, p. 288.
[63] *RGSU* 3, pp. 270–1.
[64] Knox to Castlereagh, 15 July 1803, *Castlereagh*, 4, p. 287.
[65] Drennan to M. McTier, 17 October 1800, *Letters*, p. 303.

which he suspected would be dominated by the influence of radicals like Drennan, who gave the address at its opening ceremony, the Synod ignored his warnings.[66]

Meanwhile, evangelicalism was breathing new spiritual life into the dry bones of the Synod of Ulster. Irish Presbyterians had their own tradition of evangelicalism and revivalism going back to the religious revival in the Six Mile Water valley in the early seventeenth century which had marked the beginnings of Presbyterianism in Ulster.[67] In the eighteenth century the ethos of the general Synod, the mainstream Presbyterian body, had become latitudinarian.[68] Latimer called it 'The reign of New Light'.[69] Now the Ulster Presbyterian community was beginning to feel the impact of the great evangelical revival which had begun among the displaced and persecuted Protestant minorities of Habsburg-dominated central Europe, in Silesia, Moravia, and Bohemia.[70] Just as the Irish revolutionary movement of the late eighteenth century was a facet of a wider international movement,[71] so the evangelicalism which transformed Irish Protestantism in the early nineteenth century was an aspect of a pan-revivalist movement.

Significantly the beginnings of this movement can be traced to the evangelism in Ireland of John Cennick the apostle of Irish Moravianism,[72] but it was impelled forward by the Wesleys, Whitefield, and preachers of the Countess of Huntingdon's Connexion. The great dynamic of the movement was undoubtedly to save souls but, in the context of the international revolutionary movement, evangelicalism was recognized by some and patronized as a counter-revolutionary force. As V. Kiernan has observed, 'Loyalty, conservatism, Christianity, became identical'.[73]

In the year of the rebellion an Evangelical Society of Ulster was founded with associations with the London Missionary Society in order to organize a system of itinerant evangelism in Ulster. If Drennan's sister, Martha McTier, is to be believed, the message of some of these itinerant

---

66 *RGSU* 3, pp. 452–3; Castlereagh to Peel, 9 November 1816, BL Add. MS 40182, fols 220–1; Peel to Castlereagh, 13 November 1816; *ibid.*, fol. 226.

67 W. D. Bailie, *The Six Mile Water Revival* (Belfast, 1984).

68 A. W. G. Brown, 'Irish Presbyterian Theology in the early Eighteenth Century' (Ph.D. thesis, Queen's University Belfast, 1977).

69 Latimer, pp. 370–86.

70 W. R. Ward, 'The relations of enlightenment and religious revival in central Europe and in the English-speaking world', *SCH Subsidia* 2 (1979), pp. 281–305.

71 D. Hempton, *Methodism and Politics in British Society, 1750–1850* (London, 1984), p. 23.

72 M. Hill, 'Evangelicalism and the Churches in Ulster society, 1770–1850' (Ph.D. thesis, Queen's University Belfast, 1987).

73 V. G. Kiernan, 'Evangelicalism and the French Revolution', *PP* 1 (1952), p. 45.

74 M. McTier to Drennan, 27 September 1801, *Letters*, p. 313.

evangelists was, 'a zealous religion, subtly blended with loyalty'.[74] It was this same combination which was to triumph in a bitter conflict which split the Synod of Ulster in the 1820s, when the new evangelicalism, which was to characterize nineteenth-century Irish Presbyterianism, triumphed over the latitudinarianism of the eighteenth century.[75] Henry Cooke, apostle of conservatism in religion and politics, defeated Henry Montgomery, who was not ashamed to own that his kinsmen had been United Irishmen.[76]

Cooke has often been credited or blamed with having turned the Ulster Presbyterians into Tories, but his efforts to do so were by no means successful. One of his political opponents could fairly claim in 1844:

> The Presbyterian Church is laid under a deep debt of gratitude to Dr Cooke. He was made the instrument of accomplishing a great reformation in this Church by extirpating the unitarianism which tinged and weakened the body. We shall never forget the gratitude that is due to him for this and for many other great and excellent labours. But we do not hold his political opinions. ... At the same time we have reason to believe that our opinions correspond with a large and
> · increasing majority of Irish Presbyterians.[77]

The results of the 1868 elections in Ireland vindicate this opinion, for Cooke's death-bed appeal to the Ulster Presbyterians to vote Tory and save the Church of Ireland from disestablishment fell on deaf ears.[78]

Irish Presbyterians did not abandon their basic liberalism after 1798. They did not oppose Catholic emancipation in 1829, though Cooke tried to make them do so, they were enthusiastic supporters of tenant-right and the reformist policies of governments of any party. Their political outlook of the late eighteenth century, which has been well described as 'settler radicalism',[79] did not change, but the Irish situation did.

The democratization of British politics, which, in general, Irish Presbyterians welcomed, gave a new power to the majority population in Ireland. Daniel O'Connell's campaign for Catholic emancipation had politicized that population, and his agitation for the repeal of the Union and the Irish nationalist movement which developed in the second half of the nineteenth century became almost completely identified with the aspirations of

[75] R. F. Holmes, *Henry Cooke* (Belfast, Dublin, Ottawa, 1981), pp. 31–80.
[76] *Irish Unitarian Magazine* (1847), p. 335.
[77] *Banner of Ulster*, 3 May 1844.
[78] E. R. Norman, *The Catholic Church and Ireland in the Age of Rebellion* (London, 1965), p. 351.
[79] N. Mansergh, *The Irish Question, 1840–1921* (London, 1975), p. 206.

Catholic Ireland, in spite of the efforts of the non-sectarian nationalists of the Young Ireland movement. Significantly the daughter of John Mitchel, the Ulster Presbyterian Young Irelander, converted to Catholicism, because she felt that she could not be 'thoroughly Irish without being Catholic'.[80]

Significantly, when O'Connell came to Belfast in 1841 to preach repeal it was not only Henry Cooke who opposed him but also Henry Montgomery and the *Northern Whig*.[81] Their central argument was economic—the industrial development of Belfast and the Lagan valley had forged an indissoluble link with Britain and repeal would mean ruin.[82] Thus, though they had supported Gladstone in his efforts to give peace to Ireland, in particular his disestablishment and land legislation, they parted company with him over Home Rule.

It was religion which legitimated, even sanctified, what critics saw as naked self-interest. Alan Ford has argued in his recent writings on the Reformation in Ireland that, in the seventeenth century in Ireland Protestants had found in apocalypticism and predestinarianism an ideological justification for their colonialism.[83] Such ideas disappeared from liberal or New Light theology in the eighteenth century and, in the nineteenth century, evangelicalism and revivalism modified predestinarianism for Old Light conservatives.[84] But conversionist evangelicalism easily replaced predestinarianism as an ideology of division, separating the sheep from the goats. The great Protestant missionary crusade, the 'Second Reformation', ultimately made little impact upon Irish Roman Catholics[85] and the 'Year of Grace', in which nineteenth-century evangelicalism reached its climax in Ulster, left the Catholic community largely untouched.[86] The vital difference was being underlined between Israel and the Canaanites. It may be significant that the chief Presbyterian critic of the 1859 revival, Isaac Nelson, author of *The*

---

[80] J. Mitchel, *Jail Journal*, p. 403, quoted in M. Heslinga, *The Irish Border as a Cultural Divide* (Assen, 1971), p. 186.

[81] *BNL* 4 January 1841; *The Northern Whig*, 7 January 1841.

[82] *Ibid.*, 3 January 1841.

[83] A. Ford, *The Protestant Reformation in Ireland, 1590–1641* (Frankfurt am Main, 1985), caps 8 and 9; *idem*, 'The Protestant Reformation', *Natives and Newcomers: Essays on the making of Irish Colonial Society, 1534–1641* (Dublin, 1986), pp. 66–9.

[84] J. E. Davey, *The Story of a Hundred Years* (Belfast, 1940), p. 45.

[85] D. Bowen, *The Protestant Crusade* (Dublin, 1978); R. J. Rodgers, 'Presbyterian Missionary Activity among Irish Roman Catholics in the nineteenth century' (MA thesis, Queen's University Belfast, 1969).

[86] J. T. Carson, *God's River in Spate* (Belfast, 1958), pp. 67–8.

Year of Delusion, a critique of the sympathetic account, *The Year of Grace*, later became an Irish Nationalist MP.[87]

If evangelicalism was widening the gulf between Presbyterians and Roman Catholics in one direction, ultramontanism was expanding it in the other. Presbyterians found themselves confronted by a resurgent, authoritarian, and disciplined Church in which, it seemed, the least biblical aspects of the Catholic tradition were being emphasized.[88] The confidence and claims of Irish Roman Catholicism had been transformed since the days of the United Irishmen, when it had seemed to men of the Enlightenment that it was a decaying relic of the past. The situation facing Irish Presbyterians in 1886 was utterly different from that which faced their forefathers in 1791, so their response was different also.

'The battle between Protestantism and Popery is not yet over by any means', declared a leading article in *The Witness*, the Irish Presbyterian weekly newspaper, in July 1886:

> Over! It never raged with greater violence. We do not fight now with sword and cannon. But the contest is none the less real on that account. Not in Ireland only but in all the world Rome and the Reformation are still striving for mastery.[89]

It was inevitable that the Home Rule crisis, which was about to burst, would be perceived by Irish Presbyterians in terms of 'the battle between Protestantism and Popery', that Home Rule would be regarded as Rome Rule.

There were no indications, however, in the columns of *The Witness*, in the summer of 1885, as the country prepared for a general election, that the crisis was anticipated. Referring disparagingly to 'the Parnellites', the editor took comfort from the fact that neither of the great political parties 'would pander to the Home Rulers'.[90] If they did they would deserve to be hurled from office! When, later, rumours had begun to circulate about Gladstone and concessions to the Home Rulers, *The Witness* dismissed them as unfounded.[91] Their readers were informed that, 'Presbyterians regard Mr Parnell and his followers as men who for their own selfish objects have fostered treason and goaded on the ignorant multitude to outrage and blood.' They could have no confidence that a Protestant minority would receive fair treatment at their hands.

[87] Latimer, p. 494.
[88] A. Vidler, *The Church in an Age of Revolution* (London, 1961), pp. 72–8.
[89] *Witness*, 17 July 1885.
[90] *Ibid.*, 4 September 1885.
[91] *Ibid.*, 24 December 1885.

When the reality of Gladstone's conversion to Home Rule was eventually revealed, *The Witness* expressed incredulity:

> It was the sheer inability to believe in the possibility that such rumours could have any substantial basis that prevented the inhabitants of this northern province from being roused to the very utmost by them. We could not believe that any responsible British statesman would venture to propose anything like Home Rule for Ireland.[92]

Presbyterian concern, as reflected in the columns of *The Witness*, was given official expression at a special meeting of the general assembly on 9 March 1886. There was virtual unanimity in the assembly which resolved,

> That we would deprecate in the strongest manner, as disastrous to the best interests of the country, a separate Parliament for Ireland . . . or any legislation tending to imperil the legislative Union between Great Britain and Ireland, or to interfere with the unity or supremacy of the Imperial Parliament. Legislation in any of these directions would, in our judgement, lead to the ascendancy of one class and creed in matters pertaining to religion, education, and civil administration. We do not believe that any guarantees, moral or material, could be devised which would safeguard the rights and privileges of minorities scattered throughout Ireland against the encroachment of a majority vested with legislative or executive functions.[93]

The general assembly's resolutions were seconded by Thomas Sinclair, one of the leading laymen in the Irish Presbyterian church and, hitherto, a Liberal in politics. At a Liberal demonstration against Home Rule, held in the Ulster Hall at the end of April, he asked the rhetorical question,

> Would it be a triumph of civilisation if, after having, by eighty-six years of gradual justice, transfigured the Ulster rebels of '98 into the most loyal and devoted subjects of the realm, she were now, by a grand act of injustice, to turn back the shadow on the dial and invite the return of hours of darkness and despair?[94]

This was the essence of the Irish Presbyterian explanation of the fact that the descendants of the United Irishmen of 1791 were Unionists in

[92] *Witness*, 8 January 1886.
[93] *Minutes of the General Assembly* (1886), p. 13.
[94] *Witness*, 7 May 1886.

1886. They had not changed, but circumstances in Ireland had. In a pamphlet entitled *Mr Gladstone's Two Irish Policies*, J. J. Shaw, an Irish Presbyterian academic and lawyer, and like Sinclair, a Liberal in politics, argued that they were not repudiating the United Irish tradition,

> Catholic emancipation, a reformed Parliament, a responsible executive, and equal laws for the whole Irish people—these were the declared and real objects of the United Irishmen. And it was only because they saw no hope of attaining these objects through an Irish Parliament that they took up arms.[95]

Irish Presbyterians had suffered under and rebelled against an Irish Protestant ascendancy in the eighteenth century, they were determined not to be subjected to an Irish Roman Catholic ascendancy a century later.

They did not have to resort to arms in 1886—indeed *The Witness* condemned those who talked of taking up arms[96]—for Gladstone's Home Rule bill, rejected by some of his own party, was thrown out by the House of Commons. When Gladstone lost the subsequent general election, the headline in *The Witness* was simply, 'Victory'.[97] They knew, however, that they had only won a battle and that the war would go on.

Union Theological College, Belfast

[95] Shaw, pp. 9–10.
[96] *Witness*, 21 May 1886.
[97] *Ibid.*, 16 July 1886.

POPULAR PROTESTANTISM IN ULSTER IN THE POST-REBELLION PERIOD, c1790-1810

by MYRTLE HILL

POPULAR Protestantism in Ulster in the late eighteenth and early nineteenth centuries, characterized by variety and liveliness, was directly related to events of more immediate national significance. While remaining a mere undercurrent in Irish affairs, Ulster evangelicalism in this important transitional period—shaped and moulded by the rebellion, the Act of Union, and the rise of a more articulate and assertive Catholicism—laid the foundations of a scripture-based, politically conservative Protestantism, which continues to influence the province's social and political development.

Ulster faced the new, nineteenth century, in a state of acute social and political unrest. The experience of war in Europe, revolution in France, and rebellion in Ireland combined with the social tensions engendered by economic change and a rapidly increasing population to highlight the inadequacies of the existing civil and religious institutions. Although the failure of the United Irishmen was complete, the Protestant nation was left with an anxious understanding of its vulnerability. The advancement of Roman Catholicism—in both political and religious terms—was observed, perhaps with disproportionate alarm. In the border counties of southern Ulster sectarian animosities, provoked by competition for land and jobs, remained to poison relations throughout the following century.[1]

The preface to a Dublin journal of the period stated, 'we live in an age when not only the pillars of Government, but the adamantine foundations of religion itself, shaken as it were by an earthquake, tremble to their base'.[2] Throughout Britain, indeed Europe, the whole concept of the Churches' role in society came under close scrutiny as the full implications of revolution for the old social order became apparent. Financial and legal restraints and internal tensions had limited both the pastoral and missionary zeal of the major Protestant denominations throughout much of the eighteenth century. The challenges presented by the

---

[1] See David Miller, 'The Armagh Troubles' in Sam Clark and J. S. Donnelly (eds), *Irish Peasants: Violence and Political Unrest 1780-1914* (Manchester, 1983), pp. 155-191; W. H. Crawford, 'Economy and Society in south Ulster in the Eighteenth Century', in *Clogher Record*, 7 (1975), pp. 251-8; H. Senior, *Orangeism in Ireland and Britain: 1795-1836* (London, 1966).
[2] *Ireland's Mirror or A Chronicle of the Times*, 2 vols (Dublin, 1804-5), I, p. iii.

changing social and political framework, however, altered forever their perception of their role in society. The political and social conditions which had formerly sustained them were victims of the changing circumstances. The established religion in particular had been upheld by Walpolean patronage, by the operation of discriminatory laws against Roman Catholics and Dissenters, and by a legalized recognition of ecclesiastical boundaries. In the new century the Establishment faced not only the loss of these props, but the urgent practical problems of coping with major demographic changes. The Act of Union, bringing Irish religious affairs into the domain of British party politics, subjected the Church of Ireland to unsympathetic criticism and intensified the pressures for change.

While these internal and external factors combined to highlight the inherent weaknesses of the older ecclesiastical institutions in this period, religion—Roman Catholic and Protestant—partook of the energy and the spirit of competition engendered by economic and political developments. With the established and semi-established institutions in danger of becoming irrelevant, new and popular forms of Protestantism were the major beneficiaries of such circumstances. From the mid-eighteenth century, religious sects with an emphasis on earnest pietism—from eastern Europe, America, England, and Scotland—had put down roots in the fertile soil of Ireland. Their flexibility enabled them to provide religious facilities where they were most needed, and their popular methods were both a catalyst and a product of the eighteenth-century demand for a more urgent and intense religious commitment. The events of the last decades of the century gave added stimulus to their activities.

One of the factors contributing to the religious excitement of the period was millennial expectancy. In the general atmosphere of tension and unrest, both national and international events in the secular sphere were infused with religious significance. Living in a turbulent age evoked a fear and uncertainty which proved conducive to religious revivalism.[3] Appeals to religious authority had a guaranteed emotive effect, and agrarian and political movements on both sides of the religious divide ensured a popular response by making full use of biblical imagery and indulging in interpretations of the prophecies to justify their existence and actions. The full extent and impact of millennial ideology is somewhat difficult to

---

[3] Peter Berger discusses manifestations of religious millennialism resulting from crises, disasters, and social disruption in *The Social Reality of Religion* (London, 1967); see also Susan O'Brien, 'A Transatlantic Community of Saints: The Great Awakening and the First Evangelical Network 1735-55', *AHR* 91 (1986), pp. 811-32.

ascertain. There were at least two strands—the intellectual and the popular—and, as J. F. C. Harrison points out, the latter sprang from emotional rather than intellectual roots and thus frequently lay outside the realm of conscious reasoning.[4]

Specialized intellectual studies on the approach of the millennium were the preoccupation of sections of the Presbyterian community in the 1790s, with the printing and distribution of several publications lending weight to the United Irishmen's pressure for radical political reform.[5] Millennial ideas could be used to justify the actions of any of the new political movements. In terms of an embryonic nationalism, the millennial impulse was important to the Catholic Defenders, while both David Miller and Peter Brooke see the readiness of Irish Covenanting Ministers to identify the government alongside the papacy as a force of Anti-Christ, as an important factor in the rise of United Irish support in the northeast.[6]

The scriptural interpretation of events, whether construed thus, as an academic theological exercise, or more commonly, expressed in the general linking of contemporary social upheaval with the unfolding of a divine plan for mankind, did come to have a directly spiritual as opposed to purely political significance, particularly after the disillusionment of the late 1790s. By the end of the century, the text, 'Be ye ready also, for the Son of Man cometh at an hour when ye think not', had become almost overworked.[7] During years when murder and looting were commonplace, secret societies proliferated, a repressive military presence was established, and the daily newspapers were full of the dramatic occurrences in France, references to the imminence of the Latter Days abounded.[8] Local events contributed to an anxious sense of persecution. Lord Charlemont received an alarming report from Ballymena in 1797. 'We are like Christians in the

---

[4] J. F. C. Harrison, *The Second Coming: Popular Millenarianism: 1780-1850* (London, 1979), p. xiii.

[5] David Miller, 'Presbyterianism and Modernisation in Ulster', *PP* 80 (1980), pp. 66-90.

[6] *Ibid.* and Peter Brooke, 'Controversies in Ulster Presbyterianism, 1790-1836' (unpublished Ph.D. thesis, Cambridge University, 1981), p. 35.

[7] W. S. Dickson, *Sermon on the Coming of the Son of Man preached before the Particular Synod of Belfast, at their annual meeting, November 14th 1777, Belfast* (Belfast, 1777); see also NIPRO, CR5/5A/1/ 2A, Minutes of the Associate Synod (Burgher), 1779-1814, p. 65; Minutes of the Reformed Presbytery.

[8] See the *Belfast Newsletter* of this period for the general excitement and unrest generated by political events; many examples of millennial excitement could be given, see for example, Mathew Lanktree, *Biographical Narrative* (Belfast, 1836), pp. 71, 85; *Memoirs of Francis Dobbs, also Genuine Reports of his speeches in Parliament on the subject of an union, and his Prediction of the Second Coming of the Messiah . . .* (Dublin, 1800); and the minutes of the various synods and the Methodist Conference.

first century, who every day expected the world would be at an end, and in contemplation of that great event, every idea was absorbed. So here, nothing can persuade us but that some great event is at hand.'[9] For those of evangelical faith, for whom 'moderation and gradualness did not commend themselves as virtues, but rather were signs of a lack of faith',[10] political and social events were translated into signs of the imminent arrival of the Messiah and the Last Judgement, investing all aspects of life with a compelling urgency. The Christian system of rewards and punishments acquired immediacy and a new significance in a context of social convulsion and apocalyptic expectancy.

The concentration of evangelical activity of many different kinds in the disturbed border counties of south Ulster in this period strengthens the suggestion that regional peculiarities are important factors in the fluctuations of belief and practice. But the phenomenon of revival has many strands, and while noting the aptness of the period to religious fervour, neither deeply religious nor psychological motivations should be underestimated by historians in their search for verifiable evidence.[11] The intense emotionalism generated by the preaching of the gospel message, dramatic conversions, and indeed the experience of revival itself, were self-perpetuating, with knowledge of success in one area stimulating even greater efforts in the surrounding neighbourhood.[12]

Organized sects such as Moravians, Methodists, and Seceders popularized a more enthusiastic form of religious commitment, while their flexible outreach enabled them to put down roots by filling gaps in the existing religious structures. They provided a religious outlet for the poor and isolated sections of the community who were alienated or neglected by the formalities of the traditional Churches. They responded to need—both practical and spiritual—rather than to legal or financial requirements with a pragmatism which was to become an important feature of the nineteenth-century evangelical crusade.

Methodism fitted easily into the lifestyle and world-view of the south Ulster protestant.[13] Individualist and activist, this vital and energetic faith

---

[9] *The Mss. and Correspondence of James, 1st Earl of Charlemont*, Historical MSS Commission, 2 vols (London, 1891–4), p. 303.

[10] Harrison, *The Second Coming*, p. 6.

[11] For revivalism as a frontier phenomenon, see Bryan Wilson, *Religious Sects* (London, 1970), pp. 48–51.

[12] For a graphic account of the geographical spread of revivalist fervour, see Lanktree, *Biographical Narrative*, pp. 106–7.

[13] See D. N. Hempton, 'Methodism in Irish Society, 1770–1830', *TRHS* 5, Series, 36 (1986), pp. 117–42.

reflected and promoted social and economic aspirations. The flexibility of the movement, and the active role offered to its lay supporters, could not be matched by the more rigid and institutionalized denominations, particularly in fluid settlement areas. It was not confined to church or meeting house, but reached out to, and was proclaimed from, streets, fields, and homes. Societies and classes enabled individuals to seek identity, support, and inspiration in a small religious group, which despite its intimacy and novelty, still claimed the connection with the Establishment which was so important to an inherently conservative rural population.[14] While remaining 'constitutionally' attached to a long-held tradition, the ordinary Methodist was able to challenge its authority with a sense of moral and religious superiority which focused strongly on the more extreme aspects of Protestantism. Revivals reported throughout Ireland in the 1770s, '80s, and '90s generated optimism,[15] but the rebellion of 1798 prompted a specific reaction from the Methodist authorities, with three Irish-speaking missionaries appointed to travel at liberty throughout the Kingdom.[16] The journals, diaries, and letters of these missionaries record a degree of success which is largely borne out by the statistical increases of the period 1800–02.[17] Both the missionary work and the general revivalistic atmosphere stimulated membership growth in the local societies, the number of Methodists in Ireland rising from 6,109 in 1780 to 26,323 in 1820. A more localized focus reveals that the impact of revivalism was particularly strong in south Ulster.[18]

Increased commitment to the evangelical style of religion was not only expressed through Methodism, however, particularly in the Presbyterian north. The conversionist zeal of the Methodists, their strict discipline in matters such as dress and family worship, use of pamphlets, involvement in public debate, and strong emphasis on sin expressed in days of fast and humiliation were matched in Calvinist circles by the Presbyterian Seceders and Covenanters. These bodies were likewise made up of small

---

[14] The Large Minutes according to the last edition, published during the life of Mr Wesley. Originally published under the title, Minutes of Several Conversations between the Reverend Mr. Wesley and Others, 1744–1789, included in the *Minutes of the Methodist Conference in Ireland*, 1, pp. xxix–xxx.

[15] *Minutes of the Methodist Conference in Ireland*, volume 1; Crookshank, *History of Methodism in Ireland*, 3 vols (London, 1885–8), 1, pp. 302, 392, 401; 2, pp. 174, 176, 180.

[16] *Minutes of the Methodist Conference in Ireland*, 1, p. 113.

[17] See NIPRO, CR6/3, the Journal of Gideon Ouseley, and the letters from the Irish missionaries to the missionary committee in London among the Methodist Missionary Society Archives, School of Oriental and African Studies (SOAS), London.

[18] See the tables and graphs in Hempton, 'Methodism in Irish Society', pp. 140–2.

societies, and spoke out against the spiritual complacency of their parent church, while demanding full commitment from their congregations. Although they represented only a minority of the Presbyterian strength in Ulster, their rapid expansion in this period shows that the new interest in vital faith was not confined to any one theological or denominational grouping. By 1800 the Covenanters had formed congregations in seven of the nine Ulster counties.[19] The Seceding Presbyterians increased the number of their congregations from 41 in 1770 to 91 in 1809.[20] Claiming to be the true representatives of the Church of Scotland, these bodies provided an outlet for evangelical fervour in areas traditionally hostile to Arminianism, their reforming ardour reflecting a Calvinist parallel to Methodist activity in Anglican areas. The Seceders in particular played an important early role in providing ministers and meeting houses in the more isolated Presbyterian communities. By creating a viable and theologically attractive alternative to New-Light tendencies, they also ensured that those who objected to what they saw as excessive moderation and tolerance in the Synod of Ulster could remain within the broad Presbyterian movement.

Itinerancy, however, was perhaps the most effective, and the most controversial, aspect of the evangelical movement in its early phase. Like the use of the Irish language, it was a feature of Methodism which was to become common religious practice. Popular preachers, whose commitment to 'Gospel Truth' often superseded their sense of denominational loyalty, moved outside the constraints of the diocese and the synod to engage in interdenominational initiatives such as the Dublin-based General Evangelical Society (1787), the Evangelical Society of Ulster, founded in Armagh as a direct response to the crisis of 1798, and in a variety of teaching, preaching, and Bible societies formed in the early decades of the nineteenth century. The wider context to this missionary campaign is often overlooked. For many leading British evangelicals engaged in the crusade against popery and ignorance, Ireland offered as great a challenge as far-off heathen lands, while for native preachers news of successes overseas was a heady stimulant. George Hamilton, secretary of the Evangelical Society of Ulster, pointed out that the idea to form a society to provide gospel preachers in needy areas sprang from the examples of evangelical activity in America, England, Scotland, and

---

[19] A. Loughridge, *The Covenanters in Ireland: A History of the Reformed Presbyterian Church of Ireland* (Belfast, 1984), p. 28
[20] Acts and Proceedings of the Associate Synod of Ireland: NIPRO, D1759/1F/1.

other parts of Europe which were now experiencing outbreaks of revival-ism.[21] The Second Great Awakening in America was also both an example and an inspiration.[22] Visiting preachers brought news of dramatic suc-cesses. Lorenzo Dow, who had himself taken part in the American cam-paign, converting one hundred people during a three-hour meeting at Western Up-State New York, introduced the more flamboyant style of American revivalism to rural Ireland.[23] Eccentric, superstitious, and prone to sensationalism, Dow toured Ulster in 1800 and again in 1806. Ob-servers claimed they 'had never seen any person who so much reminded them of the Lord Jesus'.[24] Letters from the many Methodist emigrants from Ulster to the New World were a further source of encouragement to local itinerants, with details of great camp meetings and mass conversions passed around the societies.[25]

The local dimension was also important, however. For if these men set out to impose their views on Irish society, they were also themselves moulded and directed by that society. The activities of the Catholic Defenders lent to the countryside around Armagh the sense of urgency and crisis so conducive to religious revivalism, and promoted the need for solidarity which transformed the theological anti-Catholicism of evan-gelical faith into straightforward sectarianism. Anti-Catholic polemics, rooted in local situations but invested with theological authority, devel-oped into the most strident aspect of Irish evangelicalism. The work of Methodist missionary Gideon Ouseley was a good example. His use of the Irish language gave him easier access to, and a decided advantage with, the illiterate peasantry owing allegiance to the Church of Rome. In true evan-gelical fashion he 'loved Roman Catholics but hated Roman Catholi-cism',[26] and his attitudes and often dramatic methods both played upon and aggravated the sectarian bitterness already prevalent in south Ulster. The actual number of converts from Catholicism to Methodism was probably never of very great significance, but reports sent to the missionary

---

[21] *Introductory Memorial respecting the Establishment and First Attempt of the Evangelical Society of Ulster* (Armagh, 1798), p. 2.
[22] O'Brien, 'A Transatlantic Community of Saints'.
[23] Lanktree, *Biographical Narrative*, pp. 156–7; Ouseley to Lanktree, March, 1805: NIPRO, CR6/3; several anecdotes concerning Dow are related in John Kent, *Holding the Fort: Studies in Victorian Revivalism* (London, 1978), p. 48.
[24] Lanktree, *Biographical Narrative*, p. 84.
[25] See for example, Letter from Ann Cooke to her mother, quoted in Lanktree, *Biographical Narrative*, p. 166.
[26] This phrase is used by David Hempton in 'Bickersteth, Bishop of Ripon: The Episcopate of a Mid-Victorian Evangelical', *NH* 17 (1982), p. 199.

committee in London emphasized this aspect of the Irish work. Claims that 'popery is falling off before us' were more optimistic than actual, but they played an important role in shaping English opinion on Irish Catholicism in general, and more particularly in promoting the belief in British evangelical circles that mass conversions were possible.[27]

The importance of individual personalities in the emotive field of revivalism should not be underestimated. Ouseley was one of Methodism's most dramatic personalities. Capitalizing on emotion and excitement, drawing large crowds and claiming many converts, his method alarmed not only the Roman Catholic priesthood, but also more conventional Methodist officials.[28] The Covenanters too were fortunate in having within their body a couple of striking personalities whose energy was committed to the extension of their cause.[29] Both the early interdenominational societies—the General Evangelical Society and the Evangelical Society of Ulster—attracted prominent revivalist preachers from the mainland. Popular and influential men, often notorious in orthodox ecclesiastical circles, they caused a considerable stir in the local religious community. Rowland Hill was refused ordination by six bishops in succession before he was finally recognized by the Anglican Church, and William Cooper was particularly noted by contemporaries for his bold efforts at converting Roman Catholics.[30] In an atmosphere of social disruption and millenarian excitement, the voices of emotional orators and extremists were more readily acceptable. Men like Ouseley, Cooper, and Hill were able to capitalize on the general aura of turbulence and unrest, and to both contribute to, and draw from, the popular anti-Catholic sentiments of the period. Such personalities

---

[27] 'No-one can have any conception of it, but those that are eye witnesses to the crowds of Catholics and others that seem to thirst for the Word', Charles Graham to Dr Coke, 30 April 1803; see also James Bell to Coke, 23 November 1802: Methodist Archive Research Centre, John Rylands Library, Manchester, MAM PLP 8-3; and Charles Graham to Coke, 11 September 1802: Methodist Missionary Society Archives, Box 74, 1802-25.

[28] Relations between Ouseley and the Methodist leaders in Dublin became more strained as the 19th century progressed, with Ouseley's flamboyance increasingly at odds with the movement's campaign for respectability and acceptance as an institution in its own right: NIPRO, Ouseley Papers, CR6/3 XXVIII.

[29] Revd S. Ferguson, *Brief Biographical Sketches of some Irish Covenanting Ministers who laboured during the latter half of the Eighteenth Century* (Londonderry, 1897); Loughridge, *The Covenanters in Ireland*, p. 50; see also 'An Elegy on the Death of Reverend William Staveley': NIPRO, D1759/1F/1.

[30] D. W. Lovegrove, 'The Practice of Itinerant Evangelism in English Calvinistic Dissent 1780–1830' (unpublished Ph.D. thesis, Cambridge University, 1980); Samuel Madden, *Life of Peter Roe* (Dublin, 1842), p. 67.

introduced vitality, and a good deal of disruption into the relatively static ecclesiastical setting.

The Evangelical Society of Ulster was a particularly important focus for Presbyterian evangelicalism in the north, although Anglicans and Methodists were also involved. Formed by five ministers of the Burgher synod, the society's proclaimed intention—to transcend denominational distinctions in the wider interests of 'the enlargement of the kingdom of Christ in the world'—was regarded as its most innovative and controversial feature in Ulster ecclesiastical circles.[31] The society lasted only three to four years, but it is more important for what it reveals of contemporary attitudes than for any particular significance of its own. Denominational tensions were particularly strong in the north, where Protestant sects operated in close—and critical—proximity, but the founders of the new society attempted to forestall criticism by stressing their desire to 'co-operate with all of evangelical mind', and by applying to already established British evangelical groups for a supply of itinerant preachers rather than provoking local opposition by undertaking this controversial step themselves.[32] Rowland Hill and William Cooper toured the north on behalf of the society in the summer of 1799, and William Gregory in 1800. Gregory was another of those intriguing, colourful characters whom the turbulence of the age produced. He had sailed to the South Seas in 1798 as one of the London Missionary Society's first ambassadors, and the story of his adventures, including capture by the French, was guaranteed to hold the attention of his listeners.[33] The reports of these missionaries are coloured by the excitement and drama of the post-rebellion period, with talk of curfews, the army presence, and a pervading atmosphere of tension. They preached wherever a crowd gathered, in fields, barns, schoolhouses, and mills—in an area within a twenty mile radius of Armagh.[34]

Their records provide an important indicator of the degree of co-operation and conflict within and between the various shades of Protestantism in Ulster. While received in parish churches and Methodist meeting houses by ministers already committed to interdenominational

---

[31] *Introductory Memorial respecting the Establishment and First Attempt of the Evangelical Society of Ulster*, pp. 7–8.

[32] *Ibid.* and George Hamilton, Armagh, to Rev. J. Eyre, London, 2 January 1799: SOAS, Missionary Papers, Box 1, Folder 6.

[33] William Gregory, 'Extracts of a Tour through the North of Ireland, engaged under the patronage of the Evangelical Society of Ulster, in the summer of the year 1800': typescript in Linenhall Library, Belfast.

[34] *Ibid.* and Hamilton to LMS, 9 October 1799, Cooper to LMS, 20 June 1799: SOAS, Missionary Correspondence, Box 1, Folder 8.

co-operation, they seem to have caused most disruption amongst Presbyterians. Their activities provoked a particularly hostile response from the Seceding Presbyterian synods who spoke out against the society's latitudinarian principles, regarding interdenominationalism as schismatic, and general itinerancy as unconstitutional.[35] The General Synod was less vehement in its opposition, and despite its reputation for lacking evangelical fervour in this period, many of its ministers appear to have opened their pulpits to the agents of the society.[36] Indeed, there seems to have been a considerable gap between the official and popular responses, with frequent clashes within the Presbyterian community. When confronted by the itinerant's request for premises from which to preach, elders clashed with ministers and congregations with elders. Ministers could find themselves locked out, or a congregation find the meeting-house doors closed against them.[37] These missionary records indicate a degree of complexity at grassroots level which is perhaps masked by the official response.

There was a similar gap between popular and official ecclesiastical responses to the variety of voluntary religious agencies which proliferated in the early decades of the nineteenth century, and in which many of these preachers were involved. Combining educational and religious principles, and with the scriptures as their major tool, they stressed the links between morality, political loyalty, and social stability. Preaching, teaching, and Bible distribution were the major, and interdependent, strands of the campaign.[38] The evangelical emphasis on conversion to Protestantism as a means of saving Ireland was reflected in the societies' exclusive use of the Bible, without note or comment, and the extensive use of the Irish language by teachers and itinerants. Such methods, however, brought the societies, and the faith they sought to disseminate, into conflict with nationalist leaders engaged in the political and social rejuvenation of Irish Catholicism. With these societies quickly becoming identified with the social and political conservatism of the alarmed Protestant nation, evangelicalism in Ireland thus became embroiled in controversial secular

---

[35] Minutes of the Associate Synod of Ireland, Burgher, 1779–1814; Acts and Proceedings of the Associate Synod of Ireland: NIPRO, D1759/1F/1.

[36] *Records of the General Synod of Ulster*, 3 (Belfast, 1898), pp. 279, 298.

[37] Gregory, 'Extracts of a Tour through the North of Ireland'.

[38] Church Missionary Society, Minute Books and Abstract Letter Books, 1814–58: Representative Church Body Library, Dublin; Proceedings of the Committee of the Irish Society, 1818–32: Trinity College, Dublin, MS 7644–76450; see the Annual Reports of the Hiberian Bible Society, the London Hibernian Society, and the Irish Evangelical Society in the Halliday Collection, Royal Irish Academy, Dublin.

issues. Accusations of proselytism, particularly in the southern border counties, complicated political and educational questions, and further highlighted the distinctive nature of Ulster's religious/cultural divide.[39]

There is thus clear evidence of a network of lively religious activity in the Ulster countryside in this period, much of it mutually reinforcing, but these more popular forms of religious expression with their flexible outreach and broadly-based appeal were both an example and a threat to the more traditional religious institutions. Their enthusiastic endeavours subjected the more orthodox religious denominations to uncommonly fervent criticism, while their overriding emphasis on personal conversion inspired a degree of Christian co-operation which threatened the old mechanisms of denominational control. While rural clergy co-operated with Methodists and evangelical individuals and organizations in preaching and Bible distribution, church leaders came to adopt a more cautious approach. Churchmen had to balance claims of mass conversions against the negative effects of public controversies and their desire to maintain their role as both social and religious leaders. The lack of restraint displayed by popular itinerants was a worrying development for those concerned to control the activities of rural clergy and maintain the dignity of the Church. The evangelical emphasis on the truths of the gospel rather than on denominational distinctions undermined both ecclesiastical authority and ministerial status. Such problems combined with internal and parliamentary pressure to propel the major denominations into a vigorous programme of reform and reconstruction in the first half of the nineteenth century.[40]

A study of this period of Ulster evangelicalism reveals a paradox. While emotive religious behaviour was regarded in official ecclesiastical circles as disruptive and radical, it was seen by many Protestants as a stabilizing force, to be promoted as an antidote to civil and political unrest. In the continuing struggle against Catholicism and secularism, both the Anglican and Presbyterian Churches came to recognize the relevance and effectiveness of at least some aspects of the evangelical campaign, and adapted

---

[39] Desmond Bowen, *The Protestant Crusade in Ireland 1800–1870* (Dublin, 1978); I. M. Hehir, 'New Lights and Old Enemies: the Second Reformation and the Catholics of Ireland, 1800–1835' (unpublished MA thesis, University of Wisconsin, 1983).

[40] D. H. Akenson, *The Church of Ireland: Ecclesiastical Reform and Revolution 1800–1885* (London, 1971); E. Brynne, *The Church of Ireland in the Age of Catholic Emancipation* (London, 1982); *Minutes of the General Synod of Ulster, 1820–40*; *Challenge and Conflict: Essays in Presbyterian History and Doctrine* (Belfast, 1981), pp. 116–47; R. Finlay Holmes, *Our Presbyterian Heritage* (Belfast, 1985), pp. 110–24.

many of their methods to their particular denominational forms. By the mid-nineteenth century Irish-speaking preachers, missions, Bible distribution, and auxiliary societies had revitalized Ulster's major churches. Much of the duality of Ulster's religious heritage—anti-Catholic vehemence and a popular religious activism—can be traced back to this turbulent period.

Queen's University, Belfast.

GIDEON OUSELEY:
RURAL REVIVALIST, 1791–1839

by DAVID HEMPTON

IDEON Ouseley was born in the year of John Wesley's second visit to County Galway, was 'converted' in the year of Wesley's death, and died on the one hundredth anniversary of Wesley's introduction to field preaching. A Methodist rural revivalist could have no better pedigree. I first encountered him, not in a dream as many Methodist contemporaries seem to have done, but in the correspondence of Joseph Butterworth, MP,[1] to whom Ouseley sent graphic details of the nature of Irish Catholicism for his controversial speeches against Roman Catholic emancipation, and in the records of the Wesleyan Methodist Missionary Society, in which Ouseley stands out as the most flamboyant missionary of his generation.[2] In terms of published works Ouseley's career can also be traced through his prolific anti-Catholic pamphleteering[3] and in the pages of William Arthur's unexceptional Victorian biography.[4] But by far the most revealing record of his life and work is to be found in the manuscripts collected by John Ouseley Bonsall, a Dublin businessman who hero-worshipped his missionary uncle.[5] The collection includes transcriptions of

---

[1] Manchester the John Rylands University Library, Methodist archives research centre MS, papers of Thomas Allan, Joseph Butterworth, and Gideon Ouseley. Butterworth was MP for Coventry (1812–18) and for Dover (1820–6).

[2] University of London School of Oriental and African Studies, Methodist Missionary Society MS, boxes 1–3 and 74–5. Additional missionary correspondence is to be found in NIPRO, Irish Wesley Historical Society MS under restricted consultation. See also Thomas Coke, *Copies of the Letters from the Missionaries who are employed in Ireland, for the Instruction in their own Language, and for the Conversion of the Native Irish* (London, 1801).

[3] Lack of space prevents a full list but the most important are; Gideon Ouseley, *The Substance of Two Letters to the Rev John Thayer, Once a Presbyterian Minister, but now a Roman Catholic Priest and Missionary. In Consequence of his Public Challenge to all Protestants* (Dublin, 1814); *Old Christianity Defended* (Dublin, 1820); *Letters to Dr Doyle on the Doctrines of his Church with an easy and effectual plan to obtain Immediate Emancipation* (Dublin, 1824); *Letters in Defence of the Roman Catholics of Ireland in which is opened the Real Source of their Many Injuries, and of Ireland's Sorrows, addressed to D. O'Connell* (London, 1829); *Letters on Topics of Vast Importance to all Roman Catholics and the State in reply to Dr Crolly's Letter to Lord Donegall* (Dublin, 1832); *An Easy Mode of Securing Ireland's Peace* (Dublin, 1833); and *A Dreadful Conspiracy against the Church of Christ Developed* (Dublin, 1837).

[4] William Arthur, *The Life of Gideon Ouseley* (London, 1876). See also C. H. Crookshank, *History of Methodism in Ireland*, 3 vols (London, 1885–8), and R. H. Gallagher, *Pioneer Preachers of Irish Methodism* (Belfast, 1965), pp. 144–7.

[5] NIPRO MS Ouseley Collection CR 6/3 ACC 13019, 28 folders of paginated MS collected and transcribed by J. O. Bonsall and enlarged by John Hay in preparation for Arthur's biography.

Ouseley's letters, reproductions of his journal—which Ouseley thought he had completely destroyed in 1814 after repeated rows with the regular Methodist preachers—and an unusual oral history dimension in the transcriptions of interviews conducted by Bonsall a few years before Ouseley's death. As a collection it is at once deeply personal in its disclosure of Ouseley's states of mind during religious conversion, illness, and death, and of much wider historical significance in its evocation of half a century of religious conflict and social upheaval in Ireland. It is also revealing of Methodism itself in its period of transition from a network of voluntary societies serviced by itinerant evangelists to a settled, chapel-based, and preacher-led denomination. But above all the Ouseley collection is a record of the remarkable religious energy of its subject in proclaiming religious certainties to a generation made anxious by revolution in Europe and Catholic resurgence in Ireland.

Ouseley was born in Dunmore, County Galway, in 1762, the son of a freethinking, anticlerical father of minor gentry status and a pious mother who introduced him to the family collection of Anglican and Puritan literature. Of English ancestry the Ouseley family was one of a declining group of substantial Protestant farmers who were surrounded by an overwhelmingly Catholic peasantry.[6] Despite his father's anticlericalism Gideon was bound for a career in the Church of Ireland, and was tutored by the local Catholic priest who had been educated in Europe. Ouseley failed to win a place at Trinity College, married into a respectable Protestant family and acquired a farm which subsequently had to be surrendered, probably unnecessarily, after a law suit. (Butterworth later alleged that Ouseley approached legal difficulties like a Calvinist waiting for divine justice rather than as an Arminian working out his own salvation.)[7] Ouseley then entered a phase of dissolute living which was dramatically brought to an end by a drunken shooting accident in which Ouseley lost an eye and very nearly his life. With Young's gloomy *Night Thoughts* as his unlikely convalescent reading, Ouseley's close encounter with death resulted in a lasting preoccupation with death and eternity.

Ouseley's first experience of evangelical religion was in the meetings conducted in a local inn by a Methodist quarter master attached to the Royal Irish Dragoons and stationed in Dunmore barrack.[8] Thus began a

[6] Ouseley Coll., II fols 1–10; III fols 1–3; IV fols 1–7.
[7] Ouseley Coll., XXVI fol. 4.
[8] The importance of the military in the early dissemination of Irish Methodism is deserving of more attention. See Ouseley Coll., XXVI fol. 10. See also IX fol. 29; XII fols 3–5; XIII fol. 16.

long and psychologically painful 'conversion' during which Ouseley encountered other Methodist itinerants and joined a Methodist society. The sense of inner struggle, anxiety, and fear of death is well conveyed in his interview with Bonsall in which he described himself as 'harassed, perplexed, and hopeless'.[9] His 'conversion' when it came was one of those characteristic two tier Methodist types in which justification preceded entire sanctification (forgiveness before cleansing) by several months. So intense was Ouseley's mental turmoil at this time that it became the emotional and conceptual foundation of much of his later preaching. Indeed so frequently did Ouseley recall in tears 'that Sunday morning' when 'I got such a sight of hell' that the more sophisticated Dublin Methodist congregations came to dread the very sight of him.[10]

Ouseley's 'conversion' in 1791, as with Wesley's in 1739, opened up the way for half a century of itinerant preaching characterized by unremitting zeal and energy. His ambition was to preach to every human settlement in Ireland in the language of the people, and it was not uncommon for him to travel 4,000 miles a year preaching 12–15 times a week.[11] Ouseley's suspicion of ecclesiastical institutions and their clergy ensured that his early itinerant labours were undertaken as a freelance evangelist subject to no outside control whatsoever. But in 1799 he was invited by the Irish Methodist Conference to be part of a team of three Irish speaking evangelists with a specific mission to the Irish Catholic poor in the wake of the Rebellion of the United Irishmen.[12] Ouseley was thereby given a degree of Conference authority and financial support without ever being taken into full connexion as a regular preacher. Indeed he refused to sign Wesley's Large Minutes as mere human compositions and jealously respected his right of independence and private judgement. In that respect Ouseley's career parallels both the American frontier preachers (Lorenzor Dow was a close friend)[13] and English revivalists, men and women, who proliferated in the quarter century after Wesley's death.[14]

---

[9] *Ibid.*, V fols 1–24; VI fols 1–20; XXVIII fol. 3.

[10] *Ibid.*, XXVIII fol. 4. See also NIPRO, Irish Wesley Historical Society MS, Gideon Ouseley to Matthew Tobias, 14 June 1820.

[11] For the flavour of Ouseley's labours see Bonsall's transcription of his journal in Ouseley Coll., IX (15 July 1802 to 15 April 1803) and X (August 1804).

[12] See 'An Address from the Irish to the British Conference (Dublin 13 July 1799)' in *Irish Conference Minutes*. For a more complete background to this venture see my 'The Methodist Crusade in Ireland 1795–1845', *Irish Historical Studies*, 22 (1980), pp. 33–48.

[13] Ouseley Coll., XI fol. 5; XII fol. 13; XV fol. 24; XXVIII fol. 43. See also Lorenzo Dow, *Works: Providential Experience of Lorenzo Dow in Europe and America* (3rd edn., Dublin, 1806).

[14] D. M. Valenze, *Prophetic Sons and Daughters* (Princeton, 1985) and W. R. Ward, *Religion and*

It is difficult to recapture the sheer colourfulness, eccentricity, and crackling energy of Ouseley's forty years as a missionary preacher in Ireland. He sang and preached, mostly in Irish, to large gatherings of people at county assizes, fairs, market days, funerals, and wakes, in prisons and outside church services, to early morning gatherings of labourers, and to travellers by the roadside. For almost half a century his life was a picaresque tale of daily adventures and narrow escapes, described by his distinguished brother Sir Ralph Ouseley as a futile assortment of wild-goose chases.[15] His preaching was unashamedly emotional and often produced disturbing scenes of physical and psychological excesses; but he had also an impish sense of humour and enjoyed a genial rapport with his audiences. If spiritually intense he was also worldly wise. He rang bells to announce his presence, stood in front of apothecaries' windows to deter missiles, used simple agrarian illustrations to engage his hearers, and often began with distinctively Catholic emphases before giving them a con-cluding evangelical twist.[16] Educated Catholics thought this was devious, but Ouseley considered it to be a justifiable form of Arminian pragmat-ism. Above all Ouseley believed in *means* as well as ends and had a lifelong dislike of a passive and providential Calvinism.[17]

Although he was occasionally victim of both episcopal prosecutions and mobs encouraged by the Established and Catholic clergy, Ouseley was not unduly restricted from itinerant preaching.[18] But in order to obtain the minimum protection from the authorities Ouseley, with regret, had to take the oaths of allegiance and abjuration and register as a dissenting preacher. Even then the cry that there was no law for the Methodists was common, at least up until 1812 when the new Methodist inspired Tolera-tion Act afforded greater protection in theory if not always in practice. Indeed Butterworth explained in meticulous detail how Ouseley might benefit from the new Act if he took proper precautions.

> It is perhaps material for you to know that we had the word 'place' introduced into the Act, instead of 'Meeting House' or 'Chapel', on

---

Society in England 1790-1850 (London, 1972), pp. 45-53. Ouseley approved of English Ranters and female preaching; see Ouseley Coll., XVII fols 9-10.

[15] Arthur, *Life of Ouseley*, p. 278.

[16] Ouseley Coll., XXVIII fols 7, 18-21, and 27-9.

[17] *Ibid.*, XXI fol. 21; XXVIII fol. 13. Gideon Ouseley, *Calvinism-Arminianism. God's word and Attributes in Harmony, being an Affectionate Attempt to Promote Union among Christians* (Dublin, 1830).

[18] Ouseley Coll., VIII fols 1 and 22-3; IX fol. 4; XVIII fols 9-14; XIX fol. 2.

purpose to protect our congregations in the *Open Air*, as well as within Doors; and wherever the Priests are troublesome by all means get the consent in writing of some occupier of a Field to hold meetings there . . . I would do all this quietly, say nothing about it, but if any priest should disturb you after you have certified the place you can punish him.[19]

When not restricted by the law, mobs, or other churchmen, Ouseley displayed all the skills of the natural outdoor orator in attracting and holding crowds. One-eyed, barrel-chested, and with a liberal dose of native humour Ouseley cut an extraordinary figure in the troubled landscape of post-rebellion Ireland. His early reports for Dr Coke, the director of the Irish mission, capture the flavour of dread and excitement.

On Monday we came to Baillieborough. The market-people were assembled when we came into the street. We did not alight, but prepared to attack the devil's kingdom which still remained strong in this town. The Methodists wished us out of the street, when they saw the manner of our proceedings, riding on our horses, with our umbrellas over our heads, the day being wet, but a young girl was so alarmed that she feared the day of judgment was at hand.[20]

We have preached two market-days and one Sabbath in the streets of Ballyshannon to vast congregations, who heard with the greatest attentions. We met with no opposition; the rich and learned seemed astonished, standing at a distance, and hearing us denounce the judgments of heaven against the crimes of a guilty nation.[21]

Ouseley's view of the Irish peasantry, who made up the bulk of his audiences, was that they adhered to a deeply pagan and superstitious form of religion upon which was grafted a veneer of Roman Catholicism that was itself superstitious and irrational. The Roman Catholic priests were therefore, in his opinion, the beneficiaries of ignorance which they had a vested interest to maintain. Likewise, poor Protestants, because of the failings of the episcopal clergy, availed themselves of Catholicized quasi-magical pratices to ward off death, demons, fairies, and banshees.[22]

---

[19] *Ibid.*, XXVI fols 4–5.
[20] *Ibid.*, VII fol. 10.
[21] *Ibid.*, VII fol. 12.
[22] *Ibid.*, XI fol. 23; XII fols 16–17; XX fol. 19.

Predictably perhaps there was a tension in his mind about the validity of supernatural occurrences. He employed a remorseless Lockean empiricism to refute Romish miracles,[23] but was quite happy to accept Methodist dreams, visions, signs, and exotic spiritual manifestations. Looked at another way this mixture of rationalism and romanticism is at the heart of Ouseley's personality, and indeed of much late eighteenth-century evangelicalism.[24] Ouseley's response to rural ignorance was to put his faith in itinerant preaching, bible and tract distribution, and elementary education. All three necessitated a strong commitment to the Irish language, predominantly but not exclusively as a vehicle for proselytism,[25] substantial support from the London-based evangelical societies, and an attitude of passive acceptance from the Roman Catholic Church and its lay representatives. The first two were more easily secured than the last.

One reason for Catholic unease was the remarkable success of the Methodist Irish-speaking missionaries in the early years of the nineteenth century, particularly in southern and south-western Ulster where numbers in Methodist societies doubled in the period 1799–1802.[26] Growth on this scale was not matched until 1819 when Ouseley was once again at the centre of revivalistic excitement in Wicklow and Carlow.[27] It now seems probable that, notwithstanding Ouseley's intention to evangelize native Roman Catholics, his greatest successes were achieved in old English settlements and among displaced Protestant minorities from Britain and Europe. Despite its original intentions, therefore, Methodism's conversionist theology introduced an element of competition into the Irish religious scene which inevitably led to deteriorating relations with the Roman Catholic Church. To an unfortunate degree the ensuing conflict dominated the second half of Ouseley's life.

Ouseley's anti-Catholicism predated his evangelical conversion and was part of a wider anticlericalism. He drew a distinction between priests and educated Catholics, who were in a position to know better, and the ordinary people, whom he regarded as victims of priestly tyranny and

---

[23] Ouseley Coll., XXVII fols 33–4. See also IX fol. 20.
[24] Roger Anstey, *The Atlantic Slave Trade and British Abolition 1760–1810* (New Jersey, 1975), pp. 157–83.
[25] For an enlightening discussion of Methodist attitudes towards the Irish language see Ouseley Coll., XI fols 18–22 and NIPRO, Irish Wesley Historical Society MS, Adam Clarke to Gideon Ouseley, 6 December 1806, in which Clarke stated that he was not 'willing that an ancient and dignified language should be lost'.
[26] See my 'Methodism in Irish Society, 1770–1830', *TRHS* 5, series 36 (1986), pp. 117–42.
[27] Arthur, *Life of Ouseley*, pp. 217–18.

unsupportable financial exactions. He thought of the Roman Church as an imperialistic force reaching out into the British Isles, North America, and the wider world; but Ireland was the battle front and the priests were his particular enemies. His experiences confirmed his prejudices. He alleged that priests incited crowds against him, burned his tracts, warned their flocks against hearing him, used public humiliation, whips, and penances if they disobeyed, offered bribes to reclaim converts and threatened eternal damnation to the recalcitrant, and systematically eroded the material, educational, and moral well-being of the Irish people.[28] To his surprise he got on well with some individual priests, but he had a particular dislike of those trained at Maynooth and stationed in Munster.[29]

Ouseley, it is clear, did not much like the Catholic Church, but his anti-Catholicism is rather more complicated than one might suppose. There are, for example, quite distinguishable phases in the development of Ouseley's anti-Catholic opinions. Between 1799 and 1807 Ouseley and his missionary colleagues experienced a number of unpleasant incidents at the hands of Irish priests but these were generally shrugged off as one of the hazards, even blessings, of missionary endeavour. Three circumstances combined to produce a more hostile climate. The first was Dr Coke's request for accurate numbers of Roman Catholic converts, presumably to stimulate fund raising for the Irish mission in England.[30] The published figures were sufficiently large to engage Catholic attention. Secondly, the reports of the Irish missionaries were reproduced in the connexional magazine and even taken direct to the secretive Committee of Privileges by Butterworth himself, with the result that both English and Irish Methodists began to ascribe a significance to the Irish mission quite disproportionate to its actual size and impact.[31] Thirdly, after a period of acute opposition from priests, Ouseley wrote a series of letters to Dr Bellew, the Roman Catholic bishop of Killala, detailing names, dates, and places of anti-Methodist persecutions.[32] Bellew's response was that since the Methodist missionaries were neither ordained nor specifically legitimized by the civil authorities then they could scarcely expect protection from a Roman Catholic bishop. As a bishop of a Church emerging from a century of penal laws, albeit loosely enforced, Bellew had no desire to clear the paths for itinerant zealots. After 1807, therefore, Ouseley was much

---

[28] Ouseley Coll., XXVIII fols 9–11.
[29] *Ibid.*, XI fol. 2 and Arthur, *Life of Ouseley*, p. 175.
[30] Ouseley Coll., XXVIII fol. 9.
[31] Hempton, 'Methodist Crusade', pp. 33–47.
[32] Ouseley Coll., XII fols 30–5.

more willing to engage in public controversies against Catholics. The thrust of his attacks also changed. Whereas earlier he had been more concerned with the social consequences of Catholic errors than with the errors themselves, after 1807 he unleashed a prolific pamphlet attack on Catholic dogma which was continued until his death.[33] The fact that Ouseley only had time to write when he was ill scarcely helped the tone of his works, which have been well described by his biographer as being full of 'home-thrusts, clever illustrations, and absurd dilemmas'.[34]

As is well known the 1820s ushered in a more aggressive era of religious conflict in Ireland with the formation of the Catholic Association on one side and the intensification of Protestant proselytism on the other.[35] Apart from his undiminished commitment to preaching Ouseley spent much of the decade publishing his own highly individualistic solution to Ireland's miseries. In a letter to the *Sligo Journal* in 1823,[36] the substance of which was reproduced in letters to Butterworth and Wellington, he complained of the unacceptable financial pressures on the Irish Catholic poor. With trade depressed and unemployment high they were nevertheless required to pay rents, tithes, church and county cess, and, indirectly, the Presbyterian Regium Donum before they could begin to meet the demands of their own Church and clergy. His remedies were more responsible land-lordism, a more equitable and rational assessment of tithes, the state payment of Roman Catholic priests without asking for a veto or any other security,[37] and an electoral register based on minimum educational standards to ensure that landlords would have to provide schools for their freeholders. Ouseley expected these proposals to loosen the bonds

---

[33] Gideon Ouseley, *The Substance of a Letter to the Rev Mr Fitzsimmons, Roman Catholic Priest on some Chief Pillars or Principal Articles of his Faith* (Glasgow, 1815); *Five Letters in reply to the Rev Michael Branaghan PP* (Dublin, 1824); *Error Unmasked. Priest Walsh's Attack on Protestantism and its clergy defeated, his Professions proved vain, and his faith deeply erroneous* (Dublin, 1828); and *A Review of a Sermon preached by Dr Peter A Baynes, Roman Catholic Bishop, at the opening of the R. Catholic Chapel, in Bradford, Yorkshire* (Dublin, 1829).

[34] Arthur, *Life of Ouseley*, p. 200.

[35] The best accounts of this important decade of religious conflict, though different in emphasis, are Desmond Bowen, *The Protestant Crusade in Ireland 1800–1870* (Dublin, 1978), I. M. Hehir, 'New Lights and Old Enemies: The Second Reformation and the Catholics of Ireland, 1800–1835' (MA thesis, University of Wisconsin, 1983), and Myrtle Hill, 'Evangelicalism and the Churches in Ulster Society, 1770–1850' (Ph.D. thesis, Queen's University, Belfast, 1987).

[36] *Sligo Journal*, 21 May 1823.

[37] Ouseley's views on this subsequently hardened as a result of the national education controversies and disillusionment with Maynooth College. In *A Dreadful Conspiracy* (1837) he stated 'what does the experience of more than forty years of Maynooth College teach? What gratitude to a Protestant Government that has hitherto been annually expending thousands of pounds in supporting it, has ever appeared?'

between Catholic priests and their flocks and to strengthen those between good landlords and their tenants. Agrarian grievances would thus disappear and the population would be delivered from Romish ignorance into truth, knowledge, equity, industry, and prosperity, all of which were linked in Ouseley's mind. Indeed there is much populist enlightenment rhetoric underpinning his more detailed proposals.

Ouseley's views were unpopular even among his friends, for few evangelicals could accept that bad means—the state payment of Catholic clergy—could ever produce a good end. If Ouseley's political views were unpopular his reputation as a second Saint Patrick in his zeal to convert pagan Ireland never stood higher. For the first quarter of a century of his itinerant labours he had been disliked by most of the Catholic clergy, the vast majority of episcopalian and Presbyterian clergy, and by a powerful group of preachers within his own connexion. He had been an embarrassment to most Protestant landlords and had posed difficult problems for the civil magistrates. But by the late 1820s he was defended by the Protestant press in Ireland, patronized by the evangelical aristocracy, on agreeable terms with the most influential Protestant clergy, and the recipient of more invitations from Britain and North America than he could ever hope to fulfil. As with Wesley before him he found that the religious world, or at least a section of it, had a soft spot for ageing evangelists.

Ouseley toured the north of England in 1828 under the auspices of the Wesleyan Methodist Missionary Society (the invitation came from Jabez Bunting) and as with his previous visit in 1818 he attracted large congregations and seemed to be particularly influential in reviving the faith and the anti-Catholicism of Irish Protestant migrants.[38] More generally he was disappointed with the level of awareness about Ireland and the Catholic question in English cities only a year before the passage of the Catholic Emancipation Act. He informed Bonsall in April 1828 that 'the Protestants this side of the water are filled with apathy about popery, as if the case were *hopeless*, or that it is not worthy of notice. The latter is it.'[39] What surprised him even more, however, was the sheer weakness of Methodism in London. Ouseley had taken orders from Methodist missionary headquarters in London for a third of a century and was perplexed to find in 1836 that there were only 20 Methodists among the 16,000 inhabitants of Wandsworth.[40] By the late 1830s Methodism was in fact

[38] Ouseley Coll., XX fols 19–21; XXI fols 7–9.
[39] *Ibid.*, XX fol. 20. Ouseley returned to England in 1836 and was much more impressed with the general public knowledge of Irish affairs.
[40] *Ibid.*, XXIII fols 14–15.

stronger in the frontier zone of southern Ulster than it was in the capital city of the Empire where it had originated a century before. Indeed it is a feature of the Ouseley papers that the evangelical grass always seemed to be greener somewhere else—in the East, on the North American frontier, or wherever—as tales of missionary expansion were circulated to keep up morale and generate funds.[41]

Ouseley's own substantial contribution to mission came to an end in 1839. Right up to his death he still preached as often as he could and still urged the Methodist Missionary Society to send out more Irish-speaking evangelists to confront 'the religion of Rome'—

> some of the professed tenets of which are exquisite, pure, and apostolic, and essentially sound Protestantism; but its practical doctrines, framed by men of great parts, and by Councils, in order to uphold the glory of the Papacy, and support of its numerous clergy, are the very reverse, and are with all diligence passed on to the credulous for divine mysteries of faith. . . . Thus are the poor, unsuspecting people taught darkness for light, and are deceived and ruined. . . . Thus is our country filled with anarchy and untold mischiefs.[42]

Apart from his remarkable contribution to the establishment of Methodism in Ireland, Ouseley is of particular interest to the historian not only because his life is unusually well documented for such a humble figure, but also because of his highly individualistic style. Defying easy categorization, he is an interstitial character, operating in the crevices of Irish society in the half century after the French Revolution. As a result his life is full of ambiguities, ironies, and paradoxes. He was a member of an English family of small landowners and military prowess, yet he was domiciled in a remote part of western Ireland among a diminishing handful of minor Protestant gentry surrounded by an overwhelmingly Catholic populace. Ouseley was the son of a pious mother and a free-thinking, anticlerical father and both influences can be detected in him. He had access to English reformation and Puritan classics, yet he was Irish-speaking and priest educated. He was a defender of the Union between Britain and Ireland, of the Protestant landed interest, and of the Church of Ireland, yet his sympathies were generally with the victims of such arrangements. But for his profound hatred of Roman Catholicism,

---

[41] Ouseley Coll., XII fol. 36. Ouseley was told that over 3,000 people had been converted at an American camp meeting.
[42] Arthur, *Life of Ouseley*, pp. 282–3.

Ouseley could easily have become a religious and political radical after the fashion of Joseph Rayner Stephens. His basic instincts were almost always populist, yet he spent his life trying to overturn the religion of the people and was rewarded with the approval of evangelical Anglo-Irish aristocrats such as Lord Farnham, the earl of Roden, and the Mountcashels.[43]

Ouseley's religious allegiances were similarly complicated. On the whole he disliked clergy and religious institutions, even of the Methodist variety. He was stoutly evangelical but intensely anti-Calvinist at a time when most Irish evangelicals were Calvinists. As a result he was never fully at home in the missionary projects of the so-called Second Reformation movement in Achill and Kingscourt, yet he was enthusiastic about the numbers of converts.[44] At the same time as his relations with the Irish Methodist elite deteriorated (to the extent that he was scarcely on speaking terms with any of the regular preachers in the last decade of his life) he became a *cause célèbre* in Britain and North America. He was a rugged individualist, a kind of religious gunfighter with his Bible in his hand and popery as the enemy. His portrait was published in the *Methodist Magazine* in 1828 and he received invitations from all over the world to preach to Irish Catholic migrants.[45] As with many such figures his reputation came to be admired more than the real person.

At the heart of Ouseley's personality and life's work is a sincere religious faith which was forged in the white heat of a traumatic and unforgettable religious conversion, and a genuine compassion for his country and his countrymen. Although persuaded that the root of Ireland's misery was religious, he was too close to the ground not to see that economic problems were just as serious. In fact much of his thinking was dominated by attempts to harmonize these apparent irreconcilables—hence the idea to pay Roman Catholic priests without preconditions. Unusually for a man of his evangelical intensity, he could see that human problems were not all caused by 'wilful wickedness', but could be the product of circumstances outside the individual's control. In a sense Ouseley too was a victim of circumstances beyond his control. He started his missionary campaign as an independent spirit, as critical of the Anglican Ascendancy as he was of the Roman Catholic Church, but after half a century of turbulent Irish history and unremitting conflict between evangelical Protestantism and a resurgent Irish Catholicism Ouseley joined the

---

[43] Ouseley Coll., XVIII fol. 7; XX fols 3 and 8–9; XXIII fol. 20; XXVIII fol. 12.
[44] *Ibid.*, XXII fols 14–17.
[45] *Ibid.*, XXVI fol. 6.

Orange Order and was warmly welcomed by the interests he had once challenged. Yet it would be to demean Ouseley's status as one of Ireland's most influential religious figures—and in however curious a way one of its best—in the post-rebellion era not to conclude that he helped initiate a new era of religious competition the legacy of which still survives in modern Ulster.

Queen's University, Belfast

EVANGELICAL CROSS-CURRENTS IN THE
CHURCH OF IRELAND, 1820-1833

by T. C. F. STUNT

IT is a commonplace to observe that the life of the Anglo-Irish community was profoundly altered by the Act of Union in 1800, but this
was particularly true in its ecclesiastical effects. Whereas in the eighteenth century the antipathy between Protestant and Roman Catholic
had diminished and even as late as 1824 the possibility of a union of the
Church of Ireland with the Roman Church was seriously being discussed
by older churchmen,[1] the effect of the Act of Union was to isolate the
Anglo-Irish. Reluctantly they had accepted the Act and now, dependent
upon it for their survival, many of them took refuge in a 'garrison mentality' which invested their ascendancy with almost sacred connotations by
which their community was transformed into a 'faithful remnant' with a
mission to bring light and truth to Ireland.

However, this sacred task was very different from the civilizing mission
of the worldly enlightenment of eighteenth-century Dublin, where the
Church seemed to have been reduced to a mere adjunct of the city's
cultural life—a situation well exemplified in the elegant buildings of
Trinity College where the chapel is externally indistinguishable from the
theatre. In contrast, any Anglo-Irish sense of mission in the early
nineteenth century appears to be predominantly a religious one and this
reflects a society on the defensive.

In spite of this growing isolation, however, there were elements contributing to spiritual renewal in the Irish Church. The Act of Union itself
had, in certain respects, inaugurated what Akenson calls 'the era of grace-
ful reform'.[2] The growing influence of evangelical clergy like Peter Roe of
Kilkenny and B. W. Mathias in Dublin was beginning to have some
impact on parish life.[3] On the other hand, the revival of an older school of
exact churchmanship emphasizing 'the quietism of contemplative devotion' and shunning the 'busy benevolence' so beloved of much evangelical

---

[1] Desmond Bowen, *The Protestant Crusade in Ireland, 1800-70* (Dublin, 1978), p. 10.
[2] Donald Harman Akenson, *The Church of Ireland: Ecclesiastical Reform and Revolution, 1800-1885*
(New Haven, 1971), pp. 79, 121 *seq.*
[3] W. D. Killen, *Ecclesiastical History of Ireland*, 2 vols (London, 1875), 2, p. 417.

piety, was also an important contributor to the increased seriousness of attitude in the life of the Church.[4]

A line of demarcation between evangelicals and exact churchmen is difficult to draw as there was more interaction btween them than one might have expected. Some evangelicals in the 1820s were beginning to take their churchmanship more seriously, while on the other side many a churchman was feeling his way cautiously towards identifying himself with evangelical concerns. Thus, George Bellett who was later anxious to keep 'a distinct line between Church and Dissent, doubting whether the means used by the Bible Society were justifiable',[5] was a member of the Society when a curate at Bandon in the 1820s and 'at that time highly esteemed' the evangelical rector of Powerscourt, Robert Daly.[6] More striking than the comparatively familiar progress from evangelical to churchman, is the passage in the other direction of a man like Henry Woodward, rector of Fethard.

In his earlier years Woodward was associated with some serious minded churchmen gathered round Archbishop Brodrick, among whom were John Jebb, the brothers Charles and James Forster, and Christopher Lovett Darby.

> [With] these good men . . . upon the subject of atonement there was somewhat of reserve. It was not denied—it was held as a part of catholic truth: it was occasionally preached, but it was not prominently put forward. From this and other causes, there had grown up in our diocese a kind of jealousy of, or rather a disposition to preserve a cautious distance from, what had begun for some time to be called the Evangelical clergy.[7]

It was only in the 1820s that Woodward began to make common cause with the evangelicals. 'Why not put up my tiny sail and catch some portion of the heavenly breeze which was blowing so strongly in their favour? . . . I joined some of the Societies in which they bore so large a share.'[8] Not all his fellow churchmen could be so enthusiastic. Jebb when writing to

[4] Mrs Hamilton Madden, *Memoir of the late Right Rev. Robert Daly, Lord Bishop of Cashel* (London, 1875), p. 34; R. S. Brooke, *Recollections of the Irish Church*, 2 vols (London, 1877), 2, p. 73.

[5] *Memoir of the Rev. George Bellett*, autobiography and continuation by his daughter (London, 1889), p. 141.

[6] *Ibid.*, pp. 78, 28.

[7] Henry Woodward, *Essays, Thoughts and Reflections and Letters*, ed. Thomas Woodward (London, 1864), p. 451.

[8] *Ibid.*, p. 457.

Peter Roe in 1809 had hoped that 'in grand essentials . . . we are agreed', and that they would not 'interfere or clash with one another', but had earlier complained strongly that Roe's piety and zeal were insufficiently conformed to the discipline of the Establishment.[9]

In fact it was a clergyman's attitude to the interdenominational societies which was becoming the acid test of the extent of his identification with the evangelical movement. Thus Thomas Kelly, who had seceded earlier because his archbishop had forbidden him to preach as he wished, wrote in 1822 that 'in the present day, attachment to the Bible Society cause goes a long way to decide the character of the individual'.[10] This was to become still more the case as other such societies proliferated during the decade.

But although involvement with ventures unsponsored by the Church was an important shibboleth in assessing a man's churchmanship, there was another equally important division though it was one of temperament rather than principle. When the flamboyant William Magee, newly appointed as archbishop of Dublin, attacked Catholics and Dissenters alike in his charge of 1822 he was inaugurating an era of pamphlet warfare and public debate.[11] This was, however, by no means the universal evangelical style. In contrast the instructions of the Scripture Readers' Society, which was formed in the same year, were most emphatic that there was to be no preaching and the readers were to 'avoid giving offence by harsh or unkind attacks upon the errors of those with whom you have to do'.[12]

This gentler variety of evangelicalism was by definition less obtrusive but very influential, especially in its pattern of domestic piety. Frances Power Cobbe looked back affectionately to 'the mild, devout, philanthropic' atmosphere in which she had grown up. Her childhood in Ireland had been 'much the same as it is physically to live in a room full of sunlight'.[13] J. A. Froude's thoughts were imilar when recalling the household of the rector of Delgany, William Cleaver, in whose home he had encountered 'a beautiful principle of unobtrusive piety'.[14] However this less

---

[9] Samuel Madden, *Memoir of the Life of the Late Rev. Peter Roe* (Dublin, 1842), pp. 180–1.

[10] Thomas Kelly to Mrs H. Crofton, 3 Oct. 1822, Dublin, National Library, Microfilm P.2936. For Kelly, see H. H. Rowdon, 'Secession from the Established Church in the Early Nineteenth Century', *Vox Evangelica*, 3 (1964), p. 78.

[11] William Magee, *Charge delivered at his Primary Visitation 24 Oct. 1822* (Dublin, 1822), p. 22.

[12] *The Warder*, 17 Feb. 1827 where the aims and constitution of the resuscitated society were published in full.

[13] *The Life of Frances Power Cobbe* by herself, 2 vols (London, 1894), I, pp. 81, 83.

[14] Waldo Hillary Dunne, *James Anthony Froude: A Biography*, 2 vols (Oxford, 1961), I, pp. 65–6. Compare this with F. W. Newman's favourable impression of Susan Pennefather [J. N.

strident form of evangelicalism was peculiarly typical of 'the special case of nineteenth-century Wicklow' where the 'siege mentality' was less acute.[15] Here, where Protestants were more numerous, the rector of Powerscourt, Robert Daly, could be uncompromisingly Protestant without at this stage being too aggressively anti-Catholic. Nevertheless even then his directness in controversy caused him to be likened to Luther while his less rigorous fellow churchmen, William Cleaver and Henry Irwin of Sandford Chapel, were seen as Melanchthons.[16]

After 1828 and the passing of Catholic Emancipation, the lines would be drawn more distinctly but in the early 1820s loyalties were more fluid. Lord Roden, later noted for his fierce anti-Catholicism, wrote surprisingly mildly in 1821 about the even more conciliatory Earl of Gosford who

> got into a serious scrape with all his friends on the subject of the Catholic Question. They say he is a dreadful *Trimmer*. I fought his battles as well as I could but I fear I have not much to say in his favour on this score—I wish I had.[17]

In 1826 it was the hope of Bishop Jebb that the 'violence on the part of some of the Bible Society' would lead to a 'coalition between the sane and safe part of the Bible Society and that for promoting Christian Knowledge', and he noted in passing that 'gymno-biblism is less in fashion'.[18] However, the political agitation of 1827 added a new dimension to the so-called 'Irish Reformation'. Whereas the meetings of the Reformation Societies had been very much the preserve of enthusiastic evangelicals, the anti-Catholic tone was becoming increasingly political. Even Robert Daly felt the need to write to the *Christian Examiner* to complain that people were 'coming forward to join the ranks of the Reformation who were never known to show any interest in spiritual objects before'. Ironically it was the high-churchman Alexander Knox who replied, maintaining that Daly's charges about political protestantism were unfounded and denying that the supporters of the Reformation Societies were 'unspiritual'.[19]

Darby's sister] and her family (wrongly assumed to be the Parnell family) in William Robbins, *The Newman Brothers* (London, 1966), p. 32.

[15] R. F. Foster, *Charles Stewart Parnell: The Man and His Family* (Hassocks, 1976), pp. xiii *seq.*

[16] *Memoir of Daly*, p. 146; *Remains of the Venerable Henry Irwin, Archdeacon of Emly and Chaplain of Sandford, Dublin*, ed. W. Pakenham Walsh (Dublin, 1858), pp. xxv, xxvii.

[17] Earl of Roden to Millicent Sparrow, 5 May 1821, Huntingdon, County Record Office, Manchester Papers, M 10A/10/3.

[18] *Thirty Years Correspondence between John Jebb, Bishop of Limerick and Alexander Knox Esq.*, ed. Charles Foster, 2 vols (London, 1836), 2, p. 245.

[19] *Christian Examiner*, 5 (Nov. 1827), p. 344; 6 (Jan. 1828), pp. 39, 103-4.

In fact the issue of Catholic Emancipation spelt the end of the era of co-operation and within two years many high churchmen seem to have washed their hands altogether of the evangelicals, claiming that in their desire to convert Roman Catholics they were ready to sacrifice the establishment. Writing to his brother, James Forster put 'the matter in somewhat lurid terms:

> The fact is, a deep laid conspiracy exists against the Church. Opposite parties, each for their respective purposes, are joined in the plot. And papists and puritans, infidels and traitors are, each in their turn fooling and fooled by their strange associates. . . . Hence it is that in the present awful crisis the ruling cant of conciliation, the pusillanimous complaisance which fears to look people in the face, have done more to sap the foundation of our ecclesiastical and civil polity than the undisguised hostility of our fiercest foes could ever have accomplished.[20]

The period before this rupture is fascinating precisely because of the kaleidoscopic interaction of these varieties of churchmanship. It was perhaps this co-operation between churchmen who at other times had little to do with each other that enabled the Establishment to contain for a while a number of uneasy evangelicals who were later, when loyalties were more clearly defined, almost inevitably to find that the logical outcome of their yearnings was secession.

According to one late nineteenth-century Irish writer, 'drawing room meetings for prayer and study of the Scriptures were then [in the 1820s] quite the rage with all serious minds',[21] and certainly this was the conclusion of the Quaker J. J. Gurney in early 1827 when visiting the home of the lawyer John Henry North. After dinner there was a sermon and 'forthwith the company dropped to their knees. . . . This description will give you some idea of the state of society in Dublin. I should imagine that these Bible readings are extensively supplanting cards and other such amusements.'[22] In addition to such occasions of domestic devotion there were more formal meetings which, following the Moravian ideal, were by no means entirely separate from the Establishment. William Russell, grandfather of the Crimean War journalist, was responsible for one of these

[20] J. W. Forster to Charles Forster, 25 Mar. 1829, Dublin, Trinity College, MS 6392, letter 10.
[21] G. T. Stokes, cited in W. B. Neatby, *A History of the Plymouth Brethren* (London, 1902), p. 6.
[22] *Memoirs of Joseph John Gurney*, ed. Joseph Bevan Braithwaite, 2 vols (Norwich, 1855), I, pp. 326–7.

communities together with Thomas Parnell, an evangelist famed for his tract distribution.[23] A similar group gathered round the striking personality of Richard Pope who had given up his position as an ordained minister, though later he was to resume it and was connected with a 'little company' in Poolbeg Street.[24] It was here in 1828 that A. N. Groves, later a Brethren missionary to Persia, was invited to preach when visiting Dublin shortly after giving up his studies at Trinity.[25]

In fact students from Trinity College were a significant element in such gatherings. Some of them attended meetings in the rooms of Fellows like Dr Joseph Singer and James Thomas O'Brien, whose Calvinist tendencies caused some anxiety to more exact churchmen.[26] Others were attracted to 'the more intimate and intense Christian fellowship' of the Bethesda Chapel where at one stage they were forbidden by their Provost to attend because of the 'Methodist' tendencies of its minister B. W. Mathias.[27] Described in The Warder as 'the sine qua non of the Bible Society—the popular pet preacher of Dublin—the man of the Christian people who worked evangelical preaching out of evil report into good report',[28] Mathias enjoyed the freedom of a proprietary chapel which allowed him to sit lightly to the traditional forms of the establishment without separating from it.

It was from these various expressions of piety, more or less loosely connected with the Establishment, that a new form of dissent was to emerge. Dr Harold Rowdon in his analysis of the Irish origins of the misnamed Plymouth Brethren, located at least three other such groups meeting in the Dublin area some of whose members were to form the nucleus of the Brethren Assembly at Aungier Street in 1830.[29] Only one of these groups had any significant dissenting element and such Plymouth Brethren leaders as J. G. Bellett, J. V. Parnell (later Lord Congleton), and William Stokes, together with A. N. Groves, were all laymen whom the Church of Ireland managed to contain in the 1820s but eventually lost. Seceding

[23] J. B. Atkins, Life of Sir William Howard Russell, 2 vols (London, 1911), 1, pp. 6–7. 'Tract' Parnell was the elder brother of C. S. Parnell's grandfather.

[24] Brooke, Recollections, 2, p. 23; see also J. J. Gurney to Joseph Gurney, 28 Feb. 1827, London, Friends' House Library, Gurney MSS 3, letter 453.

[25] Interesting Reminiscences of the Early History of the Brethren [by J. G. Bellett and others] (no date or place), p. 4.

[26] Bowen, pp. 67–8, 76–7. For anxieties about Singer and O'Brien see C. R. Elrington to Archbishop Beresford, 27 Jan. 1834, Dublin, Trinity College, Beresford Papers 112.

[27] Bowen, pp. 69, 68.

[28] The Warder, supplement July 1825, no pagination.

[29] Harold H. Rowdon, The Origins of the Brethren (London, 1967), pp. 37–47.

clergy took rather longer to decide, and this was often under the influence of J. N. Darby who for this reason was described as the 'Goliath of Dissent' though, ironically, he was one of the last to make a complete break with the Establishment.[30] A solitary individual, John Synge, the Pestalozzian educationist, remained closely associated with the seceders but still attended the Established Church and in doing so continued to pursue the comprehensive ideal of the 1820s.[31] For the many others who had seceded the 'siege mentality' of the Anglo-Irish was fast becoming a 'remnant theology'.

Stowe School, Buckingham

---

[30] Joseph D'Arcy Sirr, *A Memoir of the Honourable and Most Reverend Power Le Poer Trench, last Archbishop of Tuam* (Dublin, 1845), p. 344. See *passim*, pp. 219-20, 332-6, 343-4, 420-2. See also Rowdon, *Origins*, pp. 99-104.

[31] For the unusual career of Synge see T. C. F. Stunt, 'John Synge and the Early Brethren', *Christian Brethren Research Fellowship Journal*, 28 (1976), pp. 39-62.

JAMES MARTINEAU AND THE CATHOLIC SPIRIT AMID THE TENSIONS OF DUBLIN, 1828–1832

by RALPH WALLER

JAMES Martineau is generally known as a Unitarian divine, who in the years which followed the publication of *Origin of Species* (1859) brought his massive intellect to the defence of Christianity, especially in his debates with Henry Spencer, Professor John Tyndall, and Henry Sidgwick. What is less well-known about Martineau is that in 1828 at the age of twenty-three he began his ministry in Dublin at Eustace Street Presbyterian Meeting House. Through his 'Biographical Memoranda', a sermon preached before the Synod of Munster, and his hymn book, *A Collection of Hymns for Christian Worship* which he compiled for the Dublin congregation, we are given a glimpse of his view of Irish Christianity and see in them a reflection of his strong catholic spirit, which was confirmed and strengthened by his Dublin experience.

Martineau had been subjected to broad catholic influences long before he arrived in Ireland. He was born in Norwich in 1805 and brought up in an educated middle-class family whose social life was centred on the Octagon Chapel, dedicated to non-sectarian Christianity by Dr John Taylor some fifty years before Martineau was born. As an old man of ninety-two Martineau quoted with approval Taylor's opening address:

> We are Christians and only Christians, and we consider all our fellow Protestants in the same light, only as Christians, and cordially embrace them all in affection and charity as such. Whatever peculiar tenets they may hold, and in what respects soever they may differ from us, such tenets and such differences we consider not as affecting their Christian character and profession in general. This chapel we have erected and here we intend to worship the living and true God, through one mediator Jesus Christ; not in opposition to, but in perfect peace and harmony with all our fellow Protestants.[1]

This inclusive influence of his early childhood stayed with him for the rest of his life.

---

[1] Manuscript letter from James Martineau to the Revd V. D. Davis, 5 March 1897; Manchester College Library, Oxford.

On leaving Norwich, Martineau enrolled as a pupil at Dr Lant Carpenter's school in Bristol. Carpenter was a man of immense energy and wide interests and as such was a fine school teacher. He had a broad sympathy with those holding religious opinions at variance with his own[2] and to some extent the young Martineau inherited these views. Martineau's two years at Bristol were followed, after a short break with an engineering company in Derby, by five years at Manchester New College, then established in York. And here again Martineau's ecclesiastical sympathies were broadened by tutors who had kept in close contact with the wider Church, both in Scotland and on the Continent; John Kenrick for example had studied with Schleiermacher as early as 1818.[3]

In the summer of 1828 Martineau moved to Dublin to take up his new appointment at Eustace Street Presbyterian Meeting House, as the junior colleague of the Revd Joseph Hutton (grandfather of Richard Holt Hutton, who became one of Martineau's pupils and a close friend, and for many years was the editor of *The Spectator*). In the December of that year Martineau married Helen Higginson of Derby and settled down to his teaching and ministerial work in the hope of a long and fruitful stay in Dublin. He purchased the lease on a large house which provided a home for himself and his wife, and six students, three of whom were studying at Trinity College, and the rest under Martineau's sole tutorage. The Martineaus found Dublin society both friendly and congenial:

> In all social relations, we met with nothing but the most gracious and effusive kindness, which set us entirely at ease and especially won the heart of my wife, and still charmed her when she had learned to allow a little for national manners.[4]

The church situation was not so encouraging and although Martineau had encountered no difficulty in forming a young people's class for systematic religious instruction, the Eustace Street congregation itself was 'very small', assembled only once each Sunday, and according to Martineau endeavoured 'to give both themselves and their ministers an easy time'.[5] But as Martineau found to his cost some members of the congregation were immediately awakened from their slumbers the moment questions of religious politics or doctrinal theology were raised, when the atmosphere

---

[2] Russell L. Carpenter, *Memoirs of the Life of the Rev. Lant Carpenter* (London, 1842), p. 245.
[3] *Letters of John James Taylor*, ed. J. H. Thom, 2 vols (London, 1872), *Ibid*. 1, p. 24.
[4] M. James Martineau, 'Biographical Memoranda'; Manchester College Library, Oxford.
[5] *Ibid.*

suddenly became sensitive and highly charged. A sermon given by Martineau which mildly criticized the Arian doctrine sadly lost one of the stalwarts of the small congregation, who immediately withdrew himself and his family to another place of worship within the city. He met a similar response when he and Joseph Hutton became actively involved in the campaign for Catholic emancipation:

> A signature which with my venerated colleague, I had attached to a petition for Catholic Emancipation, brought down an explosion of wrath from a blustering but not very lucid gentleman, who 'had been credibly informed that ministers should not meddle in politics', but who nevertheless thought it our duty to sign on the other side.[6]

Martineau was also shocked and horrified by the anti-Catholic feeling he found among many of the leading people in society; people who in all other respects were kind, courteous, and fair minded. The management of a small orphanage connected to the chapel provided one such example of this extreme attitude which so impressed itself upon Martineau's mind that forty years after leaving Dublin he could still recall it vividly.

> In an endowed school connected with the Meeting House, some 40 orphans were lodged, educated and qualified for apprenticeship; the vacancies being filled up by election in open vestry. The children, it was well known, were brought up Protestants. At one of the elections a boy of very winning appearance, brought by a well-mannered father (the mother was dead), excited a prevailing interest in the members present: but it was suggested that no enquiry had been made respecting the parents' religion. The man was recalled and questioned. The mother had been a Protestant. 'And you?' said the chairman. 'I'll not be desaiving your honour,' replied the father: 'the boy may follow his mother's road; but I am bound to be a Catholic.' 'Be gone this minute,' exclaimed the Chairman, with a loud stamp of his foot upon the floor; 'how dare you show your face here? We have nothing to do with you and yours.' On my trying to remonstrate, when the vestry resumed, he lifted his spectacles and looked at me transfixed, as a naturalist would look at a live Dodo: and although there were signs of some response to my protest, he had the meeting with him in treating it as an eccentricity and passing on to the 'qualified candidates'. Yet this Chairman, apart from his Toryism and

---

[6] *Ibid.*

Protestantism, was a most estimable gentleman; of much benevolence and high honour; courteous and considerate, and in great social request for positions of trust and influence. This vestry incident however cracked the ice of a prejudice which, by repeated blows, was gradually and completely broken up: and, even 'before my return to England, a totally different temper already prevailed.[7]

One of Martineau's gifts, which he exercised throughout his long life, was the ability to make relationships with those who held opinions which differed from his own. He always tried to restrict controversy to issues rather than personalities, and it is to his lasting credit that even in his debates with Professor Tyndall and Henry Sidgwick he remained on close and friendly terms with them both. Here in Ireland he was able to exercise that same gift, even though neither the blind conservatism of the loyalists nor the radicalism of the republicans attracted him, and in one sense he always thought of himself as an outside observer of their struggles. However he certainly had friends in what he called the 'Irish Party':

It was a curious experience to pass from the society of the very decorous, loyal, semi–Orange gentlemen of whom I have given a sample, to that of the old patriot and rebel, Hamilton Rowan and his heroic wife; at whose house the conversation, when it turned upon politics, recalled the brilliancy and audacity of the Paris salons in '89. The old man himself, not otherwise particularly impressive, had eyes of a tiger: and when he was in the mood to tell the story of his adventures, they seemed to kindle and perforate you like burning glasses. His force was not intellectual, but of passion and will. . . .[8]

The tensions Martineau found within Irish society caused him to preach, before the Synod of Munster in 1829, a sermon entitled 'Peace in Division: the Duties of a Christian in an Age of Controversy'. It emerged from his own bitter experience of religious division, and was a warning against the dangers of Christian controversy and an attempt to throw some light on the duties of the Christian in such circumstances. The sermon had three main points. First, he maintained that it was the duty of every Christian to remember all the points of belief he held in common with other Christians. Secondly, he reminded his hearers of the moral innocence of mental error, and advocated the view that if a person is genuinely mistaken in his

---

[7] 'Biographical Memoranda'.
[8] *Ibid.*

opinions he is not eternally banished from God. Thirdly, he asserted that it was the duty of every Christian in an age of controversy openly to state his opinions together with the evidence which satisfied him of their truth.[9] This sermon was his first publication, and to judge by the comments in the *Monthly Repository* of 1830 it was well received in England.

His other literary achievement in Dublin which also displayed his developing catholic spirit was the publication in 1831 of his first hymn book, *A Collection of Hymns for Christian Worship*. This book contained two hundred and seventy-three hymns, five of which were written by his sister, Harriet. Its chief interest lay in the fact that it represented a much wider spirituality than previous Unitarian or Non-subscribing Presbyterian hymn books. In fact Martineau stated in his preface that previous hymn books belonging to his tradition had largely confined themselves to hymns which were paraphrases or imitations of the Psalms.[10] In compiling this collection of hymns Martineau was emphasizing the importance of the imagination and affections in true worship. In accord with his catholic ideals he tried to make the book appeal to a wide variety of theological opinion, maintaining that it was designed for the use of a society whose worship is directed solely 'to the God and Father of our Lord Jesus Christ'.[11] Here Martineau started a practice which he also used in the production of his later hymn books, that of altering some of the authors' original lines; this was not done to emphasize a sectarian point but simply to make the hymns either more devotional or to improve their imagery, thus fulfilling the inscription upon his title page, 'Sing ye praises with understanding'.

The authors represented in the book included Addison, Cowper, Doddridge, Dryden, and Bishop Heber, of whose hymns Martineau said '[they] are the unfettered composition of a deeply moved soul,—the effusions of a transparent sincerity, which reveals the graces of a pure, tender and lofty mind'.[12] Martineau also drew from the classical hymns of Luther, Milton, and Newton. It is of interest to note that the Toplady hymn he included was not the well-known 'Rock of Ages' written in defence of his Calvinism, but the more catholic but less well-known hymn which was closer to Martineau's own spirituality:

> Let party names no more
> The Christian world o'erspread,

[9] James Martineau, *Studies of Christianity* (London, 1858), pp. 480–8.
[10] James Martineau, ed., *A Collection of Hymns for Christian Worship* (Dublin, 1831), p. v.
[11] *Ibid.*
[12] *Ibid.*

Gentile and Jew, and bond and free
Are one in Christ their head.

Envy and strife be gone,
And only kindness known,
Where all one common Father have,
One common Master own.[13]

Conspicuously absent from this book are the Wesley hymns, but in later life Martineau was deeply influenced by Wesley's catholicity and liberally included the hymns of Wesley in his later books. In writing to Susanna Winkworth he confessed that Wesley was one of his sacred guides,[14] and acknowledged that his hymns came second only to the Bible itself in terms of spiritual treasure. Martineau's hymn book of 1831 and his published sermon both reveal an inclusive Christianity, which undoubtedly developed in reaction to the sectarian tension around him.

While in Ireland, Martineau was forced to consider seriously his views on the relationship of the denominational Churches to the State. This came about through the death of Philip Taylor, the retired minister of Eustace Street Presbyterian Meeting House; on Taylor's death Martineau was expected to receive the *Regium Donum*, a government grant given to Presbyterian Ministers but raised from the taxation of a largely Roman Catholic population. This situation caused a crisis in his ministry which he described some forty years later:

Before accepting ministerial duty in Ireland, I ought to have acquainted myself fully with the relations between the Presbyterians and the State, and considered whether I could make myself party to them. As however the retiring Pastor retained the *Regium Donum* attached to his office, so long as he lived, the question did not press itself upon my attention, and I ceaselessly passed it by, with a vague feeling, I believe, that nothing depended upon it beyond a little more or less of ultimate salary. Before 4 years had expired, Mr Taylor's death, devolving the grant upon me, brought the problem up for solution. Whether the theoretical objection I then felt to any organic connection between Church and State would alone have been decisive, I cannot tell. But during my residence in Ireland, the gross

---

[13] *A Collection of Hymns for Christian Worship*, no. 245.
[14] Margaret J. Shaen, *Memorials of Two Sisters: Susanna and Catherine Winkworth* (London, 1908), p. 164.

injustice involved in the relative position of the Catholic Church and the two chief Protestant bodies had become so oppressive to me that the very idea of being personally perpicipant in it affected me with shame.[15]

Martineau's immediate reaction was to write a letter to his congregation explaining why he could not accept his succession to the *Regium Donum* and offering to dispense with the additional one hundred pounds it would add to his salary. He also stated that if the members of the congregation judged that his actions would lead to a permanent forfeiture of the grant, for which they were not prepared, then he would be willing to place his resignation in their hands at an early opportunity. A meeting was hurriedly convened and a majority obtained for a resolution which promptly accepted his resignation as if it had already been tendered.

> This harsh termination of my first pastoral engagement I soon forgot in the compensating affection and generosity of the large minority, and of a numerous body that watched the struggle of principle with sympathetic interest from outside.[16]

The issue at stake over the *Regium Donum* was not simply that of the relationship between the Church and the State, but of the exclusive attitude against Roman Catholics which was inherent in the awarding of the grant. It was, he argued, a fund belonging to the whole people which had been diverted for the benefit of the few, and as such acted as a 'religious Monopoly'.[17]

Martineau's departure from Dublin was characterized by a deep sense of loss, commonly experienced by many in the nineteenth century. An important chapter of his life was over. He and his wife Helen called on their Dublin friends to say goodbye, and then stood in silence in the French churchyard by the grave of their first born child before catching the ferry to Liverpool. Financially his period of residence in Dublin had been a disaster, for not only had he taken a large cut in his salary by going to Ireland, but he had also, with the help of a substantial loan, purchased a spacious house at a cost of seven hundred pounds, which the rapid deflation of the intervening years had forced him to sell it at a greatly reduced price, thus placing him in considerable debt as he faced his uncertain

---

[15] 'Biographical Memoranda'.
[16] *Ibid.*
[17] A. W. Jackson, *James Martineau*, 5th edn. (Boston, 1900), p. 46.

future. With the termination of his ministry in Dublin went his aspirations of running a large Christian household, comprising of his own family, students enrolled at Trinity College to whom he gave extra tuition, and his resident school pupils. There was a further sense of loss in that his young adulthood had passed and with it had gone some of the youthful ideals concerning the Christian community.

Martineau set out from Dublin to embark on the most strenuous period of his life, which was to lead to the Liverpool Controversy, study in Berlin, and to becoming the Principal of Manchester New College, London; it was to lead to controversy with many of the leading thinkers of the day, and to the writing of his fine collections of sermons which exerted such a powerful influence on Bishop Colenso and the Revd F. W. Robertson of Brighton.[18] Martineau's career almost spanned the whole of the nineteenth century, with his great systematic works *Types of Ethical Theory* (1885), *The Study of Religion* (1888), and *The Seat of Authority in Religion* (1890), not being written until he was well over eighty.

However Martineau's four years in Dublin were not simply associated with a sense of loss; he had received much kindness, and moreover the spacious life surrounding his church responsibilities had provided him with time to read, to learn, and to teach. During these years his sympathies towards other Christians deepened and his catholic spirit developed. This can clearly be seen in his attitude to the restoration in 1850 of a Roman Catholic hierarchy in England. Having supported Catholic emancipation in 1829, while in Ireland, Martineau held that it was illogical to oppose the restoration of England as a Roman Catholic province. In his article *The Battle of the Churches* (1851), Martineau pointed out that the Roman Catholic Church had done nothing illegal in setting up its hierarchy; he was one of the few who argued that the most prudent response was to do nothing.[19] An indication of the strength of feeling against the introduction of a Roman Catholic hierarchy can be gauged by the reaction of the bishops of London and Durham. Charles Blomfield of London, requested his clergy to preach against the new Catholic hierarchy, and Bishop Maltby of Durham called the actions of the Pope 'insolent and insidious'.[20]

---

[18] See George W. Cox, *The Life of John William Colenso D.D.*, 2 vols (London, 1888), 1, p. 39; Jeff Guy, *The Heretic: A Study of the Life of John William Colenso* (Johannesburg abnd Pietermaritzburg, 1983), p. 162; John Hoatson, 'James Martineau and Frederic Robertson: A Study of Influence', *Expositor*, 8 (1903), p. 204; Stopford Brooke, *Life and Letters of F. W. Robertson*, 5th edn. (London, 1872), p. 418.

[19] James Martineau, *Essays, Reviews, and Addresses*, 4 vols (London, 1890-1), 2, pp. 119-95.

[20] Owen Chadwick, *The Victorian Church*, 2 vols (London, 1966, 1970), 1, p. 297.

Martineau however used the opportunity to advocate the setting up in England of a new National Church.[21] He maintained that there were two ways in which this could be achieved: either the largest of the denominations could be taken as representing the faith of the nation, or all the denominations could be viewed as contributing to the National Church, with each sect representing a partial declaration of the nation's faith.[22] Martineau believed that there were strong arguments against the first of these, for the most powerful religious community in the country might only constitute a small minority of the inhabitants, resulting in discontent among the others. The influence of his Dublin experience may be seen here, for Martineau had felt the same unease about the Church of Ireland and its relationship with the other denominations. He favoured the second approach, which he saw as closer to reality in a diverse society; this alone, he believed, would bring tranquillity back to the Church and restore it to an influential position in the world. It was his desire for inclusion and comprehension, expressed in this paper, which fired his other two major schemes for Christian Unity; The Free Church Christian Union (1869), and the National Church as a Federal Union (1887).[23]

Westminster College, Oxford

[21] James Martineau, *Essays, Reviews and Addresses*, 4 vols (London, 1890, 1891), 2, p. 189.
[22] James Martineau, *Miscellanies* (Boston, 1852), p. 463.
[23] *Essays, Reviews, and Addresses*, 2, pp. 499–524, 539–76.

THE DEMOGRAPHIC IMPACT OF
IRISH IMMIGRATION ON
BIRMINGHAM CATHOLICISM 1800-1850

by JUDITH F. CHAMP

'THE Birmingham congregation suggests what Manchester Catholicism might have looked like if Irish immigration had been a fraction of what it was.'[1] This remark of John Bossy points in the direction of a different view of the impact of Irish migration on urban Catholic congregations in England from that which has become familiar. The relationship between Irish and English Catholic population growth in Birmingham before 1850 was not straightforward and led consequently to an interesting pattern of social and religious interaction. What Birmingham illustrates in the period up to 1850 is the effect of relatively modest Irish immigration into an English Catholic congregation already well advanced in prosperity and organization. In the first half of the nineteenth century, Birmingham Catholicism was not overwhelmingly Irish, but the reception of the Irish had significant demographic and social effects on the congregation. These can be used to highlight and illustrate urban Catholic population structure, industrial enterprise, and quasi-parochial organization.

Birmingham was at the heart of early and rapid industrial and economic growth, strategically located to develop as a manufacturing and marketing centre, with easy access to coal and iron resources. It was the hub of the early industrial revolution, the link between Ironbridge and the world. By 1750 it was the fourth largest town after London, Norwich, and Bristol, and by the end of the century had a population of 70,000.[2] The 1851 census placed Birmingham fourth in size after London, Liverpool, and Manchester, with a population of 233,000.[3]

Part of this growth was an urban Catholic community of notable size, economic and social standing, and self-awareness, which was only to a limited extent the product of Irish immigration. Certainly migration into the urban centre was a vital factor in taking Birmingham's Catholic

---

[1] John Bossy, *The English Catholic Community 1570-1850* (London, 1975), p. 310.
[2] C. W. Chalklin, *Provincial Towns of Georgian England* (London, 1974), p. 43.
[3] H. Mann, *Religious Worship in England and Wales* (London, 1853), table.

population from between 50 and 100 around 1700 to about 700 in 1780,[4] however, this migratory trend was a steady one throughout the eighteenth century, stimulated by prosperity and population boom in the 1760s. Catholic migration patterns in the eighteenth century closely reflected those of non-Catholics.[5]

Indeed, the general demographic and economic profile of the Catholic population in the eighteenth century was remarkably close to that of the whole population. Pre-industrial family size has been shown to vary according to social status between 2.3 and 3.5 children.[6] Broadly speaking, the wealthier the family the larger was the group of children. Large families were not unknown, but 60 per cent of English families had 2, 3, or 4 children.[7] The English standard was 2.73.[8] Birmingham's Catholic households in the last third of the eighteenth century averaged 2.4—a little low for the status of employment categories in which Catholics were found, but not markedly so.[9]

By the 1760s Midland workshop industry was well under way and Catholics were part of it.[10] Among Staffordshire and Warwickshire Catholics there was a high proportion of workmen and craftsmen, and the Papist Returns of 1767 show that Birmingham Catholics engaged in a variety of skilled trades. They were mostly artisans, many of them in the booming metal trades.[11] The overall urban Catholic pattern was the characteristic one of early industrialization in which small one-man businesses flourished with a meaure of skill, modest premises, and an apprentice or two.

Catholics can clearly be traced among the larger and smaller businessmen of commercial and industrial Birmingham. They figured in substantial numbers in the expanding trades of metalwork, food and drink production, clothing, and building trades. As the multiplicity and diversity of trades increased so too did the number of Catholics in miscellaneous

[4] '1691 Presentation of Papists at Warwick Sessions', printed in *Worcestershire Recusant* (December 1979), pp. 7–13; Lichfield Joint Record Office, Papists Returns of 1767 & 1780, TP 1079.
[5] Judith F. Champ, 'St. Martin's Parish, Birmingham in 1767: a study of urban Catholicism', *Recusant History*, 15 (1981), pp. 342–71.
[6] P. Laslett, *The World We Have Lost* (London, 1965), p. 72.
[7] P. Laslett & R. Wall, *Household and Family in Past Time* (Cambridge, 1972), p. 148.
[8] *Ibid.*, p. 80.
[9] Judith F. Champ, 'Assimilation and Separation: the Catholic Revival in Birmingham c.1650–1850', (Birmingham University Ph.D. thesis, 1984), pp. 33–5.
[10] J. A. Lesourd, 'Les Catholiques dans la Société Anglaise 1765–1865' (Strasbourg University Ph.D. thesis, 1974), vol. 2, p. 119, table 16.
[11] Lichfield Joint Record Office, Papist Returns of 1767 & 1780, TP 1079.

trade and manufacture, and particularly in non-manual, professional, and employer categories. By the end of the eighteenth century the first wave of industrial development had created a rising class of businessmen and entrepreneurs, among Catholics as well as non-Catholics, who were the new leaders of society.[12]

The overall picture of the demography of this urban Catholic population was, until the nineteenth century, very similar to the general English picture. Legal, social, and economic pressures did not affect population structure or industrial involvement in the eighteenth century. From the early nineteenth century a very different picture emerged, but not before wealth and status had enabled the rising Catholic middle class to play a major role in the temporal and spiritual organization of urban Catholic communities. This enabled a distinctly English pattern of Catholic life to develop in Birmingham before the major influx of Irish, and facilitated the provision of much needed schools, charities and so on, at a later stage. The relatively late arrival of large numbers of poor Irish (compared to Liverpool and Manchester) and the well-developed framework of Birmingham Catholicism enabled it to absorb the problems more easily than some communities.

It was the wealthy businessmen in the Catholic community who founded the Birmingham Catholic Friendly Society,[13] and built and financed the second chapel of St Chad in 1807 with a charity Sunday School attached.[14] The day school founded in 1823 by the same middle class laity was one of the first poor schools in Birmingham.[15] Other features of parochial life included a Catholic lending library and an orphanage.[16] From the early 1830s Birmingham manifested a growing awareness of Irish social and economic problems, both in Ireland and England, and the Catholic community galvanized its own resources and organization and drew the rest of the town into its fund-raising. By then charity and the care of the poor dominated middle class English Catholic activity and organizations were ready to adopt the Irish poor and to adjust to their arrival. In 1837 a new fund was set up for 'The Children of St Patrick' to provide some outcare and to place others at the existing

---

[12] Judith F. Champ, 'Assimilation and Separation', pp. 64–6.
[13] Birmingham Archdiocesan Archives, Journal of the Birmingham Catholic Sick Club.
[14] *Ibid.*, Minute Book of the Birmingham Catholic Sunday School.
[15] J. McCave, *Catholic Education, Medieval and Modern*, an address at the annual Catholic Reunion, Birmingham Town Hall (1897), p. 12.
[16] Edward Peach, *Rules for the Catholic Library* (1809).

Catholic orphanage opened in 1832.[17] This was the first indication of special provision for the Irish in the town and was clearly designed to tug the heart strings and appeal to Irish Catholic sentiment.

However, what is under discussion here is not so much the uqestion of Anglo-Irish social and spiritual relationships, as the neglected demographic effect of Irish immigration on the existing pattern of denominational population growth. The effect of mass migration in the nineteenth century was to disrupt a well established framework of English Catholic population growth. It is this demographic effect which has received little attention and which underlies the social and spiritual disruption.

It can be illustrated in three ways: firstly, rate of population growth; secondly, average family size; thirdly, occupational distribution. From about 1800 the rate of population growth among Birmingham's Catholics was far in excess of the non-Catholic population. If the overall population had grown at the same rate, by 1851 Birmingham's population would have been not far short of a million instead of 233,000. Migration was clearly the predominant means of Catholic growth. Between 1800 and 1850 the increase in recorded Catholic baptisms was 1300 per cent but the growth in the number of identifiable families was a staggering 1700 per cent.[18]

At the same time the average number of children among Catholic families began to drop and by the 1840s was down to 1.5.[19] This was certainly linked to the overall rise in English infant mortality,[20] and to shortage of registration, but locally it was connected to a general drop in the demographic status of the Catholic population. As immigration speeded up, a greater proportion of Birmingham Catholics were in the labouring and poorer classes where infant mortality was automatically higher and family size smaller.

This is borne out by the change in occupational distribution. After 1810, while an increasing *number* of Catholics in commerce and trade can be traced, the *proportion* of the Catholic population which they represented dropped noticeably. In the eighteenth century 10–20 per cent of the Catholic population could be positively identified in the commercial community. After 1810 that figure dropped to below 10 per cent. Between 1810 and 1850 only 127 Catholics can be identified in trade directories; to have maintained their earlier proportion would have required over 400.[21]

---

[17] Birmingham Archdiocesan Archives, MSS notes of Rev. T. Leith, p. 142.
[18] Judith F. Champ, 'Assimilation and Separation', tables 11 & 12.
[19] *Ibid.*, table 9.
[20] J. F. C. Harrison, *The Early Victorians* (London, 1973), p. 25.
[21] i.e. 12% of Catholic population 1810–50 – 383.

From 1820 onwards demographic evidence indicates a larger, poorer, more mobile, less stable Catholic community in which the core of large families had shrunk noticeably. The proportion of Birmingham's wealth being shared by the Catholics had also declined. Massive growth in Catholic population continued in the town centre long after non-Catholics had begun to desert the centre and to become suburbanized. The eighteenth-century pattern of wealthy dwellers in the middle and poor on the fringes gradually gave way to the inverse pattern of the nineteenth century. Anglican registers in the town centre parishes of St Martin and St Philip reveal a slowing down in absolute growth rates, while the Catholic registers recorded growth which far outstripped non-Catholic rates. Catholic migrants continued to flood into the town centre of Birmingham long after the general growth of the town had broadened out into suburban sprawl. The fact that in the 1840s new Catholic churches (including the Oratory) were opened in the heart of the town indicates where the need continued to lie.

The role of the Irish in the changing Catholic population of Birmingham was obviously of major significance but was different from that in the northern towns. Liverpool by 1851 had 84,000 Irish, 22 per cent of its total population.[22] Manchester was 13 per cent Irish and as early as 1821 the Irish Catholics had outnumbered the English.[23] The fact that this did not happen in Birmingham and that by 1851 the population was only 4-5 per cent Irish begins to explain the remark of John Bossy with which I began. Irish immigration did give the Catholic population of Birmingham an important boost, but the town was not overwhelmed by Irish migrants nor can its Catholic population be equated directly with its Irish population.[24] The Catholic Directory of 1840 calculated 9000 communicant Catholics in the town.[25] That preceded the years of greatest Irish famine and by 1851 there were 9000 Irish in Birmingham.[26] What was the demographic relationship between Irish and English?

By examining the number of unambiguously Irish family names in the Catholic registers it is possible to show that a constant, though relatively modest, number of Irish families belonged to the Birmingham Catholic congregation between 1810 and 1850. Very few Irish names appeared

[22] G. Beck, *The English Catholics 1850-1950* (London, 1950), p. 50.
[23] G. Connolly, 'Catholics in Manchester and Salford 1770-1840' (Manchester University Ph.D. thesis, 1981), vol. 1, pt 2, pl. 410.
[24] G. Beck, pp. 80-1.
[25] *Catholic Directory* (1840), p. 60.
[26] G. Beck, p. 53.

before 1800 but over the first half of the nineteenth century approximately one third of the names in the register were clearly Irish. Two peaks occurred, in the 1820s and 1840s, when the proportion of Irish names rose to 40 per cent. There are obvious difficulties in this form of calculation. Certain names could have been as common in Ireland as England and only those unambiguously Irish have been counted. Also, counting families may undermine the impression of the overall demographic shape, as a high proportion of migrants were single or arrived with families already complete, and do not appear in the register.

Allowing a generous margin of error to cater for under-recording, perhaps half of the identifiable Catholic population was Irish. Thus the massive growth of the Birmingham Catholic population was only partially due to Irish migration and the rest was due to natural growth and immigration from the rest of Britain and abroad. Approximately 2000 'Irish' families passed through the Catholic registers between 1811 and 1851. The average number of children was only 1.5, so the family size averaged 3.5, suggesting an Irish Catholic population of 7000 over forty years. Obviously they were not all alive in 1851. It has been suggested that perhaps 75 per cent of the Irish-born recorded in the 1851 census were Catholics.[27] In Birmingham that would have been just over 7000. The Catholic population in 1851 was 15,000 so Birmingham Catholicism, even as late as 1851, was not just Irish Catholicism.

Demographically, Irish immigration certainly was a major factor contributing to the changing profile of Birmingham Catholicism from the eighteenth to the nineteenth century, but its significance may have been overemphasized in the past. However, there is a further curious demographic change which illustrates more clearly than any other the relationship between social, religious, and demographic questions, and the way in which relatively modest levels of Irish immigration disrupted the existing structures.

From 1807 there were two Catholic chapels in Birmingham, St Peter's being the older (1786) and St Chad's, the new one opened in that year. Parish boundaries were, of course, nonexistent so the only limitation was accessibility on foot. The geographical position of the churches might suggest that the town's Catholics were simply split in half, but the population structure suggests otherwise. The two congregations had distinct characters of their own, which become evident from their registers. Size was the most obvious difference. Between 1807 and 1850 four times as

[27] G. Beck, p. 53.

many baptisms took place at St Chad's as at St Peter's. The total number of families identified in the period was 6620, divided into 4654 to St Chad's and 1555 to St Peter's with 411 'floating'.

There was both a startling difference in the rate of growth within each congregation and an interesting shift, each related to Irish migration. Between 1810 and 1840 the congregation of the new chapel, St Chad's, grew at a massive rate of nearly 200 per cent in each decade. By 1820 it was already composed of nearly 40 per cent Irish families. Having absorbed the first wave of immigrants, St Chad's remained around 40 per cent Irish until 1840. During the same period St Peter's actually declined in numbers of baptisms and families in each decade. By 1820 it was only 5 per cent Irish and this rose to only 20–25 per cent by 1840. Clearly St Chad's, perhaps viewed locally as the secondary chapel, was the 'Irish' chapel. Oddly the priest at St Peter's from 1824 to 1842 was Thomas McDonnell, an active local politician and vocal supporter of the Irish cause.[28] Yet he drew only limited Irish loyalty to St Peter's. The greater numbers went to St Chad's and the simple, solidly English pastoral care of Edward Peach.[29]

By 1840, St Peter's congregation had seen little overall growth since 1810, but St Chad's had grown over five times. Suddenly in the 1840s this pattern was reversed; St Peter's congregation increased more than three-fold and by 1850 was over 60 per cent Irish, while St Chad's growth rate dropped to 50 per cent.

This reversal is not easily explained, but one obvious reason was the rebuilding of St Chad's as a cathedral in 1841. For nearly two years St Chad's was under demolition or reconstruction, which forced the congregation to use St Peter's. Some, inevitably, would not return. A large proportion of the Catholic increase of the 1840s, in the decade of deepest economic depression on both sides of the Irish Sea, consisted of very poor Irish immigrants. The new St Chad's was the first English post-Reformation Catholic cathedral, the showpiece of the Catholic revival, a centre of grand and glorious liturgy, and a mecca for visitors. It would be understandable if large numbers of poor, uneducated, ill-clad immigrants turned to the humbler fare offered at St Peter's.

Heavy immigration from Ireland and elsewhere after 1810 produced a Catholic community markedly different from that of the eighteenth

---

[28] Judith F. Champ, 'Priesthood and Politics in the nineteenth century: the turbulent career of Thomas McDonnell', *Recusant History*, 18 (1987), pp. 289–302.
[29] Oscott College Archives, Rev. G. Spencer, Funeral Oration on Rev. E. Peach, 12 September 1839.

century, with a higher proportion of new families of smaller family size and less affluence.[30] The highest proportion of new families correlated with the highest proportion of Irish family names, in St Chad's between 1811 and 1820 and St Peter's between 1841 and 1850. Family size in the community dropped generally after 1800 and was at its lowest (1.27 children) where the new families were most numerous and the proportion of Irish highest, in St Peter's 1841–50. Where new families were fewest and Irish migration weakest, in St Peter's 1811–20, numbers of children were highest (2.47).

After 1810 a greater proportion of the Catholic community were not members of the business community. Not surprisingly the largely immigrant population contained a high percentage of labourers, unskilled employees, and the poor. Certainly the commercial involvement of the Irish before 1850 was minimal; for example, the trade directory of 1843 contained two Murphys and one Kelly when the combined Catholic congregations contained 43 families of Murphys and 21 families of Kellys.[31] In general, St Peter's (the 'Irish' chapel) had a lower proportion of businessmen among the congregation. This dropped further in the 1840s when a number of wealthy families transferred their allegiance to the new cathedral. The number of known businessmen in the cathedral congregation more than doubled in the 1840s.

The demographic evidence bears out other indications of two distinct and characteristic chapels. St Chad's was the largest, fastest growing, poorest and most Irish until the rebuilding in 1841 when St Peter's took on those characteristics. From 1807 St Chad's was definitely the secondary congregation, which grew at alarming rates, largely due to Irish immigration, with an average family size suggesting considerable poverty and high mobility. The secondary chapel for thirty years was the newcomer which welcomed the newcomers, while the older, traditional leading chapel continued much in its familiar pattern.

A definite sense of separateness grew up between the two Catholic congregations, which differed in their social composition and the nature of their activities. The Irish clung to the secondary chapel, whether St Chad's or, after 1841, St Peter's, despite the counter attraction of an Irish patriot

[30] 'New' families are defined as appearing in the register for the first time in a given decade. Never less than 70% of the total, it rose as high as 95% in the 1840s.

[31] Cf. L. H. Lees, *Exiles of Erin* (London, 1979), p. 92, 'Instead of being distributed proportionately among metropolitan industries, the Irish were heavily concentrated in a few trades, in occupations which placed them amongst the lowest social and economic groups.' (Speaking of London.)

priest. For many years St Peter's was regarded as the mother church of Birmingham and the natural haven of those families who had risen in wealth and status along with their native town. The poverty of the second chapel fuelled the argument of some of the laity that Birmingham needed one large central church to unite its divided congregations.[32] When the fumbling plans for building the new church were taken in hand by Augustus Welby Pugin he changed the pecking order overnight and ended hopes of a united congregation. His insistence on building on the site of St Chad's, rather than on a third separate site, and the decision to plan it as a cathedral attracted money, publicity, and visitors to St Chad's. It drove the poorer, mainly Irish Catholics to St Peter's.

The effects of 'domination by minorities'[33] were certainly felt in Birmingham in the tensions between clergy and laity as well as in the benefits of church building, charities, and pious associations. The industrial revolution presented opportunities which placed urban English Catholics in the years 1780–1850 in a position to secure the ecclesiastical existence of Catholicism. These opportunities were taken up with conscious determination by the rising entrepreneurs who produced, in piecemeal fashion, the chapels, schools, and charities.

Birmingham's speed and relative success in its piecemeal revival was determined by four major factors. The longstanding Catholic presence in the town provided a stable base on which to build with confidence. Secondly, Birmingham's industrial and economic boom in the eighteenth century ensured a broad distribution of wealth and early immigration. Thirdly, there was no single gentry patron protecting, controlling, and insulating local Catholic activity, so the local laity and clergy were free to involve themselves and exert their influence. Lastly, the factor which has been explored here, that large-scale Irish immigration was relatively late in Birmingham, which gave the charitable and educational enterprises of the local church a chance to develop before being overwhelmed. What is clear from the demographic evidence is the strain which even moderate levels of Irish immigration placed on the population and therefore on the society, militating against the effects of the first three factors.

The rapid influx of poor, uneducated Irish Catholics, whose grasp of religion was very different from the English one, undoubtedly placed strains on the English Catholic community. It forced the English

---

[32] Birmingham Archdiocesan Archives, B157.
[33] A. D. Gilbert, *Religion and Society in Industrial England: Church, Chapel and Society 1740–1914* (London, 1976), p. 55.

community back into earlier forms of evangelical activity. English Catholicism in the towns could only hope to absorb the Irish by reverting to informality, itinerancy, and active proselytism. However, as the demographic evidence makes clear, the Irish migration may also have prevented the demise of Catholicism, along with Protestant nonconformity, into middle class 'churchiness'. The Irish removed Catholicism effectively from the nonconformist market and from the competition between Church and Chapel for the middle classes. Catholicism was rescued from the consequent loss of religious power.

The Catholic middle classes which began to develop in the late eighteenth and early nineteenth century did not become the dominant element. Catholicism failed to become a tool of Victorian respectability.[34] Disraeli commented that he would worry about the conversion of England when the grocers began to turn Catholic.[35] His scepticism was perhaps better placed than he realized. Catholic grocers never became numerous and in the changing environment of Victorian religion, neither Catholic nor any other grocers would convert England. The grocers and other urban businessmen launched the Catholic revival and in the particular circumstances of Birmingham went a long way towards seeing it bear fruit. The Birmingham congregation was better placed than many to cope with Irish immigration which infiltrated slowly into a well-developed and well-organized Catholic community. However, whatever willingness and readiness the native Catholics manifested in welcoming the immigrants, they could not avoid demographic disruption. Whatever the success of the Catholic revival in Birmingham (and it was considerable) it was powerless to prevent the average urban Catholic from being less affluent, less stable, in poorer health and housing conditions, and more divided from his fellow Catholics in 1850 than he was in 1800. The demographic evidence of the impact of Irish immigration between 1800 and 1850 points towards many of the social difficulties and religious achievements of the Catholic community in the second half of the nineteenth century.

King's College, London

[34] S. W. Gilley, 'Vulgar Piety and the Brompton Oratory', *Durham University Journal* (1983), pp. 15-21.
[35] A. D. Gilbert, p. 174.

MINISTRY AT THE ENDS OF THE EARTH:
PRIESTS AND PEOPLE IN NEW SOUTH WALES,
1830–1840

by PAUL COLLINS

CATHOLICS arrived at Botany Bay with the first fleet in January
1788. But it was not until 1820 that institutional Catholicism
arrived in the persons of two Irish priests—Fathers Philip Conolly
and John Joseph Therry. They had been appointed after considerable
negotiation between the British government, the London Vicar Apostolic,
Bishop William Poynter, the Vicar Apostolic of Mauritius, Bishop Edward
Bede Slater (in whose vast territory Australia was included), and the
Roman Congregation of Propaganda Fide.[1] In the period 1788 to 1820
sporadic priestly ministry had been carried on by three Irish convict
priests and by Father Jeremiah O'Flynn, the maverick Prefect Apostolic,
whose brief appearance in Sydney in 1817–18 was terminated by deporta-
tion.[2]

Therry and Conolly had been appointed as convict chaplains and were
paid from the police fund. Conolly worked in Van Diemen's Land and
Therry in New South Wales. Both failed to lay any lasting institutional
foundations for the Church. Therry especially was a truculent and difficult man, but he was devoted to the convicts and kind to the poor. He was
dismissed by Governor Darling from the official convict chaplaincy in
1825, but he stayed on in Sydney to create great difficulties for the two
Irish priests who followed him in that role. The Australian Church was in
the anomalous situation of being governed by a Vicar Apostolic who lived
five and a half thousand miles away in Mauritius. This bishop could exercise very little influence on events in Sydney and Hobart. It was not until
February 1833, with the arrival of the young English Benedictine, William
Bernard Ullathorne, as Vicar General of New South Wales, that the
Catholic Church began to take shape. He was the key figure in the Church
of the 1830s and I will use him as a major source. A local Vicariate
Apostolic was established in 1834 and Bishop John Bede Polding was
appointed and reached Sydney in September 1835.

---

[1] P. Collins, 'Australia's First Bishops', *Australasian Catholic Record*, 64 (1987), pp. 189–99.
[2] P. Collins, 'Jeremiah O'Flynn: Persecuted Hero or Vagus?', *Australasian Catholic Record* 63
(1986), pp. 87–95; 179–94.

These were opportune arrivals. Throughout the 1830s major economic, political, and social changes were occurring in New South Wales. The colony had broken out of the enclave that had circumscribed the first thirty-five years of its existence. New grazing lands to the west, the north, and the south were opened up in the 1820s and 1830s. The government vainly attempted to limit settlement, but squatters simply decamped on land at the expanding frontier. Seventy-three million acres were occupied between 1820 and 1850 for the raising of cattle and sheep.[3] As more and more territory was opened up, violent conflict was generated with the Aborigines whose lands were seized. This period also saw the development of calls for a more representative government and for the abolition of transportation to New South Wales—which was accomplished in 1840. From the mid-1830s onwards there was an increase in free migration.

It was against this background that the Catholic Church began to build its ministerial structure. Edmund Campion has suggested that in the period up to 1820 (before the arrival of clergy) Catholics formed 'base communities' that met for informal prayer and worship. Campion's implication is that clergy were not necessary to build a community of faith. 'Almost uniquely in the history of world Catholicism, Australia was not founded by bishops . . . not by priests but by the laity—and convict laity at that.'[4]

This suggestion needs to be examined carefully. It is quite true that there was a core of Catholic emancipists (that is, convicts who had served their term or who had been granted a pardon) who formed the nucleus of a Catholic community in Sydney. Numerically they were a small group. At best they exercised some leadership among some Catholics. But James Waldersee has shown that the majority of Irish convicts and emancipists were nominal Catholics who were uninterested in religion and who needed conventional clerical leadership to draw them back to the practice of their faith.[5] Materialistic attitudes developed among many of the settlers as they struggled to survive in an unusual and alien environment. Many had experienced the breaking of family ties and other fractured relationships as a result of transportation. Religion was not a priority for them.

However, Waldersee's assertion of wide-spread indifference to religion

---

[3] R. W. Hartwell and G. Greenwood (ed.), *Australia. A Social and Political History* (Sydney, 1955), p. 81.
[4] E. Campion, 'John Joseph Therry in 1988' in N. Brown and M. Press (eds), *Faith and Culture. A Pastoral Perspective* (Sydney, 1984), p. 3.
[5] J. Waldersee, *Catholic Society in New South Wales 1788–1860* (Sydney, 1974), pp. 186–99.

needs to be contextualized. He is reacting against the myth (perpetuated by Catholic historians such as Kenny, Moran, and O'Brien) of the pious Irish convict and emancipist suffering religious persecution from a bigoted British government.[6] While agreeing with Waldersee's demolition of the myth, I suspect that he goes too far in the opposite direction by presenting the Catholic laity as utterly materialistic and devoid of any religious motivation.[7] He paints a picture of fractious lay leaders and the Catholic lower orders sunk in vice and petty theft. A more balanced picture is given by Ullathorne. He told Bishop Morris of Mauritius in April 1833:

> Thank God we are bringing many poor wandering people to their duty. We have a number of fervent penitents who are giving great edification. . . . We had I am told more communicants on Easter Sunday than there has been hitherto in the course of a whole year.[8]

Most Irish Catholics in Australia were people wrenched out of their normal context by transportation, forced to live a socially alienated existence in a strange and difficult land among a prison population. Many would not have been practising Catholics before they left Ireland. Some of the Irish emancipists became prosperous and, as the Church was organized, were willing to support it. But as Ullathorne and Polding realized, clergy were needed as full time workers to set up the institutional structures required to underpin the ministry. The people needed conventional clerical leadership to draw them back to the practice of Catholicism.

The background to Australian Catholic religiosity was Ireland.[9] The period from the beginning to the middle of the nineteenth century was one of reform, development, and innovation in the Irish Church. This was especially true in the south east, an area of particular relevance to Australia, for it was from there that many Catholics in Australia had originated. Major social and linguistic changes were occurring: an urban Catholic middle class was beginning to emerge and English was slowly replacing Irish as the predominant language of the country. The 1820s and

---

[6] John Kenny, *A History of the Commencement and Progress of Catholicity in Australia up to the Year 1840* (Sydney, 1886); Patrick F. Moran, *History of the Catholic Church in Australasia* (Sydney, n.d. but 1895); Eris M. O'Brien, *The Life of Archpriest J. J. Therry. Founder of the Catholic Church in Australia* (Sydney, 1922).

[7] Waldersee, *Catholic Society*, pp. 191–7.

[8] D[ownside] A[bbey] A[rchives], Morris Papers.

[9] For Irish Catholicism see S. J. Connolly, *Priests and People in Pre-Famine Ireland. 1780–1845* (Dublin, 1982).

1830s saw the beginning and development of a devotional revolution in Ireland, paralleling the evangelical movement in Protestantism. This devotional change flowed into Catholic religiosity, and by the 1830s it had begun to permeate Australian Catholicism.

The early part of the nineteenth century also saw the emergence of the clergy as a professional group whose role in society was both spiritual (as leaders of worship and prayer) and practical. Priests were natural community leaders—especially in a diaspora situation like Australia. They were the celebrants of the key 'rites of transition' (baptism, marriage, death) and, at a time when morality functioned as a form of social control, they acted as 'moral police'. Ullathorne used this very term when asking Governor Bourke for an increase in the number of Catholic clergy![10] Despite Campion's search for a lay 'base community', it is hard to escape the central role of the clergy in the Australian Catholic Church from the early nineteenth century onwards.

Thus the 1830s in New South Wales can be viewed as a transitional period. The Vicar General Ullathorne was symptomatic of this transition. He was very much the well-trained professional clergyman, determined to bring order to the Church in New South Wales. He quickly gained extensive experience of the workings of the convict system and became one of its sharpest critics and a determined abolitionist. While never neglecting the convicts, he was also instrumental in re-focusing the ministry of the Church on the free population.

Since priests were increasingly important in the spiritual and moral lives of the people, the aim from the time of the appointment of the Vicar General onward was to have clergy settled in the outlying districts; periodic visits were deemed insufficient. Ullathorne told the New South Wales Colonial Secretary, Alexander McLeay in 1833:

> [Our] four clergymen are anxious to extend the labours of their ministry, as much as possible to meet the exigencies of the people, but the Catholics are too numerous and widely spread for their exertions to be extended to all. . . . It is utterly impossible to effect much permanent good unless the pastor be constantly with his flock.[11]

However, it was not until 1839 that there were sufficient priests in New South Wales for clergy to be placed permanently at the limit of settle-

---

[10] N[ew] S[outh] W[ales] S[tate] A[rchives], Colonial Secretary, 4/2175.2.
[11] DAA, Morris Papers.

ment. In the earlier part of the decade contact could only be achieved by constant travel.

Since the Church was faced with an ever-moving frontier, the aim in the early 1830s was to maintain contact by either a regular or an occasional circuit. Until Polding came to the colony, the clergy rounds were limited to a semi-circle bounded by the Illawarra district, Campbelltown, Windsor, and the Hunter River valley, with regular forays as far afield as Goulburn, Lake George, and Bathurst. These settlements lay within a 140 mile radius around Sydney. But travelling to them involved journeys through rugged, broken mountainous terrain over extremely rough tracks through unsettled country. Ullathorne also visited Norfolk Island (a sea journey of 1100 miles) and Hobart (a sea journey of 750 miles). None of these trips would have been easy. Late in 1833 the Vicar General told McLeay: 'I have had, within eight days, to travel two hundred and fifty miles, viz from Sydney to Windsor and back—to the middle of the Five Islands [an early name for the Wollongong area] and back—to Parramatta and back.'[12] Between 1833 and 1835 he also visited Newcastle, Maitland, Parramatta, Windsor, Campbelltown, and Bathurst. Therry and Polding were also great travellers. Between 1837 and 1838 the new bishop visited the Illawarra, the Hunter region, and later the southern areas, going as far as Goulburn and Yass, which was on the limits of settlement, 160 miles from Sydney. After this southern trip he reported to Father Thomas Brown of Downside Abbey that he had travelled 'upwards of 900 miles'.[13]

Ullathorne also described the way in which the clergy worked:

> Our usual mode of travelling was on horseback, a man accompanying on a second horse, carrying the vestments and the altar stone behind him. We always carried the Blessed Sacrament in a breast pocket, not knowing where we should come upon the sick and the dying. . . . Generally . . . we used the police courts for our chapels, but in Bathurst I used a ballroom built over the inn stables. At Apin [*sic*] I said Mass in a room of the tavern and preached a sermon against drunkenness.[14]

On arrival in a rural area the priest visited the surrounding homesteads, both Catholic and Protestant, inviting the Catholics to come to Mass and

[12] NSWSA, Col. Sec., 4/2175.2.
[13] Quoted in H. N. Birt, *Benedictine Pioneers in Australia*, 2 vols (London, 1911), I, pp. 337–8.
[14] W. B. Ullathorne, *From Cabin Boy to Archbishop. The Life of Archbishop Ullathorne*, ed. Shane Leslie (London, 1941), p. 68.

the sacraments, and caring for the sick. In settlements and towns Catholic innkeepers cared for the priests and their horses. In Sydney, with its large convict establishment, much of the work was concerned with the convict barracks, the jail, Pinchgut, and the Sydney, Parramatta, and Liverpool convict hospitals. The priests also attended the Female Factory and the benevolent asylum, as well as celebrating the sacraments, conducting funerals, and dealing with general administration. The Vicar General was also concerned about the very remote places: Port Macquarie and New Zealand.[15]

With the arrival of more priests in 1837–8 it was possible to station men in the country districts. However, the need for travel was not diminished. Polding's view that 'we only want priests to make this country Catholic' was taken seriously by the pioneer clergy.[16] Thus a priest-centred ministry developed in Australia in the 1830s. In this the Australian Church was in step with the rest of the nineteenth-century Catholic world.

Central to the ministry of the Church were the rites of passage. The government was also concerned with these pivotal events in the lives of citizens and the clergy were instructed to keep records of marriages, baptisms, and funerals.[17] Certificates of birth, baptism, and marriage had to be sent every month to the registrar of the supreme court.[18] Through their participation in these central rites of transition, the clergy enhanced their importance in the lives of lay people.

Birth was intimately linked to baptism. The reception of this sacrament was almost universal in Ireland. The same was true for Australia. Baptism records show that people generally waited for the coming of the priest for the sacrament to be administered.[19] The canonical enactment that children be baptized 'quamprimum' did not seem to apply in the 1830s. For instance, Ullathorne reported that he baptized three of Edward Curr's children on arrival at Circular Head in 1833. He says that two of the children '. . . were old enough to make their remarks and play with the end of my stole whilst I was administering the sacrament'.[20]

Among the clergy there was doubt about the desirability of baptizing

---

[15] Ullathorne, *Autobiography*, pp. 74–5. Port Macquarie was 220 miles and New Zealand 1300 miles from Sydney.

[16] Quoted in Birt, *Pioneers*, 1, p. 292.

[17] NSWSA, Col. Sec., 4/2224.1. Ullathorne suggested to the Colonial Secretary that printed forms be prepared and sent to the clergy.

[18] NSWSA, Col. Sec., 4/2224.1.

[19] Therry's baptismal registers illustrate this. They survive in the S[ydney] A[rchdiocescan] A[rchives].

[20] Ullathorne, *Autobiography*, p. 56.

Aborigines. The Vicar General asked Bishop Morris of Mauritius for direction and told him:

> Mr. Therry has been in the habit of baptising these [Aboriginal] children when presented by their infidel parents who are utterly dead to all religious impression, and these children are not afterwards instructed in religion or heard of any more; on the plea of their being always in danger of death from the negligence of their parents . . . I have prohibited these children to be baptised except in dangerous sickness [*sic*].[21]

Therry had been baptizing Aboriginal children since his arrival.[22] Ullathorne's view was that the only way to convert them was 'to penetrate beyond the limits of colonisation' and to assimilate them before they were corrupted by contact with Europeans. His view of the Aborigines is impressionistic and his description of their physical appearance none too flattering. But he does admit that 'We [Europeans] were the veritable intruders on their ancient demesne', and that 'Whenever the white man came, the tribe was ruined by the communication of his vices and by drink.'[23] On the question of their baptism he said that since 'We could never get from them an idea of God . . . nothing could be done for the souls of these poor creatures corrupted as they were amongst the Europeans.' After the arrival of Polding, a small group of young Aboriginal men were brought to Sydney from the interior, baptized, and given communion, but when manhood came 'they flung off their clothes, ran off to the Bush and followed their native impulse for savage freedom'. There is evidence, however, that a number of priests continued to baptize Aborigines. Among these were Therry and Father Charles Lovat at Yass, who maintained excellent relationships with the local people.[24] Polding was also in favour of baptizing Aborigines. Protestant missionaries, however, were opposed to granting them the sacrament.[25]

The second rite of transition was marriage. Here the clergy in Australia ran into many difficulties. Australia was notorious as a place of sexual promiscuity. Convicts and many free immigrants had experienced a

[21] DAA, Morris Papers.
[22] SAA, Baptismal Register.
[23] Ullathorne, *Autobiography*, pp. 66–8.
[24] W. B. Ullathorne, *The Catholic Mission in Australasia* (Liverpool, 1837), p. 47. See also Lovat's Baptismal Register, Catholic Church, Yass.
[25] Jean Woolmington, 'Missionary Attitudes to the Baptism of Australian Aborigines before 1850', *JRH* 13 (1985), pp. 283–92.

severe disruption in their lives and a complete uprooting from their traditional patterns of living. Their behaviour was no worse or better than might have been expected from people in such circumstances. The clergy seemed tacitly to understand this. They often blamed the depravity of the convicts on the conditions under which they lived. A major component of the problem was the imbalance of the population: there was a shortage of women. Drunkenness compounded the problem of promiscuity. Ullathorne paints a lurid picture of convictism especially in his books *The Catholic Mission in Australasia* and *The Horrors of Transportation*. [26] While denouncing the sexual permissiveness of the female convicts, he also speaks of the constant danger of masters seducing their female servants, especially in isolated country areas. He tells the story of one woman who always kept a carving knife beside her to ward off her importunate master! [27]

Church and State faced a common difficulty which flowed directly from the disrupted lives of many of the population: the problem of bigamy. The proclamation of banns was one way of dealing with this. The Catholic Church was always suspicious of 'vagi' (persons from outside the known environment) and there were many in the colony. [28] The government also used banns as a way of checking on people and the governor's permission was required to dispense with their publication. [29] Ullathorne complained to the Molesworth Select Committee on Transportation (1836–7) that despite attempts to establish the freedom of all prospective spouses, it was impossible to check the background of the many people wanting to marry in New South Wales. [30]

Considerable confusion reigned in the colony in the 1830s concerning the civil and ecclesiastical law of marriage. [31] It was generally accepted that the marriage laws of England applied in Australia. But there was doubt concerning one enactment: Lord Hardwicke's Act of 1753. This Act, which was aimed at clandestine marriages, stated that for validity a marriage must be celebrated by an Anglican priest in the Anglican

[26] Ullathorne, *Catholic Mission* and *The Horrors of Transportation briefly unfolded to the people* (Dublin, 1838). However, the polemical purposes of these books must be kept in mind when assessing what colonial reality might have been like.
[27] Ullathorne, *Autobiography*, pp. 111–12.
[28] See the decree *Tametsi* of the Council of Trent (1562).
[29] *Historical Records of Australia*, Series I, vol. 15, p. 153.
[30] Minutes of evidence before Select Committee on Transportation 12 February 1838, *British Parliamentary Papers. Crime and Punishment*, 3, pp. 34–5.
[31] C. H. Currey, 'The Law of Marriage and Divorce in New South Wales (1788–1858)', *Royal Australian Historical Society. Journal and Proceedings*, 41 (1955), pp. 97–114.

Church. But the statute was explicitly confined to England and Wales. Did it apply to New South Wales? It was not tested until 1836 when the Chief Justice, Sir Francis Forbes, ruled that the Hardwicke Act did not apply to New South Wales.[32] Prior to that both the Catholic and Presbyterian clergy had been allowed by the governors to celebrate marriages and this had been recognized in a local enactment of 1834 (5 Will IV, No. 2). Forbes' ruling was later overturned by a House of Lords decision and it was not until the comprehensive New South Wales marriage legislation of 1855 that the matter was settled.

However, in the 1830s the fundamental problem for the clergy was not the technical validity of marriages, but getting people married at all. Ullathorne claimed that

> Our greatest difficulty ... was to get people married, and their children baptised, especially in the interior. They had adopted the law of nature when there was scarcely a priest in the colony ... and by habit they continued in it.[33]

The Irish Catholic judge Roger Therry put it more bluntly: 'It was not until the convict element was expelled that marriage came universally to be regarded as an honourable estate.'[34] Some convict women used marriage as a way of escape from the Female Factory. Once men had been emancipated or had a ticket of leave, they could come to the Factory to obtain a wife. Many of them arrived from the frontier where men outnumbered women ten to one. It was a loveless affair, at least as Ullathorne describes it. A group of volunteer women came forth and 'The man cast his eyes over them, invited one whom he selected to a conference and after a little conversation, they were married.'[35] He admits that the majority of these marriages worked out reasonably well.

Convict women were often referred to in the colony as 'profligate' and little better than whores. As Annette Salt has pointed out, this often reflected the class prejudices of those who judged them, and she emphasizes that women in domestic service in the United Kingdom were often forced into occasional or permanent prostitution or petty crime by the economics of survival.[36] The only way that they could become

[32] J. Legge, *A Selection of Supreme Court Cases in New South Wales* (Sydney, 1898), pp. 77–85.
[33] Ullathorne, *Autobiography*, pp. 163–4.
[34] R. Therry, *Reminiscences of Thirty Years' Residence in New South Wales and Victoria* (repr. Sydney, 1974), pp. 119–20.
[35] Ullathorne, *Autobiography*, p. 112.
[36] A. Salt, *These Outcast Women. The Parramatta Female Factory 1821–1848* (Sydney, 1984), pp. 17–21; 37–8.

respectable was by marriage. Michael Sturma has shown that the behaviour of convict women in Australia reflected their British background—*de facto* unions among the poor in Britain were the rule rather
than the exception.[37] The Australian pattern followed the British until the
1830s; *de facto* unions were the norm among the poor and many of the
better-off emancipists. Both government and Church, however, encouraged marriage. Marriage and morality were coterminous, for a stable
union forced people to settle down and having a family brought a sense of
responsibility. But many of the relationships between cohabiting couples
were already permanent; it was simply that they had not been sanctioned
by a marriage ceremony. The Hardwicke legislation had been largely
ignored by the poor in England, and it would have been of little interest to
convicts and emancipists in Australia. It was only from the 1830s onwards
that the marital mores of the poor began to conform to middle class
norms.[38] By the 1830s very few middle or upper class men could afford to
live publicly with a mistress and retain their place in society. Sir John
Jameson was one of the few exceptions.[39]

Ullathorne's evidence to the Molesworth Select Committee is interesting in this regard. Answering the question 'Is there a great deal of concubinage?' he assured the Committee that when he first arrived there was
and that the cause was the lack of clergy in the interior. In order to root out
the problem he '. . . found it necessary to employ persons in whom I had
confidence to make enquiries, and to report to me the names of people
under my care who were living in a state of concubinage'.[40] Ullathorne's
solution was characteristically direct: he visited those living together and
'. . . when I found no obstacle . . . [I married] the parties or . . . insisted on a
separation'. He claimed that the appointment of priests to the interior led
to a diminution of concubinage.

One interesting statistic is the number of Catholic women in the Par-
ramatta Female Factory. There seems to be no doubt that in the late 1830s
Catholics formed at least half and possibly two-thirds of the women in the
Factory. For instance in March 1839 Polding told Archbishop Murray of

---

[37] M. Sturma, 'The Stereotype of Convict Women, 1788-1832', *Labour History*, 34 (1978),
pp. 3-10.
[38] P. McDonald, *Marriage in Australia. Age at First Marriage and Proportion Marrying 1860-1971*
(Canberra, 1974), pp. 27-57. For the whole question of marriage among the lower classes in
Austrlia see A. Atkinson and M. Aveling, *Australians. A Historical Library. Australians 1838*
(Sydney 1987), pp. 100-4.
[39] *Australian Dictionary of Biography*, 2, p. 12.
[40] *British Parliamentary Papers. Crime and Punishment*, 3, p. 35.

Dublin that two-thirds of the 600 inmates were Catholics.[41] How do we explain this large percentage? Ullathorne says that at the time of arrival Irish women convicts were more virtuous than the English women. This is probably because the Irish women's background was the tightly knit and rigid religiosity of rural Ireland. There is no doubt that there was a looser sexual code among the English urban poor. But as a result of the brutalization and sexual exploitation that some of the Irish women experienced on assignment, they reacted by going to the opposite extreme, repudiating their upbringing by a promiscuity that was fundamentally self-destructive. Drunkenness was also a major problem for the women. Sister Mary Baptist de Lacy, a Sister of Charity with experience of ministry in the Factory, told Polding in 1843 that once the women had taken the temperance pledge those who had been 'outcasts' were reformed and ready for communion and confirmation.[42]

The Catholic marriage rite itself was very informal. The ceremony was brief, generally without communion or Mass. This followed the Irish pattern. In Australia from the 1830s onwards couples tended to look for the priest to marry them. Despite severe strictures from Polding, local conditions meant that there were many more mixed marriages in Australia than in Ireland, where they were frowned upon.[43] There is evidence that the children of mixed marriages were generally brought up as Catholics. English squatters, emancipists and convicts, especially in southern New South Wales, often married Irish domestic servants. Both oral and family history tend to indicate that the mother's religion was dominant.[44] Given the social conditions of the squatting era, it was natural for the mother to be the dominant influence in a social decision such as the religion of the children.

There is a real sense in which the clergy acted as 'social workers' in early Australia. A whole range of memorials, petitions, and requests from convicts and the poor went through their hands. Ullathorne writes:

> Another field of occupation was the examining and signing of papers of the large convict population. No one of that class could obtain their ticket of leave ... or their free pardon or leave to marry, or the

---

[41] Dublin Archdiocesan Archives, Australian Collection. See also Ullathorne, *Autobiography*, p. 146.
[42] Sisters of Charity Archives, Sydney, H102/1-7.
[43] Kenny, *Catholicity*, pp. 94-5.
[44] Father P. J. Moore, in a handwritten history of Bombala parish (1911), from a study of Catholic families with English names, argues that the religion of the Irish wife was dominant in the religious upbringing of the children. MS in Canberra Archdiocesan Archives.

privilege of having their wives and children sent out at government cost, or petitions of any other description attended to unless the documents had been examined and signed by their clergy.[45]

The clergy received requests from convicts who claimed to have been falsely accused, requests from destitute people unable to get into hospital, petitions from free men asking leave to marry women from the Female Factory, and requests for tickets of leave. Letters include a request for help from a soldier's wife who had been sentenced to fourteen years at Moreton Bay for receiving stolen property, a petition from a crippled prisoner at Norfolk Island asking for mitigation of a life sentence, and a request for assistance from a destitute women with an insane, possibly epileptic, child. A sad case is that of George Hillier who arrived in 1815 with a life sentence. When he wrote to Father Therry he was sixty-four, 'an inmate of Hyde Park barracks, old, and infirm and helpless'. He claimed to have been a special constable who had captured bushrangers, but through bureaucratic bungling had received neither reward nor pardon, and was sentenced to Moreton Bay. He asked permission to build his own hut on government property at Wooloomooloo, drawing stores from the barracks. The clergy also received many letters from parish priests and others in Ireland giving character testimony to various convicts and requesting information about the welfare of those transported, especially women convicts.

In traditional societies, such as Ireland, there would have been less need for the clergy to fulfil a social welfare role. The normal structures of society were more intact and the developing religious orders of women, such as the Sisters of Charity, would have dealt with societal 'dropouts'. In Australia, where many suffered social dislocation, the Catholic clergy were called on to fulfil a mediating role between society, government, and individual. They were to carry on this role, more or less successfully, until the advent of the social work profession.

In contemporary Catholicism the sacrament of the sick has been restored to the function which it had in the early Church: it is for the *sick*. In the 1830s the sacrament was for the *dying*. That was why it was called 'last anointing' or 'extreme unction'. In early Australia priests would travel long distances to give this sacrament together with viaticum or com-

---

[45] Ullathorne, *Autobiography*, p. 73. A fascinating collection of these petitions can be found in the Therry Papers. See Mitchell Library MSS 1801/107-9 and 1810/60. See also Therry Papers in SAA.

munion for the dying. This reflected the practice of the Irish Church. To die without extreme unction was regarded as a major tragedy. 'The clergy were under the strictest obligation to attend the dying at whatever hour of the day or night they were called.'[46]

Priests in early Australia would go to tremendous lengths to respond to a sick call. Therry was often summoned on sick calls and his diaries reveal that much of his travelling was associated with care for the sick.[47] The day after Ullathorne arrived in Sydney he was called to a woman who '. . . had been living with a man who in the course of the previous night had treated her with savage barbarity'.[48] The Vicar General anointed her before she died. Several of the calls which he received were false: one took him as far as Illawarra, a seventy mile journey over a rough mountain track, and another call was to get him to reconcile a couple after a 'desperate quarrel'.[49]

Public execution was common in New South Wales in the 1830s. Ministry to the condemned and attendance at executions was one of the most onerous duties of the clergy. During the 1820s Therry had to carry out this duty. His popularity and kindness to the condemned meant that Protestants sometimes asked for his ministry.[50] In the 1830s executions were attended either by Father John McEncroe or Ullathorne; McEncroe attended seventy-five executions in his first four years in the colony.[51] Both priests maintained that many condemned convicts converted to Catholicism before they were hanged. It is hard to assess the numerical accuracy of Catholic claims and Anglican Archdeacon W. G. Broughton denied them in his pamphlet *On the True Nature of the Holy Catholic Church.* [52] However, the strongly Protestant *Colonist* admitted 'that such [conversions] occur occasionally'.[53] The attraction of Catholicism for the condemned probably lay in its ritual and tangible sacramental system and the reassuring repetitiveness of its prayers and litanies.

Michael Sturma has described hanging as 'the most dramatic and didactic' of public rituals.[54] The role of the clergy in executions was

---

[46] Conolly, *Priests and People*, p. 91.
[47] See his Diaries for 1832–3 in SAA.
[48] Ullathorne, *Autobiography*, pp. 110–11.
[49] *Ibid.*, p. 69.
[50] O'Brien, *Therry*, pp. 311–12.
[51] Ullathorne, *Autobiography*, pp. 76–8.
[52] Published by Stephens and Stokes, Sydney in 1833.
[53] *The Colonist*, 2 April 1835.
[54] M. Sturma, 'Public Executions and the Ritual of Death, 1838' in *Push from the Bush*, 15 April 1983.

multiple: they focused attention on the spiritual aspect of the action and their presence suggested that God concurred in the state's punishment of the malefactor—and this was especially true if the condemned person confessed their guilt. The confession was often read from the gallows by the chaplain. The clergy also helped to keep the prisoner under emotional control and stopped untoward situations. Describing an execution in Newcastle, Ullathorne speaks of a prisoner who

> ... wanted to harangue the [attending] convicts ... I would not let him for I knew how much vanity was displayed in these dying speeches. . . . He obeyed and attended to his prayers.[55]

Mention of execution reminds us that the Catholic clergy had come to Australia *primarily* as convict chaplains. Looming over everything that I have said so far is the fact that New South Wales and Van Diemen's Land were vast prisons. The Anglican and Catholic clergy were in constant contact with this penal reality. They encountered it in its worst form in the states and places of secondary punishment—in the chain gangs, and at Norfolk Island and Port Arthur. Ullathorne visited Norfolk Island in 1834 and again in 1835 and McEncroe was resident there from 1838 to 1843. Bishop Willson of Hobart was a frequent visitor to these places of secondary punishment from 1843 onwards. It was encounter with the penal system at this level that made the clergy, particularly Ullathorne and Willson (both Englishmen it should be noted), outspoken critics of transportation. It has taken a non-historian—Robert Hughes in *The Fatal Shore*—to bring us back to the appalling reality of the convict system.[56] He recognizes that some, perhaps even the majority of convicts, found opportunities for a new life in Australia that would never have been available to them in the United Kingdom. But Hughes relentlessly confronts his readers with the reality daily experienced by Ullathorne, McEncroe, Polding, and Therry, and the clergy of the other Churches: flogging, the abuse of the assignment system, chain gangs, execution, the endemic homosexuality and prostitution, and, especially in the penal settlements, the sadism of commandants such as Morriset and Price.

The most common form of convict punishment was flogging. David Neal had shown that in a typical year, 1835, twenty-six per cent of convicts were flogged and the average number of lashes per flogging was

---

[55] Ullathorne, *Autobiography*, p. 77.

[56] R. Hughes, *The Fatal Shore. A History of the Transportation of Convicts to Australia, 1787–1868* (London, 1987).

forty-six. 'Magistrates ordered 7103 floggings that year to a population of 27,340 male convicts (women convicts were not flogged), compared to an average of 234 floggings per year over the period 1811–27 in England.'[57] Certainly the nineteenth century was far less squeamish than we are about such realities. But it was the clergy who witnessed the worst effects of the system who emerged as the first real social reformers in Australia. It was after his second visit to Norfolk that Ullathorne began his campaign for the abolition of transportation. His constant theme was the moral degradation that flowed from the system. His pamphlets, speeches, and blunt evidence to the Molesworth Select Committee brought the issue before the public in the United Kingdom. The irony is, however, that transportation to New South Wales was abolished not because of moral degradation, but simply because it was costing too much!

Central to the worship of the Catholic Church is the celebration of the Eucharist. For the first forty years in the colony people rarely had the opportunity to attend Mass. Except for O'Flynn and the rare and brief visits of foreign chaplains, there were no priests to celebrate it. But from the 1830s onwards Mass became more important as priests moved from station to station and, after 1840, became resident in the main centres of the colony. Mass was celebrated wherever it was convenient. In the early days in Sydney and Campbelltown it was usually in the court house; in Bathurst it was in a ballroom, and at Appin the inn.[58] In Parramatta Mass was said in a dark room above the prison and the ritual was accompanied by the ribald conversation of the chain gang underneath. Churches were gradually built in the major centres of population and by 1840 Catholics could attend Mass with some regularity.

A more ornate liturgy quickly developed in Sydney once St Mary's church was completed in 1835. The arrival of Polding meant that pontifical Mass could be celebrated and the bishop loved a large clerical entourage. He was welcomed to Sydney with a 'well sung' Mozart Mass, for from Therry's time onwards there had been a strong tradition of singing. Members of the military band were often used to accompany worship.[59] Band instruments were also used to accompany liturgical singing in Ireland.[60] St Mary's became a centre for Sydney's musical life and the choir performed *The Messiah* and supporting sacred songs in

---

[57] D. Neal, 'Free Society, Penal Colony, Slave Society, Prison?', unpublished paper, 1987.
[58] Ullathorne, *Autobiography*, p. 68.
[59] See letter of Columbus Fitzpatrick in the *Journal of the Australian Catholic Historical Society*, 2, pt 1 (1966), p. 75.
[60] *Collectanea Hibernica*, 8 (1966), p. 75.

January 1838.[61] Polding preferred Gregorian chant, but it was Mozart and Haydn who dominated the Sunday services.

Thus during the 1830s the pattern was set for the development of Catholic religiosity in Australia for the next 140 years. The focus was on a practical moralistic faith directed by the clergy and the institutional Church. There was little emphasis on the laity who assumed a passive role right from the start. Generally speaking the Church was only too willing to co-operate with the State—especially if financial aid was attached! Occasionally individual Catholics made a stand against a social evil, such as transportation, but usually Catholics longed to conform and to be part of the prevailing social ethos. Australian Catholicism may have been unimaginative, but it was certainly practical.

Australian National University

[61] 'Chronicles of the Golden Jubilee of the Colony and Some Aspects of the Catholic Church There in 1838' in *Footprints*, 4, pt 12 (1983), pp. 11–16.

ENGLAND, IRELAND, AND ROME,
1847–1848*

by DONAL A. KERR

IN the spring of 1848 a number of respected English vicars-general, William Bernard Ullathorne of the Western District, John Briggs of the Northern District, and Thomas Brown of Wales decided that one of them, together with Fr Luigi Gentili, the Rosminian missioner, should proceed immediately to Rome. Their object would be to support, by personal intervention with Pius IX, a memorial drawn up by Briggs, signed by twenty Irish and three or four bishops in Great Britain, which was solemnly presented to the Pope by Thomas Grant, President of the English College in Rome. This memorial ran:

> we most . . . solemnly declare to Your Holiness that British Diplomacy has everywhere been exerted to the injury of our Holy Religion. We read in the public Papers that Lord Minto is friendly received . . . by Your Holiness. . . . At this very time, however, . . . the first Minister of the British Government, the Son in Law of Lord Minto is publicly manifesting in England, together with his fellow Ministers, his marked opposition to the Catholic Religion and the Catholic Church. Another cause of our serious alarm is the very general hostile and calumnious outcry now made in both houses of our Parliament and throughout Protestant England against the Catholic Priests of Ireland, falsely charging them with being the abettors of the horrible crime of murder whilst as true Pastors they are striving to . . . console their . . . perishing people and like good shepherds are in the midst of pestilence giving their lives for their flocks.[1]

The bishops' remarkable action was the product of a series of interconnected events in Italy, as well as in England and Ireland, during the latter half of 1847. These events and the persons involved in them form the subject of this paper. I hope, however, to indicate that if the positions adopted by those involved were reactions to the events of the day, they

---

* I am grateful to the Very Reverend Monsignor George Bradley, archivist of the Leeds Diocesan Archives, for facilitating access to the valuable papers of Bishop John Briggs, and to the Most Revd Dr Conway, bishop of Elphin, for information on the Mahon case.
[1] Briggs Papers, 1693; Dec. 1847.

reflect, too, underlying attitudes which remained constant in the relationship between the State and the Catholic Church throughout the whole period of the Legislative Union between Britain and Ireland.

In the steamy mid-July of 1847 Romans were preparing to celebrate the first anniversary of what they hailed as the dawn of liberalism for all Italy—Pio Nono's amnesty of 17 July 1846. As the pace of reform quickened and Pius granted first a Consulta and then a Civic Guard, Cardinal Gizzi had resigned as Secretary for State and the popular Cardinal Ferretti had taken his place. Suddenly police uncovered, or thought they uncovered, a plot (the so-called Gregorian plot) to overthrow the liberal regime. This shock was followed two days later by a greater one. On the very anniversary of the amnesty 860 Hungarian troops of General Radezky's army crossed the Po, entered Ferrara and marched through the streets in full battle attire. Outraged Italian patriots saw the two events as evidence of an Austrian plot to end liberal regimes. Their fears were heightened by the knowledge that they could no longer count on France, for since the Spanish marriage of Louis Philippe's daughter, France, estranged from England, had moved closer to Austria and was regarded as conniving at Austria's Italian moves. Since the two Catholic powers had taken a conservative line, Pius IX stood isolated in the summer of 1847. In a Rome tense with rumour his courageous protest to Austria brought a surge of support for him from liberals everywhere, and advice and offers of help poured in—one surprisingly from Mazzini, and in far-away Buenos Aires, Garibaldi placed his sword at the disposal of the Pope.

In England, too, The Times published an article on 5 August signed 'Angloromanus' with the stirring words: 'the feeling of the [Roman] people is strong that England, with a great and generous hand will protect them. In her unselfish policy there is great confidence that Rome will not become another Cracow.' The author of this article was believed to be Nicholas Wiseman. Wiseman was in Rome for negotiations connected with the re-establishment of the English Catholic hierarchy. Swept along by the general sympathy for the liberal Pope he assured friends on the Consulta that whatever the threats of Austria or France, England would stand by the reforming Pope. Apart from his personal loyalty to the Pope Wiseman saw his move as an opportunity for normalizing relations between England and Rome. Pius grasped at the possibility of English help and asked Wiseman to put the matter to the government. Wiseman wrote to Lord Shrewsbury, a leading Catholic peer, to approach the Prime Minister, Lord John Russell, and hurried back to England himself, to press the point. He was pushing a door already ajar. Russell had announced in the Commons in April that he was considering the renewal of diplomatic relations with Rome. Palmerston, the Foreign Secretary, had no sooner assumed office in 1846 than he had recommended such a course and in March 1847 Normanby, the ambassador at Paris, had sounded the Nuncio, Fornari, on the question. So when Wiseman came with a request for aid from the Pope Russell and Palmerston were well disposed. A positive reply would promote the onward march of liberalism and progress, halt Austrian aggression, and substitute the influence of England for that of France in Italy. An important side-benefit might follow in the form of papal support for the government's Irish policy. George Villiers, earl of Clarendon, and Lord Lieutenant in Ireland since May, was loud in his complaints that the Irish priests had intervened strongly in support of the Repeal party during the recent elections. His observation was accurate though what he failed to note was that the intervention was less an effort to defeat government candidates than to defeat Young Ireland, the more radical nationalists. When Russell, acceding to Wiseman's plea, decided to send Lord Minto, his father-in-law, and Keeper of the Privy Seal, to Rome, Clarendon took the opportunity to outline what Pius might do to ameliorate the situation in Ireland. He might prohibit the clergy from attending political meetings or joining political movements; forbid the use of chapels for political meetings or collections, and remove any bishop who resisted these orders. Palmerston agreed and told the Queen that:

> Lord Minto would endeavour to obtain from the Pope the exertion of his spiritual authority over the Catholic priesthood of Ireland to induce them to abstain from repeal agitation and to urge them not to embarrass but rather to assist Your Majesty's government in the measures which they may plan for the improvement and for the better government of Ireland.[2]

The Irish aspect of the mission, then, was twofold; by restoring better relations with the Pope, to gain his support for the government's Irish policies and to ban the clergy from involvement in politics. Minto, after visits to Switzerland, Piedmont, and Tuscany arrived in Rome on 4 November. Before he arrived events took place which affected the Irish aspect of his mission.

The first concerned the Queen's Colleges. Here a little background is in

---

[2] Palmerston to Queen Victoria, 31 Aug. 1847, Royal Archives J 1/8 in F. Curato, *Gran Bretagna e Italia nei Documenti della Missione Minto* (Rome, 1970), I, pp. 44-5.

order. In an effort to provide higher education for the Catholics and Dissenters Peel, in 1845, had decided to set up three colleges, in Cork, Galway, and Belfast. Religious instruction in the colleges was not to be endowed from public funds. Like many efforts to impose an educational compromise in nineteenth-century Ireland, this project was deeply offensive in many quarters. Robert Inglis, MP for Oxford, viewed them as 'Godless Colleges'. Daniel O'Connell and most Irish bishops, led by John MacHale, the *bête noir* of all English governments since his appointment as archbishop of Tuam in 1832, and Michael Slattery, archbishop of Cashel, denounced them as subversive of the students' faith. Pointing to the example of Trinity College Dublin, which was a Protestant college, they demanded that the Catholics, too, be given a denominational college. On the other hand, a minority led by archbishops Crolly of Armagh and Murray of Dublin, while wishing that the colleges were more Catholic, were prepared to accept them. Both sides among the bishops appealed to Rome and on the same day in July 1846 that Pius issued the amnesty, the Congregation of Propaganda, which dealt with Irish church affairs, decided in favour of the majority. Pius, however, advised by Corboli-Bussi, his liberal-minded acting-Secretary for State, withheld the condemnation. The majority bishops kept pressing for a decision and, finally, a year later he referred the question back to Propaganda for reconsideration. On 20 September 1847 it reaffirmed its condemnation and Pius ratified the decision in a rescript of 9 October. Coming when it did the rescript, which appeared to set at nought an act of Queen in Parliament and to encourage the anti-government bishops in Ireland, was viewed by Palmerston and Russell as an unfriendly act at the very time when England was coming to the Pope's assistance. Minto was convinced from his discussions with the Pope and Secretary for State, Ferretti, that if he had reached Rome earlier the rescript would never have been sent. One of Minto's first tasks would be to persuade the Pope to withdraw his condemnation.

The second event concerned the other major area now occupying the attention of the government in Ireland: the famine and the problems it gave rise to, particularly law and order. This latter problem had assumed major proportions in Ireland during the autumn of 1847. Evictions were a major cause of the trouble. The number of families evicted showed a startling increase: 3,500 families in 1846; 6,000 in 1847; 9,700 in 1848; 16,700 in 1848 to peak at the staggering total of 20,000 in 1850. The result was a sharp rise in attacks on 'land grabbers', landlords, and agents. The autumn of 1847 was marked by six dramatic assassinations in two months. One of the most sensational murders was that of Major Denis Mahon, of the 9th Lancers. Mahon, like many of the victims, was an improving landlord who, having inherited a badly-managed estate around Strokestown, County Roscommon, proposed to buy out the tenants and give them a passage to Canada. Only a minority accepted and as the rest would 'neither pay nor go' he evicted over 3,000 of them including, it was alleged, 84 widows. A more startling allegation was that the local priest, Fr Michael McDermott, declared during Sunday mass that 'Major Mahon is worse than Cromwell and yet he lives'. Not for long; within the week he was shot dead. For Clarendon, the Lord Lieutenant, who was an alarmist and had shut himself up in the vice-regal lodge, these murders were proof that 'servile war against all landlords and English rule' was about to break out. He redoubled his frantic calls for a coercion bill. Russell, who saw the landlords as the villains, and who had come to power through the rejection of the Peel's Irish coercion bill, replied sharply that:

> It is quite true that landlords in England would not like to be shot like hares and partridges. But neither does any landlord in England turn out fifty persons at once, and burn their houses over their heads, giving them no provision for the future. The murders are atrocious, so are the ejectments.[3]

English opinion, however, as expressed in both press and parliament agreed with Clarendon. When Lord Farnham raised the matter in the Commons that opinion manifested itself. Clarendon threatened to resign; Russell had to give way. Parliament and press alleged priestly collusion with assassins. Stanley declared that 'The musket of the assassin was discharged at the man whom the priest had denounced the previous Sabbath.' Palmerston's suggestion was that whenever a landlord was shot the local priest should be hanged and *The Times* announced the formation of a 'Combination of Protestants to Kill the Priest of Every Parish in which a Protestant is Killed'.[4] Such a response was not perhaps unnatural for nineteenth-century politicians schooled in the tradition of English no-popery with its gross exaggeration of the role of the priest in the Catholic community. We are perhaps now becoming aware of the centrality of anti-Catholicism in nineteenth-century English life.

[3] Russell to Clarendon, 15 Nov. 1847, PRO, Russell Papers 6G.
[4] *Hansard*, 3, xcv, pp. 680–3, 6 Dec. 1847; pp. 1208–11, 16 Dec. 1847; *Times*, 28 Dec. 1847; Palmerston to Minto, 3 Dec. 1845, Foreign Office Papers in Curato, *Gran Bretagna*, 1, pp. 240–1.

Without awaiting any verification of the charge, Palmerston told Minto to inform the Pope that 'Major Mahon who was shot the other day was denounced by his priest at the altar the Sunday before . . . that denunciation . . . made all the people in the neighbourhood think the deed a holy one. . . .' When McDermott denied the charge Palmerston, taking up some suggestions in an anonymous letter to the press signed 'An Irish Peer', wrote again to Minto that 'It seems pretty well established by what Lord Farnham said that the Reverend Mr McDermott not only incited the people to murder Major Mahon, but quibbled and equivocated in attempting to deny what he had done. He says he did not denounce Major Mahon on any Sunday, because he did it on a Monday; and he says he did not name Major Mahon, because he pointed him out by a description which rendered it needless to pronounce his name.' On 30 November Minto brought the matter to the Pope's attention. Shocked, Pius promised to do all in his power to put an end to such abuses.[5]

Was the charge genuine? Denunciations from the altar took place as is clear from church legislation to eradicate this abuse, and with the background of evictions it is possible that McDermott spoke intemperately. But Palmerston had no ground for claiming that his guilt was well established. A score of respectable parishioners solemnly swore that he had never denounced Mahon. His bishop, alarmed at the accusations in parliament and in the press, went to Strokestown to investigate and arrived at the same conclusion. McDermott in a public statement assured the public 'by the most solemn asseverations a clergyman can utter, that . . . Major Mahon was never denounced, nor even his name mentioned from any Chapel altar . . . on any Sunday before his death'. The crime was due, he said to 'the infamous . . . cruelties which were wantonly exercised . . . against a tenantry, whose feelings were already wound up to woeful and vengeful exasperation, by the loss of their exiled relatives, as well as by hunger and pestilence'. The charge made against him, he said, was a monstrous calumny and he challenged a legal process.[6] When the trial took place in July 1848 it transpired that the murder had been planned before the Sunday in question. Two men were executed and others transported but Father McDermott's name did not figure at the trial.[7] McDermott's bishop, Dr Browne, told Shrewsbury that 'he had visited Strokestown after

[5] Minto to Palmerston, Palmerston Papers in Curato, *Gran Bretagna*, 1, pp. 238–9.
[6] McDermott to editor, *Freeman's Journal*, 10 Dec. 1847; Bishop Browne to Shrewsbury, *Tablet*, 3 Jan. 1848.
[7] B. Donlon, 'The Mahon murder trials', *County Roscommon Historical and Archaeological Journal*, 1 (1986), pp. 31–2.

the murder and could never obtain the slightest information that could implicate the Rev Fr McDermott in the crimes imputed to him. The result of my inquiries has been, that he had not on Sunday, Monday, ferial or holy day, not at any time nor in any place directly nor indirectly denounced Major Mahon'. Clarendon must carry responsibility for pinning blame on him. The damning anonymous letter originated, I believe, in the Lord Lieutenant's office. After wringing his coercion bill from a reluctant Russell, he told his close friend, Henry Reeve, foreign editor of *The Times*, that Major Mahon's cousin had investigated the matter and concluded that the charge was doubtful to say the least.[8] He never publicly admitted this. Clarendon was accustomed to use the press to further his policies. As interesting as the objective truth of the charge is the fact that it was perfectly credible to Palmerston, Clarendon, and others.

Some English Catholic gentry, terribly embarrassed at their Irish co-religionists, took up the matter. In the House of Lords, Lord Beaumont took the same line as Farnham. Lord Arundel and Surrey wrote publicly to MacHale to voice his concern at 'denunciations from the altar, followed by the speedy death of the denounced'. MacHale promised that if priests were guilty they would be suspended from the exercise of the priesthood. A shriller note was sounded when Lord Shrewsbury wrote to McDermott's bishop and to Archbishop MacHale condemning the silence of the bishops. Shrewsbury had his mind made up about Fr MacDermott who 'by his denial . . . adds the sin of tergiversation to his other delinquencies'. With the encouragement of Lord John Russell, he used the occasion to detail his many grievances against MacHale and his conduct as bishop:

> it is . . . reported . . . that in what concerns religion your Grace's diocese is in a state of peculiar destitution; that you have ever debarred your poor from the benefits of education under the National System . . . that you never admitted Fr Mathew within your limits, . . . and that too many of your parishes are without a school, and some of them without a chapel, though the Repeal rent is regularly levied, and ungrudgingly paid. . . . Like Lord Arundel and Surrey, I feel too keenly the reproaches cast upon the religion which I profess in England, through the excesses of some who profess Catholicity in Ireland.

For Shrewsbury the responsibility for the famine deaths, which MacHale and other clerics imputed to the government, should be imputed instead to

---

[8] Clarendon to Russell, 10 Dec. 1847, Letterbook II; Clarendon to Reeve, 20 Dec. 1847, Clarendon Papers.

the 'unerring, though inscrutable designs of God'. God's visitation was grievously aggravated by Irish ingratitude because 'every sufficient expression of gratitude has been withheld both from the Government and the people of England'. The assassinations were part of 'one great conspiracy against property'. The Church was blameworthy for 'we are all amazed at the silent apathy which seems to reign within the sanctuary'. The English public pronounced the Church to be 'a conniver at injustice, an accessory to crime, a pestilent sore in the commonwealth; and so long will she be so proclaimed till we are shown some better reason than has yet been given us why Archdeacon Lafffan should remain unreprimanded, and why Father McDermott should still be permitted to exercise his ministry'.[9]

This indictment by the leading Catholic peer and generous benefactor shocked clergy and laity alike. MacHale made an energetic defence which took up several columns of *The Morning Chronicle*. Lucas in *The Tablet* savagely attacked what he called Shrewsbury's 'hyper-archi-episcopal' instructions to the Irish Church. The reactions of Lucas and MacHale were not unexpected, but now Shrewsbury's denunciations alarmed leading Catholics in England—Frs Pagani and Luigi Gentili, two zealous and influential Rosminian priests, and Bishops Briggs and Ullathorne. Worried at the continuous denunciations of Irish priests and suspecting government connivance, they convinced themselves of the existence of a plot to gain control over the Church. Minto's mission was to persuade the Pope, in his hour of need, to agree to a concordat or to exchange diplomats with a view to gaining control over the Church either by paying the clergy or nominating the bishops. A preliminary step would be the public discrediting of the Irish clergy who opposed such arrangements, particularly MacHale. Pagani saw Shrewsbury and Arundel as prime movers in the plot:

> That the letters of these two noblemen [Arundel and Surrey, and Shrewsbury] are addressed to Dr MacHale in order to prostrate the very head of the anti-colleges and anti-government party, nobody can question it for a moment. That the letter of Lord Shrewsbury is a defence of the present ministry, and an upholding of all their schemes against our church as the normal system, the pensioning of the clergy etc no one can doubt. That this production of the noble Lord is intended to ingratiate himself or his party with the present adminis-

---

[9] Shrewsbury to MacHale, *Morning Chronicle*, 4 Jan. 1848. Laffan made an inflammatory speech at Cashel, *Nation*, 20 Nov. 1847.

tration by countenancing their attacks against the Irish clergy and people, everyone can easily perceive; but why, one may ask, has Lord Shrewsbury taken such a course? why to make himself the champion of the British Government against the clergy and Catholics of Ireland? . . .

Part of the problem lay in the ecclesiastical politics within the Roman Catholic Church in England. English bishops, including Briggs and Ulla-thorne, as also Gentili and Pagani, feared that Wiseman identified with the Catholic aristocracy and the Oxford converts and wanted to establish close links between the government and Rome. They suspected that his ambition was to become the first archbishop of Westminster and that Shrewsbury was pushing his candidature. If he succeeded the head of the Catholic Church in England and the heads of the Irish Church (Crolly and Murray) would be united in their support of the government and its measures to control the Church in both countries. The letters, they believed, were not Shrewsbury's own but Wiseman's. Pagani answered his own rhetorical question thus:

> Your Lordship must know that the pamphlet some years ago published by Lord Shrewsbury against O'Connell was Dr Wiseman's composition, and none can believe that under the present circum-stances, and with all the links which now bind together Lord Shrews-bury and Dr Wiseman in these diplomatic transactions, Lord Shrewsbury would have published such a letter without consulting and receiving Dr Wiseman's approbation! If the head of our hierarchy in England, backed by our Catholic aristocracy and residing in London will join the government party of our Brethren in Ireland and form another party who can anticipate the result of such a union!

They must act immediately to prevent Wiseman's party getting him in as archbishop of Westminster.[10]

To some extent the incident was a phase in the power-struggle within the English Catholic Church between bishops and aristocracy. Shrews-bury subsequently told Clarendon that among his motives in continuing the controversy with MacHale was 'to vindicate the rights of the laity' and 'to prove that we are not those passive, abject slaves of our Clergy which too many suppose . . .'.[11]

[10] Pagani to Briggs, Jan. 1848, Briggs Papers, 1754A.
[11] Shrewsbury to Clarendon, 7 Feb. 1848, Clarendon Papers.

Some of Pagani's suspicions were justified. Wiseman wanted the normalization of relations between Britain and Rome and saw the importance of proper diplomatic links for furthering government policies in Ireland. He told Charles Greville, the diarist, in December that the misfortunes of the government policy in Ireland was 'all owing to there being no English ambassador at Rome, and no representative of the moderate Irish Clergy'. As for Shrewsbury's letter, although Wiseman apparently approved of it, it was not written by him. Its author was Fr Pierce Connelly, Shrewsbury's eccentric chaplain, whom Shrewsbury now sent to Rome to support the candidature of Wiseman and to discredit MacHale. A further twist in the complicated story of Roman intrigues was that although Connelly tried to discredit the Irish clergy, he also, unknown to Shrewsbury, used every effort, including canvassing Minto, to block Wiseman's candidature. Connelly, a convert American priest, disliked Wiseman intensely for preventing him seeing his wife, Cornelia Connelly, foundress of an order of sisters, and whom in 1849 he was to summon before the Court of Arches for restoration of conjugal rights.[12]

Pagani and Briggs were right in suspecting government involvement; for Clarendon remained in close contact with Shrewsbury during the controversy with MacHale, and Russell took the credit for encouraging Shrewsbury to publish the letter. Russell bears some responsibility, too, for the suspicion with which English and Irish Catholics had come to regard his government in late 1847. In the dispute over the appointment of Hampden as bishop of Hereford he openly displayed his deep-rooted aversion to Catholic influences. In a reply to the Bedford clergy in December 1847, he stated that he had maintained the appointment of Hampden despite the protests of the thirteen bishops in order to 'maintain the principles of the Reformation' and 'to strengthen the Protestant character of our Church so seriously threatened ... by many defections to the Church of Rome'. These remarks were noted with dismay, not merely by Newman but by Catholic bishops in England and Ireland, and MacHale made good use of them at Rome to disprove the assertion of the moderates like Murray of Dublin that the government was well-disposed to the Church. Briggs, Gentili, and Pagani, contrasting both the attack on the Irish clergy and Russell's anti-Catholicism at home with the friendly attitude of Minto in Rome convinced themselves that some government plot against the Church was afoot and they undertook the work of

[12] For Connelly see D. G. Paz, *Priesthoods and Apostasies of Pierce Connelly: a study of Victorian Conversion and anti-Catholicism* (1986).

uncovering it to the unsuspecting Pope. This was why Briggs felt it necessary to draw up the memorial. The replies of the Irish bishops to Briggs are extant and provide a fascinating insight into the outlook of the leaders of the Irish Church. The characteristic note was distrust of the government which is all the more striking when one takes into account the benevolence of the State towards the Church in recent years. Peel had gone quite some way towards a church endowment with no strings attached in the Bequests Act and the munificent Maynooth Grant, and Russell had sincerely sought what he called justice for Ireland. Yet most bishops signed Briggs' memorial, willingly voicing their suspicions of the government's intent. Even bishops who normally supported the moderate line of Murray, archbishop of Dublin, voiced their concern. Egan of Kerry feared that a government representative at Rome 'would not contribute to the liberty of our Churches, English or Irish. I am strengthened in the impression by the violent attacks made of late in Parliament on the Irish Priests. No doubt Lord Minto will know how to avail himself of the calumnies in circulation.' McGettigan of Raphoe declared that he had not the slightest doubt but that 'the interest now working so successfully at Rome will get the Propaganda to issue some document against the Irish priests'. Blake of Dromore, who wanted a stronger memorial, complained that 'in the midst of our utmost effort for alleviating human distress, we are assailed and calumniated in the most atrocious manner'.

The more nationalist bishops expressed their opposition in stronger terms. McNally of Clogher, put their opinion thus: 'All the Catholicity of the Empire are vitally interested. . . . Long has the English government been intriguing to obtain some interference in our religious concerns and control over the Bishops and Clergy but there can be no doubt now that they are . . . fully determined to carry their hellish schemes into effect. The calumnies so unsparingly heaped upon us will be used to a certainty by Lord Minto . . . and will be a pretext hereafter for demanding control over us.' Typical of their attitude is the reply of John Derry, bishop of Clonfert:

> I regard . . . the present establishment of diplomatic relations between the Court of Rome and the Government as an occurrence fraught with danger to Religion, the liberties and the happiness of this mis-governed country. . . . the design of its Protestant promoters is most hostile to our Faith and freedom; that the Ministers who propose it . . . do so in the hope of being able thereby to obtain a control over the appointment of the Ministers of our Holy Religion; that the tendency and almost immediate effect of such secular control and particularly

of Protestant British control, will be to alienate the People from the Pastors; that it will make the Pastors appear to the oppressed people, as stipendiary agents and agents of their oppressors; in a word, that it will utterly derange all the existing affectionate relations of Priests and People.[13]

Although admittedly these replies are in reaction to continuous denunciation of the clergy they reveal the fear and suspicion with which the leaders of the Catholic community viewed government. The Prime Minister, they believed, had made clear what they knew all along; they were living in a confessional state, a Protestant state, and vigilance was the price of their freedom.

Their fear that government diplomacy would win over the Curia appeared realized when the Pope, in response to Minto's representations, took action. On 2 January 1848 at his request, the Congregation of Propaganda wrote to the Irish archbishops:

The rumours that have for some months back been in circulation through the public journals of England, relative . . . to the abuses of some of the Irish churches, for transacting in them secular affairs . . . and also regarding the murders which are said to be repeated throughout Ireland, and are imputed to the clergy, as if they were previously planned, on account of the imprudence of some, in their preaching, or in indirect encouragement from the pulpit, or at least a wicked approval of them; such rumours ought . . . to excite the solicitude of the Sacred Congregation . . . it has deemed it an important duty to seek . . . full information, that it may be seen what credit is to be given to such defamations. . . .[14]

This letter was intended as confidential to the archbishops but Murray, encouraged by Clarendon, leaked it to the public press. The nationalists, priest and laity, were wild with anger and remonstrances poured in and protest meetings were held. Bishop Maginn of Derry appealed to the primate, in language that smacks of liberation theology, to tell the Pope that

no clergyman has transgressed the bounds of Christian duty, which makes it incumbent on every follower of the Redeemer to stand by

---

[13] The replies of 24 Irish and some English and Scottish bishops are in the Briggs Papers, nos. 1718–56.

[14] Cardinal Luigi Franzoni, Secretary of the Congregation of Propaganda Fide, to William Crolly, archbishop of Armagh, 3 Jan. 1848. *Irish Catholic Directory* (1849), p. 292.

the oppressed against their oppressors—for the poor and the needy against those that strip them. An ardent love of country for which our great Pope himself is so distinguished could not be reputed an inordinate zeal for *factious* pursuits. A desire to promote by *peaceful* and *constitutional* means, the amelioration of our *unhappy country* made by *misrule* the most wretched on *earth*, could not be considered a 'political pursuit'—nor could *in fine* the praiseworthy efforts of our clergy to check the proselytiser ... nor their earnest efforts ... to bring public opinion to bear on the ruthless extermination of their helpless starving hearers, through any malversion, be deemed criminal in them.[15]

More telling was the forty-page letter to the Pope sent by Slattery, archbishop of Cashel, a man less suspect than MacHale of extreme views. After detailing his version of the history of the Irish Church which, he asserted, had suffered since the Reformation under more than Egyptian bondage, and detailing the work of the clergy during the frightful years of famine, he traced the source of all the trouble to one cause: the English government being Protestant wanted to gain control of the Catholic Church.[16]

On the other Irish issue—the Queen's Colleges—Minto could claim initial success, for the Pope intimated his regret at having issued the rescript. Certainly, Pius was having a re-think; Newman, when taking leave of him in early December, reported that Pius was concerned and had read all that the papers had to say on the matter. He would have discussed it with him had not Newman's lack of Italian prevented it.[17] The colleges' scheme was of great concern to the government, and in particular to Clarendon who modified the religious clauses in an endeavour to make it acceptable to the bishops. His efforts brought him into contact with an unusual cleric, Francis Nicholson, coadjutor archbishop of Corfu, who offered to put the case for the colleges to the Curia. Clarendon accepted willingly, all the more so since Minto needed someone versed in the Colleges' affair to second his efforts at Rome. Clarendon provided Nicholson with a copy of the proposed revised religious statutes and a letter addressed to him, explaining why he had sought his intervention. This letter, the terms of which were drawn up by Murray and Nicholson, was to have a colourful career. All might have gone well if Nicholson had gone

---

[15] Maginn to Crolly, 21 Feb. 1848, Archbishop Murray Papers, Dublin Diocesan Archives.
[16] Slattery to Fransoni, 7 Feb. 1848, Slattery Papers, Cashel Diocesan Archives.
[17] Newman to Dalgairns, 21 Dec. 1847 in C. S. Dessain (ed.), *The Letters and Diaries of John Henry Newman* (1962), 12, p. 135.

straight to Rome. He dallied first in Dublin, London, and Paris, visiting bishops, ministers, and nuncios. His poor state of health delayed him further with the result that, although he originally planned leaving for Rome in November, he was still in London at the end of April 1848. By then events had overtaken him.

In Rome the opposition to the colleges and the defence of the clergy was organized by Dr Paul Cullen, rector of the Irish College, a cleric who combined deep-rooted suspicion of government with total commitment to the model of the Church he knew in Rome. His was the carefully thought-out votum or written advice that had convinced Propaganda to condemn the Colleges. On his return to Rome in January 1848 he used all his considerable influence and mastery of the Roman system to neutralize Minto's success. Before long he was able to report to his friends in Ireland that Slattery's letter and his own representations were bearing fruit and the Pope was more favourably disposed than he had dared to hope. Important support came early in March when Grant presented the Briggs memorandum, complete with the signature of the bishops, to the Pope. To drive home their case, however, Briggs, Ullathorne, and Gentili felt, as we saw, that some bishops should go to Rome in person. MacHale and O'Higgins decided to go and Maginn joined them later. Briggs or Ullathorne and Gentili had hoped to accompany them, but through bad communication the two Irish bishops set off on their own. Ullathorne came to Rome a few months later on a different matter, but no doubt explained Briggs' and his own position on the Irish matter and the exchange of ambassadors. MacHale and Higgins lost no time and arrived in Rome on Palm Sunday, 16 April.

Meanwhile, Minto, who had spent February and March in Naples, returned to Rome when the revolutions broke out, noting despairingly that he would have 'the mortification of finding not a trace remaining of all the labours of my outward-bound journey'. Although he stayed less than a week in Rome he found time to warn the Pope against MacHale in Ireland and Cullen in Rome, whom he accused of being 'an agency for propagating falsehood' and of sending out a 'continued stream of misrepresentation'. Pius replied that he had seen communications from Dr Cullen of a very temperate character.[18] Unknown to Minto the two opponents he warned the Pope against were about to join forces for, a few hours after Minto left by one gate, MacHale arrived by another. He immediately set to work with Cullen to undo Minto's achievements.

---

[18] Minto to Russell, 14 Apr. 1848 in Curato, *Gran Bretagna*, 1, pp. 194–6.

On 27 April MacHale and Higgins saw Pius IX and were delighted with their favourable reception. Had Pius changed his mind on the Irish question? Pius' concern was the situation in Lombardy where his army was preparing to attack the Austrians, and thither sent his best adviser, Corboli Bussi. Anguished at the prospect of war being waged in his name against a Catholic nation, and fearful that it might provoke a schism in Germany and Austria, he was reconsidering his whole attitude. The quickening pace of revolution in Rome was outpacing him. Even as the Irish prelates visited him he was finalizing the *Allocutio* of 29 April, which many took to mark the end of his liberal period. Minto's influence on Pius IX faded. The Italian liberals whom Minto and Freeborne, the English consul, patronized were now regarded as extremists. The most prominent of these was Ciceruacchio (Angelo Brunetti), whose son was to murder Count Rossi, the Pope's Prime Minister, seven months later.

In English affairs Pius had followed with dismay the debate on the Diplomatic Relations Bill. In the course of the debate in the Lords several leading politicians had made insensitive remarks about the Papacy, and Eglinton's amendment to forbid the Pope to choose an ecclesiastic as ambassador to the Court of Saint James and Wellington's amendment to deny him the title of Sovereign Pontiff were accepted. Pius' confidence in the British government's wholehearted and altruistic support was shaken.

April 15 also marks the setting out of yet another envoy to Rome. If the majority bishops sent MacHale and Higgins to counteract Minto and Nicholson, the minority bishops now sent a further agent to counteract MacHale and Higgins. When MacHale left for Rome on 1 April Murray became concerned lest he reach the Pope before Nicholson, who was still in London. He decided to send his own representative in John Ennis, parish priest of Booterstown, who had successfully represented the moderate bishops on the related question of National Education a few years earlier. Russell generously financed Ennis' mission, and Clarendon provided him with the revised college statutes concerning religion and a copy of his letter to Nicholson. To give the letter more weight Ennis changed the addressee from Archbishop Nicholson to Archbishop Murray and presented both documents to Propaganda when he arrived in Rome at the beginning of May. MacHale had Ennis' documents almost as soon as he had handed them in. His counter-measures were masterly. He immediately published the letter and the statutes in the Irish newspapers. Clarendon was doubly embarrassed. Astonished at reading his private letter in the public press he found himself denounced for underhand dealings, and his alleged anti-Catholic activities in Spain twenty years before when he was plain Mr Villiers were raked up to infuriate Catholic and nationalist opinion. On the other hand, Orangemen raised a howl of protest accusing him of submitting the statutes to the Pope for approval before presenting them to parliament. Russell had to face some difficult questions on the matter in the House of Commons. Murray, too, was wrong-footed, for the altered letter had blown his cover and shown him in league with the Lord Lieutenant behind the back of his episcopal colleagues. Embarrassed, he explained that Clarendon had never addressed any such letter to him; in turn, this denial discredited Ennis in Rome where the Curia was displeased to find that documents submitted to them had been tampered with. Finally, Nicholson, who had now reached Paris, was taken aback to discover, through the public press, that Ennis was acting in his place. This damaged the mission in Rome, for when Nicholson finally arrived there at the end of July he and Ennis became so involved in mutual recriminations that Murray was forced to recall Ennis.[19]

Having sown confusion in the enemy camp MacHale, Higgins, and Cullen, having the advantage of knowing their opponent's case, drew up an extensive criticism of the colleges' scheme. The main thrust of their argument was that when education excluded religion it would, as De Maistre had maintained, poison the whole nation. To this criticism they added a history of government antagonism, past and present, real and imaginary, to Catholicism. They cited Russell's Protestant defence of Hampden's appointment who, they told the Pope, was an intimate of Archbishop Whately and Blanco White, the one a latitudinarian the other an apostate.[20] They distributed their document to the cardinals, but so discreetly that their opponents learned of it only days before the meeting of Propaganda. An alarmed Nicholson persuaded the Pope to have the question re-examined. It was to no avail. The Curia, however, took the defensive but pastoral view that the students' faith might suffer in the Godless colleges and claiming with justification that most Irish bishops took the same view, it recommended confirming the ban on the colleges. Accordingly a rescript—the third in the same vein—was published on 11 October 1848.

MacHale and Higgins had gained their objective. On the 15 Novem-

---

[19] Russell to Clarendon, 23 Apr. 1848, Clarendon Papers, Box 43; Murray to Clarendon, 26 Aug., 2, 3 Sept. 1848, Murray Papers; Nicholson to Murray, 12 Sept. 1848, Murray Papers.
[20] *Brevi Rilievi supra il Sistema d'insegnamento Misto che si cerca di stabiliere in Irlanda nei collegi cosi detti della Regina* (1848).

ber, the eve of Rossi's assassination, they left Rome in the last public coach to leave the city. Stopped on the road to Civita Vecchia by revolutionary guards who feared that the Pope might fly the city, the bishops blustered their way past them. They returned to an Ireland which had seen the Young Ireland revolt and bloodshed since they left. His enemies blamed MacHale for being absent during these crucial months when resistance to English rule, which they accused him of fostering, found an outlet in rebellion. The rebellion saw an end to the accusation that priests promoted assassinations, for the priests, as Clarendon admitted bitterly, played a major role in preventing the spread of the rebellion.

These different British and Irish missions to Rome in the year of revolution had little permanent success. Eglinton's clause killed the Diplomatic Relations Act to the great relief of Briggs, MacHale, and Cullen. Gentili had died in September of cholera ministering to the plague-stricken poor of Dublin. The initial hopes of Pius IX and of Wiseman that Minto's mission would strengthen the Pope's position proved illusory; Metternich never really approved of Radezsky's move and an agreement was reached between Austria and the Papal government. In any case the Austrians had been effectively warned off by Palmerston's note of 11 September 1847, and Minto's mission brought no further benefit to the Pope. There was some truth in the contention of Cullen that his presence encouraged the radicals by raising their expectations of reform. In the long term Minto's mission marks the awakening of English interest in, and support for, the Risorgimento that made England ten years later (when Russell and Palmerston were again in power) one of the strongest advocates of the overthrow of the Papal States. Had ambassadors been exchanged between England and Rome in 1848 it is probable that this turn of events and the Papal Aggression debâcle might not have occurred. By November 1848 the Pope had abandoned all effort at coming to terms with the revolution and fled to Gaeta, to regain Rome only with the aid of French bayonets.

The effort to secure approval for the Queen's Colleges failed. Cullen was brought back from Rome as primate in 1849, and as papal delegate he presided over the Synod of Thurles in 1850, the first national synod since the middle ages. At this synod the bishops, by the slenderest of majorities, condemned the colleges. Government ministers dismissed the synod as a medieval farce and described the participants as the 'mummers of Thurles', language Russell was to use in the Durham Letter where he described Catholic practices as 'superstitious mummeries'. Although Russell was convinced that the desire for knowledge would not be quenched by the 'Pope's extinguisher', the bishops took the initiative and launched a Catholic University with Newman as first rector. Significantly, too, they spoke out in favour of tenant right.[21] Irish Catholicism was beginning a new and more aggressive phase in its history.

Despite the opposition of Connelly and the reluctance of his fellow-bishops Wiseman became the first cardinal-archbishop of Westminster. His flamboyant pastoral 'From out the Flaminian Gate' and Russell's over-reaction in the Durham Letter set at rest Briggs' fear of collusion between them. The 'pompous pastoral' as he called it, angered Shrewsbury. Beaumont denounced papal aggression and the Duke of Norfolk left the Church. Ironically, too, the train of events sparked off by Wiseman's action led to greater clerical intervention in politics as Catholics united in a common front against the Ecclesiastical Titles Bill. The bill and the Durham Letter destroyed the position of Murray and the moderates who had constantly protested to Rome the good-will of the government to the Church. Nicholson, who had left for Corfu a few days before the rescript had been issued, offered the Pope a refuge under the British flag either in Corfu or in Malta. After a brief episcopal career, marred by ill-health and misunderstandings with the government, he retired to Stroud in 1851.

As in many European countries, education remained a sensitive area in the relations between Church and State. The attitude adopted by the Church during these years towards non-denominational education was to endure, and still colours its attitude in Northern Ireland. Since education had at times been used for proselytism, and as government hoped that the colleges would weaken the influence of the clergy in Irish society, the bishops' outlook was coherent and understandable. They saw their attitude as the profoundly pastoral one of guarding the students' faith.

The bishops' fear of collusion between Rome and London was to endure. It had surfaced during the veto controversy in 1814, and continued later through the Parnell period and up to the Treaty of 1922. Every suspicion of negotiation between Britain and Rome alarmed Irish Catholics, particularly the bishops. In 1921 Bishop O'Doherty of Clonfert, in his capacity as secretary to the bishops' conference, wrote in careful understatement: 'We know our people and can forecast the effects of any adverse pronouncements. Irishmen would feel that as a result of threats or promises made by a great power, Rome had become the instrument of

---

[21] *Decreta Synodi Plenariae Episcoporum Hiberniae apud Thurles habitae, anno mdcccl* (1851); Clarendon to Russell, 31 Aug. 1850; Clarendon to Sir George Grey, 20 Sept. 1850; Russell to Clarendon, Clarendon Papers.

British domination here. . .'.[22] Although to the government this counter-activity of the bishops was political, in their eyes it was essentially pastoral. They were, of course, influenced by national feelings, but their priority as churchmen was to keep their flock Catholic and they feared that 'collusion' between Britain and Rome would alienate Irish Catholics from the Church. The fact that they were forced to view with suspicion certain actions of both government and curia and to follow their own counsel, helped to make the bishops the most independent hierarchy in Europe.

What this episode illustrates is the distrust each side had of one another, a distrust that was grounded in history and fostered by the religious attitude of the times: in itself an indicator of the strength of religious feelings in England and Ireland. Catholic bishops in England and Ireland for their part could suspect normal government measures as part of a plot to destroy their religion. Not only 'King Mob' but educated Protestants like Clarendon and Palmerston could believe it quite possible that Catholic priests colluded with assassins; they shared a native anti-Catholic tradition, the all-pervasiveness of which Newman in his Lectures on the Present Position of Catholics set out, in 1851, to reveal. Russell's personal commitment to the principles of the Reformation influenced his public stance as Prime Minister. Papal aggression and the Durham Letter showed that there was a limit to Whig tolerance, for the United Kingdom was still a Protestant state. Beneath sincere expressions of toleration and efforts to provide fair treatment on the part of the Liberal ministers, the bishops sensed this hostility. Some, like Archbishop Murray played it down, and, convinced of the English sense of fair play, hoped that, with the passage of time, misunderstandings would disappear. Others, like MacHale, by aggressively exaggerating this hostility appeared to justify it. Cullen, the bishop whose influence was to be the most enduring, believed in this hostility, although his attitude mellowed with time. He determined not to compromise until his Church was on a par with the Established Church.

The 1850s saw the sacking of chapels in Stockport, religious strife in city streets, and calls for investigation of Maynooth College and Catholic convents. In turn, Cullen pressed relentlessly for the disestablishment of the Church of Ireland. Victorian Britain and Ireland remained sharply interested in religious issues. Viewed from different viewpoints both whiggery and popery still flourished.

St Patrick's College, Maynooth

---

[22] Cited in D. Keogh, *The Vatican, the Bishops and Irish Politics, 1919–39* (London, 1986), pp. 69–9.

THE IRISH ABROAD: MICHAEL CONDON IN SCOTLAND, 1845–1878

by BERNARD ASPINWALL

I N May 1859, a beautifully printed card urging Revd Michael Condon
to visit 'La Plus Belle Dame de Greenock' dropped through his letter-
box. He had just arrived that day in his new parish of Cartsdyke.[1]
Given the prejudice encountered, the appalling living conditions, and the
endless demands on him and his fellow clergy, their resistance to such
charms seems remarkable. The Irish were allegedly 'liars, blasphemous,
ignorant, lying, thieving etc.'[2] And that was a Scottish priest speaking. Not
surprisingly Condon could write to a Scottish priest: 'I cannot wonder that
being treated like *a dog* by your confrere, I should be classed among dogs
by yourself.'[3]

Life had been hard. After a severe bout of fever following his early
ministry in the Glasgow slums, he had been sent to the remote crumbling
parish of Campbeltown: having transformed that church he was sent to
build a new church and school at Hamilton. His immense labours and
success there were rewarded with yet another new parish among the
Greenock poor. After over twenty years' frustration in the Western
District of Scotland, even his resilient spirit was wearing thin.

Michael Condon, one of eight children, was born at Greaves, Cool-
cappa, County Limerick in 1817. The other children who survived infancy
emigrated to America: John in 1849; Helene, the following year; his
parents went in 1852 with Anastasia and Patrick, later a renowned colonel
in the Irish Brigade in the American Civil War and afterwards a Fenian;
and finally Mary, who had served as an unaffiliated Good Shepherd sister
at Youghal, became a Dominican in 1861, and went to New York in 1867.
With no family in the old country, Condon's emotional attachment to

---

[1] Glasgow Archdiocesan Archives, Condon Diaries (hereafter cited as C.D.), 1859, p. 625. The
diaries are part later autobiography and part contemporary notes.

[2] Revd D. McNab at Bathgate, quoted *Free Press*, 3 May 1862. The Aberdeen son of a Presbyterian convert and so automatically suspect to many Irish, he later emigrated in 1867 with
some parishioners from his wealthy chapel and established a successful church in Melbourne,
Australia. He later became a missionary to the aborigines. Obituary in *Scottish Catholic Directory*
(1897), pp. 254–6.

[3] C.D., Condon to Revd C. Reid, 14 Jan. 1864; also to Revd. W. Gordon, 31 Dec. 1863; 1850, p. 37
shows Condon's frustration: 'After the fever years of Glasgow and my journeyings for
Campbeltown I fondly thought my missionary labours might end.'

Irish exiles increased. He himself was middle-aged and saw the necessity for a psychological boost for them and himself. Degraded and denigrated in their largely labouring jobs in the sugar factory and on the railways, the Irish wanted compensating recognition of their national sensibilities within the Scottish church.[4] It made sense but it held dangers.

Condon illustrates several aspects of the Irish experience in Scotland: social origins; training and pastoral attitudes; the slow development of Catholic revivalism; and Irish adjustment, assimilation or disintegration. He represents the new breed of priest who was emerging in the early nineteenth century from the poor farmer background.[5] To all these points, his didactic *Diary* with his intense personal loyalties and gentle self-dramatization provides moving documentary evidence.

His parents had struggled on the land. He himself had undergone immense hardships to acquire the education and money for his seminary training. His experience at Youghal under the rigorous ascetic, Revd John Foley, strengthened his resilient determination to succeed as a priest. His sentimentality, sense of wondrous awe and sympathy for folk religion developed alongside a rigorous almost Jansenist, puritanical ideology. His Irishness was later reinforced at All Hallows under the later Dean of Limerick, Dr Richard O'Brien.[6]

These forces shaped his critical judgements on many Scottish clergy: their shortcomings, their lack of fraternal social habits, and their lack of zeal for his Irish charges. Slipshod and self-seeking Scots compared unfavourably with Tridentine discipline. His selfless, demanding dedication invariably made his assistants' lives hard. Schooled in hardship himself, his attitudes to sexual behaviour and to temperance made him a 'modernizer' of the Irish Catholic community. With his educational drives he was equipping his co-religionists for upward social mobility and innoculating them against Scottish Protestant culture. Not surprisingly he was to be secretary of the Irish clerical complainants to Propaganda in

---

[4] C.D., 1830, autobiographical entry, and James Handley, *The Irish in Scotland* (Glasgow, 1947).

[5] See S. J. Connolly, *Priests and People in Pre-Famine Ireland, 1780–1845* (New York, 1982) and Desmond J. Keenan, *The Catholic Church in Nineteenth-Century Ireland: A Sociological Study* (Dublin, 1983).

[6] See below. Revd Dr O'Brien, 1809–85, continued his friendship in Scotland. See for example C.D., July 1846, p. 469, 24 March 1860, p. 688, 28 June, 24 August, 14 Dec., 1869. The founder of the Catholic Young Men's Society, novelist and supporter of the 1868–75 Amnesty Movement, O'Brien found his organization used as an antidote to Fenianism. See M. J. Egan, *Life of Dean O'Brien* (Dublin, 1944); R. V. Comerford, *The Fenians in Context; Irish Politics and Society, 1848–82* (Dublin, 1985), pp. 112, 143, 187; David Thornley, *Isaac Butt and Home Rule* (London, 1964).

1864.[7] Zeal, efficiency and the Irish were interchangeable notions. Ironically, the Irish church in the west of Scotland, far from following the American model, fell under Archbishop Charles Eyre, an aristocratic Englishman whose family owned considerable estates in Ireland. But that suited Condon, who under the restored Scottish hierarchy became one of the first canons of Glasgow in 1884.[8] His conservative, ultramontane, socialist, and nationalist outlook had contained more radical souls within the framework of modern Scottish Catholicism.

The uncouth image of the Irish clergy in Scotland was well established in the nineteenth century. Bishop Scott of the Western District bluntly begged the bishop of Limerick to send 'no more cabbage stumps'.[9] As early as 1835 he did not want any more priests from Youghal. Such attitudes may reflect more on Scottish and Presbyterian snobbery than on actual behaviour: Cardinal Antonelli was described as 'sprung from a family of donkey drivers'.[10] As the Irish in general were reputedly less industrious, sober, or amenable to Scottish clerical influences, their condition seemed little improved by emigration to Glasgow.[11] Scottish Catholic clergy were anxious: they wanted to maintain a quiet holding operation in the hope that the Irish would disappear. They feared virulent anti-Catholicism: they worried inordinately about finances and they sometimes despised their co-religionists.[12] Like their fellow countrymen, the apostles of the upwardly mobile, entrepreneurial society, they were apprehensive about real challenge and change within Scottish society.

While the immigrants tended to be labourers, dockers, miners, or seasonal agricultural labourers, their mobility and turnover rates seem to have been extremely high. Their upward mobility and their persistence in a district seems to have been low.[13] Effective pastoral care, institutional

---

[7] See a copy of the petition distributed with the *Glasgow Free Press*, 7 May 1864. On 'modernization' see Elizabeth Malcolm, 'The Catholic Church and the Irish Temperance Movement, 1838–1901', *Irish Historical Studies*, 23 (1982–3), pp. 1–16 and her 'Temperance and Irish Nationalism' in *Ireland Under the Union: Varieties of Tension: Essays in Honour of T. W. Moody*, ed. F. S. L. Lyons and R. A. J. Hawkins (Oxford, 1980), pp. 69–114.

[8] Obituary in *Scottish Catholic Directory*, 1903, pp. 48–54. Also see Bernard J. Canning, *Irish-Born Secular Priests in Scotland, 1829–1979* (Greenock, 1979).

[9] C.D., 1847, p. 504.

[10] Alexander Robertson, *The Papal Conquest* (London, 1909), p. 156. On the background see my 'Popery in Scotland: Image and Reality, 1820–1920', *Records of the Scottish Church History Society*, 22 (1986), pp. 235–57.

[11] See Handley, *The Irish*, and his *The Navvy in Scotland* (Cork, 1970).

[12] Edinburgh, Scottish Catholic archives, Blairs Papers contain much correspondence of Bishop Murdoch from 1848 expressing such views.

[13] See Handley, *The Irish*, and C.D., 1857, p. 442.

structures, and building developments within an increasingly assertive ultramontane enthusiasm might inculcate some emotional stability and provide a portable faith amid their wildly fluctuating personal circumstances. Epidemics, short term employment, and frequent removals provided few personal roots. Condon's genius was to meet that need in ministering to an urbanized, traumatized, ethnic group which lacked political and economic power. He gave a sense of pride in their communal achievements: in schools, churches, and organizations.

Scottish Catholicism had three distinct elements: the Irish; the largely north-eastern Scottish bishops and clergy; and the new Oxbridge converts like Robert Monteith. They were respectively the disorientated, the cautious and canny, and the zealous optimists.[14] In ministering to the Irish, Condon used ultramontane zealous optimism for his expansive and expensive strategy. To hard pressed, apprehensive Scottish bishops, such notions seemed like Irish fecklessness: Bishop Murdoch once reproached Condon for spending 4*d.* on a fare to a sick call.[15] Somewhat antipathetic to the Irish and concerned for the 'Scottish' nature of the church in a Presbyterian nation, they were reluctant developers.

Condon's training had prepared him for hardships, as Theodore K. Hoppen has suggested, he was impervious to misery and poor fare.[16] For the first twelve years of his life he was barefoot. On at least four occasions he was saved from drowning. His early chequered education came at the hands of masters who varied from excellent to appalling. The hard won family shillings went to his later residence for schooling around Rathkeale, Askeaton, Ardagh, and Shanagolden. In seeking finances for his seminary training, he himself began teaching at Kilmallock and then loyally served at Askeaton under the redoubtable archdeacon Fitzgerald: 'a man generous in all but money'.[17] His efforts to raise the £20 seminary fees proved fruitless. In 1839 in desperation and under considerable financial pressure from his ailing parents, who were now reduced to a tiny cottage, he walked 160 miles to submit a vain request for a customs post to Daniel O'Connell. Disappointed in his hopes of patronage from either

[14] See my 'The Scottish Dimension: Robert Monteith and the Origins of Modern Catholic Social Thought', *DRev.* 97 (1979), pp. 46–68, and 'The Formation of the Catholic Community in the west of Scotland: Some Preliminary Outlines', *IR* 33 (1982), pp. 44–57.

[15] C.D., 1851, p. 65.

[16] K. Theodore Hoppen, *Education, Politics and Society in Ireland, 1832–1885* (Oxford, 1984), p. 174.

[17] C.D. 1838, p. 104. Also pp. 95–104; 1830, p. 92; 1841, p. 159. Also see Alexis de Tocqueville, *Voyages en Angleterre*, ed. P. J. P. Meyer (Paris, 1958), pp. 108–11 for Fitzgerald's radical passions, which influenced Condon.

Fitzgerald, Bishop Ryan of Limerick, or O'Connell, he was shocked by his own sexual awakening. Although rejecting 'the profanity of poets',[18] he himself began writing poetry: 'I resolved to confide in no man, but to repose all my confidence in God and my own energies; to amass every trifle and to live like a recluse on anything that might sustain me and send me to college.'[19] Significantly, in 1841, Condon took the pledge from Fr Mathew and became a temperance orator.[20]

His fortunes dramatically altered. He became a teacher in Askeaton National School at £15 a year plus keep. There Fr Thomas Wallace, a priest on the Glasgow mission, told him about Fr Peter Forbes of Glasgow who had agreed to teach at John Foley's new seminary in Youghal. In exchange the first three priests would be sent to Glasgow.[21]

Foley, an ascetic and temperance zealot, had served twelve years on the continent before establishing his missionary college with lay brothers' and penitents' houses. After walking to and fro to secure admission as a £10 p.a. vegetarian man, Condon endured astonishing hardship and squalor with some of the roughest men he had ever met: with no cutlery and meals literally thrown on the bare boards before them. Dark, damp rooms, unplastered walls, leaking roof, and badly laid floors made the place 'a ventilating machine . . . as desolate as if exiled to the remotest corner of the earth . . . I was determined to weather it or die'.[22]

From 1842–4, Condon taught Classics, French, English, and Geometry to some 70 seminary students. The staff also included a bizarre Polish emigré priest, Britski, and a Frenchman, Dr Aubert, who tried to persuade Condon to join his Plymouth Oblate mission. Harsh conditions, the discrediting of alleged miracles at the seminary by *The Tablet*, and the opening of All Hallows in 1842, reduced the number of students to twenty-five.[23] But with his trust in the poor Irish as the repository of the faith, Condon remained loyal to Foley through his illness and death: 'I was now a solitary man, thrown on the bleak world again.'[24]

---

[18] C.D. 1838, p. 117, also pp. 97–8 rejecting girls.

[19] *Ibid.*, 1841, no date or page.

[20] *Ibid.*, 1841, pp. 121, 137, 174–6. Later after illness and about to depart for Glasgow he asked Fr Mathew if he might take a medicinal drink. The orator physically lifted him and literally threw him out of his Cork house, shouting that he would write to Bishop Murdoch to prevent any other drunkard going to Glasgow. Condon was terrified as Mathew came after him—to apologise for his terrible misunderstanding!

[21] *Ibid.*, 1841, pp. 137–58.

[22] *Ibid.*, no date or pagination.

[23] *Ibid.*, 1842; 1843, chapter 18.

[24] *Ibid.*, 1844, chapter 19.

Condon then went to All Hallows to join the majority of Youghal students. Fortunately, Peter Forbes and Bishop Murdoch accepted him for the Western District. That was much to the annoyance of their superior Bishop Scott in Glasgow, who wanted no further priests from Youghal.[25] The first three recruits had proved unsatisfactory. In Glasgow, Hugh Quigley had proved an embarrassing Repealer. Exiled to Campbeltown, 'the Siberia of the lowlands',[26] he had begun a pamphlet war with Bishop Scott. He was later to pursue an equally lively career in America.[27] The two others, John Scanlan and John McDermott, followed him there.[28]

Condon entered the seminary with the help of contributions from friends and clergy whom he later conscientiously repaid in full. He complained about the segregated dormitory which provided little opportunity to meet other intending Scottish missionaries. Although he had rejected a free place at Maynooth, he remained very poor: 'For weeks, if not months, my long soutane was nearly my whole dress. My shoes were worn. I had sold all my shirts but one to buy a new pair of trousers. But trousers and shirts wore away. I was cold, bore all silently and cheerfully. I knew there was a Providence.'[29]

In October 1845 he was ordained in Glasgow. His sense of isolation was intensified by the gruff, cool Scottish clergy; 'I being a teetotaller and of more retiring disposition, found little favour among them. They were civil though cold.'[30] On first meeting with Bishop Murdoch's cousin, John Bremner, at Bishop Scott's jubilee celebrations, he was told: 'the best introduction now is £1. 5s. 0d.'[31]

But he did find reassurance in ethnic solidarity: his first experience of horrifying fever calls in October 1845 'taught me the depth of faith in the Irish heart as I had never realised before'.[32] In 1847 four fellow priests died

[25] C.D., 1844, chapter 19. On All Hallows see John Tracy Ellis, *The Catholic Priest in the United States: Historical Investigations* (Collegeville, Minn., 1971), pp. 21, 305.

[26] C.D., 1842, no date, no pagination.

[27] *Ibid.*, 1842; Quigley wrote *A Series of Letters in Answer to the Rev. S. N. Berman's Letters to Archbishop Hughes* (Troy, N.Y., 1852); *The Prophet of the Ruined Abbey* (New York, 1854); *Profit and Loss* (New York, 1873); *The Cross and the Shamrock* (Dublin, 1900 edn.). He was later suspended by the Glasgow born Bishop Gilmore of Cleveland.

[28] C.D., 1850, p. 12 on Scanlan. Also *Constitutional*, 31 Dec. 1851; C.D., 1845, p. 502, on McDermott. Born 1818, he left Scotland for the U.S.A. in 1846, he wrote *Fr Jonathan or the Scottish Convert*.

[29] C.D., 1844, no date or pagination.

[30] *Ibid.*, 1848, p. 555. Also 1845, p. 457.

[31] *Ibid.*, 1845, p. 444.

[32] *Ibid.*, 15 Oct., 1846, p. 442 on his first sick call.

of fever: he himself in a typical day had 47 sick calls.[33] He confronted numerous difficulties: a demented man threatening him with a scythe in a darkened room, administering the sacrament to the sick in beds beside recently deceased corpses, to a dying woman turned out of her home with her daughter to die on a sick cart *en route* to the poor house, and many more. After two terrible years of ministry in 'coffin like apartments',[34] in back closes, and on stairwells, he was invalided out to Campbeltown.

There, still subject to bouts of fever fainting, his loyalty to church and people was tried to the limit by the notorious poverty and loneliness. A predecessor used to have to go to confession in Belfast: 'The bare mention of Campbeltown was enough to bring a refractory priest to silence and submission.'[35] The parish extended from Lochgilphead, 53 miles to the north, to Southend, 15 miles to the south, to Islay in the west and across to Ayrshire in the east. On one occasion, Condon had to travel 600 miles to make one sick call on Islay.[36] Although he had some 300–400 distillery workers and others from Rathlin and Antrim in the town, he also had some 200 farmworkers scattered through the vast area. He arrived penniless to find no money, no food, and no servant. Soon after the sheriff's officer arrived to auction off his household goods for debt. Although he himself later paid off all debts in full, in his early days he had to exist on egg flip and coffee essence.[37] His parish leaders included a customs officer, a leading local smuggler, a pawnbroker, and a petty outfitter.

Similar conditions confronted him on his arrival in Hamilton in 1850: a bare chapel, no furniture, and no school. His predecessor, a relative of the auxiliary bishop, Smith, was as 'proud as Lucifer and more profligate'.[38] His frequent lengthy absences collecting funds in England had yielded a mere £10 in six months. His incestuous sister was the rather bibulous housekeeper. On two occasions falling masonry in the ill-maintained chapel narrowly missed killing the priest and then a mother and boy. In 1859, at Cartsdyke, Condon again arrived to find no money, no furniture, no running water, and a chapel house built over an open cess pit.[39] In each

---

[33] *Ibid.*, 13 June 1847.
[34] *Ibid.*, 15 Oct. 1846, pp. 442, 484–5.
[35] *Ibid.*, 1847, p. 505, and also p. 524. His housekeeper was a Presbyterian minister's illegitimate daughter.
[36] *Ibid.*, 14 Aug. 1849, pp. 600–3.
[37] *Ibid.*, 1848, pp. 513–14, 549–50, 559, 566.
[38] *Ibid.*, 1845, p. 356 and 1850, pl. 62.
[39] *Ibid.*, 1862, pp. 605–25.

case he regenerated the parishes with improved finances, buildings, schools, and parochial organizations.

The priestly begging tour is a much neglected aspect of nineteenth-century activity. Irish priests from Sligo, Meath, and Dublin frequently appeared in Glasgow.[40] In 1848-9, Condon went on fifteen separate begging tours for his Campbeltown mission. In Edinburgh's squalid Cowgate, his 220 calls over twelve days realized £23. 19s. 11½d.[41] In Dundee, Stephen Keenan, a former Glasgow teacher and author of a renowned catechism, warmly welcomed him. He received over £20 from 387 individual contributions and 44 factory collections.[42] After further trips through Glasgow, Ayr, Dumbarton, Hamilton, Coatbridge, and Stranraer, Condon went over to Ireland for some six months until May 1850. At Ballymena, Mr Jellott, the Grand Master of the Orange Lodge, gave him five shillings. Sometimes, as in Dublin, Condon successfully competed with other Scottish clergy. In his travels through Donegal, Fermanagh, Sligo, Newry, Dundalk, Maynooth, All Hallows, Dublin, Limerick, and back to Scotland, he raised almost £220.[43] On his return he was immediately replaced at Campbeltown by a Scottish priest and transferred to Hamilton.

In August 1862, amid the Lancashire cotton crisis of the American Civil War, he went on a begging tour to Liverpool. Although competing with eight other collectors, he raised £60. Two months later he was appealing in Glasgow.[44]

These activities took place against a background of slowly developing 'Romanization' and revivalism. Bishop Murdoch and the Scottish clergy were somewhat resistant. Their cautious Scottish attitudes did not radiate exuberant notions of Catholicism. To a considerable degree, however, the church in the Western District was a laissez-faire democracy. Every priest was his own bishop. The Roman collar was rarely worn except on Sunday and parochial censuses, even if taken, were rarely sent to the bishop. Obligatory annual clerical retreats were laid down in 1839 but the arrival of the Famine Irish put an end to these and other proposals.[45] The enthusiastic John Lillis, a Youghal and All Hallows priest, who invariably preached on

[40] C.D., 1849, p. 633; 1857, pp. 498-9 and many others.
[41] Ibid., 1848, p. 558.
[42] Ibid., 1848, pp. 559-63. On Revd S. Keenan see B. J. Canning, Irish-Born Priests, pp. 168-70.
[43] C.D., 16 Nov. 1849 to 1 May 1850, pp. 615-660 as per pagination. See 4-7 Dec. 1849, p. 628 on Mr Jellott.
[44] Ibid., 1862, p. 368.
[45] Ibid., 1845, p. 438.

the Virgin Mary, was considered peculiar in his Mariolatry: the local mill girls nicknamed him, 'Father Mary'.[46]

Fears of a Presbyterian backlash made Scottish clergy reluctant to encourage the return of the Jesuits.[47] They preferred limited public visibility. St Mary's, Glasgow (1842), then the largest church in Scotland, did not have an organ, held benediction but once a month, and held no Sunday evening service except the rosary during Lent and Advent. In 1853, Condon celebrated the first choral Mass in Hamilton since the Reformation and joined in the Corpus Christi procession at nearby Carstairs House.[48] He shared Monteith's taste for emotional hymns and increasingly decorative chapels. At his Barrhead chapel, benediction began only in 1855. Bishop Murdoch objected to the cost of the sanctuary lamp for his Hamilton chapel. Only in 1866 did Condon acquire the stations of the cross for his Cartsdyke chapel.

Preaching was often ignored or left until after Mass. Condon himself was a keen preacher and was mortified when, after an early sermon, a collier slapped him on the back and said, 'No doubt about it, your reverence, it is within you, if you could only get it out of you.'[49] Later he met Ignatius Spencer, the renowned convert Passionist preacher, who was on a collecting visit to Glasgow.[50] A year later in Glenalla, Ireland, Condon was appalled by a preacher reducing his poor congregation to weeping and crying. On complaining that such techniques would lose the faith in Glasgow, the priest replied. 'I could whip them through the country and not one of them would turn on me.'[51] By contrast, a visiting Irish preacher felt Condon's congregation was hard hearted. As he said, before the sermon was 'half over I would have every soul, man, woman and child on their knees and striking their breast'.[52] In 1866, his first parish mission showed the limitations of Scottish Catholic revivalism. Amid the slow conduct of confessions, one of the Redemptorists was frequently

[46] *Ibid.*, 1850, p. 594.
[47] *Ibid.*, 1849, p. 610. Bishop Smith wrote to Condon: 'I am afraid you will discover that it is easier to contract for a *fine* church than to pay for its erection.' Also see London, Farm Street, Jesuit archives, Scottish correspondence, 1857–9 for many grudging Scottish episcopal views.
[48] C.D., 1852, p. 135; Aug. 1853, p. 206. Manning serves Condon's Mass; 11 Dec. 1853, p. 226 for the first choral Mass; 1855, p. 379, receives Monteith's translation of *The Hidden Treasure*, places Caravaggio's 'Adoration of the Magi' in the first benediction; p. 466 first sung litany.
[49] *Ibid.*, 1846, p. 453.
[50] *Ibid.*, 4 July 1849, p. 569.
[51] *Ibid.*, 1850, p. 544, Revd Driver.
[52] *Ibid.*, 9–15 Aug. 1849, Revd D. O'Keefe; 1866, p. 355. Also see J. H. Murphy, 'The Role of the Vincentian Mission in the Irish Counter Reformation of the Mid-Nineteenth Century', *Irish Historical Studies*, 24 (1984–5), pp. 152–71. The assault is in C.D., 1862, p. 394.

aroused to assault his penitents! Jesuit missions were more successful and low key.

After initial enthusiasm, Condon's efforts to establish Rosary Circles failed: 'perpetual flittings of our people break them up'.[53] His success in rallying his youth into the Catholic Young Men's Society proved equally limited. He brought his old friend and mentor, Dean O'Brien, the founder of the C.Y.M.S., to inaugurate the organization at Greenock. Its benefit society, welfare, library, and recreational facilities, could only boast 46 members in 1880.[54]

More successfully, Condon gained large support for his temperance views. As we have seen, he had taken the pledge from Fr Mathew in 1841.[55] His arrival in Glasgow followed on the successful temperance work of the Limerick priest, his friend James Enraght. With James B. Bryson, an enterprising Catholic lawyer, Condon was encouraged to go round Glasgow every Sunday to preach teetotalism to schoolchildren. That work he eventually abandoned in 1848.[56] His first act at Hamilton was to found a juvenile temperance association. Within a fortnight, Fr John Gray brought 1200 Glasgow children to his rally.[57] In Greenock later, Condon enrolled some 1100 in his temperance organization.[58]

Drink was a major Scottish problem. The Irish in Scotland were equally prone to intemperance. After 'public, universal and scandalous rows',[59] a neighbouring priest in Eaglesham had to abandon his peasant Irish as 'vilest rubbish' in 'that den of fornicators, adulterers and brothel keepers and drunkards'.[60] In adjoining Busby, the Dublin Irish were 'civilized' but still a prey to drink.[61] Condon was associated with Fr Edward Hannan,[62] the temperance founder of Hibernian Football Club in Edinburgh. It was Catholic, Irish, sober and healthy. Not surprisingly, Greenock had a strong

---

[53] C.D., 1869, p. 155; Edinburgh, Scottish Catholic archives, Blairs Papers, Bishop Murdoch to Dr Smith, 18 Oct. 1848: 'the best of our people continue to cross the Atlantic and by we will be left a congregation of beggars'.

[54] C.D., Notebook, p. 156.

[55] Ibid., 1841, p. 175.

[56] Ibid., 1845, pp. 443–53 and General Soiree and Presentation to Revd Peter Forbes, 27 April 1846 (Glasgow, 1846), p. 8 for Condon's temperance speech. Also P. Rogers, Fr Theobald Mathew (Dublin, 1944), pp. 78–80.

[57] C.D., 2 Feb., 21 July 1851.

[58] Scottish Catholic Directory (1884), p. 288.

[59] C.D., 1862, p. 524. Also see Desmond J. Keenan, The Catholic Church in Nineteenth Century Ireland, p. 105 on alcohol consumption.

[60] C.D., 1862, p. 524 citing Mission book of 1850.

[61] Ibid., 1862, p. 527 citing Mission book, 8 Feb. 1852.

[62] Tablet, Jan. 1873 and B. J. Canning, Irish-Born, pp. 134–5.

League of the Cross organization. Even so, Condon had to sack his frequently inebriated Barrhead gravedigger, a toping cleric, and, later, a frequently drunken Greenock teacher.[63] Sobriety would restore faith in God and Ireland: moral and social uplift would then follow.

His zeal for the temperance pledge brought Condon into close contact with the Revd Ignatius Spencer, the Passionist. Almost fifteen years after their first encounter in Glasgow, Spencer gave his last retreats in Greenock and Port Glasgow. In Condon's parish he enrolled some 200 young tee-totallers.[64] A few days later he died in the grounds of Monteith's Carstairs mansion. With the Monteith family, Condon also enjoyed an excellent working relationship, whether through the Catholic revivalism of processions at Carstairs House, the St Margaret Association, or the Ladies' Altar Society. In supporting less fortunate individuals or parishes, they helped to create a well organized, cohesive, disciplined, ultramontane body.[65]

That modernizing impulse was apparent as early as 1848 when Condon became a director of the Campbeltown Savings Bank.[66] In stressing self-improvement through education, better churches, reading and general uplift, Condon showed the limitations of his social criticism. In the face of overwhelming odds, he accepted a line of maximum achievement with minimum disruption within the existing order. At the same time he gave his ethnic community a psychological boost through pride in their group success.

If he endorsed neither radical structural reform nor militant Irish nationalism, he showed patriotism and considerable sympathy with the underdog. Preoccupied with maintaining dignity in poverty, he gave his little money to cholera victims and to poor miners in their 1856 strike. He listened sympathetically to the speeches of the Chartist, Feargus O'Connor[67] and the Scottish miners' leader, John MacDonald.[68] His impartiality secured industrial compensation for the miner's widow and land from staunch Protestants.[69] By encouraging the St Vincent de Paul Society, he

---

[63] *Tablet*, 11 June 1881, 19 Sept. 1885; C.D., 1862, p. 387.

[64] Revd Pius, *The Life of Fr Ignatius Spencer* (Dublin, 1866), p. 497, also p. 398; C.D., 25 July 1861, 24 Aug. 1864, pp. 771–7.

[65] *Ibid.*, 8 Jan. 1852, p. 111; 22, 25 Jan. 1853 to meet Newman at Carstairs but he was called to trial in London; 26 Sept. 1864.

[66] *Ibid.*, 1849, p. 611.

[67] *Ibid.*, 1848, p. 557.

[68] *Ibid.*, 1859, p. 500. Condon had been to the coal face. Also see Gordon Wilson, *Alexander MacDonald* (Aberdeen, 1982).

[69] C.D., Mar. 1858, widow Boyle. Also 1857, p. 447, re. Mr Stewart and allowing Mass on his property.

generated a sense of Christian security through parochial charity. Stability, well-being, and caring made for real community.

That attitude reflected several influences. He was dependent upon his poor congregations: 'the sweat of the poor labouring classes is the Californian mine that supports religion in Scotland'.[70] But he enjoyed the support of some few shopkeepers, a handful of successful entrepreneurs, and some extremely wealthy converts. In particular, the convert Princess Marie Louise of Baden, the Duchess of Hamilton,[71] was an immensely generous benefactor. She provided him with a gold chalice, church decorations, and an altar. She also used him as her private chaplain at her summer retreat, Kames Castle, Arran.

Her friends, Count and Countess Villeneuve-Arifat,[72] published an account of Condon's work in France, rallied friends in support and sent contributions. In 1853 they sent £176.[73] Another aristocratic friend, Lady Harriet Hamilton, a parishioner at Campbeltown, amid her later friendship with the Empress Eugenie, still continued her support.[74] So too did Robert Monteith. The embodiment of the Oxford movement in Scotland, the immensely wealthy friend of Tennyson and Newman, he regularly gave his support either in cash, as with £50 to Campbeltown in 1848, or with £250 for the Hamilton church debt in 1853, as well as in preventing petty bigotry in his Blantyre mill.[75] On their visits, Colonel Gerard of Rochsoles, Lady Georgiana Fullerton and Lady Augustus Craven helped.[76] The Penneys, a wealthy chemical industry family, were equally generous until they went bankrupt.[77]

Consciously or otherwise, these powerful friends may have inhibited Condon from radical social criticism. Equally, whatever his brother Patrick's enthusiasms,[78] successive Irish failures since 1829 limited his nationalist zeal. For him, Irish resurrection would follow moral

---

[70] C.D., quoting *Free Press*, 6 June 1857; 1864 addenda to Propaganda. In 1860 Condon established the Greenock S.V.P. society, pp. 711-13. See my 'The Welfare State within the State: The Saint Vincent de Paul Society in Glasgow, 1848-1920', *SCH* 23 (1986), pp. 445-60.

[71] Also C.D., 1851; 6 Dec. 1850; 1861, p. 359; *Tablet*, 15 Mar. 1851.

[72] Marie Therese de Villeneuve-Arifat, *Une Messe en Ecosse* (Paris, 1857).

[73] C.D., 1850, p. 56. Also see 1852, p. 123, £31. 16s. from France, including Henry V.

[74] *Ibid.*, 1860, p. 663. Empress Eugenie asked after Condon and his poetry.

[75] *Ibid.*, 1850, p. 38.

[76] *Ibid.*, 1851, p. 90; 3 Sept. 1858. Gerard, a convert, was the father of John, the Jesuit editor of *The Month*, and two popular novelist daughters, Dorothea and Frances.

[77] *Ibid.*, 14, 17 Dec. 1869. They had given Condon a horse in Hamilton.

[78] See various American newspaper clippings in *ibid.*, 1856, p. 446.

regeneration.[79] To that extent the myth of Irish nationality served his pastoral needs. Perhaps *his* antipathy to England lay in traditional Catholic attitudes to wealth. The alien appearance of his first collier and 'the new world' of a sugar refinery shocked him.[80] The old agrarian myth died hard.

Condon's zeal for intellectual cultivation was far more intense. If, as Peter Doyle has argued,[81] English seminaries had few books, Condon shows that independent scholarly characters could still emerge from restricted backgrounds. He frequently bought books and invariably established priests' and parish libraries.[82] He encouraged and wrote for the popular Scottish Catholic press. He even recruited at least one experienced newspaperman from Ireland. He himself published numerous poems and articles in *Duffy's Magazine*, *The Tablet*, and *The Glasgow Free Press*.[83] Some were reprinted in American journals. He attended lectures by Cardinal Wiseman, T. E. Bradley of *The Lamp*, and many others.[84] He scorned the Irish ecclesiastical critics of Newman and his Catholic University.[85] He bought himself a spinnet, furiously taught himself to play and composed music to accompany his children's songs.[86] Like a neighbouring parish priest, he saw country rambles as a search for culture, for a 'usable' Catholic past and an escape from urban depravity. Through such trips and children's revivals, rough, wild, unmanageable infants might be transformed.[87]

Education was a priority. Incensed by a snobbish Irish bishop,[88] who demanded fewer teaching duties for his nuns in Glasgow, Condon stressed education as an antidote to Ribbon 'blackguardism'.[89] In spite of Bishop Murdoch's misgivings, he even built a school in Greenock before a chapel house.[90] The prospect of government grants intensified his enthusiasm. By

---

[79] See for example Auguste J. Thebaud, SJ, *The Irish Race in the Past and the Present* (New York, 1878), especially pp. 327–73, and E. D. Steele, 'Cardinal Cullen and Irish Nationality', *Irish Historical Studies*, 19 (1974–5), pp. 239–60.

[80] C.D., 26 Jan. 1852, p. 118 and 14 Aug. 1860.

[81] Peter Doyle, 'The Education and Training of Roman Catholic Priests in the Nineteenth Century', *JEH* 35 (1984), pp. 208–19.

[82] e.g. C.D., 1858, p. 347.

[83] e.g. *Ibid.*, Nov. 1849, pp. 612, 636 and 25 Mar. 1853.

[84] *Ibid.*, 1854, p. 281 and 7, 14, 21 Jan. 1856.

[85] *Ibid.*, 20 July 1859.

[86] *Ibid.*, 1852, p. 136.

[87] *Ibid.*, 1869, p. 644. Also J. Sharp, 'Juvenile Holiness: Catholic Revivalism among Children in Victorian Britain', *JEH* 35 (1984), pp. 220–38.

[88] C.D., 23 Nov. 1847 and 1850, p. 591.

[89] *Ibid.*, 1862, p. 372. Archbishop Eyre later followed this policy.

[90] *Scottish Catholic Directory* (1881), p. 98. As usual from Condon censuses, he found a fifth of the parish was under 13 years of age.

1866 he had over 100 day pupils and fifty night school adults. By 1880, he had some 600 children of school age in the parish.[91] They were the future of the church. He sought out teaching nuns, trained staff and pupil teachers. The limitations of his lay staff were all too apparent. His first Hamilton teacher was a broken Indian army man. A Greenock teacher, well trained in Ireland and widely experienced in England, was burdened with an insane wife and three institutionalized children. He died within a year of his appointment. A convert teacher went off to the army inside twelve months. Two others died of bronchitis and alcoholism. Others emigrated to America. An ill-trained mistress had to be sent to Glasgow for music lessons. The turnover rate for his women teachers was high. Even so, his schools invariably received glowing praise for their achievements from government inspectors.[92]

If Condon had not time consuming troubles enough, his assistants sometimes proved impossible burdens. As Bishop Murdoch wrote 'between you and me, what with bad priests and useless priests, I am kept in much distress and anxiety'.[93] Though few, Condon had more than his share of them.

Quality control was not all that it might have been. His Irish predecessor in Campbeltown and Hamilton, having fathered two children, emigrated to Nova Scotia. Suspended, he then proceeded to make a fortune in California, Australia, and London. After running stark naked through the streets, he died in an asylum. Another, allegedly an anonymous Irish contributor to the *Glasgow Free Press*, fathered a child, placed the responsibility on his lay brother, and left to teach in Boston. Another spent lavishly and refused payment. A Belgian priest, outraged by Condon's puritanical attitudes to his smoking and his modest beer drinking, soon left Greenock.[94]

Condon managed to play down sectarian animosity. His positive action in local hardship assisted. He invariably gave money to disaster funds, relief in unemployment, and played a responsible role against sectarian demagogues. In Hamilton, Protestant extremists soon abandoned a planned programme of twelve anti-Catholic lectures after Condon had delivered a three hour Catholic statement.[95] Greenock did not witness any

---

[91] C.D., 1862, pp. 372, 374, 393; 28 Aug., Deery; 22 Dec. 1869, Godsil; 1, 22 Dec. 1870??
[92] Bishop Murdoch to Revd Danaher, 15 Mar. 1852 quoted in *Ibid.*, p. 263.
[93] *Ibid.*, Smith, 1850; McCafferty, 1858, pp. 475 and 507; 1859, p. 642; Adelauer, 27 Nov. 1870; 2 Jan., 2 Mar., 12 May., 8 June, 11 July, 26 Aug., 5 Sept. 1871.
[94] *Ibid.*, 1852, p. 136; 1854, p. 244 and 1855, pp. 325-6.
[95] *Ibid.*, p. 329.

repetition of the 1853 or 1855 riots in his time. For the unemployed poor, he generously supported non-sectarian soup kitchens in both Hamilton and Barrhead, where his actions were very well received.[96] In 1868, he even envisaged co-operation with Protestants in promoting the defence of religious education against radical liberals.[97]

His main differences occurred over the placement of Catholic orphans with far distant Protestant families.[98] Through his persistent objection to the high-handed behaviour of the local Greenock board, he eventually won his point. His genial but principled stands won respect from Protestant entrepreneurs, ministers, and others.

Condon's interests were wide ranging, but his prickly nature prevented relaxed relationships. Only in situations with a defined structure, as with his bishop, or the duchess, or his own parish, did he flourish. Beyond that he found fulfilment in activity. He was invariably reading, corresponding, or developing some new personal or parish initiative. Bishop Moriaty of Kerry, Dean O'Brien, Dr Cahill, and John S. McCorry,[99] the Scottish controversialist, were not infrequent visitors. He was confident in his dealings with the Duchess of Hamilton: Bishops Smith and Murdoch were far less socially assured. Smith refused to meet her and, to his astonishment, Murdoch found her as humble 'as a mill girl'.[100] Condon also travelled extensively in Ireland, Scotland, and England. In 1854 he went over to Bruges, met with Professor J. B. Robertson,[101] the Scottish luminary who contributed to the *Dublin Review*, and delighted in Memling's paintings and the continental Catholic revival. Seven years later, with his relative, Augustus Henry Keane,[102] a distinguished graduate and tutor at Newman's university, he toured Europe. From Hamburg to Dresden, through Prague, Munich, Venice, and Belgium, he fully indulged his artistic interests.

His lonely nature also pushed him into a leading role in the Irish-

---

[96] *Ibid.*, 2 April 1856, p. 336.
[97] *Ibid.*, 1869, p. 405.
[98] e.g., *ibid.*, 11, 18 Oct., 1 Nov., 20 Dec., 1862; 26 June 1877.
[99] e.g., *ibid.*, 1853, p. 195, Cahill; 1854, pp. 244, 274, O'Brien; 1855, p. 339, Moriarty. J. S. McCorry, 1812–80, founder of the Amnesty movement, 1868–75 and a voluminous controversialist, he has 16 titles in the British Library catalogue, *Scottish Catholic Directory* (1881); Monteith loathed Cahill's oratory, C.D., 1853, pp. 193–5.
[100] *Ibid.*, 1853, p. 216. Smith refused to go, 1866, p. 362.
[101] *Ibid.*, 1854, p. 300.
[102] See *Letters and Diaries of John Henry Newman*, C. S. Dessain et al. (eds), 31 vols (London, 1961–77), 18, pp. 20, 26, 410, 446, 451–52. Keane wrote numerous scholarly works, became professor of Hindustani, University of London and died unreconciled to the Church in 1912.

Scottish conflict in the 1860s. In Glasgow from the days of the Catholic Association, clerical-lay relations had been strained on occasion over cash, control and ethnicity. Condon acted against a background of the *Glasgow Free Press*, which under Augustus Keane had become the uncompromising organ of the Irish laity.[103] His virulent, almost paranoid outburst against the dominance of the 'Hielan clique' in the Western District produced a catalogue of grievances. These included Scottish financial secrecy and incompetence, the removals of Irish clergy from various parishes, and an alleged Scottish memorial to Rome against the appointment of an Irish bishop in Scotland. Keane then sent a memorial to Rome expressing Irish grievances. But Scotland was not to follow the American model: Irish 'imperialism' was to be checked. Those lay, ultra nationalist demands bedevilled other reasonable clerical grievances. Condon's simmering resentments of many years surfaced. Disappointments, petty personal slights and immense self sacrifices on a tiny income merged with popular anger at 'domineering clerical and episcopal government'.[104] He recalled the Irish priest, a fever victim of 1847, who hated the Scots, the patriotic preaching of Archdeacon McCann of Derry which outraged Bishop Murdoch, and many more. In a bitter mood, on a visit to Ireland in 1862, Condon even considered going to America.[105]

In December 1862, following a meeting of Scottish and Irish clergy, two parties developed. The anonymous *Post Prandial*[106] appeared blasting the character of several very thinly disguised Irish clergy. Allegedly financed by eighteen Scottish priests, this tract attacked them as lascivious, swindlers, and conspiratorial careerists. Some Scottish priests, it was claimed, read and distributed the tract in their churches. Several pamphlets in the same vein followed. To another Scottish priest, his Irish

---

[103] The main outlines are well known but some details here are new. See J. E. Handley, *The Irish*, pp. 199-231; D. McRoberts, 'The Restoration of the Scottish Catholic Hierarchy in 1878' in his *Modern Scottish Catholicism, 1878-1978* (Glasgow, 1979), pp. 3-29; V. A. McClelland, 'The Irish Clergy and Archbishop Manning's Visitation to the Western District of Scotland, 1867', *Catholic Historical Review*, 53 (1967-8), pp. 1-27 and pp. 229-50 and his 'Documents Relating to the Appointment of A Delegate Apostolic For Scotland, 1868', *IR* 8 (1957), pp. 93-8. A similar clash over Ireland and nationality raged around the American *Brownson's Quarterly Review* (1856-61), especially after Revd Jeremiah Cummings attacked the All Hallows clergy.

[104] C.D., 1862, p. 376.

[105] *Ibid.*, 1847, p. 516. Revd R. Kelsh; 1849, p. 633, Revd McCann.

[106] Glasgow archdiocesan archives, copy: C.D., Jottings, 1863-70. 17 Dec. 1862, 23 Oct. 1864. Bishop Gray appears as 'Mr. Peculiar' and Bishop Murdoch as 'old woman'. Passions were further heightened by the former editor of the *Free Press* being charged with drunkenness and the present editor with sexual indecency.

brethren were 'a disreputable lot'.[107] The Irish clergy, in turn, expressed their lack of confidence in the existing Glasgow administration.

Condon and his supporters wanted a more open, participatory and sensitive church: the Irish laity were the repository of faith. The whole affair convinced him 'in my theory about the necessity of calling the laity to a participation in the discipline of the Church. In no other way can the many disorders of the Church be cured ... only the people directly ... through public opinion and the priesthood can heal the wounds of the Church.'[108] To hear them reciting the rosary in a mission chapel revival gave Condon 'a clear, full conception of the majesty of the faith'.[109] Such optimism contrasted with the cautious pessimism of their Scottish brethren. Their call for an Irish bishop was partly an ethnic demand for identity in the Church. The laity were 95 per cent Irish. More Irish clergy would reduce the awesome burdens. The Church belonged to all, as Archbishop Hughes of New York said, 'as much as the sunbeams of heaven'.[110] Outraged by the exclusion of Irish hymns from the hymnals, they saw an exclusive Scottish church would not retain the Irish. An Irish bishop was both necessary and expedient. Hardwork alone was inadequate: 'were he St Paul, he could not do all the work of the vicariate. We need some organisation to reduce our complex elements to order.'[111] Effective, assertive leadership under a restored Scottish hierarchy would give Irish pastors canonical rights in their parishes, regulate salaries, and prevent abuses; regular ecclesiastical conferences would follow; and better financial organization would be targeted to clear common objectives. It was a demand for greater professionalism.

In March 1864, Condon sent a memorial to Rome[112] in which 22 Irish clergy of the Western District protested against its improvident, insensitive administration. Significantly, at least two thirds of the memorialists came from All Hallows. They further protested against the secret selection of Scottish bishops and the arbitrary removal of successful Irish priests in favour of Scottish clergy. To Condon's dismay, amid these

---

[107] As above. C.D., Revd S. Reid cited in letter, Condon to Revd P. Forbes, 23 Feb. 1864, also 4, 11 Dec. 1864. I have been unable to find Revd J. Dowd's two scurrilous anti-Irish pamphlets.

[108] *Ibid.*, 1862, p. 405.

[109] *Ibid.*, 1857, p. 435.

[110] *Ibid.*, 1864, Addenda, summarizing the submissions to Cardinal Barnabo, Propaganda and Condon to Bishop Murdoch, 4 Mar. 1864. The Western District, with only one priest per 5,000 Catholics, still refused to recruit any more All Hallows' priests however cheap their provision.

[111] *Ibid.*, 1864, annual clerical meeting.

[112] *Ibid.*, 1864, entry summarizing submissions.

controversies, Patrick Lavelle,[113] the militant Irish nationalist priest, descended upon Glasgow to publicly flay the Scottish clergy. Denounced by Cardinal Cullen, his incipient Fenianism might blight their case in Rome.

Scottish clannishness seemed accurate. The bishops of the Western District were invariably related to each other. Of the 96 priests in the Western District, 42 were Irish by birth or parents. Only 36 were Scots.[114] Holding executive positions as bishops or trustees of institutions, the Scots refused to recruit much-needed clergy from Ireland. They were indifferent to the dangers confronting poor law children. Even the Catholic reformatory was staffed entirely by Scottish priests and their lay relatives: its low quality, condition, and management were questioned.[115] But where the *Free Press* saw 'imaginary debts',[116] Condon welcomed debts. Building schools was preferable to cautious savings 'against some future and probably imaginary want'.[117] Such investments provided a parochial focal point. Unimpressed, Cardinal Barnabo of Propaganda rebuked their 'uncanonical' attack on their bishop.[118]

Two years later, Condon approached Rome with a similar catalogue of defects and demanded the appointment of a 'neutral' to the Western District.[119] Even he was not above using scurrilous rumour to curb Scottish dominance. Bishop Murdoch's successor, Gray, was a 'nonentity' and some of his entourage scandalous.[120] Whatever the truth, he effectively undermined likely Scottish nominees. Eighteen months later, he could congratulate Barnabo on the appointment of the unfortunate Irish Vincentian, Dr Lynch as bishop in Glasgow.[121]

The general crisis persisted, intensified by Fenianism, real and alleged, until the *Free Press* finally closed in 1868.[122] At the same time the clerical

---

[113] C.D., 29 Marc., 3, 17 May, 27 Sept. 1862. On Lavelle, a priest of Tuam under Archbishop MacHale, see R. V. Comerford, *The Fenians*, pp. 113-14. He wrote *The Irish Landlord Since The Revolution* (Dublin, 1870).

[114] C.D., 1862, p. 381. Also Memorial to Cardinal Barnabo, 4 Mar. 1864.

[115] *Ibid.*, Correspondence, Barnabo to Condon, 19 April 1864.

[116] *Ibid.*, 1861, and Handley, *The Irish*, pp. 213-22.

[117] C.D., 23 Nov. 1864, petition notes.

[118] *Ibid.*, Barnabo to Condon, 19 April 1864.

[119] *Ibid.*, Correspondence, Cardinal Barnabo, 7 Mr. 1866.

[120] *Ibid.*, 1845, p. 355, 9 April, 2 Sept. 1867. The character assassination of Revd Alexander Munro, a Presbyterian convert, is atrocious. Condon himself had been similarly accused in his early days. Part of the explanation may be Munro's Scottish misgivings about Irish nationalism.

[121] *Ibid.*, 9 April 1867, letter to Cardinal Barnabo.

[122] See Handley, *The Irish*.

divisions received attention. Archbishop Manning came, interviewed Condon among others, and reported to Rome. The Englishman, Charles Eyre, was appointed to Glasgow, a prelude to the restoration of the hierarchy. Under this like-minded cleric, Condon became one of the first canons of the restored chapter in 1884. With recognition, his career continued the same committed way in his St Patrick's parish, Glasgow until his death in 1902.[123]

He had served the west of Scotland well through the period of immigration, growth, adjustment, and restoration. From personal contact and commitment to charismatic clergy like himself, the Church moved on to a more institutional, rigid structure. With the development of political pressure groups and newspapers, the emerging Catholic middle class was mobilized.[124] The Irish laity had been disciplined and their nationalism contained. They had been reduced to a supportive role under professionalized priests.

The Church in Scotland had neither become an Irish preserve, as in America, nor a subordinate of Cardinal Cullen. It was more Scottish than it knew. Organization, professionalism, and the definition of roles in a clericalized Church produced effective infrastructures in chapels, schools, seminary, and the like. Caring and compassionate, like Condon himself, it was none the less somewhat remote from its clients. Increasingly occupied with committees on schools, fund-raising and the like, he was now a middle manager in an ultramontane corporation as it developed its spiritual and material riches.[125] As with leaving Ireland, the gains were considerable and so were the losses.

University of Glasgow

---

[123] Obituary in *Scottish Catholic Directory* (1903).

[124] Condon lists six Glasgow pastorals condemning Irish revolutionary bodies, C.D., 1870. Also see J. F. McCaffrey, 'Roman Catholics in Scotland in the Nineteenth and Twentieth Centuries', *Records of the Scottish Church History Society*, 21 (1983), pp. 275–300 and his 'Politics and Catholic Community since 1878' in McRoberts (ed.), *Modern Scottish Catholicism*, pp. 140–55. As in Ireland, Fenian weakness was related to the strength of the priests and parochial activities. See K. R. M. Short, *The Dynamite War: Irish-American Bombers in Victorian Britain* (Dublin, 1979), pp. 103–53; Oliver MacDonagh, *States of Mind: A Study of Anglo-Irish Conflict, 1780–1980* (London, 1983), pp. 99–103; R. V. Comerford, *The Fenians*, p. 112. On the ambivalence of the Church see J. Newsinger, 'Revolution and Catholicism in Ireland, 1848–1923', *European Studies Review*, 9 (1979), pp. 457–80.

[125] C.D., 3 May 1870, schools, 12 Oct. 1876, bazaar organizer. He notes his brother, Patrick, at the Hayes' White House, 13 Mar. 1877. The later brief entries suggest a parish priest in a new bureaucracy.

'TOO PECULIARLY ANGLICAN': THE ROLE OF THE ESTABLISHED CHURCH IN IRELAND AS A NEGATIVE MODEL IN THE DEVELOPMENT OF THE CHURCH MISSIONARY SOCIETY'S COMMITMENT TO INDEPENDENT NATIVE CHURCHES, 1856-1872

by C. PETER WILLIAMS

HENRY Venn, the CMS[1] honorary secretary between 1841 and 1872, is rightly regarded as the great exponent of self-supporting, self-propagating, and self-governing churches. I have argued elsehwere that his principles took many years to assume their final shape and that, when they did, they contained what was regarded as an ecclesiological anomaly—that there should be separate bishops for different races in the same geographical area.[2] Between about 1856 and 1872 Venn became increasingly daring in his proposals, abandoned his support for the idea of a single European bishop wherever there were European settlers and was instrumental, not only in having Samuel Crowther appointed as the first black bishop in West Africa or in responding positively to suggestions of an Indian bishop for South India, but also in proposing, both in India and in China, that the needs of a truly culturally integrated independent 'native' church demanded that its structures should be separated from those of the imported European church.

There were many factors which caused Venn to move decisively in such directions. Disillusionment with paternalistic missionaries who constantly undermined the potential of their converts was a major one. There was furthermore a climate of opinion favourably disposed to disengagement. In 1865 Parliament declared that Britain's objective for West Africa was the encouragement of those qualities 'which may render it possible for us more and more to transfer to them the administration of all the Governments, with a view to our ultimate withdrawal from all, except,

---

[1] Church Missionary Society (MS, London, CMS and Birmingham, University of Birmingham).
[2] C. Peter Williams, 'The Ideal of the Self-Governing Church: An Examination of the Official Policies of the Church Missionary Society in Relation to the Development of Self-Governing Churches, with Special Reference to Creating an Independent Native Episcopate from c.1850–c.1910' (Ph.D. thesis, University of London, 1986), cap. 1.

probably Sierra Leone'.[3] There were finally severely practical reasons. The high death rate amongst missionaries, combined with a distinct falling off in recruitment in the sixties,[4] made it possible to speculate that the tendency of missionaries to smother by over-pastoring was being 'providentially corrected'.[5]

If these were the major factors in creating a context in which such thinking could be accepted without undue difficulty, I want to suggest that a particular understanding of the failure of the Established Church in Ireland as a missionary force in its own country was sufficiently cogent, especially in the depressing decade leading up to disestablishment,[6] to act as convincing supportive evidence from church history. The interpretation, echoed by modern historians,[7] was a simple one—the Established Church failed in Ireland because it did not identify itself sufficiently with the indigenous people and their culture and institutions. It had the even greater disadvantage of being the creed of a conquering and hated race. Only if missionary strategy could learn from such failings could there be any hope of missionary advance in the 'heathen' world. Venn did not himself speak of Ireland to any degree. He was given to writing terse memoranda without a great deal of historical illustration. Indeed his most recent biographer, Wilbert Shenk, rather unfairly I think, argues that he never approached the key question of missionary bishops 'biblically, theologically, or on the basis of early church history'.[8] Leaving aside the fact that Venn's little known biography of Francis Xavier represented an important quarrying of church, if not early church, history,[9] the role of the influential CMS journal the *Intelligencer* must be considered. It was edited from its launching in 1849 almost to Venn's death by a graduate of Trinity

---

[3] Winfried Baumgart, *Imperialism: The Idea and Reality of British and French Colonial Expansion, 1880–1914* (Oxford, 1982), p. 15.

[4] C. Peter Williams, 'The Recruitment and Training of Overseas Missionaries in England between 1850 and 1900' (M.Litt. thesis, University of Bristol, 1976), pp. 6–7.

[5] *Church Missionary Intelligencer* (hereafter *CMI*) (1862), p. 123; (1869), p. 98.

[6] From 1856 Irish Roman Catholics favouring disestablishment made links with the Liberation Society in Britain and the strength of the case grew through the sixties. See Kevin B. Nowlan, 'Disestablishment: 1800–1869' in Michael Hurley (ed.), *Irish Anglicanism, 1869–1969* (Dublin, 1970), pp. 10–17.

[7] Desmond Bowen, *The Protestant Crusade in Ireland, 1800–70: A Study of Protestant-Catholic Relations between the Act of Union and Disestablishment* (Dublin, 1978), pp. 73–4, 246–7.

[8] Wilbert R. Shenk, 'Henry Venn as Missionary Theorist and Administrator' (Ph.D. thesis, University of Aberdeen, 1978), p. 258.

[9] Henry Venn, *The Missionary Life and Labours of Francis Xavier Taken from His Own Correspondence with a Sketch of the General Results of Roman Catholic Missions among the Heathen* (London, 1862).

College, Dublin,[10] the Reverend Joseph Ridgeway. Ridgeway frequently took up the issues with which Venn was dealing and provided biblical, historical, and theological arguments to bolster the analysis. Ireland obviously engaged his passions and, through much convoluted prose, metaphor and simile, he provided a convincing historical rationale for the emerging CMS approach to self-governing churches and, in so doing, showed that evangelical Anglican assessment of the Established Church in Ireland was by no means uniform.

From 1856 the Society for the Propagation of the Gospel had been pressing for the extension of the episcopate in India. It was much influenced by the Tractarian conviction that bishops should be part of the missionary operation from its beginning. Venn and the CMS opposed the proposals,[11] but in a way which advanced their own thinking significantly. They grounded their case partly on a fear of episcopal tyranny (particularly where there were no clear canons to control any abuse of authority); partly on the judgement that Indian lay opinion was not sufficiently developed to have the restraining hand on any episcopal excesses which it had in England; partly on the appropriateness of evangelists preceding bishops—a bishop's functions (confirming, ordaining, superintending, and encouraging) could only be exercised after the Church had been properly established,[12] and partly on the conviction that, if a European bishop was appointed, it was likely to impair the development of the true objective of missionary work—'the euthanasia of the Mission and the establishment of a Native Church, under Native Pastors *and a Native Episcopate*'.[13]

This was a major development in Venn's thinking and leads Gavin White to suggest that some credit for his position as the revered prophet of the autonomous independent church 'may belong to those High Churchmen who spurred him to study the relationship of bishop and church in the mission field'.[14] Some credit for the acceptance of these ideas

---

[10] *CMI* (1871), p. 193.
[11] T. E. Yates, *Venn and Victorian Bishops Abroad: The Missionary Policies of Henry Venn and Their Repercussions upon the Anglican Episcopate of the Colonial Period, 1841-1872* (London, 1978), pp. 99-109.
[12] G/AZ/1/1, no. 92, 14 April 1856, 'Memorial of the Church Missionary Society upon the Extension of the Episcopate in India'; *ibid.*, no. 93, 13 April 1857, another Memorial with the same title; *ibid.*, no. 98, 12 April 1858, 'Letter to a Friend with the Views of the Committee of the Church Missionary Society on the Extension of the Episcopate in India', Henry Venn.
[13] 'Letter to a Friend', p. 2 [my italics].
[14] 'The Idea of the Missionary Bishop in Mid-Nineteenth Century Anglicanism', MST, General Theological Seminary, New York (1968), p. 86.

within the evangelical world must also go to Ridgeway and his *Intelligencer* articles, where the arguments from Irish history figure prominently, and to these we must now turn.

Ridgeway argued that the New Testament showed evangelism taking place in Antioch without apostolic command but as a result of '*individual earnestness*'.[15] The evangelist, in other words, preceded the bishop. Certainly the bishop could also be an evangelist but if he acted in the way typical of bishops he would expect 'deference to his views', with the unfortunate result that the whole mission would be 'cast into the mould of his idiosyncracy' and its work would consequently be cramped.[16] He went on to press the case for native clergy pointing out that St Paul had ordained local elders within a short period of time—in sharp contrast to contemporary practice. Native pastors were now being used and, if that was the right way forward, and if there was belief in the power of the Holy Spirit to transform, then 'it is indispensible that when the Episcopate be permanized among them, it be, because of the same reasons precisely, native—not European'.[17] This was not only because of the cultural affinity it would bring, but also because a European bishop would be regarded as superior and thus would not be subjected to the 'wholesome check' on his power which mixing with equals in Britain brought. The danger would be especially great in India where a besetting weakness of the Indian character was undue servility. The Gospel must ever attack such servility but, he asked, if episcopacy was transferred from England to a simple native church, would 'the native clergy ever divest themselves of the consciousness of immeasurable inferiority, or approach the bishop, except in a servile and almost abject manner?' The English bishop enjoyed 'temporal rank'[18] but any measure of transfer of such secular power in India would 'have a most ruinous effect, and the progress of the native pastorate towards manliness of character, candour in the avowal of their real sentiments, straightforwardness and self-reliance in action, would be grievously hindered, if not precluded altogether'.[19]

If any proof of this was required, he went on, you need look no further than the Established Church in Ireland. It was weak and this was because its sees were filled 'not by individuals raised up from the body of the church itself, but by Englishmen, who could only imperfectly adapt them-

[15] *CMI* (1858), p. 162.
[16] *Ibid.*, p. 163.
[17] *Ibid.*, p. 172.
[18] *Ibid.*, p. 173.
[19] *Ibid.*, pp. 173–4.

selves to the English speaking clergy and congregations over whom they were to preside, but who with the mass of the Irish-speaking people had no sympathy whatever'. Not only did they not speak Irish, they were pledged to its abolition. They were frequently ignorant of the country and 'laboured to advance rather the interests of England, than the interests of the Gospel'. From this analysis, which also held true, he contended, of the Welsh Church, Ridgeway felt confident to reach powerful conclusions:

> Place a foreign Episcopate over a native church, and then will follow, unavoidably, such an infusion of the foreign element into the clergy of that church as will lessen their sympathy with the native element, and unfit them for usefulness. Affinity and power of assimilation will be seriously interfered with. . . . the result will be, the isolation of the church from the native community around it, and the cessation of all action on its part as a Missionary church.[20]

In brief, 'To permanize a native church under the continued superintendence of a foreign episcopate, would be to stunt its growth' and prevent its proper independence. The objection would always be brought against such an episcopate that it was not 'homogeneous with the church'.[21]

It has to be granted that though Ridgeway's arguments were against European missionary bishops, they were only in favour of indigenous bishops in the future.[22] Even then 'native' bishops could only be appointed where there were no considerable body of Europeans, else there would be introduced 'into our ecclesiastical arrangements a principle adverse to that amalgamation of races in which alone there is security for permanent peace and true prosperity . . .'. In other words the primary target for such an experiment was somewhere where there were very few Europeans, such as Tinnevelly in South India.[23] This concern that the Church should unite different racial groups, under a European bishop, was in keeping with most church tradition and is therefore, in many ways, unremarkable. It did not however fit very easily with Ridgeway's critique of Irish history. This demanded Irish bishops and yet the fact of a substantial English presence, on the amalgamation of races argument, justified English bishops. The challenge of the next decade was to move that reasoning dramatically.

[20] *Ibid.*, p. 174.
[21] *Ibid.*, p. 38.
[22] *Ibid.*, p. 176.
[23] *Ibid.*, p. 171.

Partly as a consequence of Venn's opposition,[24] the idea of missionary bishops in India was postponed but the issues it raised had been placed firmly on Venn's agenda. By the sixties he was emphasizing that the whole notion of European superintendence should be dropped to be replaced by 'Native and European *Association*'.[25] He consequently sought, by every means at his disposal, to allow the indigenous church a greater independence. In his famous 'Second Paper' of 1861[26] he suggested a means by which missionaries would hand over to the local church and made it absolutely clear that 'a native Episcopate' was the objective.[27]

The *Intelligencer*, under Ridgeway, provided powerful support for a native episcopate, again using Ireland as the prime historical sobering case study. Ordinary Indians expected that converts would be 'denationalized'. In order to avoid this 'the native character of the new churches must be carefully and jealously preserved. They must remain homogeneous with the masses around.'[28] They must strike a root in the native soil and not, like lichens, provide their own soil. The Reformation in Ireland, with the appointment of English bishops and the commitment to the English language, was a good example of the unfortunate denationalizing process. As a result 'no active sympathies were permitted to be formed' between the Irish people and the Established Church.[29] It was 'a thing of lichen growth. It was in no union with the people, and received no welcome there.' 'Are', Ridgeway asked rhetorically, 'the native churches in India to be similarly dealt with? A theory of secular policy wrought the mischief in Ireland; a theory of ecclesiastical policy may do the same for India.' Having waxed once again on the adverse effects of the interaction of European episcopal ideas and Indian servility,[30] he observed that the Established Church in Ireland was disliked, not merely for cultural reasons, but because it was the church of the conqueror. 'If the Hindu thinks that, with a change of faith, national essentials must be changed, he will decline having to do with an

---

[24] There were other powerful opponents including Bishop Tait of London. See Randall Thomas Davidson and William Benham, *Life of Archibald Campbell Tait: Archbishop of Canterbury*, 2 vols (London, 1891), 1, p. 329.

[25] C A3/L1, p. 65, 23 May 1860, Venn to Crowther. See also CN/L6, pp. 384–8, 8 June 1860, Venn and W. Knight's instructions to the Revd and Mrs J. W. Gedge.

[26] Venn wrote three papers on the organization of the native church (1851, 1861, and 1866) and these, together with his 1868 paper on nationality, contained the core of his thinking on this subject. They can be found in W. Knight, *The Missionary Secretariat of Henry Venn, BD* (London, 1880), pp. 282–92, 305–21.

[27] Knight, *The Missionary Secretariat*, p. 313.

[28] *CMI* (1861), p. 274.

[29] *Ibid.*, p. 275.

[30] *Ibid.*, p. 276.

element so disturbing.' What he wants to see is whether Christianity 'can leave behind English materiality, and, as a simple spiritual system, enter into the Hindu, and deal with Hindu materiality as it has done with that which is English.' If the church is to act as 'leaven' on the people, it must be 'homogeneous.' Thus, he postulated optimistically, 'for each distinct nation a different leaven is being provided, and Christianity is being clothed with that language and form which will enable it to act . . .'. Import an English bishop, paid from England, and you will have someone 'naturalized as regards England' but 'an alien to them'. Indeed he prophesied in conclusion, 'Commence with an Anglican Episcopate over a native church, and there never will be a native Episcopate.'[31]

The way forward then was clear. It was to avoid the Irish failure and to seek to integrate the Church fully with its own culture. What Venn and others began to discern more distinctly was that the great obstacles to this were the settlers and, perhaps even more so, the missionaries. One blatant example of this was the missionaries' refusal in West Africa to accept Bishop Crowther's superintendence.[32] Venn consequently responded positively to a proposal from Bishop Cotton, the Metropolitan of India, that an Indian bishop should be appointed in South India. Significantly, the proposal originated with a Celtic missionary, the Welshman John Thomas. His biographer speculates, 'Possibly he knew how the Church in Wales in the past had suffered from the neglect of the native ministry, and through foisting on the people not a few pastors who could not speak their language, and who neglected to study their characteristics. . .'.[33] Venn welcomed the proposal and quoted Crowther as saying that it would be better if missionaries were regarded as 'separate from the native church not under his jurisdiction but rather as *amici curiae*'. He went on:

> My own lengthened experience of Missions, in all parts of the world, strongly impels me to the conclusion that the European element in a native church is the great snare and hindrance to its growth: and that if native churches were kept separate with a complete organization of Bishop, priest and Deacon they would exhibit a more firm and rapid development.

Venn was quite aware, and willing to face up to the fact, that his proposal would 'violate the principle of geographic Dioceses'.[34] It was a radical

[31] *Ibid.*, p. 277.
[32] C A2/o49/65, 15 November 1864, the Revd David Hinderer to Venn.
[33] A. H. Grey-Edwards, *The Life of a Great Missionary; Memoir of the Revd John Thomas, CMS Missionary at Megnanapuram Tinnevelly, South India, 1836-1870* (London, 1904), p. 148.
[34] C I1/L6, pp. 430-1, 26 December 1864, Venn to Bishop Cotton.

proposition, so radical that some modern historians, who wish to present Venn as a properly orthodox churchman, follow Stock in dismissing any apparent evidence for separate episcopal oversight as an exception.[35] That Venn remained consistent to this policy cannot be argued here,[36] except to say that when the question of creating a new diocese in China arose his preferred solution was separate bishops for the Chinese and English, even though this would produce overlapping episcopates.[37]

In connection with China Ireland comes into this story again. Ridgeway, in an article in 1869,[38] offers another prolonged investigation of the organization of the 'native' church. The dangers of Anglicization, and of denationalization were once more underlined. How 'prejudicial' it would be if the Chinese came to regard Christianity 'as essentially Anglican in its character and destructive in the influence which it exercises' on 'their national distinctiveness and independence'.[39] Clearly the CMS was much influenced by the unsettled political state in China and was alert to the dangers of converts becoming 'in some way detached from their native rulers, and under European protection'.[40] Ireland illustrated a policy to be avoided. Used in relation to the Chinese context, there was an even greater emphasis than with respect to India on the harm that had flowed from the connection between ruler and religion. The policy of the English government to the Irish Protestant Church 'constituted a most grave impediment to the progress of Protestant Christianity in that country'. Having dealt again with the misguided attitude to culture and language, Ridgeway stressed that great care must be taken 'to eliminate from Christianity everything of mere national peculiarity which might excite prejudice and obstruct progress'. The essential principles of the Christian faith were like 'bare grain', but this grain must be allowed to grow in the soil of the countries in which it has been planted. The soil will 'modify the product' in a way which will be in sympathy with 'the

---

[35] Yates, *Venn and Victorian Bishops Abroad*, p. 131; for Stock see Williams, 'The Ideal', pp. 66, 69–70, 108–9, 344–5.

[36] See Williams, 'The Ideal', pp. 50–76.

[37] *Ibid.*, pp. 63–73.

[38] The article, like the others considered, was not signed by Ridgeway but Eugene Stock, who was in the best position to know, attributes the 1858, 1861, and 1869 articles tohim, see *CMI* (1901), p. 261 and *History of the Church Missionary Society*, 3 vols (London, 1899), 2, p. 590.

[39] *CMI* (1869), p. 99.

[40] Papers on Africa, Mauritius, China, and New Zealand, no. 37, August 1872 'Memorandum on the Need of Some Modification of an Order in Council, May 1848, Respecting the Jurisdiction of the Bishop of Victoria (China)', p. 2.

national peculiarities'—'. . . we must be careful to avoid in any wise so dealing with them as to lead the people to think, that, in becoming Christian, they have become less native, and are not so entirely and identically national as they were.'[41] This risk was particularly great where, as in Ireland, conqueror and conquered had not been assimilated. This lesson underlined the importance of avoiding any suggestion that becoming a Christian is 'incompatible with loyalty to their own rulers'.[42] What must therefore be accepted is that the independent native church will, very probably, be quite distinctive in appearance, rather like the difference in looks between mother and daughter—'one characterized by many and by no means unpleasing variations'.[43]

The implications of such reasoning for China and elsewhere are clear. 'If we would propagate Christianity amongst the natives, we must be prepared to let them have it without its Anglicanism, which, however valuable for us, is unsuitable for them',[44] and this might mean, for example, a radical rewriting of the Prayer Book. 'It is impossible to doubt', he wrote of India, 'that a liturgy might be found which would be better adapted for it than that of the Church of England.'[45] Hence in China it was crucial to appoint a missionary bishop who knew the language[46] and who was 'prepared to lay aside, before he enters the gate of independent China, whatever of authority and jurisdiction may have been super-added to his office by the Crown of England, and, reducing himself to the simplicity of a primitive Bishop, go forth in the exercise of that power which is derived from Christianity alone'.[47] Though Ridgeway does not give much attention to the question of whether the bishop should have a geographic diocese, he is clear that he should not be tied down by 'territorial jurisdiction',[48] and that he would have a very different sort of relationship to his clergy, who should not, for example, be required to make promises which suggested obedience to a political authority which underpinned the ecclesiastical. Indeed the whole ordination service was 'too peculiarly Anglican to be proposed without manifest impropriety to members of an independent state . . .'.[49] Though

[41] *CMI* (1869), p. 99.
[42] *Ibid.*, p. 100.
[43] *Ibid.*, p. 104.
[44] *Ibid.*, p. 105.
[45] *Ibid.*, p. 317.
[46] *Ibid.*, p. 106.
[47] *Ibid.*, p. 312.
[48] *Ibid.*, p. 106.
[49] *Ibid.*, p. 105.

the missionary bishop would have to be a European for the moment as there were as yet only two Chinese deacons,[50] the object was a mature independent, 'native' church with its own distinctive institutions and, as soon as possible, a 'native' bishop.[51]

The story of Anglicanism in Ireland thus became part of a very radical argument for the ecclesiastical, liturgical, and cultural independence of those churches established through European missionaries. There is one final example of Ridgeway using this story as a negative model. In the following year he spoke in Ireland 'under', notes Stock, 'the shadows of Disestablishment'.[52] There the themes, we have noticed, are recounted again, though put in a wider context. Paul had been committed to founding national churches 'built up, not of strangers, but of indigenous materials ... the Christians being homogeneous with the heathen around, and therefore well fitted to reproduce amongst the masses of their countrymen the new influence of which they had become, in the first instance, the recipients'.[53] He chose elders from the young churches refusing to appoint them from longer standing churches, even though this meant a loss in knowledge and experience, 'but these were defects which time would correct, while that they were of the people amongst whom they were to labour was an advantage of primary importance'. Likewise, he claimed, the CMS had been 'careful not to Anglicize the Christian churches' which they had established 'but to conserve their nationality'. In contrast, the Church of Ireland had been 'disadvantaged by the adoption of a system the reverse of this'. Consequently it had been distrusted because it had been perceived to be 'Anglican' and the 'race-prejudice' of the Irishman had 'made him cling more tenciously [sic] to the Romish faith, which, however debased by superstition, was presented to him through the medium of his native tongue'.[54] Ridgeway asked, allowing his missiological logic to outweigh his evangelical tribalism, might disestablishment not be for the good 'so that the church, cast off by the State of England, shall no longer be regarded as Anglican, but as Irish?'[55]

---

[50] Lambeth Palace Archives, Tait Papers, vol. 169, fol. 313, 14 May 1870, Bishop Alford to Archbishop Tait.

[51] *CMI* (1869), pp. 106, 316.

[52] *History*, 2, p. 425.

[53] *CMI* (1870), p. 230. Again the article is anonymous but Stock (*History*, 2, p. 425) makes it clear that it is by Ridgeway.

[54] *CMI* (1870), p. 231.

[55] *Ibid.*, p. 232; see also *CMI* (1869), p. 102. On contemporary evangelical attitudes to disestablishment see A. Bentley, 'The Transformation of the Evangelical Party in the Church of England in the Late Nineteenth Century' (Ph.D. thesis, University of Durham, 1971), pp. 24–30.

What we have been arguing is that the historical analysis of the Established Church in Ireland gave additional support, likely to be influential because it concentrated on an area of unease high in the contemporary awareness of evangelical Anglicanism in general and of the 3000 subscribers to the *Intelligencer* in particular,[56] to conclusions (reached mainly for other reasons) about the need for churches which were self-governing and genuinely reflected indigenous culture and institutions. Perhaps because the question of the failure of Irish Anglicanism was less prominent within evangelicalism after disestablishment, or perhaps because Ridgeway died in 1871, the example of Ireland does not seem to have been used very much in subsequent discussions about the shape of the native church. It is, none the less, an example of that creative capacity to question established wisdom which dissatisfaction with one's own world and the exposure to other worlds sometimes brought to those passionately concerned with the missionary undertaking.

Though it is impossible to make more than modest claims for the impact of the Irish dimension on the case for creating self-governing churches, it is important to note in closing that the policy which emerged at this time was much more central and durable than is often thought. Ridgeway was clear in 1869 that the questions, forced to the fore in China because it was outside the Empire and because its people had such natural independence, must also be asked of India, else the Church there might 'degenerate into an excrescence, something growing on the living body, and yet not part of it'.[57] It is in keeping with this that in 1872, before the death of Venn, it was being argued that the Church in India should be reconstituted 'on an independent organic basis of its own', in a close relationship with its mother church, but standing 'as the Native Church of India' and not 'merely a poor and feeble imitation of a far distant church across the seas'.[58] By 1877 it had become formal CMS policy that it was looking for an independent native church, with its own bishops, who would exercise 'Episcopal functions in the Native Church independently of the existing Diocesan Bishops'.[59] That was to

---

[56] *Conference on Missions Held in 1860 at Liverpool* (London, 1860), p. 77.

[57] *CMI* (1869), p. 316.

[58] 'Pamphlets and Papers on India, Educational etc.', n.d., no. 13, 'Native Church Organization', p. 3. M. A. C. Warren, in his index on North India, p. 85, deposited in CMS London, speculates that this may have been from an 'associate' or 'disciple' of Venn's or even a final memorandum from him. It was in fact published in the *Madras Church Missionary Record* in 1872 and is quoted extensively by Sir Bartle Frere in *Church Congress Report* (London, 1882), pp. 531–3.

[59] See the 'Memorandum upon the Resolutions Passed at the Conference of the Bishops of the Province of India and Ceylon' etc., and bound into *CMI* (1877), p. 7.

remain official policy until the early twentieth century when integration across racial boundaries once again became the accepted objective.[60] In the early evolution, propagation, and acceptance of such a radical strategy, based, as it was, on a deeply controversial ecclesiology, the perceived failure of the Established Church in Ireland had a not insignificant part.

Trinity College, Bristol

[60] Williams, 'The Ideal', cap. 5.

THE IRISH PRIEST IN NORTH AMERICA

by OWEN DUDLEY EDWARDS

TO assert at the outset of this study, as I do, that the task before me is both impossible and essential, may be justly proclaimed a proceeding both cowardly and obvious. We are principally concerned with the nineteenth century, but the twentieth century prolonged many of the features of Irish Roman Catholic clerical identity of the nineteenth, in North America as elsewhere. Vitally important patterns and castes (social and mental) were established in the eighteenth century, and the first Irish-American Roman Catholic priest of major significance in the United States, John Carroll (1735–1815), first Roman Catholic bishop in the U.S.A. and first archbishop of Baltimore, owed his American birth initially to migration of his father's kinsmen in the late seventeenth century. Anglophone North America from 1783 consisted of two political obediences, with similarities and contrasts both subtle and, at least superficially, forceful. The huge and consistently expanding area of white settlement in North America in which the Irish Catholic clergy participated, created other great divergences: when American historians at the end of the nineteenth century under the influence of figures as divergent as Frederick Jackson Turner of the 'frontier thesis', Ulrich Bonnell Phillips of slavery apologetics, and Alfred Thayer Mahan of sea-power celebration, looked to environmentalism as the chief explanation of the American past, they may have oversimplified—indeed, they did oversimplify—but their sheer preoccupation with the question gives its own warnings against a filio-pietism which chooses to see an Irish ethnic character resolutely asserting itself to the third, fourth, and even later generations.

Irishness in the Roman Catholic clergy, as in the laity, owed much of its perceived identity among its votaries to cards of identity often dealt by North American non-Irish observers, whether friendly or hostile, critical or exploitative. Such observers leaned to the assumption of stereotypes, but those among them who looked closely were often startled by the radical contrasts which asserted themselves. H. L. Mencken, writing in the Baltimore *Sun* for 5 July 1927, commented on the dangers for Al Smith, the Roman Catholic Governor of New York, in his candidacy for the White House to be decided the following year:

> the great ecclesiastical organization of which he is an humble satellite may say or do something so inept and preposterous that his chances,

and those of every other Catholic, will go down to zero for another generation.

. . . The Catholic hierarchy in America, at the present moment . . . can show no leader comparable to Archbishop Ireland, and none even remotely comparable to Cardinal Gibbons. . . . Can you imagine Cardinal Gibbons calling in the police to rough a meeting of birth-control fanatics, as was done by certain eminent ecclesiastical dignitaries in New York a couple of years ago—to the scandal of the church and the mirth of the town? . . . Can you imagine him letting one of his parish priests set off such an orgy of wowserism as now disgraces Boston? If so, you can imagine more than I can.

. . . As one who would be delighted to see [Smith] in the White House, if only as a merited rebuke to the Methodist-Baptist tyranny which now oppresses the Republic, I confess frankly that my hopes are cooled every time I contemplate William Cardinal O'Connell and Patrick Cardinal Hayes.

Environmentalists might make something of that: O'Connell (1859–1944) of Boston and Hayes (1867–1938) of New York were from North-Eastern Irish Catholic ghetto cultures whereas James Gibbons (1834–1921) of Baltimore might be felt to reflect the gentility of Catholic-founded Maryland, and John Ireland (1838–1918) of St Paul might equally seem to embody some of the frontier compromises of Minnesota. But it was the products of the less Irish-dominated backgrounds who had personal Irish antecedents, the Baltimore-born Gibbons having been brought back to Ireland for several boyhood years, while Ireland did not reach Minnesota until his twelfth year having been born in Ireland in the ominously-named Burnchurch.[1]

---

[1] The work of John Tracy Ellis dominates the whole subject, and anything he has written or influenced is invaluable to the student, from the *Catholic Historical Review* during his editorship and subsequently, to the *New Catholic Encyclopedia* whose editor for American Catholic history, Mother Mary Peter, OSU, was a distinguished pupil of his and whose contributors, as I can personally testify, had so many reasons to bless him and her. His *Life of James Cardinal Gibbons* (2 vols, Milwaukee, 1952) is both in subject and in treatment the great exemplary work on a North American priest; his *The Formative Years of the Catholic University of America* (Washington, D.C., 1946) opens up a host of major problems; his 'American Catholics and the Intellectual Life', *Thought*, 30 (1955), pp. 351–88, inspired a most constructive debate; his *American Catholicism* (Chicago, 1955) is a profoundly judicious survey; his *Documents of American Catholic History* (2 vols, Milwaukee, 1961, Chicago, 1967) is a mine of rich material and abounds in pointers for different areas of future investigation; *The Catholic Priest in the United States*, Collegeville, Minn., 1971) edited by him contains his 'The Formation of the American Priest: An Historical Perspective', pp. 3–110, which was the main intellectual stimulus for the present essay. Ellis quietly but firmly forces the thought of students of American Catholicism,

Al Smith himself raises another symbolic question. Mencken, like all of Smith's contemporaries (and apparently Smith himself) took the ill-fated Democratic Presidential nominee of 1928 to be Irish-American; it was only after Smith's death that he was discovered to be but one-quarter Irish. The maternal grandfather who helped bring him up established him in his own Irish mould; Smith's other grandparents were Italian (name altered by U.S. immigration authorities), Austrian, and English. He 'passed for Irish'. So did many others who knew that the most politically influential non-Protestant ethnic group offered advantages in socio-political better-ment. Equally, many Irish would Anglicize their names and mute their Irish links whether or not they renounced Catholicism. Priests would be less likely to exhibit such chameleon methods, but variants of them seem possible, especially when, as in Smith's case, the decision to proclaim or disown Hibernicity had been made for them.[2]

---

whether Catholic or not, American or not, out of their personal blinkers, and was most unusual among American historians in taking account of Canadian developments. Arthur P. Monahan, 'Canada' in Patrick J. Corish (ed.), *A History of Irish Catholicism* (Dublin, 1971), 6, pt 3, is useful if largely a simple charting. Jay P. Dolan, *The American Catholic Experience* (Garden City, N.Y., 1985), is an interesting reappraisal. The *Dictionary of American Biography*, *Who Was Who in America* (especially the Historical first volume 1607-1896), *Encyclopedia Canadiana*, *The Harvard Encyclopedia of American Ethnic Groups* (1980), abound in helpful material. Thomas N. Brown, *Irish-American Nationalism 1870-1890* (Philadelplhia, 1963) marks the Copernican revolution in Irish-American lay historiography. Lawrence J. McCaffrey, *The Irish Diaspora in America* (Bloomington, 1976) is a challenging if somewhat defensive presentation by a scholar of authority in Irish history on both sides of the Atlantic. The various studies and historio-graphical surveys by David Noel Doyle are most instructive, for which most recently see *Irish Historical Studies*, 23 (1982-3), pp. 254-83. The chief influences on my remarks on Ireland are the writings of Patrick J. Corish, Maureen MacGeehin (later Wall), S. J. Connolly, and in certain respects Emmet Larkin; and the essay by Brendan Bradshaw in this volume. I had the advantage of a lifetime's instruction from my father, R. Dudley Edwards, on the questions raised herein: his last words of advice to me were given while the essay was in final draft, and he died a few hours before its last pages were written (he would not have wanted me to go to his obsequies without finishing my text). It is thanks to him that I owe my first instruction from my old tutor at University College Dublin, John A. Watt, in whose honour this in-adequate tribute has been written, and to him also the first basis of understanding with my all too generous and patient editor, W. J. Sheils. If this essay, even in a very small way, reflects some of the excitement and enthusiasm with which Professor Watt galvanized his students, I have succeeded in what I tried to do.

The quotation from Mencken was reprinted in his *A Carnival of Buncombe*, ed. Malcolm Moos (Baltimore, 1956), and may be conveniently found in its latest edition (Chicago, 1984), pp. 141-2.

[2] Smith's ancestry seems to have been discovered by Frances Perkins, his former supporter and then Roosevelt's Secretary of Labor, when she was working on the biography of Smith she did not live to write. (Information from his subsequent biographer, Matthew Josephson: H. and M. Josephson, *Al Smith: Hero of the Cities* (London, 1970)).

What was Irishness? In North America its situation initially was as much a compound of negatives as of anything positive. The Irish in this somewhat resembled the modern Canadians whose consciousness of identity so often seems to be primarily a matter of being non-British and non-American. Canadian identity in more positive terms is powerful enough, but all identity asserts itself most conspicuously at conflict-point, and Canadians seem at their most culturally forceful in indicating what they are not. Within Canadian identity today further negative points of identity are made: most obviously non-Francophone, or non-Anglophone. Canada is a society which deliberately acknowledges, as it is forced to acknowledge, that it is no 'melting-pot' (however illusory the United States 'melting-pot' myth may actually have been); and by comparison it thereby gives us some purchase on a North American past when assurance of ultimate Irish assimilation was far from certain on either side of the 49th Parallel. The Irishman in eighteenth-century North America knew himself to be non-British: his caste in Ireland told him how far his concealment of his non-Britishness was an option—the Irish Protestant Episcopalian in America having many opportunities to deHibernicize, the Irish Presbyterian having fewer, the Irish Catholic fewer still. But up to the Great Famine Irish self-identification in America seems to have been primarily by caste and county rather than by nationality. It was often his North American hosts who bore his Irishness upon the Irish immigrant. Sometimes they did not make much of it: the Irish Protestant Episcopalian immigration seems easily to have merged with its new surroundings. The Irish Presbyterians in eighteenth- and early nineteenth-century North America were much more conspicuous: their self-consciousness in a tradition usually hostile to Episcopalian Government in Ireland and to the aboriginal Catholics made much of its origins on the Anglo-Scottish borders. As a community in the North Atlantic, the Irish Presbyterians seem to have maintained much closer links than any of their Irish colleagues, especially in the late eighteenth century. Their most conspicuous political figures were noted for noisy involvement in Democratic-Republican politics. The Irish Catholics whose social leaders in the eighteenth century were much more naturally conservative, found themselves being given a radical political identity by the early nineteenth century by the American notions of an Irish stereotype, and for all of the awareness of their deep difference in identity from the Presbyterians, Irish Catholics in the United States accepted identification with the Ulster Presbyterian Andrew Jackson (who had escaped birth in Ireland by a few months).[3]

---

[3] Some of these ideas were stimulated by conversations with Thomas N. Brown and David N. Doyle.

The Irish Roman Catholic clergy in North America differed from their coreligionists in being much more aware of their identity, and much less inclined to have it circumscribed by outsiders. And they were conspicuously less likely to walk in Presbyterian political footsteps. But they also lost something of the propensity of Roman Catholic clergy in Ireland to think of themselves in contrast to their Irish non-Catholic fellow-clergy. Officially Irish Roman Catholic priests in Ireland made few direct allusions to their Protestant counterparts, but they thought of them a great deal and often surreptitiously modelled themselves on them. If anything in North America the converse was true in that, towards the end of the nineteenth century, North American Protestant clergy of Irish origin began to imitate their Irish Roman Catholic rivals in helping to whip up support for their Unionist fellow-Protestants in Ireland who felt threatened by the North American Irish Catholics' support for Parnell and Home Rule. But this last development among the Presbyterian and evangelical clergy of Irish origin never reached anything like the proportions of Irish Catholic clerical support for Home Rule and, earlier, Daniel O'Connell's Repeal movement, or even his crusade for Catholic Emancipation: the reason was simple—for all of their original community spanning the Atlantic, the Presbyterians and evangelicals from Ireland had largely merged with too much success among their fellow-Protestants. Where they preserved a distinctive identity in the United States, it was largely in rural, somewhat mountainous terrain, where they were cut off from metropolitan, let alone cosmopolitan, links. In the cities 'Scotch-Irish' societies, historical and otherwise, grew up in the late nineteenth century, but as a rule they led rather than followed their clergy in any Irish political preoccupation which went beyond the cultural, the ceremonial, and, above all, the business fellowship. In Canada the Irish Protestant identity, conscious of its socio-political strength in the assertion of identity with the British Crown, obtained considerable if fluctuating power through Orangeism and its offspring institutions; but here again the clergy were more in attendance than in the leadership.[4]

Irish priests in Canada might be more inclined to model themselves on, or differentiate themselves from, fellow-clergy of Irish Protestant origins, but in Canada even more than in the United States most Irish priests seem to have worked out their identity principally in opposition to their non-Irish co-religionists. They were not Scots; they were not Germans; they

---

[4] I am grateful to John J. Appel particularly with respect to conversation on Scotch-Irish historical societies in America.

were not English; above all, they were not French. The beginnings of widespread Roman Catholicism in the United States were marked by a pattern of hostility between French and French-educated clergy on the one hand, and Irish clergy on the other though, when the Irish clergy were French-educated, loyalties often became confused. The French clergy in the U.S.A. were doomed by time, however. French culture seems to have extraordinary powers over alien populations with only the thinnest mingling of French-born among them: but so tiny was French migration to the U.S.A. that French Catholic clerical dominance in America was bound to become anomalous. Moreover its conservatism sat uneasily with United States liberal ideologies, and it was also increasingly at odds with developing patterns in Frence itself. The spiritual power of France outside Louisiana (not the great territory, purchased in 1803, but the state, admitted in 1812) gradually shrank, for all of the initial achievement of French clergy in, for instance, Kentucky: Louisiana, holding a large population of French origin, retained much of its original culture and was benevolently recognized as 'Gallican' by highly anti-Papal American nativists. Canada, having a far greater French population than Louisiana, kept Irish Catholic clerics perpetually on the defensive: with such notable results as the French-inspired hierarchical condemnation of the Irish-led Knights of Labour in Canada during the 1880s when the organization was protected in the U.S.A. from Papal condemnation.[5]

As stated above, Irish Roman Catholicism was a popular religion, sometimes populist; but the Irish Catholic clergy had marked features distinguishing them from their flocks, apart from their spiritual calling. The most obvious would be literacy and education, decidedly higher among the clergy in both eighteenth and nineteenth centuries. The priest both in Ireland and in North America acted as letter-writer for many parishioners. Irish emigrant letters must often have been a matter of priests in one country writing letters which would ultimately be read by priests in another, although the ostensible writers and recipients would be lay persons.

A critical point in the separation of Irish Catholic clergy and laity in North America lay in the priests' not having migrated with their flocks, unless, like Archbishop Ireland, they migrated, or, like Cardinal Gibbons,

---

[5] The major source on the contrasting fortunes of the Knights of Labor with respect to U.S. and Canadian authorities is still Henry J. Browne, *The Catholic Church and the Knights of Labor* (Washington, D.C., 1946). A note on the Louisianian exception to pro-slavery nativism can be found in my article 'NATIVISM (American)' in *NCE*.

they remigrated, before entering the priesthood. Roman Catholicism in Ireland had become definitely a religion of the poor by 1750, but it still was, as a universal religion, a Church which thought of itself in terms of social as well as spiritual hierarchies. Hence the movement of priests, however close their relationship to their flocks, had to be independent of them. North America had its Catholic hierarchies; Ireland had its. For a priest to transfer from one jurisdiction to another meant decisions taken by higher ecclesiastical authority. There was no way in which a parish priest or curate in Ireland might lead a migration to North America, as happened in the British Isles with Presbyterian communities, or in Norway or the Netherlands with Lutheran or Calvinist ones. Irish Catholic migration to North America in the nineteenth century was not a religious migration in the sense of religion being the chief motive of departure. Nor did it have such motivations as indignation at the treatment of a dissident religious minister, such as one can notice in Dutch and Scandinavian transplantings: if a Roman Catholic priest were similarly disgraced by the ecclesiastical authorities his leadership by religious definition was over. Occasional schisms, arising from conflict between individual priests and repressive bishops, caused rifts in North American Catholicism, but the incidence of such seems to have been exceptionally low in Irish congregations in contrast with German, Polish, Ukrainian, and even Italian Catholics.[6]

This is not to say that there have not been dissident Irish-American priests, some of whom have become conspicuous in bitter recrimination against the Church which condemned them. In 1785 a Capuchin from Ireland named Charles Maurice Whelan (1741–1806) was appointed by Carroll to minister to St Peter's, New York; complaints arose from his inability to preach (his first and second languages were probably Irish and French), and he was deserted by many parishioners in favour of another Irish Capuchin, Andrew Nugent. The congregation was divided into factions. Carroll was obliged to transfer the faithful Whelan, and to suspend the more mutinous Nugent, but while some turbulent followers supported the latter his most important votaries quickly swung into line behind Carroll. Outbreaks of this kind were inevitable in a tiny and far-flung Catholic community, but the only major Irish Catholic clerical rebellions seem to have taken place in the last hundred years. Father

[6] I thank Dr Pieter Stokvis of the Netherlands American Studies Association on this matter, and see his and other essays in Rob Kroes (ed.), *American Immigration: Its Variety and Lasting Imprint* (Amsterdam, 1979).

Edward McGlynn (1837-1900) supported the land and labour theories of Henry George, and was excommunicated in 1887 at the instance of Archbishop Michael Corrigan (1839-1902) of New York: he had a considerable following, all the more because Corrigan was suspected of a timely support for Tammany Hall whose candidate for Mayor of New York City had been in grave danger of defeat by George. But McGlynn was known to have sympathy from Gibbons, and in 1892 was restored to his sacerdotal functions (Corrigan first learning of this in the newspapers). The Canadian-born 'radio priest' Charles E. Coughlin (1891-1979) had a huge following in the 1930s for his demagogic demands for social reconstruction, but although protected by his local bishop in Detroit was ultimately silenced by his ecclesiastical superiors in the early 1940s by which time he had lost much of his following and his message had become one of anti-Semitic near-Fascism: on the whole, his followers, other than his immediate entourage, preferred to forget that his disappearance from their sight and hearing had been at episcopal command, and he made no attempt to counter it. Irish-American doctrinal orthodoxy ultimately found its own extremist outlet in Father Leonard Feeney (1897-1978), who founded the Slaves of the Immaculate Heart of Mary, an order unrecognized by the Church. Feeney, of Harvard, Mass., was excommunicated in 1953 for proclaiming that no salvation could exist outside of the Roman Catholic Church, thus denying the doctrine of 'invincible ignorance' which protected non-Catholics. Feeney retained some disciples, but since his excommunication placed him, on his own logic, in a condition of damnation, he failed to hold most of them, remarkable though his command of unclerical language was: he made his peace with Rome in 1972. But the whole concept of rigid obedience to Catholic hierarchical and Papal assertions was called into question for many liberal American Catholics, Irish-Americans noteworthy among them, by the events of the 1960s in religion and politics: and since that time dissidence from practising Catholics is often great, and their capacity for influencing their clergy considerable.[7]

If Irish-American clerical schisms were few, the Irish clergy in North America would seem to have shown itself a body of remarkable heterogeneity. The first half of the twentieth century admittedly reflected a strong institutional conservatism: there were remarkable administrators,

[7] Some of the material relating to Coughlin comes from oral testimony collected by the BBC Radio producers Daniel Snowman and David Perry and communicated to me, as well as from abusive mail directed to me personally, by Coughlin supporters. Invaluable personal recollections of Feeney were supplied by the late Kenneth Wiggins Porter, my colleague at the University of Oregon, to whose beloved memory I owe countless tributes.

church-builders, political lobbyists, Catholic evangelists, but relatively few intellectual leaders and independent thinkers. But the nineteenth century showed a wide spectrum of social and political views among the Irish-American priests. Mencken's moroseness in contemplating Cardinals O'Connell and Hayes had something of a lament for the passing of a great tradition with the deaths of Gibbons and Ireland: he would have found similarities to Hayes and O'Connell in Corrigan and his ally Bishop Bernard John McQuaid (1823-1909) of Rochester, to say nothing of the formidable Archbishop John Joseph Hughes (1797-1864) of New York, but he would not have had cause to complain of the absence of alternative ecclesiastical voices. In certain respects the change in Irish-American Catholicism after Gibbons reflected the new conformism of Roman Catholicism in the twentieth century inaugurated by the Pontificate of Pope St Pius X. Nineteenth-century Papal conservatism had no such reasons for assurance in dealing with Irish North American Bishops: Archbishop Peter Richard Kenrick (1806-96) of St Louis, Bishop Edward Fitzgerald (1833-1907) of Little Rock, and Archbishop Thomas Louis Connolly (1814-77) of Halifax, Nova Scotia, were prominent opponents of the definition of Papal Infallibility at the first Vatican Council, and all three were born in Ireland. Mencken's view was taken at the first point of Irish-American Catholicism's attempt to assert its United States acceptability at the highest level, and yet its clergy had least to offer other than self-confidence. There was little apparent change when the first Irish-American Catholic reached the Presidential goal in 1960: again, administrative accomplishments were matched by little intellectualism. Francis Joseph Spellman (1889-1967), Cardinal Archbishop of New York, was a byword in financial skill, administrative authority, and flamboyant reaction. Yet he lived to see his cause for complacency shattered, above all for his own ethnic group. And the explosion indicates how much such figures as Spellman had deceived themselves and others in playing the ecclesiastical politics of conformity: a great deal of rethinking had evidently taken place in silence, secrecy, and prayer.[8]

Mencken's shrewd political assessment that either through ignorance or through indifference Hayes and O'Connell would not allow circumspection on behalf of Smith curb their excessive pastoral zeal, reminds us that the Irish clergy in North American Catholicism operated in politics

---

[8] It is useful to mention here the value for me of the generosity in time and scholarly information of Monsignor Ellis, but his personal communications of knowledge and insight inform the whole essay.

very independently of the laity. It was notorious in 1960 that Spellman, as a Republican, was personally opposed to the candidacy of the ultimately successful Democrat, John Kennedy (for all of his common ideological ground with Kennedy's father Joseph): Archbishop Ireland had also been Republican, and in his day the Irish laity, at least those east of the Mississippi, were taken to be habitual Democrats. Archbishop Hughes tried to found something like a Catholic party in New York, and ended his days as an unofficial diplomat for Lincoln in Europe. The Civil War especially had some effect in closing ranks, but in sometimes unexpected ways. Bishop Patrick N. Lynch (1817-82), Irish-born like Hughes, resembled him in undertaking European diplomatic service during the War—but, his see being Charleston, South Carolina, he acted for the Confederate States of America. Bishop James Whelan (1822-78) of Nashville so openly opposed the C.S.A. and welcomed the Union officers invading Tennessee that the hostility of his flock forced him into retirement in May 1863. The Revd Abram Joseph Ryan (1838-86) became the leading Confederate poet. The Irish-born Archbishop John Baptist Purcell (1800-83) of Cincinnati, was a forceful supporter of Lincoln and his Emancipation Proclamation in a diocese bordering on slave soil: he was unpopular but probably influential none the less. The Irish-born Archbishop Francis Patrick Kenrick (1796-1863) of Baltimore—in a Maryland trembling on the verge of secession to the C.S.A. in 1861—was known to support the Union, but permitted pro-Confederate propaganda to flourish in the local Catholic press, read the prayer for the Union in Church when his pro-Confederate priests would not, and carefully avoided any egregious symbolism. Whatever the individual motivations of all of these varieties of political stance during the War, none shared that of James Augustine Healy (1830-1900), who would be appointed bishop of Portland, Maine, in 1875: his father was indeed Irish-born but his mother was a mulatto slave. But apart from the special courage and solitude demanded of Healy, the independence of the Irish clergy from their often highly political flocks is striking.[9]

This independence may in part have owed something to the appearance of Irish issues on which no wise priest or bishop would wish to be

[9] Ellis, *American Catholicism* should obviously be taken as source for almost the whole essay, but his discussion of this point (pp. 91-6) is obviously seminal. I have also benefited from Madeleine Hooke Rice, *American Catholic Opinion in the Slavery Controversy* (New York, 1944), and from the Ph.D. dissertation by my student Douglas Cameron Riach (Edinburgh University, 1975) on 'Ireland and the American Anti-Slavery Movement'. Joseph M. Hernon, Jr., *Celts, Catholics and Copperheads: Ireland Views the American Civil War* (Columbus, Ohio, 1968) shows how far the Irish in Ireland had moved from Daniel O'Connell on the slavery question.

taken for granted: they might or might not support Irish nationalist sentiments as adumbrated in North America, and they might vary between
hostility and neutrality to occasional extreme cases of sympathy for
violence, but they had to prove themselves capable of making a decision
rather than being openly manipulated, otherwise their pastoral authority
was thrown into danger. The decision of how much support to give, to
what, and where, had to be balanced against considerations of non-Irish
reactions, reflections as to who was the local activist for the issue in question and whether that person should best be encouraged or deflated, caution as to how much a commitment given at one time gave hostages to
more perilous future commitments. When Charles Stewart Parnell came
to the U.S.A. in 1880 to solicit philanthropy for the starving Irish peasants
and the Land League agitation, bishops and priests responded in all kinds
of different ways, including McQuaid who initially opposed Parnell (and
his influential sponsor the leading Rochester Catholic newspaper-owner)
but who, on fresh information from episcopal informants in Ireland,
announced characteristically but apparently inimitably that he had been
wrong. Many other clerics would trim their sails on Irish issues as their
popularity and respectability fluctuated, but without McQuaid's massively confident self-criticism. It would be most unfair, however, to assume
that responses were simply conditioned by consideration of Irish, non-
Irish, and part-Irish North American popular opinion: and the exhibition
of that was far from predictable. Parnell was received fairly coldly by New
York and its prelate, John Cardinal McCloskey (1810-85), but drew
powerful support from Mid-Western dignitaries, lay and clerical, Protestant and Catholic, Irish and non-Irish; and the proportion of Irish-born or
Irish-descended in Kentucky or Indiana was infinitely smaller than New
York. Irish-American clergy might stir up less resentment among non-
Irish for their support of Irish issues where the proportions of Irish in both
the Catholic and the general population seemed less threatening.

The entire picture assumes striking differences in Canada, where the
support of Irish nationalist sentiment expressed alienation from the Royal
Government in at least some degree. Roman Catholic clergy had always to
be aware that their obedience to the Pope implied a division in their
political loyalties, and usually these doubts as to their patriotism were
interpreted with much exaggeration and confusion as to what obedience
to the Pope meant. In the United States support for a further non-
American cause was a luxury which might be dangerous, increasing
doubts as to loyalty, but it might also have the reverse effect, especially in
years such as 1844, 1861, 1866, 1870, and 1920 when Anglophobia ran

high. In Canada ostentatious Catholic clerical Hibernophilia was certain of increasing the condition of security risk. As the nineteenth century advanced, the increase of Irish power was all the more resented by the still predominant French clergy and populace, and in Quebec the excessively Hibernophile cleric ran foul of two cultural loyalties. In some respects it was sauce for the gander: the Irish journalist John Francis Maguire, MP, Knight Commander of St Gregory, noted in his invaluable travel book *The Irish in America* (1868) that the Irish-born priests Patrick McMahon (died 1851) and Patrick Phelan (1795-1857), later bishop of Kingston, Ontario, had used their considerable oratorical powers against the Canadian insurgents of 1837 which proved 'a very natural cause of prejudice' against the Irish, evidently still a sore point thirty years later.[10]

Irish bishops and priests in North America who took up Irish issues invited subsequent backlash against Catholicism in general. There was an obvious identity of Irish and Catholic political interests in the American support for Daniel O'Connell in the Catholic Emancipation struggle; but support for his cause of Repeal of the Union, reasserted by mass agitation in the 1840s, induced some bitter divisions among Catholics. O'Connell's courageous and outspoken hostility to American slavery and open refusal of financial support from pro-slavery bodies caused much hostility to him North and South including a bitter attack from Archbishop Hughes of New York. O'Connell's obvious influence on William Lloyd Garrison and Wendell Phillips led Garrison to champion Repeal of both Unions, linking the O'Connell campaign with Garrison's conviction that the American Union must be dissolved rather than continuing to tolerate slavery, and he burnt the Constitution on Boston Common in the same spirit. Patriotic Northerners, let alone the pro-slavery white Southerners, were naturally repelled. The Young Irelanders who reached the United States after 1848 were if anything pro-slavery, a linkage with Irish politics which in its turn caused dissidence, more particularly after John Mitchel (Protestant, but deeply identified with Catholic nationalists), vehemently defended slavery, settled in the South and ultimately supported the

---

[10] I base myself here on a study of the American press in general during Parnell's American mission of 1880. I am grateful to my student Dr Christopher McGimpsey for material on United States Protestant backlash in the 1890s. The backlash of the 1920s and its origins are studied in Edward Cuddy, 'The Irish Question and the Revival of Anti-Catholicism in the 1920s, *Catholic Historical Review*, 67 (1981), pp. 369-85. Maguire, *Irish in America* (London, 1868), pp. 98-9, is an admirable, if ostentatiously pious, compilation of tradition and history, as well as personal observation, on the whole North American scene, and is particularly noteworthy on the Canadian side: my father first brought its merits home to me.

Confederacy. Hughes initially supported Young Ireland's attempt at insurrection in 1848, though he later opposed it when the immigrant Young Irelanders gave fraternal status to the anti-clerical Louis Kossuth of Hungary, whose defeat by the Austrians brought Papal rejoicing. Nevertheless, he permitted the lying-in-state of the Young Irelander Terence Bellew Mac-Manus, whose death in 1860 proved the first formal assertion of Fenian power. Bishop John Bernard Fitzpatrick (1812–66) of Boston was more cautious, but he too gave some support which also soured when confronted by Young Ireland incursions into Boston Catholic journalism. It is noteworthy that the three greatest outbreaks of anti-Catholicism in the United States should have followed the collapse of clerically-supported Irish nationalist agitation there: Repeal and Young Ireland were followed by the Know-Nothing movement of the 1850s; Parnell's decade of triumphant American support ended in the abrasive split of 1891 and the subsequent decade saw the rise of the widely-based and highly influential anti-Catholic American Protective Association; and the vehement campaign for the Irish Republic in 1919–21 largely dissolved by the Irish Civil War of 1922–3 was succeeded in America by the fiercely anti-Catholic agitation of the Ku Klux Klan and others in the mid-1920s. Modern scholarship has linked injudicious Catholic clerical support for the Irish cause to the resurrection of popular anti-Catholicism: Hayes and O'Connell had been outstanding in indiscretion, and Mencken doubtless was thinking of their public outbursts in support of Irish-related agitations and riots when he complained in 1927 that 'The Catholic hierarchy in America, at the present moment, ... has ... few statesmen, and the few do not seem to be in high places.' Gibbons, throughout his long archiepiscopate, had responded to Irish agitation with a humane and constructive caution. In the long run Irish-born and Irish-descended clerics who indulged themselves in filio-pietistic displays cost North American Catholicism dear.[11]

But these intermittent excesses may have hardened Irish North American clerical control over at least their fellow-Irish Catholic laymen. Maguire contrasted the Irish support of the North American Catholic clergy with the 'comical absurdity which I heard uttered in no less important a place than the House of Commons—that the Irish were rushing to America in order to get rid of their priests!' and later ironically recalled:

> It has been confidently stated that the moment the Irish touch the free soil of America they lose the old faith—that there is something in

---

[11] I have benefited from Dr John Sweetman's work on comparative controversies arising from Irish clerical controversies on Irish national questions in Australia and New Zealand.

the very nature of Republican institutions fatal to the Church of Rome.

James Anthony Froude, as fervent an enemy of Roman Catholicism as Maguire was its votary, made the same point over a decade later:

> That their religion would survive the change was expected by no one. Their own clergy dreaded the effect upon them of contact with American liberty. The Americans themselves thought that they could absorb and assimilate these ignorant millions of ragged wretches as easily as a shoal of sprats are swallowed and digested by a whale. 'How long does it take', I once asked a distinguished gentleman in New York, 'to make an Irishman into an American?' 'How long?' he said; 'h'm! well, about half an hour.' The answer, unfortunately, was more epigrammatic than true. . . .
>
> In this as in some other points the fine confidence of the Americans in the effect of their institutions has been disappointed.

Both Maguire's Parliamentarian acquaintance and Froude's somewhat less well documented 'no one' symbolize English wishful thinking of the same order and from the same places as those which had long predicted the demise of the United States, a circumstance of which Irish publicists enjoyed reminding the Americans. But however suspect the initial incorrect prediction, the Irish clergy in North America had saved—in all senses, they believed—their own. In the nineteenth century they fended off a potentially anti-clerical challenge from alienated intellectuals, partly by the backing and filling in response to Young Ireland. The German intellectuals of 1848 who arrived in the United States proved a dangerous, and at times lethal, source of opposition to the German-American Lutheran clergy. Jewish intellectuals responded to Rabbinical and parental orthodoxy by rebellion and defection. Irish Catholic American clergy had various controversies with Irish Catholic American journalists, but a *modus vivendi* was obtained, particularly during the age of Gibbons. The most forceful Irish-born journalist critic of the Gilded Age, John Boyle O'Reilly, denounced it *inter alia* for

> The organized charity, scrimped and iced,
> In the name of a cautious, statistical Christ

and remained Boston's leading Roman Catholic layman until his death in 1890. The Revd Robert Emmett Curran, SJ, sees the McGlynn affair as a turning-point for American Catholic conservatism which thenceforward trusted less in American Catholics' capacities to settle their own differences and more in a stress on the authority of Rome. While Gibbons lived, Rome might seem cosmopolitan to young Catholic intellectuals like F. Scott Fitzgerald. But a narrow, and increasingly monarchical American cult of the Papacy especially after Gibbons's death simply made Rome reveal itself as the supreme parochialism. The postponed revolt of the Irish-American Catholic intellectuals played its part in the general alienation of American intellectuals in the 1920s, Fitzgerald among them.[12]

In a few cases, Canada acted as a means to drain off dissidents in ways Turner would later over-optimistically ascribe to the United States open frontier. The Young Irelander Thomas D'Arcy McGee after clashes with Hughes and subsequent ill-success in Boston journalism went to Canada, became a famed advocate of Canadian confederation and opponent of the Fenians, and was assassinated in 1867, apparently by their sympathizers: his funeral Mass was celebrated by his close friend in the Canadian hierarchy, Archbishop Connolly of Halifax. For at least one Irish Catholic the Canadian balance among negatives produced the identity he sought, as it would do for U.S. dissidents, including some Catholics of Irish descent, in the 1960s.[13]

The Western expansion in North America posed alarming prospects for the Irish clergy. Froude's

> distinguished gentleman ... went on to explain that they would be scattered over a vast extent of country, where their priests could not follow them—a man could not remain a Roman Catholic to any purpose without priest, sacrament, or chapel—if the parents continued, for their own lifetime, to pray to the Virgin and the saints, the American schoolmaster would take care to enlighten their children.

---

[12] Maguire, *Irish in America*, pp. 106, 346. Froude, 'Romanism and the Irish Race in the United States', *North American Review*, 129 (1879), pp. 521-2. Apart from the indignation this engendered it proved an involuntary source for Irish nationalist agitators, Parnell quoting it in favour of the Land League cause in his address to the United States Congress, 2 February 1880. O'Reilly's lines come from his poem 'In Bohemia'. Robert Emmet Curran, SJ, 'The McGlynn Affair and the Shaping of the New Conservatism in American Catholicism, 1886-1894', *Catholic Historical Review*, 66 (1980), pp. 184-204. On Scott Fitzgerald, see my essay on the revival of his Irishness and Catholicism under the influence of Gibbon's protégé Monsignor Cyril Sigourney Fay, in A. Robert Lee's forthcoming collection of essays on Fitzgerald.

[13] On D'Arcy McGee, apart from obvious sources, see Thomas N. Brown, 'The Irish Layman', in Corish (ed.), *A History of Irish Catholicism*, 6. McGee, *The Irish Position in Britain and in Republican North America* (Montreal, 1866), contains observations worthy of respect for its perception as well as for its courage.

His identity is a little suspicious, since Froude could not have met him in New York before 1872. If indeed he ever existed he must have been remarkably successful in resisting the invasion of his distinction and gentility by vulgar facts, for the Irish-American Roman Catholics were by then firmly established in the West and conspicuous for their religious tenacity. In any case Froude himself was incredibly ignorant, even for him:

> ... the immigration of Irish peasantry ... began on a large scale in 1866–'67.... The immigration from Ireland has almost ceased.

The Irish immigration in the late 1840s and early 1850s to the U.S.A. was well over a million, and reached a quarter-million in one year. It was rising sharply once more as Froude was writing, and shortly afterwards reached over 80,000 in one year. But to refute Froude is, in a metaphor from the world he loved, shooting a sitting duck—and a straw duck at that. However he misdated the misgivings on the survival of Catholicism in the West, they had existed. On 26 March 1857 Hughes had opposed a suggestion for Catholic settlement in the West:

> ... the idea of disturbing the minds of those who may be already established, whether in the East or in the West, by a gilded and exaggerated report of theoretical blessings, which are in reserve for them, provided they can acquire the nominal ownership of 60 or 100 acres of uncultivated land, not unfrequently teeming with fever and ague—remote from the church—remote from the school—remote [from] the Post Office—remote from the physician—remote from the neighbors—this idea is dangerous, just so far as any Catholic emigrant is liable to be misled and deceived thereby....
>
> ... the hundreds and thousands who, in New York, Boston, Philadelphia, and New Orleans are living in the proverbial wretchedness usually associated with the idea of a residence in cellars and in garrets ... could not but improve their condition by a change to the open fields of the rural districts. But ... A great majority of them are entirely unfit by any sudden transition to enter on the multifarious industry which a settlement on wild land pre-supposes. They know not how to use the axe, if the land is to be cleared of timber. They know not how to hew and shape the logs necessary for the construction of their first rude cabin. They know not how to guide the plough in the prairies. They are inexpert in almost every element necessary to carry out the impractical ideal of their Buffalo advisers.

Passing over the detail that the Buffalo proposal had emanated from, amongst others, Hughes's old enemy D'Arcy McGee, Hughes's attitude proved highly influential and played its part in ensuring that very many of the Irish immigrants who went Westward would seek urban destinations, however small, in preference to the new rural society for which their Irish experience must have prepared them better than he was ready to concede. His method is instructive. He says nothing about dangers to fidelity of religion, apart from a fleeting allusion to remoteness from church swallowed up in his litany of other necessary resources such as school, post, and doctor (this last already high-lighted by the omnipresence of fever and ague). The Irish Catholics were not to be insulted by a suggestion that they would prove less than fervent in their religion under any circumstances: to do so would have been to prompt the answer that they came of stock who had retained their Catholicism in Ireland in a far harsher climate. The fear of souls lost to the Church—something for which Hughes, like all other bishops and priests, would have held himself to be accountable on the Day of Judgement—animated the attack, but was not permitted to exhibit itself. The shepherd would guide his sheep according to unexceptionable wisdom of a kind both startlingly secular and strongly persuasive. Froude's gentleman was late in his diagnosis as well as in its timing. Hughes and others like him maintained their ascendancy by anticipating the 'American schoolmaster' with a local worldly wisdom which amounted to a decisive pre-emptive strike. Froude saw what was happening as part of one process in Ireland and America:

> The Irish peasant has suffered so long for his religion that it is in the granules of his blood. Roman Catholicism, which grew sick and stagnant in power and prosperity, has in Ireland been braced in vigor by calamity. Like the mythological monster, it has been in contact with the hard soil of fact, and has gathered fresh life from it. With an energy infinitely creditable to them, when they reached the New World, the Irish clergy and people set themselves to meet their new circumstances. There was money in plenty. The old sixpence-a-day wages of Ireland was turned into as many shillings, and out of the shillings the Irish boys and girls parted cheerfully with as many as were needed for a faith which was a second nature to them. Thousands, perhaps tens of thousands, were lost at first in the huge cities of the enormous continent, but the Church soon overtook its straying sheep. It watched over their marriages: the Irish in America marry wholly among themselves and within their own creed.

Bishop Healy would have surprised him.

> It kept its hold on the children, and furnished them with antidotes to
> correct the poison of the secular schools. . . . The Irish in America . . .
> preserve the abstinence from sexual vice which distinguishes them so
> honorably at home, and this is favorable to large families.

This last seems a basis for the oft-repeated Irish Catholic clerical insistence
that Protestants have dirty minds; but Froude was perfectly correct in seeing education as a critical point in Catholic clerical attempts to retain
control of the laity. Nevertheless the parochial school, while strongly
championed by Hughes in New York, and Purcell in Cincinnati, took
many years to become nation-wide. Froude assumed extensive and vigorous parish work for the consistent affirmation of Catholic values, and
even in his assumption that the result was a separateness of Catholics from
ordinary Americans, he was less inaccurate than his critics maintained.[14]

It says much for the confidence with which his attack was met that his
chief adversary, the non-Irish bishop of Peoria, John Lancaster Spalding
(1840–1916) rightly saw Froude's most vulnerable point in his lack of a
sense of humour:

> He has heard that the Yankees are a dyspeptic race, and, as his power
> of accounting for things is unlimited, he straightway seeks and finds
> the cause, which of course can be none other than 'the growth of the
> Irish element'. 'They have absorbed', he says, 'a substance which they
> have been unable to assimilate, and it interferes with their digestion.'
> Now, I doubt whether there is in all this great country a medical prac-
> titioner who will say that this diagnosis is correct. It is not the growth
> of the Irish Catholic element that makes the Yankees dyspeptic—it is
> doughnuts and apple-pies. 'The growth' of almost anything is pre-
> cisely what your genuine American most delights in. He has the
> greatest country, the longest rivers, the highest mountains, the broad-
> est prairies, the most thundering cataracts, and the largest cities of any
> man who walks the earth. . . .

Yet Froude had been timely in seeing a growing fear within the pride in
growth, and when the frontier whose opportunities delighted Spalding as
much as Turner was officially closed, the A.P.A. arose. Spalding was

[14] Froude, 'Romanism and the Irish Race', pp. 521–2. Ellis (ed.), *Documents of American Catholic History* (1966), I, pp. 317–21: 99. Archbishop Hughes' Opposition to Western Colonization for Catholic Immigrants, March 26, 1857.

shrewd in noticing that Froude was a much more dubious defender of American values than were the Irish immigrants:

> . . . suicidal strife is precisely what Mr Froude desires to stir up among us; and it may fairly be doubted whether this loyal Englishman would be most pleased by the destruction of the republic or the ruin of the Church.

But while Spalding could hit Froude hard by exhibiting his ignorance on the non-Irish element in American Catholicism, he was not altogether happy in his ridicule:

> 'Every true Catholic is bound to act and think as his priest tells him.' Is this a fair statement? Do good Catholics believe that they are bound to consult their priests as to how they shall carry on their business, or how they shall vote, or what legitimate pursuits they shall engage in? Do they believe that it is their duty to ask their priests what they are to think concerning the cause of yellow fever . . . ?

Perhaps they did not, in Spalding's multi-ethnic flock around Peoria, Illinois, but Hughes's warnings tell a different story of the Northeastern Irish ghettoes, and Spalding, desperately trying in 1879 to offset the still powerful influence of that dead shepherd in the matter of Western colonization, would have been foolish not to know that it was precisely the kind of ascendancy of which Froude complained which had given Hughes his hold. Indeed there seems a Freudian admission here: Hughes had found the West to be a cause of fever. As for politics, Hughes had been ready in emergency to dictate the voting patterns of his flock, and the Irish who had come to political sophistication in Daniel O'Connell's Ireland were regularly accustomed to clerical direction on such matters. They might not always heed it, although while O'Connell remained at the helm they seem to have done; and Hughes had assumed as much. He had tried not to overdo his direction. Seven years after Froude's article, Corrigan would be trying a more underhanded variant of the same methods against Henry George's Mayoralty candidacy of 1886. For the most part immigrant urban machine politics did not rely on open endorsement by the Catholic clergy: the boss merely took the trouble to be seen in clerical circles at appropriate public occasions. In the ghetto, symbolism was everything.[15]

[15] Spalding, 'Mr Froude's Historical Method', *North American Review*, 130 (1880), pp. 293, 287, 295. (Froude had produced a second instalment in the issue of January 1880 which need not concern us here. Charles Stewart Parnell, 'The Irish Land Question', *ibid.* (1880), pp. 388–406, is also an answer to, and still more an exploitation of, the questions raised by Froude.)

The Canadian experience, as so often, raises questions of its own, throwing sidelights on the American. Archbishop John Joseph Lynch (1816–88) of Toronto came to his bishopric (upgraded to an archbishopric in his tenure) in 1860 after service in Texas, Missouri, and Buffalo, N.Y. (a reminder that the Irish, like other Catholic clergy in North America, moved and still move frequently across the border during their training). Lynch did what he could for impoverished Irish Catholics in Toronto but for most of his career was vehement in discouraging Irish emigration to the New World, stating in a pamphlet for Irish consumption *The Evils of Wholesale and Improvident Emigration from Ireland* (1864) that the Irish were 'obligated to look for the cheapest lodgings in the city . . . such places are the haunts of vice. The consequence is that they and their children are lost to morality, to society, to religion, and finally to God.' The Vatican, presumably sequacious of Irish furtherance of Catholicism in the New World, expressed its displeasure, and Lynch made it clear in reply that he was attacking immigration to cities, not to the land. His fellow Irish-born archbishop, Peter Richard Kenrick of St Louis, agreed with his analysis. John Ireland's efforts beginning in 1876 to settle Irish immigrants in Minnesota stimulated Lynch to take up a project of the same kind in Manitoba. Canadian-fashion, it relied on British Governmental support. Lynch was a friend and political supporter of the Canadian Conservative premier John A. Macdonald who strongly encouraged the scheme, but despite his entertainment in England by the Catholic Duke of Norfolk he was frustrated by new hostility from Gladstone's government in the aftermath of the Phoenix Park Murders of 6 May 1882. Apparently the resolution carried through both houses of the Canadian parliament in favour of Irish Home Rule, and Lynch's known sympathy for such a measure played a part in the rejection. Lynch then fell out with Macdonald. The 'New Ireland' proposal was turned over to another Irish-born Canadian bishop, John Walsh (1830–98) of London, Ontario, later to succeed Lynch at Toronto, but the foundering of other colonization projects in the Canadian Northwest seems to have led him to drop it. Lynch reverted to opposition to immigration, refusing to accept women from Irish workhouses into Toronto as he insisted they tended to immorality. He told the then Parnellite archbishop of Cashel, Thomas Croke, that the Irish were an

> intelligent and warmhearted and impulsive people degraded and impoverished into the prox lieus of the cities of Great Britain, the United States and Canada where their children were obliged by necessity to be reared from their infancy in the proximate occasion of vice

and stressed that those staying at home were

> proving their love of God and country by their gallant efforts to save the remnant of their people.

Lynch's Home Rule sympathies were consistent with his social attitudes, and he deserves the lonely credit for facing realities: 'Your statement was rather defective than exaggerated' Kenrick had said to him in 1864, 'for the whole truth could not well be told.' Hughes had chosen to transfer to the unknown his fears as to the destinies of Irish immigrants, fears which were more relevant to those remaining under his jurisdiction than he admitted. The numbers of Irish Catholic observants in North America held up, but as Spalding grimly declared in answer to Froude, having disposed of his nonsense about Irish exclusiveness in marriage:

> 'The lapses from the faith', he continues, 'once relatively large, have by now wholly ceased.' This too, I regret to be compelled to say, is false. The number of those who fall away from the faith is smaller in proportion to the Catholic population than it was twenty-five years ago, but to affirm that defections have wholly ceased is to be regardless of facts.

But Irish clerical domination often refused to partake of Spalding's compulsion. If religious lapse, or moral collapse, was presented as a rarity, it could be endowed with taboo, and those who fell into it excluded from future reference. The Vatican clearly encouraged such wishful thinking and social controls. It is hard to avoid sympathy for Lynch's honesty which met with such ill-success at Rome, London, and Ottawa; it is also hard to avoid sympathy for the Irishwomen left in the workhouses.[16]

Attention has here been drawn specifically to the many Irish-born clerics. In the early nineteenth century their situation was to be expected, and those trained before the Reign of Terror in the French Revolution would probably have had their formal education in France. Their advent brought some resentment from non-Irish clergy and laity, and at the beginning of the nineteenth century Archbishop John Thomas Troy of Dublin seems to have had ideas of commanding the choice of United States bishops from Ireland. This was effectively countered from the American clergy, but from 1842 Irish priests were specifically trained at All Hallows' College Dublin for American service, and it was sometimes

---

[16] Gerald J. Stortz, 'Archbishop Lynch and New Ireland: An Unfulfilled Dream for Canada's Northwest'), *Catholic Historical Review*, 68 (1982), pp. 612-24.

asserted in both Ireland and North America that those selected were of third-class quality; the first-class, trained at St Patrick's College May-nooth, being potential Irish bishops, and the second-class, trained at diocesan seminaries, being intended for Irish parish priests. Within North America the obvious ethnic rivalries and hostilities usually masked another basis for controversy but did not silence it: Irish-born priests were often recognized as a different breed from American-born clergy of however recent Irish descent. (Gibbons rather neatly straddled both categories, with his American birth and his Irish primary education.) It might well be that the Irish-born had reached the New World at a com-paratively early age, and hence that formative years were dominated by North American and not Irish perspectives: yet at flash-points of collision it was the Irish birth rather than Irish education which was made the touchstone of controversy. We must remember that two distinct phases are in question: the first, when Irish priests were literally missionaries, fre-quently nomadic, especially in the infant United States with a tiny Roman Catholic population. Then the Irish Catholics began to come in numbers, and wanted priests who like themselves had been brought up in Ireland. The appalling psychological dislocation of emigration was in part eased by the presence of guides in the most basic internal forms of identity. There would also have been a language question. The really active decline of the Irish language in Munster, Connaught, and western Ulster was an early nineteenth-century phenomenon. Emigrants from Catholic Ireland seem to have been chiefly Anglophone, or bilingual, until the Famine which struck in 1845: many—it could even be most—of the Famine emigrants were probably at least primarily Gaelic-speaking, although they lost the Irish language rapidly in North America in the search for survival at the lowest possible economic level of society. Priests who could speak Irish would have been as welcome to those whose spiritual reflection would have been in that language as they would have been unwanted by persons to whom Irish was irrelevant and arcane. It was enough trouble keeping some grip on the Latin language of the Mass without having to make allowance for clergy whose grasp of English might be enfeebled by their retention of Irish. This problem declined as the century advanced, and it seems probable that the education of the Irish clergy meant that those priests who received the Famine immigrants in North America, even those of them who made the voyage during the Famine years, were usually much less proficient in Irish than many of their new parishioners. But the new Irish immigrant still wanted his or her Irish-born priest. We must remember that the highest total of Irish-born persons in the United States was the 1,872,000 recorded in 1890. By 1900, when only 50 per cent of U.S. Catholics were Irish, 62 per cent of the bishops in the United States were Irish, and more than half of them Irish-born.[17]

Accordingly the retention of ecclesiastical positions of command by the Irish-born in North America was a considerable factor throughout the nineteenth century. For example, the first vicar-apostolic of St John's, Newfoundland, was installed in 1797, and both he and the ensuing five vicars-apostolic and bishops were Irish-born, the sequence only ending in 1893, with the appointment of a native Newfoundlander. The Irish-born gave way grudgingly. Patrick Augustine Feehan (1829-1902), Irish-born, was the first archbishop of Chicago, appointed in 1880. In 1901 Peter J. Muldoon (1863-1927) was appointed his coadjutor, and the ensuing fracas, particularly associated with the Revd Jeremiah J. Crowley, parish priest of St Mary's Church, Oregon, Illinois, resulted in Crowley's excommunication and something of a schism on the issue of Muldoon's not being Irish-born (he was in fact born in California). It seems probable that the objection to Muldoon's native place had a useful symbolic quality and was not the real cause of clerical outrage, however successful it may have been for whipping up the indignation of Irish-born Catholic lay persons. Muldoon had not been Feehan's first coadjutor: Alexander Joseph McGavick (1863-1948) was the initial choice, but ill-health apparently dictated his replacement. McGavick had been a parish priest appointed to All Saints Church in 1887 and subsequently at St John's Church. Muldoon had been appointed Feehan's Chancellor in 1889. McGavick had not been Irish-born either. The problem would seem to have been that Muldoon had encountered some clerical hostility during his term of office, and was regarded as having won his preferment because of Feehan's personal regard for him. Accordingly the issue may really have been one arising from some priests' hostility to Feehan himself, and his Irish birth was used to cloak rebellion in the guise of personal loyalty. Muldoon's appointment invited the presumption of his succession, and hence the probable continuation of Feehan's reign beyond his own death. In the event, when

---

[17] Apart from the relevant articles in *NCE* (by Thomas N. Brown and others), Patrick J. Blessing, 'Irish' in Stephan Thernstrom (ed.), *Harvard Encyclopedia of American Ethnic Groups*, pp. 524-45, is generally helpful here, as is Dolan, *American Catholic Experience*, pp. 143-4, and more generally 127-57. But the question of Irish-speaking immigration to North America is still only in its historiographical infancy, the most important recent work being that of Dr Cormac Ó Gráda from whom a major summation on the whole matter is shortly to appear, one hopes. Somewhat less scientific work had been carried out on the question by Proinnsias Mac Aonghusa in various lectures in Irish and English which rightly point to the contrast between users of Scots-Gaelic and Irish-Gaelic in Canada as a useful basis for future study.

Feehan died suddenly the year after Muldoon's consecration, the un-welcome coadjutor was passed over, only receiving some compensation in 1908 with appointment to the bishopric of Rockford, Illinois. James Edward Quigley (1854–1915) was made archbishop of Chicago: ironically he was not a native-born American either, having drawn his first breath in Oshawa, Canada, a few years before his family settled in the U.S.A. He seems to have cleared up the divisions fairly effectively. As for McGavick, his health did not prevent him from outliving them all. In 1909 he published a book with the appropriate title for a business-conscious society *Some Incentives to Right Living*, and in 1921 he was made bishop of La Crosse, Wisconsin, which he governed for a quarter of a century. The episode, then, seems complex enough to provide material for an American Catholic Anthony Trollope, but it is significant that the question of an archbishop of Irish birth was recognized as an appropriate ground of agitation.[18]

To assign an identity for the North American Irish clergy, whether Irish-born, American-born or Canadian-born, may seem absurd in the light of the varieties encountered so far. Yet some points suggest them-selves. The Irish clergy in North America, whether immigrant or native to it, would naturally have made what they could of their ethnic traditions. They would have had reservations: the Irish immigrants, apart from the pioneers, would have had to overcome their repugnance towards Irish-American assumptions which had evolved in ways different from those in which Catholicism in Ireland was adjusting itself to its emancipation and its place in a bourgeoisifying society now a part, however alienated, of the United Kingdom of Great Britain and Ireland in existence since 1 January 1801; the Irish clergy born in North America had to come to terms with newcomers from a world celebrated by parents or grandparents but seem-ing remote in the extreme from a New World expanding its white settle-ment with almost unbelievable rapidity. Externals would have hardened the polarization of representatives of the two groups as they first encoun-tered one another. The newcomer often arrived with convictions of enter-ing a childlike society, deceiving itself by a physical growth far outstripping its intellectual and spiritual maturing. The Irish indigenous to North America would have shared in the common views of Europe as mired in an earlier phase of history. Their remote common origins would at first seem less important than the vast differences in human experience

---

[18] 'Chicago', *NCE*, and other articles; also *Dictionary of American Biography*, *Who Was Who in America*, 1.

which had intervened. Yet it is clear that they knew how to talk to one another. It is not only a giant such as Gibbons who showed himself capable of comprehending Irish realities in Ireland: very different North American Irish clerics such as McQuaid of Rochester or Lynch of Toronto found themselves aware of a largely common framework of reference in their dialogues with Irish-domiciled counterparts. Moreover all parties needed to adjust themselves to the needs of immigrant and local-born Irish Catholics as quickly as possible. They faced a growth rate which was simply terrifying. About 20,000 Irish reached the United States in the 1820s. 70,000 came to North America in the twenty years before the Famine. 1,300,000 arrived in the United States between 1847 and 1854. The Irish immigrant total as late as 1880–90 came to 626,604. American-born clergy had to discover the latest meanings of Irishness. Irish-born clerics had to recognize they had arrived in a country where an Irish identity did not mean, as they had hitherto usually assumed, a primary loyalty to Ireland, but to the United States or to Canada.[19]

The Irish priests in North America derived from a clerical tradition which had taken its form in the eighteenth century at whose mid-point a judge on the Irish bench had declared the law did not presume such a thing as an Irish Roman Catholic to exist. Thanks to the splendid work of the late Maureen Wall we now know that the savage penal laws bit less than they barked where Roman Catholic clergy were concerned. But the memory of that symbolic degradation and its accompanying deprivation has continued to fuel Irish sectarian conflict to the present day. What it means for the clergy was that for the first half of the eighteenth century all save a very few were illegal: and these 'illegals'—the modern American term is useful—included bishops, friars, and most particularly Jesuits. Before 1766 every Roman Catholic bishop, by a Papal courtesy, was appointed by the man most Irish Catholics thought of as James III: and to his credit he seems to have chosen men of religious rather than political priorities who, if they ever arrived, would see to the needs of their flocks as best their fugitive existences permitted, rather than furthering the Stuart cause by injudicious agitation. But the nomadic friars, sometimes bishops themselves, were the mainstay of a Church whose votaries were largely constant but whose religious observance had to be extremely intermittent. After 1750 new regulations from Rome curbed the independence of the friars and in particular their recruitment into their ranks within Ireland itself: European training would henceforth be required for any novices.

---

[19] Brown in *NCE*; Blessing in *Harvard Encyclopedia of American Ethnic Groups.*

The parish became a reality. Bishops began to reside openly, at first permitted by the Protestant authorities tacitly, then in the last quarter of the century explicitly. But it made for a singular pattern. The Roman Catholic Church, accustomed to flourish under secular governmental auspices, maintained its existence in Ireland by the fidelity of supporters who had deliberately chosen all the disadvantages of adherence to an outlaw institution. Observance, normally the statistician's prime yardstick, had little relevance here. Having made the sacrifice of being Catholic was what distinguished Irish Catholics. Hence the fact that before the American Civil War more than 50 per cent of Irish Catholics in New York were not regular church attenders carried less weight than their insistence that they were Catholics. The tradition going back to the penal laws also meant that Irish Catholics regarded priests with reverence but not with an automatic assumption of their being essential. The Irish clergy in North America had to come to terms with their status as venerated outsiders. It was a Church based on its people, but it would differ from Presbyterianism and other popularly-based Churches in that the priest never gained full acceptance as one of the people. They were placed on an open pedestal: it was also something of an open prison. Their education distanced them, and here again the tradition had been that it did so literally; above all when education meant going to France, most frequently by a smuggler's boat. Folk-memory survived even when the causes of common attitudes had been forgotten: to encounter a priest was often thought of as unlucky, to entertain a priest partook of an ordeal, in part deriving from times when ill-luck or inquisition from governmental hands might result from such activities. The priest was extremely influential: but it was the influence of a superior, not of a person sharing the common experience or assumptions and projected thence into leadership.[20]

There is another side to the folklore of priests as symbols of ill-luck: Celtic folklore has come down a very long way in some of its manifestations, and the ill-luck from the chance encounter with men of the spirit may in part derive from pre-Christian times, with legends of effective curses from a pagan priest. Sir Samuel Ferguson in his 'The Burial of King Cormac' rather neatly blended his own Protestant reactions to the rising power of the Irish Catholic priests in the nineteenth century by a vigorous account of the pagan priests cursing the High King Cormac Mac Airt for attacking them in the light of his discovery of Christianity long before the advent of St Patrick:

[20] Patrick J. Corish, *The Irish Catholic Experience* (1987), *passim*.

They loosed their curse against the king,
    They cursed him in his flesh and bones;
And daily in their mystic ring
    They turn'd the maledictive stones,

Till, where at meat the monarch sate,
    Amid the revel and the wine,
He choked upon the food he ate,
    At Sletty, southward of the Boyne.

High vaunted then the priestly throng,
    And far and wide they noised abroad
With trump and loud liturgic song
    The praise of their avenging God.

And, with a significance his Irish Protestant readers at least would not miss, Cormac is vindicated when his orders for burial in Rossnaree where he was converted to

'One, unseen, who is God alone'

are flouted by his courtiers but carried out by that future symbol of victorious Protestantism, the river Boyne.

While, as a youth with practised spear
    Through justling crowds bears off the ring,
Boyne from their shoulders caught the bier
    And proudly bore away the king.

The attack on polytheism is in subtext an attack on the Roman Catholic devotion to (which Protestants termed 'worship of') the Virgin Mary, the Saints and Angels. The warriors defeated by the Boyne are not odious, as the priests are: they are presented as heroic if misguided. Ferguson had hopes of conversion of the heroic if misguided Irish masses of his own day by the rising tide of evangelicalism from England. So, according to him, had the dying Cormac:

'His glory lightens from the east;
    His message soon shall reach our shore;
And idol-god, and cursing priest
    Shall plague us from Moy Slaught no more.'

For Moy Slaught, read Maynooth. Ferguson's Protestant contemporaries were reinforced in their conviction of the Catholic priesthood's ready recourse to cursing as a means of keeping their hold on the people. The great reporter of Catholic peasant life, William Carleton, later enlisted in the cause of Protestant evangelical propaganda, gave forceful instances of priests reducing dissidents to obedience by threats that they would take away the power of their arms or legs. The point was that Catholics did take the priest's curse seriously. A very learned theologian, a Kerry priest, told me once that the way for the clergy to have really effective results in ostracizing the Provisional I.R.A. was solemnly to curse them. A solemn curse, he believed, could be much more successful than the rite of excommunication, and would entail no demand for any physical consequences.[21]

Whatever the extent of the power of clerical cursing, it showed few signs of being transported to North America. I have made so much of it because of this. If Froude's insistence on North American Irish clergy reasserting controls has some justice, it entailed the loss of certain powers. Cursing in America simply became a synonym for profanity. Even its secular consequence of social ostracism was somewhat muted in America. The boycott, given North American publicity by James Redpath when so vigorously carried out against Captain Charles C. Boycott (the parish priest even coined the name in response to Redpath's demand for one), was quickly taken over by the American labour movement of the 1880s, but its use in the community seems to have been sporadic, local, and difficult to pin down. In a tightly-knit parish, especially in the early twentieth century, apostates might find themselves ostracized, but any activity of the priest in the proceedings would have been very private. Priests who lapsed, and more specifically, priests who lapsed publicly and became distinguished for diatribes against their former faith, simply became nonpersons as far as American Catholics were concerned. Orthodox priests would quietly advise parishioners not to speak of them. Excommunication, on the other hand, seems to have been of only limited success in America as in Ireland: it did not silence the Irish Catholic followers of Edward McGlynn, and apparently it did not still the supporters of Jeremiah Crowley in Chicago until Quigley, using conciliatory methods, was firmly in control of the archdiocese. It would be easy to assume this was a product of the American experience, with its hostility to church interference in state matters—pro-McGlynn cartoons showed Tammany

---

[21] Griogóir Ó Dúbhghaill has in preparation a study of Ferguson which is to explore some of these points further. My own reading owes something to the insights of Conor Cruise O'Brien. The poem appears in many anthologies, most recently in Thomas Kinsella, *The New Oxford Book of Irish Verse* (Oxford, 1986), pp. 288–91.

Hall using the Pope as a puppet while McGlynn paraded his rights as an American citizen—but it was frequently ignored in Ireland as well, again where the motives seemed political, as in its use against the anti-Treaty forces in 1922.[22]

In any case Irish Catholic priests in Ireland from the eighteenth century onwards were largely distinguished by their hostility to superstition, not by their exploitation of it. If Irish Catholics in America did not appear particularly superstitious—save to a vigorous Protestant to whom their whole creed was superstitious—it may have owed something to this. Catechetical requirements in the eighteenth century involved very serious cross-examination in the confessional as to the penitent's deference to superstition. This was not a matter of waiting until the penitent brought such matters forward. Priests were to question penitents on a whole range of possible transgressions by superstitious observance, and make their wholehearted hatred of such actions very clear. The inference would seem to be that the Irish Catholic clergy in the eighteenth century strongly suspected the real danger to their under-ministered flocks would not be in the alien new faith they had so conspicuously rejected, and whose own torpor on the proselytizing front contrasted strongly with the Protestant evangelical energy of the next century, but in the indigenous old faith. They were as worried about paganism as any Protestant, and the sneers of Protestants kept them up to the mark. If Archbishop Hughes knew of Thomas D'Arcy McGee's poem 'The Celts' (and in view of its celebrity he probably did) with its lines luxuriating in the pagan deities of the ancient Irish, it would have done nothing to increase his enthusiasm for the Young Irelander: in D'Arcy McGee's *Canadian Life*, his flights of poetic fancy seldom took themselves beyond Catholic contours apart from suggestions that the Indians might have a natural creed bearing strong marks of Christian monotheism. In the twentieth century Irish priests on either side of the Atlantic continue to express their hostility to superstitious fashions, from horseshoes to horoscopes—and, it would seem, with some justification.[23]

Historical record has naturally preserved little of pastoral instruction

---

[22] Redpath, *Talks About Ireland* (New York, 1881). The Georgist paper the New York *Standard* is a useful source for anti-clerical comment on the McGlynn affair in early 1887.

[23] The catechism chiefly in use was that by the Revd Andrew Donlevy (1694?-1761?), *The Catechism, or Christian Doctrine, by way of Question and Answer, drawn chiefly from the Express Word of God, and other Prime Sources* (Paris, 1741, in Irish; 3rd edn., Dublin, 1848, bilingual). See also Patrick J. Corish, *The Catholic Community in the Seventeenth and Eighteenth Centuries* (Dublin, 1981), pp. 111-12.

in eighteenth-century Ireland, but our one major source, the *Sermons* (1736) of Bishop James O'Gallagher (Raphoe, 1725–37, translated by James III to Kildare and Leighlin 1737–51), repays close study. O'Gallagher, a Dominican, was probably an exceptional preacher and an outstanding man—James's second selection of him, for promotion to a see near Dublin, suggests as much, as does his own decision to take the risk of publishing while an outlaw—but if he was far above most of his fellow clerics they would have been influenced by his methods and attitudes in the absence of anything comparable. The *Sermons* were in Irish. They speak of a very dark world, one reflecting God's bitterness at His Son's Crucifixion. He is not presented as a very loving God. Mary, His creature and inferior, is loving, and by her intercession He may be led to show mercy: a mother-figure, even of a murdered Son, is forgiving of the penitent, a father-figure is less likely to be so, at least on His own. O'Gallagher in fact gave his congregation images which their own human experience would bear out. Faction-fighting and vendetta in Irish Catholic rural life was as a rule sustained by men, and frequently deplored by women. His Christ returning to judge the world on the Last Day is a terrifying figure, particularly in the look on His face. He is to catalogue the sins of those whom He intends to condemn, and O'Gallagher made their applicability very explicit. Other improving Catholic devotional works in Irish show signs of a Parisian origin in discussing sins few Irish Catholics would have had anything like the necessary money to commit. O'Gallagher applied the judgement of God to the sins they would be likely to commit. Christ would point out that, like Joseph, He was sold by His brethren, and for what?

> *sibhse lucht na drúise, dhíol sibh mise ar aoibhneas gearr*
> *sibhse lucht na meisge . . . dhíol sibh mise ar buidéal uisge beatha*

> You yourselves the people of the lust, you sold myself for a short
>   pleasure
> You yourselves the people of the drunkenness . . . you sold myself
>   for a bottle of whiskey

People who cheated or extorted money unjustly, especially from the poor or destitute 'you sold myself for fourpence or for sixpence'; women who cheated poor customers in selling cottage-made goods 'you sold myself for a little snap of thread'. He made much more of the drunkards than of the fornicators, savagely placing them in their excess below the brute creation. It is government by fear rather than love. But it is also a brilliant pin-pointing of the utter meanness of sin. As I said, he repays close study.[24]

There is one very startling applicability of O'Gallagher's Irish to the North American linguistic experience. The Gaelic languages have made little impact on American usage. But the American word for a business transaction, 'deal', seems directly derived from the Irish word 'díol' (sell) as used here by O'Gallagher. Its links with the deal of card-playing are far more tenuous: a deal in cards is a giving from one person to another and is separate from any pecuniary transaction that may or may not be part of the game. A business deal involves sale and price, and frequently has sordid implications. It is ironic that the charge against the inappropriate-ness of the Irish language for modern industrial life—O'Connell's phrase 'Irish never sold the cow'—should coexist with the sacrosanct position of the chief Irish commercial verb in the vocabulary of the world's principal centre of capitalism. To stress this is not to say that the word had auto-matic reference to sin in the minds of those who used it. But *díol* crops up again and again in eighteenth-century Irish spiritual and patriotic poetry: Christ was sold, Ireland was sold. The ugly power given to eighteenth-century informers (to which O'Gallagher himself was so vulnerable) hardened community ranks against any potentially profitable action breaking an individual from community observance of totem and taboo. The Irish clergy could enforce obedience on spiritual issues from their flocks by stressing that sin made one a traitor like Judas, whose rapacity and selfishness brought about the crucifixion. The more they talked, as O'Gallagher had talked, within the framework of normal human be-haviour under economic and social deprivation, the greater their hold. They also kept the possibility, indeed the probability, of hell before their people's eyes. The early Irish Catholic immigrants to North America went through quite enough hell in their new life without wanting any prolon-gation of it for eternity.[25]

---

[24] E. B. Fryde *et al.* (eds), *Handbook of British Chronology* (3rd edn, London, 1986), pp. 411, 432, 441 (where the name appears variously 'Gallagher' and 'O'Gallagher', hardly surprisingly since his own first language was evidently Irish which knows no distinction between these forms). A bilingual edition by Canon Ulick J. Bourke of *Sermons in Irish-Gaelic by the Most Rev. James O'Gallagher, Bishop of Raphoe* (Dublin, 1879) carries a 'literal idiomatic English translation on opposite pages' but I have found it necessary to supply translation more literal still: see espe-cially pp. 40-1. In some ways 'a short sweetness' may convey O'Gallagher's meaning even better than 'a short pleasure'.

[25] *Oxford English Dictionary* (Oxford, 1933), 3. 66 ("Deal. sb.² 4) simply assumes the North American usage derived from the Teutonic root meaning 'part' or 'amount', and its *Supple-ment* (Oxford, 1972), I. 745, follows suit. But this makes no sense. The first recorded U.S.

There has been much fashionable discussion of the possible effects of European culture, notably French, on Irish Catholicism: was it Jansenist, or Gallican, or baroque? No doubt these things had some influence here and there. I would argue that the real strength of the continuing appeal was its applicability to the personal experience of the Irish themselves. They knew their world to be a dark one, but it did not lead them into dread of frequent Communion, or beliefs that some of them were automatically saved and others automatically damned. They thought of themselves as a race apart, with strong and unpleasant reason, but they did not seek state control of their religion, even when it might seem advantageous to do so. They went in for little cults of angels (especially the military victor Michael) and saints (especially the unhappy immigrant Patrick), and above all the Virgin Mother whom their poetry described following the bloodspots that led her to her crucified Son; but their religion centred firmly on the passion and death of Christ, a fate worse than their own but in its loneliness and poverty not remote from theirs. It was not a religion of complacency. It made no attempt to minimize their own misfortunes, and it does not seem to have suggested these were the direct results of their sins—others who had evidently committed greater sins were in high places—but it was unsparing in its demands for consciousness of sin. These things lay ready for their priests to invoke. The Irish immigrant priests in North America would have been thrown back on Irish tradition in one important particular. In Ireland they were largely from the communities in which they worked; in America they found fellow Irish, but usually would have had little chance of finding any significant number of common local roots.[26]

The social effects of the Irish priests' perpetuation of their ascendancy offer easy targets: it may therefore be useful to cite an unexpected witness to their beneficent consequences. James Joyce defected from Roman Catholicism but unlike many, perhaps most, of its intellectuals who

---

usage is the New York banker John Rathbone (1834), the first Canadian is the writer T. C. Haliburton (1838), both of whom would be witnesses to the progress of such a word from usage by Irish servants.

[26] The Jansenist thesis has been most notably put forward by Sean O'Faolain, *The Irish* (Harmondsworth, 1969), pp. 104-11. The whole book is well worth reading in any of its editions. Professor Emmet J. Larkin adumbrated the Gallicanism thesis informally in Dublin in the late 1950s but it seems with some modifications to underly most of his subsequent books on Irish Church-State relations. Dolan, *American Catholic Experience*, pp. 33-4, succinctly outlines the baroque thesis. I base myself on O'Gallagher, Donlevy and various Irish poems reprinted in Pádraig Ó Canainn (ed.), *Filidheacht na nGaedheal*.

apostatized, he did so with little bitterness. His cold observation and keen power of ridicule made him an unsympathetic but not a hostile reporter. *Dubliners* includes two stories, 'Grace' and 'Counterparts', which may seem to imply absurdity in recourse to Catholicism—the invalided drunkard is subjected to pious drivellings about 'Lux upon Lux' and 'Crux upon Crux' as supposed symbols of the Pontificates of two Popes, the wretched child who has forgotten to provide food for his job-oppressed father screams a hopeless offer to say 'Hail Marys' to prevent corporal punishment—but the drunkard does at least temporarily reform to the considerable increase in his family's happiness, and the miserable father who brutally ignores his child's offer of prayers is rejecting the gift that would compensate for all his misfortunes, the love of his child. We may apply these reports on Irish Catholicism in the bourgeoisifying process to comparable situations when that process is examined in North America. The work of the Irish priests in keeping religion before the eyes and within the minds of their fellow immigrants made an inhumane existence acquire at least some forms of humanity. They also strengthened the bonds of marriage, which the nomadic requirements of employment had placed under great strain among labourers in the late eighteenth century. Many more Irish fathers abandoned their families in North America than filio-pietistic historians cared to admit, but the idea of family solidarity took increasing hold as the power of the clergy asserted itself more and more, and seems to have put the Irish achievement in this respect rather higher than is to be found in other comparably circumstanced ethnic groups at the same period.[27]

The Irish priests are not known to have sought to arouse much sentiment against Protestants, although when O'Connell and his associates gave them the opportunity at the time of Catholic Emancipation they moved rapidly and skilfully to displace the Protestant landlords in so far as they could from social control of the voters. Many of them would subsequently play a critical part in Parnell's time to break the power of the landlords for good, including at the end the most famous Irish landlord of all, Parnell himself. In the United States a few Irish-born priests played a part in attacks on Irish and American capitalists, usually Protestants: John Joseph Keane (1839–1918), successively bishop of Richmond, first Rector of the Catholic University of America, and archbishop of Dubuque, Iowa, who shared with Gibbons the credit for preventing a Papal condemnation

---

[27] J. A. Joyce, *Dubliners* (London, 1914). I am grateful to my Edinburgh University students in Modern Irish History for stimulating discussions on these questions.

of the Knights of Labor; Thomas James Conaty (1847-1915), a major figure in the American Land League supporting Parnell in the Irish land war and subsequently Keane's successor at the Catholic University whence he became bishop of Monterey and Los Angeles; and Father Peter Christopher Yorke (1864-1925) of San Francisco, a major labour leader in California. Father John Joseph Curran (1859-1936) became the great advocate of the miners of Pennsylvania, mediating to their advantage with President Theodore Roosevelt in 1902; Father Thomas H. Malone of Denver, Colorado, was a vigorous supporter of American Irish trade unionists; and Father Thomas J. Hagerty of New Mexico became an outstanding socialist orator with some influence on the birth of the I.W.W. before leaving the priesthood and Church.[28]

But memories, and indeed witness, of Irish sectarian conflict had effects on Irish priests in North America in directions very different from Socialism. John Hughes had returned to his native Ireland in 1840 when co-adjutor bishop of New York at a time when the bitter tithe war had only recently ceased. Up to that time, Catholics were forced to give tithes to Church of Ireland rectors in addition to supporting their own clergy, as were nonconformist Protestants. The atmosphere of sectarian hostility hardening with Catholic violence against Protestant tithe-proctors, who made a profit as the rectors' agents, boded little good to the recently-established state education for all religions. The Catholic archbishops of Dublin and Armagh sought to support the idea of 'mixed education', but it was coming under fire from the formidable Archbishop John MacHale of Tuam. Hughes's entry into the controversy about public education in New York began with his letter of 1 June 1840 from Dublin:

> ... nothing can be more just than that Catholics should receive benefit of taxes, to which they contribute like other citizens. And, if the common school system is injurious to the religion of Catholic children it should be reformed—or else Catholic citizens should be exempted from the obligation of contributing to its support. Nothing could be more cruel or unjust in principle, than to tax the Catholic father for a fund which is to be expended in perverting his child, under the name of public education.

He warned strongly about the issue's becoming entangled in politics, and

---

[28] Dolan, *American Catholic Experience*, pp. 329-41. See also the pioneer study by James J. Green, 'American Catholics and the Irish Land League, 1879-1882', *Catholic Historical Review*, 35 (1949-50), pp. 19-42.

on his return highly politicized it and turned against the system to build parochial schools. The result would be a significant division of the formative years of an increasingly large number of Catholics, Irish and other, but especially Irish, from the American norm. Suspicion of state schools had existed in Boston and New York among Catholics before Hughes, but it seems likely that his incursion was animated by the Irish atmosphere of retrospective resentment and present questioning of government policy.[29]

Hughes's activities did not involve conflict against the Whig party, for all of the somewhat unjustified Irish Catholic suspicion that it was the guardian of anti-Irish prejudice maintained by well-established American businessmen. On the contrary, he built up an excellent understanding with the Whig Governor William H. Seward who was engaged in a perceptive and moderately enlightened bid for New York Irish votes. But Ireland was by now witnessing a strong Protestant counter-attack on the sectarian neutrality within the state system, and Hughes remained thereafter very suspicious of the growth of New York evangelicalism and the several reform movements into which it projected its energy. Hughes also inaugurated a fairly positive alienation from government control of education. As a result Irish Catholics in particular acquired strong cultural and religious barriers against absorption into the American educational and intellectual mainstream. Without going the length of Froude's attempts to insist that Irish Roman Catholicism in America remained alien and separate, one can diagnose tendencies in restraint of a process of full immigrant assimilation. There is also a darker point. Catholic emphasis on separate education sought in compensation to show enthusiastic American patriotism within classroom instruction, but it also deepened Irish Catholic sectarian doubts as to the acceptability of key American standards. Visibly, Irish Catholics wanted to climb in society to the status of the leading Americans. Spiritually, their conviction was reinforced that their somewhat frosty involuntary hosts in American higher echelons were either damned—a fairly strong unspoken presumption of Judgement Day as described by the late Bishop O'Gallagher and his imitators—or else were saved by 'invincible ignorance'. In this respect at least Irish Catholics believed themselves superior to that into which subsequent historians have taken them to seek assimilation. Hughes's personality ensured a clear pattern of Irish leadership in American Catholicism. Other Catholic

---

[29] Henry J. Browne, 'Public Support of Catholic Education in New York, 1825–1842: Some New Aspects', *Catholic Historical Review*, 39 (1953–4), p. 18. See also T. Ó Raifeartaigh, 'Mixed Education and the Synod of Ulster', *Irish Historical Studies*, 9 (1954–5), pp. 281–44.

ethnic groups followed the Irish lead in at least this respect. That the Chinese held to their culture in a conviction of its superiority to the American is famous, and at least on aesthetic grounds they had a strong case. But in spiritual terms the Irish Catholics had also little desire to stoop to conquer. They would go to many lengths to prove their American credentials, or happily to assert an identity with American priorities on such fine points as strong common reasons for suspicion of British intrigue or soft cultural infection. On a spiritual level they would demand that Americans accept their standards. Translated into the material world, it bred a readiness to see in Boston Brahmins and New York high society the kin of the Irish shapers and upholders of the penal laws. Those Irish who studied American colonial history—and the parochial schools at least tried to look at its Catholic elements—would find ample warrant for such identification in the anti-Catholic penal legislation of all thirteen colonies apart from Maryland (when not under Protestant domination) and Pennsylvania.[30]

It is essential to see the history of Irish-born priest and priests of Irish descent in North America as part of a continuing process, with frequently altering consequences of their intermingling in the nineteenth century, when each of them could see greater and greater possibilities of Irish Catholic power whose divergences across the Atlantic they did not always fully appreciate. If the Irish-born priests in the parishes of North America could never hope to reach the automatic place they held in the local community at home, they won a different primacy in the actual creation of new communities, particularly in Canada where the 'Irish priest', as Nicholas Flood Davin put it in *The Irishman in Canada* (1877), 'followed his people wherever they went, and had, sometimes, preceded them into the wilderness as missionaries to the Indians, as was the case with the Revd Edmund Burke, the bishop of Halifax' (1753-1821). And it was British North America, not the United States, which received and kept most Irish immigrants until the 1840s. In the smaller population the Irish clerical leadership could be both more notorious in eccentricity and have disproportionately stronger influence. The Irish-born Bishop John Thomas Mullock (1807-69) was credited with ensuring that the Atlantic cable would operate via his see of Newfoundland, while also winning celebrity for his impassioned conviction as to the antisocial effects of Newfound-

---

[30] Theodore Maynard, *The Story of American Catholicism* (New York, 1941) offers a convenient presentation of the traditional picture of American Catholicism, but Ellis, *Documents*, is necessary to see the reality in depth.

land dogs. By the mid-nineteenth century the Irish in Canada were taken to be more numerous than the English or the Scots. Landholders were a far higher percentage among the Irish in Canada—75 per cent in 1866, claimed Thomas D'Arcy McGee—but as Lynch's experience would testify the priests' new fields for pioneer work would then be in the ever-expanding urban population. As D'Arcy McGee put it, 'Never, in the world's history, were a purely agricultural population so suddenly and unpreparedly converted into mere town laborers.' Ireland had seen individually electrifying clerical reformers, such as the temperance advocate Father Theobald Mathew: the U.S.A. welcomed him, but his lone efforts on tour there before the Civil War were, for all their courage, dwarfed by the mighty organization of the Catholic Total Abstinence Union of America, founded after the war in 1872. The U.S.A. justly incurred reproach for its failure to grapple with the assimilation of immigrants on a level of public and private philanthropy during the famine, Edward Everett Hale being a lone crusader among American reformers: but in good American style the ethnic group itself moved into the field with the largest of all nineteenth-century immigrant charitable organizations, the Irish Catholic Benevolent Union, founded in 1869 and numbering a membership of 30,000 in 1876. For all of the famous emphasis on increasing Irish leverage in United States politics, this type of enterprise contrasted strongly with dependence on government for action which so much dominated Irish and Canadian reform movements. And there is a startling contrast in the 1860s between the prestige held by Lynch of Toronto, Hughes of New York, and Lynch of Charleston among their respective ruling political elites, and the Irish bishops' deployment of Irish politicians at Westminster into the cul-de-sac of 'The Pope's Brass Band' crudely shouting for Pius IX against the prevailing English storm of enthusiasm for the Risorgimento.[31]

It seems appropriate to single out in conclusion the two leading examples of Irish-descended and Irish-born clerics in the United States, as they reflected the impact of Ireland. John Carroll was justly sympathetic to the condition of his co-religionists in the home of his paternal ancestors. He kept in close touch with Archbishop Troy of Dublin and with

---

[31] Davin, *The Irishman in Canada* (Toronto, [1877]), p. 101. D'Arcy McGee, *Irish Problem*, p. 7. J. F. Maguire's position as one of the 'Brass Band' seems to lend a slight note of wistfulness to his description of the more substantial accomplishments of his fellow-Irish coreligionists in North America. On these questions in general I have said a word in my 'The American Image of Ireland: a Study of its Early Phases', *Perspectives in American History*, 4 (1970), pp. 241-82.

Charles Plowden, brother of the Catholic historian, to whom he wrote in 1797 during the danger of French invasion of Ireland

> I long to hear, that all threatening appearances, which hang over England, are dispersed; but I wish at the same time, that the just demands of Irish Catholics may be satisfied. If not, the justice of heaven will one day inflict some dreadful punishment on your country for that most iniquitous & immoral system of legislation, which has oppressed Ireland so long.

With bitterness he concluded in 1804 that 'there is no great hope of a restitution to the Irish Catholics of their political rights'. To Troy in 1810 he wrote:

> I have noticed in the public prints that the Catholics of Ireland are to be joined this year by those of England in their annual petition; but your King, it is presumed, will be persuaded to persevere in his rejection of the prayer of it. Should not every thinking man be struck by comparing the peaceable demeanour of Catholics under the injustice done to them, and the violence which would be openly pursued by reformers, if, having a physical force such as that of the Catholics of Ireland, their demands were rejected with the contumely and scorn affected in the Houses of Parliament?

To the Irish hierarchy he formally stated the same year:

> You occupy episcopal sees distinguished by the virtues of a long series of holy bishops, your predecessors. To you has been confided a people confirmed in the old faith, and in virtue revealed in word and good works. In conjunction with your flocks you offer a singular, perhaps a unique, example of unconquerable fortitude in defending and spreading Catholic dogma, despite the obstacles of every human device originating in deceit and violence.

When the question of a British Governmental veto over Irish Catholic episcopal appointments looked like winning Papal support in 1815 he acknowledged Papal precedent in dealing with other 'uncatholic states' but was dubious about it and advised Troy:

> The reasonable distrust, founded on past experience, which attaches itself to the promises of British Protestant ministers, to the R.C. of Ireland, forbid, that the concession of a *Veto* will not be abused. . . .

And he told the English Jesuit Joseph Tristram the same year, clearly in opposition to attempts at compromise:

> Whatever opinion individuals may adopt, I trust that the Society [of Jesus], in England and Ireland will not embrace any of the contested points on the subject of a limited Veto, which shall be maintained by them, as their standard doctrine, nor with the zeal of partizans. Ireland has too much reason to distrust the promises of a British Protestant ministry: and both English and Irish Catholics may find in their own histories the evils of internal division.[32]

But Carroll's views of Irish priests, although he had to welcome many of them, showed that he was all too well aware of the consequences of oppression on the integrity of its victims. Individual Irish priests in America accepted his hospitality and patronage, and then intrigued against him using his former Jesuit status as an Achilles heel when the Jesuits were in eclipse. 'Of Irish clergymen I am afraid', he bluntly informed Charles Plowden in 1802:

> for tho we are blessed with some worthy & able men from that class, yet many have caused disorders here; and in many parts of the country have excited prejudices against them very difficult to be removed.

He kept a good sense of humour about it, however, when he noted in 1815 that one gesture of philanthropy in the direction of an Irish cleric would result in

> emboldening others in Ireland to leave their country for America, under an expectation, that they will be maintained till the end of their Theology. It is said, that there are not less than 30 students in Divinity at Kilkenny alone, who are ready to come and offer themselves as Candidates for Holy Orders; and, no doubt every one, whose name is Carroll, will call himself my relation.[33]

---

[32] Carroll to Plowden, 7 July 1797, in Thomas O'Brien Hanley, SJ (ed.), *The John Carroll Papers* (Notre Dame, 1976), 2, p. 217. Carroll to Plowden, 7 December 1804 (*ibid.*, 2, p. 462). Carroll to John Troy, 21 March 1810 (*ibid.*, 3, p. 116). Carroll to the Hierarchy of Ireland, 11 November 1810 (*ibid.*, 3, po. 126). Carroll to Troy, n.d. (*ibid.*, 3, p. 312). Carroll to Tristram (*ibid.*, 3, p. 352).

[33] Carroll to Plowden, 12 March 1802 (*ibid.*, 2, p. 383). Carroll to Enoch Fenwick, 10 September 1815 (*ibid.*, 3, p. 358). Dolan, *American Catholic Experience*, 103-24, is stimulating on Carroll, and Annabelle M. Melville, *John Carroll of Baltimore* (New York, 1955) is useful, but the *Papers* must be the most profound source.

On the other hand, the unfortunate examples of Irish-born priests and bishops in the United States in Carroll's day were decisively obliterated by the remarkable character of such figures in the next generation as Bishop John England (1786-1842) of Charleston. Professor Patrick Carey has produced a most judicious and thought-provoking recent study of him, *An Immigrant Bishop: John Enlgand's Adaptation of Irish Catholicism to American Republicanism* (1982) which delves much deeper than previous historiography into the Irish roots of the expanding American Church. England, transplanted to Charleston as bishop at the age of 34, arrived with vigorous experience of support for Daniel O'Connell's political evangelism of the Irish Catholic populace. Dr Carey is alive to the problems caused by the background:

> When Irish immigrants like John England came to the United States carrying their traditions with them, they were not always accepted, to say the least, as genuine liberals. Not only did their identification of republicanism with Catholicism irritate many of the American Protestant nativists, but their aggressive manner in doing so also disturbed many of their American Catholic neighbors who preferred a low-profile Catholicism in a Protestant country. . . . Even though as the majority of the population in Ireland they had suffered from the penal laws imposed upon them by the Protestant minority, the Irish liberals like England had never experienced a minority status in Ireland. Thus, they did not properly appreciate their role as a minority in the United States and, particularly in England's case, failed to understand the persistence of American hostility to Catholicism.

But the penal laws also gave Irish Catholic clergy an unexpected advantage in understanding certain American peculiarities:

> Living under such circumstances, Irish Catholics actually experienced a separation of church and state . . . that no other Christian community which represented a majority of a country's population had ever experienced. . . . After 1766 . . . the Catholic Church enjoyed in Ireland a greater freedom from state interference in its own internal operations (particularly in the selection of clergy and the determination of ecclesiastical policies) than it did in all other European countries.
>
> The experience of the penal system, furthermore, encouraged Irish Catholics to perceive the union of church and state as inimical to

their own interests. The practical experience of such a union ...
gradually induced them to develop liberal principles of religious
liberty and separation of church and state. ... they also enjoyed common bonds between the clergy and the laity, voluntaryism, and
separation of church and state—all of which ... prepared them for
accommodating themselves to American principles and practices.[34]

As the Veto question reminded England and his fellow-clerics in Ireland, the Papacy primarily considered the surviving numbers of Catholics
in their island as a means by which the far greater prize of the larger and
adjoining island could be recovered. Concessions to the British government made sense to Popes who still thought in terms of repossession of the
state religion. In the United States and in Canada the Roman Catholic
Church was one of many in the religious market-place. Nobody could
win, and no compromises with Protestant rulers were therefore on offer.
Both the American-born and the Irish-born had every reason to rejoice in
religious freedom, however suspicious local Protestants might be of their
motivation. There were other compromises to be made: fearful of splitting
Catholic ranks, Carroll, England, Hughes, and many others would
temporize on the slavery question. Initially Irish-born Catholic priests
voiced criticisms of the slaveholding Carroll (the archbishop gave support
to gradual emancipation and freed his own slave in his will). England, desperately seeking to augment his pygmy church in the American South as
slaveholding sentiment grew stronger, saw his work of salvation as thrown
away were he to make the question of slavery a moral one, although he did
quietly but firmly make it clear that he personally disliked the institution.
In the years before the Famine many Irish priests were sent to work in the
South and followed England in refusing to put their mission at risk over
slavery. The hostility of Pope Gregory XVI to slavery was set aside by
American bishops such as Hughes in the North as well as by the Southern
Catholics. On the other hand, within the Catholic Church in North
America itself Irish-born priests looked in general with suspicion on all
other ethnic groups within the Church, and here as elsewhere throughout
the world Irish episcopal rule often virtually assumed two classes of
Catholic: the Irish, and the rest. To this extent they perpetuated the less
desirable features of the caste system in Ireland, save that it was made one
of ethnicity rather than of sect.[35]

[34] Carey, *An Immigrant Bishop* (Yonkers, N.Y., 1982), 6, p. 7.
[35] *Ibid.*, *passim.* England to the Cardinal-Prefect of Propaganda, 30 January 1833, in Peter
Guilday, *The Life and Times of John England* (New York, 1927), 1, p. 531.

The Irish priest in North America might seem to have as many faces as the appearance of Junius in Byron's 'The Vision of Judgment'. Nevertheless the roots in eighteenth-century Ireland require more study if any common heritage is to be appreciated and its various different epiphanies are to be construed sensibly. But we must also remember that the inheritance from oppression is but one part of the story: the other is the place of Irish-descended Catholics such as John Carroll among the formal makers of the American Revolution, and of many others among the many different evolutions that went to make up the great totality of Canada.

University of Edinburgh

POPULAR CATHOLICISM IN IRISH
NEW YORK, *c* 1900*

by HUGH McLEOD

I N 1905 was published one of the most interesting books ever written
about New York. It was a study by Elsa Herzfeld of twenty-four
working-class families living on Manhattan's West Side. All too
briefly, yet with many tantalizing quotations and anecdotes, she discussed
a whole series of themes that most previous students of New York life had
taken for granted, or perhaps regarded as too trivial to be worth recording:
the pictures people had on their walls, the music they liked, relations
between spouses and between parents and children, beliefs about good
and bad luck, funeral customs, and attitudes to physicians and hospitals.
The families all included at least two generations, the older of which was
predominantly European born. Most were of Irish or German descent.
The purpose of the volume was to identify the distinguishing characteristics of what it termed 'Tenement-House Man'. There is thus a tendency to
stress what is common to the families studied, and to suggest a shared pattern of life. Time and time again, though, there are hints that religion was
a differentiating factor within this allegedly homogeneous culture. In particular there are frequent references to Catholics as in some sense a group
apart—a very large group apart, as they made up about 40 per cent of the
city's population at that time.

Here are some of the references I found in the book to behaviour and
attitudes regarded as distinctively Catholic:

> 'In every Irish Catholic home the colored religious print is always
> found. . . . In every Catholic home there are crucifixes either of light
> wood, black ebony, enameled or white glass. There are frequently
> china figures representing the Virgin Mary and the Christ child,
> colored in bright reds and blues with golden halos.'
> 'The Catholics spoke with pride of their fine church choir.'
> 'In Catholic families the child is christened before the end of the first
> week, until then "it is not safe from harm".'
> 'If possible Catholic families send their children to one of the two
> parochial schools in the district.'
> 'The Catholics especially dwell on the future state in their talk.'

* I wish to thank the British Academy and Social Science Research Council for research grants.

'The Irish Catholic mother believes that praying over a sick child will cure it, and placing "holy bones" on the body of a crippled child will make it whole.'
'If the relative is dead, the Catholic will give his name [to a child] only if another is added for good luck.'

There are also various references to beliefs and practices which are evidently distinctively Catholic, although this is not explicitly stated: for instance, the wearing of scapulars, or the claim that 'A child born in May is always lucky'. Equally revealing are the reports of anti-Catholic prejudice and of the ill-feeling cause by mixed marriages.[1]

Herzfeld never explicitly discusses the extent or significance of sectarian divisions, and in this she was no different from other members of the first generation of sociological observers of New York life, most of whom either ignored religion or assumed that it was of diminishing relevance.[2] While I would not wish to go to the opposite extreme by exaggerating the strength and centrality of Catholic loyalty,[3] I would argue that there is very considerable evidence for the existence in working-class districts of turn-of-the-century New York of a popular Catholic culture, distinguished by patterns of behaviour and belief that were in important respects different from those of Protestants, Jews, and unbelievers belonging to the same social class. I shall analyse the characteristics of this culture under three headings: first, aspects which seem to me uniquely Catholic; second, those that represent distinctly Catholic variants of ways of thinking and acting found more generally in the popular religious culture of America at this time; and third, those that represent distinctly Catholic versions of ways of thinking and acting that were generally current in the 'secular' culture of working-class and lower-middle-class New Yorkers.

At the start of this century, about half the Catholics in New York City were of Irish descent. The public face of New York Catholicism was even more Irish than this might suggest,[4] since the Irish were over-represented both among the clergy and among those lay Catholics who attended mass regularly, and every archbishop, from Hughes in the 1850s to O'Connor

[1] E. Herzfeld, *Family Monographs* (New York, 1905), pp. 15–28, 118, 120, 139.
[2] See for instance P. Goldmark (ed.), *West Side Studies*, 2 Vols (New York, 1914); T. J. Jones, *The Sociology of a New York City Block* (New York, 1904), pp. 95–7, 116.
[3] Parish histories often present the period c. 1880–1930 as a golden age of New York Catholicism. See G. A. Kelly, *The Parish* (New York, 1973).
[4] See H. McLeod, 'Catholicism and the New York Irish 1880–1910', L. Roper, J. Obelkevich, and R. Samuel (eds), *Disciplines of Faith* (London, 1987), pp. 337–50.

in the 1980s, has been of Irish background. In illustrating my argument I shall limit myself to Irish examples. However, I am not claiming that there is anything uniquely Irish about the patterns of thought and behaviour that I shall describe. On the contrary, I would argue that these are broadly characteristic of working-class and lower-middle-class Catholics of all ethnic groups, though there were certainly important differences of emphasis between, for instance, Irish and Italians or Irish and Germans.

I

The later years of the nineteenth century were those in which the champions of a fortress-like American Catholicism gained a clear ascendency over those who wanted to build bridges between the Church and surrounding society.[5] In part, the existence of a Catholic culture reflected the success of the clergy in inculcating a highly-developed sense of religious identity, reinforced by ideas and institutions that emphasized the boundary-lines between Catholic and non-Catholic. Yet the many Catholics whose contacts with the clergy were very infrequent often shared in this culture. So it was maintained by several partly independent factors. First, with the encouragement of the hierarchy, there was a proliferation of specificially Catholic organizations, intended to provide for as many as possible of the Catholic's social, recreational and educational needs within an environment shaped and controlled by the clergy. Second, Church teaching of this period laid special stress on doctrines and practices that were uniquely Catholic, and repudiated by other Christians. Third, Catholicism was tightly bound up with the culture and identity of specific ethnic groups: the importance of inter-ethnic conflict in New York during this period tended also to strengthen Catholic consciousness. And fourth, Catholicism was learnt not only in the church but also in the home, and many of those who were in the Church's eyes 'bad Catholics' continued to be in their own eyes loyal Catholics, to practise their religion in their own way, and to pass it on to their children.

The institutional basis of American Catholic culture was being firmly laid in the later nineteenth century by bishops anxious to protect the faith of their people from Protestant or secularizing influences. The Third

---

[5] R. E. Curran, *Michael Augustine Corrigan and the Shaping of Conservative Catholicism in America* (New York, 1978); H. McLeod, 'Building the "Catholic Ghetto": Catholic Organisations c.1870–1914', *SCH* 23, pp. 411–44. See also the excellent new general history, which is relevant to many of the themes in this paper, J. P. Dolan, *The American Catholic Experience* (New York, 1985).

Plenary Council of American bishops at Baltimore in 1884 marked the definitive triumph of those who regarded the parochial school as the only acceptable educational environment for the young Catholic (though lack of money meant that the ideal of a school in every parish never came near to being achieved). This was also a boom period for Catholic publishing, with growing numbers of newspapers, magazines, devotional books, and even novels being produced for a specifically Catholic market (as well as ethnic newspapers, many of which gave considerable space to church affairs).[6] From about 1880 parish organizations of all kinds were also proliferating. At first confraternities outnumbered recreational clubs. But by the 1900s increasing numbers of parish societies were being formed explicitly for athletics, billiards, dramatics, literary discussions, and the like. Dances, outings, and fairs were also bulking large in the parish calendar. So, for the more parish-oriented Catholic, the Church offered a complete way of life, with specifically Catholic versions of most of the amenities available to the non-Catholic public from charities or commercial undertakings.[7]

The doctrinal underpinnings of Catholic exclusiveness were also being strengthened in this period. The definitions of the doctrines of the Immaculate Conception of the Virgin Mary (1854) and Papal Infallibility (1870), the Syllabus of Errors (1864), the condemnations of 'Americanism' (1899) and 'Modernism' (1907), as well as the continuing teaching of 'No Salvation outside the Church', all served to provide a theological rationale for self-separation.

But the popular Catholic culture described in this paper was by no means limited to those Catholics who were actively involved in the life of their parish. Especially in the centres of south Italian settlement, such as East Harlem, observers were faced with the apparent paradox of a community that was overwhelmingly Catholic in affiliation, where very few converted to Protestantism or secularism, where observance of certain saints' days was very widespread and enthusiastic and religious symbols often filled the home, but where the prestige of the clergy was low and few people attended mass.[8] While formal religious practice was certainly much higher among the Irish than the Italians in New York, there were many among the poorer Irish whose contacts with the Church were fairly

---

[6] For Catholic novels see P. Messbarger, *Fiction with a Parochial Purpose* (Boston, 1971); for the Catholic publishing boom more generally, A. Taves, 'Relocating the Sacred: Roman Catholic Devotions in mid-nineteenth-century America' (Ph.D. thesis, Chicago University, 1983).

[7] Dolan, *Catholic Experience*, pp. 205-6.

[8] See especially R. Orsi, *The Madonna of 115th Street* (New Haven, 1985).

spasmodic.[9] The rhythms of regular devotion prescribed by the Church fitted better into a regime where income and hours of work were regular and predictable than into the hand to mouth existence of the poorer working class. Moreover, regularity of practice was often stimulated by the quest for respectability, a status for which most of the poor were ineligible. This did not mean, however, that they were in their own eyes any less Catholic than their more formally devout neighbours.

II

The culture of Catholic New Yorkers diverged most sharply from that of their non-Catholic contemporaries in the comprehensiveness of their effort to rank all times, places, objects, and people on a scale of holiness, and in the pervasive presence in their lives of the symbols of the holy. The holy was that which brought Catholics out of the workaday world, and closer to the supernatural world. In doing so, it offered them the prospect of benefits of many different kinds—from the strengthening of their faith, or courage to resist temptation, to safety in the face of danger, alleviation of pain or success in business or exams. The most visible symbols of the holy were the huge Catholic churches which were among the most prominent landmarks in the tenement districts of New York—Most Holy Redeemer on the German Lower East Side, St Paul's on the Irish West Side, Our Lady of Mount Carmel in Italian East Harlem, St Stanislaus Kostka in Polish Greenpoint, and so on. But more important than sheer size was the idea of the holy that these buildings embodied. Everything in the church was intended to stand in the starkest possible contrast to the surroundings in which New York tenement-dwellers lived the rest of their lives. Over against the dull matter-of-factness, the chaos and the squalour of everyday life, the churches were places of mystery and ceremony, and were lavishly decorated. The marble and the carved wood, the music and the incense, the stained glass windows, the priests in vestments speaking Latin, all combined to shut out the workaday world, and to create an atmosphere in which, it was believed, it was easier to feel the presence of God. A powerful expression of what Catholics felt about their churches was that by a West Side woman in reply to a questionnaire about the history of her parish. She wrote that her church 'has always been and always will be a place of refuge for me. I draw whatever strength I need from it—it isn't

[9] McLeod, 'New York Irish', pp. 343–4; Jones, *New York City Block*, p. 116.

just a place of worship, it's Sacred Heart—full of wonder, hope, faith, mystery, and yes, miracles'.[10]

Next to the church on the scale of holiness was the home. In some respects, the two were in complete contrast. The church was, after all, treasured so much partly because it offered escape from the noise, smell, and clutter of the tenement flat. Yet there also were parallels. If the streets, the workplace, and the places for drinking and entertainment belonged wholly to the workaday world, and if the churches belonged wholly to the world of set-apart holy things, the home was the point of intersection between the two. One parallel between church and home is indicated in the Irish custom of procuring holy water when moving into a new flat, and sprinkling it around each room.[11] On entering the church, a holy place, the church-goer, as a sinful human being, needed holy water; by contrast there was nothing holy about a tenement flat, but it was a place where a home was to be established, where people would be born and would die, and to be fit for this dignity the place needed to be cleansed of the association with whatever evil or unhappy events had happened there in the past. The parallels between church and home were more directly apparent in the multiplicity of sacred pictures that filled Catholic homes— though the position of the home as point of intersection between different worlds is reflected in the juxtaposition of a variety of apparently divergent themes on the crowded walls of the Catholic home. The most detailed description we have is Herzfeld's account of a 'typical' Irish tenement flat—three rooms occupied by a middle-aged couple and their six children. The wholly mundane is represented by insurance, grocery, and brewery calendars. The obviously sacred is represented by the family shrine (a brown wooden box with a slanting roof, in which there is an image of the Virgin, over whom is hung a rosary), by a crucifix and a plaster image of the Virgin holding the infant Jesus, and by pictures of Christ healing the sick and of Saints Benedict and Anthony. In intermediate categories might be placed portraits of Popes Leo XIII and Pius X, by which the family may be said to have declared their common identity as Catholics in a Protestant-dominated society, together with the family portrait gallery (apparently a general feature of West Side tenement flats, and including in this instance a photograph of a family tombstone in Ireland), and pictures of a child praying and of a mother and child under a shower of apple blossoms. Above the clock hangs the motto 'God Bless Our Home'.[12] If there is an overriding theme, it would seem to be the link between the two most sacred forms of obligation—to God and to one's family. At the same time, the multiplication of sacred images might be seen as a recognition of the knife-edge on which the home was balanced, and an attempt to mobilize all the available resources of supernatural support in order to assist its survival.

The clergy laid a heavy stress on the sacredness of the home and of family obligations, sometimes showing a realistic appreciation of the difficulties in converting ideal into reality, but sometimes conveying the message in purely ideal terms, as in the following parallel between earthly home and heaven:

> [The home] stands at the end of each day's labour, and beckons us to its bosom; and life would be cheerless and meaningless, did we not discern across the river that divides us from the life beyond, glimpses of the pleasant mansions prepared for us. . . . Just as there is no happiness to compare on earth with that which consecrates the home, so there is no misery equal to that growing out of dispositions that desecrate it.[13]

The converse of this stress on the sanctity of church and home was the relegation of work, politics, and leisure to a secular sphere, about which Catholicism had relatively little to say. This did not of course mean that the Church was uninvolved in any of these areas. When the bishops believed that the Church's vital interests were affected they had no hesitation about intervening in elections. When strikes broke out in their parishes, priests frequently got involved, whether in support or opposition.[14] Parishes frequently had their own gyms, billiard tables, basketball teams, and other facilities. But all of these were regarded as wholly secondary to the Church's main business, which was the worship of God, and the saving of individual souls. The Catholic Church did not in this period follow the many Protestants who were beginning to preach a

---

[12] Herzfeld, *Monographs*, pp. 44–6.

[13] *Calendar* of the Church of St Paul the Apostle, January 1908. (Copies at the church.)

[14] For discussions of the role of clergy in strikes, covering favourable, hostile, and ambiguous responses, see C. Shanabruch, *Chicago's Catholics* (Notre Dame, 1981), pp. 150–1; V. R. Greene, *The Slavic Community on Strike* (Notre Dame, 1968), pp. 106–7, 167, 192; J. J. Bukowczyk, 'Steeples and Smokestacks: Class, Religion and Ideology in the Polish Immigrant Settlements of Greenpoint and Williamsburg, Brooklyn 1880–1929 (Ph.D. thesis, Harvard University, 1980), pp. 173–80.

'Social Gospel', according to which Christianity was as much about transforming society as saving individuals, and no area of life was to be seen as
merely 'secular'.

Catholics were not of course alone in setting apart certain times as
more sacred than others. Jews and Protestants had their Sabbaths, and
Jews, Lutherans, and Episcopalians also attached a great deal of significance to certain annual festivals. Catholics, however, had their own
distinctive way of organizing time, and they also did it in greater detail
than any other major religious group.[15] In the first place, rather than a
simple dichotomy between Sabbath and workdays, Catholics had a hierarchy of days, with Sundays certainly at the top, though less pre-
eminently so than among Protestants, but with Friday not too far
behind, and Thursday and Saturday also having some claims to sanctity.
Secondly, while Catholics shared with members of some other Churches
the practice of celebrating a variety of festivals and seasons, they were
alone in organizing the months of the year into a hierarchy of holiness,
identifying each with specific saints or with other devotions. May, the
month of Mary, was at the top of the list, but a number of other months,
notably March, June, and November, also became associated in the
minds of devout Catholics with particular aspects of their faith. Thirdly,
the celebration by Catholics of large numbers of saints' days introduced
an attractive elective element into this organization of time. The saint's
festival, and often the eve of the festival, or even the nine days preceding,
became a time of mass celebration for the saint's devotees, who might
vary from those who had been or hoped to be healed by the saint, to all
those living in a parish named after the saint, to all the New Yorkers
originating from a town or a nation of which that saint was patron. The
most obvious example of the latter was St Patrick's Day, with its typical
mixture of religious rites, public parades, patriotic speeches, and eating
and drinking, which was a major event in the city's calendar. But many
other saints' days were important local events within particular sections
of Manhattan or Brooklyn.

The saints played a crucial role in popular Catholicism, of which more
will be said later. Equally significant as a reflection of the all-pervasive
sacred/secular dichotomy was the deep divide between priests and nuns
on the one side and, on the other, lay people. Attitudes to religious profes-
sionals were complex and ambivalent, and there were important ethnic
differences. The status of nuns seems generally to have been high among

---

[15] The best discussion of this is Taves, 'Relocating the Sacred', pp. 44–9, 72–5.

American Catholics,[16] whereas that of priests varied, being highest among the Irish, but considerably lower with some nationalities, notably the Italians. Common to all ethnic groups was the frequency with which priests occurred, whether in heroic or in villainous roles, in the folklore of the community;[17] individual priests, and the clergy as a body, provoked extreme emotions, some coming to be regarded as saints, while others were attacked or even murdered by disappointed parishioners.[18] One reason for this was that the Irish, in particular, but also many Catholics belonging to other ethnic groups, saw the priests as touchstones by which the whole Catholic community was judged. Thus, the supreme test of the quality of a parish was the number of vocations it had produced. For a devout family there could be no greater source of pride than a child who became a priest or a nun—nor any source of shame more poignant than if the child were subsequently to abandon that vocation. Anniversaries, jubilees, or special distinctions conferred on the priests of a parish were occasions for memorable celebrations.[19]

Priests and nuns belonged to the sacred rather than the secular domain. But here too there was a scale of holiness. At one extreme were those who violated the law of celibacy. Priests could be criticized for many other things—addiction to money, power, drink, or golf being the most common accusations.[20] None of these addictions disqualified a man from being a priest, though very heavy drinkers were sometimes suspended from their offices. But even a single breach of the prohibition on sexual activity fatally compromised the priest's status as a man set apart for the

---

[16] Orsi, *Madonna*, pp. 84–5; H. R. Diner, *Erin's Daughters in America* (Baltimore, 1983), p. 130; Dolan, *Catholic Experience*, p. 290.

[17] The contrast is illustrated in the W.P.A. collection on New York City Folk Lore (Library of Congress Folk Music Division, Washington D.C.), which includes jokes and songs current in the various ethnic communities. An elderly Slovak woman told a series of stories in which priests were presented as seducers or money-grubbers. However, a collection of songs that had been popular with Irish immigrants *c.* 1900 included one entitled 'Father O'Flynn', which is about an idealized country priest from County Kerry, and concludes 'Och, Father O'Flynn, you've a wonderful way with you.' See Mary Swenson and Patrick Quinlan folders.

[18] P. J. Murnion, 'Towards Theopolitan Ministry: The changing Structure of the Pastoral Ministry, New York 1920–1970' (Ph.D. thesis, Columbia University, 1972), pp. 86–7, 132–3.

[19] *Ibid.*, pp. 3, 132–3 and *passim* provides a useful discussion of the role and status of the priest in New York in the 1920s.

[20] The 'Studs Lonigan' novels of J. T. Farrell present a brilliant (and totally unflattering) picture of the Irish Catholic community in Chicago in the 1920s. The main criticism of the clergy that was openly voiced by the characters was that they were obsessed with money. The main criticism implied by the author would seem to be lack of sincerity. They are prosperous and prestigious figures, more or less of a kind with politicians, but with no hint of spirituality about them.

service of God. It was celibacy that separated them unmistakably from the workaday world, and was a necessary precondition for holiness. Accusations of unchastity thus became deadly weapons in clerical infighting; an accusation that would stick was known as the most effective means of discrediting an opponent in the eyes of his supporters.[21] At an intermediate point in the scale of holiness were those whose competence and worthiness were not in doubt, and who commanded immense respect, but scarcely love. Priests of this kind were fairly numerous at a time when the pastor of a parish was a powerful and prestigious figure, especially in Irish districts of the city. Many of them cultivated a formidable and somewhat aloof image, and were accustomed to wield the big stick—metaphorically, or even literally.[22] However, there also were priests who came to be revered. Even in their lifetimes, special powers were often attributed to them, and after their deaths they came to be regarded as saints.[23]

III

While the forms of popular Catholicism were distinctly and uniquely Catholic, much of its style was less far removed from that of revivalist Protestantism. The appeal of both, and their common ability to hold the loyalty of a vast working-class and lower-middle-class constituency, lay partly in characteristics that they shared, and which made them equally objectionable not only to secularists and the religiously luke-warm, but also to many devout 'mainstream' Protestants. Both were highly dogmatic, and emphasized the boundary-lines between Church and world; both appealed very directly to emotions of fear and hope, hate and love; both thrived on their internal dramas—the mission or revival meeting, with its straight-from-the-shoulder hell-fire preaching, the death-bed conver-

---

[21] During the great conflict between Archbishop Corrigan and the radical New York priest, Fr Edward McGlynn, Corrigan tried hard, though with inconclusive results, to prove that McGlynn had had at least one child and solicited women in the confessional. See Curran, *Corrigan*, pp. 276–86.

[22] See reminiscences of a West Side priest who was said to tour his parish at night armed with a horse-whip, to be used on prostitutes and drinkers, and of an English-born priest who liked preaching on hell. H. J. Browne, *One Stop above Hell's Kitchen: Sacred Heart Parish in Clinton* (Hackensack, 1977), p. 61; P. J. Dooley, *Fifty Years in Yorkville* (New York, 1917), pp. 103–5, 148.

[23] The most explicit example I have seen concerns a German priest who worked in a Lower East Side parish from 1866 to 1894. See Chronicles of Most Holy Redeemer Parish, Vol. 2, pp. 68–9 (Archives of the Redemptorist Fathers, Brooklyn). However, there are strong hints of a saint-cult in the kind of devotion inspired by Fr Edward McGlynn (though I know of no reported miracles). See my paper on McGlynn in S. P. Mews (ed.), *Modern Religious Rebels* (forthcoming).

sions of atheists and hardened sinners, or (in the case of Catholicism) the race to bring the last rites to the victims of accidents. I would argue, therefore, that in spite of their mutual antipathy, ultramontane Catholicism and evangelical Protestantism owed an important part of their appeal to similar factors, and might be seen as alternative forms of a wider popular religious culture in turn-of-the-century America.[24] I want to lay special stress here on one of the most important features of this culture, namely the sense of the nearness of the supernatural world. As with many evangelicals, this meant that Catholics prayed very frequently, and often for apparently trivial ends, and that they lived in constant expectation of miracles. The distinctly Catholic form of this popular supernaturalism was the highly personal relationship between Catholics and their saints.[25]

Unlike God, the saints could be portrayed in statues or paintings in church or home, or in little pictures that their devotees carried around. Unlike Jesus, they represented ideals of humanity that were in principle attainable, and because they were fully human they appreciated the temptations and difficulties to which ordinary people were subject, and they could identify with their devotees in their times of trouble. Yet because they were saints they could intercede effectively with God on behalf of those less holy than themselves. At the same time, an important attraction of the relationship between Catholics and their saints lay in its conditionality—the very reverse of the unconditional faith in God taught by orthodox Christian theology (though not so different from the more pragmatic faith of many laypeople). The saints offered help in return for the performance of tasks that were often onerous, but were none the less limited and clearly defined. If the saint failed to keep his or her part of the bargain, the trust would be broken, and the devotee would turn elsewhere.

While, therefore, many of the clergy presented the saints primarily as exemplars,[26] it was above all as miracle-workers that they were honoured by the people. Catholics believed that God continually intervened in everyday life to heal the sick, to bring peace to divided families, to change the hearts of drunkards and thieves, and to convert heretics and

---

[24] Similar points are made in J. P. Dolan, *Catholic Revivalism* (Notre Dame, 1978), pp. 185–203, and Taves, 'Relocating the Sacred', pp. 258–61.

[25] A useful general study on this issue is S. Wildon (ed.), *Saints and their Cults* (Cambridge, 1983). Specifically on later nineteenth-century America, see Taves, 'Relocating the Sacred', pp. 132–3, 148–60.

[26] Parish magazines often carried articles about saints. These tended to stress their virtues, wise sayings associated with them, or causes of which they were patrons. *Calendar* of the Church of St Paul the Apostle, November 1886; *Church Bulletin* of St Ignatius parish, March 1905 (copies in parish library).

unbelievers. These miracles could ultimately be traced back to the prayers of the faithful, who entreated the saints to intercede with God. The records of New York churches during this period include many references to this quest for miracles. Some New York churches won such formidable reputations as places of miracles that they attracted the sick from all over the city, or from all parts of the north-eastern United States. St Ann's on the Lower East Side held a novena in honour of their patron saint every July, which attracted enormous congregations (and solved the parish's financial problems). In the 1920s it was claimed that 40,000 people had the relic applied to them in a year. Even more famous were the relics of St Ann held by the Blessed Sacrament Fathers at their church of St John the Baptist on the Upper East Side—and in fact one of the West Side Irish families studied by Herzfeld had a child who had been cured at that church. The cult began in May 1892, when a relic was temporarily lodged at the church while *en route* from Rome to Montreal:

> In the interval between Mass and Vespers word spread that the relic was to be exposed, and that afternoon the church was packed to the doors. Eager crowds thronged the little structure long after the usual hour, and throughout the three days following an unending stream of ill and needy petitioners came to the then quiet and out-of-the-way church.

The Fathers subsequently obtained their own relic, and a regular programme of devotions was instituted.[27] The search for miraculous cures was the most visible aspect of these shrines, for those who visited them were often obviously disabled, and some churches displayed wax arms, legs, etc., given by the grateful recipients of favours, in order to show the parts of their body that had been cured. But a much wider range of problems were brought to the saints. They were seen as friends with whom troubles could be shared.[28]

Popular Catholicism had important affinities not only with certain aspects of popular Protestantism, but also with the 'secular' culture of working-class and lower-middle-class New Yorkers—that which transcended the differences of ethnicity and religion. The themes I want to

[27] H. J. Browne, *St Ann's, New York City* (New York, 1952), pp. 41–9; Herzfeld, *Monographs*, p. 19; R. L. and H. F. Woods, *Pilgrim Places in North America: A Guide to Catholic Shrines* (New York, 1939), pp. 108–9.
[28] Analysis by Taves ('Relocating the Sacred', pp. 148–9) of thanks for favours received that were published in the Catholic papers, *Ave Maria* and *The Messenger of the Sacred Heart*, shows that prayers were most frequently for cures and conversions. Other subjects of answered prayers included the resolution of family difficulties, the reform of drunkards, and happy deaths.

explore here are beliefs about good and bad luck; the significance of 'friendship' and patronage networks; and the sharp dichotomy in working-class New York between male and female worlds. I will argue that one factor in the popular appeal of Catholicism lay in the ease with which it adapted itself to certain very deeply rooted ways of thinking, which Protestantism had much greater difficulty in accepting.

The way in which New York working-class life was permeated by beliefs about good and bad luck was well illustrated by Herzfeld's study, where such beliefs are specifically referred to in relation to sixteen of the twenty-four families, with Protestants and Catholics, immigrants and 'Americans', people of English, Irish, and German descent, all being included among the most 'superstitious'. There is no evidence that Catholics were more prone to such beliefs than were Protestants, Jews, or unbelievers; the difference was that the latter tended to hold beliefs about luck that were independent of or even in contradiction to their religious beliefs, whereas the Catholic practice of ranking all aspects of the world on a scale of holiness provided an essential basis for their beliefs about luck. While the secular world was neutral, holy places, times, objects, and persons were potent whether for good or for evil, depending on how they were used, or on the sources of their sanctity. As one example, Friday, as the day when Jesus was killed, was a day of ill omen;[29] May, as the month of Mary, was of good omen; whereas Monday had no particular significance either way. The clergy were subjects of many such beliefs, though in this case there was no consensus as to the likely consequences of contact with them, and different sections of the Catholic population had their own traditions. For instance, it was reported in East Harlem in 1930 that Italian families with members who were sick did not send for the priest, as they believed that to be visited by a priest brought bad luck. This may be a rationalization of the anti-clericalism that was widespread in the first generation of Italian-Americans—though a Brooklyn Irishman, born in 1922, reports that his Mayo-born grandmother held the same belief, tempered in her case by the claim that it also brought bad luck to speak ill of the cloth.[30]

The performance of Catholic rituals was even thought to bring good

---

[29] This belief was sufficiently widespread to be singled out for criticism in an article on 'Superstition' in the *Calendar* of the Church of St Paul the Apostle, August 1898. The severest condemnation was of those who consulted fortune-tellers.

[30] M. C. Marsh, 'The Life and Work of the Church in an Interstitial Area' (Ph.D. thesis, New York University, 1932), p. 439; T. C. Wheeler (ed.), *The Immigrant Experience* (New York, 1971), p. 21.

luck in the pursuit of activities that Catholic morality condemned. An autobiography by a reformed criminal, written in the 1920s, recalled among the author's former associates a Roman Catholic safeblower called Danny, who told him: 'If ye said a prayer once in a while ye would have better luck.' Danny never missed mass, and gave a considerable part of his winnings to priests and charities. He liked buying clothes and toys for poor children. 'The conviction that he could steal forever so long as he prayed ultimately became an obsession with him. He took chances that the ordinary crook wouldn't think of taking and then later in his career he grew ambitious and desperate.'[31] In the Studs Lonigan novels of J. T. Farrell, also set in the 1920s, the assorted layabouts, hoodlums, and drunks with whom the hero hangs around mostly believe that Catholicism brings good luck, although their religion has little other effect on their behaviour. Thus, when the gang are *en route* to a brothel and speakeasy in the suburbs of Chicago on Christmas Eve, the driver of the car is worried by an outburst of bad language in the back, believing that swearing on Christmas Eve is likely to bring bad luck—a belief that is borne out by events, as the house is raided by the police, and most of the gang spend the night in jail. Studs Lonigan himself, who wants to volunteer to fight in World War I, but is worried about the risk of being killed, is reassured by the belief that if he wears a scapular he will be safe, and will live to enjoy his fame as a war-hero.[32]

At the individual level, beliefs about good and bad luck were an important means of coming to terms with the dangers and uncertainties of life in the poorer districts of New York. At the collective level, the main response was the concept of 'friendship' and the networks of 'friends' who supported one another in many different ways by doing favours.[33] Most crucially this included the ties of mutual dependence between kin, neighbours, and immigrants who had come from the same town or district. At a more organized level this included benefit societies, political parties, and churches. While most ties of 'friendship' were between social equals, it was also important to secure the 'friendship' of patrons, of men who

[31] J. Callahan, *Man's Grim Justice* (New York, 1928), pp. 68–9.

[32] J. T. Farrell, *The Young Manhood of Studs Lonigan* (New York, 1977), pp. 288, 163 [first published 1934].

[33] For discussion of kinship and neighbourhood ties, see Herzfeld, *Monographs*, pp. 33–5, 58–9; and on ways that these related to political attitudes, see M. Simkhovitch, *The City Worker's World in America* (New York, 1917), p. 182. For a somewhat earlier period, see K. A. Scherzer, 'The Unbounded Community: Neighbourhood Life and Social Structure in New York City 1830–1875' (Ph.D. thesis, Harvard University, 1982). The classic statement on the role of 'friendship' in policies is W. L. Riordon, *Plunkitt of Tammany Hall* (New York, 1905).

carried influence. This meant, above all, politicians. But priests and pastors (and indeed, the saints) were often seen in the same light. With social equals one could reciprocate favours by doing the same kind of service when occasion arose. With patrons too it was necessary to show gratitude, but this was done in different ways—by, for instance, voting for the politician, regularly attending the priest or pastor's church, or performing acts of devotion to the saint. My argument here is that there were strong affinities between the kind of Catholicism prevalent in New York at this time and the view of the world that was embodied in the concept of friendship.

One parallel has already been hinted at. The idea of 'friendship' was already built into the Catholicism of the time in the form of the cult of the saints. It may also be noted that the authoritarian style of clerical leadership prevalent at the time fitted the clergy well for the role of patrons, and that the many formal requirements laid on the Catholics of the time (for instance, attendance at mass every week) made it easy for the people to show their gratitude for favours in an easily recognizable way. However, there are two other points that I want to stress.

The first is the very strong sense of Catholic identity which many of the people had, and the heavy emphasis on loyalty to the Church in much of the clergy's teaching. Among the Irish, especially, religious and ethnic identity came to be completely intermeshed ('Be proud you're Irish' was the title of an article in a New York parish magazine in 1908),[34] and the public practice of Catholicism became the generally accepted means of establishing insider status. As Dick Butler, a West Side politician, wrote in a volume of memoirs that is largely a record of chicanery of various sorts, his regular attendance at mass made it clear that he was 'a right-hander in religion'.[35] It means that he was a loyal member of the Irish Catholic community, and recognized the obligations that this entailed, and that was more important in winning trust than, for instance a reputation for rigid honesty. The keen awareness of the boundary-lines between insiders and outsiders was characteristic of the Catholicism of this period and equally typical of the various systems of 'friendship' in the city, of which the most

---

[34] *Calendar* of the Church of St Paul the Apostle, March 1908. Notices given at mass in Sacred Heart church during 1919 included: information about a meeting in the church hall in support of Ireland's claims at the peace conference, and a meeting of the Robert Emmett Society to call for recognition of the Irish Republic; announcement of a book, *Ireland's Case*, available from the church office; and an appeal to contribute to the Irish Victory Fund, a collection for which was being held in the church vestibule after mass. See the Notice Book (Sacred Heart rectory).

[35] D. Butler, *Dock Walloper* (New York, 1931), p. 40.

famous was that focused on Tammany Hall, the headquarters of New York County Democratic Party. In both instances one can see a tripartite division. There were 'friends' (or 'good Catholics') who commanded loyalty, and must be helped when they needed it; there were outsiders (equivalent to Protestants and Jews), towards whom feelings were fairly neutral, but towards whom one had no obligations; and there were former friends (equivalent to apostate or disloyal Catholics) who were regarded with deep resentment. A journalist explained the hold exercised by Tammany Hall in the following terms: 'The real thing in Tammany's eyes is friendship. That is the great virtue, and that is why ingratitude is the blackest sin. The common people believe this implicitly, and it is consequently true that Tammany is strong in the hearts of the people.'[36] Similar themes occur widely in the literature produced by New York churches. Thus an article denouncing apostasy made God sound like a Tammany leader who, after doing all sorts of favours for his people, discovered that they had gone and voted for a rival: 'God abandons them who abandon Him.'[37]

The second point I want to stress is the close relationship between the Church and Tammany Hall and the acceptance by the majority of the clergy of New York's patronage-based system of politics. Largely eschewing the politics of moral crusading practised by many Protestant ministers, they used their political contacts to gain favours for the Church and for their parishioners. The clergy sometimes reciprocated directly by urging parishioners to vote 'the straight Democratic ticket', by condemning rival parties, or by expressions of approval for individual Tammany politicians. Equally important to the politicians was the respectability, the access to constituents, and the reputation for being 'one of us' that was made possible by their participation in church activities and their generous contributions to church funds. The Church in turn had its reputation as a place of power and influence re-inforced by the fact that the most obviously powerful members of the community seemed so often to be identified with it.[38] The relationship was not indeed entirely smooth. Clergy were aware of, and suspicious of, the motives for many politicians' piety.[39] Moreover, some of the methods by which Tammany men enriched themselves were unacceptable to the Church. None the less,

---

[36] H. Hapgood, *Types from City Streets* (New York, 1910), p. 57.
[37] The *Parish Monthly* of Our Lady of Good Counsel Church, February 1905 (copies in New York Public Library).
[38] Browne, *Sacred Heart*, pp. 60–71; McLeod, 'New York Irish', pp. 346–7.
[39] D. N. Doyle, 'Catholicism, politics and Irish America since 1890: some critical considerations', *Irish Studies*, 4 (1985), pp. 192–230 stresses the tensions between priests and politicians.

co-operation between priests and politicians was assisted by similarities in style and thinking. Particularly relevant here was the dominant Catholic theology of the time with its doctrine of 'No salvation outside the Church'. This meant that the Church had an obligation to maintain its power, influence, and resources at a maximum level, as these were all means by which the greatest possible number of children could be educated in Catholic schools, that the sacraments could be brought to the greatest possible number of Catholics, and the greatest possible number of heretics and unbelievers preached to and perhaps converted. This type of theology, which legitimated a dominant concern with maintaining the Church's institutional interests, tended to lead to a pragmatic form of politics, in which the Church was willing to ally with whatever political party seemed to offer the Church the best kind of deal, and all issues that did not relate directly to the Church's interests were given a minor priority.[40]

I shall mention one other area of congruence between the assumptions inherent in the Catholic teaching of the time and in the 'secular' culture of working-class New Yorkers. There was in working-class areas of New York a deep divide between male and female worlds.[41] Not only did men work with men and women with women: in the rare hours that they could call their own, both women and men tended to relax with members of their own sex. Most forms of work were regarded as the exclusive preserve of one or other sex; the benefit societies, which were the most widespread form of working-class organization, catered very largely for men, and women members generally belonged to all-female branches. The Catholic Church rejected certain aspects of the existing relationships between women and men—for instance, it criticized men for spending too much time in saloons and neglecting their families.[42] However, the Church continually emphasized that the two sexes *were* essentially different in

---

[40] For a wide-ranging discussion of this theme see J. H. Whyte, *Catholics in Western Democracies* (Dublin, 1981), a study of Catholic politics in thirteen countries, mainly between 1870 and 1960, which shows how the primary goal of protecting Catholic interests led the Church into a wide variety of alliances determined by the circumstances in specific countries. See also a valuable local study by S. J. Fielding, 'The Irish Catholics of Manchester and Salford: Aspects of their Religious and Political History 1880-1939' (Ph.D. thesis, University of Warwick, 1988), p. 263. Contrasting Catholicism with Nonconformity, he concludes that Catholicism 'was a pragmatic religion which gave rise to a pragmatic politics'.

[41] Herzfeld, *Monographs*, pp. 50-2; K. Peiss, *Cheap Amusements: Working Women and Leisure in Turn-of-the-Century New York* (Philadelphia, 1986), pp. 16-33.

[42] C. McDannell, '"True Men as we need them": Catholicism and the Irish-American Male', *American Studies*, 27 no. 2 (1986), p. 29.

character and vocation, and in doing so it helped to provide a rationale for the existing divide. Catholic services vividly illustrated the dichotomy, offering as they did the sharp contrast between the exclusively male priests and servers at the altar and the mainly female congregation in the body of the church. Parish magazines defined more explicitly the contrasting spheres of men and women. Articles on 'Woman in the Home' stressed that the home was woman's special domain, and women were advised against seeking employment in offices, except when driven by dire financial necessity; at the same time, the husband was definitely the head of the household and men were urged to take this duty more seriously.[43] Boys and girls needed a different type of education, because of the essential differences in the character of the two sexes: males were by nature aggressive and energetic, whereas 'To bring out the womanly character sweetness and light are absolutely necessary. . . . In women is developed the fundamental instinct of race preservation, the mother instinct that will sacrifice everything, even life, for the good of the child.' The Church also stressed the practical advantages of the existing sexual division of labour: if the home was to be a haven of cheerfulness and rest for tired bread-winners and a place for the Christian nurture of children, it needed a skilled (female) home-maker.[44]

Some of these points would have been accepted by many Protestant and secular moralists, but the Catholic Church was unusually consistent in the way that it demarcated male from female spheres—for instance, by the turn of the century, many Protestant ministers advocated women's suffrage, whereas very few Catholic priests did so.[45] But in one respect the Catholic Church was uniquely effective as a proponent of sharply separated sex-roles: its ability to offer clearly juxtaposed role-models. At the ideal level there was the contrast between Jesus and Mary, and at the more mundane level that between priests and nuns. In particular, the constant reference in the Catholic teaching of the time to the example of Mary had the effect at one and the same time of enhancing the dignity and status of women, and of emphasizing the fact that they enjoyed this status only within the context of ultimate subordination.

---

[43] *Calendar* of the Church of St Paul the Apostle, March 1899, July 1898; McDannell, '"True Men"', p. 28.

[44] *Church Bulletin* of St Ignatius parish, March 1905; McDannell, '"True Men"', p. 28. See also Taves, 'Relocating the Sacred', p. 175.

[45] A. S. Kraditor, *The Ideas of the Woman Suffrage Movement 1890–1920* (New York, 1965), p. 94; T. J. Kenealley, 'Catholicism and Women's Suffrage in Massachussets', *Catholic Historical Review*, 53 (1967), p. 54.

In everyday Catholic life, the separation of spheres found its chief expression in a way that was not entirely welcome to the clergy: religion came to be seen as primarily a part of the female sphere. To some extent this followed naturally from the fact that women had most practical responsibility for the running of the home. It was inevitably women who taught the children their prayers and who decorated the walls with portraits of the Pope and pictures of the Sacred Heart. But in the Catholic Church, more than any other in New York, attendance at church services became a mainly female affair. The Manhattan church census of 1902 showed that 73 per cent of the adults attending Catholic services were women. The larger Protestant denominations all had a female majority, but the gap was considerable narrower: 66 per cent of Episcopalians were women, 59 per cent of Lutherans, 58 per cent of Presbyterians, and 55 per cent of Methodists.[46] In particular, Catholicism came to be closely bound up with the Irish-American ideal of motherhood. In memoirs of Irish-American life around the beginning of this century, an almost stereotyped 'Mom' inevitably stands out for her piety and devotion to her children, while 'Dad' often remains a much more shadowy figure.[47] In some cases, no doubt, guilt, loneliness, or nostalgia led the memoir-writer to invest Mom with virtues that she never possessed. But a rather similar view emerges from some more disinterested sources such as the autobiography of a German immigrant, who came to the Upper East Side around 1900 and remembered a neighbouring Irish family as the first to befriend him:

> Mother of seven children, poor and plain, burdened with the care of a large family, the wife always found time to take a sympathetic interest in other people's troubles. To me she personified the spirit of universal motherhood, unselfishly taking care of every weak creature that crossed her path. ... Pious, rigidly observing all the tenets of her church, she once told me how much the good sisters had done for her relatives and family during one of the periodic famines in Ireland. She hoped that one day she could come into some money and would be able to do something for the good gray nuns.[48]

---

[46] H. McLeod, 'Weibliche Frömmigkeit—männlicher Unglaube?', U. Frevert (ed.), *Bürgerinnen und Bürger: Geschlechterverhältnisse im 19. Jahrhundert* (Göttingen, 1988), p. 137.
[47] The most vivid example is in the autobiography of a Boston-born criminal, Callahan, *Grim Justice*, pp. 2–3.
[48] F. Hackenburg, *A Solitary Parade* (New York, 1929), p. 30.

IV

New York offers only one of the more striking examples of a wider phenomenon: the relative success with which Roman Catholicism survived the mass migrations of the later nineteenth and early twentieth centuries, and became established as a major force in many of the cities and industrial regions of Europe and North America. Particularly notable was the degree to which Catholicism held the loyalty of large numbers of working-class people, at a time when Protestantism was becoming largely a middle-class religion. Relatively well known are the ways that Catholics as a body related to the wider society during this period:[49] the discrimination suffered by Catholic minorities, and the importance of religion as a symbol of identity in an ethnically heterogeneous urban environment; the multiplication of Catholic organizations; and, particularly, the formation of Catholic political parties, and the considerable success that they frequently enjoyed. However, the internal culture of Catholicism has been little explored.[50] One point is fairly well established: the popular appeal of certain aspects of Catholicism (notably, the belief in, and constant expectation of miracles) that played little part in the 'mainstream' Protestant Churches, and were largely the preserve of more plebeian sects. Equally relevant, though, to Catholicism's capacity for survival may have been those areas of belief and practice that were relatively independent of the clergy. In New York, it would seem that Catholicism could easily be adapted to, or expressed in terms of, such central concepts of popular culture as the belief in 'friendship' and in 'luck'. The results caused great indignation or amusement to Protestants, and sometimes exasperated the clergy, but this adaptability no doubt added to Catholicism's popular appeal. How far can this point be applied to cities other than New York? A second point is certainly of wider application: the importance of certain largely private forms of religion, especially devotion to the saints, even in sections of the city where the clergy enjoyed little influence and involvement in the public life of the Church was low. It seems likely, therefore, that in countries such as France where formal religious practice is low, too much attention has been paid to attendance at mass as the principal indicator of religiosity. This suggestion gains support from a recent study

---

[49] See, for instance, McLeod, '"Catholic Ghetto"', which includes references to much of the recent literature.

[50] The outstanding essays on Catholicism by Connolly, Gilley, and Samuel in R. Swift and S. Gilley (eds), *The Irish in the Victorian City* (London, 1985), mark an important step in this direction. See also Fielding, 'Catholics of Manchester'.

of the cult of the saints in the churches of central Paris, which argued that it was precisely in the working-class districts, where formal Catholicism was weakest, that this cult was most flourishing.[51] It may be, therefore, that Catholicism, apparently the most clerically-dominated form of religion, owes an important part of its capacity for survival to forms of devotion which are distinctively and uniquely Catholic, but can largely be practised without reference to the clergy.

University of Birmingham

[51] Wilson, *Saints*, p. 257.

NEW ZEALAND CATHOLICISM AND
THE IRISH ISSUE, 1914–1922

by RORY M. SWEETMAN

RECENT biographies of Archbishops Mannix and Duhig have shown how those doughty warriors for the Catholic faith in Australia faced a rising tide of anti-Catholicism in the period 1916–23. Studies of Australian society and politics during and after the First World War have dwelt at length on the sectarian impulse. The conflict between Catholic and Protestant has even been cast by Professor Manning Clark as the central theme of Australian history.[1]

By contrast New Zealand historians have neglected the Catholic minority as a subject for historical examination. Yet, in these years, the latter country witnessed an outburst of sectarianism quite as bitter as anything seen across the Tasman. The wartime controversy over the conscription of priests and religious left the New Zealand Catholic leadership convinced that there was a plot afoot to rid the country of the Catholic clergy. A Protestant Political Association, launched in 1917, conducted a virulent campaign against 'Romanism' at home and abroad, and managed to secure the passage through Parliament, from 1920, of a string of measures penalizing Catholic rights. In that year New Zealand became the only part of the Empire to pass legislation against the supposed effect of the decree *Ne Temere*.

The period 1916–23 in Australia witnessed a belligerent Irish Catholic challenge to the Protestant establishment, orchestrated by the archbishop of Melbourne, which claimed its most stunning victory in the defeat of conscription in successive wartime referenda. The New Zealand Catholic hierarchy, however, welcomed the passage of the Military Service Act in 1916, and had no doubts about Catholic commitment to the war effort. Yet, by 1922, relations with the Protestant community had soured to the extent that the Catholic body saw its leader, James Liston, coadjutor bishop of Auckland, facing imprisonment on a charge of sedition. Nothing so embarrassing ever happened to Daniel Mannix—and the purpose of this paper is to help to explain this seeming paradox.

The standard explanation for this sectarian explosion involves a

[1] T. P. Boland, *James Duhig* (Brisbane, 1986); C. Kiernan, *Daniel Mannix and Ireland* (Dublin, 1984); B. A. Santamaria, *Daniel Mannix* (Melbourne, 1984).

deterioration in inter-denominational relations from the turn of the century; a gradual build-up of tension and hostility, with the Catholic Federation, symbol of a growing Catholic assertiveness, cast as devil figure.[2] Established in 1913 to act as a pressure group for a variety of Catholic interests, the Federation was a power more apparent than real. The leaders of the long-running campaign to have Bible reading introduced into the State Schools might have found in Catholic opposition a convenient scapegoat for its repeated failures, but the clear majority registered against the League's proposals in Parliament was confirmed by the result of the general election of 1914.

The coincidence of a Catholic, Sir Joseph Ward, serving as Liberal Prime Minister from 1906–12 revived talk of Catholic favouritism in the public service. The hierarchy was less impressed by Ward's credentials or his performance, and the educational gains made by Catholics in the pre-war years were thanks to the new Reform Government, led by an ex-Grandmaster of the Orange Order, William Massey.

Evidence of Catholic unpopularity was not lacking. Contagion from Australia of a certain type of sectarian agitation, and often of the agitator himself, caused recurrent squabbles and helped to fill the correspondence columns of New Zealand's many newspapers. Catholic positions on prohibition, gambling, mixed marriage, as well as the Bible in schools question, were uncompromising and won few friends. There was tinder aplenty for any future conflagration. I believe that the influence of Old World politics, and above all of the corrosive Irish issue, provides the key to explaining the dramatic turn in the Dominion's hitherto cordial community relations.

The din of battle in Ireland in the nineteenth century had echoes at the Antipodes. There was a comic opera 'Fenian Rising' on the West Coast of New Zealand's South Island in 1868. The violence associated with the Land War divided even the Catholic community. Home Rule was widely seen as a threat to Imperial unity. The tide of Irish ecclesiastical imperialism, which engulfed the Benedictine mission in Australia, had not fully reached New Zealand. The Society of Mary, a French Order with strong English connections (though increasingly Irish in personnel), continued to dominate New Zealand Catholicism. The appointment of English bishops by Rome encouraged the emergence of a conservative, integrationist hierarchy.

---

[2] Cf. P. S. O'Connor, 'Sectarian Conflict in New Zealand, 1911–1920', *Political Science*, 19 (1967); '"Protestants", Catholics, and the New Zealand Government, 1916–1918', in G. A. Wood and P. S. O'Connor (eds), *W. P. Morrell: A Tribute* (Dunedin, 1973), pp. 185–202.

Perhaps this was just as well. Catholics numbered only 14 per cent of the population, and were largely to be found in the humbler occupations. They had few representatives in positions of authority, and with the decline of the Liberal Party had lost a valuable political lever. Gentle persuasion, rather than aggressive demand, was the order of the day. The bishops supported compulsory military training, condemned Socialism, and trumpeted their Imperial loyalties.

The foremost exponent of this art of accommodation was Henry William Cleary, editor of the sole Catholic journal, the *New Zealand Tablet*, from 1898 to 1910. Wexford-born, with Australian pastoral experience, Cleary was well suited to cope with the potentially explosive Irish issue. He had shown marked skill as a controversialist. His first book, a lengthy attack on the Orange Order, had gone through eleven editions on its publication in 1895, and he refuted well-worn tales of 'Irish outrages' in *An Impeached Nation*, published in 1909.

He was always careful to stress the unifying potential of Ireland's national struggle. The centenary of the 1798 rebellion was celebrated, to Cleary's design, with the enthusiastic participation of Protestant clergymen. Clearly wanted unity in Irish ranks at home and abroad. He wrote to John Dillon in December 1898 of the need to

> put an end to a disunion which has been the despair of our people in these colonies for many years past. . . . I have not permitted the insertion of any letters, news, or correspondence that could create divisions here on the question of Irish politics.[3]

Fears of the threat to Imperial unity posed by Irish ambitions were gradually soothed away. The warm reception accorded to successive Irish Parliamentary delegates in 1907, 1911, and 1914 was in stark contrast to the hostility which greeted the Redmond brothers in 1883. The visitors, generally on fund-raising tours, were careful to cut the cloth of Irish political ambitions to a New Zealand measure, and Home Rule gradually came to resemble a respectable old acquaintance, who had outlived a wild youth. Politicians, both lay and cleric, queued to grace the delegates' platform.

With the re-emergence of Home Rule as a live political issue, after the elections of 1910, Ireland soon came to dominate the cable news. Each act in the lengthy drama was vicariously replayed in the Dominion. There was vocal and influential support for the Ulster resistance. Prominent

---

[3] Cleary to John Dillon, 21 December 1898, Dillon Papers, Trinity College, Dublin.

citizens in Wellington cabled their sympathy and support to Carson. The debate had some of the divisive effects caused later by the rise of Sinn Fein. The coincidence of Irishmen leading both the major New Zealand political parties led to a careful choice of words. When the real war broke out the local partisans quickly sank their differences in a chorus of patriotic harmony.

The Catholic body went to war with gusto. Father Coffey of Dunedin had great hopes of this flowering of Catholic loyalty to the Empire. He wrote of

> the silver lining that may be seen through the dark war cloud which hangs above. The patriotism of Catholics is clearly seen in . . . their willingness to fight for a King who is a Protestant while the Protestants say they would dethrone their King if he became a Catholic. . . . This is seen and must produce its effect.[4]

Catholic leaders spoke in favour of conscription, once they were assured of the effective exemption of the clergy and religious.

Cleary, who had been appointed bishop of Auckland in 1910, spent some months in Flanders as an army chaplain and wrote fulsomely of the unity between Catholic and Protestant in the trenches. The Irish question would be solved there, he predicted. The ready co-operation he received in his chaplaincy mission from the New Zealand authorities confirmed Cleary's good opinion of the establishment—at the very time when his episcopal colleagues in New Zealand were becoming totally alienated by what they saw as institutionalized sectarianism.

At home, community camaraderie was wearing thin. As wartime tensions grew and casualty lists lengthened, the search for scapegoats began. Anti-German feeling was accompanied by dark suspicions about Papal sympathies. The *Tablet* was kept busy refuting accusations of poor Irish recruiting figures. The visit of a papal delegate in early 1916 provoked the first outburst of local bigotry which would scar the body politic for the next few years.

The Rising in Dublin came to many as confirmation of suspected Irish Catholic disloyalty. It was condemned by the *Tablet* as 'a made in Germany rebellion', and hurried cables were sent to Redmond assuring him of continued support. Nevertheless, the daily press was scathing in its denunciation. The occasional public defence of Sinn Fein by Catholic

---

[4] Coffey to P. J. O'Regan, 1 August 1916, O'Regan Papers, Alexander Turnbull Library, Wellington.

spokesmen provoked considerable bitterness. Irish priests were reported to the Defence department for seditious speeches which allegedly harmed recruiting and helped the Kaiser.

In early 1917 the government's maladroit handling of the issue of clergy conscription, and some hypersensitivity by an inexperienced Catholic leadership, brought on the crisis. It was made to appear that the Catholic Church was attempting, by some unscrupulous means, to avoid her equal share of sacrifice. Catholic indignation at what was seen as the government's deception was matched by Protestant outrage at its truckling to Rome. The hierarchy was soon convinced that the whole affair had been engineered by bigots who aimed to drive the priests out of New Zealand.

Catholic opposition to conscription in Australia had helped to raise the temperature in New Zealand, but by mid-1917 events in the Dominion were being cited by Australian anti-conscriptionists as a reason why Catholics should vote 'No' rather than put their faith in the false promises of politicians. Statistics showed that the Catholics were not slow or averse to joining the colours, but this fact was lost in the outcry at 'secret deals'.

Catholics had further offended by seeming to press for sectional advantage, in the form of educational concessions, during the national crisis. The Catholic Federation had a stormy interview in late 1916 with an unyielding Minister of Education. The equal blood sacrifice made by the Catholic body sharpened the sense of grievance at the disabilities suffered by their schools. Cleary assured the rest of the hierarchy of his amicable dealings with Massey and Ward in London—the poisoned atmosphere of sectarian bitterness which they experienced on their return to New Zealand in mid-1917 came as a shock to all three leaders. Dr James Kelly announced in the *Tablet*, 'Mr Massey and Sir Joseph may thank their stars that news of a rebellion in New Zealand did not reach them in England.'[5]

It is time to meet Dr James Kelly—the villain of the piece according to most New Zealand historians, who have agreed to share out his sins among the Catholic bishops. Dr Kelly has been depicted as the voice of the hierarchy, chosen to articulate an aggressive new departure involving a head-on confrontation with the state.[6] This interpretation does less than justice either to Kelly or to his ecclesiastical superiors. On 22 January 1917, one month before Kelly was appointed editor of the *Tablet*, Archbishop

[5] *New Zealand Tablet*, 12 July 1917.
[6] P. S. O'Connor, 'Sectarian Conflict . . .'; R. P. Davis, *Irish Issues in New Zealand Politics 1868–1922* (Dunedin, 1974), cap. 9.

Redwood sent a cautionary note to the administrator of Auckland diocese, regarding the Catholic Convention soon to be held there: 'During this terrible war time we must be careful not to offend people. . .'. His coadjutor, Thomas O'Shea, chimed in,

> I am afraid that we have been devoting too much time to hostile criticism of the Government and of individual Ministers, and not enough to constructive policy. . . . Some people are inclined to think that we are seeking to take an unfair advantage at such a time as the present . . . we must not go in for too much criticism during the war, or appear to be trying to make capital out of the country's present difficulties.[7]

Kelly went south with other exhortations ringing in his ears than those of prudence. As the *Tablet*'s managing director later explained to an irate Bishop Cleary,

> Before he [Kelly] came down here he was urged by the vast majority of the priests to adopt a strong aggressive policy. In fact they told him as some of them told myself that if the 'Tablet' did not drop its jingoism they would turn it out of their parishes.[8]

Kelly needed little encouragement to challenge the anti-Irish bias of the daily press, and to educate the Catholic community on the real aims and nature of Sinn Fein. It was only four years since he had left his native Wexford, where he had been involved in the Gaelic League and, he claimed later, had known the Sinn Feiners well. He had helped out with *Tablet*'s editorial work in late 1915, but, as he complained to John Hagan, the vice-rector of the Irish College, Rome, 'They will not allow me to write on the war owing to my having revealed tendencies to show fair play.'[9]

The crisis over conscription gave Kelly the perfect issue with which to radicalize the Catholic body. He told Hagan,

> My first trouble was with the Government which broke its pledges to us and in obedience to the Protestant bigots tried to drive our clergy and students out of the country. I . . . fought hard against the Ministers of the Government who were frankly opposed to us and in order

---

[7] Redwood to Mahoney, O'Shea to Mahoney, 22 January 1917, Cleary Papers, Auckland Catholic Diocesan Archives.
[8] Coffey to Cleary, 24 November 1917, *ibid.*
[9] Kelly to Hagan, 16 February 1916, Hagan Papers, Irish College Rome.

to stir up our own people and to unite them I had to speak out very plainly in telling them what sort of tricks our foes had resorted to.[10]

Kelly's talent to abuse now had free rein, despite repeated cautions from an exasperated hierarchy. His articles on the war were provocative, and the name of England was denounced as 'a synonym for oppression and tyranny'. Kelly raged against what he termed 'the heresy of conciliation', and especially resented the curbs placed on him by Bishop Brodie, who was attempting to reach a compromise with the government. Sinn Fein would save Ireland, he announced, and perhaps even New Zealand.

Not by relying on worthless promises, not by wasting our time in conciliation, not by supporting politicians who have not the courage of their convictions, but by *ourselves alone* will we succeed.[11]

Subscriptions rose, sheaves of letters supporting his policy poured in, but there was a price to be paid.

The conscription crisis also helped to spawn the Protestant Political Association, an offshoot of the Orange Order, which was launched amidst a storm of controversy in July, 1917. Its leader, Howard Elliott, an Auckland Baptist minister, toured the country reciting a litany of Catholic misdeeds—the Pope's neutrality, or his German sympathies; he had caused the war, he was delaying the peace; the civil service was stuffed with Catholics, the Marist Brothers were shirking, Irish priests were out to destroy the Empire, and the Catholic Federation was running the country. Dr Kelly came to Elliott as the answer to a prayer. The P.P.A. could manufacture its propaganda simply by reprinting the choicer extracts from *Tablet* editorials. In the issue of 1 November 1917, Kelly surpassed himself by referring to the late Queen Victoria as 'a certain fat old German woman'.

By the end of 1917 the P.P.A. claimed to have almost 20,000 members.[12] Cleary's return from Europe, however, marked the end of its unchallenged run. Taking the high moral ground, Cleary appealed successfully to the public repugnance at this deplorable importation of sectarian bitterness. In an exhaustive propaganda campaign, a repeat of his pre-war efforts against the Bible in Schools party, he worked to win back the sympathy of the secular press and to repair the rift between government and hierarchy.

[10] Kelly to Hagan, 16 May 1918, *ibid.*
[11] *New Zealand Tablet*, 22 November 1917.
[12] *Evening Post*, Wellington, 12 December 1917.

Cleary acted swiftly to curb the excesses of Dr Kelly's prose and to distance the Catholic Church from his opinions. He forced the removal from the *Tablet*'s front page of its title as 'sole organ of the Catholic body in New Zealand'. His setting up of a rival paper, the *Month*, orchestrated protests to the *Tablet* directors by the hierarchy, and successive appeals to the apostolic delegate, drew repeated promises of reform from the editor, all of which were soon broken.

Elliott's disgrace during the Post Office Inquiry, set up by the government to investigate his charges of a Catholic conspiracy, was compounded by Cleary's skilful use of published 'challenges' which highlighted P.P.A. scurrility. On Cleary's representations, the government prohibited the importation of sectarian literature, and the end of the war brought the promise of a restoration of peace on the home front.

However, the Irish issue could not be so simply contained. 'The end of the year has brought our justification', Kelly announced when the news of Sinn Fein's electoral victory arrived.[13] The encouragement of Archbishop Redwood, who proclaimed himself a Sinn Feiner, and the outcome of Archbishop Mannix's Irish Race Convention, held in Melbourne in late 1919, emboldened the editor. 'The Convention was a great success and was wonderfully enthusiastic,' Kelly informed Hagan, 'It pledges Australasian friends of Ireland to Sinn Fein, and in this way was no slight vindication of my attitude and a strong rebuff for the Cleary-Brodie clique of seonini.'[14]

Taking advantage of Dr Kelly's notorious scorn of New Zealand's Imperial loyalties, the P.P.A. launched a powerful new campaign, with the 1919 elections in view. The New Zealand voters were exhorted to oppose the triple menace of 'Rum, Romanism and Rebellion'. While Dr Kelly roused the Catholics to agitate in favour of Irish self-determination, Howard Elliott portrayed Ireland as the front line in the defence of Protestant liberties against Roman aggression. The Governor General informed the Colonial Office in June 1919,

> The situation in Ireland and its future is considered of far more vital importance to the Empire than the possession of Samoa, however much New Zealand may desire to see her flag flying over those Islands ... the Protestants in this Dominion are organizing under a distinctive League to oppose everything pertaining to the Roman

---

[13] *New Zealand Tablet*, 26 December 1918.
[14] Kelly to Hagan, 3 January 1920, Hagan Papers, Irish College Rome.

Catholics. The cry is that it is the fault of the Roman Catholics that we are in the position that we are as to Ireland, and that what they have done in Ireland they will try to do in this Dominion. The Roman Catholics are stigmatised as not to be trusted, possibly by some, disloyal. At all events Mr Massey is a strong Orangeman, Sir Joseph Ward a Roman Catholic, and it would take very little to inflame the minds of the people. . . .[15]

The importation of Irish quarrels was equally embarrassing to Massey as to Ward. The former certainly enjoyed the support of Elliott's organization at the polls, and rewarded him in 1920 by granting several of the P.P.A.'s anti-Catholic wishes—the Marriage Amendment Act which struck at the decree *Ne Temere*, the cessation of free railway travel and withdrawal of scholarships from Catholic schools, accompanied by threats to rate Catholic schools and enforce coventual inspection. However, after the elections of 1922 had revealed the P.P.A.'s waning influence, Massey broke with Elliott.

In the general election of 1919, Ward lost his seat and his party was decimated. The real gainer from the divisive Irish issue was the emergent Labour Party. Opposed to conscription and sectarianism, the Party was anathema to the P.P.A. Labour's espousal of advanced Irish nationalism helped to cement the informal alliance with the largely working-class Catholic body. Dr Kelly gave his enthusiastic editorial support, and by 1922 Bishop Liston was publicly rejoicing that, 'Thanks be to God, the Labour people, our friends, are coming into their own—a fair share in the Government of the country.'[16]

In the meantime the Reform Government, with the P.P.A., was in the saddle. As evidence of a legislative anti-Catholic drive became incontrovertible, Cleary redoubled his efforts to have Dr Kelly silenced. He was convinced that much of the hostility to the Church stemmed from the constant stream of ridicule and insult which the *Tablet* directed at what it called the 'Messey' or 'P.P. Ass' government. He strove to limit the damage caused by the deteriorating situation in Ireland. Cleary would have no collections for an Irish Republic taken up in his diocese, and no Sinn Fein flags or emblems decorating the St Patrick's Day march. The national anthem was to be played at all Catholic concerts. His journal, the *Month*, dwelt on the evils in Ulster rather than on any southern righteousness. In

---

[15] Secret Affairs Report, 5 June 1919, PRO, Colonial Office Papers, 209/300.
[16] *Auckland Star*, 13 December 1922.

1921 Cleary was reluctant to sign the joint episcopal welcome to the returning Archbishop Mannix until the laudatory reference to his opposition to conscription was deleted.

Powerless to control the contagion of sectarian bitterness from across the Tasman, Cleary had the courage to break ranks and disavow the sectarianism of his own side. His journey to Europe late in 1921 had as its ostensible object the recovery of his health, but was more concerned with securing Roman censure of Dr Kelly and his tactics. In his absence the divisions over Irish politics reached a climax with the trial on a charge of sedition of his coadjutor, James Liston. In his speech at the Auckland St Patrick's night concert in 1922 Liston was reported as describing those killed in Ireland since 1916 as having been 'murdered by foreign troops'.

Cleary was able to intervene on Liston's behalf through the Irish and British governments. The Irish question he saw as a stick which was being used to beat the Catholics, and he welcome its solution in the foundation of the Irish Free State. However, the identification of the Catholic Church with any recognized political party was completely abhorrent to him, and the action of his coadjutor in publicly praising Labour caused a serious breach between them. Steps had been taken in Rome, on Cleary's representations, to prevent Dr Kelly from pursuing this very policy. While the Massey party was so firmly in power, the abuse and scorn of the government by the *Tablet* faction could only harm the Church's vital interests, especially in the field of education.

There is evidence that the rest of the hierarchy was less than convinced of Massey's essential good faith. Cleary's conviction that a bigoted minority was enjoying a temporary ascendancy, largely through Dr Kelly's misdeeds, was to prevail over the advocates of a militant challenge to the established order. The outbreak of civil war in Ireland, the appointment of a bishop in Dunedin (after a vacancy of two years), and Dr Kelly's reluctance to follow Daniel Mannix in embracing the anti-Treaty cause, all helped to resolve the dilemma. When the archbishop of Melbourne paid his first visit to New Zealand, in 1924 for the celebration of Archbishop Redwood's jubilee, he was astonished to find his host taking him aside and asking him to refrain from making any political speeches.[17]

Peterhouse, Cambridge

[17] Diary of P. J. O'Regan, 1 March 1924, O'Regan Papers, Alexander Turnbull Library, Wellington.

THE HUNGER-STRIKE OF THE
LORD MAYOR OF CORK, 1920: IRISH, ENGLISH
AND VATICAN ATTITUDES

by STUART MEWS

O
N 25 October 1920, a new name was added to the martyrology of Irish nationalism. On that date, the Lord Mayor of Cork, Alderman Terence MacSwiney, died in Brixton prison after a hunger-strike which had lasted 74 days. He had held office for little more than six months, his predecessor having been roused from sleep and shot, most Irish people believed, by plain clothed policemen.[1] MacSwiney had succeeded not only to the symbolic positions of head of the municipality and titular chief magistrate, but also the less decorative but potentially more deadly positions of president of the Cork branch of Sinn Fein and commandant of the First Cork Brigade of the Irish Volunteers.[2] Brought up in the full flood of the Catholic spiritual and Gaelic cultural revivals,[3] MacSwiney had a long record of active commitment to the struggle for Irish independence. He had been imprisoned by the British in 1916 in the aftermath of Dublin's Easter Rising which he had watched from Cork in an agony of indecision, developing in one English historian's view 'a guilt complex which he was later to expiate in the grimmest possible way'.[4] In August 1920, only days after the introduction of courts martial to replace civilian courts in Ireland, he was arrested in the City Hall, while presiding over a meeting of the Brigade Council. Proclaiming his allegiance to the Irish Republic, the Lord Mayor challenged the right of the British Army to detain him, and immediately commenced a hunger-strike. Charged with the unauthorized possession of a secret police cypher, he denounced the proceedings as unconstitutional, declined to offer any defence, and was

---

[1] Charles Townshend, *The British Campaign in Ireland 1919–1921* (Oxford, 1975), p. 96; Archbishop's House, Westminster, Bourne MS Bo 5/36, D. Cohalan to A. C. Dunlop, 19 November 1920; H. W. Nevison, *Last Changes, Last Chances* (London, 1928), p. 175.

[2] Moirin Chavasse, *Terence MacSwiney* (Dublin, 1961). But James Healy has implied that Mrs Chavasse has played down MacSwiney's commitment to physical force: 'Hunger Strikes: Other Ethical Reflections', *Milltown Studies* 15 (1985), p. 100.

[3] F. S. L. Lyons, *Culture and Anarchy in Ireland 1890–1939* (Oxford, 1982), pp. 79 *seq*; Tom Garvin, 'Priests and Patriots: Irish separatism and fear of the modern, 1890–1914', *Irish Historical Studies*, 25 (1986), pp. 67–81.

[4] Charles Townshend, *Political Violence in Ireland* (Oxford, 1984), p. 300.

sentenced to two years imprisonment. 'I shall be free, alive or dead within a month', he vowed.[5]

The hunger-strike was a device which had come to public notice with the pre-war suffragette movement (at least 22 women were on hunger-strike in Irish prisons between 1912 and 1914) and it was the tactic adopted to secure their release by the syndicalist socialist James Connolly in 1913 and the anti-First World War pacifist Sheehy Skeffington in 1915.[6] It was a stratagem ripe for exploitation in the nationalist cause. At relatively little personal cost, the British state could be challenged by republican enthusiasts drilling illegally and provocatively, often under the noses of the police. When arrested, they would hunger-strike to secure treatment as 'political prisoners', despite the fact that 'none of us knew what political prisoner status meant'.[7] Hunger-striking, as David Fitzpatrick has pointed out, 'gave new dignity to the concept of imprisonment which had been debased somewhat by the evident enjoyment derived by many post-Rising internees from their overseas holidays' in British gaols.[8] It also tapped a deep current in the Irish tradition of ascetic spirituality.

Terence MacSwiney had first embarked on a hunger-strike during his second prison sentence in November 1917. Two months earlier, Thomas Ashe, one of forty Republican prisoners on hunger-strike in Mountjoy prison, had died following forced feeding.[9] His death produced such an outcry and roused such popular emotions in Ireland that the authorities had abandoned forced feeding and began the early release of hunger-strikers under the 'Cat and Mouse' Act. After only four days without food in 1917, MacSwiney had been set free, but was re-arrested four months later to complete his sentence. Whilst in Lincoln prison, the 'Coupon' election of 1918 had been held, and MacSwiney found himself elected unopposed as member for Mid-Cork. He was released on parole when his wife became ill during the influenza epidemic in the winter, but was never required to return to gaol. When he chose to hunger-strike in 1920, therefore, MacSwiney was repeating an action which had secured his speedy

---

[5] An account of the trial taken from the *Cork Examiner* is printed in P. S. O'Hegarty, *A Short Memoir of Terence MacSwiney* (Dublin, 1922), p. 90.

[6] Healy, 'Hunger Strikes', p. 100; C. Desmond Greaves, *The Life and Works of James Connolly* (London, 1972), p. 311; Leah Levenson, *With Wooden Sword. Portrait of Francis Sheehy Skeffington, Militant Pacifist* (Boston, 1983), pp. 175–83.

[7] Typed statement of Michael Brennan, quoted in David Fitzpatrick, *Politics and Irish Life 1913–1921: Provincial experience of war and revolution* (Dublin, 1977), p. 149.

[8] Fitzpatrick, *Politics and Irish Life*, p. 149.

[9] Sean O Luing, *I die in a good cause. A study of Thomas Ashe, idealist and revolutionary* (Tralee, 1970).

release previously, but which on this occasion was, for several reasons, destined to have a tragic ending.

The British cabinet was thrown into confusion by MacSwiney's decision. 'The English public do not like his dying of starvation', Lloyd George told H. A. L. Fisher, the historian turned cabinet minister.[10] Appeals for the Lord Mayor's release came from most of the British press, the T.U.C., Labour, and Liberal parties, F. B. Meyer, secretary of the National Free Church Council, some Catholic bishops (most notably, indefatigably and tactlessly, Peter Amigo, bishop of Southwark), even the King and Queen.[11] The King favoured some form of house arrest outside Ireland, where MacSwiney could be with his wife.[12] The archbishop of Canterbury, according to his biographer, 'refused to intervene',[13] but that is not quite accurate for he did send a cautiously-phrased telegram to the Home Secretary which referred to the pleas to him to urge the Government to show mercy. He maintained that the problem 'lies quite outside my range of detailed knowledge', adding that he would 'personally approve if Government decided on release'.[14] A more passionate plea, uttered with deeper insight into the Irish mentality came in a letter to the *Manchester Guardian* from the young classical scholar E. R. Dodds:

> Let him die and before the month is up he will be a legend, a symbol, a ghost haunting the secret thoughts of every Irishman. In Ireland a legend has the power of many bayonets; and ghosts live longer than men.[15]

When ministers met on 25 August, the Home Secretary Edward Shortt argued that a strong case could be made for giving MacSwiney his liberty. Government officials in Dublin Castle were already describing him as a political prisoner which had created a difference of perception in the minds of the British public. The Lord Mayor's physical condition did not allow him to be forcibly fed and the 'Cat and Mouse' Act could not be used this time because he was adamant that he would only resume eating

---

[10] Oxford Bodleian MS, H. A. L. Fisher diary, 9 September 1920.
[11] *The Times*, 28, 30 August 1920; Archbishop's House, Southwark, P. Amigo to D. Lloyd George, 5 September 1920, P. Amigo to Sir Edward Troup, 5 September 1920, P. Amigo to A. Bonar Law, 7 September 1920, P. Amigo to Sir Hamar Greenwood, 14 September 1920.
[12] Robert Rhodes James, *Memoirs of a Conservative: J. C. C. Davidson's Memoirs and Papers 1910–37* (London, 1969), p. 98.
[13] G. K. A. Bell, *Randall Davidson*, 2 vols (Oxford, 1935), 2, p. 1058.
[14] House of Lords, Lloyd George MS F/3/5/†13, R. T. Davidson to E. Shortt, n.d. (27 August 1920?).
[15] *Manchester Guardian*, 26 August 1920.

if given a written statement offering unconditional freedom. A. J. Balfour, now Lord President of the Council, was as vehemently opposed to conciliation as he had been in 1887 when he became known throughout Ireland as 'Bloody Balfour'. Ministers, however, were moving in the direction of release, but felt that they should first seek the opinion of Sir Neville Macready, general in command in Ireland.[16] Fearing the collapse of the morale of his men, Macready was, in Fisher's words, 'dead against release'.[17] But before the general's advice could be considered by the cabinet, its hand was forced by a telegram to the British press from Lloyd George, holidaying in Lucerne, which rejected absolutely any possibility of a change of heart. He later explained to Bonar Law that he had been swayed by military advice, but apparently had received no information from the Irish Office[18] about the political factors which might be involved. Thus as a modern Conservative historian, Robert Rhodes James, has argued, 'the commonsense and humanity of the King were superior to those of his ministers'[19] and this episode came to merit the words which Kenneth O. Morgan has used to describe the Coalition's policy towards Ireland: 'a monument to ignorance, racial and religious prejudice, and ineptitude'.[20]

The consciences of British ministers were eased somewhat when a fortnight later, the Prime Minister showed Fisher a medical report on the Lord Mayor's condition: 'He is sitting up in bed!' This led Lloyd George to conclude that 'he has clearly been fed through the sacrament'.[21] The tone of Fisher's diary entry suggests that Lloyd George believed that it was MacSwiney and his collaborators who were responsible for this deception. However in 1924, Thomas Jones, one of the civil servants most closely involved, was told by Sir George Newman, Chief Medical Officer at the Ministry of Health, that Lloyd George and Bonar Law had 'begged him to use every effort' to keep the Lord Mayor alive. He had been thirty days into his fast when this plea was uttered and 'Newman kept him alive for another forty-two!'[22]

---

[16] Lloyd George MS F/31/1/40, Memorandum by J. C. C. Davidson; Thomas Jones, *Whitehall Diary III, Ireland 1918–25*, ed. Keith Middlemas (Oxford, 1971), pp. 35–7.

[17] Fisher diary, 9 September 1920.

[18] House of Lords, Bonar Law MS 101/4/83, A. Bonar Law to Lord Stamfordham, 26 August 1920; Lloyd George MS F/51/1/44, D. Lloyd George to A. Bonar Law, 4 September 1920.

[19] Rhodes Jones, *Memoirs of a Conservative*, p. 98.

[20] Kenneth O. Morgan, *Consensus and Disunity: The Lloyd George Coalition Government 1918–22* (Oxford, 1979), p. 132.

[21] Fisher diary, 9 September 1920.

[22] Thomas Jones, *Whitehall Diary I 1916–25*, ed. Keith Middlemas (Oxford, 1969), pp. 279 *seq.*

MacSwiney's ordeal evoked world-wide interest and sympathy. In the U.S.A. reports of the deterioration of his condition are said to have been followed with more concern and curiosity than the presidential election campaign, while in London, a young Vietnamese washing dishes in the Carlton hotel is said to have burst into tears. 'A nation which has such citizens', cried the young Ho Chi Minh, 'will never surrender'.[23]

Not all witnesses of the macabre spectacle were as favourably impressed. 'The truth is', asserted the *Spectator* shortly after the hunger-strike had begun, 'that Mr MacSwiney, to his other crimes, is trying to add the crime—legally recognized as such—of committing suicide'.[24] An Anglican paper, the high church and high Tory *Guardian*, reported on 29 October that 'the Lord Mayor of Cork has succeeded in his prolonged attempt to commit suicide'.

But this interpretation of the Brixton tragedy did not appear to be shared by the authorities of the Roman Catholic Church. Throughout his fast MacSwiney had been accompanied by his chaplain, Father Dominic, who gave him communion every morning. His visitors included Dr Cohalan, bishop of Cork, Archbishop Mannix of Melbourne, and four other bishops. After his death, the body was taken to Southwark Cathedral where it was received by the bishop, Peter Amigo, and Archbishop Mannix. It was mildly ironic that the presence of an archbishop had only been made possible by the British government. The government had long had its eye on Mannix, who was still held responsible by them for rousing Australia against conscription in 1916.[25] He was only in England in 1920 because the government was determined to keep him out of Ireland, even to the extent of sending a destroyer to intercept his ship and convey him to a more placid place, namely Penzance. What the government did not realize was that the south-west was the one corner of England with Irish-born bishops,[26] and William Cotter of Portsmouth soon

---

[23] A. G. Gardiner, 'Ireland an American Question', *Literary Digest*, 6 November 1920, pp. 20–1, quoted Alan J. Ward, *Ireland and Anglo-American Relations 1899–1921* (London, 1969), p. 229; P. Beresford Ellis, *A History of the Irish Working Class* (London, 1972), p. 254.

[24] *Spectator*, 28 August 1920.

[25] Lloyd George MS f/28/2/2, W. M. Hughes to D. Lloyd George, 17 August 1917; Nial Brennan, *Dr Mannix* (London, 1965); Thomas E. Hachey, 'The Quarantine of Archbishop Mannix: A British Preventive Policy During The Anglo-Irish Troubles', *Irish University Review* (1970), pp. 111–30.

[26] During Cardinal Vaughan's archiepiscopate (1892–1903) not a single Irish-born bishop had been appointed to a diocese in England. In 1920 apart from the antique Bishop Lacy of Middlesborough, appointed in 1879, Cotter of Portsmouth and Keiley of Plymouth were the only two Irish bishops.

made himself responsible for stage-managing a tour of the principal Irish settlements.

The MacSwiney funeral provided an obvious setting for a personal appearance by the archbishop. The body lay in state for 24 hours, during which time it was seen by 30,000 people, and then an episcopal high mass of requiem was celebrated by Cotter with the assistance of Mannix, while Amigo presided and gave the absolution. Then the coffin, escorted by a guard of honour in the uniforms of the Irish Volunteers and followed by Mannix and Cotter, a large number of priests, and 10,000 people, was taken in procession to Euston station 'amid the respectful silence of the English crowds'[27] to be taken for burial to Cork. In the City Hall, the radical journalist H. W. Nevison joined the crowds who filed past the corpse and viewed 'the exposed face of the dead man . . . yellow-pale, wasted to extreme thinness, but fine and resolute—the face of a poet as well as a patriot'.[28] The inscription on the coffin proclaimed the Irish interpretation of the cause of death: 'Terence MacSwiney, murdered by the Foreign enemy, in the Fourth Year of the Republic'.

English observers found different levels of significance in the funeral procedures. 'It was openly a Republican demonstration' claimed the New Statesman, of the march through London.[29] As such it was castigated by the Spectator. Under the heading 'The Roman Church and the Crimes of Sinn Fein', the journal claimed that 'because it suited a certain part of the Roman Church in Ireland and apparently also a section of Roman ecclesiastics in England to 'boom' the suicide of the Lord Mayor of Cork as a martyrdom suffered at the hands of the British Government, we have seen the suicide's funeral converted into what we might almost call a festival of the Church'.[30] It went on to assert that such events highlighted the essential difference between Roman and Anglo-Catholicism. The latter 'may seem Roman in its views, but thank God, it has never sacrificed truth on the altar of casuistry'.

Despite its whole-sale condemnation, the Spectator had been right in referring to 'a section of Roman Catholic Ecclesiastics in England', because the Catholic community was deeply divided over the moral questions posed by the hunger-strike and the elaborate display in Southwark Cathedral. After Bishop Cohalan's visit to MacSwiney, one English

[27] H. W. Nevison, Last Changes, p. 175.
[28] Ibid., p. 175.
[29] New Statesman, 30 November 1920.
[30] Spectator, 6 November 1920.

Catholic wrote to *The Times* to enquire whether the bishop had said any-thing to dissuade the lord mayor 'from the terrible deed of self-slaughter which he has in hand?' According to Catholic doctrine, continued the puzzled correspondent, suicide is a mortal sin:

> It does not cease to be so when, as in this case, the perpetrator per-suades himself that he is doing a noble act. God, not the human con-science, is the author of the moral law. . . . It is inexplicable and a scandal that a poor misguided man, now starving himself, should be encouraged in his wrong-doing by the ministers of the Church—by the priest who administers the sacraments to him, and by the bishop who paid him a visit of sympathy, but apparently did not explicitly and urgently teach and exhort him to desist from the sin which he is committing.[31]

The letter in *The Times* was reprinted in the *Tablet* which in the same number published the reaction of the most popular Catholic preacher of the day, Father Bernard Vaughan, a younger brother of the previous arch-bishop of Westminster. He acknowledged the existence of different opinions but asserted that it would not be proper to give the last sacrament to a hunger-striker.[32] Once the subject had been broached in the pages of the *Tablet* a battle-royal began which revealed not only that the Catholic community held different interpretations of the moral teaching of their Church and its application to hunger-strikes, but emphasized also the political divisions which at that time were never far below the surface.

Father W. H. Kent of Birmingham, who had shown where his sym-pathies lay by attending a reception in London for Archbishop Mannix, came out against Vaughan on the grounds of patristic precedent, citing the case of St Eusebius of Vercelli who had refused to take food from the hands of his Aryan jailers. Another defence of MacSwiney came from an Irish Jesuit, Father P. J. Gannon, who also contributed a long article on the ethics of hunger-striking to the Dublin review, *Studies*.[33] 'It may happen', he wrote,

> that a person can be in perfect good faith even where objectively the act is not conformable to divine law. In such a case the relations between the Creator and His creature are decided by the subjective

---

[31] *The Times*, 31 August 1920.
[32] *Tablet*, 4 September 19820.
[33] *Ibid.*, 11 September; P. J. Gannon, 'The Ethical Aspect of the Hunger Strike, *Studies*, 9 (1920), pp. 448–54.

dispositions of the latter, and sincere good faith redeems from guilt an act that may perhaps in itself harmonise but ill with the divine law. That the Irish hunger-strikers are in this disposition is too evident to need elaboration.

To the defence of his brother came John Vaughan, assistant bishop of Salford. 'There is much difference of opinion still among priests and theologians', he wrote, but 'I must confess that I have met many more who differ from the learned Jesuit [Gannon] than who agree with him.'[34] In reply to six questions posed by Bishop Vaughan, Father Gannon returned to the fray with an insistence that the omission of taking food was not the positive and direct cause of death, and may on occasion be justified. 'The question then turns on the nature and sufficiency of the motives.'[35] But as Father Nicholas Lawless wrote 'no writers in all the correspondence give the same motives' for MacSwiney's action:

glowing reasons were given about Ireland's freedom to be won in right chivalrous fashion by a solitary hunger-striker! Others argued from the natural desire of a prisoner to escape from a sentence he deemed unjust—no very noble motive, and hardly to be balanced against death. Others still seemed to think it useless to put the motives before stupid Englishmen who could not understand the deep spirituality of it all.

Father Lawless quoted from the report of the inquest which stated that the hunger-strike had been begun as a protest against arrest by what MacSwiney regarded as an alien power with no legal authority over him. Lawless spelled out the implications:

If the Lord Mayor might hunger-strike unto death for the reason given, why not any other of the Sinn Fein prisoners awaiting court-martial, especially those expecting a capital sentence or already under it? It is to be feared just now that many of our young men would prefer death from starvation to death on the gallows.[36]

From September to December 1920, the debate continued in the *Tablet* drawing in contributions from Catholics from Cairo to Canada. Much of the discussion was highly academic involving ingenious applications of

[34] *Tablet*, 6 November 1920.
[35] *Ibid.*, 20 November 1920.
[36] *Ibid.*, 6 November 1920.

obscure passages in the writings of St Thomas Aquinas and his later commentators, especially the Spanish Dominican, Dominic Soto, Imperial Theologian at the Council of Trent, and August Lehmkuhl, the leading German Jesuit moralist of the day. It was left to another Catholic correspondent of *The Times* to point out that 'for Irish Catholics the question is a closed one'. He pointed out that when forty Republican prisoners had gone on hunger-strike in Mountjoy jail in 1917 the standing committee of the Irish hierarchy had pronounced that their deaths would be the responsibility of the government. That pronouncement had never been withdrawn, and the writer held that as the hierarchy was the maker and interpreter of church law for Ireland, the question of suicide did not arise.[37] In fact the position of the Irish bishops was rather more complicated. Over thirty years later, the bishop of Galway, Michael Browne, in private letters to Moirin Chavasse, who had submitted to him parts of the manuscript of her new life of MacSwiney, recalled that the morality of the hunger-strike had been the subject of intense debate in Irish Catholic theological circles. 'The spearhead of the theological objection,' he recalled, '. . . came from Clonliffe College, the theological seminary in Dublin', in the form of articles in the *Irish Ecclesiastical Record* in 1918 from Father John Waters, chaplain to Mountjoy (a man dismissed by Mrs Chavasse as 'pro-British'), and in the *Irish Theological Quarterly*.[38] But these theological and moral arguments were balanced in the pronouncements of the bishops by the realities of the political situation. It has more recently been argued that the Irish hierarchy was not willing to condemn the hunger-strike because their more immediate aim was to lead their people away from guerilla tactics—the armed ambush, the bullet from behind the tree. In comparison, the hunger-strike was a form of passive resistance, and as such the lesser evil. In any case, before MacSwiney, it had been an exercise in brinkmanship, which had never led directly to death.[39] This line of thought would give some consistency to the position of Daniel Cohalan, bishop of Cork, who in the autumn of 1920 supported

[37] *The Times*, 20 September 1920.
[38] University College, Dublin MS P 48c/123, Michael Browne to Moirin Chavasse, 22 February 1954. See John Waters, 'The Morality of the Hunger Strike'), *IER* 12 (1918), pp. 89–108; Patrick Cleary, 'Some questions regarding the morality of Hunger Strikes', *IER* 12 (1918), pp. 265–73; John Waters, 'The Morality of the Hunger-Strike: A Rejoinder', *IER* 13 (1919), pp. 14–26; Patrick Cleary, 'Some further questions regarding the Morality of the Hunger-Strike', *IER* 13 (1919), pp. 219–29.
[39] David W. Miller, *Church, State and Nation in Ireland 1898-1921* (Dublin, 1973), pp. 401 *seq*; Dermot Keogh, *The Vatican, the Bishops and Irish Politics 1919-39* (Cambridge, 1986), pp. 60 *seq*.

MacSwiney, then in December, publicly attacked and threatened with excommunication, those who used terrorist methods.[40]

If by 1920 the question was closed for the bishops in Ireland, what about England? Bishops Amigo and Cotter were members of the English hierarchy. Where did the English bishops stand, and where did their leader, Cardinal Bourne, archbishop of Westminster, stand? This question troubled many English Catholics, especially those who were horrified by the resort to arms of the Irish Republican Brotherhood. 'I wonder if the Cardinal realizes how, by the ignorant, he is blamed and held responsible for the actions of the other bishops?' enquired a lady from Southwark.

> Cannot the Cardinal who we all love for his loyalty and sense of duty speak out and say he is on the side of law and order. His silence is interpreted as giving consent. . . . Murders, suicide and endless crimes seem mixed up with masses, rosaries, Holy Communion and the sympathy and help of the clergy.[41]

There was no doubt about the position of the president of the Catholic Union, an organization of middle- and upper-class Catholics. Admiral of the Fleet Lord Walter Kerr wrote to England's other cardinal, Aidan Gasquet in Rome, to tell him 'how deep is the feeling among English Catholics on this painful subject'. In the light of the theological disputes, he did not object to the last rites having been given to MacSwiney, 'but I do submit that it is deplorable that any bishop should have officiated at a solemn funeral in his honour'. Considerable pressure had been put on Kerr to organize a formal and public protest but he thought it 'unseemly in a lay body to publicly censure bishops for action taken in the discharge of purely spiritual functions'.[42] Such considerations did not, however, inhibit some members of the congregation of Southwark Cathedral. Four of them signed a protest objecting 'to the anti-English spirit manifested by Bishop Amigo, and the desecration of St George's Cathedral for Sinn Fein use':

> We intend approaching Parliament with a view to getting English Bishops and English priests for England . . . we do not see why we should be called upon to support Seminaries and Training Colleges to

---

[40] Miller, *Church, State and Nation*, pp. 465 *seq*; Keogh, *The Vatican, the Bishops and Irish Politics*, pp. 60 *seq*.

[41] Westminster Diocesan Archives, Bourne Papers 5/36; B. Basset to A. Jackman, 7 November 1920.

[42] Downside Abbey MS 917A: Lord W. Kerr to F. A. Gasquet, 7 November 1920.

fill England with Irish priests and bishops and foreign hostile men like Peter Amigo. . . . It is doing horrible harm to the Conversion of England, and brings scandal on our Church.[43]

Bishop Amigo was predictably the recipient of many letters and post-cards of puzzlement and protest from the outset of MacSwiney's tribulation. A Catholic layman from Hove was desperately troubled about the moral issue: 'we have consulted priests but get different replies'. Reading the opposing views of the bishop of Cork and Father Vaughan had brought matters 'to an acute point', he wailed. What answer could be given to the challenge of non-Catholic friends?[44] The *Universe* also sought a statement to dispel the bafflement of a priest in Southwark whose parish 'is seething with discussion'.[45] Amigo acknowledged the complexity of the situation but 'knowing as I do the circumstances of this particular case, I am convinced that MacSwiney is not committing suicide'.[46] After the funeral, he sent one of his most revealing justifications to James Hope, a Catholic Unionist MP, cousin of the Duke of Norfolk, and resident in the diocese. The bishop argued that he could not have refused the use of the cathedral for the lord mayor when Westminster cathedral had been made available for the funeral of Sir Daniel McCabe, ex-Lord Mayor of Manchester.[47] In agreeing to the request of the relatives, he had been able to keep some control over the proceedings. No political demonstrations had been a condition, there had been no sermon, and he had not walked in the procession. The bishop's trust had, nevertheless, been abused, he considered, when the Irish Volunteer uniform had been placed over the dead body.[48]

If the entire Catholic community had shared the views expressed by Amigo's critics, Cardinal Bourne's path would have been relatively easy. But if English Catholics were in revolt in the diocese of Southwark, Irish Catholics were in revolt in Westminster. On 23 September, a great reception had been given for Archbishop Mannix by priests of the dioceses of Westminster, Southwark, and Brentford. 'All pretence about an ecclesiastical function was thrown aside', reported the editor of the *Universe*, 'and the thing was a Sinn Fein demonstration of the most insolent kind'.

[43] Bourne Papers 5/36, James Dredgfer *et al.* to F. Bourne, n.d. (postmark 27 October 1920).
[44] Archbishop's House, Southwark, N.S. Marchant to P. Amigo, 25 September 1920.
[45] *Ibid.*, H. S. Dean to P. Amigo, 9 September 1920.
[46] *Ibid.*, P. Amigo to N. S. Marchant, 28 September 1920.
[47] *Ibid.*, James Hope to P. Amigo, 5 November 1920, P. Amigo to James Hope, 8 November 1920.
[48] Chavasse, *MacSwiney*, p. 185.

Bourne had sent his apologies but Bishop Cotter referred to Amigo's presence as 'amply "filling a gap"(!!)'.[49] One of the Westminster priests who attended and was also nauseated by Cotter's behaviour complained later that 'this Irish-born Prelate has not only conducted his Irish campaign . . . in this diocese, but has also let his political tongue run riot about His Eminence'.[50]

With emotions running at such a level, Bourne was probably wise to keep silent. But while he never spoke out on the questions raised by the MacSwiney affair, he did make certain gestures in an attempt to satisfy some of his critics. As archbishop of Westminster, Bourne had three main tasks: to keep his flock together, to demonstrate to the general public that Catholics were loyal and responsible citizens, and to keep on good terms with the government. Amigo was only interested in the Catholic community. He ignored public opinion and deeply disliked the government. One of his many complaints about Bourne (and there was no love lost between them) was that 'he is very friendly with Lloyd George but I am sorry that he trusts this Prime Minister who will use him without helping us'.[51] But this was a serious underestimation of Bourne's political skill; which had been first demonstrated when he outwitted Asquith in 1908, and was to be finally revealed in 1926 during the General Strike.[52]

In private, Bourne had already taken steps to attempt to defuse the situation in England, and unite the Catholic community, by encouraging in August the establishment of the Committee of British Catholics for Reconciliation. The initiative had come from Father Charles Plater of the Catholic Social Guild. Plater explained that:

> Our working people, being mainly of Irish blood are incensed against the Government because of its treatment of Ireland. They are therefore against the Government on every issue that arises whether it be an industrial question or a question of foreign policy. This brings them into company with and into sympathy with revolutionaries and all sorts of extremists. . . . If it were not for the aggravation of the Irish question the masses of Catholic workers in this country would be a solid conservative force. As it is their support is largely given to extremist elements, not because they are socially revolutionary but

---

[49] Bourne MS 5/36, H. S. Dean to A. Jackman, 24 September 1920.
[50] Ibid., 5/36, Basil Baston to A. Jackman, 28 April 1921.
[51] Downside Abbey MS 917A: P. Amigo to F. A. Gasquet, 25 February 1920.
[52] Stuart Mews, 'The Churches', The General Strike, ed. Margaret Morris (Harmondsworth, 1976), pp. 330–2.

because they hate the British government which, as they think, is the oppressor of Ireland.

Plater went on to describe working–class Catholic suspicions that their better–off co-religionists were 'no friends of Ireland'. Their fears had to be allayed if the Catholic community was to be saved from disruption and extremism stopped before it went too far.[53] He suggested a united appeal for peace and reconciliation to be signed by both Catholic Unionists and Sinn Feiners. Both Bourne and Mannix approved the memorial and it was published at the end of October. Any good that it might have done was obliterated by the MacSwiney affair, and the community became even more polarized. The time for joint action was now past. The need now was to reassure English Catholics without unnecessarily alienating the Irish, and to offset the unfavourable publicity of the Southwark ceremony.

A month later an opportunity arose to accomplish these objectives. On 21 November, Dublin's 'Bloody Sunday', fourteen British officers were shot in their beds. Three of them turned out to be Catholics and Bourne made sure that they had an impressive requiem in Westminster Cathedral, a gesture which drew a public letter of thanks from Lloyd George.[54] The Westminster requiem gave considerable satisfaction to English Catholics, while the premier's letter demonstrated that although the government might have lost all patience with the Irish hierarchy, it still had some confidence in the Catholic leadership of England. Moreover it has now become apparent that Lloyd George hoped for more than just a mass from his Catholic friends.

In 1961, Moirin Chavasse was able to reveal the suspicions of Michael Curran, Vice-Principal of the Irish College in Rome, that during MacSwiney's fast, Cardinal Gasquet, the English Benedictine working in Rome on revision of the Vulgate, was secretly in correspondence with the Secretary of State, Cardinal Gasparri, in an attempt to get the Vatican specifically to condemn the Lord Mayor's actions. Hearing rumours that a papal pronouncement was in the offing, Curran rushed to Archbishop Cerretti, secretary of the Congregation for Extraordinary Ecclesiastical Affairs, and pleaded for consultations with the Irish hierarchy.[55] The story

---

[53] Bourne MS 5/36, C. Plater to Edward Eyre, 31 August 1920; F. Bourne to E. Eyre, 8 September 1920; Henry Somerville to F. Bourne, 20 October 1920.

[54] James Gleeson, *Bloody Sunday* (London, 1962); Tom Bowden, 'Bloody Sunday—a Reappraisal', *European Studies Review*, 2 (1972), pp. 25–42; Charles Townshend, 'Bloody Sunday—Michael Collins speaks', *European Studies Review*, 9 (1974), pp. 377–85; Bourne MS 5/36, D. Lloyd George to F. Bourne, 29 November 1920.

[55] Chavasse, *MacSwiney*, p. 159; Keogh, *The Bishops, the Vatican*, p. 250.

has the ring of truth. The members of the Irish College in Rome had long suspected Gasquet, who was a fervently patriotic Englishman. He had been in Rome throughout the First World War and done everything in his power to advance the British cause and counter German and Austrian influence. On 12 April 1921, Gasquet learned that 'the most absurd things were being said by the Irish. Inter alia that I was receiving £700 a year as agent of the British government and Father Philip [his secretary] £300 for propaganda.'[56] In 1920 Gasquet was in England from 1 July to 23 October, and having left his diary in Rome, there are no entries for that period. He later inserted a paragraph summarizing his travels. These did include four meetings with Lloyd George which suggests something more than a courtesy call and the fact that he returned to Rome on 23 October when MacSwiney was visibly weakening and had an audience with the Pope on 28 October when they had a long talk about England and Ireland, gives some credibility to Mrs Chavasse's claim.

It is obvious from the Foreign Office papers that the Vatican was intrigued, puzzled, and disturbed by the MacSwiney affair. A fortnight after the funeral, the British representative, Count de Salis, had an interview with the Pope who referred to overtures which had been made about hunger-strikes. His Holiness according to the Count, had doubts about them, and was convinced that MacSwiney must have taken food to survive for so long. He also expressed surprise at the excessive ostentation of the funeral. 'There was a certain element of farce with it all.'[57] This aspect was also raised shortly after by Cerretti. 'And all the time', mused de Salis, 'the Holy Office was considering whether the unfortunate man was or was not a suicide and entitled at all to a Christian burial.'[58] But did the request for a consideration of the case by the Vatican come from the British government, or from the English Catholic hierarchy?

The British government clearly wanted the death condemned as suicide, and de Salis took comfort from a conversation which Gasquet had had with Cardinal Merry del Val, the former Secretary of State and now secretary of the Congregation of Propaganda Fide. But del Val had lost most of his influence on Vatican policy and his view that MacSwiney's death 'was clearly to be treated as one of suicide' was evidently a private opinion.[59] By this time, Gasquet should have known that a condemnation

---

[56] Downside Abbey MS 917A, Diary of F. A. Gasquet, 12 April 1921.
[57] PRO, FO 380/31/433/20, de Salis to Curzon, 13 November 1920.
[58] Ibid., 380/31/458/20, de Salis to Curzon, 28 November 1920.
[59] Ibid., 380/31/433/20, de Salis to Curzon, 13 November 1920.

would not be forthcoming. In his papers there is a letter from Cerretti which refers to some correspondence with Gasparri. It leaves no doubt that at an early stage in the hunger-strike, Gasquet had requested a verdict from the Vatican and that the case was being considered by three consultors. But if Father Curran is correct, by the time the letter was sent, 3 October, the Irish College had already intervened and made sure that Rome did not reach a speedy decision. Indeed Cerretti's letter with its reference to Father Gannon's defence of the hunger-strike was obviously meant as a warning to Gasquet that Rome would not necessarily see things from his point of view. The Vatican might have been willing in the 1880s to condemn boycotting, but the situation in Ireland was now totally different. And though Bishop John Vaughan might conclude his debate in the *Tablet* with the assertion that 'it is on such occasions as the present that one appreciates the supreme authority of Rome. May we soon cry out: "Roma locuta est, causa finita"', Archbishop Cerretti was reminding Gasquet that '*Roma e eterna*', and that 'you may be sure that if the Lord Mayor of Cork is not dead when a decision in his case will be given, he will never die!'[60]

University of Lancaster

[60] *Tablet*, 27 November 1920; Downside Abbey MS 917A, B. Cerretti to F. A. Gasquet, 3 October 1920.

AN IRISH BENEDICTINE ADVENTURE: DOM FRANCIS SWEETMAN (1872–1953) AND MOUNT ST BENEDICT, GOREY

by DOMINIC AIDAN BELLENGER

O N 11 January 1913 the following article, signed by 'Me Fein', appeared in an Irish periodical of pronounced nationalist views under the heading 'Wexford Again. More Language Compulsion':

Compulsion in educational matters seems to revolt some good souls in Wexford, and the following flash will possibly electrify Mr Fanning of the County Council of that model county. (By the way, it seems to be rapidly becoming the 'model county' for Irish Ireland wobbling and drunkenness prosecutions.) A school has been established at Gorey for some years by the Benedictine Fathers, for the better class young Irishmen, and it will be of interest to note some features of that educational establishment.

The staff is absolutely recruited from Oxford and Cambridge! There is not one Irish University represented in the list of the staff set forth in the syllabus, not even Mr Minch's Trinity gets a look in. So young Irishmen of the better class will be trained (one cannot say educated) on purely English University ideals; also, no Irish University is qualified to furnish a Professor for the Benedictine Fathers in County Wexford. The only member of the staff who stands apart is the matron, a Miss *K'Eogh*, who is apparently of French extraction! So much for the staff.

The curriculum announces that 'All modern languages are taught in the Direct Method'. (There is a Gaelic League ring about that. But, oh! Reader, wait for the next.) *'French is compulsory throughout the school.'* French compulsory throughout a County Wexford school! Where now are Mr Fanning, of County Wexford County Council, and Mr Minch, of Kildare County Council, and the other sham educational, anti-compulsory Irishmen? Now is the time, and here is the place to denounce compulsion. Irish boys compelled to learn French in a school staffed from the English Universities! The curriculum proceeds: 'From time to time a party of older boys is formed to go *abroad* and visit various places of historic interest on the Continent.'

(The Italics are, of course, mine.) One must conclude that for Irish boys of the better class there are not any places of historic interest in Wexford—(are there Mr Fanning?)—or in Limerick, or at Athlone, or in Donegal; or if there be, that they are not of any value. In this projected tour the students are recommended to avoid English routes; but the Irish-speaking districts are utterly ignored in this Franco-English curriculum. The young gentlemen in this educational institution will be reared up by an English University staff in compulsory French, and nourished by trips on the Continent. The names of some of the students are Comerford, McCann, Murphy, Mahony, Joyce. Of course, for those who like that sort of thing it is just the sort of thing they would like. But what has Mr Fanning, and those who think with him, to say of compulsory French in a Wexford school? What will the Wexford County Council, that would not keep the bargain made by its accredited delegate on behalf of Essential Irish, do with a foreign body in its midst that is expatriating Irish students? Shaun Dillon, son of John Dillon, M.P., spent some time at this school, and then passed in due course to Downside, England, the parent establishment. Let Mr Fanning, of Wexford, and Mr Minch, of the 'Freeman's Journal', *'et hoc genus omne'*, contemplate and ponder over the problem of John Dillon's son at an English school! One begins to enquire, can Shaun Dillon's term at this school, and the English University Benedictine establishment at Gorey help in any way to explain the tergiversation of the Wexford County Council? The Headmaster of the Franco-English School is the Rev. J. F. Sweetman, O.S.B. Any relation to John of that ilk? Oh! Wexford; and oh! Sinn Fein.[1]

This piece is worth quoting in full as it provides a good example of standard anti-English propaganda of the time. It identifies the school at Mount St Benedict, Gorey, County Wexford, as an outpost of the British Empire as represented by Downside Abbey. Such an identification, never convincing, was to become absurd, as we shall see, in the years that followed. The first Benedictine 'monastic' school to be established in Ireland became increasingly implicated in the struggle for Irish freedom which coincided with the First World War, and its presiding genius, Dom Francis Sweetman, came to be recognized as a great patriot.

Benedictine monasticism, except in its Cistercian guise, did not take root in post-Reformation Ireland until the settlement of the women's

[1] *The Leader*, 11 January 1913, p. 548.

monastery at Kylemore, County Galway (1922)[2] and the foundation of the community at Glenstal, County Limerick (1927).[3] Even in medieval Ireland the number of Benedictine houses was 'comparatively small'[4] and the Irish Benedictine houses on the continent, the so-called *Schottenklöster*, founded in the Middle Ages, became more Scottish (in the modern sense) than Irish before their dissolution.[5] Mount St Benedict, Gorey, bore little resemblance to a conventional monastery in either its medieval or modern manifestation. For most of its history it had more about it of the hermitage than the *cenobium*.

John Sweetman (in religion, Dom Francis), was Gorey's founder and its continuing inspiration. He was born at Clohammon, County Wexford, on 22 May 1872, the third son of Walter and Mary (née Butler) Sweetman, prosperous landowners.[6] He was educated for two years (1889–91) at Downside in England. Downside was then a small monastic school, domestic in atmosphere, attached to the Benedictine monastery of St Gregory the Great. The Gregorian *conventus* had been established at Douai in Flanders in 1607 and its school, one of the more successful of the exiled educational ventures of the English Catholics, opened soon after. It was re-established at Downside near Bath in Somerset in 1814 following the French Revolution. At Douai, at least until the last quarter of the eighteenth century when the number of French pupils increased, most of its *alumni* had been the sons of the English Catholic landed classes. At Downside its clientele was more eclectic and in Sweetman's time, more than a generation before Downside evolved into a great 'public school', it was one of the most popular English schools for the sons of Irish gentlemen.[7] The political standpoint of these Gregorians (as Downside monks and boys are known) was generally moderate and loyalist. This can be shown in the career of one of the most distinguished of them, the Right Honourable Charles Owen,

---

[2] The community of nuns now resident at Kylemore were founded at Ypres in the Low Countries in 1665 and remained there until they were shelled out in 1914. They fled to England and then to MacMine, County Wexford. In 1922 they moved to Kylemore Castle where they conduct a school. See P. Nolan, *The Irish Dames of Ypres* (Dublin, 1908).

[3] Glenstal was founded in 1927 from the abbey of Maredsous in Belgium as a memorial to the great Irish Benedictine abbot of Maredsous, Dom Columba Marmion (1858–1923). Glenstal started life as a priory with an 'arts and crafts' school attached. This school was closed in 1945 and the monastery became an abbey in 1957. The abbey school proper was first opened in 1932.

[4] A. Gwynn and R. N. Hadcock, *Medieval Religious Houses, Ireland* (London, 1970), p. 103.

[5] For a discussion of the Schottenklöster see M. Dilworth, *Scots in Franconia* (London, 1974).

[6] Biographical details of Dom Sweetman come from the various memoirs referred to later in the notes and from the MS *Fasti Gregoriani 1793-1932*, Downside Abbey Archives (henceforth D.A.A.) which has brief lives of all monks of Downside.

[7] See H. N. Birt, *Downside* (London, 1902).

O'Conor Don, who was at Downside in the 1850s. He was MP for Roscommon, 1860–80, introducing a Bill to extend the Industrial Schools Act to Ireland which became law in 1867. He was a Privy Councillor from 1881 and was Chairman of the Royal Commission on the financial relations between England and Ireland in 1896. He served as Lord Lieutenant of County Roscommon from 1888 until his death in 1906. He had a great attachment to the Irish past—he was, for example, President of the Society for the Preservation of the Irish Language—but was always loyal to the Crown. In 1902, he bore the standard of Ireland at the Coronation of King Edward VII.[8] Such men were Sweetman's fellow Gregorians.

Sweetman entered the Downside community on leaving school and made his profession in 1892. He spent the years 1893–7 in Rome as an ecclesiastical student. An anecdote from those years reveals several of his abiding characteristics—an open-hearted attitude towards non-Catholics, an independence of mind, and a tendency to alienate superiors. Sweetman was delegated to show Lord Halifax the city on one of the Anglican peer's visits, perhaps his first, to Rome. They attended a Candlemas ceremony and Sweetman gave Halifax a lighted candle. The 1890s were not ecumenically auspicious times and one of the members of the Commission on Anglican Orders, Dom Aidan Gasquet (not yet a Cardinal), heard of the Candlemas incident. Gasquet had once been Prior of Downside. Gasquet, in Sweetman's telling phrase, was barking round the young monk's knees. Sweetman looked down on the other man and said, in a very lordly way to the short but rather important Gasquet; 'When any gentleman, whether Catholic or Heretic, asks me for a light either for a candle or a cigar, I always give it to him.'[9]

Sweetman was ordained priest at Downside in 1899. In 1900 he went to South Africa as a Chaplain to the Forces during the Boer War and was badly wounded in the leg. It is said that he crossed the lines many times to learn about growing tobacco, a lifetime's interest. He had already made up his mind that Downside should make an Irish foundation. 'His reason for accepting a military chaplaincy was that on active service it is easy to save money and he was even then planning to have an Irish school. However, his Abbey of Downside insisted, he told me, that some of it should be spent on hanging a bell in their tower. He treasured a newspaper cutting of

---

[8] See *DRev* 33 (1914), p. 216.
[9] D.A.A. VII.A.3 e (III) Mount St Benedict's, Gorey, Co. Wexford. Copy of a personal memoir of Dom John Sweetman by Dean C. M. Gray Stack given to Old Wexford Society in March 1978, p. 72.

his bell being hit by lightning. Apparently the Order of St Benedict is said to be preserved from such accidents but this happened when he considered that Downside was treating him and the Mount with some asperity.[10] His return to Downside where he taught in the school after his South African experience was not prolonged and in 1906 (by which time he had also served for a short time as assistant priest at St Mary's, Liverpool), he went to Ireland. He was to remain there for all but a few months of his long life.

In 1925, when giving evidence in reply to alleged (mainly political) charges against him, Father Sweetman summarized the aspirations of his foundation:

> Mount St Benedict, Gorey, is a Benedictine school, founded by Downside Abbey, Somerset, England, some twenty years ago. The project originated amongst certain Irish monks in the Downside community who were anxious to work in Ireland, and was warmly welcomed by leading Irish Catholic Laymen, many of whom had been educated in Benedictine schools abroad, and wished for the same opportunity for their sons in Ireland. Such schools play a conspicuous part in Catholic education at the present time in Italy, Austria, France, England, Belgium, America, and other countries, and if any other proof of the value attached to the Benedictine training and spirit were needed it could be found in the history of the Order during the past 1400 years. Numerous Popes and not less than 200 Cardinals have been chosen from its ranks, 37,000 monasteries have been established, and the memorials of its activities are scattered over the face of Europe. The work of reconstructing and evangelising Europe after the collapse of the Roman Empire was, in conjunction with our own Irish monks, largely the work of the Benedictines. To this day, Boniface, Willibrord, and to some extent Augustine, are revered as the apostles of Germany, Sweden, and England, respectively.
>
> The monasteries which the monks established became centres of progress and work, especially in the education of the young, and agriculture. The monk, following St Benedict's precept to live by his own labour, became an example of industry. No work is foreign to Benedictine life, but from the very character and spirit of his Rule, which

---

[10] *Ibid.* Copy of unpublished typescript, originally intended for publication in a series produced by the Catholic Truth Society of Ireland entitled *Great Educators*, *Adventure in Education Father Sweetman & Mount St Benedict* by M. Dillon, O.S.B. (henceforth *Dillon*), p. 73.

aims at common family life with the permanent attachment of the monk to his monastery, the first call on his labour was the development of the neighbourhood in which his monastery was built. The Benedictines carry the idea of home life into their schools, and it is a special feature of Benedictine education that boys are given a wide measure of freedom in order that, by being trained in habits of personal responsibility, they may be fitted to exercise the greater freedom of the University and after life.

It was with such objects in mind that the monks of Downside Abbey, recognising the debt of Catholic England towards Ireland in the past, obtained permission from Dr Browne, the then Bishop of Ferns, to establish a school, and ultimately a monastery, in his Diocese, and sent three of their number, with Dom Sweetman, a native of Wexford, as Superior, and Dom Cuthbert Butler, a native of Dublin, as his assistant, to carry out the foundation. The money necessary for the purchase of suitable premises was lent by Mr John Sweetman, of Dublin, and at no subsequent date has financial assistance been sought from Downside.[11]

Preliminary soundings about the Irish foundation had been made in the spring of 1905 when the abbot of Downside, Dom Edmund Ford, wrote to the bishop of Ferns, Dr James Browne. Ford informed the bishop of his intention 'to open a school' which he hoped 'might gradually develop and enable us to establish a priory'. This school, he continued, 'is intended for the class of boys who are now sent to England'.[12] Browne was cautiously welcoming in his response. 'If you will not interfere with our diocesan school or with parochial work and rights', he replied, 'we can have no possible objection to your founding a monastery in this diocese.'[13] The property selected for the foundation (after a temporary billet at Ballinapierce, Enniscorthy) was Mount Nebo near Gorey and by the autumn of 1907 negotiations for its purchase had been completed. It had been bought on behalf of Downside by Mr John Sweetman, of Drumbaragh, County Meath, Father Sweetman's cousin. The direct family involvement in the purchase of the property and the fact that Mr Sweet-

---

[11] D.A.A. VII.A.3 e (III) Abbot's Archives, Gorey Files. Printed 'Evidence' 'in reply to alleged charges against Father Sweetman; taken on 19 April 1925, in the presence of Mr Gavan Duffy, B.L., Count O'Byrne, and Arthur Cox, Solicitor for Father Sweetman' (henceforth *Evidence*), p. 5.

[12] *Ibid.* VII.A.3 e (i) Copy of letter from Abbot H. E. Ford to Bishop J. Browne, 7 April 1905.

[13] *Ibid.* Letter from Bishop J. Browne to Abbot H. E. Ford, 10 April 1905.

man was a founder-member of Sinn Fein were indications of some of the difficulties which were to ensue. In 1907, however, all seemed bright for the Mount's future.

It was a very fine property ideally suited for the purpose. There was a good house and about five hundred acres of land. There was also a large steward's house which was to be known as St Michael's or the Lodge and which housed some of the staff and later provided single and double rooms for the senior boys. His Reverence immediately began to build and added a chapel and refectory to the main house. Later he built another wing which consisted of three class rooms on the ground floor and the seven rooms passage on the floor above. It seems that the original plan was that Mount St Benedict should be primarily a preparatory school for Downside and that the boys would go on there when they reached the appropriate age, but His Reverence [as Sweetman was always known at the Mount] did not approve of boys going to school in England and, as boys and parents were enthusiastic about the new school, there was no difficulty in arranging that they should stay on and complete their education under the guidance of His Reverence.

His Reverence's connection with Downside naturally attracted the more anglophile section of the community and in the early days the majority of the boys came from families in that tradition. On one occasion a lady called to inspect the school with a view to sending her boy there. She was pleased with all that she saw, but before coming to a decision she raised the objection that she had been told, though she could hardly believe it, that Fr Sweetman had accepted the sons of 'that rebel' John Dillon. 'Oh, he had a boy here once', said his Reverence, 'but I don't care for that type of person.' ('There were three of you here at the time', he added, when telling me the story, 'but you have to exercise a bit of tact when you are a schoolmaster.') The lady, reassured, sent her boy and apparently never adverted to the fact that he was exposed to such dangerous company.[14]

The school took its tone from its founder. 'He was not so much a teacher as a leader. He was not deliberately teaching boys a code of behaviour but rather communicating naturally his own code.'[15] It was never a large establishment—in 1909 it had a staff of four, three classrooms and

[14] *Dillon*, p. 7.
[15] *Ibid.*

perhaps fifty pupils—and its administration was personal and somewhat eccentric. Sweetman was no ordinary schoolmaster.

> Like Dr Johnson, he loved conversation and would sit in the guest room, as his study was called, for hours talking to anyone whom he could find to talk to him. It might be a visitor, one of the old boys, or a senior whom he might have met in the passage and led in for a chat. He had the embarrassing habit of falling asleep during these conversations and the unhappy visitor or boy would be left sitting there wondering whether he should slip away or wait patiently till His Reverence would wake up.[16]

The teaching staff, too, were not altogether commonplace.

> Greek and German were well taught, but the Irish and Science were not taken very seriously. Irish when I arrived, was in the hands of an elderly English man, Victor Collins, who had spent a year or more on the Aran Islands learning Irish. He used to tell us that the islanders were amazed that anyone could stay there so long and learn so little Irish. Their amazement was fully justified.[17]

Examinations were not always taken seriously. Life was austere despite the ready access to tobacco; Sweetman conducted a tobacco factory (which gave much-needed local employment) as well as running a school. Despite its eccentricity, Dom Matthew Dillon, a pupil at the Mount and afterwards a monk of Glenstal, regarded Mount St Benedict as a great educational experiment in which an emphasis on self-reliance and freedom of choice brought something new into Irish education.

> It has been said that true education is teaching people to live and in the Mount we were certainly taught that. You might hear boys complain about the cold, they might sometimes grumble about the food, but no one ever complained of being bored. Life had its hardships but from the first day of term to the last it was an adventure and a very enjoyable adventure.[18]

But it was not as an educational institution, despite its famous old boys, who include Sean MacBride, the Nobel prizewinner, that the Mount

[16] *Dillon*, p. 16.
[17] *Ibid.*, p. 25.
[18] *Ibid.*, p. 36.

became famous (or notorious) but as a centre for political activity. It is as a patriot that Sweetman is remembered.

Matthew Dillon's brother James in his memoirs, quoted in *The Irish Times* in 1981, reflected that when he first met Father Sweetman he found him 'most enthusiastic to persuade anyone who was available to join the British Army'. Later, he continued, probably about 1916, 'he became strongly anti-British, and it was from then on that he became more violently Sinn Fein'.[19] Father Sweetman himself wrote later:

> During the subsequent struggle of the Irish people for independence against England, Father Sweetman and the monks identified themselves with the National movement, in particular against Conscription. As a consequence the establishment began to receive constant attention from the Black-and-Tans. Many raids were carried out, at one of which, Miss Keogh, the Matron, was arrested (subsequently sentenced to two years' imprisonment), the workmen's savings robbed, boys' property looted, and one British officer, after gathering the school-boys, aged 9 to 17, and male staff into a classroom, threatened that anybody who moved would be shot.
>
> As a further consequence of the National leanings of the monks, some of the boys' parents who were not in sympathy with the movement began to remove their boys, causing serious financial loss, and effort had to be directed more to saving the existence of the school than to its expansion. Efficiency suffered inevitably.
>
> When it became known that a determined effort was being made to have Mount St Benedict closed, many prominent persons in Ireland, and amongst them Mr John Dillon, Mr George Russell, Mrs Stopford Green, Mr Justice O'Connor, the Wexford County Council, the local administrative bodies, Rural District Council, Board of Guardians, and the Labour organisations, all combined in sending strong remonstrances to Rome against what they considered would be a calamity.[20]

Sweetman's activities were undoubtedly political. He attended the funeral of Thomas Ashe, the first Irishman to die on hunger-strike, and was present at the first meeting of the Dail. He retained, however, a tolerance of other people's views—he was prepared to allow Dom Patrick Nolan, a monk of Maredsous who resided at the Mount, to continue to

[19] B. O Cathaoir, 'Father Sweetman and Mount St Benedict', *The Irish Times*, 16 September 1981.
[20] *Evidence*, p. 20.

express support for the Free State, a position he personally found untenable[21]—and a distance from the most extreme 'direct action' politics. Rumours abounded, however, about his activities and it became necessary in the battles with ecclesiastical authority in which he became involved to deny many accusations and to call upon witnesses of all sorts to clear his name. Peter Connolly, an I.R.A. man, gave his testimony on 19 April 1925:

> I was Adjutant in the I.R.A. at the outbreak of the Civil War, and later on was Commandant of the area in which Mount Benet is. I remained in command until the end. Any important meetings held in my area would have been known to me. I never heard of a Republican meeting being held at the Mount, and no meeting was ever called to be held there to my knowledge. I didn't know of Miss Comerford coming to Mount Benet. If she was there it must have been for private reasons. I had nothing to do with it. I never heard that Father Sweetman held a meeting at Mount Benet and exhorted people to join the I.R.A. until recently when I heard the gossip going around. Such a thing didn't happen to my knowledge.
> The first time I ever spoke to or had any communication with Father Sweetman was in August, 1924, when he sent for me to do some painting. I knew he was a Republican politically but he never had anything to do with the I.R.A. at all. Mount Benet was not used by us at all during the Civil War.[22]

More evidence was provided on the same day by an English officer, Captain S. Godfree, resident in the vicinity:

> I live at Preshute, Carnew, Co. Wicklow, and have resided there during all the troubled period. I never heard that Mount Benet was used as a centre of Republican activity. I knew that Father Sweetman sympathised with the Republican movement. I never heard that he had harboured stolen goods at Mount Benet. I never heard that he had a stolen motor car there, and allowed it to be used by Miss Comerford for the purpose of raids. I never heard that Father Sweetman asked anyone to fight for the Republic, nor that he administered an oath. I never heard that he took any part in the military side of the movement. I never heard that he allowed any meetings of Republican troops or a Republican Council to be held at Mount Benet. I think it

[21] *Dillon*, p. 24.
[22] *Evidence*, p. 18.

410

would be a great loss to the locality if the place were closed down, and it would mean a good deal of unemployment. The closing down of the school would also be a very serious loss.

I am an Englishman, and Master of the Island Foxhounds. During the troubles my area was very quiet. Hunting never stopped. I only heard two shots the whole time. If anyone asked me to take in a car I should have done so.

I am prepared to swear to the truth of the foregoing at any time.[23]

The rumours of extremist tendencies at the Mount were fuelled by the actions of the Matron, Miss Aileen Keogh, whose personality was almost as dominant as Father Sweetman's.

She too was a very formidable character but a very competent nurse. She wore her hair close-cropped like a boy, which was very unusual in the early years of this century. As a relaxation she would take an axe and sally forth to the woods to fell a couple of trees, smoking the while one of His Reverence's pungent cheroots. She had one other weakness which we did not discover till after we left the school; she had a passion for Wild West stories and kept a magnificent collection of them in the privacy of her room.

She held very extreme political views, and on the outbreak of the Rebellion in 1916 she mounted her bicycle and set out for Dublin to play her part. She was arrested and brought into the guard room at Trinity College, where, the story is told, an old boy of Mount St Benedict was in command. He had fought the Germans in France and was quite prepared to face all the normal risks of warfare but in this emergency his courage failed him, and he fled and remained under cover until Miss Keogh had been removed to another place of detention.

She was again arrested during the Black-and-Tan period and lodged in Mountjoy. After a few weeks there she escaped over the wall with the more or less open connivance of the warders. An old boy was waiting with a car outside and she was driven back to the Mount. The authorities made no effort to recapture their prisoner.

Although she took a very strong view about those who did not share her political loyalties, her loyalty to Father Sweetman and the Mount took precedence even over her devotion to the Republic, and she was prepared to receive and even to welcome people whom she regarded

[23] *Ibid.*

as politically unsound provided they were faithful to His Reverence. She was an amazing example of unselfish devotion, and the survival of the Mount through the difficult years which followed the closing of the school was largely due to her determination and unremitting work.[24]

The controversy of the twenties, which led, in 1925, to the closure of the school was not, however, only a political conflict. It had about it various elements familiar to students of ecclesiastical institutions throughout Christian history. In summary, three themes predominate. First, there was the conflict between a local bishop and an 'exempt' religious house. Secondly, there was a disagreement between an abbey and a dependent house particularly in the areas of administration, finance, and ownership. Thirdly, and related to the second, was the problem of the obedience of a monk to his religious superior and the overriding demands of conscience.

Dr William Codd, who had succeeded Dr James Browne as bishop of Ferns, formally requested the abbot of Downside to suppress the Mount in 1919. In the bishop's opinion the Mount was interfering with the local church by taking congregations away from the local parishes and by suggesting by its very existence that secondary education was not sufficiently provided for in the diocese.[25] The dispute went to Rome and the judgement, which was deliciously ambiguous, suggested that Mount St Benedict should continue but not as it existed under Sweetman and with a resident community of six. Despite Sweetman's frenetic activities in supporting the establishment and his attempt—which reached Cabinet level[26]—to get government support for the school, Abbot Leander Ramsay of Downside wrote to Dr Codd indicating that the Mount would close:

> As it is impossible for me to comply with the condition laid down by the Holy See that a sufficient number of monks should be sent to Mt S. Benedict, Gorey, to constitute a *domus formata*, I have informed Father Sweetman that the house must be closed at the end of the Summer term of this year. I trust that your Lordship will have no further trouble or annoyance in the matter. It is to me a subject of great regret that we have not been able to make a foundation calculated to

---

[24] *Dillon*, pp. 4–5.
[25] D.A.A. VII.A. 3 e (II) ('First draft—not put in at Rome' of 'Comments on Rt Rev. Bishop of Fern's [*sic*] petition on Gorey), 8 November 1920.
[26] S. O'Buachalla, 'Education in the First and Second Dáil'; *Administration* (Journal of Irish Public Administrators), 25 (1977), pp. 64–5.

serve the best interests of religion and to deserve your Lordship's approval. But circumstances have been against us throughout, and it is literally impossible for me to spare the men who would be needed. I have every hope that Father Sweetman will give your Lordship no cause for complaint in the final stages, but if it should be otherwise, *quod absit*, I trust you will not hesitate to communicate with me without delay.[27]

Sweetman was not so easily dispatched. A letter from the abbot to the bishop a few months later was more explicit:

I duly received your letter of the 19th ult. with enclosures, and I hasten to express my regret that Father Sweetman should have given ground for complaint by his indiscreet utterances. With the unanimous consent of the Council held yesterday I am writing to him by this post, giving him the following instructions:

(1) That he should at once take steps to wind up the business of the house—financial and other:

(2) That he should be in residence at Downside not later than August 15:

(3) That no public Mass is to be said at Mount S. Benedict after Sunday, Aug. 2:

(4) That the administration of the property will be placed in the hands of solicitors from the date at which he leaves the house.

I have also instructed him from this time forward to refrain from making any public statement, either verbally or through the press, in connexion with his hopes that the Benedictines may still find a home at Mount S. Benedict. I have told Father Sweetman that I am writing to you in this sense.

On your side your Lordship will doubtless take any further steps which you may deem necessary.[28]

Father Sweetman, at first, seemed willing to abide by these instructions from his abbot and went to the United States—safely out of the way as far as the authorities were concerned—to 'find a community of Benedictines who will be able and willing to establish a foundation at Mount St Benedict, Gorey'.[29] When, however, Sweetman heard that the property was to

[27] D.A.A. VII.A. 3 e (ii), Abbot H. L. Ramsay to Bishop W. Codd, 30 April 1925 (printed letter).
[28] *Ibid.*, 2 July 1925 (printed letter).
[29] *Ibid.*, C. D. Goolden, OSB, writing to *The Irish Independent*, 20 October 1926 (reprinted and appended to letters referred to in notes 27 and 28 above).

be disposed of he returned to Gorey from St Mary's, Liverpool, where he had gone on his return from the U.S.A., to sit it out. He was to remain there, in what amounted to internal exile, until his death in 1953.

The years 1925–39 were spent under ecclesiastical ban. He made several attempts to make peace with his abbot and bishop—who had suspended him for his stubborn resistance to leaving the Mount—while the authorities at Downside made many attempts to sell off the property, attempts always frustrated by the fact that the property was held in the name of Mr Sweetman. A prayer to St Jude was printed 'for the Restoration of Mount St Benedict'. Father Sweetman attempted to have himself secularized and released from his monastic vows. Throughout, Sweetman remained certain that he was the aggrieved party and that he had a conscientious obligation to keep the Mount manned. His anomalous position was akin to that of his very different confrère, Dom David Knowles, who felt that the 'monasticism of the soul' took precedence over community and ecclesial regulations. Dom Sigebert Trafford, who became abbot of Downside in 1938, had Sweetman's position regularized and granted him permission to continue to reside at the Mount in 1939.[30]

Sweetman, even during the worst years of ecclesial estrangement, had never lost his commitment to the people of Ireland and their freedom. In 1935, for example, he had spoken clearly and with great fervour against what we would now call big-business interference at a meeting at Clauhganny, County Carlow, provokingly entitled 'Who Rules this country? The President or the bankers?' which was printed and circulated.[31] With his ecclesiastical ban lifted, he began to enter into more practical schemes. In 1940 he attempted to reopen the Mount on 'agricultural and industrial lines' for 'future leaders',[32] before being told by the bishop, by then Dr James Staunton, via the abbot that he 'would not and could not give the necessary consent to his proposal'.[33] In 1942 he began the organization of a 'Hollyfort Helpers Guild' which brought relief to the local poor. His tobacco factory continued to operate until the late '30s.[34] He always hoped that the Mount would once again open its doors to pupils.

---

[30] The conflicts of these years are chronicled in D.A.A. both in VII.A.3 e (ii) & (iii) and in Abbot's Archives, Gorey Files. The papers preserved include letters, accounts and newspaper cuttings. Mount St Benedict remained in Downside's possession until 1977. For David Knowles see A. Morey, David Knowles (London, 1979).

[31] D.A.A. Abbot's Archives, Gorey Files. The speech was delivered on 8 September 1935.

[32] Ibid. Copy of letter from J. F. Sweetman to Bishop J. Staunton, 17 March 1940.

[33] Ibid. Letter from Bishop J. Staunton to Abbot R. S. Trafford, 29 March 1940.

[34] See article in Enniscorthy Guardian, 28 February 1970, announcing the formation of a committee to erect a suitable monument to Father Sweetman.

Dom Francis Sweetman

Sweetman remained a great character in the locality until the end. When he returned to begin his long vigil at the Mount in the mid-twenties, he was greeted at the train at Gorey Station by a crowd who lifted him into a carriage and accompanied him all the four miles back to his residence. He was very Irish in his love of his home and hearth. Irish religion is at its most characteristic when it is domestic. He was in many ways a figure out of time, a feudal lord in a world where feudalism was becoming a dirty word, an old Benedictine missionary in a monastic climate where the 'primitive observance' was becoming the norm. He was the victim of many cross-currents in Irish society. He was seen as a member of the Sweetman clan and regarded by those who opposed him as nothing better than a revolutionary. He was in the midst of the bad-feeling and vendettas which followed the Civil War. He became alienated from his monastic family. And yet, when all is said and done, he can be seen as a modern representative of the great tradition of the Irish holy man with his equal passion for his homeland and his religion.

I knew him in his late sixties, when he had mellowed, and had put most of his personal problems behind him. He had much cause for bitterness and recrimination, but he never indulged in self-pity, at least not in spoken words. He was very much a priest, and also a monk. His monastic stability was centred on the Mount, which he considered his home and his monastery. It was quite fitting that the Mount became his last resting-place.[35]

Downside Abbey, Stratton on the Fosse

[35] M. Tierney, 'The Mount during the War Years', *The Gorey Detail*, 7 (1983), unpaginated.

ABBREVIATIONS

AHR	*American Historical Review* (New York 1895–)
An Bol	*Analecta Bollandiana* (Brussels 1882–)
BL	British Library, London
Cal.Pap.Let.	*Calendar of Entries in the Papal Registers relating to Great Britain and Ireland*, 15 vols (London/Dublin 1894–)
CalSPD	*Calendar of State Papers: Domestic* (London 1856–)
Cal.SPI	*Calendar of State Papers relating to Ireland, Henry VIII, Edward VI, Mary and Elizabeth*, 11 vols (London, 1860–1912)
CSer	*Camden Series* (London 1838–)
DNB	*Dictionary of National Biography* (London 1885–)
DRev	*Downside Review* (London 1880–)
Emden (O)	A. B. Emden, *A Biographical Register of the University of Oxford to 1500*, 3 vols (London 1957–9); *1500–40* (1974)
HBC	E. B. Fryde, D. E. Greenway, S. Porter, and I. Roy, *Handbook of British Chronology* 3rd edn (1986)
HJ	*Historical Journal* (Cambridge 1958–)
HMC	Historical Manuscripts Commission
HZ	*Historische Zeitschrift* (Munich 1859–)
IER	*Irish Ecclesiastical Record* (Dublin 1864–)
IR	*Innes Review* (Glasgow 1950–)
JEH	*Journal of Ecclesiastical History* (London 1950–)
JRH	*Journal of Religious History* (Sydney 1960–)
JSRAI	*Journal of the Royal Society of Antiquaries of Ireland* (Dublin 1871–)
LThK	*Lexicon für Theologie und Kirche*, ed. J. Höfer and K. Rahnes (2nd ed. Freiburg-im-Breisgau 1957–)
MIOG	*Mitteilungen des Instituts für österreichische Geschichtsforschung* (Graz/Cologne 1880–)
MS	Manuscript
NCE	*New Catholic Encyclopedia*, 15 vols. (New York 1967)
NH	*Northern History* (Leeds 1966–)
NIPRO	Northern Ireland Public Record Office, Belfast
ns	new series
PP	*Past and Present* (London 1952–)
PRIA	*Proceedings of the Royal Irish Academy* (Dublin 1936–)
PRO	Public Record Office
QFIAB	*Quellen und Forschungen aus Italienischen Archiven und Bibliotheken* (Rome 1897–)
SCH	*Studies in Church History* (London 1964–)
SS	*Surtees Society* (Durham 1835–)
STC	*A Short-Title Catalogue of Books Printed in England, Scotland and Ireland and of English Books Printed Abroad 1475–1640*, ed. A. W. Pollard and G. R. Redgrave (London 1926, repr. 1945, 1950)
TCD	Trinity College, Dublin

ABBREVIATIONS

TRHS	*Transactions of the Royal Historical Society* (London 1871–)
Wilkins	*Concilia Magnae Britanniae et Hiberniae A.D. 446–1717*, 4 vols, ed. D. Wilkins (London 1737)
YAJ	*Yorkshire Archaeological Journal* (London/Leeds 1870–)